# Military Politics,
# Islam, and the
# State in Indonesia

The **Institute of Southeast Asian Studies (ISEAS)** was established as an autonomous organization in 1968. It is a regional centre dedicated to the study of socio-political, security and economic trends and developments in Southeast Asia and its wider geostrategic and economic environment. The Institute's research programmes are the Regional Economic Studies (RES, including ASEAN and APEC), Regional Strategic and Political Studies (RSPS), and Regional Social and Cultural Studies (RSCS).

**ISEAS Publishing**, an established academic press, has issued more than 2,000 books and journals. It is the largest scholarly publisher of research about Southeast Asia from within the region. ISEAS Publications works with many other academic and trade publishers and distributors to disseminate important research and analyses from and about Southeast Asia to the rest of the world.

# Military Politics, Islam, and the State in Indonesia

## From Turbulent Transition to Democratic Consolidation

**MARCUS MIETZNER**

ISEAS

**INSTITUTE OF SOUTHEAST ASIAN STUDIES**

*Singapore*

First published in Singapore in 2009 by
ISEAS Publications
Institute of Southeast Asian Studies
30 Heng Mui Keng Terrace, Pasir Panjang
Singapore 119614

*E-mail*: publish@iseas.edu.sg    • Website: bookshop.iseas.edu.sg

The responsibility for facts and opinions in this publication rests exclusively with the author and his interpretations do not necessarily reflect the views or the policy of the publisher or its supporters.

**ISEAS Library Cataloguing-in-Publication Data**

Mietzner, Marcus.
  Military politics, Islam, and the state in Indonesia : from turbulent transition to democratic consolidation.
  1. Indonesia—Politics and government—1998-
  2. Muslims—Indonesia—Politics and government.
  3. Indonesia—Armed Forces.
  I. Title
DS644.5 M63            2009

ISBN   978-981-230-787-3 (soft cover)
ISBN   978-981-230-788-0 (hard cover)
ISBN   978-981-230-845-0 (PDF)

Typeset by International Typesetters Pte Ltd
Printed in Singapore by Utopia Press Pte Ltd

# CONTENTS

*Preface*　　　　　　　　　　　　　　　　　　　　　　　　　vii

*Glossary*　　　　　　　　　　　　　　　　　　　　　　　　　xi

### INTRODUCTION
Militaries in Political Transitions: Theories and the Case of Indonesia　　1

### PART ONE: HISTORICAL LEGACIES, 1945–97

1　Doctrine and Power: Legacies of Indonesian Military Politics　　37

2　Islam and the State: Legacies of Civilian Conflict　　68

### PART TWO: CRISIS AND REGIME CHANGE, 1997–98

3　Regime Change: Military Factionalism and Suharto's Fall　　97

4　Divided Against Suharto: Muslim Groups and the　　146
　　1998 Regime Change

### PART THREE: THE POST-AUTHORITARIAN
### TRANSITION, 1998–2004

5　Adapting to Democracy: TNI in the Early　　195
　　Post-Authoritarian Polity

6    New Era, Old Divisions: Islamic Politics in the Early          251
     Post-Suharto Period


     PART FOUR: DEMOCRATIC CONSOLIDATION, 2004–08

7    Yudhoyono and the Declining Role of State Coercion             291

8    Stabilizing the Civilian Polity: Muslim Groups in              329
     Yudhoyono's Indonesia


                              CONCLUSION
Controlling the Military: Conflict and Governance in Indonesia's     360
Consolidating Democracy

*Bibliography*                                                       384

*Index*                                                             411

# PREFACE

This book is the result of more than ten years of intense engagement with Indonesian politics and its actors. I began research for my Ph.D. dissertation in Indonesia in 1997, when the New Order regime started to crumble. Since then, I have lived in the country for most of the time, witnessing at first hand many of the events that shaped the post-Suharto polity. Based on these direct observations, this book covers one of the most eventful decades of Indonesian modern history, from the end of authoritarian rule to the phase of democratic consolidation from 2004 onwards. Of course this latter phase is far from completed, and the outcome of the political reform process still uncertain.

A great number of people have assisted me during my research for this book, both directly and indirectly. First and foremost, Harold Crouch has been a great influence on my scholarly and personal development since I began my Ph.D. candidature at the Australian National University (ANU) in 1997. I was deeply impressed by the warmth and dedication that Harold showed towards his students, providing significantly more assistance and support than his position as a university professor would have required. Even after I completed my doctoral studies, Harold continued to comment on my academic writings, including the last two chapters of this book. Without Harold's willingness to introduce me to senior military officers and politicians, his constant encouragement and advice, and his intellectual guidance, this book would not have been possible. In the same vein, I am indebted to Greg Fealy, also of ANU, who played a big role in the production of this book as well. His friendship and uncompromising scholarly advice have accompanied my life for the last ten years. I have become a great admirer of his strong academic ethics, his command of a precise but colourful language, and his unique sense of humour. Special thanks are also due to Merle Ricklefs, of the National University of Singapore, who continued to read my drafts after his departure from the ANU in 1998 and provided invaluable comments and insights.

Other scholars, journalists, diplomats, and analysts have influenced this study through long discussions over breakfast, lunch, dinner, or coffee, mostly in one of Jakarta's hotels or meeting places. Edward Aspinall, Rodd McGibbon, and Sidney Jones have influenced my views on Indonesian politics to an extent that they are probably not aware of. Douglas Ramage, David Engel, Ken Ward, Bill Liddle, Andrée Feillard, Greg and Sarah Moriarty, Jamie McAden, Joe Judge, Ambassador Michael Green, Ken Brownrigg, Alan Roberts, Justin Lee, Eunsook Jung, Michael Buehler, Lisa Misol, Dave Jensen, John Subritzki, and David di Giovanna have shared important information and analyses with me, and often hosted greatly entertaining gatherings that turned into heated debates on the ins and outs of the Indonesian political elite. John McBeth, David Jenkins, Adam Schwarz, Hamish McDonald, Jose Manuel Tesoro, Jeremy Wagstaff, Vaudine England, Erhard Haubold, and Michael Vatikiotis contributed greatly to this study, both through personal discussions and their fine journalistic work. In addition, I would like to thank Donald Emmerson, Greg Barton, Martin van Bruinessen, Daniel Ziv, David Pottebaum, the late Geoff Forrester, David Blizzard, Michael Stievater, Terry Myers, Oren Murphy, Vishalini Lawrence, Ignacio Sainz, and Michael Malley for much needed assistance in the preparation of this study. I am also humbled by the interest that some of the "elder statesmen" of Indonesian studies have taken in my research, among them Jamie Mackie and the late Herbert Feith.

This book would not have seen the light of day had it not been for the great patience of Indonesians who, despite their busy schedules, always find time to explain their country to outsiders like myself. The Centre for Strategic and International Studies (CSIS) was my host during my fieldwork in Indonesia in 1998 and 1999. Clara Joewono, Hadi Soesastro, Harry Tjan Silalahi, and Rizal Sukma made my stay at the Centre most enjoyable and productive. In 2006 and 2007, I was a Senior Visiting Fellow at the Indonesian Institute, and this fellowship allowed me to research and write the final two chapters of this book. At the Institute, Jeffrie Geovanie and Anies Baswedan were great sources of information and inspiration, and Jeffrie's failed candidacy as vice-governor of Jakarta in 2007 provided me with original insights into the workings of Indonesian electoral politics ten years after Suharto's fall. Other Indonesian scholars who have shared their knowledge and expertise with me included Ikrar Nusa Bhakti, Andi Widjojanto, Kusnanto Anggoro, Cornelis Lay, Humam Hamid, Edy Prasetyono, the late Munir, Fajrul Falaakh, Hari Prihatono, Aribowo, Muhammad Asfar, and the late Riswanda Imawan.

In the military, several generals have devoted considerable time to answer my questions on their institution, most notably Lieutenant General

Agus Widjojo, General Endriartono Sutarto, Lieutenant General Djadja Suparman, Major General Sudrajat, and the late Lieutenant General Agus Wirahadikusumah. Among the Muslim leaders and politicians who were always prepared to discuss the complexities of their religion and its political manifestations were Abdurrahman Wahid, Muhaimin Iskandar, Habieb Syarief Mohammad, Saifullah Yusuf, Zulkieflimansyah, Mustafa Zuhad Mughni, Din Syamsuddin, and Djoko Susilo, as well as the late Cholil Bisri and Matori Abdul Djalil.

I would like to express my gratitude to the East-West Center Washington for allowing me to use some of their copyrighted material. Parts of Chapter 5 of this publication were originally published in "The Politics of Military Reform in Post-Suharto Indonesia: Elite Conflict, Nationalism, and Institutional Resistance", East-West Center Policy Studies 23.

I would also like to thank Triena Ong at the Institute of Southeast Asian Studies in Singapore for helping me throughout the process of publishing this book. She has exercised motherly patience whenever other commitments forced me to delay the submission of the manuscript, and provided indispensable technical guidance. At the Department of Political and Social Change of the ANU's Research School of Pacific and Asian Studies, Claire Smith and Bev Fraser have also helped with various technical and administrative aspects associated with my dissertation, which formed the basis of this book. I am also indebted to my parents, Peter and Karin Mietzner, who have provided significant financial assistance to my studies. Without their help, I probably would have never been able to go to Australia and complete my doctoral degree. I am deeply grateful to them. Finally, I thank my partner Samiel Laury for his love and support. Despite his dislike for politics, he has been a source of constant encouragement and inspiration.

A short note on spellings and the use of names is also in order. Generally, I followed the spelling standardized in the Indonesian press or used by the person concerned. In some cases, however, I followed the preferences of international publishers. This means, I used "Suharto" instead of the Indonesian version "Soeharto", and "Sukarno" instead of "Soekarno". In other instances, I maintained the original spelling, particularly if the name was internationally not widely known. I applied a similar approach to the problem of family and first names. In the Indonesian press, first names are mostly used to represent the full name, i.e. "Amien" for "Amien Rais". The international media, however, would refer to Amien as "Rais". In this context, I have followed majority usage and my intuition rather than a clear rule. For instance, the use of "Wahid" for Abdurrahman Wahid and "Yudhoyono" for

Susilo Bambang Yudhoyono has become widespread in the Indonesian press after these figures assumed the presidency. By contrast, no Indonesian paper would use "Sukarnoputri" for Megawati Sukarnoputri, but would invariably stick to the popular use of "Megawati". In the same vein, no Indonesian analyst would understand the use of "Subianto" for Prabowo Subianto. Consequently, I have adopted those names that are most widely used in Indonesia and the academic community of Indonesianists.

# GLOSSARY

| | |
|---|---|
| *abangan* | nominal Muslim(s) |
| ABRI | *Angkatan Bersenjata Republik Indonesia*, Armed Forces of the Republic of Indonesia |
| Akabri | *Akademi Angkatan Bersenjata Republik Indonesia*, Academy of the Armed Forces of the Republic of Indonesia |
| *amar ma'ruf nahi munkar* | Qu'ranic command to do good and prohibit evil |
| Ampera | *Amanat Penderitaan Rakyat*, Mandate of the People's Suffering |
| ANU | Australian National University |
| APEC | Asia-Pacific Economic Cooperation |
| ASEAN | Association of Southeast Asian Nations |
| Babinsa | *Bintara Pembina Desa*, NCOs for Village Supervision |
| BIA | *Badan Intelijen ABRI*, ABRI Intelligence Agency |
| BIN | *Badan Intelijen Negara*, National Intelligence Agency |
| BKSPPI | *Badan Kerja Sama Pondok Pesantren Indonesia*, Cooperation Body of Indonesian Islamic Boarding Schools |
| *bughot* | rebel; person who takes up arms against the legitimate government |
| *bupati* | district head |
| CSIS | Center for Strategic and International Studies |
| *dakwah* | Islamic predication |
| Darul Islam | lit. "Abode of Islam" |
| DDII | *Dewan Dakwah Islamiyah Indonesia*, Indonesian Council for Islamic Predication |

| | |
|---|---|
| DPD | *Dewan Perwakilan Daerah*, Regional Representative Council |
| DPR | *Dewan Perwakilan Rakyat*, People's Representative Council |
| Dwi Fungsi | Dual Function |
| FBR | *Forum Betawi Rempug*, Betawi Brotherhood Forum |
| *fikih* | Islamic jurisprudence |
| FKPPI | *Forum Komunikasi Putra-Putri Purnawirawan Indonesia*, Communication Forum of Sons and Daughters of Indonesian Veterans |
| Forki | *Forum Kerja Indonesia*, Indonesian Working Forum |
| FPI | *Front Pembela Islam*, Front for the Defenders of Islam |
| FPK | *Front Pembela Kebenaran*, Front of Defenders of the Truth |
| GAM | *Gerakan Aceh Merdeka*, Free Aceh Movement |
| Giyugun | volunteer army (during the Japanese occupation) |
| Golkar | *Golongan Karya*, Functional Group(s); government party during the New Order |
| GPB | *Gerakan Pembela Bangsa*, Movement of Defenders of the Nation |
| *hajj* | annual Islamic pilgrimage to Mecca |
| *haram* | prohibited (according to Islamic law) |
| Heiho | auxiliary troops (during the Japanese occupation) |
| ICMI | *Ikatan Cendekiawan Muslim se-Indonesia*, Indonesian Association of Muslim Intellectuals |
| *ijtihad* | independent judgment, based on recognized sources of Islam, on a legal or theological question |
| Ikhwanul Muslimin | Muslim Brotherhood |
| IMF | International Monetary Fund |
| IPNU | *Ikatan Pelajar Nahdlatul Ulama*, Nahdlatul Ulama Students Association |
| IPPNU | Ikatan Pelajar Putri Nahdlatul Ulama, Nahdlatul Ulama Female Students Association |
| Jemaah Islamiyah | lit. "Islamic Community" |
| JPPR | *Jaringan Pendidikan Pemilih Untuk Rakyat*, People's Voter Education Network |

| | |
|---|---|
| *ka'abah* | lit. "cube"; a cuboidal building inside the al-Masjid al-Haram mosque in Mecca |
| KAMMI | *Kesatuan Aksi Mahasiswa Muslim Indonesia*, Indonesian Muslim Student Action Union |
| *kekaryaan* | lit. "work"; temporary assignment of officers to non-military posts |
| *kiai* | lit. "noble"; title of religious scholar or leader |
| *kiai khos* | lit. "venerable Islamic scholars" |
| KISDI | *Komite Indonesia untuk Solidaritas Dunia Islam*, Indonesian Committee for Solidarity with the Muslim World |
| KNIL | *Koninklijk Nederlandsch-Indisch Leger*, Royal Netherlands East Indies Army |
| Kodam | *Komando Daerah Militer*, Regional Command |
| Kodim | *Komando Distrik Militer*, District Command |
| Komando Jihad | lit. "Holy War Command" |
| Koramil | *Komando Rayon Militer*, Sub-district Command |
| Korem | *Komando Resort Militer*, Resort Command |
| Kostrad | *Komando Cadangan Strategis Angkatan Darat* (Army Strategic Reserve Command) |
| Kowilhan | *Komando Wilayah Pertahanan*, Territorial Defence Command |
| Laskar Jihad | lit. "Holy War Fighters" |
| Lemhannas | *Lembaga Ketahanan Nasional*, National Resilience Institute |
| LIPI | *Lembaga Ilmu Pengetahuan Indonesia*, Indonesian Institute of Sciences |
| LKKNU | *Lembaga Kemaslahatan Keluarga Nahdlatul Ulama*, Institute for the Benefit of Nahdlatul Ulama Families |
| LSI | *Lembaga Survei Indonesia*, Indonesian Survey Institute |
| MAR | *Majelis Amanat Rakyat*, Popular Mandate Council |
| Masyumi | *Majelis Syuro Muslimin Indonesia*, Indonesian Muslim Advisory Council |
| *mazhab* | Islamic school of law |
| MK | *Mahkamah Konstitusi*, Constitutional Court |
| MPR | *Majelis Permusyawaratan Rakyat*, People's Consultative Assembly |

| | |
|---|---|
| MPRS | *Majelis Permusyawaratan Rakyat Sementara*, Provisional People's Consultative Assembly |
| MUI | *Majelis Ulama Indonesia*, Indonesian Council of Muslim Scholars |
| Muspida | *Musyawarah Pimpinan Daerah*, Consultation of the Regional Leadership |
| Nasakom | Sukarno's acronym for the combination of Nationalism (*Nasionalisme*), Religion (*Agama*), and Communism (*Komunisme*) |
| NATO | North Atlantic Treaty Organization |
| New Order | The political order in Indonesia under Suharto's rule (1966-98) |
| NII | *Negara Islam Indonesia*, Islamic State of Indonesia |
| NKRI | *Negara Kesatuan Republik Indonesia*, Unitary State of the Republic of Indonesia |
| NU | *Nahdlatul Ulama*; lit. "Revival of the Islamic Scholars" |
| PAN | *Partai Amanat Nasional*, National Mandate Party |
| Pancasila | lit. "The Five Principles" |
| Parmusi | *Partai Muslimin Indonesia*, Indonesian Muslim Party |
| Partai Bulan Bintang | Crescent and Star Party |
| Partai Demokrat | Democratic Party |
| PBM | *Pasukan Berani Mati*, Troops Ready to Die |
| PBR | *Partai Bintang Reformasi*, Reform Star Party |
| PDI | *Partai Demokrasi Indonesia*, Indonesian Democratic Party |
| PDI-P | PDI-Perjuangan, PDI-Struggle |
| Pertamina | *Perusahaan Tambang Minyak Negara*, State Oil Company |
| Perti | *Persatuan Tarbiyah Indonesia*, Islamic Education Association |
| *pesantren* | traditional Islamic boarding school |
| Peta | *Tentara Pembela Tanah Air*, Army for the Defence of the Homeland |
| PK | *Partai Keadilan*, Justice Party |
| PKB | *Partai Kebangkitan Bangsa*, National Awakening Party |

| PKI | *Partai Komunis Indonesia*, Indonesian Communist Party |
| PKNU | *Partai Kebangkitan Nasional Ulama*, Party of the Islamic Scholars' National Awakening |
| PKPI | *Partai Keadilan dan Persatuan Indonesia*, Party of Indonesian Justice and Unity |
| PKS | *Partai Keadilan Sejahtera*, Prosperous Justice Party |
| PKU | *Partai Kebangkitan Umat*, Party of the Awakening Umat |
| PLA | People's Liberation Army |
| PMB | *Partai Matahari Bangsa*, Party of the National Sun |
| PMII | *Pergerakan Mahasiswa Islam Indonesia*, Indonesian Movement of Islamic Students |
| PNI | *Partai Nasional Indonesia*, Indonesian Nationalist Party |
| PNU | *Partai Nahdlatul Umat*, Revival of the Umat Party |
| PPDK | *Partai Persatuan Demokrasi Kebangsaan*, United Party of National Democracy |
| PPP | *Partai Persatuan Pembangunan*, United Development Party |
| PSI | *Partai Sosialis Indonesia*, Indonesian Socialist Party |
| *putihan* | lit. "the white ones"; devout Muslims |
| *Rais 'Aam* | Chairman of the Religious Council of Nahdlatul Ulama |
| *santri* | devout Muslim(s) |
| *shirk* (or *syirk*) | idolatry, polytheism |
| SUNI | *Solidaritas Uni Nasional Indonesia*, Solidarity of the National Indonesian Union |
| *syariat* (or *sharia*) | Islamic law |
| *syubhat* | dubious, questionable (according to Islamic law) |
| TII | *Tentara Islam Indonesia*, Islamic Army of Indonesia |
| TKR | *Tentara Keamanan Rakyat*, People's Security Force |
| TNI | *Tentara Nasional Indonesia*, Indonesian National Military |

| | |
|---|---|
| *ulama* | Islamic scholar(s) |
| *umat* | Islamic community |
| UN | United Nations |
| UNICEF | United Nations Children's Fund |
| UUD 1945 | *Undang-Undang Dasar* 1945, Constitution of 1945 |
| *waliyul amri* | de facto holder of interim power (according to Islamic |
| *dlaruri bissyaukah* | jurisprudence) |
| Dharmais | *Dharma Bhakti Sosial*, Social Service |
| Supersemar | *Surat Perintah Sebelas Maret*, Order of March the Eleventh |

# INTRODUCTION

## MILITARIES IN POLITICAL TRANSITIONS
### Theories and the Case of Indonesia

> One of our greatest challenges now is to sideline the military from politics. They have dominated our political system, our society, our economy for too long.... It is now time for us civilians to take charge and reform the foundations of this nation.
>
> Amien Rais, June 1998[1]

> My party cannot rule this country alone. I need a partner ... with a wide network to win the people's hearts, somebody strong and with charisma. He has to be from TNI. My second reason for choosing a military man to run as my vice-presidential candidate is to safeguard the national integrity of the whole of Indonesia's wide territory.... We are really grateful to TNI.
>
> Amien Rais, September 2003[2]

Indonesia's political system has undergone dramatic structural change since the 1998 downfall of the New Order regime that had ruled the country for more than three decades. A multitude of political parties has replaced the tightly controlled three-party system; free and fair elections were held that resulted in three successive coalition governments with a weakening presidency; political power was transferred from the once omnipotent centre into the regions; the previously sacrosanct constitution was extensively rewritten; civil society organizations have mushroomed; and one of the most diverse media landscapes in Asia has emerged. One area that has seen some of the most significant changes is the security sector. Indonesia's armed forces (TNI, *Tentara Nasional Indonesia*) had to give up their institutional engagement in politics, accept their removal from the DPR (*Dewan Perwakilan Rakyat*, People's Representative Council) and the MPR (*Majelis Permusyawaratan Rakyat*, People's Consultative Assembly),[3] and were mandated by law to reduce their role in domestic security affairs. The police, formerly a part of the armed forces, were separated from the military and assigned the task of managing internal security.

The extent of institutional reform affecting Indonesia's security sector has led some observers to the conclusion that "the civil-military balance has tilted against the military, and state-soldier relations are in the midst of substantial change" (Alagappa 2001*a*, p. 16). In this view, the reform movement has weakened the armed forces substantially, rushing in a new class of civilian politicians that has taken charge of the country. Yet other analysts have stated as recently as 2006 that "there is a widespread belief that military reforms have so far only been superficial and that further reform would require a more committed leadership than the one currently in power" (Nyman 2006, p. 168). Such highly diverse assessments, which are also reflected in veteran politician Amien Rais's conflicting statements cited earlier, are not only an expression of disagreements between scholars in evaluating the successes and failures of military reform efforts after 1998. More importantly, they suggest that the process of military reform in Indonesia has been anything but a linear and stable development. Apparently, there were remarkable fluctuations in the quality of democratic civilian control of the armed forces in different periods of the post-Suharto era, mirroring the ebbs and flows of the reform process as a whole. Influenced by a variety of internal and external factors, the pace and scope of change within the armed forces differed under each of the four post-Suharto governments. Yudhoyono, for example, exercised significantly better control over the armed forces than his predecessor, Megawati Sukarnoputri. Exploring the reasons for these differences and fluctuations will be a major purpose of this book.

The complexity of the military's new role in the post-Suharto polity does not only pose difficult challenges to Indonesia's democratic governments, but also to the theoretical debate on democratic transitions in general. The existing literature on civil-military relations in post-authoritarian states has found it difficult to grasp the oscillating dynamics of military influence on evolving democratic polities. Classic theories on military intervention in politics have largely focused on open interventions by the armed forces and the formal mechanisms of their political participation. These theories are insufficient, however, to describe the fluid power relations in emerging political systems, with militaries often using their non-institutional powers to gain access to political and economic resources. More recent models, on the other hand, have used a predominantly normative approach, proposing reform steps that countries in post-authoritarian transitions have to introduce in order to establish democratic control over their militaries. Theorists of this school have set the concept of democratic governance of the security sector as a normative ideal that allows them to identify diversions (and their causes) in particular countries. The ideal often proves difficult to achieve, however, with even some developed democracies failing to meet the benchmarks set up by the theorists. This creates problems in defining the very specific conditions faced by countries that have only recently emerged from decades of military-backed rule. Thus while both the classic and normative theories have captured some important aspects of the role militaries can play in post-authoritarian politics, it appears necessary to expand the existing models to tackle the complex case of Indonesia.

This book is a study of civil-military relations in post-Suharto Indonesia. It discusses the causes and consequences of the country's problematic attempt to establish democratic control of the armed forces as a major agenda of its post-authoritarian reform programme. The book is structured in four main parts, each containing parallel chapters on developments in military politics and civilian affairs. The idea to structure the narrative and analysis chronologically in parallel military and "civilian" chapters was born out of my intense engagement with the literature on civil-military relations. As this introduction will show, the outcome of civil-military transitions is not only determined by internal military reforms and the changing attitudes in the officer corps. Developments within civilian politics are equally important, with the quality of democratic governance, the level of intra-civilian fragmentation, and the use of state coercion playing a huge role in shaping civil-military relations. Accordingly, this book analyses the two sides of civil-military relationships in separate yet parallel discussions. In order to further narrow down the focus, I chose to analyse developments in political Islam as a means to demonstrate general patterns of civilian politics in Indonesia's transition. Many of these patterns are visible in other segments of the civilian polity as well, such as the internal dynamics of secular-nationalist or non-Muslim groups, but the choice of intra-Muslim affairs as a case study offered numerous opportunities to highlight broader trends in civilian constituencies that impacted on the quality of Indonesia's civil-military relations after 1998.

In this context, it is important to note that this book is *not* a study of the special interaction between the military and political Islam. The fact that the armed forces and their individual officers occasionally forged alliances with Islamic leaders and groups to serve their vested interests is touched upon in this study, but it does not constitute its main focus. Instead, the book emphasizes how developments *within* the Muslim community have influenced civil-military relations. In particular, it points to political, ideological, and social divisions between Islamic groups that have destabilized civilian politics both before and after the 1998 regime change, allowing the armed forces to consolidate their position. The book also demonstrates, however, how the declining tensions between Muslim groups after 2004 contributed to the stabilization of the civilian polity, which consequently translated into improved civilian democratic control of the armed forces under the Yudhoyono presidency. Accordingly, while the manipulation of both extremist and mainstream Muslim groups by the armed forces during the New Order and in the early post-Suharto transition is an interesting phenomenon and deserves detailed scholarly attention, it is marginal to the theme explored in this book.

The discussion of the literature on civil-military relations presented in the following section also led to three additional propositions that shaped the structure of this book. First of all, the insight that the level of engagement of the armed forces in political affairs rises and falls with fluctuations in the effectiveness of civilian governance suggested that a chronological approach is best suited to capture the erratic developments in Indonesia's post-1998 civil-military affairs. The quality of democratic civilian control over the military differed greatly under Presidents Habibie, Wahid, Megawati, and Yudhoyono, and only a chronologically structured analysis can pinpoint the causes for these differences.

The second important proposition emerging from the review of the literature is the importance of historical legacies for current civil-military affairs. As a result, the first part of this book (Chapters 1 and 2) discusses the historical background of Indonesian military politics and intra-Islamic developments respectively, and although the two parallel chapters do not present new research material, they provide readers with the necessary information to contextualize the discussion of more recent events in the subsequent parts.

Finally, the significance of the character of regime change for the dynamics of post-autocratic civil-military relations requires that this study provide a detailed analysis of the events that triggered the democratic transition in 1998. Thus the second part of the book (Chapters 3 and 4) examines the 1998 transfer of power from Suharto to his successor, and its consequences for the pace and quality of the post-authoritarian transition. As further explained in this introduction, the discussion of the regime change is followed by parts three (Chapters 5 and 6) and four (Chapters 7 and 8) of the book, which analyse both Indonesia's transition between 1998 and 2004 and the phase of democratic consolidation after Yudhoyono's rise to power.

## DEMOCRATIC VS CIVILIAN CONTROL

Democratic control of the armed forces is one of the key factors in successful transitions from authoritarian rule to democracy. Militaries that have supported, participated in, or dominated authoritarian regimes are likely to be crucial players in the transition, trying to preserve as many of their previous political and institutional privileges as possible. In order to minimize the military's influence on the shaping of post-authoritarian political structures, it is a major challenge for civilian forces to quickly initiate the establishment of constitutional mechanisms that put democratically elected, civilian state institutions in charge of all aspects of governance, including the security sector. While O'Donnell and Schmitter (1986, p. 32) have asserted that it is "civilian control" that is most important in democratic transitions, recent discussions put more stress on the quality of civilian control, and how it is achieved and exercised. Cottey, Edmunds, and Forster (2001, p. 4), writing on transitional processes in Eastern European states and the former Soviet republics, propose that what really matters is the "control of the military by the legitimate, democratically elected authorities of the state". Accordingly, it "concerns more than the simple maximization of civilian power over the military, and is fundamentally about the democratic legitimacy, governance, and accountability of a state's civil-military relationship". Democratic control of the military is, therefore, best understood as an inter-institutional process in which legitimate state bodies authorize the structure, size, function, and use of the armed forces (Callaghan and Kuhlmann 2002, p. 4). Civilian control, on the other hand, can be undemocratic if exercised by civilian forces not sufficiently legitimized through proper democratic procedures. In some cases, the establishment of civilian control by only one dominant civilian element in the post-authoritarian transition can reinforce the very manipulability of the armed forces that the regime change aimed to remove.

The distinction between "civilian" and "democratic" control of the armed forces will prove crucial in discussing the Indonesian case. The transitional process in Indonesia has seen several presidents making attempts to use the armed forces in the competition with their political opponents. Such examples underline the necessity of further defining what exactly democratic control of the armed forces entails. The first level of explanation concerns the decision-making on military policy. In a democratic state, such decisions are made by the openly and freely elected executive in coordination with the legislature. By entrusting the decision-making process to an institutionalised system of checks and balances, the possibility that a single political actor can gain monopolistic power over the military is reduced. Parliamentary oversight of the armed forces is the most crucial element in this level of democratic control, with the legislature approving defence-related policies, adopting legislation, and allocating the budget for the military (Born 2003). Countries in transition often face difficulties in empowering their legislatures to exercise these control functions properly, due to a variety of reasons ranging from lack of expertise in military affairs to divisions within the political elite. The second level is related to the implementation of decisions made by political authorities through the bureaucracy. As Edward Page (1992, p. 174) has outlined, the adequate implementation of political decisions made by state institutions is a major element of functioning democracies. In terms of controlling the military, the department of defence is the bureaucratic tool through which policy decisions are translated into concrete action on the ground. In military-backed authoritarian regimes, armed forces officers thus often seek to establish unchallenged dominance over the defence bureaucracy. This deliberate exclusion of civilian defence officials can lead to serious problems in the subsequent democratic transition (Fedorov 2002, p. 16), and post-Suharto Indonesia is a case in point. Finally, the third level of democratic control highlights the importance of societal scrutiny of the armed forces, largely exercised through civil society groups and the media. Their participation in the management of defence policy and its implementation are crucial additions to the traditional concepts of "civilian control".[4]

The extent of military adherence to these three levels of democratic control is determined by the quality of the civilian institutions that oversee them. Successful empowerment of civilian leaders, and effective cooperation between them, is likely to result in the acknowledgement of democratic control by the military leadership. On the other hand, problems in the establishment of civilian state and societal institutions, whether provoked by sabotage, inter-civilian disputes, indifference, or lack of expertise, are almost certain to encourage the armed forces to disobey or ignore orders by civilian control authorities. This inter-connectivity between empowerment of civilian state institutions and democratic control of the armed forces has led most recent authors on the subject to integrate democratic control into the broader concept of "security sector reform" (Ball 2001; Bland 2001; Smith

2001). The inclusion of democratic control into the concept of security sector reform is important for the clarification of two major issues. First, it defines military reform as part of a larger process of reforming not only other security institutions (police, armed militias, forces of executive agencies), but the system of governance as a whole. It links the success of establishing democratic control of the armed forces with the levels of consolidation shown by both the democratically authorized state institutions and those security agencies charged with carrying out the functions previously monopolized by the military. Second, it clarifies that the "key civil-military problem in the post-authoritarian state" is not only, as Alagappa (2001b, p. 54) put it, "the need to curb the military's political power", but also to guarantee that this reform process does not result in an erosion of general security conditions. Such erosion is likely to undermine the project of democratic consolidation, and includes the possibility that the public will demand the retention of military powers unless other credible alternatives are presented.

The expansion of traditional theories on "civilian control" to the more comprehensive concepts of "democratic control" and "security sector reform" carries significant methodological consequences for this study, and has played an important role in defining its scope. It suggests that the interaction between civilian forces, i.e., their struggle for control of the political institutions and the fora of civil society, are as important to the outcome of the civil-military reform process as the classic concentration on corporate interests of the military.[5] Accordingly, it will be one of this book's tasks to analyse how the relationships and rivalries between civilian groups have affected the chances of establishing democratic control of the armed forces. At the same time, the application of the concepts will provide important normative evaluation tools regarding the reform steps Indonesia has taken in its process of democratic consolidation. Where the notion of "civilian control" would fail to grasp the complexities of the relationship between the executive, the military, and other civilian forces, the norms and standards enshrined in the model of democratic control are much more likely to identify those areas where the reform efforts have produced insufficient results to carry the process forward, and are therefore more useful in determining Indonesia's place in the comparative scheme of civil-military transitions.

The discussion so far has identified democratic control of the armed forces as a crucial element of security sector reform and, ultimately, processes of democratic transition and consolidation. The literature on this topic is of a largely normative nature, with authors giving recommendations to countries in transition regarding reform measures they are expected to take and the risks they should avoid. In contrast, the academic exchange on the causes and dimensions of military interventions in politics has been vast, and filled with numerous case studies from the 1950s to the 1990s. Samuel E. Finer (1985, pp. 23–24) argued that theories on military intervention in politics could be negatively applied in order to explain military non-intervention or "extrusion". While this is not entirely true, the description of the various causes of military intervention in politics, the different models of military-state relations, and the theoretical approaches to the downfall of military-backed regimes provide an important background for this book. In particular, the analysis of the last area, the disintegration of authoritarian governments, not only delivers invaluable insights into the socio-political patterns of regime change, but can also explain their repercussions for the ensuing periods of democratic transition and consolidation.

## AREAS OF MILITARY ENGAGEMENT

Before discussing the various models of military intervention in politics, it is important to introduce the political, economic, institutional, and socio-cultural sectors of state organization in which militaries traditionally seek to exert influence. The description of these areas, and the opportunities of intervention they offer, will make it easier to identify diversions from the normative model of democratic control of the armed forces, and will provide analytical tools for the analysis of the Indonesian case. First, and most important, is the participation of the military in the political institutions of the state. In countries where democratic control of the armed forces has been established, the military is part of the political process only in terms of submitting policy options if the civilian authorities ask for such advice, and implementing the policy militarily once the relevant decisions have been made. Military officers may, of course, exert political influence by voting in general elections, lobbying politicians, shaping public opinion by engaging with the media, or aligning themselves with civil society organizations or think tanks. Such interventions remain, however, within the democratic political framework. In non-democratic states, on the other hand, militaries have not only tried to influence the decision-making process, they have used coercion to put pressure on state institutions, have pushed for participation in legislatures and executive bodies, and, in some cases, have taken over government. Koonings and Kruit (2002, p. 19) have outlined two major motivations for military interventionism in political institutions:

> First, there is the notion that the military institution is exceptionally well placed not only to defend but also to define the essence of the nation by birthright and competence. Second, the military "knows" that "civilians",

that is to say, civilian politicians, the institutional framework of civic governance, the actions of societal interest groups, and the overall political culture tend to be inadequate to address the needs of the nation.

These interventions transform the armed forces from an advisory and executive instrument of the state into a decision-making institution, with the corporate interests of the military becoming an important element in general governance. As a result, the institutional set-up of the state is fundamentally changed.

The second area where militaries tend to seek involvement in is the economic sector. George Philip (2001, p. 74), for example, pointed to the importance of "economic fiefdoms" for "bureaucratically autonomous and politically interventionist" militaries in South America between 1925 and 1982. In this field, analysts have differentiated between two types of intervention: first, the economic activities aimed at raising funds for the operational costs of the military and the personal enrichment of its officers; and second, the engagement in national development projects, boosting the political legitimacy of the armed forces and institutionalizing their role in governance. The first type of engagement includes military-owned businesses and cooperatives, stakes in large conglomerates that seek security and political protection in return, illegal activities such as extortion, drug trafficking, backing of prostitution and gambling, and involvement in natural resource-extraction (Diamond and Plattner 1996, p. xix). The second type of socio-economic activity is of a developmentalist nature: the military participates in programmes such as the building of crucial infrastructure, family planning and public health, management of sports and youth organizations, education in rural and remote areas, and disaster relief. These activities grant the armed forces access to non-military items within national and regional budgets, increase the participation of military personnel in governance, and help to legitimize political intervention in the eyes of society. The Indonesian military has been deeply involved in both types of economic activity, complicating attempts to subordinate it to democratic civilian control after 1998. In Indonesia as well as in other countries with problematic militaries, the extent to which the armed forces are independent from financial resources provided by the state is reflective of the position military officers can assume in their interaction with civilian state institutions (Brömmelhörster and Paes 2003, p. 16).

The third field of military intervention is related to the institutional and organizational autonomy of the armed forces. Often the involvement of militaries in the two areas mentioned earlier — the participation in political institutions and the economy — are functions of the inherent tendency of the armed forces to protect and expand their institutional autonomy. Military officers are inclined to view issues of defence management, such as force structure and size, purchase of equipment, senior appointments, and the development of military strategies, as matters of internal organization rather than policy fields directed by civilian authorities. This belief is based on what Peter D. Feaver (2003, p. 68) called the "information asymmetries in civil-military relations", which points to a level of technical expertise of the armed forces in the "management of violence" that civilian controllers do not possess. The drive for institutional autonomy can lead militaries to seek direct participation in or control of state institutions in order to limit their intervention opportunities vis-à-vis the armed forces (Nordinger 1977). Similarly, the involvement of militaries in the economic sector is often motivated by their desire to remain financially independent from the control institutions of the state.

There are, however, two areas of institutional autonomy in which even participation in political institutions or budgetary independence can prove insufficient to prevent interference by civilian forces: first, the authority over senior appointments and second, decisions on major defence and security policies made by civilian state institutions. In many post-authoritarian states, the control over appointments constitutes the only civilian bargaining power in the interaction with militaries that have preserved large elements of their institutional and organizational powers built up under the previous regime. The confrontation between civilian appointment authority and the institutional power of the military often leads to civil-military negotiations over the terms of the transition (Hernandez 1996, p. 72). These negotiations can result in alliances between civilian power-holders and military leaders aimed at establishing new forms of semi-authoritarian rule. Alternatively, civilians may concede organizational autonomy to the armed forces in exchange for their support of the democratic transition, just as Presidents Habibie and Megawati did in Indonesia after the 1998 regime change.

Besides institutional autonomy, militaries also often seek jurisdiction over the formulation and implementation of defence and security policies. In his study on the armed forces of Chile, Gregory Weeks (2003, p. 15) described this area as "highly salient" for the military. Many militaries view it as their prerogative to manage the security of the state, insisting that civilians are politically too divided or do not possess the necessary skills to be left in charge of national security issues. In transitional states, militaries tend to utilize their organizational autonomy to obstruct decisions on security matters made by civilian authorities. Unable to influence the decision-making process itself, and aware that overthrowing the government is politically unfeasible, the armed forces may run counter-operations that undermine the goal of the policies set by the executive. In Indonesia, the armed forces formally endorsed the decision by the Habibie government to hold a referendum in East Timor, but immediately began to support the build-up of pro-integration militias assigned with sabotaging the process. In addition to the control of defence and security policies, militaries often demand legal jurisdiction over their own personnel. In post-authoritarian states, the armed forces may insist on the autonomy of their legal systems in order to fend off demands for legal inquiries into crimes and violations that occurred under the previous regime. While such investigations are often essential for the success of democratic transitions, civilian authorities may find it necessary to reach compromises with the military, resulting in *de facto* amnesties for incriminated officers. The ability of militaries to sabotage and obstruct the implementation of government directives in other policy fields is the major consideration behind such compromises. Once again, Indonesia has had significant difficulties in this area during the transition.

The fourth area that militaries traditionally attempt to participate in or establish control over is the socio-cultural sector. Civil society and its socio-cultural expressions, including the media, are important elements in stabilizing or undermining political structures, and their control and manipulation is a major component of regime maintenance in authoritarian states. Not only does military surveillance of cultural activities dampen criticism of the regime, but the armed forces may also initiate or support religious events, literary works, ideological indoctrination courses, theatre plays, media features, or concerts aiming to influence public opinion on policy issues in general or the role of the military in particular. The socio-cultural sector is in fact the most difficult to establish definite control over, and the decline of authoritarian regimes often begins with subtle manoeuvres by protagonists of cultural life to voice the very opposition towards the government that formal institutions were unable to express. Intellectuals, writers, artists, and musicians have often had a larger impact on the fate of regimes than politicians, either in destabilizing or legitimizing them (Bodden 1999, pp. 155–56). The interaction of the armed forces with civil society and the cultural sphere is often overlooked in studies on civil-military relations, with the main focus remaining on state institutions and military participation in them. The widened concept of democratic control of the armed forces, however, acknowledges the importance of non-political actors in the civil-military equation, and looks critically at how socio-cultural factors either catalyze democratic consolidation, or on the contrary, help the armed forces in preserving their privileges.

## TYPOLOGICAL MODELS OF MILITARY INTERVENTION

After having identified the areas in which military intervention occurs, it is important to describe the various typological models that have dominated the discourse on civil-military relations in authoritarian states so far.[6] Although these models are less precise in analysing civil-military dynamics in transitional states, they are helpful in picturing the level of military intervention a particular state had to overcome when the democratic transition began.

The most extreme form of military intervention in politics has been termed as "praetorian" rule. In praetorian models of governance, the military is the main component of the regime, and all other forces and institutions are under its control. Executive, legislature, and judiciary are either directly occupied by members of the armed forces or by loyalist civilians. Praetorian regimes often rule under emergency regulations or legislation passed under their supervision. Many of the Latin American and African states that were the focus of the classic studies on military interventionism in the 1950s were countries under praetorian rule. In the 1970s and 1980s, South Korea and Bangladesh had praetorian regimes, and Burma still falls under this category today. A second model is that of "participant-ruler", describing countries with direct military participation in, but not full control of, government bodies. The armed forces may form alliances with or serve the interests of a particular civilian elite, and receive government participation and control over security policies in return. The Philippines under Marcos, Thailand for much of the 1980s, and the majority of communist states were examples of this type of state-military relations. Communist leaders in particular may have calculated that the inclusion of the military in governance would not only bind the armed forces to the ruling elite and neutralize the potential for opposition, but also transform the military into one of the main pillars of the regime.

In the model of "guardian" rule, on the other hand, militaries do not necessarily have to participate in or dominate the government. They have enough institutional powers to judge the performance of civilian governments and remove them if deemed necessary. Such militaries define themselves as protectors of national values and goals, whether it is to preserve the territorial integrity of the state or the adherence to a specific national ideology. Turkey has been a classic example of the guardian model, with the military now staying out of most government institutions, but still powerful enough to successfully challenge any government viewed as violating the principles of secularism or not doing enough to contain the Kurdish threat to Turkey's borders.[7] In contrast to this, the "referee" model describes the role of militaries in countries with high levels of political competition, where the armed forces act as "king-makers". The backing by the military may decide the power struggle in favour of a certain group, and the top brass will receive concessions for its support. Such concessions can take the form of regime participation or other privileges serving the military's interests. Of particular importance in this model are the non-political powers possessed by militaries, whether based on coercion or collective acknowledgement by civilian forces. The notion of the military as a "referee" suggests, however, that the armed forces are a neutral mediator in political conflict, which is rarely the case. Huntington therefore introduced the concept of a "praetorian society", in which no single force is able to exercise full authority, including the military.

Most countries with long histories of military intervention have found themselves changing from one model into another at various stages of their development. Arguably, Indonesia went through all four paradigms since the 1950s. The role of the armed forces under parliamentary democracy conforms to the guardian model as the military helped to terminate the democratic system amidst threats to Indonesia's territorial integrity. During the Sukarno regime of 1959–65, the armed forces were participant-rulers, sharing power with the president and confronting the rising influence of the communists. The army intervened in 1965, establishing a praetorian regime with military control of all state institutions. By the early 1990s, however, the increasing stake of civilian elements in the New Order reduced the military's role in state institutions again to that of a participant-ruler. The armed forces were increasingly critical of the more sultanistic aspects of the president's rule,[8] but withdrew their support only after a public uprising had cornered him. The "referee model", finally, is able to describe some phenomena of the early post-Suharto transition. Especially in the 1999–2001 period, the armed forces were able to position themselves as a power broker between the competing civilian forces, gaining substantial concessions in return. The model is less suitable, however, to grasp the dynamics of later stages of the transitional process. It is difficult to argue, for example, that the military today still has the power to engineer the appointment of governments and influence key policies, particularly since Yudhoyono's direct election in 2004 and the subsequent resolution of the Aceh conflict. While no longer possessing "veto powers", however, the armed forces have been able to cling on to several of their institutional privileges, including *de facto* legal impunity from legal investigations, the territorial command structure, and the system of military self-financing. Evidently, the existing models for military intervention are poorly equipped to explain these dynamics of post-authoritarian transitions.

## ANALYTICAL EXPLANATIONS FOR MILITARY INTERVENTION

The various models of military intervention in politics have been linked to different sets of explanations. The question why some militaries intervene in politics and others do not, and which factors influence the level of intervention, has been the focus of numerous case studies and theoretical discourses. Three approaches stand out as the most prominent ones, and they are discussed shortly in this section: first, the classic Huntingtonian notion of professional militaries versus non-professional ones; second, the reference to internal and external threats as a major determinant of military engagement; and third, the linkage between the functionality and legitimacy of civilian institutions on the one hand and the intensity of military involvement on the other.

The proposition of a nexus between military professionalism and the involvement of the armed forces in politics has been challenged by new theories and contradicting evidence, but it remains a prominent school of thought in the study of civil-military relations. Huntington asserted that a professional military is certain to maintain its neutrality and isolate itself from the temptations of political interference. Militaries that concentrate on the development of technical expertise and the fulfilment of their institutional responsibilities, said Huntington (1957), are very likely to obey policy decisions made by civilian authorities. Professional militaries allow for what Huntington (1957, p. 121) calls "objective civilian control", a concept that in its substance comes close to what has been introduced above as "democratic control" of the armed forces, but lacks its procedural understanding. Unprofessional militaries, i.e. those that do not focus on skills development, technological innovations, and improvement of strategic thinking, are prone to become interested in practical politics. David Shambaugh (2002, p. 13), commenting on the reform process of the Chinese PLA (People's Liberation Army), used Huntington's theory to describe the depoliticization of the PLA in the second half of the 1990s:

Senior PLA officers ... are now promoted based on meritocratic and professional criteria, while political consciousness and activism account for little. The officer corps is thus becoming increasingly professional, in classic Huntingtonian terms.... The military's mission today is almost exclusively external, to protect national security, rather than internal security. The role of ideology is virtually nil, and political work has declined substantially....

Huntington's model continues to be influential in the field of foreign military assistance to countries in transition, where many donors believe that professionalization of the armed forces is a precondition for establishing democratic control. Accordingly, large parts of the available funds are being allocated for training officers in classic military courses, with the expectation that this may instil sufficient levels of interest in their military profession and, at the same time, reduce their desire to intervene in politics.

The problem with Huntington's assertion lies, of course, in its definition of "professionalism". The concept of "professionalism" does not exclude the possibility that militaries acquire professional skills that may encourage intervention in politics. Stepan's notion of a "new professionalism" captures this possibility, and identifies internal security and national development as the two areas in which militaries have increased their professional skills, driving them into the political arena (Stepan 1986; Danopoulos 2002). Stepan argued that the expansion of military professionalism into areas of non-military expertise, such as economic management and community development, has increased the dependence of civilians on the advice of the armed forces in various fields of governance. In addition, a series of case studies has also questioned Huntington's findings. In his study on the armed forces of Pakistan, Pervaiz Iqbal Cheema (2002, p. 157) maintained that the military "played a very important role in the Pakistani polity and no significant decision was taken, in domestic or security affairs, without the military's input". Yet he also concluded that the armed forces are "disciplined and well-trained" (Cheema 2002, p. xiii). Military professionalism in praetorian states? The majority of academic research suggests that such cases exist, casting doubt on the very linkage between professionalism and levels of military intervention that forms the essence of Huntington's model.

Besides the issue of professionalism, the discussion on the causes of military intervention in politics has concentrated on internal and external threat levels in particular states. While there is agreement that high levels of internal threat (political conflict, social inequalities, ethnic rivalries, separatism, lawlessness) lead to increased political intervention of the armed forces, the literature remains divided on the consequences of high levels of external threat (wars, international terrorism, piracy). Some, like the proponents of the "garrison state", have argued that the constant threat of war may lead to the institutionalization of the military's role in politics (Lasswell 1941). Others, such as Andreski (1954), have maintained exactly the opposite. They have explained that external threats keep militaries occupied and, therefore, out of politics. Hunter (1996), writing on civil-military relations in Latin America, even asserted that deepening the engagement of post-authoritarian militaries in external defence cooperation helped to reduce their political ambitions. Further developing this argument, Michael Desch (1999) introduced a model that analyses the interplay between external and internal threats on the one hand and the quality of "civilian" control of the military on the other. He suggested that high levels of external threat and low levels of internal threat result in "stronger" civilian control; high levels of external threat and high levels of internal threat lead to "poor" civilian control; low levels of external threat and high levels of internal threat produce the "worst" civilian control; and low levels of external threat and low levels of internal threat are likely to see "mixed" civilian control. Desch's theory, particularly its proposition that low levels of internal conflict produce stronger civilian control, will be significant for the discussion of Indonesia's civil-military relations after the successful implementation of the Aceh peace agreement in 2005.

Theories that link the levels of internal and external threat with the extent of military intervention in politics are of significant descriptive value, but they have one crucial analytical weakness. They tend to view levels of threat as objective facts, established by scientific means and under conditions of political neutrality. The reality is, of course, quite different. There is sufficient evidence that militaries have not only created public perceptions of threat levels that consolidated their political positions, but have also actively engineered conflict situations that increased the levels of threat, both internally and externally. Threat levels are part of the political discourse within societies, and their interpretations are therefore informed by the vested interests of particular groups and institutions (Mares 1998, p. 9). Militaries may give their assessments of threat levels not only based on objective facts, but also from the perspective of how such an analysis can generate additional funding and other institutional privileges for the armed forces. In the same context, militaries may stimulate, create, or prolong conflicts, particularly in the domestic arena, if such acts of manipulation are deemed favourable to their interests. In Indonesia, many observers have argued that while the secessionist movements in Aceh (before 2005) and Papua have constituted serious threats to the state, their operations have been partly encouraged by elements of the military in order to highlight its indispensability as the guardian of national unity. This problem of manipulability exposes threat level theories to another analytical question: what has made militaries in a small number of states so powerful that they can control the public perception of threat levels, and even create conflict situations to increase them? With this, the threat level theories may arrive back at the very question that they claimed to answer.

A third school of thought has highlighted the quality of civilian state institutions as an important factor in determining the extent of military involvement in politics. Finer (2003, pp. 86–89) laid the grounds for this model by asserting that countries with a "developed political culture" are more likely to see strong civilian control over the military than those with low levels of societal respect for the governmental and legal institutions of the state.[9] Militaries tend to seek political participation, and ultimately control, if state institutions lack the legitimacy and functional strength to run effective and stable administrations. In this view, the failure of civilian governments to maintain political stability, manage security threats, deliver economic growth, and uphold law and order has "forced" militaries to intervene. However, Finer's argument carries the risk of being tautological: military non-intervention does not only result from a developed political culture, it is in fact one of the preconditions for the latter to emerge in the first place. The importance of Finer's theory, therefore, is less based on its explanatory strength than its ability to shift the analytical emphasis from the military-focused professionalism and threat-level theories to the discussion of political culture. For Finer, the key to understanding the reasons for involvement of the armed forces in politics lies as much in society as in the institutional interests of the military.

In this context, several authors have looked at levels of economic development as indicators for the likelihood of military intervention.[10] Proponents of development-based theories have argued that higher levels of economic development produce new political actors with increased demands for participation in state institutions, challenging traditional players such as the bureaucratic elite, large business corporations, and the military. For example, the emergence of a new middle class in Asia in the late 1980s has been credited with the removal of the military from power in South Korea and Thailand. There, economically inspired demands for free markets, eradication of corruption, abolition of monopolies, and the impartiality of the legal system formed the conceptual core of the oppositional movements.

As one observer of Thai politics noted, the 1992 uprising was "not so much pro-democracy, as it is often claimed, but rather a movement opposed to the possibility of a new alliance of the military and business leading to a dictatorship" (Samudavanija 1997, p. 63). There are more complex examples, however. The military in Indonesia did not only survive three decades of economic growth without major challenges to its privileged position, but has drawn its political legitimacy from it. It was precisely when the economic boom ended, and the new middle class was thrown into crisis, that the armed forces had to accept Suharto's departure and the subsequent democratic reforms. It appears, therefore, that it is not always economic development as such that erodes military interference in politics. Rather, it is often a sudden downturn after long periods of growth that increases the likelihood of opposition by the middle class to the very authoritarian rulers that facilitated its rise.

The theories that focus on society, the economy, and institutions of the state as key indicators for military interventions in politics have considerable advantages over the models based on military professionalism and the various levels of threat. They establish an important (and so far missing) link between the quality of governance as a whole and the political intervention opportunities of militaries, and analyse the issue of civil-military relations in the wider institutional framework of the state. Substantial weaknesses remain, however. To begin with, the issue of weak civilian institutions cannot be debated in a political vacuum. Militaries may have the power to weaken institutions of the state in order to prepare their own rise to power. This is particularly relevant for countries in which political institutions are in an early stage of their development and thus vulnerable to outside interference. Daniel Lev (1994, p. 39), for example, has argued that the disintegration of Indonesia's parliamentary democracy in the late 1950s was the result of political manoeuvring by the army: "Why? In part because it could, but also because it had compelling interests in a quite different political system." Conceptually, the identification of weak civilian institutions as a factor in motivating military intervention in politics raises new questions related to the causes for such weaknesses, and the institutional interests of the military may well be part of the answer. A second problem is the omission of international factors. The shifts in policy priorities after the Cold War, the role of international donors, and the increased importance of human rights since the 1990s have, however limited in scale, influenced the political aspirations of militaries in developing states. While insufficient to form a theoretical model on their own, arguments centring around international factors have to be taken into account when explaining the elements that facilitate political involvement of militaries or force them to disengage.

## THE FALL OF MILITARY REGIMES: FACTORS AND CONTEXTS

The discussion of the causes of political interference by militaries leads into the debate about their "extrusion" (i.e., their departure) from politics. Consequently, this section will examine the reasons for the disintegration of military-backed or military-dominated regimes, and build analytical bridges to the study of civil-military relations in transitional states.

Some of the theories developed to explain the downfall of military regimes deal specifically with the unsustainable aspects of military rule, while others propose more general explanations for the end of authoritarian governments. The notion of an inherent non-sustainability of military rule has traditionally been based on the inability of the armed forces to explain their political engagement beyond the short-term legitimacy of emergency intervention (Alagappa 2001*b*, pp. 50–51). Militaries tend to intervene in times of political and economic crisis, claiming that civilian authorities have failed to protect the interests of the state. Such an intervention may be popular for as long as the emergency persists, but becomes problematic once stability is restored and the role of the military is institutionalized. Some militaries can argue that their institutional engagement is necessary to prevent the reoccurrence of the very emergency situation that provoked it to intervene, but such situational frameworks of legitimacy are unlikely to sustain military rule for a longer period of time. Accordingly, some militaries have expanded their basis of legitimacy to include national development, the defence of particular ideologies or, more generally, the maintenance of national unity. The link between military legitimacy and the achievement of certain goals, however, has thrown the armed forces into what Huntington called a "performance dilemma". If they fail to achieve their self-set targets, societies are likely to seek a quick end to military rule; if, on the other hand, the goals are achieved, the reasons for continued military intervention may be questioned as well. Sustained economic growth, the unchallenged dominance of a particular ideology, or the permanent neutralization of threats to national unity remove not only the emergency context under which militaries came to power, but also erode their claim to institutionalized rule. Theories of disintegrating military regimes have therefore concentrated on the linear process of emergency intervention, expansion of legitimacy claims, and subsequent erosion of the regime by either performance failures or, on the contrary, the long-term consequences of its successes. This erosion can facilitate a change of regime, and in some cases initiate post-authoritarian transition.

One important factor in limiting the lifespan of military regimes is the growing distance between those officers who staged the initial emergency intervention and assumed executive powers of government, and those who are in charge of the day-to-day management of the armed forces. In addition to these two major factions, Stepan (1988, p. 30) emphasized the importance of military intelligence operators, or the "security community", as a third group with specific interests. Military leaders in positions of political power may, like Indonesia's Suharto, try to create factionalism within the armed forces in order to prevent a challenge to their rule. These efforts of weakening potential rivals for political power are closely related to the issue of succession (Brooks 1998, p. 20). Only very few military regimes have seen non-violent changes in leadership, with coups and internal elimination of competitors the most common way of transferring governmental authority. The ouster and arrest of Burmese Prime Minister Khin Nyunt in October 2004, for example, illustrated the non-institutional character of succession in military-dominated states. Similarly, Thailand has seen a series of coups within its military regimes between the 1930s and the early 1990s, and rumours of a counter-coup from within the armed forces also circulated widely after their most recent overthrow of a civilian government in September 2006. It was partly this prospect of being violently deposed and persecuted that has discouraged military-backed rulers like Suharto from addressing the issue of succession at all. Instead, they tended to postpone the topic for so long that society began to turn not only against them, but against the system of military-based governance itself.

While there are some military-specific aspects in the downfall of regimes controlled or backed by the armed forces, most of the factors that lead to the erosion of such polities can be applied to other forms of authoritarian rule as well. Alagappa (2001b, p. 53) divided the possible explanations for the breakdown of authoritarian governments "into two categories: international factors (war, conquest, changes in the global material and normative structure, changes in the global economy, changes in the foreign policy of major powers), and domestic factors (economic crisis, loss of legitimacy, conflict within the ruling bloc, growing public opposition, civil war, internal conflict)". Apart from very obvious cases where regimes are overthrown by external military intervention (such as the U.S.-led invasion of Iraq and subsequent removal of Saddam Hussein from power), there seem to be very few cases in which international factors played the lead role in bringing authoritarian reigns to an end.[11] International economic crises, multinational alliances, and development aid may, in fact, stimulate and sustain authoritarian interventions as much as they can help remove autocratic regimes. The role of international donors in the Indonesian crisis of 1998 is a case in point: while the credits extended by the International Monetary Fund (IMF) had the potential of saving Suharto's rule, it was the president's mishandling of the aid package that fuelled opposition to the continuation of his government. It appears, therefore, that the major causes of the disintegration of authoritarian regimes lie in the domestic area. Regimes become vulnerable if they are no longer able to serve the interests of the societal groups that originally benefited from authoritarian rule, triggering a series of phenomena that ultimately cause the regime to fall: internal splits within the elite, the revitalization of opposition groups through new power configurations, societal protest against the inefficiency of government, and conflicts within the military. While all these developments take place within an international context, and may well be influenced by it, they follow the inherently domestic logic of the contested regime and the opposing forces it has produced.

As demonstrated in the course of this introduction, the literature on civil-military relations has been expansive on the areas in which militaries seek intervention; on the various models of military participation in politics; on the reasons that cause some militaries to intervene and others to stay disengaged; and, finally, on the explanations for the downfall of military regimes. Among the presented theoretical approaches and models, however, there were very few that could capture the dynamics of the role militaries play in post-authoritarian states. The classic categorizations of military intervention (praetorian, participant-ruler, guardian, referee) have proven too general to describe the complexity of civil-military interactions in transitional states, and the various reasons linked to them (lack of professionalism, internal and external threat levels, quality of state institutions) are limited in their scope and explanatory power. The theories on the fall of military regimes, on the other hand, do not extend to the residual powers the armed forces may use in post-authoritarian transitions, or the way they may assimilate to new democratic frameworks. According to Robin Luckham (2003, p. 11), the fluid contexts of political transitions have created "new problems for analysis, including how to decipher underlying shifts in military power relations when these are no longer flagged by open military intervention". The following section will, therefore, look at the very limited number of studies that have attempted to describe the nuances of civil-military relations in transitional states, and will then discuss a recently developed model that may be of help to investigate the subject of this study, the civil-military relations in post-Suharto Indonesia.

## MILITARIES IN TRANSITIONAL STATES

Most of the recent case studies on civil-military relations in post-authoritarian states have used classic models in order to explain the complexities of new contexts. This leads to problems in connecting the theoretical model with the empirical material, and may even result in inconsistencies between the model-based argument and narrative-based conclusion. Herbert C. Huser's study on civil-military relations in Argentina, for example, uses the Finerian model of "political culture" to explain the military's exit from politics after 1983. Using Finer's notion of legitimacy as the major element of a developed political culture, Huser (2002, p. 23) maintained that

> Argentine politics may be characterized as different sources of legitimacy being advanced, simultaneously and exclusively, by groups in contest. In other words, democracy is not a given in the political culture, and a single rule of legitimacy does not apply; fragmented legitimacy and conflicts are apparent.

In Finer's model, such a diversity of competing legitimacies, reflected in a lack of respect for the existing institutions, would lead to increased levels of military intervention. Yet Huser (2002, p. 196) concluded that "the historical role of the military as an autonomous political contender appears to have run its course, as have the contests between the military and the civilian government for legitimate political authority". Apparently, the evolution of civil-military relations in post-authoritarian Argentina was much more complex than Finer's model would suggest; Huser described the persistence of important differences between the civilian forces over the legitimacy of the political framework, but at the same time reported substantial progress in depoliticizing the armed forces. This disconnect between theoretical assumption and the presented material points to the ineffectiveness of classic models in capturing the nuances of developments in transitional states.

Other authors have approached the problem of civil-military relations in post-authoritarian states in a very normative way. They identify democratic control of the armed forces as a substantial element of successful democratic transitions, and describe the conditions countries have to fulfil to achieve this goal (Fitch 2001, pp. 61–63). These conditions read like the reversed catalogue of the reasons classically given for military intervention: empowerment of civilian institutions of the state, reducing the use of coercion in managing political conflicts, installing democratic paradigms into the mindset of the officer corps, professionalization of the armed forces and their concentration on external defence matters, restructuring of the security sector, and isolation of the old top brass from the political process. There is some disagreement about the importance of reform initiatives taken in the early phase of the transition. O'Donnell and Schmitter have argued that the process of reforming the military is a generational project, and that initial institutional changes may have only limited impact. Aguero (1995, p. 39), on the other hand, has asserted that "the initial conditions are critical in shaping the first transition outcome". Among others, he named civilian control over the reform agenda as a crucial element of the transitional process. The widely held view that democratic transitions in general and establishment of democratic control of the armed forces in particular are long-term developments likely to proceed for decades, has discouraged most observers from analysing the early period of the transition in much detail. This study will argue that many of Aguero's "initial conditions" are determined by the character of the regime change from authoritarian rule to the new government, as well as by developments in the early days of the democratic era when the political landscape takes shape. This focus will help to identify the extent to which the normative conditions for initiating democratic control of the armed forces were addressed at an early stage, and where delays and omissions have caused serious problems in later phases of the transition.

Besides the concentration on classic models and the proposition of normative conditions, another prominent approach has been the analysis of transitions as interplays of competing political and economic interests. Such a model, which authors such as David Pion-Berlin (2001, p. 18) have called a theory of "strategic action", allows for a high extent of analytical flexibility, and calls for case studies to explain the specific situations of particular countries. The downside of this approach is, of course, that it is largely self-evident. There is little doubt that the scale and the outcome of the competition between interest groups over political privileges and economic resources have a major impact on transitional processes, including on the evolution of post-authoritarian civil-military relations. The strength of this model, therefore, lies more in its ability to concentrate its analytical focus on what it views as the primary source of conflict in transitions and draw attention away from secondary factors such as conflicting value systems and long-term structural change. With its emphasis on politico-economic conflicts between key actors, the interest-based approach is less an explanatory theory than a methodological guideline for the description of particular transitions.

It is interesting to note that even proponents of structuralist explanations of democratic transition, while rejecting the interest-based model as narrow and ignorant of global dynamics of change, tend to describe the conflicts in transitional states as power struggles between old elites and new political forces, between "predatory" and "neo-liberal" interests. Richard Robison (2002, p. 95), for example, criticized the interest-based approach as the product of "rational choice theorists" who explain democratic transitions as processes "driven by the rational calculations of rising and declining elites facing rising costs of suppressing opponents and forced to seek a new political format that, while second best, is preferable to mutual destruction". His own analysis of the Indonesian transition, however, describes the post-1998 events as "the struggle to shape the institutions that define the new democracy", involving "alliances and coalitions of state power and social interest" connected to the Suharto regime on the one hand and the "reformist camp" on the other (Robison 2002, p. 93). While contextualised in a framework of capitalist expansion, it appears that even structuralist approaches like Robison's rely heavily on the analysis of competing interest groups to make their case.

The multitude of theoretical approaches introduced so far has indicated that particular aspects of some models may be helpful in capturing the dynamics of civil-military relations in post-authoritarian states. Several authors have tried, therefore, to combine the various theories into a single model that can address the specific conditions of democratic transitions, and explain why some civil-military reform projects succeed while others run into serious obstacles. Alagappa (2001b, p. 29), for example, has amalgamated the most influential writings on civil-military relations into one inclusive "analytical framework". The downside of such eclectic models is their vagueness and generality. Forced into a united theoretical approach, most of its components lose their sharp analytical edge and explanatory power. Accordingly, the following section discusses one model that tries to integrate diverse aspects of the existing civil-military literature without insisting on their analytical combination. Andrew Cottey, Tim Edmunds, and Anthony Forster, writing comparatively on civil-military relations in post-authoritarian transitions in Eastern Europe and the former Soviet republics of Central Asia, have designed a model that appears to be well equipped to explain the fluid state of civil-military relations in post-Suharto Indonesia.

# CRITIQUE: THE TWO-GENERATION MODEL

The model developed by Cottey, Edmunds, and Forster integrates normative and empirical elements into one comprehensive framework of gradually evolving civil-military relations in transitional states. They recognize the establishment of democratic control over the armed forces as a crucial component of democratic consolidation, and assert that the academic discourse on such issues has been misguided by its narrow focus on the circumstances, traditions, and histories of Western states (Cottey, Edmunds, and Forster 2001, p. 2). Traditional theories of civil-military relations developed in the West have often stressed the likelihood of the armed forces seizing political power, instead of explaining the wide spectrum of intervention levels between the extremes of democratic control and praetorian rule. Not only have most Western models proven ineffective in capturing the dynamics of civil-military relations in post-authoritarian contexts, they have already moved on to paradigms of a "post-modern military". Analysts such as Charles Moskos have characterized the post-modern military by its increasing "interpenetrability" between civilian and military spheres; its internal modernization in terms of gender equality and acceptance of different sexual orientations; its involvement in non-traditional operations such as peacekeeping; and its integration into supra- or multinational command structures (Moskos, Williams, and Segal 2000, pp. 6–9). Obviously, such models have little relevance for transitional states struggling to build workable institutions of governance and reduce military intervention in politics. Cottey et al. tried to address the ineffectiveness of both traditional theories and post-modern models by developing an approach that fits the political circumstances of post-authoritarian transitions, and also allows for sufficient levels of analytical flexibility to establish differences between particular countries.

The explanatory focus of the model is directed towards security sector governance, a process of multi-level interactions through which democratic control of the armed forces is exercised. This approach investigates the relationship between state institutions (executive, legislature, bureaucracy), the security forces (armed forces, paramilitary forces, police, state-legitimized armed formations), and civil society — defined by Linz and Stepan (1996, pp. 7–8) as the arena in which "self-organizing groups, movements, and individuals, relatively autonomous from the state, attempt to articulate values, create associations and solidarities, and advance their interests". The quality of this relationship determines whether countries are successful in their attempts to establish democratic control over the armed forces, or whether problematic civil-military interactions become obstacles to further democratic consolidation. Specific indicators are the extent to which the democratically legitimized executive is able to formulate and implement policy decisions on foreign relations, the deployment and use of force, and defence management; the effectiveness of parliamentary oversight of the armed forces; and the involvement of civil society groups with expertise in defence and security affairs (which make up what Cottey et al. call the "non-governmental security community") in the formulation of defence policy.

The most significant contribution of the Cottey et al. model to the debate on civil-military relations in post-authoritarian states is the introduction of a two-generation model of reform phases in democratic transitions. According to Cottey et al., most countries that have initiated democratic reform after long periods of military-backed, authoritarian rule begin the transitional process with changes to their institutional framework: abolition of security institutions associated with the old regime, establishment of new civilian bodies to control the armed forces, changes to the command system, and empowerment of parliament. This first phase of institutional measures is what Cottey et al. (2001, p. 5) called the "first generation" of civil-military reforms. The first generation of reforms is important for the dismantling of old power structures as well as for the definition of what the end goal of the democratic transition should be. It is insufficient, however, to address capacity problems of the newly created institutions, and to control residual powers the armed forces may be able to exercise through non-institutional political networks (Betz 2003, p. 2). Political institutions, as well as civil society groups, can only function properly if they have the capacity to fulfil their tasks. Lack of expertise, experience, funds, infrastructure, supporting staff, technology, and information can cause even highly sophisticated institutional frameworks to collapse or simply become dysfunctional.

Accordingly, the "second generation" of reforms is crucial. The second generation consolidates the frameworks created in the first; it provides the democratic substance to the structures established by laws and political decisions. The challenge of the second-generation reforms is centred around building capacity of both state institutions and civil society, and it concerns three main areas: first, the "development of working mechanisms for the implementation and oversight of defence policy". Second, the establishment of "effective systems of security sector governance, which allows a country's defence and security requirements to be adequately assessed, reassessed, and addressed". And third, "the engagement of 'civil society' as a core component of oversight and accountability in defence and security matters" (Cottey, Edmunds, and Forster 2001, p. 5).

Cottey, Edmunds, and Forster used their two-generation model to evaluate processes of civil-military reform in numerous states of Eastern Europe and Central Asia, most of which had highly politicized armed forces during decades of communist rule. Their assessment of the reform processes concludes that despite strong traditions of military praetorianism in most of the investigated countries, and despite the chaos of post-communist transition, none of the states has seen the recurrence of military rule. However, the experiences of the researched states with their military reform projects have been highly diverse, ranging from considerable successes to failure to launch reform initiatives at all. Cottey et al. have developed four categories of countries, each defining the position of a particular state on the two-generation scale of civil-military reforms.[12] The first group consists of states that have largely addressed the first-generation agenda, but in some cases have experienced problems in implementing second-generation reforms. In their research, Cottey et al. have identified eleven states that belong to this group, among them Bulgaria, Estonia, the Czech Republic, and Hungary. The second type is characterized by countries that have faced persistent problems with the first-generation agenda, although some civil-military reforms have been initiated. This group contains two countries: Russia and the Ukraine. The third group of countries is made up of states that have not even seen first-generation measures of reforms. There are seven countries in this group, including Turkmenistan and Belarus. The fourth category, finally, describes states that have initiated both first and second-generation reform steps but were too weak to sustain them, leading to either stagnation or collapse of the reform process. This group consists of seven states, among them Armenia, Georgia, and Tajikistan.

In order to explain why some countries have progressed further than others in the process of civil-military reforms, Cottey et al. (2002, pp. 10–14) have developed five explanatory propositions: first, the historical legacy of military engagement in politics under previous regimes can influence the pace and scope of military reform in post-authoritarian transitions. While transitions are not predetermined by historical contexts of the preceding regime, the persistence of its power structures may play an important role in the emerging democratic polity. Second, the state of civil-military relations is a reflection of the democratization process as a whole. Countries in which alternatives to liberal democracy have largely been delegitimized have seen more significant moves towards establishing democratic control over the armed forces than states in which the principles of political organization are still contested. Third, international incentives have had a major impact on the willingness of states to pursue civil-military reforms. The majority of

Central and Eastern European countries have established democratic control over their armed forces as a precondition for acceptance into NATO and the European Union. The economic and political advantages offered by membership in these multinational associations have even convinced the more conservative militaries in the region to comply with the normative standards of the organizations they sought to enter. Fourth, the depth of domestic institutional reform in the security sector can be an important factor for the state of civil-military relations. Consolidated institutional reforms "reduce the vulnerability of civil-military relations towards the vagaries of domestic political change" (Cottey, Edmunds, and Forster 2000, p. 3), while artificially implemented reforms are unlikely to be sustainable over longer periods of time. Fifth, specific "military cultures" can support or obstruct the efforts of establishing democratic control. In this regard, the level of professionalism (understood as "the extent to which the military view their core mission as to undertake in a professional manner the military tasks defined for them by civilian political leaders")[13] is of crucial importance.

The Cottey et al. model leads to important insights regarding the case of Indonesia. To begin with, it delivers an explanatory framework for the preliminary analysis that despite a series of institutional reforms, Indonesia's armed forces have retained considerable privileges that have made it difficult for the state to establish effective democratic control. The model suggests that Indonesia has experienced serious difficulties in completing the first-generation reforms and/or initiating second-generation measures. The two-generation categorization allows for a much more precise identification of Indonesia's place in the comparative scale of countries with transitional civil-military relations than the traditional models of praetorian, participant-ruler, guardian, and referee levels of military intervention. In addition, it also points to the wider context of democratization in Indonesia, and requires the study of the correlation between institutional military reform and the political discourse on competing models of governance. Such a focus may help to discover the extent to which political disputes between major political forces have obstructed the process of institutional military reform and, therefore, delayed its second-generation consolidation. Furthermore, the model highlights the absence of international affiliations and alliances that could have forced Indonesia to pursue military reforms faster and with more depth. Finally, the emphasis on institutional reform questions the degree to which the structures of Indonesia's security sector were reformed after 1998. In this context, the persistence of the entrenched territorial command structure suggests that the process of institutional reform remains incomplete.

Despite its explanatory advantages over other models of civil-military relations, the Cottey et al. approach shares one fundamental weakness with most of its counterparts: it says very little about the factors that obstruct the empowerment of civilians to control the security sector. Cottey et al. tended to focus on the lack of technical expertise and infrastructure, and pay only secondary attention to the dynamics of post-authoritarian power struggles among civilian forces. In a rather cursory manner, they concede that there is significant "willingness of some civilian elites to try and draw the armed forces (or elements of the armed forces) into politics in order to gain their support in what are primarily civilian, domestic political conflicts" (Cottey, Edmunds, and Forster 2001, p. 4). This is an important assessment, and deserves further analysis. In his study on the Nigerian military, 'Emeka Nwagwu (2002, p. 73) focused on tribalism and regional conflicts as the main reasons for military intervention in African politics. Similarly, Indonesia's social, religious, and political landscape is a complicated web of long-standing alliances and rivalries, with the conflict over the role of Islam in politics standing out as one of the primary sources of tension in the civilian sphere. In fact, the impact of inter-civilian disputes on the pace and quality of civil-military reforms appears to be one of the most important explanatory components of the two-generation model, and should have been integrated into the catalogue of causes for successful, failed, or stalled transitions. Accordingly, while the Cottey, Edmunds, and Forster model covers a wide range of analytical indicators and explanatory propositions, it provides ample opportunities for improvements, additions, and alterations. The aim of this book is, therefore, not only to test existing models in the context of civil-military relations in post-authoritarian Indonesia, but also to expand such theories with the lessons learnt from the Indonesian case. This expectation is reflected in the structure of the book.

## THE STRUCTURE OF THIS BOOK

As indicated earlier, the review of the scholarly literature on civil-military relations has led to important insights that consequently determined the structure of this book. First and foremost, the discussion above demonstrated that neither Huntington's focus on military professionalism nor Finer's emphasis on political culture and the quality of civilian governance are — as isolated analytical approaches — sufficient to explain the extent to which militaries engage in political affairs. In order to present a full picture of civil-military relations in transitional states, the analysis must take account of internal developments in the military *and* in civilian politics. Accordingly, this book divides its attention equally between military affairs and the dynamics within civilian groups, presenting parallel chapters that allow for in-depth analysis of both fields. In terms of civilian politics, this book stresses the impact of conflicts between key civilian constituencies on intervention opportunities of the armed forces in political affairs. It will show that whenever the level of intra-civilian conflict was high, democratic oversight the armed forces was weak. By contrast, when tensions between civilian groups declined, as they did in Indonesia after 2004, the quality of democratic control improved. In this context, I chose the controversy within the Muslim community over the role of Islam in political life as a case study to highlight general patterns of intra-civilian conflict in Indonesia. Historically, Muslims with secular-nationalist attitudes have been engaged in heated debates with more devout followers of the faith over the relationship between the state and religious affairs. Equally important, however, are divisions within the community of devout Muslims itself, with modernist and traditionalist groups split over doctrinal, social, and political aspects of their religion. These conflicts have stretched from the colonial period over parliamentary democracy and two authoritarian regimes to the current phase of democratic consolidation, making them suitable for a long-term study on the correlation between levels of civilian fragmentation and military engagement in politics.[14]

The second important conclusion drawn from the discussion of the existing scholarly literature for the structure of this book relates to the fluctuation in the quality of democratic control of the armed forces. If the effectiveness of oversight depends on the level of intra-civilian conflict and the overall stability of the civilian polity, we should expect significant variations in different phases of the transition. Indeed, Indonesia has seen highly diverse trends in civil-military relations under Presidents Habibie, Wahid, Megawati, and Yudhoyono, reflecting both their individual approaches to the military and different dynamics in civilian affairs. Thus in order to identify events and developments that caused these fluctuations in the process of military reform, a chronological approach is imperative. Based on this insight, the book is chronologically structured in four parts, with parallel chapters on military and Muslim affairs covering different periods in Indonesia's modern political history. Closely related to this, the academic discourse on civil-military relations in transitional states has pointed to the importance of historical legacies for the course of military reform under post-authoritarian rule. Cottey, Edmunds, and Forster asserted that in countries where military ideologies and power structures were imposed by historical coincidences and/or external force, their disintegration was fast and complete. The armed forces in such states found it easy to support post-authoritarian polities as their identification with the deposed power-holders was artificial. If, on the other hand, military dominance of political institutions was deeply entrenched in society, transitional processes were much more problematic. For that reason, the first part of this book discusses the historical legacies of military involvement in Indonesian politics and, parallel to that, the divisions within the civilian sphere that helped to sustain it.

The last key conclusion from the theoretical discussion that informed the structuring of this book is concerned with the impact of the character of regime change on transition outcomes. Aguero's emphasis on the "initial conditions" suggests that the analysis of events that marked the transfer of power from the *ancien régime* to the post-authoritarian polity is essential for the understanding of civil-military transitions. The second part of this book is therefore devoted to the discussion of the 1998 regime change in Indonesia. It shows that the roles played by the armed forces and key civilian groups during the political crisis of 1997 and 1998 assisted elements of the New Order to extend their influence into the post-authoritarian era and obstruct efforts for wider institutional reform in the early period of the transition. The chapters on historical legacies and the character of regime change subsequently provide the analytical and empirical background for the explanation of civil-military developments in the post-Suharto transition, which are covered in the third and fourth part of the book.

In summary, the four parts of the book, which comprise two chapters each, combine a historical approach with contemporary political analysis. The first part focuses on historical legacies that have had a profound impact on the state of Indonesian civil-military relations. Chapter 1 discusses the history of military politics, the structural entrenchment of the armed forces in society, and ideological developments within the officer corps. Chapter 2, for its part, highlights the divisions within Indonesia's Muslim community as one of the primary sources of conflict in the civilian political sphere. The chapter explains the religious, social, and political gap between secular-nationalist and devout Muslims on the one hand, and the conflicts between traditionalist and modernist Islam on the other. The second part of the study describes the regime change of 1998 and its repercussions for the civil-military transition after Suharto's fall. Chapter 3 argues that moderate elements in the armed forces helped to negotiate an intra-systemic transfer of power from Suharto to his deputy, avoiding a more radical break with the authoritarian past. The diverse attitudes of key civilian forces and figures towards the disintegrating regime are the subject of Chapter 4, with the main focus on the divisions between the largest Muslim groups. The inability of civilian elites to form a united

front against the regime and assume control of the government facilitated
the emergence of the student movement and popular resistance as the
main vehicles of opposition. The collapse of the regime amidst violence
and societal protest left a power vacuum that was filled by residual components of the New Order, with serious consequences for the democratic
transition.

The third part of the book discusses the dynamics of civil-military
relations in the post-authoritarian transition between 1998 and 2004.
Against this backdrop, Chapter 5 evaluates the process of military reform
in the early post-Suharto period in the context of its high levels of political
uncertainty. Subsequently, Chapter 6 maintains that in the early phase of the
transition, the intense rivalry between important Muslim leaders and their
constituencies offered the armed forces frequent opportunities to intervene
in the political process. Most importantly, TNI determined the outcome of
the 2001 fight over the Wahid presidency, which had involved the followers
of Indonesia's two largest Islamic organizations. Finally, the fourth part
concentrates on the period of democratic consolidation which began with
Yudhoyono's election in 2004. Chapter 7 argues that Yudhoyono's decision
to sideline conservative officers from the armed forces and settle the Aceh
conflict peacefully contributed to the improvement of civilian oversight
of the military after 2004. In the same vein, Chapter 8 explains the
interrelationship between the declining political tensions in the Muslim
community, the general stabilization of the civilian polity, and the
marginalization of the military from political affairs under Yudhoyono's
presidency. The conclusion then pulls the various narrative and analytical
tracks together, reflecting on the state of civil-military relations in Indonesia
ten years after Suharto's fall and pointing to the implications of the findings
of this book for the theoretical discourse on the role of militaries in political
transitions.

## Notes

1   Amien Rais at a public rally in Bandung, 5 June 1998, personal notes by the
    author.
2   "Amien Rais Pilih Wapres dari Kalangan TNI", *Kompas*, 13 September 2003.
3   The DPR is Indonesia's parliament, while the MPR is nominally the highest
    institutional authority in the country. Under the New Order, the MPR consisted
    of the members of the DPR, regional representatives, and functional groups.
    Every five years, it elected a president and vice-president, and issued policy
    directives for the government in the form of decrees and regulations that ranked

higher than the legislation passed by the DPR. As a result of the constitutional amendments adopted in 2002, however, the MPR has lost its electoral powers and its legislative authority. It now comprises the members of the DPR and the DPD (*Dewan Perwakilan Daerah*, Regional Representative Council), a senate-like body consisting of representatives from Indonesia's provinces. The post-2002 MPR only swears in the president elected directly by the people, and can be part of impeachment proceedings if initiated by the DPR.

4   This element of democratic control has been referred to as "horizontal control", as opposed to the "vertical control" exercised by formal state institutions (Born, Caparina, and Haltiner 2002, p. 11).

5   For theories that emphasize the corporate interests of the military, see Abrahamson (1972), Perlmutter (1977), and Alagappa (2001c).

6   The following typology of states with different levels of military intervention is largely based on Perlmutter (1977) and Nordlinger (1977).

7   Gareth Jenkings (2001, p. 84) has asserted that by "January 2001, the military continued to insist that the twin threats to Kemalism from Kurdish nationalism and radical Islam had been contained rather than defeated". In 2007, the Turkish military temporarily prevented the election of a devout Muslim as head of state, but could do nothing to stop his party from winning the subsequent parliamentary elections, which was widely interpreted as an act of popular defiance against the military.

8   Linz and Stepan (1996, pp. 52–53) defined sultanism as a form of government in which "there is high fusion by the ruler of the private and the public. The sultanistic polity becomes the personal domain of the sultan. In this domain there is no rule of law and there is low institutionalization." Linz and Stepan contrasted sultanistic rule with authoritarianism, in which "there may or may not be a rule of law, space for semi-opposition, or space for regime moderates who might establish links with opposition moderates...."

9   Larry Diamond (1994, pp. 7–8) has defined political culture, based on Finer's assumptions, as "a people's predominant beliefs, attitudes, values, ideals, sentiments, and evaluations about the political system of its country, and the role of the self in that system".

10  In some of his later works, Huntington (1996, p. 9), for example, has postulated a correlation between per capita income and the possibility of military coups. Countries with a per capita gross domestic product of US$3,000 or above are very unlikely to witness successful coups, while countries with per capita levels of below US$500 are extremely prone to such forms of military intervention.

11  Samuel Decalo (1998, p. 199), for example, doubts the effectiveness of the "economic deterrence of the West in case of military coups". While it helped in the short term to create some of Africa's "New Democracies", its failures are clearly "visible in the pattern of mutinies and attempted coups that have punctuated the rhythm of political life in the 1990s".

[12]  A summary of the country classifications can be found in Herd and Tracy (2006, pp. 552–53).

[13]  This definition is presented in Cottey, Edmunds, and Forster (2002, p. 14).

[14]  There are, of course, other important reasons for choosing Muslim groups as the main focus when studying conflicts in Indonesia's civilian realm. First, Islamic groups represent the largest segment of Indonesian society, both numerically and in terms of political significance. Consequently, the study of their interests, relationships, and conflicts will reflect general patterns of political interaction in Indonesia. Second, the discussion of Indonesia's civil-military affairs between 1998 and 2008 will point to the critical relevance of the Wahid presidency in the transitional process. Wahid's rise and fall was closely related to the factionalism and alliance-building between Islamic groups, and facilitated intervention opportunities for the armed forces that led to a consolidation of military interests under the Megawati presidency. Third, the study of intra-Islamic relationships and conflicts will inherently extend to other socio-political segments. The central position of Islamic forces in Indonesia's political landscape makes them a main target for the build-up of cross-constituency coalitions. In fact, Islamic forces and secular-nationalist groups have cooperated more often than Muslim-based groups among themselves. The role of secular-nationalist constituencies is, therefore, an integral part of any study of the relationship between forces of political Islam.

# PART ONE

# Historical Legacies, 1945–97

# 1

# DOCTRINE AND POWER
## Legacies of Indonesian Military Politics

Cottey, Edmunds, and Forster have identified the historical legacy of the armed forces, especially their relationship with the previous regime, as one of the main factors determining the quality of post-authoritarian civil-military relations. This legacy is particularly relevant for states in which controversial debates about the military's past continue throughout the transition. Patricio Silva (2001, pp. 1–2), writing on South America, asserted that

> deep divisions between the military and the civilian world remain. The clearest expression of this lies in the existence of two conflicting and mutually excluding readings about the recent authoritarian past. On the one hand, the military and their civilian supporters in countries like Argentina, Uruguay and Chile argue that the armed forces actually saved their nations from complete chaos and disintegration. On the other, the left and human rights organizations blame the armed forces for having destroyed the old democratic system and for the systematic use of state terrorism against their opponents. The passing of time has definitely not reduced the enormous breach between these two interpretations.

Similar tensions exist in contemporary Indonesia. There are five aspects of TNI's historical legacy that possess analytical significance for the study of post-Suharto civil-military relations. First, the military's perception of itself as a "people's army" that — in contrast to civilian nationalist leaders — made no compromises in their fight against Dutch colonial forces and led the country to independence in 1945. Still popular in today's officer corps, this belief has supported both a sense of entitlement to participate in government and an engrained disdain for civilian politicians. Second, there is a widespread view in the Indonesian military that democratic civilian rule in the 1950s failed to establish good government and produced regional revolts that threatened to bring about the disintegration of the nation. The third legacy relates to the gradual evolution since the 1950s of a doctrine to justify military involvement in government, followed by the creation of an organizational format to support such an involvement. This doctrine — later known as Dual Function (*Dwi Fungsi*) — and the accompanying territorial command structure provided the foundation for the New Order regime after 1966. Fourth, the deep penetration by the military into civilian institutions under the New Order between 1966 and 1998 entrenched the armed forces in the infrastructure of the state. The TNI's participation in government and society was so extensive that the post-authoritarian reform of civil-military institutions would have to go much deeper than in other countries with more elite-oriented regimes. Finally, the broadening of Suharto's power base during the late New Order and the increasingly sultanistic character of his rule led to a growing gap in the 1990s between the ageing president and the military. This gap had considerable consequences for the character of the 1998 regime change and the role of the armed forces in it, as well as for the development of civil-military relations in the post-Suharto era.

## TNI AND INDONESIAN INDEPENDENCE: BETWEEN MYTH AND LEGACY

The Indonesian armed forces view themselves as a "people's army". The idea that the military was born out of a revolutionary struggle for national independence has constituted a central element in the political thinking of the armed forces since the 1940s, crediting the people with TNI's creation rather than the civilian political leadership at that time. Propagating the concept of "being one with the people", the military has invariably maintained that it was the decisive force in the fight for independence. The events during the guerrilla war against the Dutch between 1945 and 1949, or the military's historiographical interpretation of them, have served to legitimize the armed forces' claim that Indonesia's civil-military relations are fundamentally different from those in other countries. In fact, some generals have traditionally rejected the term "civil-military relations" as a Western concept aimed at creating an unpatriotic "dichotomy" between the military and its people (Maliki 2000, p. 90).[1] In 1999, the then Commander of the Armed Forces General Wiranto (1999, p. 85) emphasized that

> ABRI[2] views itself as the creation of the people's army that gave birth to the state.... This was the situation that led to the character of ABRI's roles and perceptions in society until today. The differences of opinion between TNI and the politicians in several historical events strengthened TNI's perception that differentiated between armed struggle and political-diplomatic struggle. Out of this historical perception grew ABRI's self-perception that Indonesia's independence was more determined by armed struggle than by the diplomatic struggle.

Believing that the armed forces "gave birth" to the nation, TNI concluded that it was destined to guard the integrity of the nation state (McGregor 2007, p. 220). Subsequently, the military's sense of historical mission combined with its derogatory view of civilian achievements to form the core of TNI's political perceptions and interpretations. While it is politically irrelevant if these self-perceptions are based on accurate historical facts, it is nevertheless important for the understanding of TNI's politico-ideological identity to provide a brief assessment of the most crucial historical events that led to the military's creation and entrenchment in Indonesian society.

The Indonesian armed forces were founded in October 1945 as TKR (*Tentara Keamanan Rakyat*, People's Security Force).[3] The nationalist movement under its popular leader Sukarno had declared independence in August 1945 after the Japanese capitulation, but Dutch colonial forces soon returned to Indonesia, where they met with fierce opposition by a wide range of local guerrilla forces.[4] The TKR was tasked with coordinating the operations of these militias, but in reality it exercised little authority over them. The situation was further complicated by the fact that many of the militias were linked to political parties and charismatic local leaders. As rival groups struggled for power, civil-military conflicts were inevitable. For example, the leftist politician Amir Sjarifuddin, who became minister of defence in November 1945, attempted to enforce civilian control over the TKR (Leclerc 1993, pp. 20–21). Wiranto's speech (1999, p. 84) identified Sjarifuddin's moves as the beginning of TNI's "involuntary" engagement in politics:

> TNI's involvement in politics began as a reaction against efforts by politicians to control or at least subordinate TNI, which since its founding had been relatively independent in its internal affairs, to

their political influence. The efforts to control TNI became especially apparent when Amir Sjarifoedin became minister of defence ... and established an armed wing of leftist groups named TNI of the People (TNI-Masyarakat). He tried also to ... create splits within TNI through all sorts of slander and intrigues.

The determination of the armed forces to manage their own affairs and resist civilian intervention is a major concern of militaries everywhere, and has been described by authors such as Nordlinger as a key motivation for military participation in politics. Evidently, Wiranto's recollection of civilian interference in matters of military organization was not disinterested historiography but intended as a less-than-subtle contribution to the civil-military debate in the post-Suharto era. In the turmoil of the armed struggle against the Dutch, the armed forces had even defied the civilian government by electing its own commander, the legendary Sudirman (Cribb 1991, p. 19; McFarling 1996, p. 37). Sudirman would remain the only TNI chief directly elected by his fellow officers, making him an iconographic reference point in TNI history. In 2003, the governor of Jakarta, himself a retired military officer, inaugurated a statue of Sudirman, overlooking the capital's main boulevard named after the general as well. While widely considered a national hero for his achievements during the war of independence, for Indonesia's military Sudirman has been primarily a symbol of military autonomy, heroic defiance of misguided civilian leadership, and absolute self-sacrifice for the sake of the nation, beyond and above the intrigues of divisive politics (Hamid 1997, p. 129).

Highlighting the institutional autonomy of the armed forces, Sudirman frequently disregarded the political strategies set by the civilian government. Most importantly, he insisted on the continuation of the military struggle at all cost, while the war cabinet favoured negotiations with the Dutch and continued diplomatic engagement with international powers as the best way to achieve independence. Neither of the two strategies appeared to be successful, however. Negotiated agreements with the Dutch were short-lived and regularly followed by Dutch offensives against the remaining Indonesian positions. The military, for its part, was unable to resist the growing military dominance of the Dutch, and the area controlled by the Republican government shrank rapidly as a result. Nevertheless, military officers were outraged at what they saw as the cowardice of Sukarno when the latter allowed himself to be captured by the Dutch in December 1948, and consequently regarded the civilian leadership as frail and ineffective. In the view of the armed forces, this contrasted sharply with their own determination to continue the fight.

In the end, however, it was the international outcry over what increasingly looked like an anachronistic and brutal colonial war that convinced the Dutch to give in (Taylor 1960, pp. 171–72). At a round table conference in the Netherlands, Dutch and Indonesian negotiators agreed on the transfer of authority to the United States of Indonesia in late 1949.[5]

The military rhetoric of unrivalled sacrifice could hardly hide the fact, however, that the armed forces had been just as weak and divided as their civilian counterparts. For instance, the military's rationalization programme, which aimed at bringing the various militias and regional units under the control of the centre, led to conflicts within the ranks (Kahin 1982, p. 17). In addition, regional sentiments created considerable tensions between military units operating in particular territories. There was little communication between local commanders, complicating larger operations that required cooperation beyond the boundaries of their designated areas. Finally, the endless string of defeats damaged the military's reputation, and even triggered doubts about the armed forces' capacity to continue the armed struggle. George McTurnan Kahin (1952, p. 228) reported that Sukarno only agreed to sign a major agreement with the Dutch because field commanders had told him how bad the military situation was, especially in terms of ammunition supplies. Sudirman even felt the necessity to issue an official denial regarding such rumours (Said 1992, p. 70). Episodes of internal fragmentation, regional splits, military shortcomings, and implicit acceptance of the strategy of negotiations do not figure prominently in TNI's official historiography, however. Instead, the major stress is laid on either TNI's defiance of civilian orders to surrender (illustrated by Sudirman's rejection of Sukarno's order to remain in Yogyakarta after the 1948 attack),[6] or its reluctant acceptance of policy directives (exemplified by TNI's compliance with some of the agreements negotiated with the Dutch).

The extent to which the guerrilla war contributed to the defeat of the Dutch invasion has been the subject of intensive debates in Indonesia's civil-military discourse (Harvey 1996, pp. 79–80). These controversies have little to do with an analytical assessment of historical incidents, but more with the contested legitimacy of military participation in politics. President Suharto, for example, insisted that the armed struggle was the key to independence, thus legitimizing the political role of the armed forces in his regime. In fact, he considered the historiography of the 1945–49 period as such an important element of political legitimacy and regime stabilization that he ensured that his own personal role in it was not overlooked. The Republican attack on Yogyakarta in March 1949, during which army troops managed to recapture the city for several hours, was re-interpreted by New Order historians to portray Suharto as the main strategist and executor of the operation.[7] Annual memorial services reminded the public of Suharto's role in the military campaign, and even the dates of political events were tailored around the anniversary of the attack.[8] Only after Suharto's fall did relatives of the Sultan of Yogyakarta have the courage to credit Hamengkubuwono IX with the initiative for the military action, and describe Suharto's participation in it as rather marginal.[9]

However, despite its importance for TNI's self-perception, the role of the armed forces in the war does not provide a strong explanation for Indonesia's tradition of military intervention in politics. As Alagappa (2001*b*, p. 63) pointed out, "that a military did or did not participate in the struggle for national liberation or won or lost the war is by itself unimportant as an explanation". He stressed that neither the Indian nor Pakistani military participated in the struggle for independence, yet the former has consistently stayed out of political affairs, while the latter has dominated politics for most of Pakistan's post-colonial history. Similarly, the Burmese military, the Chinese People's Liberation Army, and the Vietnamese People's Army have all played crucial roles in their respective independence wars. But while the Burmese armed forces have run a series of praetorian regimes, the Chinese and Vietnamese militaries have remained subordinated to their communist leaderships. The reference to major historical contributions of militaries has, therefore, rather limited relevance in explaining the level of their intervention in politics. In combination with other factors, however, the claim to a unique historical role, often intertwined with corresponding missions and mandates, can consolidate and sustain military intervention in politics for a remarkable period of time.

## PARLIAMENTARY DEMOCRACY:
## OVERTHROWN OR ABANDONED?

The interaction between the military and civilian authorities during the period of parliamentary democracy from 1950 to 1957 is of particular relevance to contemporary perceptions of civil-military relations. Critically, the failed experiment with liberal democracy in the 1950s was Indonesia's only experience of non-authoritarian rule before the fall of Suharto in 1998. In comparative terms, the dynamics of that period were similar in important respects to those emerging after the demise of the New Order, with unregulated activity of political parties, free elections, wide-ranging parliamentary powers, strong regionalism, and a pluralist press driving the political process. This period was therefore the only historical reference point for both the post-Suharto leadership of the armed forces and civilian politicians in anticipating the character of civil-military relations after 1998. The period gains additional significance from the widely held view that parliamentary democracy did not fail due to its own weaknesses alone but was deliberately undermined by the armed forces. If true, the involvement of the military in bringing down a democratic regime comparable to that established after Suharto's resignation could constitute a critical historical precedent in the minds of military officers, and thus affect the ongoing process of democratic consolidation.

The armed forces leadership during the time of parliamentary democracy had manifold reasons to be dissatisfied with the political system. General A.H. Nasution (1963, p. 213), who was army chief of staff during most of the 1950s, blamed the rise and fall of a series of cabinets, anti-centralist sentiments in the regions, and the spread of corruption on "the parties and groups [which] fought for all sorts of principles and goals, namely a variety of –isms". This aspect of the military's political memory of parliamentary democracy has remained influential to this day. In his 1999 speech (pp. 85–86), Wiranto repeated Nasution's interpretation of liberal democracy in an almost unchanged anti-pluralist thrust:

> The fear that the Republic could fall apart amidst the various conflicts between political parties motivated TNI in the 1945–57 period to take measures with political nuances, which were outside of its role as an instrument of defence and security. The events of 17 October 1952, when the military asked President Sukarno to dissolve parliament and take over the government, form the most outstanding example of the anger of TNI officers over the manoeuvres of political parties, which they viewed as the main reason for the instability of the nation and the short-lived rule of several governments.[10]

An equally important source of dismay within the armed forces, however, was their sense of political marginalization. Nasution (1963, p. 205) complained that "when we lived under the atmosphere of liberalism, TNI slowly but steadily lost its identity". According to Nasution, the military "operated in a very limited environment, namely only in the sector of its military duties, and was nothing more than a dead instrument like the previous KNIL". Evidently, the civilian view that the post-war military was merely a tool of the state to achieve military goals and had no particular role to play in times of peace differed immensely from TNI's self-perception. Furthermore, the military also felt that civilian leaders tried to subordinate the armed forces to the interests of political parties (Crouch 1988, p. 31). In the view of the top brass, politicians sought alliances with individual officers mostly to serve their own political purposes, threatening the unity of the officer corps as a result.

Civilian intervention in military affairs was not only driven by vested interests of politicians, however, but was also the result of internal divisions within the armed forces. The differences between officers mostly concerned appointments and structural reforms. Officers who had been part of the former Japanese auxiliary forces claimed that a new promotion system discriminated against them by requiring educational qualifications that they did not possess. It was this dissatisfied group within the military that lobbied both politicians in parliament and the president to overturn the recruitment regulations, providing a significant "pull" factor for civilian interference from within the armed forces (Suryohadiprojo 1997, pp. 155–57). In addition, the various factions in the military also disagreed over the general political direction of the country and the role TNI should play in politics. Some regional commanders toppled provincial governments in Central and South Sumatra in December 1956, and in Sulawesi in March 1957. The military leaders in these provinces demanded more rights for the regions, and the return of Vice-President Mohammad Hatta, who had resigned over differences with Sukarno, to the helm of government. Nasution, on the other hand, sought more institutional powers for the armed forces but without a coup and without challenging Sukarno. Nasution, who after a three-year break had resumed his post as army chief of staff in 1955, joined forces with the president to launch a military campaign against the rebellious officers in Sumatra and Eastern Indonesia, which ended in mid-1958 with the complete victory of Nasution's forces. The end of the regional rebellions consolidated Nasution's leadership and strengthened his concept of institutional participation in politics without praetorian dominance (Crouch 1988, p. 33). Furthermore, the political turmoil created by the unrest had produced a political landscape in which Nasution's ideas were likely to find quick application.

The defeat of the regionalist forces was followed by a power-sharing agreement between Nasution and the president that established an autocratic regime under Sukarno's leadership (named "Guided Democracy") and granted the military an institutional role in politics. In July 1959, Sukarno decreed the return to the 1945 constitution, with the armed forces represented in the new regime as a "functional group".[11] The question of how much the armed forces contributed to the downfall of the parliamentary system has not only been discussed by historians, but is also of importance for the theoretical discourse on the prospects of democratic control of the military in Indonesia. As mentioned earlier, Daniel Lev argued that the armed forces sabotaged liberal democracy simply because "it could". Lev's assessment was echoed by Jamie Mackie (1994, p. 36) who stated that "the roles played by Sukarno and the Army in pressing for substantial changes in the political system, culminating in the 1958–59 drive to 'return to the UUD 1945', were crucially important in undermining popular support for the parliament and parties at that time". Robert Elson (2001, p. 58), on the other hand, balanced the "destructive" role of the military with the political context that made this destruction possible: "Together, Sukarno and the Army conspired to deliver the 'death blow' to parliamentary democracy, in the face of only token opposition by the political parties — a sign of the flaccidity of party politics and the fact that, in their discredited position, they were no longer the pivot of politics." Similarly, Herbert Feith (1967, p. 322) asserted that "constitutional democracy was both overthrown by its opponents and abandoned by those who had earlier upheld it". This diversity of views exposes the problematic nature of theoretical models that view military intervention in politics only as a result of failing state institutions; there appears to be equally convincing evidence for military-driven acts of sabotage against civilian bodies in state and society. Feith's analysis suggests, however, that the two approaches are not mutually exclusive. Failing institutions do not necessarily lead to military rule unless the armed forces make use of the presented opportunity, while military sabotage of governments has a greater chance of succeeding when state institutions are already dysfunctional.

The period of parliamentary democracy in Indonesia constituted a failed post-authoritarian transition, and as such can be analysed by the comparative models introduced earlier to cope with the phenomena of the post-Suharto era. Applying the model proposed by Cottey, Edmunds, and Forster, Indonesia's democratic regime in the 1950s belonged to the group of states in which first and second-generation reforms had been initiated, but failed due to the weakness of the state. Post-independence Indonesia had established the structures for effective democratic control of the military (civilian department of defence, parliamentary committees, free and critical press), but they disintegrated under the pressure of rapidly spreading political conflicts. Accordingly, Indonesia failed to meet most of the conditions that Cottey et al. outlined as crucial for successful transitions. To begin with, there was a variety of alternatives to liberal democracy in circulation. The political spectrum reached from communism and nationalist authoritarianism to proposals for the establishment of an Islamic state. With only a few supporters left, liberal democracy proved unsustainable. Moreover, the political system had to deal with the legacy of military prominence during the revolutionary period. Ultimately, the transition from protagonist of the armed struggle to neutral instrument of civilian authorities proved too big a leap for a military unfamiliar with processes of political change. Finally, there was very little international support for the struggling democracy and, implicitly, the establishment of democratic civil-military relations. The Dutch refusal to transfer West Irian to Indonesia was one of the factors that fuelled the divisions within the political elite and encouraged military demands for a larger political role. The United States, on the other hand, supported the regional rebellions against the central government, expecting them to topple the left-leaning Sukarno. This policy, however, effectively provided the opportunity for the military to expand its influence and remove what was left of liberal democracy.

## NASUTION AND THE "MIDDLE WAY"

The evolution of what later became the military's "Dual Function" (*Dwi Fungsi*) constitutes another influential legacy of post-independence military politics. Increasingly alienated from the principle of civilian-led democratic governance, the military in the 1950s began to devise a doctrine that could be used to justify military involvement in political affairs. Although the "Dual Function" doctrine was only formulated in those terms after the military took full power in 1966, its origins went back to the "Middle Way" concept proposed in the late 1950s. Most importantly, the search for a suitable doctrine was accompanied by the development of the territorial command system that anchored TNI firmly in local politics.

The philosophical justification of military involvement in the political system was authored mainly by Nasution during the political crisis of the mid-1950s, and it has impacted on the doctrinal thinking of military officers ever since. Nasution was influenced by the writings of Karl von Clausewitz, a nineteenth century military strategist from Prussia. Clausewitz's notion of the inseparability of military affairs and politics provided the conceptual basis for Nasution's drive for deeper political involvement of the armed forces, and developments in other countries served as useful reference points:

> In defending TNI's position, I have strong arguments based on the history of struggle and the practice in Eastern European countries, where it is not the separation between the military and civilians that is being highlighted, but the totality of the participation of all elements of society and the people.... I lean towards the Eastern interpretation that ... finally, the political, military, economic, and cultural strategies have to come together into one concept of 'great politics'....[12]

Nasution argued that the military had to participate in politics in order to avoid coups such as those that had occurred in South American and Middle Eastern countries throughout the 1950s. Suggesting that Indonesia might well be the next in line in terms of military takeovers, Nasution offered institutionalized power-sharing with the armed forces as the only solution to satisfy the military's inherent drive for political leadership. In November 1958, he finalized his ideas in the concept of the Middle Way between praetorian dictatorship on the one hand and the Western ideal of non-participation of the military in politics on the other. Nasution stressed the urgency of his proposal by issuing a barely veiled threat: TNI had to be given its share in governing the country, he said, "because to hold it back is like putting a cork on the volcano of Merapi, which certainly will erupt at some stage".[13]

Nasution's model encapsulated the sentiments of many within the officer corps who instinctively felt that the armed forces had a legitimate right to political power but were unable to formulate a conceptual justification for that claim. The importance of Nasution's ideas for the development of TNI's political identity was recognized in Wiranto's speech (1999, p. 86), in which he maintained that the armed forces had learnt from Nasution that TNI was

> not only an "instrument of the government" like in Western countries; also not an "instrument of one party" like in communist countries; and of course not some sort of "military regime" that dominates the state. TNI is an "instrument of the people's struggle", as one of the national political forces, and with its participation in political life, TNI will never remain inactive.

The model of the Middle Way was gradually implemented throughout the second half of the 1950s, affecting three major areas. First, the military's participation in policy-making was institutionalized through the establishment of the National Council in May 1957, with the chiefs of staff of all services represented on the body. The Council had the task of finding a new format for the post-democratic polity, and provided Nasution with a platform to present his ideas. Second, the army was given more access to the economic resources of the state. In December 1957, Nasution decreed military control over a large number of Dutch businesses that had been occupied by workers protesting against the inactivity of the UN vis-à-vis the West Irian issue. Third, the implementation of the Middle Way in the sector of state bureaucracy was supported by the declaration of martial law in March 1957 (Crouch 1988,

p. 33). Through this declaration, Nasution and his commanders obtained extra-constitutional powers, and many officers were put into leadership positions of local administrations, particularly in West Java and the Outer Islands (Legge 1961, p. 219). Most importantly, their assumption of civilian powers did not end with the lifting of martial law. As Feith (1967, p. 333) observed, "these incursions were difficult to reverse; the army's actual role did not diminish significantly when its formal powers were reduced by a change in the martial law level in a particular region".

Closely related to the development of the Middle Way doctrine was the consolidation of the army's territorial command system, which would turn into a major legacy for the evolution of Indonesia's current civil-military relations. The structure of TNI's territorial commands was first put in place in Java after the Dutch attack on Yogyakarta in December 1948, but its expansion and consolidation as a permanent form of military organization was carried out only in 1957 and 1958. Nasution contended that Indonesia's geographical, demographic, and financial condition did not allow for a highly concentrated military with modern equipment and rapid deployment capacities. Instead, the country would have to rely on a network of military micro-units with strong roots in the local population, collecting intelligence, preparing for warfare, and mobilizing the people should need arise. The units were placed alongside the hierarchy of the civilian administration, so that every military command had a civilian counterpart.[14] Consequently, the military became an influential political and economic player in local affairs, even in areas not under martial law.

The most critical aspect of the territorial command system, as far as democratic civil-military relations are concerned, was (and still is) its principle of self-financing. Military commanders during the war rarely received official contributions from the central government; mostly, they raised funds from local sources, including small businesses. After the end of combat operations in 1949, the government was supposed to provide the armed forces with a regular defence budget. However, the limited availability of state monies and the ongoing political conflicts within the elite convinced the armed forces to continue with their own fund-raising efforts. Moreover, the unsuccessful attempt by some officers to dissolve parliament in 1952 persuaded the legislature to further cut the military's budget, which had the unintended effect of driving regional commanders into sensitive areas of smuggling, rent-seeking, extortion, and business alliances with local entrepreneurs. Subsequently, the increasing financial independence of military commanders at the grassroots was one of the factors that led to the regional rebellions of 1956–58 (Kahin and Kahin 1995, p. 55). After Nasution had defeated the rebellion, he split the regional commands into smaller territories in order to reduce the danger of political adventurism by regional military leaders, but their budgetary autonomy was maintained. In consequence, the territorial command structure became the institutionalized instrument for mobilizing the economic resources of the regions for the operational costs of the armed forces and the salary supplements of their officers.[15] This financial autonomy of the military made it extremely difficult for future civilian governments to establish control over the armed forces. Militaries that can determine their own budgets simply have fewer reasons to subordinate themselves to democratic control than those that depend on budget allocations approved by civilian authorities, and Indonesia's armed forces were a case in point.

## PRAETORIAN RULE:
## TNI AND THE EARLY NEW ORDER

Writing in 1963, at the height of Sukarno's Guided Democracy, Herbert Feith reflected upon the question why Indonesia's armed forces, despite their obvious privileges and powers, had not sought exclusive dominance over the government. Internal military conflicts were Feith's (1967, p. 329) first possible answer, but he suggested that there were more fundamental reasons:

> Secondly, there is fairly widespread opposition among civilians generally to the idea of government by the army. This is partly a reflection of the army's unpopularity, which has grown markedly since the army began its large-scale movement into politics and administration in 1957–58. In addition, it reflects a common view that military rule is the very antithesis to democracy and sovereignty — very much more so than, for instance, rule by a single party or national movement. Thus the advocates of an army take-over are told that it would be hard to find acceptable justifications for this, that they would gain only grudging support from civil servants and the people generally, and so be forced to govern by something more like naked force. Neither General Nasution personally nor the army leaders as a group are seen as having an inborn or acquired right to rule Indonesia.

Only two years later, the armed forces assumed authority over the government, institutionalized their rule by revamping the political system, and expanded Nasution's Middle Way to become the Dual Function as a model of military dominance over the state. The New Order would last for more than three decades, and despite its various internal transformations, it remained a military-backed regime throughout its history.

The ascendancy of the armed forces to direct political rule was preceded by growing tensions between Sukarno and the senior military leadership. Several factors were responsible for this. Most significantly, Sukarno was increasingly leaning towards the Indonesian Communist Party (PKI, *Partai Komunis Indonesia*) for political support in order to keep the military in check. The majority of officers had been staunchly anti-communist since a failed coup by the PKI in Madiun in 1948, which military leaders saw as a betrayal of the nationalist struggle against the Dutch (Kahin 1952, p. 303). Consolidating its grassroots support throughout the early 1960s (Hindley 1964, p. 300), and enjoying political protection from the president, the PKI had emerged as a serious challenger to the armed forces as a main component of Sukarno's Guided Democracy. As the president grew older, speculation about communist ambitions for a post-Sukarno takeover of the government was rampant. Moreover, from the early 1960s onwards, Sukarno appeared determined to assert his control of the armed forces by placing loyalists in key military positions (Legge 1990, p. 326).[16] This produced tensions within the ranks, as some officers approached either Sukarno or the PKI to promote their career interests. Finally, the armed forces became increasingly concerned about Indonesia's international isolation. Sukarno's course of confrontation with the West, culminating in his campaign against Malaysia in 1963 and the withdrawal from the United Nations in 1965, had severe political and economic consequences for the country. While supporting the *Konfrontasi* campaign against Malaysia in public, senior officers worked behind the scenes to de-escalate the situation (Mackie 1974, pp. 213–24).

Despite strong dissatisfaction with Guided Democracy, nurtured by rapidly declining economic conditions and escalating political conflicts at the grassroots, there was very little societal support for the idea of military rule. Thus the quest for erecting a military regime had to be driven by naked force, just as Feith had predicted. The opportunity for assuming political control by force emerged on 30 September 1965. On that day, six of the highest-ranking armed forces officers were killed in what the army called a communist coup attempt. Major General Suharto, the commander of Kostrad (the Army Strategic Reserve) and one of the top officers not arrested and killed in the abortive coup, brought the situation under control within a day. Hundreds of thousands of suspected PKI followers were murdered or arrested in the months after the September incident, with the army using paramilitary groups affiliated with Muslim organizations to carry out most of the killings (Roosa 2006). Sukarno, suspected of involvement in — or at least knowledge of — the alleged coup attempt, never regained control. In March 1966, he was forced to handover effective government authority to Suharto, and was gradually stripped of his presidential insignia. Finally, in March 1968, Suharto was appointed by the MPR to become the second president of Indonesia.

The purge against the PKI and political activists suspected of association with it removed violently what Feith had referred to as "widespread opposition among civilians" to the idea of military rule. Despite the crucial role of coercion, however, several other factors were equally essential for the establishment of praetorian control. To begin with, non-communist political groups offered little resistance to the ascendancy of the armed forces. In fact, many societal leaders supported the military in its campaign against the PKI, and the remaining political parties helped to create the legal framework for institutionalized military rule. The divisions between communists on the one hand and Islamic forces on the other had been so deep that many Muslim groups prioritized wiping out their PKI rivals over questioning the political intentions of the armed forces. In addition, the economic decline had reached alarming levels, and the existing civilian groups appeared poorly equipped to overcome the crisis. According to Hal Hill and Jamie Mackie (1994, p. xxiv), "the economy was in chaos, with inflation headed towards 1000 per cent, while [the] central government was unable to maintain even the most minimal standard of administrative services". After years of political cleavages, social tensions, and declining living standards, many Indonesians seemed willing to accept a limited period of military rule. Finally, the armed forces partially succeeded in avoiding the impression of a military dictatorship. The gradual transfer of authority from Sukarno to Suharto extended over a period of two and a half years, pointing to the effort of the armed forces to portray their ascension to power as a constitutionally legitimate change of government (Djiwandono 1998, pp. 52–53). It was this combination of force, civilian fragmentation, economic decline, and manipulated public images of the new regime that drove the process of entrenching praetorian rule, which was largely completed by 1968.

Having grabbed power amidst the political turmoil of the mid-1960s, the armed forces spent much of their early years in government consolidating the military's long-term claim to national leadership. The military placed its officers in senior political positions in the central and local administrations, and kept civil society and potential political players of the post-Sukarno era under tight surveillance. In addition, the officer corps also sought ideological confirmation of its new dominance by adjusting the military's doctrine at a seminar in April 1966. The involvement of the armed forces in political and economic development, their role as a guardian of the state ideology Pancasila,[17] and the upholding of the 1945 constitution became the core elements of the military's new doctrinal concept, the Dual Function. The conclusion of the seminar was an ideological justification for praetorian rule (Seskoad 1966, p. 10):

> Recently, all hopes of the people have been directed towards the armed forces in general, and the army in particular, to lead it to prosperity. Accordingly, there is only one alternative for the armed forces, and that is to implement what has been entrusted to them by the people. Based on all of this, the armed forces have an interest in taking part in the formation and guidance of a government that enjoys respect, a government that is strong, and a government that is progressive.

Arguing that the emergency situation forced the military to increase its representation in the bureaucracy, the seminar suggested that it was the army's duty to support the Ampera cabinet — the post-coup government formally headed by Sukarno, but in practice led by Suharto. In fact, the military's evolving doctrine legitimated retrospectively what had already been implemented — twelve of twenty-nine ministers of the Ampera cabinet were military officials, and a rapidly increasing number of officers assumed senior positions in local bureaucracies.[18]

By the early 1970s, the armed forces had taken either control of, or established dominance over, the four major areas in which militaries traditionally seek to involve themselves: the political sector, the economy, military organization, and the socio-cultural arena. In the political field, the armed forces were especially well entrenched in the executive branch of government. Supported by the doctrinal concept of *kekaryaan* (the secondment of officers in non-military posts), the military leadership filled the most senior positions of the regime. Suharto controlled the administration as both head of state and head of government, and military officers held key cabinet posts, including the ministries of defence and security, home affairs, and the state secretariat. Even in departments led by civilians, a military officer routinely held the post of secretary-general. In addition, generals also "usurped the top strata of the diplomatic and consular corps" (Sundhaussen 1978, p. 51). Military officers ran the national logistics board (the institution in charge of distributing basic food items such as rice) and controlled the government's news agency. In the provinces, eighty per cent of governors were officers, and an equally high percentage held positions as district heads.

On the legislative side, seventy-five officers were delegated to parliament, and more were appointed to the MPR. General Nasution, the former leader of the armed forces who had been "honourably" sidelined by Suharto, presided over the MPR that dismissed Sukarno, inaugurated Suharto, and adopted major changes to the political system. Military dominance of the national and regional legislatures was also exercised through the crucial role its officers played in the government's electoral machine Golkar,[19] which won the 1971 elections with the help of massive military intervention and intimidation. Significantly, Suharto had a threefold grip over the legislatures: as supreme chairman of Golkar, he had the authority to select the party's parliamentary candidates; as head of the armed forces, he was authorized to exclude parliamentary nominees of both Golkar and the other parties if he thought they posed a risk to national security; and as head of state, he had the right to select representatives of functional groups for the MPR. Two years after the 1971 elections, the remaining political parties were merged into two, the secular-nationalist PDI (*Partai Demokrasi Indonesia*, Indonesian Democratic Party) and the Islamic PPP (*Partai Persatuan Pembangunan*, United Development Party). Both parties were heavily supervised and their leaderships screened before being allowed to compete in general elections.

The third branch of state administration, the judiciary, saw similar levels of military intrusion. The attorney general's office came quickly under military control, as did the courts, while the police remained one of the four services of the armed forces. This allowed the military to maintain supremacy over all aspects of legal investigations and proceedings.

Political control was reinforced by increased participation in the economy. The intervention in economic affairs was an integral part of the Dual Function, which called on the armed forces to provide the necessary conditions for economic growth (Honna 2001, p. 55). Moreover, it delivered increased income opportunities for the military as an institution as well as its officer corps. Military officers had held senior management positions in several state enterprises since the late 1950s, but their number grew rapidly under the New Order. The national oil company Pertamina, for example, provided substantial contributions to the budget of the armed forces and its military directors (Iswandi 1998, pp. 146–51). Regional commanders also forged business alliances with local entrepreneurs, offering a service that Robert Lowry (1996, p. 141) called "facilitation". In addition to obtaining business licences, this covered assistance "in resolving land disputes, calming labour unrest, overcoming bureaucratic obstacles, relocating squatters, and so on". The business elite, Lowry concluded, found it "prudent to keep the local military on side against the day when social unrest might threaten their lives and property".

Politically, the military's new grip over local administrations, legislatures, and political parties handed it a virtual monopoly in brokering business deals and implementing projects. In order to institutionalize these newly acquired economic privileges, the military established a large number of companies, foundations, and cooperatives that managed its increasing business interests. The officers in charge of these business operations had, according to Richard Robison (1986, p. 252), "now almost unlimited access to the resources and facilities of the state and power to influence allocation of import/export licences, forestry concessions and state contracts". This was particularly evident after the economy began to recover in the early 1970s, and foreign investment entered the country. Not surprisingly, the military viewed the economic boom as a result of its political intervention and, as one officer put it, believed it had a legitimate claim on "its share of the cake".[20]

The commercial involvement of the armed forces did not only impact heavily on the institutional standing of the military vis-à-vis other socio-political groups, it also changed the social profile of its officers, and created additional incentives for them to defend the praetorian regime. Military commanders, often coming from lower-middle-class families, suddenly enjoyed the prospect of rapid social advancement. In fact, a successful career in the New Order officer corps virtually ensured entry into the most exclusive elite. Senior officers often owned several houses in elite compounds and luxury cars, travelled widely and sent their children to expensive universities abroad. Ibnu Sutowo, the army officer in charge of Pertamina, purchased Indonesia's first and only Rolls Royce in the early 1970s, symbolizing the extent of self-enrichment within the officer corps. In later periods of the New Order, sponsors would provide officers with credit cards for use at their convenience, or accompany them on shopping trips to attend to their wishes and consolidate the relationship.[21] Suharto himself handed out substantial gifts to his senior officers or made sure that his business associates did. The prospect of a rapid rise up the social ladder drove more and more young men to seek entry into the military academies. Between 1970 and 1975, an average of nearly 400 officers graduated from Akabri, the armed forces academy. In 1963, only 113 graduates had been listed.[22]

The hegemony of the armed forces delivered a multitude of post-retirement opportunities for officers and their families. If retiring military leaders were not placed in military-run enterprises or state companies, they were almost certain to receive offers from private business corporations. Expected to use their past connections to gain access to the ruling armed forces elite, military retirees were provided with offices and considerable salaries. Wiranto gave an illuminating insight into this phenomenon. After his retirement, Wiranto called in some of his tycoon friends and asked who had office space available for him. All hands went up. When he asked further who among them had no bad debts with the state, only two entrepreneurs still felt qualified. Wiranto finally chose one among the last two offers.[23] This special treatment of senior officers contrasted sharply with the retirement packages for lower ranking personnel, creating additional pressure to seek civilian positions before reaching pension age or to use all possible means to achieve a rank that would encourage interest from the business sector.

The increased economic powers of the armed forces also strengthened their organizational autonomy. The unprecedented flow of off-budget funds into the military allowed it to exercise a high degree of managerial autonomy, with unit commanders now also functioning as heads of rent-seeking foundations and cooperatives. Suharto encouraged this trend (Anderson 1990, pp. 117–18), despite obvious fears that the armed forces might grow too independent from his executive control. Drawing from his own experience as regional commander in the late 1950s, he apparently believed that granting senior officers access to additional sources of funding would strengthen their loyalty towards him as the patron of the system that made such self-service possible. In order to anticipate any challenges to his regime from inside the ranks, however, Suharto also introduced wide-ranging changes to the command system. At the core of his reform programme was the integration of the services into a strong central command under ABRI headquarters and the department of defence and security. Suharto downgraded all service commanders to chiefs of staff, thus depriving them of direct command over troops, and stripped them of their cabinet status. He also reduced the powers of the regional commanders, creating a system of coordinating commands overseeing several military territories (*Komando Wilayah Pertahanan, Kowilhan*). While this led to some tension within the armed forces, there was no doubt that their leadership for the first time since Sudirman's election enjoyed complete jurisdiction over internal military affairs.

The fourth arena of military intervention is in the socio-cultural sector. It is in this area that militaries typically face the most serious difficulties, and Indonesia's military was no exception. The early New Order regime was relatively tolerant towards expressions of criticism from the media and the arts, largely because different factions in the military were still using the press for their own purposes and Suharto appeared anxious to avoid the impression of a military dictatorship.[24] This changed, however, from the early 1970s onwards. The government established a system of tight censorship regulations for the media and cultural activities. At the same time, it encouraged the development of an official culture consistent with the leadership principles of the regime. Barbara Hatley (1993, p. 50) explained that the key element of that culture was the

> celebration of conservative, hierarchical values. The central state
> — Java-based and Javanese-dominated — supports Javanese culture of
> a particular type, that of court tradition. Images of noble grandeur and
> hierarchical social order serve to display and confirm the authority of
> the contemporary state and its officials.

The indoctrination of the New Order masses with officially sanctioned forms of artistic expression was successful on the surface, but did not manage to penetrate all segments of the cultural sector. Many writers, painters, cartoonists, musicians, and journalists continued their critical work, and some went to jail or suffered intimidation and social marginalization.[25] The majority of them, however, developed a highly sophisticated system of self-censorship, producing language and art forms that would be understood by the audience as being critical, but deliver no legal pretexts for the New Order apparatus to take action.

The historical legacy of the early New Order period for the development of civil-military relations in the post-Suharto era consisted of three major components. The first and most important element was the evolution of the military's role from earlier forms of political participation into direct praetorian control, establishing the Dual Function as the leading guideline for the Indonesian armed forces, state, and society. Despite the military's efforts to portray its takeover as constitutionally legitimate, the new doctrinal guidelines issued in August 1966 provided philosophical justifications for political hegemony over the state. Furthermore, the entrenchment of the military in state institutions and civil society was so extensive that any successor regime would have difficulties in disengaging the armed forces from the areas they had intruded. Military involvement in local politics and businesses, its expansion into the state bureaucracy, legislature, and the judiciary, its surveillance of civil society, press, and arts — all these institutional manifestations of praetorian rule would shape long-term perceptions of political culture, both within the elite and the wider population. Finally, the successes of the authoritarian regime in stabilizing the economy and controlling political conflicts persuaded many Indonesians that non-democratic forms of government were best suited to secure economic development.[26] This widely held view posed very serious challenges to the process of democratic consolidation in the post-authoritarian transition, including the propagation of democratic civil-military relations.

## SUHARTO'S AUTOCRACY AND THE
## MILITARY IN THE 1970s

The successful establishment of a praetorian regime, however, exposed the New Order to divisive dynamics that affect all military-dominated governments. Alagappa (2001*b*, pp. 51–52) pointed out that

> once the military rulers begin to govern, fissures develop between those who govern and those who command the troops, especially the field commanders.... To consolidate their control and prevent counter coups, military leaders at the political helm may hold on to senior positions, appoint loyalists, create counter-balancing factions, develop patronage networks, develop extensive surveillance and intimidation mechanisms, or remake the political center by co-opting potential challengers. Despite these measures, the contradiction between military as government and military as an institution is a fundamental and inescapable contradiction that ultimately leads to disunity and breakdown of the military regime.

The phenomenon described by Alagappa was present in Suharto's regime even in its very early phase. In formulating policy directives and creating the fundamentals of the political system, Suharto relied heavily on long-time friends from the army who worked on the SPRI, the private staff of the president. Officers at armed forces headquarters observed this concentration of power in Suharto's private circle with suspicion. Moreover, regional commanders as well as service heads affected by the structural reforms to the military hierarchy expressed concern over their loss of influence.[27] Their dissatisfaction, however, was reduced by the collective feeling within the ranks that Suharto's regime generated unprecedented political and material advantages for the armed forces as an institution and the individual interests of their officers.

The divisions between Suharto's inner circle and the armed forces intensified when the political system of the New Order was fully erected after the 1971 polls and the 1972 re-election of Suharto. It had become apparent to many officers that Suharto was about to install an institutional mechanism for the perpetuation of his personal rule, and that he viewed the military only as the stabilizing framework for his autocracy (Jenkins 1984, pp. 255–56). The growing awareness within the officer corps that the political interests of Suharto were gradually separating from that of the armed forces left a deep mark on TNI's institutional memory, and would form an important element in the complex of historical legacies relevant for the post-New Order period. In his 1999 address, Wiranto (1999, p. 88) admitted that in the New Order era under President Soeharto, we saw ABRI playing its most extensive socio-political role; according to some ABRI seniors who participated in developing the concept of Dwifungsi, this role even exceeded the proportions intended at the time when Dwifungsi was born. In this context, we arrive at the conclusion that the concept of Dwifungsi cannot anticipate the possibility that the office of president is held by someone with a direct position in the system of the command hierarchy, and who manipulates his influence on the command hierarchy for his own socio-political interests.

Throughout the 1970s, there were challenges from within the armed forces to the exclusivism of Suharto's rule, but the president was able to contain them by using his direct control over the military commands. He was still an active member of the armed forces for most of the 1970s, creating the impression that many of the disputes were linked to intra-military conflicts rather than the growing gap between the presidency and the army elite. In 1974 and 1978, Suharto struggled to fend off threats to his regime launched by critical student groups, which claimed to have received support by some elements within the armed forces (McDonald 1980, pp. 136, 246–47). Many of the student leaders were arrested and jailed, while the officers linked to the movement were relieved from their command positions and subsequently sidelined.[28]

Another cause for the increasing tensions between Suharto and his military was the president's effort to establish an independent network of financing sources for his political operations. Throughout the 1970s, Suharto set up a large number of foundations, requiring state banks, companies, and wealthy taxpayers to donate money to them (Vatikiotis 1994, pp. 51–52). For example, beginning in 1978, state-owned banks had to give 2.5 per cent of their profits to Suharto's *Dharmais* and *Supersemar* foundations. While officially handing out scholarships and delivering social services, large parts of the collected money were used by Suharto to reward political allies and co-opt potential foes, including in the armed forces. Suharto signed each cheque above US$50,000 personally, reminding the recipients that their affluence depended on his individual patronage rather than on the institutional mechanisms of the regime. In 1978, Suharto's foundations took over the previously private Bank Duta, using it as their main instrument for business ventures. The gradual expansion of Suharto's personal economic empire cut deeply into the military's institutional business interests, and made senior officers dependent on Suharto's favours. Suharto was now not only the political, but also the monetary epicentre of the New Order regime.

Suharto's re-election to a third presidential term in 1978, and his retirement from active duty in the army, did away with all remaining doubts that he would be more than just the replaceable leading officer of a military junta. Significantly, Suharto's consolidation in the presidency was accompanied by generational changes in the armed forces. As Kammen and Chandra (1999, p. 8) noted, "by the early 1980s the ... 1945 generation that had fought in the Indonesian revolution against the Dutch had retired, passing the leadership to a post-war generation of officers". The retirement wave removed both trusted associates and critics of the president from the military elite and redefined the relationship between the regime and the armed forces. With Suharto firmly established in the centre of a personalized autocracy, and a new type of officers in charge of the armed forces, the praetorian regime was about to undergo substantial change.

## THE LATE NEW ORDER: PRAETORIAN REGIME OR SULTANISTIC RULE?

The legacy of the later New Order period that would impact most significantly on the character of post-Suharto civil-military relations was shaped by two critical developments. Most importantly, there was a gradual reduction of the role of the armed forces in politics from the mid-1970s to the late 1990s. The number of military officers in cabinet, governorships, the legislatures, and senior bureaucratic positions declined, and so did the influence of the armed forces on matters of general policy. While in the early 1970s around eighty per cent of the gubernatorial posts were held by active or retired military officers, that figure shrunk drastically to forty per cent by the late 1990s. Executive positions were increasingly given to civilians whom Suharto had integrated into the foundations of his regime: technocrats, Muslim leaders, technology experts, business executives, and Golkar politicians. In addition, Suharto also reshuffled the composition of his inner circle, replacing confidants from his days in the army with business cronies and members of his own family. Despite the reduction of their political powers, however, the armed forces remained the backbone of the regime, and Suharto continued to command their loyalty by handpicking the top brass and distributing material rewards to the officer corps.

The second element was the gradual change in societal perceptions of the armed forces. The decline in formal regime participation allowed ABRI to deflect much of the growing public criticism of the government onto Suharto's personal leadership style. Throughout the 1980s until the early 1990s, the military elite had been a central target of widespread dissatisfaction with the repressive policies of the regime. During the final years of the New Order, however, the discontent in many segments of society with economic favouritism, political stagnation, and tight social control was increasingly addressed to Suharto and his family. Many even started to view the armed forces as much a victim of Suharto's manipulative tactics as they considered them a crucial component of his regime (Dhakidae 2003, pp. 256–57).[29] This dualism of continued loyalty towards the regime and declining formal engagement with it was reflected in the doctrinal development of the armed forces in the 1990s. Military attitudes ranged from hard-line responses vis-à-vis the challenges of socio-political change to critical reflections on the excesses of Suharto's rule (Honna 2003, p. 113). The prominence of non-military protagonists in the late New Order, and the development of a critical discourse within the armed forces, dissociated the military to some extent from the failures of the regime. This disassociation, or the perception that the Indonesian public had formed of it, would have a profound impact on the character of the 1998 regime change.

Suharto actively contributed to the impression of a growing distance between himself and the armed forces mainstream through a series of controversial military appointments in the 1980s and 1990s. Most importantly, in February 1988 he dismissed ABRI chief Benny Murdani, whose independent political operations had attracted deep suspicions on Suharto's part. Murdani, a Catholic, had fiercely defended the secular orientation of the regime against the rising influence of Muslim activists, and had not been hesitant in protecting the political and institutional interests of the armed forces. Following Murdani's dismissal, Suharto apparently concluded that he had to broaden his civilian power base and curb the autonomy of the military elite (Said 2001, p. 79). Thus from the late 1980s onwards, he encouraged Muslim leaders and intellectuals to intensify their socio-religious activities and become part of his regime — a development that will be discussed further in Chapter 2. In appointing the post-Murdani top brass, on the other hand, Suharto applied two major criteria. First, candidates for leadership positions had to be firmly opposed to the Murdani group. Accordingly, officers with devout Muslim backgrounds, who had seen their promotions held up under the Murdani reign, were now given special consideration.[30] Second, future military leaders qualified for speedy promotion if they were members of Suharto's wider family, had strong relationships with it, or had recently served as his adjutants and commanders of the presidential security squad.

Suharto's new approach turned the immediate military leadership into an exclusive circle of the president's most trusted cronies, relatives, and subordinates, attracting extensive cynicism from both the rank and file and society as a whole. The post of army chief of staff, for example, was held in the 1990s consecutively by the brother-in-law of Suharto's wife, a close confidant of his daughter Siti Hardiyanti Rukmana, his former adjutant and, finally, the former chief of the presidential security squad. At the same time, Suharto's son-in-law and several other ex-adjutants filled senior positions. Suharto apparently came to believe that only officers with direct links to his personal fate would develop the kind of allegiance that was necessary to sustain the regime. The political repercussions of this nepotistic transformation of the top military elite were tremendous, however. Many younger officers began to demand that ABRI distance itself from Suharto and the regime, leading to the emergence of critical discussion groups in the military's educational facilities in Bandung in the early 1990s. Moreover, society figures, intellectuals, and politicians no longer saw the armed forces as an independent political entity — instead, they viewed ABRI as Suharto's manipulated instrument of power maintenance. For that reason, the president was increasingly seen as directly responsible for all its actions, including the brutal repression of regime dissidents that Suharto previously could blame on Murdani and his group.

The New Order state of the 1990s had undergone substantial social and political change since its formation in the early 1970s and its consolidation in the 1980s. The reduction of military participation in governance, the inclusion of various civilian groups in its power structure, and the increased concentration of political and economic powers in Suharto's family circle gave the regime an image significantly different from the praetorian rule it had exercised throughout the 1970s. Edward Aspinall (2000, p. 6) argued that "by the mid-1990s, Suharto's regime was undergoing a process of sultanization, in which the dominance of the president, and that of his family and inner circle, was becoming increasingly venal and all pervasive". Accordingly, while the armed forces still enjoyed the profits distributed by Suharto's patronage network, they were now severely impaired in their ability to function as an autonomous political actor. David R. Mares (1998, p. 7) saw the military in the late New Order, similarly to the armed forces under Chile's Pinochet, "relegated to agent status along with the rest of society".

The decline of the armed forces' influence was evident in all four areas in which militaries traditionally involve themselves. In the political arena, besides witnessing the formal reduction of military representation in the executive, the legislature, and the judiciary, the armed forces also had to concede the leadership of Golkar to civilian politicians (Hadad 1996, p. 72). In its relations with Suharto, the military suffered a series of defeats, and was only rarely able to translate its crucial importance for the maintenance of the regime into concrete political gains. In 1993, the military forced its vice-presidential candidate, General Try Sutrisno, on Suharto, but the president retaliated by isolating Try and replacing him after one term in office. In the economic field, the armed forces had to surrender some of their privileges to businesses controlled by the Suharto family and civilian entrepreneurs protected by the state secretariat (Pangaribuan 1996, p. 57). The ongoing economic boom, with growth rates of around seven per cent each year in the early 1990s, ensured that the military still had considerable income opportunities, but the increase in the number of actors resulted in a reduction of its total share (van Langenberg 1990, p. 128).

The most drastic reduction of the military's influence, however, occurred in the sector of its organizational autonomy. Suharto, now a civilian with a complex web of political interests and support groups, had almost complete control over appointments and matters of internal management. Generals with links to the Suharto family or a history of personal service at the palace rose rapidly through the ranks, creating discontent within the corps. Many officers with outstanding professional qualifications felt that they had to make way for those with better political connections.[31] Finally, in the socio-cultural sector, the military faced increasing difficulties in controlling public expressions of disappointment with the regime. Responding to demands for fewer restrictions on the freedom of opinion, the New Order declared a new era of openness (*keterbukaan*) in 1989. During that period, the press was temporarily able to raise several sensitive issues, including the role of the military and the business connections of senior officials. However, this experiment ended abruptly in 1994, when Suharto ordered the closure of Indonesia's leading news magazines. Now convinced that even cautious political liberalization was incompatible with his ambition to sustain the regime, Suharto further tightened his grip on the political system and society. The dissatisfaction among ordinary Indonesians, on the other hand, continued to grow. Aided by newly available technology, dissidents established underground information networks that published newsletters on the Internet or shared information through short messaging services on mobile phones. The military found it hard to identify and neutralize these unconventional opposition circles, which quickly spread from Jakarta to other urban centres both on Java and the Outer Islands (Nyman 2006).

The reduction of the military's involvement in the four areas mentioned above underscored the change in the character of the regime. The late New Order polity could no longer be described as a praetorian state. The armed forces did not have full control of the government as they had in the early period of the regime. In the traditional scheme of civil-military relations, Indonesia's armed forces in the 1990s played the role of participant-ruler. They supported the political interests of an increasingly sultanistic civilian leader, and received substantial political and economic concessions in return. Writing in 1997, the last full year of Suharto's presidency, Anders Uhlin (1997, p. 58) contended that while "the military is obviously an important power center and many powerful ministers have a military background, ... the New Order is not a pure military regime". The government, Uhlin explained, "uses military force to rule but its first concern is not the interests of the military, but the protection of the political and economic interests of the Soeharto family and the big Chinese conglomerates associated with Soeharto". This ambivalence of its role as a beneficiary and mishandled tool of the regime created uncertainty within the military about its institutional interests in the late New Order. Obviously, the armed forces were dissatisfied with their loss of political powers since the 1980s. But there was also widespread anxiety in the ranks that the fall of the New Order regime might end the military's role in politics altogether. The present arrangement, with all its shortcomings and frustrations, still appeared to many officers as more attractive than an uncertain future.

The historical complex of institutionalized power structures, ideological self-perceptions, and societal interpretations of the armed forces' intervention in politics forms the background for the analysis of the political crisis that unfolded in 1997 and led to the post-authoritarian transition in the years after 1998. The debate over the role of the military in achieving national independence; the experiences with liberal democracy in the 1950s; the evolution of the Dual Function; the institutionalization of military powers in the early New Order period; and the eroding identity between Suharto and the armed forces in the 1990s all constitute elements of an influential historical legacy. The strength of this legacy would become evident in the early phase of the post-New Order transition, impacting considerably on the characteristics of its civil-military relations.

## Notes

[1]    Interviews with Major General Suwisman, assistant for territorial affairs to the army chief of staff, Jakarta, 28 November 2000; Lieutenant General Agum Gumelar, governor of Lemhannas (*Lembaga Ketahanan Nasional*, National Resilience Institute), Jakarta, 9 June 1998, and Lieutenant General Soeyono, secretary-general of the department of defence, Jakarta, 15 October 1998.

[2] ABRI (*Angkatan Bersenjata Republik Indonesia*, Armed Forces of the Republic of Indonesia) was the term used for the military from the 1960s until the early post-1998 polity.

[3] In January 1946, Sukarno changed the name of the TKR to Armed Forces of the Republic of Indonesia (*Tentara Republik Indonesia*). At the same time, he ordered the restructuring of the military's organization (Kodam VII/Diponegoro, pp. 71–73). In June 1947, the name changed again, this time to TNI (*Tentara Nasional Indonesia*), marking the integration of former paramilitary groups into the official hierarchy of the army (Dinas Sejarah TNI Angkatan Darat 1979, p. 8).

[4] The militias consisted of elements from the former colonial army KNIL (*Koninklijk Nederlandsch-Indisch Leger*, Royal Netherlands East Indies Army), auxiliary forces trained by the Japanese (*Heiho*, *Giyugun* and *Peta*), and locally recruited Islamic and ethnic armed groups, the *lasykar* (Muhaimin 2002, pp. 31–34).

[5] The army had been reluctant to acknowledge the UN-sponsored negotiations with the Dutch, reminding the government of former agreements broken by the former colonial power. Sudirman wrote in April 1949 that if the negotiations were to be successful, the Indonesian side had to be represented by the "real fighters" in the struggle, i.e. the army ("orang jg benar2 berdjoeang pokoknja"). Instead, Indonesia's delegation was made up of the very civilian leaders who, in the eyes of the military, had unnecessarily surrendered to the Dutch in December 1948 (Tjokropanolo 1993, p. 253).

[6] This line was presented by, among others, Syarwan Hamid (1997, pp. 129–30).

[7] George McTurnan Kahin (1952, p. 411), for instance, made no mention of Suharto in his description of the attack.

[8] Most of the sessions of the MPR during the New Order, for example, would start on the 1 March, the date of the attack, and end on 11 March, the day Sukarno handed over power to Suharto in 1966.

[9] "Soeharto Bukan Penggagas Serangan Oemoem 1 Maret 1949", *Kompas*, 1 March 2000.

[10] The "17 October Affair" had been triggered by a parliamentary motion criticizing the armed forces for, among other things, their internal promotion system and the alleged intervention in the formation of cabinets. Outraged by this move, officers close to Nasution confronted Sukarno and demanded the dissolution of parliament and fresh elections. The president refused, and Nasution and his supporters within the army had to resign (Sundhaussen 1982, p. 65; Idris 1997, pp. 136–42).

[11] Sukarno had promoted the concept of functional groups as an alternative to the political party system. Douglas Ramage (1995, p. 22) has noted that the army, on the other hand, saw the concept as a welcome "way to legitimize military participation in political life".

[12] Quoted in Supriyatmono (1994, pp. 103–04).

13  Quoted in Supriyatmono (1994, p. 114).

14  The territorial command system, as it evolved under the New Order, is
    comprised of Regional Commands (*Komando Daerah Militer*, or *Kodam*), which
    corresponds to either one large province or a number of smaller provinces;
    Resort Commands (*Komando Resort Militer*, or *Korem*), covering the boundaries
    of the old Dutch regencies, often one smaller province or a number of
    *kabupaten* (districts); District Commands (*Komando Distrik Militer*, or *Kodim*),
    corresponding to districts; Sub-district Commands (*Komando Rayon Militer*,
    or *Koramil*), supervising the *kecamatan* level; and the NCOs for Village
    Supervision (*Bintara Pembina Desa*, or *Babinsa*), responsible for *kelurahan* and
    *desa* (villages).

15  Immediately after Nasution announced the formal structure of the territorial
    system, regional commands set up special offices assigned with fund-raising and
    establishing business cooperatives (Limbagau 2000, p. 236).

16  Sukarno also began to dismantle Nasution's network in the military. Nasution
    was replaced as army chief of staff in July 1962 and "kicked upstairs" to serve as
    minister of defence. He also became chief of staff of the armed forces, a largely
    ceremonial post vacant since the 1952 events.

17  Sukarno had announced five ideological principles in June 1945, which he
    believed were suitable to reflect the ideals, customs, and convictions of all
    Indonesians. The five principles, collectively called Pancasila, were: nationalism,
    internationalism (or humanitarianism), democracy (or consent), social prosperity,
    and belief in one God. The Pancasila guidelines were designed to overcome
    the ethnic, religious, social, and political differences within Indonesian society.
    However, the principles were also subject to diverse, politically charged
    interpretations, with different groups and regimes attempting to use Pancasila
    in their struggle for political hegemony. The New Order would be no exception,
    launching Pancasila as its main ideological instrument to maintain political
    stability, eradicate extremism, and limit individual freedoms. In doing so, the
    Suharto government claimed to have saved the state ideology from the political
    manipulation it suffered under the Sukarno reign (Nasution 1966, p. 24).

18  Suharto had formed the Ampera cabinet after the Fourth General Session of
    the MPRS (the provisional MPR) in July 1966. In its sessions, the MPRS had
    legalized the transfer of executive authority to Suharto as well as the banning
    of the PKI, and had stripped Sukarno of the title President for Life (McFarling
    1996, pp. 84, 87).

19  Golkar was established in October 1964, when a large number of pro-military
    functional groups were merged into one organization. The merger was conducted
    in response to a government regulation that required all members of the National
    Front (a body of mass organizations established in 1959) to seek affiliation with
    existing political parties or to merge into one organization. Accordingly, the
    anti-communist members of the National Front established a joint secretariat
    of functional groups, or Sekber Golkar. Fifty-three of ninety-seven founding

members were army-sponsored trade unions and civil servants organizations (Suryadinata 1989, p. 13).

[20] Interview with Major General Sudrajat, senior staff to the commander-in-chief, Jakarta, 28 November 2000.

[21] Confidential interview with a weaponry contractor, Jakarta, 29 April 2003.

[22] The number of graduates dropped by 75 per cent, however, in 1975–76. While no official explanation was provided for this decline, it is likely that recruitment was reduced after the New Order had consolidated its position, and most *kekaryaan* positions were already filled (Kammen and Chandra 1999, p. 35).

[23] Interview with General (ret.) Wiranto, Jakarta, 13 October 2000.

[24] The armed forces had two newspapers of their own, *Berita Yudha* and *Angkatan Bersenjata*, both established in 1965. The military also played a dominant role in the Golkar newspaper, *Suara Karya* (Hill 1994, p. 36).

[25] Those Indonesian authors who had gained international reputations for their literary work were the most difficult to control, even for the armed forces. Y.B. Mangunwijaya, for example, was one of the most vocal critics of the military's Dual Function during the New Order. His collection of articles, expressing indirect criticism through historical comparisons and philosophical contemplations, can be found in Mangunwijaya (1999).

[26] In September 2003, a poll conducted by the independent research institute LSI (*Lembaga Survei Indonesia*, Indonesian Survey Institute) showed that 56.4 per cent of the Indonesian electorate believed that the system of the New Order was more efficient than the current polity. At the same time, 65 per cent of voters identified the economy as the most serious problem facing the government. "Menguat, Dukungan terhadap Tentara, Orba, dan Partai Golkar", *Kompas*, 29 September 2003.

[27] Written communication with General (ret.) A.H. Nasution, Jakarta, 11 December 1997.

[28] General Sumitro, the most prominent officer to lose his job over the 1974 events, has credibly maintained that students misunderstood his attitude towards their protests. "You guys were wrong", he later told the students. It is indeed unlikely that Sumitro thought he could bring down Suharto at that stage. He was, however, strongly opposed to the SPRI officers in Suharto's inner circle (Cahyono 1998, p. 1).

[29] Dhakidae lamented the weakness of the armed forces, and their deliberate misuse as "guards of Soeharto's personal interests, and that of his cronies".

[30] Interview with Lieutenant General (ret.) Sayidiman Suryohadiprojo, Jakarta, 4 December 1997. Despite the increased numbers of devout Muslim officers in the military elite, however, Suharto did not exclude non-Muslim and secular Muslim officers from the promotion cycle. In fact, there appears to have been a delicate balance between the appointments of officers with devout Muslim backgrounds on the one hand and commanders with non-Muslim and secular profiles on the other. This dualism led some observers to conclude

that ABRI was divided into a "green" (Muslim) faction and a "red-and-white" (nationalist-secular) camp. As will be argued later in this study, this division was superficial and reflected political calculations rather than ideological or religious dispositions.

31  Interview with Major General Agus Wirahadikusumah, commander of the army staff and command school, Jakarta, 8 November 1998.

# 2

---

# ISLAM AND THE STATE
## Legacies of Civilian Conflict

The military quest for political participation is one important aspect of the civil-military equation, and its historical manifestations and legacies in Indonesia have been discussed extensively in Chapter 1. Authors such as Samuel Finer asserted, however, that the quality of civilian political leadership is equally crucial for the outcome of civil-military interactions. Solid civilian state institutions, consensus among important groups in society over the foundation of the system of government, and low levels of political conflict combine into what Finer called a "developed political culture". States with sophisticated political cultures are much less likely to experience military intervention in politics than those with weak institutions and fragmentation among major civilian groups.

For much of Indonesia's post-independence history, fissures within the civilian polity have had an obstructive effect on the development of strong democratic institutions. Conflicts among influential societal groups have weakened the civilian capacity to run stable governments, eroding the confidence of the public in political parties and democracy. Significantly, the intra-civilian fractures contributed to an environment in which the armed forces were presented with numerous opportunities for political intervention. This chapter focuses on divisions within the Muslim community as a case study to highlight both general patterns of intra-civilian conflict in Indonesia and their impact on the levels of military intervention in political affairs. Disputes among key constituencies over the role of Islam in state and society as well as over its diverse doctrinal, cultural, and political interpretations have marked Indonesian politics since 1945. The historical legacies of these debates and conflicts had, as will be shown in the course of this study, important implications for the development of civil-military relations after 1998.

In discussing the fragmentation within the Muslim community, this chapter draws attention to three main areas. First of all, there have been stark differences between groups favouring a strong role for Islam in politics and those that promote a nationalist vision of the state without distinguishing between followers of different religions. The controversy between these two camps over the formal role of Islam in the state dominated the Indonesian polity from the mid-1940s to the late 1950s and played an important role in the decline of liberal democracy. Second, the rivalry between traditionalist and modernist Muslim groups over religious, social, and political questions concerning the interpretation of the Islamic faith has been equally significant. Both currents developed a deeply antagonistic relationship, fed by bitter experiences of failed cooperation during liberal democracy in the 1950s and mutual accusations of betrayal during decades of authoritarian rule. Third, the existence of small, but influential groups at the militant fringes of political Islam posed security threats to civilian governments in the 1940s and 1950s and served as a legitimazing threat for the New Order in the 1970s and 1980s. Developments in all three areas undermined the standing of civilian leaders and strengthened the role of the military in politics, and despite strong fluctuations in their conflict potential at various stages of modern Indonesian history, they would play a critical role in shaping the political landscape of the early post-Suharto era.

## THE CLEAVAGES IN
## INDONESIA'S MUSLIM COMMUNITY

Indonesia has the largest Muslim community in the world, with 88.6 per cent of its population, or 195.8 million people, identifying themselves as followers of the Islamic faith.[1] There are significant divisions within the umat,[2] however, which are reflected in different practices and doctrinal beliefs, regional variations, and conflicting political viewpoints. The most important of these divisions have been the split between *santri* and *abangan* on the one hand, and between traditionalist and modernist Muslims on the other.

The scholarly differentiation between *santri* and *abangan* was an influential typology in the 1960s and 1970s, distinguishing devout from less pious Muslims.[3] *Santri* were defined as devout Muslims who adhere strictly to the rituals prescribed by scripture, such as praying five times a day, fasting during the month of Ramadhan, avoiding alcohol and gambling, as well giving alms to the poor. Therefore, this group of pious Muslims initially called themselves *putihan*, or "the white ones" (Ricklefs 2007, p. 49). In contrast, *abangan* Muslims — "the red or brown ones" — were described as less strict in their practice of Islamic rituals, or as engaging in religious practices that combined elements of the Islamic faith with those of other religions, mostly Hinduism and Buddhism. In this context, the more "lax" *abangan* do not view orthopraxy as a matter of importance for them, while the syncretistic *abangan* often adhere devoutly to a set of rituals developed through an amalgamation of local beliefs and Islamic regulations. The distinction between *santri* and *abangan*, introduced by the anthropologist Clifford Geertz in his classic text "The Religion of Java" (1960), has been widely criticized as inapplicable to a larger Indonesian context and changing socio-demographic trends (Hodgson 1974). The categories have remained helpful, however, to grasp the political preferences of voters with divergent religious profiles. In the 1950s and 1960s, for example, *santri* typically supported Islamic parties with clearly defined demands for the introduction of Islamic law and state structures, while *abangan* voted for secularly oriented parties (nationalist, communist, and socialist) that opposed the idea of an Islamic state. While the cultural features of the *abangan-santri* divide have undergone important changes, its political dimension continues to influence voting behaviour to this day. Anies Baswedan (2004), for example, has convincingly demonstrated that voters who switched parties in the 2004 elections largely did so within the Islamic and nationalist blocks respectively, and only rarely moved from one camp to the other.

In the *santri* community, there are two major currents: modernism and traditionalism. The two groups have significant differences over issues of doctrine, religious practices, and their relations with the state. In matters of doctrine and jurisprudence, the traditionalists almost invariably follow the Syafi'i school, one of the four main Sunni law schools (*mazhab*).[4] Traditionalist *ulama* or *kiai*[5] often blend local influences into their religious practices, leading to forms of syncretism that the modernists view as deviations from the "true" Islam (Fananie and Sabardila 2000, pp. 1–3). The leaders of traditionalist communities are revered by their students as sources of clerical expertise collected over the centuries, placing them at the apex of their respective local hierarchies and handing them a degree of social control over their constituency much greater than that exercised by modernist *ulama* (Turmudi 2004, p. 42). Doctrinally, modernists refer primarily to the Qur'an and the Sunnah (compendia of the exemplary behaviour of the Prophet Mohammad), and are opposed to religious practices not based on strict Islamic prescriptions. Modernists promote *ijtihad*, the individual reasoning to understand the Qur'an, which grants Muslims the freedom of adopting or rejecting aspects of the *mazhab* (Hidayatullah 2000, pp. 2–3). These doctrinal differences are also reflected in socio-economic and regional splits. The traditionalist community has its strongholds in the rural areas of Central and East Java, with its members living in or around Islamic boarding schools (*pesantren*) and working in lower-class jobs as farmers, small traders, and labourers. The modernists, on the other hand, are largely urban-based, better educated, typically work as traders, entrepreneurs, and professionals, and are particularly strong in the Outer Islands.

The two groups differ not only in their religious practices and socio-economic profiles, but also in their concepts of the relationship between the Muslim community and the state. The two constituencies use different reference sources in determining their position vis-à-vis state authorities and therefore often develop very different attitudes towards incumbent regimes. The basis for the spiritual and political behaviour of traditionalist leaders is the *kitab kuning*, commentaries on medieval Sunni jurisprudence. As explained by Greg Fealy (1998, pp. 50–68), the main sources of this compilation are texts of Middle Eastern scholars and jurists written between the tenth and fifteenth centuries, such as al-Baghdadi (d. 1037), al-Mawardi (974–1058), al-Ghazali (1058–1111), Ibn Jama'a (d. 1333), and Ibn Khaldun (d. 1406). These texts reflect the political decline of the Abbasid caliphate. The caliphs, traditionally the political as well as the religious heads of the Islamic community, lost their powers gradually to a succession of foreign invaders and local warlords. This forced the jurists of the caliphate to adjust their religio-political theories to reflect the shift in power. The majority of the *ulama* opted to avoid conflict with the new power-holders by declaring social order as the priority of the Islamic community (Fealy 1998, pp. 51–52). In their view, violent opposition against the government would disrupt the very political stability that the philosophers asserted was the precondition for the enforcement of God's law (Daman 2001, pp. 87–88). This jurisprudential focus allowed the followers of the powerless caliph to avoid risks to the *umat* by collaborating with the new regime. The upholding of a strong government, regardless of its religious orientation, was seen as preferable to anarchy, which was synonymous with the betrayal of Muslim interests.

The political experience of the Sunni theorists supported the accommodative nature of traditionalist legal-political theory. Like the caliphs, the *kiai* felt responsible for the spiritual *and* material well being of their followers (Sukamto 2003, pp. 84–97). And, like the philosophers and jurists of the caliphate, the *kiai* feared that a possible breakdown of political order would diminish their privileged place in the social hierarchy. This concept of avoiding risks in the interests of the *umat* was also expressed in the traditionalist interpretation of the Qur'anic injunction of *amar ma'ruf nahi munkar* (enjoining good and preventing evil). Sunni theorists frequently used the injunction to justify their concept of choosing compromise with the power-holders over the risk of challenging them.[6] The judgement about what exactly constituted danger and what suitable compromise rested with the *ulama*, and formed a large part of the *fikih* discourse (the study of Islamic jurisprudence). In later discussions about *amar ma'ruf nahi munkar*, traditionalist leaders laid the main stress on the obligation of the *kiai* to cooperate with the government, give advice to those in power, and thereby protect their own communities.

The modernists, on the other hand, intended not only to reform Islam as a faith by challenging the validity of the medieval sources used by traditionalists, but also to make Islam relevant and competitive in the modern world. One of the leading questions for Indonesian modernists has been: "Why are the Muslims backward while the infidels are affluent?" The Egyptian thinker Amir Shakib Arsalan, one of the most prominent intellectuals of the global modernist movement, published a book of that title in 1930. The book was widely read in the Middle East and in Indonesia, and Arsalan claimed that it was an Indonesian scholar who had put the question to him (Dhofier 1990, p. 170). The improvement of social and economic conditions for the Muslim community, the quest for technological innovations that would close the growing gap with the West, and the mobilization of resources to recruit traditionalist Muslims to their cause became central issues in the theological and political agenda of the modernists.[7] As far as their relationship with the state was concerned, modernist intellectuals had considerable differences among themselves, but agreed that it had to be defined through references to original sources of the Islamic faith. Robert Hefner (2000, p. 40), for example, pointed out that modernist thinkers of the pre-independence period differed on the question of the Islamic state, but they did so in reference to their different readings of the Qur'an. The traditionalists, by contrast, could formulate their attitude towards models of state organization on the basis of what was best for the political interests of the *umat* at that particular point of time.

The religious, socio-economic, and political interests of the modernist and traditionalist communities have been represented since the 1910s and 1920s by two major and a number of smaller organizations. The main traditionalist organization is Nahdlatul Ulama (NU, Revival of the Islamic Scholars). It was founded in 1926 and currently claims a membership of over 35 million, with the majority of its followers concentrated in East and Central Java. The *ulama* or *kiai* have traditionally dominated the religious and political course of the organization, with its executive board assigned to carry out the directives of the clerics. There are a number of smaller traditionalist organizations such as *al-Jamiyatul al-Wasyliah* and *Persatuan Tarbiyah Indonesia* or Perti (West Sumatra), *Mathlaul Anwar* (West Java) and *Nahdlatul Wathan* (Lombok), but their influence is limited to their local contexts. The largest modernist organization is Muhammadiyah, with a membership of around 25 million. Founded in 1912, it drew its members from the urban upper and middle classes, providing the organization with considerable funds to develop a wide network of schools, libraries, and hospitals (Noer 1994, p. 95). Professionals, university lecturers, and bureaucrats have played a large role in Muhammadiyah's leadership (Alfian 1989, p. 189). Other modernist organizations include *Persatuan Islam* and *al-Irsyad*, but they are much smaller both in membership numbers and political significance. NU and Muhammadiyah have for much of Indonesia's political history succeeded in defending their status as the main representational bodies of their communities in national politics.

## COMPETING FOR HEGEMONY: MUSLIMS AND THE STATE

The religious and social divisions within the Muslim community resulted in stark political differences. Fealy (2003, p. 153) asserted that "when it came to politics, each stream had major differences over ideology, policy and leadership style, and each used different aspects of Islamic thought and tradition to legitimate their particular approach to politics". Most of the controversies focused on the structure, identity, and resources of the state. In this respect, there were two main areas of debate: one that concerned the formal role of Islam in the state, while the other related to the function of the state as the main distributor of funds, positions, and privileges to particular constituencies.

The controversy over the role of Islam in the state has created substantial fractures in Indonesia's civilian polity. In June 1945, when a committee for the preparation of Indonesian independence discussed the issue, there were fierce debates between those who wanted to see *syariat*, or Islamic law, recognized in the constitution and those who argued for a religiously neutral state. Non-Muslims and *abangan* nationalists warned that the inclusion of *syariat* in the constitution would encourage predominantly non-Muslim areas to secede from the nation state, and some *santri* politicians agreed (Sekretariat Negara Republik Indonesia 1995, pp. 213–14). The representatives of Muhammadiyah and NU, however, insisted on an explicit role for Islam in legal and political affairs. On 22 June 1945, the delegates reached a compromise: the preamble of the constitution, or Jakarta Charter, would include a seven-word clause which translated as: "with the obligation for adherents of Islam to practise Islamic law" (*dengan kewajiban menjalankan syariat Islam bagi pemeluk-pemeluknya*). The exact meaning of this clause remained open to dispute, however, especially as far as its legal consequences were concerned. Muslim delegates pointed out that the state was given no authority to enforce the regulation, and demanded that, at the very least, the president had to be a Muslim in order to ensure that *syariat* was observed. Sukarno, the main nationalist leader, convinced Christian delegates to accept this proposal, and it was adopted as an additional paragraph in the draft constitution (Boland 1982; Basalim 2002).

The compromise did not last long, however. Delegates from the predominantly Christian areas of Ambon and the Minahasa reported that significant segments of their societies threatened to separate from the Indonesian Republic if the Jakarta Charter came into effect. In fact, the split of the Republic into a large number of smaller states was exactly what the returning Dutch forces were hoping for (Chauvel 1990, p. 198). Against this background, secular nationalists under the leadership of Hatta convinced the proponents of the "*syariat* clause" on 18 August to drop their demands, and the constitution was subsequently passed without the "seven words" and the stipulation that the president had to be a Muslim. In consequence, Islamic leaders were deeply disappointed by what they saw as an unbalanced political compromise. They consoled their supporters, however, by claiming the first principle of the Pancasila ideology, the "belief in Almighty God" (*KeTuhanan yang Maha Esa*), as the result of their insistence on monotheism. Moreover, Muslim politicians also considered the compromise to be temporary, and intended to reopen the debate once the struggle against the Dutch was over. Expecting to win sufficient majorities in the post-independence elections, they were confident that they could implement Islamic law through legislation and the anticipated revision of the constitution.

Developments after 1949, though, failed to satisfy the expectations of Islamic leaders. The elections of 1955 did not produce the majority for Islamic parties that their leaders had predicted. Combined, parties with explicitly Islamic profiles won only 43 per cent of the votes, denying them the necessary numbers to push *syariat*-based laws through parliament. In addition, the constitutional assembly, the body tasked with producing a new constitution from 1956 onwards, deliberated for three years on the reintroduction of the original Jakarta Charter without reaching agreement on the issue. The secular-nationalist parties, backed up by Sukarno and the armed forces, were opposed to its reinstatement, and in a series of votes in May and June 1959, the supporters of the Charter failed to reach the necessary two-thirds majority (Nasution 1992). On the other hand, the non-Islamic parties proposed to return to the presidential constitution of 1945, but did not manage to gain a majority either. As a result, the assembly was deadlocked. The inability of Indonesia's political parties to compromise on the future constitution added to the increasing impatience of the public with the parliamentary system (Feith 1967, p. 361). In contrast to 1945, when the goal of independence and the threat of the returning Dutch had forced key societal forces to cooperate and compromise, the constitutional debates of the late 1950s deepened the political divisions and accelerated the decline of the democratic polity. On 5 July 1959, Sukarno dissolved the assembly and declared the return to the 1945 constitution, marking the end of the parliamentary system.

The debate over the role of Islam in the state polarized civilian politics along secular-nationalist and Islamic lines, but the Muslim forces were deeply divided as well. Their conflicts focused largely on the second issue in Islam-state relations: the function of state bodies as the largest distributor of institutional and material privileges. In this regard, the department of religious affairs was, and still is, of crucial importance to both traditionalist and modernist constituencies. It has responsibility for central aspects of Islamic life, including religious education, authority over marital, inheritance, and divorce laws, as well as *hajj* affairs.[8] For NU particularly, the department has been the predominant vehicle of patronage and material advancement for its supporters.[9] It offers civil service positions to both *kiai* and *pesantren*-educated *santri*, and its control of funds, contracts, and licences has given NU much needed access to the economic infrastructure of the state. While modernists tend to posses the necessary educational backgrounds to gain employment in other ministries as well, NU politicians typically had to focus on the department of religious affairs as their sole source of bureaucratic power (van Bruinessen 1994, pp. 79–80). Accordingly, the struggle to control the department has created serious tensions between modernist and traditionalist organizations and parties for much of Indonesia's modern history, including the transition after 1998. It was a critical issue in the formation and disintegration of cabinets in the 1950s, and provided the authoritarian regimes of Sukarno and Suharto with a welcome tool to lure Muslim groups into backing their rule.

## CONFLICT AND DECLINE: ISLAMIC POLITICS IN THE 1950s AND 1960s

The fight for the reinstatement of the Jakarta Charter was one of the few political issues that traditionalist and modernist Muslim politicians agreed on. The differences over other doctrinal, social, and political questions were substantial, and ultimately caused the failure of attempts to create and maintain a single Islamic party. In 1945, most Islamic organizations had united to form the party Masyumi (*Majelis Syuro Muslimin Indonesia*, Indonesian Muslim Advisory Council). Tensions within Masyumi grew continuously after 1949, however, when younger modernist politicians took control of the party and demanded that it acquire a more "rational" and "modern" outlook. In the following years, the political authority of the NU-dominated supervisory board was gradually reduced in favour of the central board led by the modernist Mohamad Natsir, resulting in a widespread feeling of marginalization within NU.[10] The number of Muhammadiyah representatives in the party leadership increased steadily, from under 30 per cent in 1949 to around 50 per cent in 1952 (Syaifullah 1997, p. 190). Many of the old animosities between traditionalists and modernists re-emerged during the conflict over the party leadership, with modernists portraying their traditionalist counterparts as obstacles to political reform and social modernization, and the traditionalists fearing that their rivals wanted to erode their authority over the NU *santri*. The control of the department of religious affairs was an equally contentious issue in the party. Consequently, it was a conflict over the department in 1952 that escalated tensions within Masyumi. When modernist elements claimed the ministry for themselves, NU declared its separation from Masyumi and the establishment of its own party.

The secession of NU from Masyumi convinced both communities that political representation of their interests through an Islamic umbrella organization was impossible. As a result, each constituency felt that they needed their own party in order to compete in politics, catalyzing a tendency for particularism in the Muslim community that would, much later, cause the proliferation of Islamic parties in the post-Suharto era. The split also sharpened the specific profiles of the parties used by the various groups. NU established itself as a Java-centric, pragmatic party that sought to protect the interests of the traditionalist community by approaching politics in a flexible, moderate, and compromise-oriented fashion. Its populist sentiments brought it close to the Sukarnoist PNI (*Partai Nasional Indonesia*, Indonesian Nationalist Party), which in turn was attracted by NU's sympathies for syncretistic religious practices. The modernist Masyumi, on the other hand, pursued political and economic modernization in a "rational" and technocratic manner, and rejected NU's compromise-seeking policies as lacking conviction and conceptual thinking. This rationalist interpretation of politics allied Masyumi with socialist and non-Muslim parties which, like Masyumi itself, had their strongholds in the Outer Islands. The political and regional preferences of the Islamic parties and their secular counterparts were highlighted by the outcome of the 1955 general elections. Masyumi gained 20.9 per cent of the vote, and emerged as the dominant political force in the Outer Islands. NU came third with 18.4 per cent, with its supporters largely concentrated in Central and East Java. On the secular-nationalist side, PNI became the strongest of all parties with 22.3 per cent, and the PKI took the fourth place with 15.4 per cent. The split between Java-based parties, like NU and PKI, and the parties dominating the Outer Islands, had a significant impact on political developments in the post-election period (Feith 1957).

Both NU and Masyumi were drawn into the spiralling political crisis of the mid to late 1950s. As the strongest party in the Outer Islands, Masyumi played a major role in the regional uprisings on Sumatra and Sulawesi in 1956–58. There, several regional administrations were toppled by alliances between Masyumi politicians critical of the centralist policies of the Jakarta government and local military commanders dissatisfied with the dominance of army headquarters over their affairs. The rebellions were defeated militarily, discrediting Masyumi in the eyes of the political elite and making it largely ineffective in defending the increasingly embattled parliamentary system. Combining with widespread societal apathy towards liberal democracy and its parties, the regionalist insurgencies provided Sukarno and the armed forces with welcome arguments in their lobbying for an authoritarian solution to the crisis (van der Kroef 1957, pp. 49–54). NU, for its part, appeared unwilling to resist the mounting calls for replacing the democratic system. The 1955 result for the PKI had come as a shock to many NU leaders, and the communists had improved their position further in local elections on Java in 1957. If the PKI was able to sustain this trend under the existing democratic polity, it might have emerged as the largest political party at the next national election. The prospect of having an atheist party dominating parliament and government, and the fear that communist grassroots leaders would expand their influence at the expense of the *kiai*, undermined the support of NU politicians for parliamentary democracy. Thus when Sukarno erected his Guided Democracy, Masyumi and NU were incapable or reluctant to offer meaningful resistance (Lev 1966).

The imposition of Guided Democracy marked the beginning of almost four decades of authoritarian rule and political marginalization of Islam. The early phase of Sukarno's regime saw the evolution of a general pattern that exploited the divisions between Islamic groups as an instrument of political legitimacy and regime maintenance. Based on the presumption that any form of non-democratic rule in Indonesia needed the endorsement of at least one of the two major currents of political Islam, Sukarno invited NU to join his regime, but deliberately excluded Masyumi. In the lead up to his 1959 decree, Sukarno had observed that NU was reluctant to support Guided Democracy, but appeared ready to compromise. Masyumi, on the other hand, was unwaveringly opposed to the authoritarian shift (Maarif 1996, p. 54). The difference in NU's and Masyumi's attitudes towards Guided Democracy contributed significantly to the consolidation of non-democratic rule. Fealy (1998, p. 223) suggested that "had NU joined Masyumi in rejecting the Konsepsi and Karya cabinet, Sukarno would have been forced to abandon or moderate his plans".[11] After long internal debates, NU accepted Sukarno's invitation, and in exchange retained the department of religious affairs and significant representation in the restructured parliament.[12] The main argument of the NU board for joining Guided Democracy was to ensure that Muslim interests were sufficiently represented, and that participation in the regime was necessary to control the expansion of the PKI (Haidar 1994). Masyumi, by contrast, was banned in 1960, and two years later many of its leaders were arrested and imprisoned (Mrazek 1994, pp. 463–64).

The differences within Islamic groups over their attitude towards Guided Democracy not only helped Sukarno and the armed forces to establish and sustain their authoritarian rule, but also had long-term effects on the relationship between civilian forces and non-democratic polities. Nahdlatul Ulama's acceptance of Sukarno's regime in exchange for political concessions signalled that representation in government was more important to its institutional interests than the nature of the political system it participated in.[13] The support for democratic principles of state organization appeared to be negotiable if authoritarian actors offered the same political resources that otherwise were only accessible after intense competition in parliamentary systems. NU's indifference towards the destruction of Masyumi by the authoritarian regime also gave rise to a sense of bitterness in some sections of the modernist community, aggravating the tensions within the *umat* and allowing future non-democratic rulers to manipulate them for their political purposes. The prioritization of regime engagement over democratic values and the growing intra-Islamic antagonism developed into important elements of Indonesia's political culture, and they would impact significantly on the early period in post-Suharto politics between 1998 and 2004.

## FRUSTRATED EXPECTATIONS: MUSLIM GROUPS IN THE EARLY NEW ORDER

Suharto's rise to power in 1965 further marginalized political Islam. This was a big disappointment to Muslim groups, who had hoped for increased regime participation after assisting the army in its purge of the PKI. In fact, in the years preceding the military takeover, some Islamic leaders had entered into an informal alliance with anti-communist segments within the armed forces. Traditionalist *kiai* in particular had been concerned that the rapid expansion of the PKI into rural areas could threaten their dominance over Nahdlatul Ulama's core constituency.[14] They established militias to defend their interests, which in turn sought contacts with and advice from military officers.[15] The political turmoil surrounding the events of 30 September 1965, during which the army claimed to have aborted a communist coup attempt, led to almost institutional cooperation between the armed forces and Muslim groups in eradicating the PKI. Islamic youth organizations, mostly but not exclusively NU-affiliated, played a major role in destroying the infrastructure of the PKI and killing probably several hundred thousand of its members. In many cases, the army rounded up suspected communists, loaded them on trucks, and delivered them to a location where members of Muslim militias stood by to kill them (Young 1990, p. 79). The involvement of civilian groups in the killings not only fulfilled logistical purposes, however. More significantly, it made a large number of civilians dependent on the establishment and continuation of a regime that would prevent investigations into the legality of these actions. The New Order was such a regime, offering protection to those involved in the unlawful killings and asking for political support in return.

While neither the traditionalist nor the modernist Muslim groups intended to facilitate the rise of a military-run dictatorship, they assisted the army in dismantling the political structures of Guided Democracy and establishing the New Order polity. By doing so, they demonstrated that under conditions that threatened their core interests, key civilian organizations were prepared to accept military intervention in politics as a legitimate instrument for settling societal disputes. Like most political actors at that time, Islamic organizations and parties believed that interference by the armed forces in politics was temporary, and that the regime emerging from the post-coup turmoil would serve their interests better than previous political systems. The modernists expected to end their marginalization from political life and return to the arena of the leading societal forces. Nahdlatul Ulama politicians, on the other hand, hoped that the post-Sukarno state would reward them for their close cooperation with the army in destroying the PKI. Accordingly, NU members of parliament played a crucial role in Sukarno's political demise and Suharto's ascent to the presidency (Feillard 1996).[16] In the same vein, modernist student leaders were at the forefront of the movement that demanded Sukarno's resignation, allowing Suharto and the armed forces to consolidate their grip on power. It was only by 1967 that Islamic leaders began to realize that their support for the army had not only resulted in the collapse of Sukarno's pro-communist regime, but also in the creation of another authoritarian polity with equally strong reservations towards political Islam (Wahid 2000, pp. 74–75).

The optimistic atmosphere of cooperation among Muslim groups that had accompanied the decline of Guided Democracy and the rise of the Suharto regime dissipated soon after the new rulers had consolidated their position. With the PKI destroyed, the single most important bond of solidarity between Islamic organizations had vanished, and their diverging interests began to dominate the political attitudes within the *umat* once again. Faced with an unsympathetic regime, the two currents of Indonesian Islam competed for the few privileges and resources available under the new polity. In doing so, they were likely to develop highly diverse attitudes towards the regime in order to outplay each other, offering Suharto opportunities to demonstrate the powers of retribution and patronage at his disposal. Like Sukarno's Guided Democracy, Suharto's regime was aware that it was crucial to gain the support of at least one of the two major Islamic groups to legitimize its authoritarian rule. In theory, the integralist nature of the New Order sought the cooperation, and eventual cooptation, of both constituencies, but in the reality of pragmatic power politics, the support of only one stream was sufficient. For Suharto, however, the most important goal in this regard was to prevent both constituencies from uniting against the government and withdrawing the Islamic credentials they supplied to the regime.

As anticipated by most observers and Suharto himself, the modernist and traditionalist groups indeed used different approaches in defining their relationship with the new regime. In fact, their attitudes towards the early New Order were a direct reversal of their roles in establishing Guided Democracy. This time, NU chose a more confrontational strategy. The reason for this was not so much opposition towards the non-democratic nature of the regime, but its gradual exclusion from it. NU lost the department of religious affairs in 1971, was severely intimidated by the military in the elections of the same year (Ward 1974), and had to give up its status as an autonomous political party in 1973 when it was merged into the all-Islamic PPP under modernist leadership. By the mid-1970s, Suharto counted NU among the opponents of his regime, and removed most of its officials from public office.[17] The modernist community had a more diverse approach, but none of its key groups chose to confront the New Order state. Arguably, it was the bitter experience of marginalization under Guided Democracy that led most modernist organizations to drive an accommodationist course. Muhammadiyah decided at its 1971 congress to eschew active politics, followed by an influx of bureaucrats into the national and regional leadership boards.[18] A substantial proportion of them would later become members of Golkar. By the 1990s, 78 per cent of Muhammadiyah's leadership personnel were state bureaucrats (Nashir 2000, p. 8). Many former modernist politicians, on the other hand, joined Parmusi (*Partai Muslimin Indonesia*, Indonesian Muslim Party), the Islamic party sanctioned by the government after it had objected to the rehabilitation of Masyumi in 1967 (Ward 1970; Anwar 1995, pp. 27–28; Thaba 1996, pp. 246–52). At the same time, prominent members of Masyumi founded *Dewan Dakwah Islamiyah Indonesia* (DDII, Indonesian Council for Islamic Predication), which assembled modernists with a more scripturalist understanding of Islam. It concentrated on missionary and social work (*dakwah*) in order to avoid open confrontation with the increasingly repressive regime (Liddle 1996; Abdillah 1999, pp. 261–62).

The reversed intra-Islamic power relations under the early New Order pointed to the continued divisions between the modernist and traditionalist constituencies. Many of the doctrinal and socio-cultural differences remained relevant, and the key organizations Nahdlatul Ulama and Muhammadiyah still viewed each other as competitors in the struggle for religio-political hegemony and access to the socio-economic infrastructure of the state (Azra 2000, p. 371). Just as Nahdlatul Ulama had reacted with indifference to the destruction of Masyumi in 1960, and had accepted regime participation in return, so did modernist elements in the 1970s and early 1980s tolerate, or even applaud, the marginalization of NU from the political arena. In fact, modernist politicians actively sidelined NU representatives from the leadership of PPP, assisting the regime in maintaining high levels of conflict between modernists and traditionalists throughout the New Order period. The internal competition within PPP not only allowed the regime to hand out rewards to loyalists and retaliate against opponents but also reduced the capacity of the party to challenge Golkar at the general elections (Haris 1991, pp. 98–106). The intra-Islamic fragmentation, therefore, served to stabilize the authoritarian regime, which both created and cultivated the divisions to prolong its rule.

## ADAPTATION AND CONFRONTATION: THE LATER NEW ORDER

The capacity of the regime to distribute favours and inflict punishment encouraged modernist and traditionalist intellectuals to reformulate the political and ideological guidelines for their relations with the state. This led to significant changes within the ideological frameworks of both Islamic constituencies from the early 1970s onwards. In the pre-New Order period, traditionalist thinkers had defended NU's endorsement of regimes that differed from the ideal of an Islamic state by referring to the accommodationist principles of Sunni theology. The modernists, on the other hand, had accepted the parliamentary system of the 1950s only as a means to achieve their ultimate goal, the establishment of an "Islamic democracy", and had refused to cooperate when Guided Democracy put an end to that option. By contrast, in the early 1970s some Muslim intellectuals and politicians began to question the benefit of elite politics as such, using the banner of the "reform movement" (gerakan pembaruan), and in later years, "cultural Islam" (Islam kultural). These new conceptual patterns were motivated by three major conclusions related to the history of Islamic politics in Indonesia: first, the major Muslim parties had failed to achieve any of their goals. They had not gained a majority in elections, had not succeeded in implementing syariat, and had created anything but unity within the umat. Second, the partial confrontation with the New Order had only worsened the situation of Muslims. Finally, the concentration on political competition had distracted Muslim leaders from further developing the intellectual, cultural, and doctrinal principles of Islamic life.

The intellectual reform movement in the Islamic community called on Muslims to practise their faith in a manner that was not only concerned with formal fulfilment of religious regulations, but emphasized the doctrinal substance of Islam: justice, social equality, and human dignity. While "cultural Islam" appeared to mark the departure from Islamic politics, it in fact paved the way for increased participation of Muslim organizations in the structures of the New Order by shifting their attention from the ideal of an Islamic state to the religious and social goals achievable under existing political regimes (Effendy 1998, pp. 189–93; Anwar 1995, p. 240). In the modernist discourse, the young intellectual Nurcholish Madjid called for the depoliticization of Islamic theology, proposing that Muslims concentrate on the application of basic Islamic values in the context of modern, industrializing states.[19] In the framework of the New Order and its booming economy, this stress on Islamic principles such as social equality created a strong incentive for modernists to cooperate with the regime instead of pursuing the ideal of an Islamic state or society from the political margins. For example, the modernist intellectual Adi Sasono (1995, p. 31) legitimated interaction with the state as an instrument to propagate economic redistribution of resources from well-connected Chinese tycoons to Muslim entrepreneurs:

How can you change the situation without power? You can become someone at the periphery whose job it is to read poems. But power is not the same as government. Om Liem [the Chinese tycoon Liem Soei Liong, M.M.] is not the government, but who would deny that he has power?

This concept saw engagement with the regime not as an act of transitional cooperation in times of emergency, but as a legitimate effort to improve the social conditions of Muslims and to uphold justice. Similar processes of theological modernization occurred in the traditionalist community. Under the leadership of Abdurrahman Wahid, who became chairman of Nahdlatul Ulama in 1984,[20] young NU intellectuals began to review the sources of traditionalist thinking. They argued that the *kitab kuning* had to be reinterpreted in order to fit into the contexts of modern state organization (Aleana 2000, p. x). In their view, cooperation with unsympathetic power-holders was not, as the Sunni theorists had proclaimed, a necessity in times of exceptional circumstances, but an integral part of the political process.

Despite reservations from more scripturalist Islamic scholars, the new doctrinal frameworks eventually allowed traditionalist and modernist organizations to compete openly for the resources and institutional privileges that the state had at its disposal. After having suffered from continued economic isolation throughout the 1970s, NU dramatically improved its relationship with Suharto in 1984 by endorsing the government's controversial plan of prescribing Pancasila as the sole ideological principle for all mass organizations. In an interview with John Bresnan (1993, p. 240), an NU leader, presumably Abdurrahman Wahid, left no doubt about the motivation behind NU's decision to seek cooperation with the regime:

> I reached an agreement with the government. They agreed that all NU people who had been civil servants, and left the civil service to take political posts with PPP would be reinstated. They also agreed they would give preference to NU people in making new appointments to the civil service, assuming they met the necessary requirements. The government also agreed that NU would receive licences for economic activities, so we can support ourselves by our own efforts.

Under Wahid's leadership, NU declared its departure from party politics, withdrawing its organizational support from PPP and opening the traditionalist constituency for Golkar's electoral efforts.[21] The modernists, on the other hand, were pleased with a series of political moves by Suharto, from the late 1980s onwards, that indicated his willingness to revise some of the restrictions on political Islam. Suharto initiated a number of laws strengthening Islamic courts and educational institutions, went on a much-publicized *hajj*, and approved the foundation of a modernist-dominated organization of Muslim intellectuals, ICMI (*Ikatan Cendekiawan Muslim se-Indonesia*, Indonesian Association of Muslim Intellectuals).[22] Under the leadership of Suharto's trusted Minister of Research and Technology B. J. Habibie, ICMI became the main political vehicle for government bureaucrats and modernist leaders for promoting explicitly Islamic policies in the field of economic distribution and socio-religious representation (Susanto 1995, pp. 35–36; Karim 1999, p. 229).

The increased integration of modernist Muslim figures into the regime led to fresh tensions between the traditionalist and modernist currents of Indonesian Islam. Abdurrahman Wahid (1995, p. 20) was highly critical of ICMI and warned that it could facilitate the rise of "sectarianism". In order to counter the political manoeuvres of modernist politicians and activists, Wahid began to forge alliances with opponents of ICMI, including nationalist intellectuals, politicians in the PDI, and military officers close to Benny Murdani. The regime retaliated by challenging Wahid's leadership of NU. In 1994, Wahid was able to fend off a regime-sponsored attempt to unseat him as NU chairman (Fealy 1996; Wahid, Ghazali, and Suwendi 1999, p. 28). The government continued to apply pressure on NU's branches, however, withholding economic resources and marginalizing NU officials from political life. By 1995, Nahdlatul Ulama was confronted with a similar situation to that of the early 1980s, when the economic problems of many *pesantren* communities had forced the NU leadership to reconsider its stand towards the regime. Left with very few political options, Wahid reconciled with Suharto in 1996, much to the pleasure of local NU leaders who saw an immediate change in the attitude of government offices and the security forces towards their organization (Sujuthi 2001, p. 121). Just like in the post-reconciliation period of the mid-1980s, previously withheld funds for the *pesantren* were made available, and regime support for anti-Wahid elements within NU was suspended. The 1997 elections consolidated the accord, with Wahid introducing Suharto's daughter to key *pesantren* leaders and helping to secure an unprecedented electoral triumph for Golkar.

NU's reconciliation with the regime coincided with a sharp decline in the relationship between Suharto and senior modernist leaders. Muhammadiyah chairman Amien Rais,[23] a senior member of the ICMI leadership, started criticizing the president in late 1996 on a wide variety of issues, ranging from the businesses run by Suharto's family to his failure to provide a schedule for his departure from politics. Once a staunch supporter of regime accommodation in order to defend the interests of political Islam from within the administration, Amien now believed that the New Order had gained more from this cooperation than the Islamic forces he represented.[24] The government responded to Amien's criticism by mobilizing its well-established mechanisms of regime exclusion, socio-political isolation, and the creation of internal divisions. Amien was forced to resign from ICMI, and calls for him to stand down from the Muhammadiyah chairmanship were heard from within the organization. The very policies of repression and intimidation that were lifted from NU branches and their affiliated *pesantren* in late 1996 began to impact on Muhammadiyah and its network of educational institutions.[25] As the 1997 elections approached, the key figures of traditionalist and modernist Islam found themselves, once again, in diametrically opposed positions vis-à-vis the regime.

The fact that the political antagonism between key Muslim groups persisted despite the gradually narrowing doctrinal and cultural gap was largely related to the absence of unifying themes of all-Islamic concern in the late New Order. Ironically, the support of the Suharto regime for the process of cultural Islamization, and the concessions it had made to some of the legal-political demands of the *umat* since the late 1980s, had taken away the few opportunities in which major Muslim organizations could demonstrate the potential strength of Islamic solidarity. In 1973 and 1978, modernists and traditionalists had united to oppose new marriage laws and an MPR decree on the role of syncretism, forcing the regime to revise some of its positions. These moments of Islamic unity had become rare, with the regime allowing for a larger role of Islam in society and granting rewards to those organizations that supported its rule. In fact, the pro-Islamic policies of the regime in the early 1990s proved to be a divisive factor in intra-*umat* relations. While Wahid was opposed to state support for the Islamization of society, and viewed religious practice as a personal matter, the modernists threw their full support behind Suharto's new approach. The policies of retribution and patronage exercised by the regime on the one hand, and the continued rivalry between its leaders on the other, sustained the disharmony between the modernist and traditionalist communities and impaired their ability to formulate an alternative to the non-democratic polity of the New Order.

The New Order left important legacies that highlighted and consolidated the linkage between political conflict and military intervention in politics: first, the support for the army by key Muslim organizations in the turmoil of 1965 and 1966 defined the conditions under which major civilian groups viewed military intervention in politics as an acceptable form of political interaction. The massive threat of the PKI towards the religio-political privileges of both the traditionalist and modernist communities legitimized, in the eyes of Muslim leaders, temporary praetorian rule. When Islamic groups realized that the armed forces had no intention of handing back power to civilian actors, the authoritarian regime was already deeply entrenched in the political system. Second, the emphasis that civilian groups put on gaining representation in and resources from the New Order government suggested that they interpreted politics largely as a quest for regime participation rather than for a democratic system in which different concepts and ideas compete for acceptance at the ballot box. Allan A. Samson (1978, p. 200) concluded that "Nahdlatul Ulama is not so much a goal-centered political party as it is a religious welfare organization governed by a confederation of religious and political notables." The focus on constituency welfare made the form and quality of the political system in which it was achieved an issue of secondary concern, allowing Islamic groups to accept military-backed authoritarian rule as long as it paid attention to their interests. Third, the continued divisions between modernist and traditionalist groups provided the regime with the opportunity of using its instruments of retribution and patronage in order to secure the cooperation of and legitimation by at least one of the major Islamic groups at any given time.

## ISLAMIC MILITANCY: SECURITY THREAT OR POLITICAL MANIPULATION?

The differences between Islamic and secular groups on the one hand and the divisions within the *umat* on the other had a significant impact on the political landscape of Indonesia. The divisions led to tensions and self-destructive behaviour within the civilian sphere of politics, affected the institutional functionality of liberal democracy, and provided opportunities for non-democratic actors to seize power and sustain it for extended periods of time. These conflicts were, however, of a largely political nature, and provided indirect "invitations" for the armed forces to intervene. In contrast, the existence of a small, but militant segment of political Islam has constituted a direct security threat to all regimes from the emergency governments during the guerrilla war to the incumbent Yudhoyono administration. The intensity of this threat has varied greatly in the different periods of Indonesia's modern history, but it has occasionally resulted in extensive security operations that widened the political space of the armed forces, the police, and the intelligence apparatus. The rise of Islamic militancy in the post-New Order environment, particularly between 2000 and 2005, and the fact that most of these groups have their roots in radical movements under previous regimes, requires a closer look at the historical legacies of Islamic radicalism in Indonesia, and their impact on democratic consolidation in the post-Suharto era.

Extremist Islamic groups in post-colonial Indonesia first emerged during the guerrilla war against the Dutch, with Muslim clerics and leaders mobilizing militias consisting of their students and followers. Given the only rudimentary administrative control of the Republic over its territories, these militias exercised considerable authority in areas with ongoing combat operations. In West Java, a former Masyumi politician by the name of Sekarmadji Maridjan Kartosuwirjo led one such militant group, the *Darul Islam* ("Abode of Islam"). In early 1948, he declared the establishment of the Islamic Army of Indonesia (*Tentara Islam Indonesia*, TII) and subsequently refused to acknowledge the central command authority of the national army under Sudirman. By early 1949, there was open war between *Darul Islam* and the Republic. When the Republic's Siliwangi division marched into West Java after the Dutch attack on Yogyakarta in December 1948, their leaders met with heavy resistance from TII fighters (Kahin 1952, p. 409):

> Their way was bitterly contested not only by the Dutch but by the troops of Darul Islam as well, with as many casualties being lost to the latter as to the former. (This was totally unexpected, many Siliwangi units being caught completely off guard, for at the time they set out they had believed Darul Islam still backed the Republic.) Wherever the units of the Siliwangi went, they were enthusiastically received by the local inhabitants as deliverers not only from the Dutch, but from Darul Islam as well.

Despite the decimation of his forces by government troops, Kartosuwirjo announced in August 1949 the creation of the Islamic State of Indonesia (*Negara Islam Indonesia*, NII), which claimed authority not only over West Java, but the entire Indonesian territory. But except for regionally limited rebellions in South Sulawesi and Aceh, which were temporarily part of the *Darul Islam* movement, Kartosuwirjo's rebel state never gathered much support outside of its West Java strongholds. The armed forces had to allocate substantial resources to suppress the insurgency, however, and only in 1962 did the army manage to capture Kartosuwirjo. He was put on trial and executed later that year.

While the *Darul Islam* rebellion had been a serious threat to the authority of the government and the capacity of the armed forces, several actors in Indonesian politics were able to use the insurgency for their ideological and political purposes. For the nationalist groups, references to the militancy of the movement served to fend off demands for an Islamic state (Gunawan 2000, p. 39). Opponents of parliamentary democracy pointed to the failure of a series of governments to end the rebellion, calling for more "decisive" leadership and regime change. Muslim grassroots leaders, while not sympathetic to the rebels, considered *Darul Islam* a potential counterweight to the expanding mass organizations of the PKI. And the armed forces, finally, enjoyed increased political support, operational autonomy, and budget allocations to destroy *Darul Islam*, exposing the indispensability of the military to any incumbent regime.

Given this political instrumentalization of Islamic militancy in the 1950s and 1960s, it was not surprising that some factions in the intelligence services of the New Order too tried to utilize it to consolidate their grip on power. In 1977, the government announced that it had uncovered a conspiracy by former *Darul Islam* figures to regroup under the name of *Komando Jihad* ("Holy War Command"). Many leaders of PPP felt that the announcement constituted a deliberate effort by the intelligence apparatus to undermine the chances of that Muslim-based party at the approaching general elections.[26] Ali Murtopo, a senior military officer entrusted by Suharto with "special" intelligence operations, was widely believed to have engineered the emergence of *Komando Jihad*, and even some of his colleagues in the intelligence community confirmed this (Jenkins 1984, p. 57):

> So, for instance, you talk about Komando Jihad.... [Ali Murtopo] had the opinion that we must create issues. He said, 'One time we will have to use this' and so on and on. Let's say it's always in his mind.

In the wake of the *Komando Jihad* affair, the government clamped down on several other militant groups. Abu Bakar Ba'asyir, a leading member of one such group, was arrested in November 1978 and sentenced to prison for subversion (Awwas 2003, pp. 89–202). Ba'asyir would later come to prominence in the post-Suharto era as the spiritual head of *Jemaah Islamiyah* ("Islamic Community"), a terrorist group that carried out a series of bombings throughout the archipelago, including the Bali attacks of October 2002.

The political manipulation of radical Islam helped the New Order regime to broaden its legitimacy base and to justify the continued use of repression against opponents. After a decade of political consolidation, and the almost complete destruction of the communist network, the regime had to remind the public that its main mission was to defend the Pancasila state against extremist threats from both ends of the ideological spectrum.

This manipulative use of Islamic militancy, however, achieved significantly more than was initially envisaged. Sidney Jones, in an International Crisis Group report (2002, pp. 8–9), pointed to the "unintended consequences" of Murtopo's intelligence operations:

> It renewed or forged bonds among Muslim radicals in South Sulawesi, Sumatra, and Java. It promoted the idea of an Islamic state that the original Darul Islam leaders had perhaps not intended, and in doing so, tapped into an intellectual ferment that was particularly pronounced in university-based mosques. That ferment was only beginning when Komando Jihad was created, but through the late 1970s and early 1980s, it was fuelled by the Iranian revolution, the availability of writings on political Islam from the Middle East and Pakistan, and anger over Suharto government policies.

The regime began to feel the consequences of this ferment in September 1984, when Muslim demonstrators clashed with army troops in the Jakarta harbour district of Tanjung Priok. The unrest was sparked by soldiers who had entered a mosque without removing their shoes, tearing down Islamic posters they viewed as critical of the government. When troops opened fire on the protesting crowds, at least thirty-four people were killed, but unofficial reports put the number of deaths in the hundreds (Pusat Studi dan Pengembangan Informasi 1998). The incident was followed by a series of bomb explosions on Java, including the January 1985 bombing of the Buddhist temple of Borobudur, one of Indonesia's cultural landmarks. Four years later, army troops under Colonel Hendropriyono, who later became the head of intelligence under the Megawati government, attacked a group of Muslim militants in Way Jepara, Lampung. The group had attracted followers from Java, offering an "authentic" Islamic lifestyle isolated from government intervention and secular influences. When the military sought to disperse the compound, around 100 people were killed.

The late New Order saw a drastic decline in violent Islamic activity. By the late 1980s, most of the radical leaders with roots in the *Darul Islam* movement had either been imprisoned or fled the country. Abu Bakar Ba'asyir, for example, went to Malaysia and developed a new militant network from there. The younger generation of extremists, on the other hand, chose to study in Pakistan or join the guerrilla war in Afghanistan as well as the Muslim insurgency in the Southern Philippines. Moreover, Suharto's efforts to increase Muslim participation in his regime, and his support for cultural Islamization policies, made it unnecessary (and even counterproductive) for the government's intelligence apparatus to continue manipulating violent

Islamic movements as an ideological deterrent. Finally, some of the ultra-modernist Islamic groups that had withdrawn into *dakwah* activities in the late 1960s and early 1970s began to reconcile with the New Order. While not directly linked with the most militant of the groups, *Dewan Dakwah* leaders had considerable influence over those elements of radical Islam that opposed the regime but were unwilling to use violence to achieve their goals. Since the early 1990s, some of these clerics and activists developed ties with central figures of the regime, in particular with a group around Prabowo Subianto, Suharto's son-in-law and seen as a rising star in the armed forces (Hefner 2000, p. 201). With the relationship between the government and the most radical elements of the modernist mainstream considerably improved, many Islamic militants temporarily suspended their opposition to the regime.

The activities of militant Islamic groups throughout Indonesia's post-independence history have left important legacies for the current democratic transition. These legacies are largely related to theories of threat levels as explanations for military intervention in politics. Authors such as Michael Desch identified high levels of internal threat as incentives for military intervention, with security operations against insurgencies and terrorist cells providing the armed forces with expanded resources and authority. As the introduction has shown, however, the threat level theories are vulnerable to cases in which regimes or elements within them have an interest in creating artificial threats in order to serve their political purposes, such as the justification of repressive measures against dissidents or higher budget allocations for security forces. Evidently, the history of Islamic militancy in Indonesia is a case in point. On the one hand, the military campaign against the *Darul Islam* rebellion in West Java confronted a "real" threat to the stability of the state and strengthened the armed forces vis-à-vis civilian politicians as a result. On the other hand, the case of the *Komando Jihad* campaign in 1977 exposed the importance of manipulated images of militant Islam for purposes of power maintenance and regime legitimation.

This chapter discussed societal divisions over the role of Islam in the state as a case study of intra-civilian conflict in Indonesia. The severity of these splits has assisted non-democratic actors, including the armed forces, to gain political control and sustain decades of authoritarian rule. The internal fractures within the Muslim community between traditionalists and modernists have been a particular source of instability in the civilian realm. Despite the gradual reduction of doctrinal and socio-cultural differences, the cleavages have remained politically volatile. In addition to the political conflict between mainstream constituencies, the existence of a tiny, but high-profile extremist segment of Islam destabilized the civilian polity. The political impact of these tensions both weakened the civilian capacity to establish strong governance and aggravated the domestic security situation. Consequently, Indonesia became a classic example of a state in which serious conflicts between key civilian forces and rising internal threat levels resulted in increased military intervention in politics. The legacy of this civilian fragmentation, which stretched from the colonial period to the late New Order polity, was about to leave its mark on the 1998 regime change and extend into the subsequent post-authoritarian transition.

## Notes

1   These figures are based on the registration of voters conducted by the central statistics board in 2004, which concluded that the total population stood at 220,953,634, and the census of 2000, which established the percentage of religious affiliations.

2   The term "umat" (Ar. *umma*), literally "community", "people" or "nation", is in the Islamic context used to describe the community of believers, i.e. Muslims.

3   The following paragraphs on the doctrinal and social differences between Muslim groups are largely based on Fealy (2003, pp. 150–68).

4   See, for instance, van Bruinessen (1996, p. 168) and Zayd (1997, p. 3).

5   The terms "ulama" and "kiai" are not differentiated in this book, describing religious scholars and leaders. However, some authors have pointed out that *kiai* typically are heads of Islamic boarding schools or *pesantren*, while *ulama* do not necessarily fulfil that function.

6   This guideline was also reflected in the premise *dar al-mafasid muqoddam 'ala jalb al mashalih*, which prioritizes the avoidance of danger over the quest for advantages that carry higher risks (Jamhuri 1998, p. 61).

7   In the eyes of the modernists, the traditionalist leaders were not only competitors for resources and leadership over the *umat*, they also represented the very backwardness of the Muslim community that the modernists hoped to leave behind. The traditionalists had, in their view, allowed non-Islamic elements to intrude the sanctity of their faith, and had therefore to shoulder the blame for its demise.

8   *Hajj* is the pilgrimage to the holy site of Mecca. It is required for all Muslims who can afford it.

9   While *kiai* raise some of the funds necessary to run their boarding schools from the payment of tuition fees and businesses, many *pesantren* are dependent on outside funding (Dirdjosanjoto 1999, pp. 151–53).

10  Even decades later, there was still a strong sense within NU circles that modernist politicians in Masyumi had betrayed them. An NU-sponsored pamphlet of 2002 recalled that "… Masyumi successfully cheated NU. At the beginning, activists

who had initiated Masyumi lured NU leaders to support Masyumi because the latter controlled large masses, with the promise of strategic positions like chairman of the Advisory Board or 'Consultative Council' with full authority to determine the course of Masyumi. It is indeed true that K.H. Hasyim Asy'ari became chairman of Masyumi's Advisory Board. But unfortunately, his role and functions were 'sterilized'. His talks were never given attention. His *fatwa* were always ignored" ('Ulum 2002, p. 34).

[11] Sukarno had presented his idea (*konsepsi*) of "burying the political parties" and erecting a "guided democracy" in October 1956. In response, Natsir contended that "if the parties are buried, democracy will be buried automatically". In April 1957, Sukarno installed the Kabinet Karya, a "business cabinet", replacing the last democratic government elected by the 1955 parliament (Feith 1962, p. 518).

[12] In the Sukarno-appointed parliament, NU had 51 seats (1955: 45 seats). As Masyumi had no representatives at all, however, the total number of Islamic members was only 67 out of 283, giving the nationalists a comfortable majority.

[13] The allegations of political opportunism, directed against NU by a variety of political forces, were reflected in the derogatory reference to NU's spiritual leader, Wahab Chasbullah, as "Kiai Nasakom" (Ma'shum 1998, p. 151). Sukarno had promoted Nasakom as an all-encompassing ideological concept, combining Nationalism (*Nasionalisme*), Religion (*Agama*), and Communism (*Komunisme*).

[14] In 1963, the communists had started a campaign, named the "unilateral action" (*aksi sepihak*), for the immediate implementation of land reform legislation introduced in 1960. As owners of *pesantren* and agricultural land attached to it, *kiai* became targets of the campaign (Kasdi 2001, pp. 230–31).

[15] The NU youth activist Subchan ZE became one of the main contacts between NU militias and military officers (Mandan 2001, p. 50).

[16] In contrast to the younger NU politicians, however, the "old guard" under NU General Chairman Idham Chalid supported Sukarno until it became evident that the latter's decline was irreversible.

[17] Young NU activists even suspected that the government wanted NU to "disappear", and called this period a time of "NU phobia" (Anam 1990, pp. 128–29).

[18] The regime had banned civil servants from joining political parties, so former Muslim politicians keen on keeping their jobs in the bureaucracy saw Muhammadiyah as their primary option for remaining active in Islamic affairs.

[19] A major focus of the new generation of Islamic intellectuals was the refutation of claims that industrialization led to the decline of religiousness (Madjid 1987, p. 149).

20   Abdurrahman Wahid, born in 1940 and popularly known as "Gus Dur", is the grandson of the NU founders Hasyim Asy'ari and Bisri Syansuri, and son of Wahid Hasyim. In 1953 he was with his father when the latter died in a car accident. After spending several years in various *pesantren* in Java, Wahid left for Cairo in 1964, and later for Baghdad. In 1971, he went to Europe fur further studies, but returned to Indonesia soon afterwards, teaching in his hometown of Jombang. Wahid moved to Jakarta in 1978, founded his own *pesantren* in Ciganjur, and became active in NU's executive board as well as in a wide range of cultural organizations. In 1984, he was nominated by a number of senior *kiai* to take over the chairmanship of NU. Prior to his election, Wahid had attracted Suharto's sympathies by proposing the "pribumization" of Islam, meaning the adaptation of Islamic teachings to national Indonesian culture. He also called attempts to confront Islam with Pancasila "stupid", paving the way for NU's endorsement of Pancasila as its ideological guideline (Isre 1998).

21   This policy shift was rewarded with the very material concessions that Wahid had hoped for: the civil service was opened for NU cadres; leading bureaucrats took senior positions in NU's regional chapters; government officials resumed handing out donations to *pesantren*; and the army extended training to NU's security forces organized under its youth wing Ansor (Feillard 1997, p. 139).

22   For these developments, see Hefner (1997, p. 11).

23   Amien Rais was born in 1944 in Solo, Central Java. Active in several modernist student organizations, he pursued an academic career that led him to doctoral studies in the United States. He graduated from the University of Notre Dame with a Masters degree in 1974 and received his doctorate from the University of Chicago in 1981. Despite his long periods of study in the West, he was highly critical of the United States and Europe for what he viewed as their pro-Israel policies. He became a specialist in Middle East politics at the University of Gadjah Mada in Yogyakarta, engaging in research projects such as "Zionism: Its Meaning and Function". Amien joined ICMI in the early 1990s and became an increasingly important figure in Muhammadiyah. In 1994, he was appointed as its chairman (Uhrowi 2004).

24   Interview with Amien Rais, Yogyakarta, 27 November 1997.

25   Despite these acts of intimidation, many Muhammadiyah branches encouraged Amien to continue his confrontation with the regime. He received numerous invitations to speak at branch activities and on Muhammadiyah campuses (Wahyudi 1999, pp. 123–24).

26   Shortly after announcing that the security forces had rounded up the *Komando Jihad*, Admiral Sudomo, the head of the all-powerful security agency Kopkamtib (*Komando Pemulihan Keamanan dan Ketertiban*, Command for the Restoration of Security and Order), declared that there were four major limitations on campaigners for the general elections: first, no attacks on political opponents;

second, no offences to the dignity of the government and its officials; third, no attempts to destabilize national unity; and fourth, no criticism of government policies. This catalogue of limitations virtually paralysed the PPP campaign, which had planned to ride to victory on a wave of widespread disenchantment with the Suharto regime. Despite these obstructive measures introduced by the government, however, PPP won nearly 30 per cent of the vote (Liddle 1992, p. 67).

# PART TWO

# Crisis and Regime Change, 1997–98

# 3

# REGIME CHANGE
## Military Factionalism and Suharto's Fall

The introduction to this book has presented a number of theoretical approaches to explain possible complications in establishing democratic controls over the armed forces in transitional states. Most of these models suggested that historical legacies play an important role in prefiguring the shape of civil-military relations in post-authoritarian polities, which made it necessary for the first part of this study to examine the historical roots of both military politics and intra-civilian conflict in Indonesia. The introduction also emphasized, however, that the character of regime change is an especially crucial element of the "initial conditions" of civil-military reform processes, and thus deserves separate discussion. For example, the violent overthrow of a repressive regime by popular protests can have a different impact on post-authoritarian polities than a pacted transition, in which the transfer of power occurs as a result of elite negotiations. In discussing the nature of regime change and its repercussions for military reform in democratic transitions, the role of the armed forces in the handover of authority from the previous government to its successor is of particular interest. In Indonesia, the engagement of the armed forces in the events leading to Suharto's resignation has been critical in two aspects. Both of these aspects are closely related to the dynamics of military factionalism, but concern different analytical areas.

In more general terms, the success of compromise-oriented military officers in negotiating an intra-systemic transfer of authority from Suharto to his deputy helped to prevent the very breakdown of the regime that is typically associated with the fall of sultanistic systems. Linz and Stepan (1996, p. 70) asserted that sultanistic polities "present an opportunity for democratic transition because, should the ruler (and his or her family) be overthrown or assassinated, the sultanistic regime collapses".[1] One possible explanation for the fact that this total disintegration of the regime infrastructure did not occur in Indonesia is Aspinall's proposition that Suharto's system was not purely sultanistic but included strong authoritarian features. Aspinall (2005c, p. 269) suggested that the combination between sultanistic and authoritarian characteristics resulted in a democratic transition that occurred in a tumultuous way and witnessed "dramatic breakthroughs", but was also marked by "a high degree of continuity between the new democratic politics and those of the authoritarian past". This chapter will argue, however, that in addition to such structural factors, the political behaviour of military leaders willing to desert Suharto was equally crucial in producing a regime change that avoided the complete collapse of the existing system. Consequently, the first post-Suharto government consisted of figures associated with the New Order regime, impacting on the pace and depth of reform efforts in the early phase of the transition, including in the area of civil-military relations.

The second important influence of military factionalism on the character of the 1998 regime change is related to societal perceptions of the armed forces during the political crisis leading to Suharto's overthrow. The failure and eventual dismissal of hardline military officers such as Prabowo, who had proposed a crackdown on oppositional forces and demanded that martial law be declared, not only defused political tensions and paved the way for the intra-systemic regime change discussed above. The outcome of the factional dispute also gave rise to the public impression that the post-New Order military leadership was in the hands of those officers who had endorsed the people's call on Suharto to retire, while the most hawkish generals associated with Prabowo and his circle had been successfully marginalized. This perception of an effective "cleansing" of the military of its most notorious Suharto loyalists and human rights abusers temporarily satisfied some of the immediate societal demands for change in the post-authoritarian armed forces. Public pressure for more wide-ranging reform decreased as a result, and the majority of generals groomed under the New Order were allowed to keep their posts. The following chapter develops the two main arguments outlined above by discussing the factionalism that marked the political behaviour of the military and its individual officers during the crisis of 1997 and 1998. Interpreting military politics within the context of Suharto's rapid political decline, the chapter points to the consequences of the intra-military conflicts for the nature of Indonesia's regime change and the evolution of civil-military relations in the early phase of the post-authoritarian transition.

## COMPETITION AND LOYALTY: MILITARY FACTIONALISM IN THE NEW ORDER

In his work on the role of militaries in praetorian states, Muthiah Alagappa (2001*b*, pp. 51–52) asserted that splits between the governing generals and the field commanders are an inevitable consequence of the inherent tension between the military as government and the military as institution. In many cases, the ruling military junta even creates further splits in order to stay in power. For much of his thirty-two year rule over Indonesia, Suharto was a skilful strategist of military factionalism and patronage, using already existing cleavages to his advantage and creating new ones in order to extend his grip on power. In this context, numerous intra-military divisions related to ethnicity, unit membership, functional role, and religion offered Suharto plentiful opportunities to apply his tested tactics of *divide et impera*. To begin with, there were important ethnic differences, with Javanese officers and those from the Outer Islands competing for key posts. Rivalries also occurred between soldiers attached to the various regional commands, especially the Siliwangi, Diponegoro, and Brawijaya units in Java.[2] Moreover, generational differences created tensions between the "generation of 1945", the transitional officers, and the "younger" generals trained in the military academy in Magelang. Also, officers from the intelligence services were engaged in conflicts with the rest of the armed forces as well as among themselves. Furthermore, the "financial" officers, who spent most of their time and energy on running business-related and political operations, had major differences with more "professional" military leaders. Religio-political divisions were equally relevant, as was evident in the controversy over *abangan* "syncretism" in Suharto's inner circle in the 1970s, the prominence of Christian officers in the 1980s, and the perceived split between "Islamic" and "nationalist" commanders in the 1990s. Finally, personal patronage networks were also important, such as the close ties of some officers to the palace that marked most of the intra-military rivalries in the mid-1990s.

In many other states with military-backed governments, similar cleavages within the armed forces have played an important role in the destabilization, and ultimately degeneration, of authoritarian rule. The divisions within the Brazilian armed forces between moderates and hardliners, for example, contributed significantly to the erosion of the military government in the early and mid-1980s (Koonings 2001, pp. 147–48). In the same vein, severe regional splits within the Nigerian and South Korean militaries accompanied the rise and fall of several authoritarian regimes in these countries (Nwagwu 2002, p. 73; Jun 2001, p. 124). In Indonesia's New Order, on the other hand, Suharto was mostly able to manage the ethnic, regional, and generational divisions by centralizing the command structure and increasing the frequency of reshuffles in the officer corps (Kammen and Chandra 1999, p. 83). In fact, by the early 1980s, factionalism in the Indonesian armed forces had largely turned into an instrument used by Suharto to consolidate his rule. The creation and cultivation of intra-military competition ensured that no camp within the armed forces grew strong enough to challenge Suharto's presidency. This competitive atmosphere also encouraged rival groups to report indications of disloyalty on the side of their opponents directly to Suharto, feeding the intelligence network developed by the president with invaluable material on potential threats to his regime. The positions of ABRI commander and army chief of staff were at the centre of Suharto's efforts to engineer conflicts over authority and resources, with the incumbents in both posts seeking presidential backing to decide the competition in their favour. In major reshuffles, Suharto paid careful attention to the "equitable" distribution of key positions among competing factions, balancing their interests and ensuring their loyalty to his government.

One of the most important elements of New Order military factionalism was the formation of strategic alliances between competing officers and civilian socio-political forces. Military leaders sought to advance their interests by cultivating civilian support groups, hoping that their attachment to and influence on key political constituencies would convince Suharto of their indispensability in mobilizing support for the regime.[3] These attachments were not necessarily of an ideological nature, but reflected perceptions within the competing military groups of Suharto's changing political priorities. The formation of alliances between senior officers and ultra-modernist Islamic organizations in the late 1980s and early 1990s, for instance, was a direct reaction to Suharto's campaign against Murdani. Other officers believed, however, that Suharto had no intention of "Islamizing" the armed forces and instead was determined to keep a stable balance within the military. Accordingly, these officers aligned themselves with civilian opponents of modernist groups, largely in the traditionalist Muslim community. Geoffrey Robinson (2001, p. 239) has maintained that the formation of civilian-military alliances caused by intra-military factionalism has "enhanced the power of civil society", and sometimes even allowed civilians to "challenge the military or the regime itself". This enhancement of civil society may have occurred occasionally as a by-product, but in most cases, the alliances focused on promoting the interests of both partners within the regime by gaining access to Suharto's patronage system. In the very few instances that civilian-military alliances carried ideas of reform, these were largely aimed at weakening competitors within the New Order state rather than at presenting conceptual alternatives to Suharto's rule.

It was this successful isolation of reformist ideas from intra-military competition that had allowed Suharto until very late in his rule to avoid the kind of regime-destructive repercussions of military factionalism that had undermined the praetorian regimes of Brazil, Nigeria, and South Korea. Instead, he had been able to use factionalism in the armed forces as an instrument of regime maintenance. While criticism of Suharto's sultanistic leadership emerged in the lower and middle ranks in the mid-1990s, it was not part of the competition within the elite. The various factions in the top brass, despite their concerns about the military's loss of political influence and widespread dissatisfaction with the government, still viewed Suharto as the key to advancing their careers, and feared the complete collapse of the Dual Function should he be removed from office. Accordingly, it required a change in the substance and quality of intra-military divisions for them to pose a serious threat to the regime. Suharto's control over the armed forces was in danger if one or more of the competing factions utilized reformist ideas, and ultimately notions of regime change, as instruments of inter-elite conflict, and if alternatives to Suharto's leadership began to offer higher rewards than continued loyalty. The increasing social and political tensions of the late New Order provided the platform for such a scenario, but it needed the dramatic shock of the crisis unfolding in the second half of 1997 to elevate previously isolated discourses on political reform to the centre of intra-military rivalries.

## THE INTRA-MILITARY DEBATE
## ON THE 1997 ELECTIONS

The political landscape of Indonesia ahead of the 1997 elections showed classic indicators of an autocratic regime that was approaching its end. To begin with, Suharto's age (he had turned seventy-five in 1996) played a crucial role in fuelling expectations that his political departure was near. In addition, while still exercising tight and effective control, Suharto suffered from a number of personal and political setbacks from the beginning of 1996 (Fealy 1997). Crucially, his wife and key political confidante Siti Hartinah, popularly referred to as Tien Suharto, died in April 1996. Shortly afterwards, Suharto spent some time in Germany for medical treatment, sparking speculation about his health and possible succession scenarios. The sudden vulnerability of Suharto's rule encouraged critical forces both within and outside the government to intensify their political activity. Most significantly, the chairwoman of the secular-nationalist PDI, Megawati Sukarnoputri, openly challenged her replacement by a regime-appointed party official. With public protests against Megawati's removal providing a platform for criticism of Suharto's leadership, many previously cautious dissidents began to demand a clear schedule for the president's exit from the political scene. In July 1996, after several weeks of anti-regime speeches in front of Megawati's PDI headquarters in Jakarta, the military mobilized thugs and supporters of the new, government-backed chairman to storm and occupy the party offices. The attack led to the worst rioting in the city since 1974, leaving at least five people dead and sending hundreds of Megawati followers to prison.[4]

The unrest not only indicated the increasing opposition towards the repressive methods of the regime, but created cracks within the political system of the New Order. Megawati's call on PDI members to ignore the instructions of the new party leadership was largely obeyed, undermining the very three-party system that had supplied Suharto's regime with a modicum of formal legitimacy. In addition, a series of ethnic, religious, and social riots and clashes occurred throughout 1996 and 1997, with government offices, banks, and Chinese businesses being the primary targets (Purdey 2006; Sidel 2007; van Dijk 1997, p. 12). The power erosion typical for late sultanistic regimes, coinciding with ruptures in the previously static polity and increasing levels of social unrest, challenged the key components of the New Order, including the armed forces, to define their level of commitment towards the embattled ruler. With the 1997 general elections approaching, these political protagonists faced the difficult task of having to make decisions that would neither threaten their position in the regime nor exclude them from participation in a possible post-Suharto government.

## Military Factionalism Ahead of the 1997 Elections

The internal military discourse on the 1997 general elections provided the first indication that political reform was about to become an element of military factionalism in the late New Order. The controversy did not yet lead to the establishment of clear-cut factions, but individual officers began to take on ideas of change to compete for influence in the armed forces. Catalyzing already existing differences between senior generals, the debate concerned the extent to which the armed forces were prepared to support Golkar in the upcoming polls. In this dispute, some officers demanded unconditional military support for Golkar's electoral machine and viewed any criticism of Suharto's leadership as an act of subversion. Blaming the increasing societal dissatisfaction with the New Order on internal and external provocateurs, these officers proposed that the security forces prepare for an uncompromising crackdown on dissidents. Guided by a militaristic paradigm of solving political conflicts, their conceptual thinking rejected institutional changes to the New Order system for the foreseeable future and saw a reduction of military engagement in politics as neither necessary nor appropriate. While not aligned in one faction and even frequently engaged in deep personal conflicts among themselves, officers who subscribed to such hawkish views included Army Chief of Staff General Hartono, a close confidant of Suharto's daughter and leading Golkar politician Siti Hardiyanti Rukmana; ABRI Commander General Feisal Tanjung; and the head of Kopassus (Special Forces) Major General Prabowo Subianto, Suharto's son-in-law.[5] The three generals had separate and often antagonistic patronage networks below them, with a large number of regional commanders, staff officers, and intelligence operators depending on their favours and protection. Despite their fierce rivalry over appointments and resources,[6] however, there were also important connections between these highly conservative officers. One important bond was their cooperation with ultra-modernist Muslim organizations, aimed at building up constituents willing to defend the regime against mounting societal dissent. In addition, they were strongly opposed to former ABRI chief Benny Murdani and his patronage of non-Muslim officers, a policy that many of them felt had hampered their careers in the past.

While many officers pleaded for a repressive approach to the emerging societal criticism of the regime, other generals favoured a more compromise-oriented strategy. Although they shared their fellow officers' intolerance towards the militant fringes of the opposition, some commanders believed that there were legitimate complaints over the static nature of the New Order and its inability to accommodate public calls for institutional change. Believing that political problems needed political solutions, these officers also had a mixed opinion on the role of the armed forces in the regime. While they agreed that regime participation was important for political stability and the institutional interests of the military, they feared that too close an identification with the government could damage the reputation of the armed forces. Accordingly, such officers argued against open support for Golkar in the 1997 elections, insisting that it was not the mission of the armed forces to back a particular political party. There was no factional association between generals who supported this view, and they included officers with such diverse personalities as Chief of Staff of Socio-Political Affairs Muhammad Ma'ruf; Chief of Staff of General Affairs Soeyono; and Wiranto, then commander of Kostrad. Wiranto's position on this issue was particularly important, given his influence in the ranks and exclusive access to Suharto. Having served as Suharto's adjutant for four years, he was seen as destined to replace Feisal Tanjung as head of the armed forces when the latter's term expired in 1998.[7] Wiranto felt a deep personal affection for Suharto, but understood that the longevity of his rule was a source of concern among ordinary Indonesians. The fact that even presidential loyalists such as Wiranto and his inner circle proved susceptible to societal pressure turned them into a good barometer of the political mood in the military and the country as a whole. If societal resistance to the continuation of Suharto's rule remained low or manageable, these officers were certain to continue their support for him; on the other hand, a possible drop in public backing for the president was likely to reduce their willingness to defend the regime at all cost.

In addition to the hawkish and more restrained generals, there was also a small number of officers who developed sharp critiques of the New Order government and its policies. Arguing that the armed forces needed to return to their professional roots, these officers were mainly interested in shielding the military from the growing discontent with Suharto's government. Expecting that regime change would most likely occur through the president's death or voluntary resignation, this tiny minority of military "reformers" projected its idea of opening up the tightly controlled political system into the post-Suharto polity. While stopping short of proposing an unrestricted democratic system, the "reformist" officers were prepared to introduce more political rights and greater institutional transparency. Regarded as "intellectuals", many of them had served for long periods at the military's staff and command schools in Bandung, providing them with the time, resources, and distance to reflect on the future of ABRI's engagement with the regime (Honna 2003, pp. 74–81). Furthermore, they also tended to have extensive foreign experience, including study in the United States, and most had begun their careers in the seventeenth airborne infantry brigade of Kostrad in West Java.[8] Despite their similar views, however, these younger officers were far from forming a coherent and solid faction. Ironically, some of the most antagonistic relationships in the armed forces occurred among the "reformers", which included Susilo Bambang Yudhoyono, the regional commander in South Sumatra; the assistant to the ABRI commander, Agus Widjojo; and another staff officer, Agus Wirahadikusumah. Mostly occupying junior staff positions, the "intellectuals" had little influence on the policies of the military elite, with their opinions voiced in military seminars, discussion circles, and private conversations rather than at official leadership meetings that determined ABRI's political strategy vis-à-vis Suharto and his regime.

## The Intra-Military Debate on Golkar

The dispute over the role of the armed forces in the 1997 general elections brought the differences within the armed forces into the open. Lieutenant General Soeyono, then chief of staff of general affairs, recalled how the two diametrically opposed opinions on ABRI's relationship with Golkar clashed at an armed forces leadership meeting in October 1995. At that gathering, Chief of Staff of Socio-Political Affairs Muhammad Ma'ruf openly challenged Hartono's proposal to support Golkar in the upcoming ballot. Demanding that the military remain neutral, Mar'ruf's remarks triggered an angry response by Hartono, who argued that ABRI had a historical obligation to support the party it had helped to create. The debate became so tense that other senior officers had to mediate between the two.[9] The incident did not convince Hartono to moderate his views, however. On the contrary, he subsequently stepped up his efforts to strengthen ABRI's institutional ties with Golkar. In March 1996, he declared his "personal allegiance" to Siti Hardiyanti in her capacity as deputy chairwoman of the Golkar central board. He began to tour several *pesantren* at Siti Hardiyanti's side, wearing Golkar's yellow uniform jacket, and giving campaign-like speeches (Supriatma 1996, p. 158; Butarbutar 2003, p. 113). In late 1996, he played a significant role in organizing the reconciliation between Abdurrahman Wahid and Suharto, and successfully lobbied the NU leader to open his community to the Golkar campaign. By early 1997, the army chief of staff was seen as a key political player, skillfully balancing his contacts to the Muslim community, Golkar politicians, and the presidential family.

The controversy between proponents of political neutrality and officers propagating institutional support for Golkar provided invaluable insights into the politics of factionalism within the armed forces. Most importantly, officers on both sides exercised considerable pressure on their subordinates to endorse their individual viewpoints. They offered speedy promotion in case of obedience, and threatened to obstruct the careers of disloyal commanders. Djadja Suparman, then chief of staff at the South Sumatran Sriwijaya command, reported that the pro-Golkar generals were particularly active in calling up influential officers to demand loyalty and explain possible sanctions if they did not sign up to their political agenda.[10] The second element in the intra-military competition was association with civilian partners in order to build societal support and launch attacks against rivals. Hartono, for example, supported the Center for Policy Development Studies (CPDS), a think tank staffed largely with researchers from a modernist Islamic background. Ahead of the 1997 elections, the organization published a paper that accused Wiranto of planning Suharto's downfall.[11] Wiranto, for his part, commented that the paper "contained nothing but lies and garbage".[12] The bad-mouthing of competitors had, as the incident showed, turned into an important feature of internal factionalism in the armed forces in the late 1990s.

The militancy of some of the pro-Golkar generals convinced the more critical and "intellectual" officers to intensify their activities and turn their thoughts into coherent concepts. Wirahadikusumah, for example, organized an army seminar in June 1996, at the height of the PDI crisis and Hartono's campaign for Golkar. The seminar criticized the political "superstructure", i.e. the government, for its excessive intervention in socio-political life, nepotistic and corrupt practices, and inconsistency in policies. Significantly, papers presented at the seminar suggested that the armed forces mediate between the "superstructure" and society, effectively defining ABRI as a non-participant in the New Order regime (Honna 2003, pp. 81–86). Based on this analysis, some of the reform-minded officers, including Yudhoyono, developed a new doctrinal concept for ABRI, which was discussed within the ranks in the first half of 1997. The concept contained four points: first, ABRI had to accustom itself to the idea that it was not always to be at the forefront of political developments; second, the concept of "occupying" would be transformed into a concept of "influencing"; third, ABRI's method of exerting influence would be changed from a direct to an indirect way; and fourth, ABRI was ready for political role-sharing with civilian forces.[13] The four suggestions added up to what its authors called the "New Paradigm of ABRI's Dual Function". While the paradigm was drafted to undermine the pro-Golkar officers, many of their adversaries, such as Wiranto, did not endorse the concept. Despite their deep antagonism towards Hartono and other proponents of ABRI's role as the guardian of Golkar's political predominance, Wiranto and his circle saw no reason to reformulate the military's doctrine. The political and economic situation still seemed sufficiently stable, and as long as this did not change, officers close to Wiranto chose the status quo over the uncertainty associated with a possible revision of ABRI's role.

The marginality of reformist thinking in the officer corps was reflected in the military's preparations for and its conduct of the general elections. In February 1997, shortly before the polls, Feisal Tanjung emphatically rejected the results of a study conducted by the Indonesian Institute of Sciences (LIPI, *Lembaga Ilmu Pengetahuan Indonesia*), in which it had proposed the gradual disengagement of the military from political affairs.[14] In addition, the continued dominance of repressive security paradigms in the military elite also became apparent at an ABRI leadership meeting in April 1997. There, the military top brass condemned the emergence of new social organizations with leftist orientations, the uncontrolled circulation of pamphlets, the publication of books not in line with Pancasila, and the proliferation of NGOs with a tendency to "political adventurism".[15] Apparently, none of the criticisms raised at the 1996 seminar had made it into ABRI's official language. The only success at this gathering for the "intellectual" officers and the proponents of the military's political neutrality was the abortion of Hartono's campaign for direct electoral support of Golkar. Announcing the compromise between the various viewpoints, Feisal Tanjung suggested that the relationship between individual officers and the government party was of a personal rather than an institutional nature. The armed forces subsequently extended indirect support to Golkar, however, by helping to remove one of the greatest obstacles to another landslide victory for the regime: the "Mega-Bintang" movement.[16] The initiative, which was strongest in Central Java, had been launched by PPP officials who hoped to attract the support of pro-Megawati voters determined to endorse neither the government-sanctioned PDI nor Golkar. The movement gained considerable momentum in the national media and some urban centres, but the security apparatus dispersed Mega-Bintang crowds wherever they emerged (Thoyibi 1999, p. 43). Towards the end of the campaign, the initiative had largely collapsed, and the way was open for Golkar to claim its sixth successive triumph in New Order electoral history.

## Triumph or Decline? The Post-Election Landscape

The result of the 1997 general elections exposed the growing gap between the political sentiments in large sections of the population and the "theatre politics" performed by the New Order establishment. Despite high levels of social unrest, widespread criticism of corruption, and the inability of the elite to absorb demands for reform, Golkar won 74 per cent of the votes and the largest majority in parliament since the creation of the New Order. Golkar chairman Harmoko presented the outcome of the polls as an unprecedented vote of confidence in the regime, but in reality it delivered the ultimate proof of its inherent failure to accommodate change (Srengenge 1998). The clearest indication of this failure was not the ridiculously inflated result for Golkar, however, but the almost complete disappearance of the PDI. Only 3 per cent of the electorate supported the party, a decline of almost 12 per cent. Evidently, the majority of nationalist voters had expressed their resentment of the government intervention in PDI's affairs by withdrawing their support not only for the proxy backed by the regime, but for Suharto's restricted party system as a whole. Even the president appeared to be uncomfortable with the election results and the way several government officials claimed credit for them. Only one week after the elections, Suharto dismissed Harmoko from his post as minister of information, and filled the vacancy with General Hartono.

Hartono's departure from the army was followed by the most extensive reshuffle in the armed forces since early 1995. The reshuffle improved the position of those officers who had opposed supporting Golkar in the general elections, with Hartono replaced by Wiranto as army chief of staff. Subagyo H.S., who was appointed as Wiranto's deputy, and Sugiono, who became commander of Kostrad, had also propagated ABRI's neutrality in the polls, although they held rather hawkish views on other political and social issues. The defenders of a repressive approach to regime opposition maintained their grip on key positions, however, with Feisal still in command of ABRI headquarters and Prabowo retaining his control of Kopassus. In addition to balancing diverse patronage networks and different political viewpoints, Suharto had once again used personal loyalty to him as the most crucial criterion for promotion. Officers who had served in the palace either as adjutant (Wiranto), in the presidential security squad (Subagyo), or both (Sugiono) were elevated in the reshuffle,[17] and Prabowo together with the head of the national police, former presidential adjutant General Dibyo Widodo, remained central figures in the security apparatus. Hence there was no doubt that despite their severe factional and personal divisions, the armed forces were in the hands of officers with long-standing personal ties to the Suharto family and its cronies.[18]

The contrast between the mechanical conduct of the elections and the general mood in the country pointed to signs of decay within the regime. The cracks in the elite that O'Donnell and Schmitter (1986, p. 19) have identified as the major cause for degenerating authoritarian systems were clearly visible. In addition, the destruction of the PDI in the elections exposed ruptures not only in the elite, but in the political framework as a whole. With the credibility of the New Order's political system at an all-time low, Suharto's re-election through the MPR scheduled for March 1998 was overshadowed by uncertainties concerning his future. Moreover, the divisions in the armed forces over their political stance in the 1997 elections had, for the first time, triggered the emergence of a reformist discourse at the fringes of the officer corps that even involved images of an Indonesia without Suharto. While unable to penetrate the decision-making process of the military elite in 1997, these ideas had the potential of attracting officers in the army mainstream who had opted for neutrality in the Golkar dispute and appeared to prefer a political approach to regime opponents over sheer repression. These officers, which included generals as influential as Wiranto, had so far extended firm support to Suharto, but a further destabilization of the New Order polity was likely to change that.

## MILITARY FACTIONALISM IN A DECLINING REGIME: ABRI AND THE CRISIS

The New Order state of mid-1997 was crippled by inter-elite conflict, social unrest, and political stagnation. Despite old divisions and newly emerging ruptures in its political system, however, the Suharto regime appeared stable enough to neutralize serious threats to its rule. The single most important factor in this was continued economic growth. The New Order's rise to power in 1966 had been underpinned by promises of political stability and economic development, and for most of the time, the government had delivered. Anne Booth (1999, p. 129) contended that "whatever its exact dimensions, a prolonged and broad-based improvement in living standards under the New Order did take place". In the eyes of many Indonesians, the robust economic growth had justified restrictions on political activities and individual freedoms, and even supported certain levels of tolerance towards corruption in the elite. The economic strength of the regime, however, made it politically vulnerable. With the legitimacy of the government tied to its economic performance, any significant disruption in the economy was certain to alter the political attitudes of Indonesian society.

The view that economic development legitimized non-democratic forms of governance was a central theme in the political thinking of the armed forces elite, but it played an even more important role in the logic of Suharto's sultanistic rule. With the armed forces slowly disengaging from formal politics since the 1980s, it was Suharto who personally exercised almost absolute control over political institutions, society, and the economy. Consequently, the public was much more likely to identify Suharto as the main cause of economic difficulties than any other component of the regime. The business empire of the presidential family had been exposed to sharp criticism for some time, but was certain to become the focus of societal outrage if economic conditions deteriorated (Habir 1999, p. 86). The emergence of a regime-critical discourse in segments of the armed

forces provided the public with additional reasons for differentiating between
the president and the institutions he used to stabilize his government. Thus,
when the economic crisis began to affect Indonesia in July 1997, following the
float of the Thai baht and the fall of the Malaysian ringgit, Suharto was the
most vulnerable target in the search for the causes of this downturn (McIntyre
1999). The crisis, which initially appeared to have hit the monetary sector
only, soon spiralled into political dimensions. Economic observers noted
that Suharto's anachronistic system was incompatible with the requirements
of global markets, and pointed to the uncertainty of Suharto's succession as
a major reason for the massive capital outflow. The dramatic drop in the
stock market and the Indonesian currency paralysed the real sector, with
foreign debts increasing, investment projects cancelled or postponed, and
consumption declining. Unemployment rose, the numbers of corporate
bankruptcies exploded, and inflation reached levels last seen in the mid-
1970s. By the end of the year, the free fall of the economy was accelerated
by a severe drought that led to a disastrous decline in agricultural production
(McLeod 1998, pp. 37–38).

## Crisis and Competition: The Wiranto-Prabowo Rivalry

While critics largely focused on the institutional inflexibility of Suharto's rule,
the economic decline also affected the legitimacy of military participation in
politics. The armed forces had traditionally presented their role in securing
economic growth as a key reason for their political engagement, but the
sudden downturn in the economy challenged this claim. The tight control
of society, previously viewed as an important factor in containing political
conflicts, was now widely blamed for the lack of creativity and competitiveness
of Indonesian businesses. With central components of ABRI's doctrine eroded
by the crisis, senior officers and their patronage networks were confronted
with difficult strategic choices as far as their relations with Suharto were
concerned. For the time being, unconditional defence of the president
appeared as the only realistic option for most generals, regardless of whether
they supported uncompromising repression of dissidents or pleaded for less
draconian responses. From their perspective, the risk that Suharto's fall would
end the Dual Function was seen as more harmful than the political cost
of maintaining the regime. The "intellectual" officers, on the other hand,
were not in a position to influence the decision-making in the top brass.
Yudhoyono was promoted in August 1997 to the post of assistant to the
chief of staff of socio-political affairs, but was still unable to implant ideas
of substantial reform into the political attitudes of the most senior military

elite. Agus Wirahadikusumah, then deputy assistant of general planning, felt frustrated by the conservatism of his superiors:

> The world was collapsing around them, but the military leadership did nothing. Nothing! They just could not connect the dots. Suharto was clearly responsible for what was happening, but all they talked about was giving him his fifth star, an honorary star for all his extraordinary achievements! I couldn't believe it.[19]

Before conferring a fifth star on Suharto and declaring him a "Grand General" in early October,[20] the ABRI leadership had announced in August that it would re-nominate Suharto for the presidency. Outgoing Chief of Staff of Socio-Political Affairs, Lieutenant General Syarwan Hamid, explained that ABRI had decided to put its trust in the president as the majority of Indonesians wanted to see a continuation of his rule.[21] At the same time, ABRI backed Suharto's request for the restitution of a 1988 MPR decree giving the president special powers to deal with security threats in emergency situations.[22] Furthermore, ABRI rejected suggestions to limit presidential terms to two periods, the idea coming closest to public criticism of Suharto at that early stage of the crisis.[23]

The caution exercised by generals from diverse factional backgrounds suggested that the system built by Suharto was still strong enough to detect and prevent disloyalty towards him. Evidently, the norms and rules of that system continued to dictate the dynamics of intra-military conflict. In the second half of 1997, competition within the armed forces focused on the position of ABRI commander. Feisal Tanjung was expected to be replaced soon, and there were only two prospective candidates for the job: Wiranto, the army chief of staff, and Prabowo Subianto, who was still only a two-star general, but had significantly more influence within ABRI than his rank suggested.[24] Obviously, this competition was not only a personal rivalry, it also concerned the future attitude of the military to regime opposition and the continuation of Suharto's rule. Throughout August and September, rumours supported Prabowo's hopes of a promotion to chief of staff of general affairs and a third star, therefore qualifying him for the top post.[25] But the promotion never came. Prabowo later reported that the chemistry between him and the army chief of staff was bad, blaming the stark contrast between Wiranto's Javanese village background and his own origin from a Western-educated, intellectually sophisticated family.[26] Despite the relevance of Prabowo's observation, it appears that their antagonism had less to do with cultural or educational differences than with the high stakes involved in the appointment of the ABRI chief: as Suharto rarely changed ABRI commanders before the end of their five-year term, only one of them could make it to the top, with the loser likely to be sidelined under the leadership of the winner.[27]

The competition between Wiranto and Prabowo over the armed forces leadership was accompanied by the same features of military factionalism that had marked the intra-military conflicts of the 1990s: the promotion of loyalists to key positions, the establishment of links with civilian supporters, and the bad-mouthing of competitors. The crisis, however, catalyzed the political relevance of the rivalry. It was obvious that Suharto would look favourably upon military officers whose political activities and interactions assisted him in addressing the growing problems. Prabowo apparently believed that Suharto wanted to shift the blame for the crisis to Chinese tycoons and confront his critics with repression rather than persuasion. Accordingly, Prabowo strengthened his links with Islamic groups on the far right of the political spectrum, and encouraged them to promote their traditional views that Chinese rent-seekers undermined the Indonesian economy.[28] At the same time, he ordered a special unit in Kopassus to prepare for the kidnapping of several political activists who had spoken out against the re-election of Suharto. Wiranto, on the other hand, consolidated his relationship with the main opponent of Prabowo's civilian allies, Abdurrahman Wahid. Wiranto viewed the alliance with the moderate Muslim leader as an effective instrument to appease the critics of the regime and demonstrate its openness towards ideas of change. According to Wahid, Wiranto was not convinced that Suharto endorsed Prabowo's tactics of political radicalization and physical violence against opponents to re-stabilize the regime. Wiranto thus sent envoys to Wahid, asking him to help the president restore order by calling on Indonesians to remain calm.[29] Despite their close ties with Suharto, however, neither Wiranto nor Prabowo could predict with absolute certainty the strategies and methods the president had in mind for overcoming the mounting difficulties. For that reason, the political manoeuvres of both officers were conducted in secretive ways for most of the first period of the crisis between July and December 1997.[30]

The divisions between Prabowo and Wiranto were not, despite claims by many observers, an indication of a religious split within the military. Robert Hefner (2000, p. 151), for example, suggested that Prabowo was a member of the "ascendant 'Islamic' wing of the armed forces". Opposed to this "green" faction was the "red-and-white" group, which Hefner identified as "nationalist". It appears, however, that the political alliances both Prabowo and Wiranto built were to a much larger extent shaped by their divergent views on how to deal with regime opposition than by individual religio-ideological preferences. The major difference between these two paradigms was the degree to which the military was prepared to nurture and mobilize militant societal elements in defence of the regime, and was only superficially related to the role of Islam in society or politics. Prabowo was hardly an Islamic radical, with his family rooted in the former PSI (*Partai Sosialis Indonesia*, Indonesian Socialist Party), ideals of Western education, and acceptance of non-Muslims.[31] Prabowo had learnt, however, that Islam could be a powerful instrument of political engineering, using it in the early 1990s to confront the remnants of the Murdani group.[32] Wiranto, on the other hand, was a practising Muslim, and not opposed to a greater role of Islamic groups in political life. What the two officers fought over at this stage of the crisis was the most suitable strategy to contain the mounting opposition to Suharto's presidency, and they were bitterly opposed in their competition for the armed forces leadership. So far, neither Prabowo nor Wiranto had contemplated political alternatives beyond Suharto's rule to advance their interests. It needed a further escalation in the crisis to not only raise the stakes of the intra-military conflict, but to also link the rival officers with Suharto critics both inside and outside the armed forces.

## THE CRISIS ESCALATES:
## BETWEEN REPRESSSION AND DIALOGUE

The second phase of the crisis, beginning in December 1997, saw a serious deterioration in economic and political conditions. Suharto suffered a mild stroke in early December, sparking fresh speculation on the issue of his succession.[33] The news led to negotiations between oppositional forces over forming an alliance in case sudden opportunities should arise, with several prominent figures coming forward to question Suharto's continued rule. Amien Rais had already declared his willingness to run for president in September, breaking the New Order taboo against proposing Suharto's replacement. By January, Megawati joined the chorus, offering to lead the country if nobody more appropriate was found. While his re-election was openly challenged, Suharto aggravated the economic decline by presenting a highly unrealistic state budget in early January.[34] The subsequent free fall of the rupiah caused widespread panic, with supermarkets emptied by customers worried about the escalating prices of basic food items. Only days later, the IMF intervened, forcing Suharto to sign a second letter of intent after he had failed to meet the benchmarks set in a similar document agreed upon in October (Eklöf 1999, pp. 122–23). At the same time, Suharto shocked the political elite by announcing his vice-presidential candidate for the 1998–2003 term: B.J. Habibie, his minister of research and technology, who was well known for spending big on ambitious, but dubious development projects. Domestic political actors were stunned at this choice, as were international investors, who sent the rupiah to another all-time low (Schwarz 1998).

## Blaming the Chinese: Prabowo's Strategy of Radicalization

The nomination of Habibie sharpened the factionalism within the officer corps. While he was disliked by the armed forces mainstream for his interference in ABRI's procurement procedures and his political affiliation with Islamic groups, Habibie had several military associates. Feisal Tanjung, Syarwan Hamid, and the then Chief of Staff of Socio-Political Affairs Yunus Yosfiah were known to be close to Habibie, but his most influential ally was Prabowo. Their relationship was mutually beneficial. On the one hand, Prabowo opened access for Habibie to ABRI's formal command structure, helping him to mitigate deeply entrenched sentiments in the officer corps against the civilian technology expert. He also provided Habibie with an additional link to the presidential family, as some of Suharto's children did not approve of the close relationship between their father and his favourite minister. On the other hand, Prabowo hoped that the vice-presidential candidate would pave his way to the top post of the armed forces, either through input given to Suharto or by succeeding the latter. According to Prabowo, Habibie used to dream aloud of his future presidency, under which Prabowo would be "armed forces chief, you'll be four-star" (Tesoro 2000). It was this promise that formed the core of their alliance. It provided a crucial incentive for Prabowo to secure Suharto's re-election and, inseparably linked to it, the installation of his associate in the vice-presidency. Significantly, Habibie supporters sent out public signals that seemed to confirm Prabowo's hopes. A.M. Saefuddin, a close Habibie confidant in the PPP faction and later minister of agriculture in his cabinet, predicted during the crisis that Suharto would use special powers handed to him by the MPR to make Habibie president in 2000, with Prabowo filling the then vacant vice-presidency.[35]

Opposition to Habibie's nomination was strong, however, and Prabowo played an active role in regime efforts aimed at defusing it. The international and domestic business community, especially Chinese conglomerates, objected to Habibie's lack of economic credentials and his open support for indigenous, Muslim entrepreneurs. The campaign against Habibie was initiated by Sofyan Wanandi, a leading Chinese businessman and a central figure at the think-tank CSIS (Center for Strategic and International Studies), in which the retired Benny Murdani still maintained an office.[36] One week after Habibie's likely nomination made headlines, Sofyan's name was suddenly implicated in a bomb explosion in a low-class apartment in Central Jakarta. In the course of the investigations under Prabowo's friend Sjafrie Sjamsoeddin, "evidence" was found that linked the incident to Sofyan. Sofyan was investigated, but the widely expected questioning of Benny Murdani was called off.[37] Violent demonstrators appeared at the CSIS building for two consecutive days, on 26 and 27 January, demanding that Sofyan be brought to court and CSIS shut down. According to one leading CSIS executive, the demonstrations only stopped after he called Zacky Anwar Makarim, Prabowo's associate in command of the military intelligence agency, BIA: "We knew who was behind the mobilization of the crowds that threw stones at our office, and I told Zacky that this madness had to end, otherwise we would make the involvement of senior officers in the whole affair public."[38] If Prabowo and his associates had cornered CSIS, Wiranto pledged to protect it. Wiranto ordered the police to secure the CSIS offices, and the protests quickly died down.

The campaign against CSIS signalled the beginning of Prabowo's accelerated efforts to mobilize the Muslim majority against what he portrayed as a Chinese conspiracy to bring down the New Order. On 23 January, Prabowo and his ABRI associates met with prominent modernist intellectuals and *kiai* at a large fast-breaking gathering at the Kopassus headquarters. While his staff distributed books containing data on the Chinese dominance of the Indonesian economy, Prabowo called on the participants to unite against those who threatened the stability of the nation (Cohen 1998*a*).[39] After the sharp devaluation of the rupiah in the first week of January, Suharto had privately spoken of machinations of the financial markets to undermine his authority, but after the next rapid drop following Habibie's nomination, the president made his suspicions public. Officers close to Prabowo interpreted Suharto's remarks as an endorsement of his son-in-law's confrontational approach, and they acted accordingly. Feisal Tanjung phoned thirteen ethnic Chinese tycoons in mid-January, asking them for "donations" in order to overcome the economic crisis,[40] and he led the anti-Sofyan chorus in ABRI headquarters.[41] Prabowo's double strategy of aggravating political conflicts and conducting covert operations to confront the opponents of the regime was gradually adopted by other officers in the military elite, particularly those with a reputation for hardline views and an immediate interest in Habibie's ascension to the vice-presidency.

## Mitigating Tensions: Wiranto and the "Intellectuals"

Wiranto countered Prabowo's strategy of radicalization and mobilization with an approach of mitigation, offering the critics of the regime dialogue and ordinary Indonesians empathy for their suffering caused by the crisis. This did not reflect a particular "soft-line" element in Wiranto's political character, but rather the insight that Suharto had a greater chance of staying in power by defusing than by fuelling societal tensions. While Wiranto had previously made few efforts to conceptualize his thoughts and reflect on their political consequences, Prabowo's divisive strategies for defending the regime convinced Wiranto that he needed to consolidate both his strategic thinking and his team of advisers. It was in this environment of competition with Prabowo that Wiranto began to link up with the military "intellectuals", who in the past had isolated themselves from the army mainstream by propagating ideas of reform and long-term regime change. Wiranto now began to seek their advice, and slowly but steadily their language and argumentation started to impact on Wiranto's:

> Of course the crisis changed us a lot. It forced us to reconsider the principles of our political beliefs. I include myself in this.... We had to go out to people and signal that we understood their problems, and that we were ready for change. That did not mean toppling Suharto, but constituted an invitation to society to work with us to overcome the crisis — not pinning the blame on certain groups and then taking profit from it. That was certain to lead to disaster.[42]

The paradigmatic difference between Wiranto's conciliatory approach and Prabowo's strategy of escalation was reflected in the meetings that the army chief of staff organized with influential society figures. In discussions with Muslim leaders on 18 and 25 January, Wiranto stressed the necessity to defuse tensions, asking the *kiai* to assist the government in fighting against what he called "destructive rumours".[43] One of Wiranto's allies, Chief of Staff of General Affairs Lieutenant General Tarub, even launched an indirect attack on Prabowo and Feisal by suggesting that their accusations against the Chinese tycoons were baseless. Alluding to Feisal Tanjung's remark that Chinese corporations had done nothing at all to help stop the economic decline, Tarub asserted that the media simply might not have covered the advice given by leading tycoons on how to solve the crisis.[44] Stating that there should be no differential treatment of the Chinese entrepreneurs as the crisis called on all Indonesians to do their duty, Tarub could not have drawn a sharper demarcation line to Prabowo and his circle.

In addition to Wiranto's efforts to convince important societal constituencies to be patient and allow the government to overcome the economic difficulties, some of his associates established contacts with critics of the regime. Major General Agum Gumelar, then chief of the Wirabuana command in Sulawesi, spoke regularly with Amien Rais:

> We exchanged information with Amien. He told us things, we told him things. For instance, when some within the government thought Amien should be arrested for treason, we told him to slow down. [Yudhoyono] also knew Amien well, so we had pretty good relations with him.[45]

The polarization between those officers determined to suppress oppositional groups by force, and other military leaders prepared to open a dialogue with dissidents, pointed to the rapidly changing nature of intra-military competition. In the past, the logic of New Order military factionalism had required competing generals to demonstrate maximum levels of loyalty towards Suharto. The divisions emerging amidst the political and economic decline of the regime in 1997 and 1998, however, had much stronger conceptual features, and none of them looked particularly promising for the president. Prabowo's manoeuvres in defence of the regime were aimed at securing the election of Habibie to the vice-presidency, and he offered few indications about his plans beyond that date. Wiranto, on the other hand, believed at that stage that Suharto's regime was reformable, and he was determined to win wide-ranging societal support for this view (Sulistyo 2002, pp. 190–92). Given Suharto's fierce resistance towards reform, however, the officers around Wiranto increasingly opened up to the very ideas of political change that had been discussed by the military "intellectuals" since 1996. The ultimate conclusion from this gradual adaptation process within the Wiranto group was instinctively felt by the officers associated with it, but they were reluctant to express it openly: Suharto had to resign, and the main task of the armed forces was to secure an honourable and orderly departure of their patron.

## FINAL ELECTION, FINAL RESHUFFLE

Military factionalism had been a major element of regime stabilization throughout Suharto's rule. Balancing rival groups and distributing important positions among them, Suharto granted rewards and punished disloyalty. The fact that Suharto did not deem it necessary to sideline either of the two major patronage networks competing for hegemony in early 1998, and used the last reshuffle of his presidency to allocate key posts proportionally between officers associated with Wiranto and Prabowo, indicated that the embattled leader was still convinced of the continued loyalty of his military elite. Suharto appeared to trust the public assurances given by both Wiranto and Prabowo that they were determined to keep him in power, and seemed unaware of Prabowo's understanding with Habibie on the one side and the growing influence of the idea of regime change in Wiranto's circle on the other. Consequently, he appointed Wiranto as ABRI chief and Prabowo as commander of Kostrad in February 1998. Susilo Bambang Yudhoyono, who as one of the "intellectuals" felt closer to Wiranto's approach to the crisis than to that favoured by Prabowo, became chief of staff of socio-political affairs, handing compromise-oriented officers a crucial military portfolio to begin negotiations with regime dissidents. As compensation, however, Major General Muchdi Purwopranjono replaced his friend Prabowo as head of Kopassus. Subagyo H.S., for his part, was promoted to army chief of staff.[46] The reshuffle left supporters of Wiranto and Prabowo with roughly equal control networks within the armed forces: Wiranto headed ABRI headquarters, with key allies holding important regional commands and most positions in the military's socio-political branch. Prabowo, on the other hand, had direct control of, or influence over, the brigades of the capital, Kopassus, the ABRI intelligence agency, and his own unit, Kostrad.

The reshuffle pointed to Suharto's inability to adapt to the radically changed political context created by the crisis. In the same way that he applied conventional strategies to address untraditional economic and political threats to his regime, he appeared to believe that the well-tested approach of engineered factionalism in the military would carry him through the turmoil (Mietzner 1999). Suharto had obviously failed to notice that the character of this factionalism had changed substantially, and that it, for the first time, included scenarios of a post-Suharto military. The paradigmatic shift became evident in Wiranto's first major policy speech after his appointment on 23 February. Openly contradicting the position of his hawkish predecessor Feisal Tanjung that the country's problems had been instigated by "provocateurs",[47] Wiranto conceded that Indonesia faced a political, economic, and security crisis. The complexity of this crisis, Wiranto explained, affected all aspects of life. The middle class was losing its competitive talents and its vitality, while the lower classes saw their purchasing power declining. Unemployment was up, social inequality widened, and crime was increasing, with the vast majority of Indonesians experiencing a drastic drop in living standards. In such a situation, Wiranto said, it was understandable that the people felt helpless in facing realities.[48] While he signalled that ABRI was prepared to stop potential "troublemakers" from exploiting the crisis for political gains, Wiranto's empathy for those socially affected by the crisis marked a significant breach with Feisal's approach to security politics. His analysis of the problems echoed many of the critical ideas discussed in the 1996 army seminar, and indicated how far the thinking of the "intellectuals" had penetrated the views of Wiranto and his circle. It was this increasing susceptibility to rising societal demands for change that slowly eroded Wiranto's institutional loyalty to Suharto, and not, as O'Rourke (2002, p. 113) suggested, the predilection of the ABRI chief for Javanese "tales of kings being overthrown by their trusted advisors, lieutenants or even their own brothers".

## Frustrated Hopes: Suharto's Inability to Reform

The mounting tensions caused by the factional differences in the officer corps came into the open on the day of Wiranto's speech. During the handover ceremony of the post of army chief of staff from Wiranto to Subagyo, Agum Gumelar asked his fellow regional commanders as well as the heads of Kostrad and Kopassus to join him in declaring an oath of loyalty to Wiranto.[49] Agum was one of the core members of Wiranto's circle, and his dislike for Prabowo was well known.[50] The oath was a clear warning to Prabowo and his associates, with Agum keen to "make sure that everybody understood who the new commander was, and that was Wiranto".[51] The now publicly exposed splits within the military provided strong indications for the political elite and the broader population that some elements in the armed forces were prepared to reconsider their support for Suharto. This perception had a significant impact on the character of subsequent events leading up to Suharto's fall. The removal of the president had been the primary target of oppositional forces for some time, but now these groups turned to lobbying military leaders to achieve their goal. Marking the beginning of the third phase of the crisis, students began to organize and demonstrate in late February against Suharto's re-election, but at the same time they distributed flowers to soldiers and police officers who showed a much less repressive approach to their protest than some had feared.[52] Wiranto's concept to contain and de-escalate the protests rather than to violently disperse them helped to convince key government critics that the political attitude of some senior military officers was indeed undergoing substantial change. That other elements in the military still favoured the traditional security approach only reinforced the interest of regime dissidents in establishing contact with commanders thought to be more open towards the idea of regime change.

The public interpretation of the intra-military conflicts as a competition between moderate officers and more hardline generals favoured Wiranto's group as far as societal support for its approach was concerned. The kidnappings of student activists, labour leaders, and other dissidents, starting in February and widely linked to Prabowo, accelerated this polarization and provided Wiranto with further arguments for his policy of de-escalation. It was unclear, however, whether Suharto would appreciate Wiranto's non-confrontational approach as much as large segments of society did. Given the risk that the president might view Wiranto's tolerance of societal protest as an indication of declining loyalty towards him, the ABRI commander had to strike a delicate balance between accommodating public discontent and maintaining the political hegemony of the regime.

The intra-military debate on Habibie's nomination for the vice-presidency delivered a welcome opportunity for Wiranto to express his continued loyalty to Suharto. The press had speculated that Wiranto would overturn Feisal's earlier decision to back Habibie, with many retired officers publicly encouraging him to do so. Wiranto, however, made it clear that ABRI stood by its endorsement of Habibie.[53] The armed forces leader saw little value in seeking an open confrontation with Suharto, and Wiranto also did not believe that Habibie's election would significantly alter the power balance in the military. In fact, he insisted that his personal relationship with Habibie was good. They had become acquainted during Wiranto's time as presidential adjutant, when they discovered some similarities in their family's origins: Wiranto's wife was from Gorontalo, as was Habibie's father, and Habibie's mother was from Yogya, like the ABRI chief himself.[54] Discounting the warnings from colleagues that Habibie would promote Prabowo's interests in the armed forces if elected as Suharto's deputy, Wiranto assured Habibie of his support. Habibie's appointment as vice-president was confirmed by the MPR in mid-March, and Suharto was handed his seventh term in office. Many observers believed that Suharto had no intention of resigning any time soon, and therefore did not view Habibie's election as a final decision on the matter of succession. Some even suspected that Suharto had chosen a controversial deputy in order to deflect demands for his departure from politics. If that was indeed Suharto's intention, it provided further evidence for his declining political instincts. Despite the smooth procession of Suharto's re-election in the MPR and the theatrical celebrations of his achievements, the political cynicism in both the elite and the general population continued to grow.

The officers supporting a non-repressive approach to the crisis had hoped that Suharto would use his re-election to begin reforms aimed at overcoming the stalemate and stabilizing the political situation. Even the most progressive and liberal of the "intellectuals", who were deeply sceptical about Suharto's ability to bring about major change, examined the president's every statement and political manoeuvre for possible signals of his willingness to reform. However, their search returned nothing, as Wirahadikusumah recalled:

> We thought he still might have a last chance, if he just offered something to calm down the protesters. Anything, really. More political parties, more freedoms, maybe early elections. Or a clear plan for his retirement. But there was just a big zero.[55]

Suharto, in delivering both his accountability and acceptance speech at the MPR, had not only failed to offer concrete reforms, but had presented an analysis of the situation that indicated his increasing isolation from political realities. Against the background of economic crisis, political stagnation, social riots, and demonstrating students, Suharto read out economic statistics that compared the 1993–94 period with that of 1997–98, stressing the successes of his government in raising per capita income, life expectancy, and the value of exports.[56] Mentioning air crashes, train and ship accidents, as well as the ongoing drought, he described the events of 1997 as a chain of unfortunate incidents, ultimately culminating in the economic crisis, which he largely blamed on the IMF. Suharto promised to serve out his full term, and made no reference to political reforms or a controlled transfer of power to his successor. The president's political immobility came as a great disappointment to the officers around Wiranto. Agum Gumelar, asked by the ABRI faction to present the response of the armed forces to Suharto's accountability report, declined because "people would hate me for that sort of hypocrisy".[57] ABRI's response to the president, eventually read out by the police chief, reflected a compromise between Suharto's view of the economic crisis as a technical matter and the position of the compromise-oriented officers that political change was inevitable. According to ABRI's official statement, two things were important: first, overcoming the economic crisis, and second, reform of the political system, the economy, and the judiciary. While the first agenda was of an "actual" and "situational" character, the second was more "fundamental, structural, and cultural". In other words: while solving the economic crisis was the priority, political reform was only a long-term project.[58]

## Wiranto and the Inevitability of Regime Change

The image of Suharto's progressing political calcification was aggravated by the announcement of the new cabinet shortly after the MPR session. Filled with loyalists, the cabinet featured the president's decades-long friend and tycoon Bob Hasan in the crucial department of industry and trade. In addition, Siti Hardiyanti became minister for social affairs, in a promotion that many saw as the initial step to a dynastic solution to the succession problem (McBeth 1998b).[59] The hawkish former general Hartono was appointed minister of home affairs, and Wiranto Arismunandar, the brother of Tien Suharto's brother-in-law and notoriously harsh rector of the Bandung Institute of Technology, became minister of education.

The composition of the cabinet signalled Suharto's unwillingness to reform the political system, and it had an immediate, radicalizing effect on the student movement and other oppositional forces. Amien Rais, who had earlier softened some of his criticism of the regime following Habibie's selection as vice-president,[60] resumed his role as the intellectual leader of the reform movement, travelling to campuses and providing political guidance to the previously disorganized student groups. The new radicalism not only facilitated the spread of the student protests from the cities of Java to other areas of the archipelago, it also questioned the effectiveness of Wiranto's concept of de-escalation. Wiranto's approach had been based on efforts to convince the protesters of the inherent ability of the New Order to reform itself, and had offered dialogue as a way of integrating the critics back into the regime. However, by insisting that no political reform was necessary, Suharto eroded the most important precondition for the successful implementation of Wiranto's strategy. With Suharto incapable of delivering prospects for change, and the students determined not to give up before the president resigned, the outbreak of violent confrontation was only a matter of time. The escalation of the conflict would, eventually, expose as unworkable and outdated the attempts of officers in Wiranto's circle to offer change within Suharto's political framework. Thus the resignation of the president, both unthinkable and unacceptable for many officers close to Wiranto only a few months ago, increasingly appeared to them as the only possible solution to the crisis.

The generals in favour of negotiations with the opposition moved closer to dissociating themselves from Suharto after the escalation of violence on the campuses in mid-March 1998. On 17 March, 103 students were seriously injured during a confrontation with security personnel in Solo. As a result, universities in Jakarta, Lampung, Bandung, Yogyakarta, Surabaya, and Makassar saw the number of protesters increasing by the day. Wiranto had earlier signalled that the armed forces would tolerate demonstrations on the campuses, but were determined to prevent them from taking to the streets. This warning was increasingly ignored, aggravating the tensions between student leaders and the local security apparatus.[61] In early April, apparently violating Wiranto's orders, security forces attacked the Gadjah Mada University campus in Yogyakarta, leaving scores wounded and seriously damaging ABRI's reputation. The clashes increased fears within Wiranto's circle that the strategic goal of the protests might shift once again, and this time include the role of the armed forces as a major focus of criticism. Suharto's removal had become the main theme of the protests, but the more the armed forces were viewed as being inextricably tied to the regime, the more likely they were to be targeted by the oppositional demands for change. Wiranto was well aware of this risk, and responded by offering an open discussion forum between ABRI and the student movement on political reform issues. Student leaders, however, were in no mood to compromise and boycotted the ABRI-sponsored dialogue scheduled for 18 April. It was at this juncture of the crisis that Wiranto realized the failure of his conciliatory approach and, by implication, the impossibility of defending Suharto:

> Frankly, I thought we had reached a dead end. The students were very stubborn, and there was no movement on the political side either. I told my staff that all we could do was try to prevent people from getting killed. Because once a student gets shot, they will have a martyr, and then we will lose control.[62]

Wiranto's impression was confirmed by his intensifying contacts with NU leaders and Amien Rais, mostly through Yudhoyono. NU was publicly calling on ABRI by mid-April to "support the reform process", and Amien left no doubt about his intention to continue the criticism of the regime until substantial change had been achieved.[63]

The gradual separation of reform-minded generals from Suharto's political interests was in no sense a linear process, however. Suharto's system of patronage and personal loyalties had been weakened, but still proved forceful enough to prevent officers from openly demanding his resignation. Confronted with the choice of assisting in Suharto's removal or applying the coercive force of the military to contain the opposition, Wiranto avoided a clear-cut decision. He tried to combine both approaches in order to buy time, and temporarily damaged his reputation as a result. But just as the paradigmatic demarcation lines in the military between the proponents of change and the supporters of a repressive approach began to blur, Prabowo and some similarly hawkish generals reinforced them once again. Throughout the month of April, victims of the kidnapping campaign ordered by Prabowo re-emerged and identified the latter publicly as the brain behind the operation (McCohen 1998*b*). In addition, Hartono and Feisal Tanjung, now coordinating minister for political and security affairs, underscored their hardline images by openly sabotaging Wiranto's initiative for dialogues between students and the government. Asked in late March why Suharto was ready to meet farmers while refusing to receive student representatives, Feisal Tanjung replied that if the students would behave themselves like the farmers, they would get a chance to see the president.[64] In early April, Hartono opined on the same topic that a meeting between Suharto and students would create the false impression that the students had aspirations worth listening to.[65] By contrast, Wiranto's ally Agum Gumelar called the student's aspirations "right, pure, and positive, and representative of the society as a whole".[66] If there had been any doubts about the existence of fundamental intra-military differences between consensus-seeking officers and those propagating a crackdown, such statements served to both confirm and aggravate the cleavages.

While the students were critical of his swaying between dialogue and regime loyalty, Wiranto remained the best hope for those oppositional forces that tried to encourage the armed forces to side with the movement. This view was also shared by most of the "intellectual" officers who advised Wiranto during the crisis. Yudhoyono, for instance, recalled that although Wiranto "was close to the power centre", he "wanted to seek a wise solution to this hard political conflict" (Chrisnandi 2005, p. 52). Significantly, Suharto also contributed to this public perception of Wiranto's position. On 16 April, Suharto threatened to send Kopassus troops to deal with the unrest, implying that security forces so far had been too soft in their approach to the protesters.[67] The prospect that Kopassus soldiers under the command of an officer known for his hardline views could replace organic troops on the ground put the sharp criticisms of Wiranto into a wider context, and helped to repair some of the damage he and his circle had suffered as a result of the increasing violence. In this regard, William Case's assessment (2002, p. 62) that Wiranto had "retreated to a more hard-line posture" neither captured the grave tensions between the ABRI chief and those officers demanding a security crackdown nor Wiranto's growing awareness that repression alone would not be able to address the reasons for the protest.

With the country locked in a stalemate between calls for Suharto's departure and the intransigence of the president, the compromise-oriented generals in the armed forces suddenly saw a tiny glimpse of hope for a breakthrough when Suharto ordered Indonesia's political elite to the palace on 1 May for a major policy speech.[68] Many no longer believed that Suharto would finally offer reforms, but others expected him to launch a last-minute effort to save his presidency. According to Zarkasih Nur, the chairman of the PPP faction in the DPR who was present at the meeting, the atmosphere in the palace was one of tense expectation:

> Personally, I did not have much hope. But I thought "Who knows? Suharto had saved his head so many times in the past, why not this time?" … But he offered nothing. Actually, it was worse than nothing.[69]

Much to the disappointment of the audience, Suharto suggested that Indonesians start thinking about political reforms for the time after 2003. This announcement provided the final confirmation of Suharto's failure to grasp the urgency of the crisis that had engulfed him. It also served as a further motivation for the officers around Wiranto to increase their engagement with the opposition in order to assess the chances of granting Suharto a graceful departure from office. This approach was in line with what William Liddle (1999a, p. 28) called Wiranto's "pattern of reaction instead of action", with growing societal pressure forcing the ABRI chief into the gradual endorsement of regime change. Even within Prabowo's circle, however, preparations for a post-Suharto regime were under way. Prabowo and his associates expected that a possible Habibie presidency might facilitate their rise to the helm of the armed forces, and they began to use their contacts with Islamic groups to prepare the necessary societal support for this scenario. The nature of military factionalism — initially created by Suharto to sustain his rule — had ultimately been transformed in a way that encouraged competing officers to develop political plans for a future without him. When the crisis approached its next, and final, phase of escalation, none of the patronage groups in the armed forces was prepared to follow Suharto into the political abyss.

## NEGOTIATING SUHARTO'S EXIT: WIRANTO PREVAILS

After the 1 May announcement had underlined Suharto's unwillingness to offer reform, the crisis entered into its fourth and, as far as the New Order was concerned, its last phase. On 4 May, the government announced that fuel subsidies would be drastically reduced, fulfilling one of the conditions set by the IMF for further financial assistance. The subsequent sharp rise in electricity and petrol prices led to violent demonstrations in Medan, escalating

into three days of rioting in the North Sumatran capital. The clashes in
Medan triggered a chain reaction, radicalizing the student demonstrations
in the rest of the archipelago (Denny J.A. 2006, pp. 112–14). The unrest
involved more and more non-academic protesters, ranging from small traders
and workers to street criminals who hid behind a political agenda to loot
unprotected shops. With Medan in flames, important elements of the regime
made their first public moves to desert Suharto. Harmoko, now chairman
of the DPR and MPR, declared on 4 May that the parliament welcomed
the students' aspirations and would therefore consider revising the political
laws on which the New Order regime was based.[70] In the same vein, ICMI
called for a special session of the MPR on 6 May.[71] The non-governmental
elite, in turn, also accelerated its dissociation from the regime. NU stated on
11 May that it was preparing its own reform agenda, and Amien announced
on the same day that he would form a *Majelis Kepemimpinan Rakyat*, a
People's Leadership Council, by the end of May.[72] With alternative political
institutions in the making, the various patronage groups in ABRI had to
respond quickly. On 7 May, Wiranto announced the establishment of an
ABRI team under Yudhoyono to work out concrete proposals for reform.
While officially still rejecting a special session of the MPR to replace Suharto,
Wiranto opened the door for "gradual and constitutional change".[73]

Despite the vagueness of their public references to reform, the officers
around Wiranto worked intensely behind the scenes to win societal approval
for their efforts to allow Suharto a graceful departure from office. The input
from non-military groups on this matter was not only designed to increase
the acceptability of ABRI's proposals, but also to shield the compromise-
seeking officers from possible retaliation by Suharto. Accordingly, Yudhoyono
consulted various intellectuals and asked them to prepare concepts for political
reform. Among them was Nurcholish Madjid, who enjoyed Suharto's respect
and was therefore well placed to develop a schedule for the latter's retirement.
Nurcholish, for his part, saw the armed forces as the key to solving the
stalemate:

> Just look at Thailand, the Philippines, and South Korea. There
> the cooperation of the military was crucial in initiating democratic
> change. So we had to win ABRI's support for reform. If they remained
> obstructive, no change would have been possible.[74]

The president, meanwhile, took the risky step of leaving the country on
9 May for an international conference in Egypt, demonstrating, according to
Robert Elson (2001, p. 290), that he "was still unable to grasp the significance

of the mounting movement against him". His absence gave both formerly loyal associates and fierce opponents the chance to draft a political map for a future without Suharto. With the travelling head of state cut off from his network of informants and thus largely dependent on Wiranto's telephone reports, ABRI headquarters could promote Yudhoyono's initiative without the fear of presidential intervention. The dynamics created by Yudhoyono's project and Nurcholish's input would play a crucial role in shaping the events leading to the president's resignation.

Before Nurcholish could present his proposal to ABRI headquarters, however, developments took yet another escalating turn. The conflict between officers associated with Wiranto and Prabowo erupted in dramatic fashion, and the chaos arising from this split made Suharto's position increasingly vulnerable. When Suharto cut short his trip and returned to Jakarta in the early morning of 15 May, the New Order was in ruins.

## The Regime Disintegrates: Trisakti and the May Riots

The escalation of violence in Jakarta began with the fatal shooting of four students during a demonstration at Trisakti University on 12 May 1998. Public speculation immediately connected the incident to army units loyal to Prabowo who was already widely known to have masterminded the kidnappings of activists. Obviously aware of the accusations against him, Prabowo visited the parents of one of the Trisakti victims on 17 May, explaining that he felt the duty to pay his respects because the student's father was a military veteran. He insisted that he be allowed to prove his innocence by pledging an oath on the Qur'an, and after the distressed parents had refused three times, the victim's mother finally gave in. Prabowo subsequently swore that he "knew nothing about the incident nor had given any orders" (Pattiradjawane 1999, p. 163). For many, however, the fact that Prabowo deemed it necessary to issue a public denial of his involvement in the shooting only added to the widespread suspicions (Hadikoemoro 1999, p. 141). The Trisakti tragedy led to the eruption of long-established intra-military conflicts, with Wiranto apparently suspecting that Prabowo aimed at escalating the situation in order to convince Suharto that the ABRI chief was incapable of securing the capital:

> I do not know who was behind the shootings and the violence that followed, but one thing was obvious: I was commander of the armed forces, Suharto was away. If anything happened during his absence, it was clear that my opponents would try to blame it on me.[75]

The riots that broke out on the day after the Trisakti killings were accompanied by city-wide looting, burning, and occasional rapes. The carnage went on for nearly two days, on 13 and 14 May, leaving up to 1,200 people dead and Chinese business centres devastated. Other cities, mostly on Java, were affected as well. Solo, for example, experienced one of the worst riots in its long violent history.[76] While even ten years after the unrest Indonesians continue to seek final clarity about the actors and motivations behind the events, public opinion at that time saw Prabowo and his associates as the main beneficiaries of the turmoil (McBeth 1998a). The chaos in Jakarta cornered Prabowo's rivals in the military and brought him one step closer to a Habibie presidency, under which he could expect to be "four star" and eventually chief of the armed forces.

The suspicion that Prabowo had an active interest in the spread of violence was largely based on the inactivity of the security forces vis-à-vis the rioters. Troops from the Jakarta garrison, Kostrad, and Kopassus, all under the command of Prabowo or officers associated with him, remained conspicuously indifferent towards the unrest sweeping through the city. Prabowo later gave conflicting explanations for the insufficient number of troops and their reluctance to face the rioters, which contrasted sharply with his previous insistence on stern measures against regime opposition. On the one hand, Prabowo recalled his surprise at noting the absence of troops on Jakarta's streets, and claimed to have reminded his friend and commander of the Jakarta garrison, Sjafrie Sjamsoeddin, that "there are no troops" (Tesoro 2000). According to Prabowo, Sjafrie and he then inspected Jakarta's main protocol road, and upon establishing that there was indeed an acute lack of soldiers, decided to move some troops from the defence ministry to the city centre. On the other hand, Prabowo maintained that the soldiers were hesitant to "fire at housewives and children looting the shops" because they shared the same low-class background: "I think that was psychological."[77] Most confusingly, despite admitting that he ordered the transfer of troops from the defence ministry to other parts of Jakarta, he insisted during most of his later testimonies on the riots that he had no influence over, or knowledge of, troop deployments during the unrest, pointing at Sjafrie and Wiranto instead.

Regardless of the reasons and motivations for the inactivity of ABRI's troops, Prabowo clearly understood that the riots could accelerate Habibie's rise to the presidency, and therefore lead him to the top post in the armed forces. At the height of the rioting, Prabowo went to see Habibie and discussed possible succession scenarios and, most importantly, what they meant for him. Habibie seemed ready to claim the presidency, but was less forthcoming about his plans for Prabowo. In contrast to previous talks between the two men, Habibie no longer promised to make Prabowo ABRI commander. Describing the conversation with Habibie, Prabowo stated that "I should have noticed the shift.... He said: 'If your name comes up, I will approve.' There's a big difference there" (Tesoro 2000). The mounting public criticism of Prabowo and his hawkish friends in the armed forces was probably the main reason for Habibie to reconsider his alliance with the Kostrad chief. However, Habibie's changing position on Prabowo's future role was only the first in a series of setbacks for the latter that would tip the power balance decisively in favour of Wiranto and his plans for Suharto's orderly and self-determined departure.

The dramatic change in Prabowo's fortunes was caused by a combination of factors. First of all, Wiranto had the advantage of delivering regular telephone briefings to Suharto in Egypt, conveying his version of events before the president could gather information from other sources. Moreover, the ABRI chief was able to blame the indolence of the troops on Sjafrie and appear as a decisive leader when he intervened on 14 May to order the immediate deployment of new units. According to Wiranto, he threatened to dismiss Sjafrie and take direct control of all troops if his directives were not heeded.[78] Wiranto also won the support of several regional commanders, among them Djadja Suparman in Surabaya, Djamari Chaniago in Bandung, and Ryamizard Ryacudu, the chief of the Kostrad division in Malang. Marines were flown in from Surabaya on 14 May, helping to end the riots within a day and supporting the perception that the situation had only stabilized after Wiranto had assumed authority over the operation. Moreover, Prabowo's support base in the civilian realm was disintegrating rapidly. Amien Rais, whom Prabowo counted among his allies in the modernist Muslim constituency, distanced himself publicly from the Kostrad commander.[79] Habibie, for his part, had ended the cooperation with his former key partner in the military, and Muslim student groups that had previously thought about cooperating with Prabowo now threw their support behind Amien. Desperate to recruit new political friends, Prabowo even visited his long-time critic Abdurrahman Wahid, but after allowing the three-star general to massage his feet for a while, the NU leader sent him home without promises of support.[80]

## Suharto's Path to Resignation

Prabowo and his associates in the military sought to counter the erosion of their political power base by trying to convince Suharto that Wiranto was about to betray him. The reform proposals developed by Nurcholish for Yudhoyono delivered one such opportunity. In his report, Nurcholish recommended fresh elections in January 2000 and a special session of the MPR three months afterwards, implying that Suharto should not stand for re-election. Furthermore, Nurcholish demanded that Suharto return his illegally obtained wealth and apologize to the nation for his mistakes:

> Yudhoyono really liked the concept. But he suggested that I drop the demands related to Suharto's wealth and the apology.... Prabowo, on the other hand, called the paper "crazy". And I am sure he let Suharto know what Wiranto's people were doing behind his back.[81]

Besides reporting the Nurcholish initiative to the president, Prabowo also informed Suharto about a statement issued by ABRI headquarters on 16 May, which seemed to indicate that the armed forces supported calls for the resignation of the president.[82] Although the statement had clearly not intended to endorse demands for Suharto's departure, Prabowo presented it to his father-in-law as final proof for Wiranto's hidden plans to get rid of him. In addition, Prabowo and his circle also raised questions about Wiranto's trip to Malang on the morning of 14 May, taking with him almost the entire military leadership, including Prabowo, at a time of rioting and political turmoil (Zon 2004, p. 117).[83] The accusations launched by Prabowo caused serious doubts on Suharto's part about Wiranto's intentions, encouraging the president to investigate the claims and call his former adjutant in for clarification. In this encounter, Wiranto offered his resignation, which Suharto rejected (Wiranto 2003, p. 81). While the information supplied by Prabowo was insufficient to convince Suharto that he had to sack his top general, it nevertheless persuaded him to consider ways of preventing Wiranto from concentrating too much power in his hands (Hafidz 2006, p. 92).

Suharto's attempt to limit Wiranto's authority, however, only provided additional evidence of the extent to which the riots and their political implications had strengthened the position of the compromise-oriented officers in the armed forces. The president told his advisers on 15 May that he planned to establish a new security command that was to play a role similar to that of Kopkamtib in the 1970s and 1980s. The idea of reinstating one of the most notorious New Order instruments of repression signalled Suharto's determination to apply a more confrontational approach towards the unrest. Suharto stressed that he intended to hand the top post of this new body to a military officer other than Wiranto, as the latter was "too busy" (Wiranto 2003, p. 77). The creation of a dual hierarchy within the armed forces would have weakened both Wiranto and the military as an institution, allowing the president to gain more direct control of the security operations against the protesters. Wiranto, however, opposed the plan, and Subagyo, whom Suharto proposed as head of the agency, declined the offer (Sukmawati 2004, p. 174). Subagyo, although very tempted, was apparently aware that leading a security body specifically tasked with quelling popular protest to defend a doomed regime carried high risks for his career, and he was also not prepared to confront Wiranto over the issue. The incident confirmed that Suharto's authority over the military and its officer corps was declining dramatically. Rebuffed by his senior generals, Suharto called off Subagyo's already scheduled inauguration and instead drafted a presidential instruction on 18 May that appointed Wiranto to lead the agency, while Subagyo was only named as its deputy head.

The diminishing of Suharto's influence was accelerated further when student activists occupied the parliament complex in the early morning of 18 May. The symbol of the New Order's manipulation of formal democracy was now in the hands of disrespectful youths who camped on its roof and bathed in its decorative fountains (Aritonang 1999, p. 204). How exactly the initially moderate influx of protesters was able to pass ABRI's security apparatus remains unclear. Prabowo later claimed that Wiranto had promised student leaders to provide them with transportation for their planned march to the parliament, and Sjafrie confirmed that he was asked by two Wiranto aides to prepare military vehicles for the demonstrators (Tesoro 2000). While most of the students refused to accept the free ride, Sjafrie allowed them to enter the DPR complex as long as they came on wheels. On the morning of the occupation, Amien Rais addressed a public hearing at parliament, repeating his demand that Suharto handover his mandate.[84] This was followed in the afternoon by a press conference in which the DPR leadership, "encouraged" by hundreds of fanatical students, called on Suharto to resign. The fact that Syarwan Hamid, the deputy speaker of parliament and most senior military legislator, endorsed the statement was interpreted by many within the political elite as the official termination of ABRI's support for Suharto, triggering a series of defections of long-time loyalists from the New Order state (Sinansari 1998, p. 83). It is likely that Syarwan only sought to disengage himself individually from a polity with little prospect of survival, but the societal repercussions of his move were tremendous. Although Wiranto denounced the DPR statement as an "individual opinion", Suharto's regime was now in a process of rapid disintegration (Hamid 1999, pp. 92–96; Luhulima 2001, p. 150).

Suharto's failure to push the armed forces into a more confrontational stand against the protest movement — coinciding with the decay of the regime from within — forced the president to launch a final promise of reform. He received Nurcholish Madjid to discuss the timetable for political change the latter had presented to Yudhoyono, and arranged for a meeting with several Muslim leaders to announce his plan for early elections and the establishment of a "reform council". The gathering of Muslim figures at the palace on 19 May did not bring the breakthrough that Suharto had hoped for, however. Nurcholish, who was part of the group, thought that his own proposals had already been overtaken by new developments, and now demanded elections within six months. Suharto, for his part, only agreed to the formulation "as soon as possible", provoking the Islamic leaders to rule out their participation in the reform council or the new cabinet the president planned to form (Pour 1998, pp. 131–32). During the next two days, Suharto's office contacted numerous societal leaders with the offer to join the council, but only received rejections. In addition, fourteen of his ministers sent a letter to Suharto, declaring their resignations and refusing to serve in the next cabinet if it was still led by him. With oppositional forces unprepared to cooperate, and regime loyalists deserting their patron, Suharto's position had become untenable.

The gradual demise of Suharto further undermined the influence of those officers in ABRI who were in favour of a security crackdown. With the president increasingly deprived of his tools of political intervention, it seemed less and less likely that he would be willing or able to order the suppression of the protest movement. Despite his weakened position, Prabowo on 18 May tried to convince Siti Hardiyanti for a last time that her father had to dismiss Wiranto or declare martial law. Suharto, however, neither had the intention nor the political power to take such a huge and possibly disastrous step. Although both Wiranto and Yudhoyono feared that they could be arrested if Suharto decided to accept Prabowo's proposal (Usyam 2004, p. 341), there are no indications that the isolated president seriously considered it. The successful opposition to his plans of recreating Kopkamtib had demonstrated to Suharto where the new power centre in the armed forces was located, and had made him realize that he was in too vulnerable a position to challenge it. The prospect of martial law did not offer a realistic chance of stabilizing his regime either, with the inevitable escalation of violence certain to close the option of a negotiated withdrawal from the political stage. Wiranto, on the other hand, was loyal enough to Suharto to shield him from threats to his personal safety and ensure that his interests were considered when arrangements for the transfer of power were made. On 20 May, Wiranto concluded that Suharto had to resign immediately:

I knew since April that Suharto had to announce his resignation at some stage in order to calm down the protesters. But I had hoped for a transitional period.... After the meeting with the Muslim clerics, however, and the public reactions to it, I knew it was a matter of days rather than months or years. But at the same time, Suharto's dignity had to be maintained.[85]

The concern for Suharto's "dignity", based on years of personal attachment and the ingrained military sentiment against popular uprisings, led Wiranto to ban a mass demonstration planned for 20 May, which was supposed to be headed by Amien Rais and bring millions of protesters to the streets. Amien ultimately called the rally off after receiving strong hints from within the military that it could result in massive bloodshed. At the same time, however, Wiranto worked towards Suharto's retreat. On the same day, he convened a meeting of several academic experts in his office, making it clear that within three hours he expected from them a convincing concept for Suharto's resignation.[86] Several options were discussed, from endorsing Suharto's reform committee to military intervention, but only one looked politically and constitutionally reasonable: Suharto had to resign in Habibie's favour.[87] With this concept, Wiranto left to see Suharto.

## The Final Act: Suharto's Exit

The conversation that took place between Suharto and the head of his armed forces on that night of 20 May 1998 has been the subject of much speculation, focusing on the question of how much this discussion contributed to Suharto's decision to lay down the presidency. Takashi Shiraishi (1999, p. 82) claimed that after the meeting with Wiranto, "Soeharto chose not to test the military's resolve and resigned the following day." It is more likely, however, that Suharto had already made up his mind to resign when Wiranto, together with Subagyo and the Commander of the Presidential Security Squad Endriartono Sutarto, arrived at Suharto's residence. The DPR had set Suharto an ultimatum for 23 May to step down or face impeachment, and he had unsuccessfully tried to form a new cabinet and establish the reform council. Against this background, Wiranto explained to Suharto that the use of violence in order to defend the government would most likely make matters worse:

Personally, I think he agreed with this assessment. He didn't want a repetition of Tiananmen either.... Did my reminder play a role in his resignation? I don't know. I believe he was tired and had enough, he just wanted to get it over with.[88]

Suharto's immediate acceptance of both Wiranto's political analysis and the recommendation it implied suggested that the president had arrived at the same conclusion. More than three decades earlier, Suharto had witnessed the fruitless attempts of an ailing and politically doomed president to regain control over the military and the political system, ending in disgrace and personal decline. Suharto must have been well aware of the historical parallels between Sukarno's eroding powers in 1966 and his own loss of authority in the last days of his regime. Rather than being stripped of his presidency by the MPR (a procedure that Sukarno had suffered at the initiative of his eventual successor), Suharto agreed to surrender the presidency to Habibie and retire from political life. And as if to further highlight the similarities with the beginnings of the New Order, Suharto handed both Wiranto and Subagyo letters that would have allowed them to take power — evoking memories of March 1966, when Sukarno had been forced to give Suharto a comparable letter to legalize his takeover. Neither Wiranto nor Subagyo ever made use of the letters, however, instead sticking to the previously agreed solution of allowing Habibie to assume the presidency (Sukmawati 2004, p. 176).

Suharto publicly announced his resignation the following morning at the palace, and Habibie was sworn in only minutes later. When the ceremony was over, Wiranto informed the nation that ABRI supported the new president fully, but warned that the armed forces were determined to guarantee the "dignity" of "all former presidents and their families". The warning pointed to Wiranto's conservative understanding of the regime change that he had helped to negotiate: the transfer of power facilitated the replacement of the political leadership in order to accommodate demands for reform, but did not constitute a complete break with or denunciation of the New Order regime. This view had placed him among the politically moderate generals in the lead up to Suharto's fall, but set him on a path of conflict with more radical oppositional forces in the post-authoritarian transition. Before facing the difficulties of the post-Suharto era, however, Wiranto was forced to engage in a final struggle with his adversaries in the New Order military.

Encouraged by Habibie's ascension to the presidency, Prabowo and his associates believed that they now had a unique opportunity to reverse their misfortune of the past weeks and sideline Wiranto once and for all. Despite the growing distance between the two men, Prabowo apparently hoped that Habibie could be convinced to promote him and his allies to higher posts in the armed forces. For that reason, Prabowo went to see Habibie only hours after his inauguration, and according to the latter's chief of staff,

Prabowo came straight to the point. He proposed to promote Subagyo as ABRI commander, and leave Wiranto only with his ministry. Of course, he thought of himself as the next army chief. He said all this in such an intimidating manner that Habibie began to have concerns about having such a guy in his military — at all.[89]

Following this tense meeting, the new president received information that Prabowo was moving his troops around the capital, and that some of them were marching towards the palace and Habibie's private residence (Habibie 2006, p. 102). Now completely convinced of his unreliability, Habibie not only decided to deny Prabowo the promotion he sought, he also had him relieved of his Kostrad command. Habibie instructed Wiranto to ensure that Prabowo handed over command authority within a day, and that all Kostrad troops immediately returned to their bases. It appears that Habibie, Wiranto, and the Suharto family had all agreed that Prabowo could not stay on. Suharto's children believed that it was Prabowo who had provoked the unrest that had led to their father's ouster (Rinakit 2005, pp. 87–88); Habibie viewed the ill-tempered officer as a potential source of instability for his government; and Wiranto used the welcome chance to remove his most serious competitor for the military leadership.

When Prabowo learnt of his dismissal on 22 May, his allies in the armed forces encouraged him to disobey the order and lead an open challenge against Wiranto:

> I met some generals who were my supporters. Their message was: Let's have a confrontation. I said: Just keep quiet.... I knew that many of my soldiers would do what I say. But I did not want them to die fighting for my job. I wanted to show I placed the good of the country and the people above my own position (Tesoro 2000).

While Prabowo obviously had at least contemplated resisting his removal, it remains unclear how far he and his associates were prepared to go. Undisputed is the fact that Prabowo went to see Habibie at his home to receive a personal explanation for the decision to dismiss him, and that his appearance was so threatening that Habibie had his family airlifted to the palace. Habibie indicated in his 2006 autobiography that Prabowo may have intended to launch a coup against him, but it is more likely that the notoriously hot-blooded general simply wanted to extort concessions from a man he once considered his political ally. Had Prabowo seriously planned a coup, he would have been better prepared and would not have given up so quickly: after Habibie rejected repeated requests to leave him in command for "another three months or at least three days" (Habibie 2006, p. 102), and after Subagyo endorsed his dismissal, Prabowo offered no further resistance. He was assigned to head the ABRI staff and command school in Bandung, leaving him without troops and isolating him from political events in Jakarta. The conflict between the two major patronage groups within the armed forces that had marked many of the political events during the final months of the Suharto regime had come to a dramatic and abrupt end.

The outcome of the factional dispute within the military in favour of Wiranto and the compromise-seeking officers was determined by a combination of internal and external factors. Most importantly, the growing intensity of popular protest since March 1998 had made an effective hardline response to the crisis virtually impossible. The economic collapse drove more and more ordinary citizens onto the streets, joining a student movement determined not to relent before Suharto resigned. By May, the societal protest had spread throughout the archipelago, and even if Suharto had decided to violently confront it, the overstretched resources of the military would have been incapable of managing all trouble spots at one time. Moreover, Prabowo's circle of officers was increasingly isolated from the political elite and influential societal forces. As the media accused Prabowo of involvement in severe human rights violations, regime figures such as Habibie and oppositional leaders like Amien Rais began to distance them-selves from the Kostrad commander and his faction. With only tiny ultra-modernist Islamic groups left to provide societal legitimation for a possible declaration of martial law, such an option had become unsustainable. Finally, Suharto's decision not to order a last crackdown on his opponents and to hand in his resignation instead played an important role in deciding the intra-military competition. Although his political instincts had failed him throughout the crisis, he sensed correctly on 20 May that there was no way out for him. He knew that his power had all but evaporated, and had little interest in clinging to his office as Sukarno had unsuccessfully tried three decades before him. The inevitability of regime change, the public discrediting of Prabowo, and Suharto's relatively quick surrender gave the officers supporting a political solution to the crisis the decisive edge over their opponents.

## MILITARY FACTIONALISM, REGIME CHANGE, AND DEMOCRATIC TRANSITION

In the introduction to this book, the review of the academic literature on transitional civil-military relations suggested that the character of regime change plays a significant role in creating the "initial conditions" for military reform processes in democratizing states. One of the major issues in this regard is the extent to which the old repressive order is able to extend some of its features into the new polity. States in which the authoritarian infrastructure of the predecessor government collapses during the regime change seem to have better chances of short-term successes in their democratic transition and consolidation than countries that begin their reform efforts with much of the autocratic system intact. Aspinall (2005c) argued that Indonesia's regime change of 1998 resulted in both fundamental changes and considerable continuity between the New Order and its successor regime, which he explained by pointing to the fact that Suharto's state had exposed a mixture of authoritarian *and* sultanistic characteristics. Complementary to Aspinall's structuralist argument, however, this chapter has shown that divisions within the armed forces during the late New Order period were equally responsible for the ambiguous character of the 1998 regime change, which despite widespread social unrest ended with the controlled transfer of power within the constitutional format of the regime. To a significant degree, it was a circle of compromise-seeking officers that negotiated the handover from Suharto to Habibie, sidelining more hawkish generals in the process. Pursuing a pacted transition that aimed at the involvement of the opposition rather than its destruction, the steps taken by some senior generals avoided the complete breakdown of the New Order system and instead assisted some of its key figures in entrenching themselves in the first post-authoritarian government.

It is difficult to overestimate the impact of this intra-systemic regime change on the early phase of Indonesia's political transition and its efforts to establish democratic civilian control over the armed forces. As a direct result of the rise to power of Suharto's handpicked successor, core elements of the New Order, including the armed forces, were able to defend and maintain many of their institutional privileges throughout the first years of the democratic polity. This aspect of the victory by "dovish" officers becomes evident if contrasted with the potential consequences of a triumph by those generals who had favoured a repressive approach to the mounting regime opposition. The declaration of martial law, as demanded by Prabowo, would have almost certainly led to a further escalation of protests and increased use of military coercion against demonstrators. This scenario was unlikely to prolong the life of the New Order, with more deaths on the side of the protesters set to increase the radicalism and popularity of the opposition while irreversibly discrediting the government and its security agencies. Despite the undoubtedly higher number of victims and the more chaotic nature of the regime change, however, the violent overthrow of the New Order would arguably have created more favourable "initial conditions" for Indonesia's political transition than the relatively smooth transfer of power within the framework of the authoritarian system. The disintegration of New Order institutions would have been faster, and the armed forces in particular would have found it much more difficult to recover from the damage to their reputation caused by an ultimately unsuccessful crackdown on the democratic movement. Most importantly, the complete breakdown of the old regime would have allowed members of the opposition to form the first post-Suharto government, presumably leading to a cabinet with less interest in preserving the privileges of the military than shown by the eventual Habibie administration.

Instead, the defeat of the military hawks created the impression within society and the political elite that reforming the armed forces in the post-Suharto era was less urgent than initially thought. The removal of those officers viewed as responsible for the kidnappings and the May riots temporarily satisfied public demands for change in ABRI and eased societal pressure for a more wide-ranging replacement of the New Order military leadership. Wiranto and his associates had, after all, helped to negotiate Suharto's resignation, and thus were initially not counted among the most challenging hurdles for a successful democratic transition. This interpretation distracted from the fact, however, that there were substantial fissures in the group of officers now in charge of the post-Suharto military. Wiranto had only in the escalating stages of the political crisis integrated ideas of regime change into his conceptual thinking. Before that, he had viewed the reform-oriented officers, or the "intellectuals", as helpful allies in the competition with Prabowo, but had considered their ideas of political liberalization and disengagement from the regime as too radical. For Wiranto, the leap from defending his patron to assisting in his resignation had exhausted much of his willingness to accommodate political change. Beyond that, he had not paid much thought to the political format of a post-authoritarian system and the way the military would operate in it. Some of the reform-minded officers around Yudhoyono, Wirahadikusumah, and Widjojo, on the other hand, had developed ideas for political reform since the mid-1990s, and despite the suddenness of Suharto's demise, they appeared better prepared than Wiranto to engage with the new polity. The dividing lines between officers in support of different degrees of reform would define newly emerging military factions in the post-Suharto era, with each group developing highly diverse responses to the political change occurring around them.

## Notes

1   Linz and Stepan (1996, pp. 52–53) explained that the low level of institution-alization in sultanistic regimes makes them particularly vulnerable to violent overthrows, and power is typically transferred to provisional governments composed of non-regime forces. In contrast, the stronger roles of political institutions under authoritarian rule, both within and outside the regime, provide the preconditions for a negotiated, institutional transfer of power to a successor government.

2   These regional rivalries did not always coincide with ethnic identities, however. In the Siliwangi command of West Java, for example, many non-Sundanese officers occupied central positions.

3   Officers were under strong pressure, however, to provide evidence to Suharto that their alliances with civilians served the interests of the regime and were not designed to undermine it. Particularly in the 1970s and 1980s, Suharto was highly suspicious of military officers who built support bases outside the military to pursue their own interests more than those of the government. The increased integration of civilian groups into the New Order in the 1990s eased some of these concerns, but Suharto remained alert to indications that officers might turn their cooperation with civilians against him.

4   The number of victims who died in the actual attack on the party offices remains in dispute. According to estimates from the PDI faction led by Megawati, twenty-three people were "unaccounted for" after the incident. See "Alex Litaay: Kasus 27 Juli, Ada Korban yang Hilang", *Kompas*, 5 September 2003, and Luwarso (1997, pp. 14–42).

5   Prabowo had a reputation of being a highly professional but ill-tempered soldier. Coming from a well-connected political and diplomatic family, he had grown up abroad and spoke several languages fluently. His tendency for emotional outbursts, however, was the subject of extensive discussion within the ranks and the political elite. In 1974, he graduated from his military academy class with a one-year delay because of a conflict with a superior. After marrying into the Suharto family, he became widely known as the president's "special envoy" for sensitive political and military tasks, dealing with officers and affairs way above his rank. For Prabowo's reputation in the political elite, see Friend (2003, p. 324).

6   The most important of these divisions was that between Feisal and Hartono. Despite their very similar views on how to deal with opposition to the regime, they cultivated an intense personal rivalry over the position of ABRI commander. Hartono was widely known to be interested in the job, and with his retirement age approaching, he needed a quick decision on the matter. Feisal, on the other hand, was determined to stay on at least until March 1998, when he could expect a cabinet appointment.

[7]   Wiranto had been presidential adjutant between 1989 and 1993. After his term in the palace, his career skyrocketed. The soft-spoken, low-profile officer became chief of staff of the Jakarta command in 1993, its commander in 1995, and commander of Kostrad in 1996.

[8]   Interview with Agus Widjojo, Jakarta, 15 August 2007.

[9]   According to Soeyono, besides himself and Ma'ruf, officers who supported ABRI's neutrality against Hartono in the meeting included the head of ABRI Intelligence (BIA, *Badan Intelijen ABRI*), Major General Syamsir Siregar, and the Governor of Lemhannas, Lieutenant General Sofian Effendi. Interview with Lieutenant General Soeyono, Jakarta, 15 October 1998.

[10]  Interview with Lieutenant General Djadja Suparman, Bandung, 21 June 2000.

[11]  "Analisis Perkembangan Sosial-Politik Menjelang Pemilu 1997 dan SU-MPR 1998", unpublished paper.

[12]  Interview with General (ret.) Wiranto, Jakarta, 13 October 2000.

[13]  "Paradigma Baru Dwifungsi ABRI", *Tiras*, 24 April 1997.

[14]  Interview with Ikrar Nusa Bhakti, Jakarta, 23 September 2003. Bhakti was a member of the research team.

[15]  "Rapim ABRI Bahas Pemantapan Stabilitas Menjelang Pemilu", *Pikiran Rakyat*, 4 April 1997; "Ada Kelompok yang Mencoba Bangkitkan Paham Komunisme", *Kompas*, 4 April 1997.

[16]  The term "Mega-Bintang" suggested an alliance between Megawati's PDI and PPP. The Islamic PPP had adopted the "Bintang" (Star) as its party symbol in the 1980s.

[17]  Subagyo had been in the presidential security squad since 1986 and left the service only in 1993 as commander of its Group A. In 1994, he was appointed to head Kopassus before becoming commander of the Central Java Diponegoro command in 1995. Sugiono, also a former presidential adjutant, commanded the presidential security squad from 1995.

[18]  In a separate reshuffle a month after Hartono's replacement, Syarwan Hamid left his post as chief of staff of socio-political affairs. He was sent to parliament and finally became deputy speaker of the House in October. Syarwan's replacement in ABRI was Lieutenant General Yunus Yosfiah, an officer with an openly expressed admiration for Habibie who, like him, originated from Sulawesi. He thought that Habibie's contribution to the nation's development was "extraordinary". Interviews with Lieutenant General Yunus Yosfiah, Jakarta, 22 November 1997 and 6 December 2006.

[19]  Interview with Major General Agus Wirahadikusumah, Jakarta, 12 November 1998.

[20]  "Penganugerahan Bintang Lima: Tidak Ada Motif Politik", *Kompas*, 3 October 1997.

[21]  "ABRI Juga Dukung Pak Harto", *Kompas*, 2 September 1997.

[22]  "Pak Harto Hanya Minta Dipertimbangkan", *Kompas*, 16 August 1997; "Pangab: 'Tap VI Hanya untuk Berjaga-jaga'", *Jawa Pos*, 15 August 1997.

23  "Pangab: 'ABRI Tak Ikut-ikutan'", *Jawa Pos*, 30 August 1997. Suharto himself made his rejection of any restriction on presidential terms very clear. Like ABRI, he referred to the constitution that included no such limits.

24  In September, Prabowo's close friend Sjafrie Sjamsoeddin had been promoted to Jakarta commander, and other Prabowo allies led several regional commands. Sjafrie Sjamsoeddin was a classmate of Prabowo, graduating from the military academy in 1974. From 1974 to 1984, Sjafrie served in the presidential security squad, and returned to command its Group A in 1993. Another Prabowo ally in an important position was Zacky Anwar Makarim as head of the military intelligence agency BIA, who was appointed in August 1997.

25  "Wajar jika Prabowo Kasum ABRI", *Suara Merdeka*, 7 September 1997.

26  Jose Manuel Tesoro, "The Scapegoat?", *Asiaweek*, 3 March 2000.

27  ABRI commanders were typically replaced shortly before or after the five-yearly sessions of the MPR. That was the case with M. Yusuf (1978–83), Benny Murdani (1983–88), and Try Sutrisno (1988–93), with the only exception of Edi Sudradjat, who spent a short time in the post in 1993 before being transferred to the department of defence and security.

28  According to Fadli Zon, one of the key contact persons between Prabowo and Islamic groups, Prabowo increased the frequency of his meetings with ultra-modernist organizations as the crisis intensified, citing his "concern for the future of the nation". Interview with Fadli Zon, Jakarta, 14 April 1999.

29  Interview with Abdurrahman Wahid, Jakarta, 17 December 1997.

30  Interview with Abdurrahman Wahid, Jakarta, 17 December 1997. Wiranto asked Wahid to keep their communication and cooperation confidential until the MPR session scheduled for March 1998.

31  Prabowo's Islamic allies frequently noted his rather erratic observance of Muslim rituals, and wondered why he had chosen them as political associates. They agreed, however, that such considerations were secondary as long as Prabowo protected their interests. See "Mengapa Prabowo Mendekat?", *Sabili*, 2 September 1998.

32  Interview with Lieutenant General (ret.) Z.A. Maulani, Jakarta, 5 December 1997.

33  "Mensesneg Moerdiono: Presiden Perlu Istirahat Penuh", *Kompas*, 6 December 1997. A few days later, there were even rumours that Suharto had died. See "Presiden Tersenyum Saat Diisukan Wafat", *Kompas*, 10 December 1997.

34  Suharto announced that economic growth would slow down to four per cent in the year 1998–99, while most observers expected zero growth or even a contraction. The rupiah was calculated at 4,000 to the dollar, although the currency was close to double-digit figures. See "Disiapkan 7 Program Reformasi Ekonomi", *Suara Merdeka*, 7 January 1998.

35  "Hanya Sekali Yang dengan Catatan", *Jawa Pos*, 3 March 1998.

36  CSIS was founded in the early 1970s by intellectuals of largely Catholic-Chinese descent and intelligence officers close to Suharto, among them Ali Murtopo

and Sudjono Humardhani. It was widely viewed as being behind the anti-Islamic policies of the government of the 1970s and much of the 1980s. The relationship between CSIS and the regime declined drastically, however, after Suharto marginalized Benny Murdani in the late 1980s.

37   The press had speculated about a possible investigation of Murdani after Prabowo's private talk about it had been leaked to journalists. See "LB Moerdani tidak akan Diperiksa", *Kompas*, 5 February 1998; "Wartawan Terkecoh Isu Klarifikasi LB Moerdani", *Republika*, 5 February 1998.

38   Interview with J. Kristiadi, deputy executive director of CSIS, Jakarta, 3 September 1998.

39   Kholil Ridwan, chairman of BKSPPI (*Badan Kerjasama Pondok Pesantren Indonesia*, Cooperation Forum for Islamic Boarding Schools in Indonesia), gave the main speech of the evening. In line with Prabowo, he stressed that if ABRI and the Muslim community united, this would create a power capable of overcoming any element that trys to destabilize the country. See "Umat Islam dan ABRI harus Bersatu", *Republika*, 26 January 1998.

40   Feisal argued that the tycoons had received government facilities for the last thirty years, and that it was now time for them to return the favour. See "Panglima ABRI Telepon 13 Konglomerat", *Kompas*, 15 January 1998.

41   "Pangab: Sofyan tak Bertanggung Jawab", *Republika*, 5 February 1998.

42   Interview with General (ret.) Wiranto, Jakarta, 13 October 2000.

43   "KSAD Minta Ulama dan Santri Tenangkan Masyrakat", *Media Indonesia*, 19 January 1998; "KSAD Minta Ulama dan Umaro, Harus Saling Menasihati", *Media Indonesia*, 26 January 1998.

44   "ABRI Sumbang Uang dan Emas kepada Pemerintah", *Kompas*, 27 January 1998.

45   Interview with Lieutenant General Agum Gumelar, Jakarta, 8 June 1998.

46   Yudhoyono, Prabowo, and Muchdi were to take up their new positions after the session of the MPR, while Wiranto and Subagyo were installed in their new posts shortly after the announcement was made.

47   On 7 February, Feisal had spoken in front of 25,000 security personnel in Senayan. Using traditional New Order rhetoric, he threatened to deal harshly with those who wanted to disturb national stability and the proceedings of the MPR session. He claimed that the phenomena of the current crisis, such as unrest, mass movements, radicalization, and terror were all products of instigation by those who aimed to obstruct the MPR session. See "ABRI Siapkan 25 Ribu Personel", *Jawa Pos*, 8 February 1998; "ABRI Chief Warns of Mass Unrest", *Straits Times*, 8 February 1998.

48   "Seluruh Panglima Dukung Pangab", *Kompas*, 24 February 1998.

49   "Seluruh Panglima Dukung Pangab", *Kompas*, 24 February 1998.

50   Interview with Lieutenant General Agum Gumelar, Jakarta, 8 June 1998.

51   Interview with Lieutenant General Agum Gumelar, Jakarta, 8 June 1998.

52   The 3,000 students rallying at the campus sang "Do not hurt us. We are your friends. We are on the same side." See "Students Urge Riot Troops to Join Demonstration", *Sydney Morning Herald*, 27 February 1998.

53   "ABRI Denies it was Forced to Nominate Habibie", *Straits Times*, 26 February 1998.

54   Interview with General (ret.) Wiranto, Jakarta, 13 October 2000.

55   Interview with Major General Agus Wirahadikusumah, Jakarta, 12 November 1998.

56   "Pidato Pertanggungjawaban Presiden/Mandataris Majelis Permusyawaratan Rakyat Republik Indonesia, Di Depan Sidang Umum Majelis Permusyawaratan Rakyat Republik Indonesia, 1 Maret 1998", *Media Indonesia*, 2 March 1998.

57   Interview with Lieutenant General Agum Gumelar, Jakarta, 8 June 1998.

58   "F-ABRI: Reformasi dan Restrukturisasi Ekonomi Suatu Keharusan", *Kompas*, 10 March 1998.

59   Siti Hardiyanti produced a comical moment when she claimed that the new cabinet was in line with Golkar's commitment to "anti-corruption, anti-collusion, and anti-nepotism". See "Tutut: Saya Memang Antinepotisme", *Kompas*, 18 March 1998.

60   Amien and Habibie had cooperated closely in the 1990s in ICMI. Their relationship, and Amien's changing attitudes towards the regime, will be discussed in detail in Chapter 4.

61   The students of the Bandung Institute of Technology (ITB, *Institut Teknologi Bandung*), one of the most prestigious universities in the country and therefore one of the most watched by both the media and the military, left their campus for the first time on 9 April.

62   Interview with General (ret.) Wiranto, Jakarta, 13 October 2000.

63   Amien got Yudhoyono into trouble by claiming that the latter had "asked" him to continue his criticism, insinuating that ABRI was happy with his attacks on Suharto. Yudhoyono clarified Amien's statement the next day, saying he had only expressed ABRI's appreciation for academic criticism as long as it remained academic. Interview with Amien Rais, Surabaya, 10 May 1999; "Kassospol Minta Amien Tetap Kritis", *Jawa Pos*, 28 March 1998, and "Kassospol: Kritis Boleh, Kebablasan Jangan", *Jawa Pos*, 29 March 1998.

64   "Tak Ada Dialog dengan Presiden", *Jawa Pos*, 27 March 1998.

65   "Mendagri Tolak Dialog Mahasiswa-Presiden", *Jawa Pos*, 6 April 1998.

66   "Pangdam Wirabuana: Aspirasi Mahasiswa Benar dan Mewakili Masyarakat", *Suara Pembaruan*, 25 April 1998.

67   Suharto delivered the warning in a statement read out at the forty-sixth anniversary celebrations of Kopassus. The president expressed "hope" that "the people, local officials, and police can maintain national security and order without the involvement of Kopassus troops". See "ABRI Can Now Take 'Repressive' Action", *Straits Times*, 18 April 1998.

68    Invited to the "consultative" meeting with Suharto were the DPR/MPR leadership, the leaders of the DPR factions, officials of the political parties, ministers related to political and security issues, the chiefs of staff of the three military services, and the head of the police.

69    Interview with Zarkasih Nur, chairman of the PPP faction in the DPR, Jakarta, 10 February 1999; "Reformasi Politik Tahun 2003 ke Atas", *Kompas*, 2 May 1998.

70    "Harmoko: DPR Siap Ubah UU Politik", *Jawa Pos*, 5 May 1998. These laws, mostly passed in the 1980s, concerned the general elections, political parties, the composition of the DPR and MPR, and mass organizations.

71    "Buka Kesempatan Sidang Istimewa dan Reshuffle", *Jawa Pos*, 7 May 1998.

72    "Amien Rais: Tunggu Akhir Mei", *Bernas*, 12 May 1998.

73    "Army Moves to Defuse Unrest", *Sydney Morning Herald*, 8 May 1998.

74    Interview with Nurcholish Madjid, Jakarta, 27 May 1998.

75    Interview with General (ret.) Wiranto, Jakarta, 13 October 2000.

76    The most prominent target of the Solo riots was the house of Harmoko in the elite area of Solo Baru. See "Terakhir, Harmoko Menginap Desember Lalu", *Bernas*, 17 May 1998.

77    See Prabow's testimony to a team of investigators in September 1998, in Sinansari (1999, p. 184).

78    Interview with General (ret.) Wiranto, Jakarta, 13 October 2000.

79    Amien rejected a suggestion by ABRI's ailing "elder statesman" Nasution, who had proposed that Amien and Prabowo take the lead in reforming the country. In front of some of his Christian friends, who were particularly suspicious of Prabowo, Amien insisted that he had never made any political arrangement with the former, earning him enthusiastic applause from the audience. See "Para Tokoh Bentuk Majelis Amanat Rakyat", *Kompas*, 15 May 1998.

80    Interview with Abdurrahman Wahid, Jakarta, 26 May 1998, and Al-Zastrouw Ng, Jakarta, 26 May 1998.

81    Interview with Nurcholish Madjid, Jakarta, 27 May 1998.

82    Wiranto later disclosed the background of the press release. After a meeting with NU chairman Abdurrahman Wahid, Wiranto had asked the Assistant for Socio-Political Affairs Major General Mardiyanto to draft a press release about the outcome of the discussion, namely an agreement of mutual support between ABRI and NU. Mardiyanto drafted the paper, expressing ABRI's backing for a lengthy NU statement issued the day before, unaware that one of the points in the NU declaration could be read as an implicit call for Suharto's resignation. Mardiyanto gave the ABRI release to the press without consulting Wiranto. Prabowo got hold of the paper long before it reached the newsrooms of the media, leading Wiranto to believe that officers from his own staff had brought the release to Prabowo's attention. Interview with General (ret.) Wiranto, Jakarta, 13 October 2000.

83  The question of why Wiranto insisted on leaving for Malang in the morning of
    14 May remains one of the many mysteries of the May riots. Prabowo claimed
    to have reminded the ABRI chief several times that it would be wiser to stay
    in the capital. While the Prabowo supporters continue to interpret Wiranto's
    stubborn insistence on leaving Jakarta as an indication that he planned to blame
    the spreading riots on Prabowo, Wiranto's associates explained that the ABRI
    commander went to Malang in order to bring loyal troops from the Brawijaya
    command with him back to the capital. Wiranto himself insisted that it was
    Prabowo who had asked him to go to Malang to preside over a ceremony that
    marked the transfer of regional command authority from the first Kostrad
    division to the second, and claimed he had received no warnings from Prabowo
    to cancel the trip. Wiranto also saw no problem in leaving the capital for three
    hours as the command was in the hands of the Jakarta commander and the police
    chief. Wiranto did indeed order marine troops from East Java into the capital
    on 14 May, but insisted that this was done through phone communication.
    Interviews with General (ret.) Wiranto, 13 October 2000, and Major General
    Agus Wirahadikusumah, Jakarta, 12 November 1998.

84  "Amien Rais Minta Presiden Serahkan Mandat", *Bernas*, 19 May 1998.

85  Interview with General (ret.) Wiranto, Jakarta, 13 October 2000.

86  Interview with Salim Said, Jakarta, 23 November 1998. Salim was one of the
    academics consulted by Wiranto.

87  The military option would have seen Habibie resigning with Suharto, bringing
    in a triumvirate of ministers, with Wiranto as minister of defence and security
    in effect dominating the new government until new elections could be held.
    Wiranto rejected this option, and he later often referred to this decision as the
    moment when he could have taken power easily but did not do so in order to
    avoid a bloodbath (Roestandi 2003, p. 132).

88  Interview with General (ret.) Wiranto, Jakarta, 13 October 2000.

89  Interview with Lieutenant General (ret.) Z.A. Maulani, Jakarta, 26 May
    1998.

# 4

---

# DIVIDED AGAINST SUHARTO
## Muslim Groups and the 1998 Regime Change

One of the main arguments of this book is that developments within the civilian political realm are as crucial for the shape of transitional military politics as the internal dynamics within the armed forces themselves. More specifically, I submit that the level of military participation in political affairs tends to rise and fall proportionately to the intensity of intra-civilian conflict. Accordingly, after the previous chapter discussed the role of leading military officers in negotiating a regime change that left the fundamental infrastructure of the New Order state intact, it is now necessary to examine the extent to which disagreements between civilian groups contributed to this intra-systemic transfer of power in 1998. Using the analysis of Muslim affairs as a case study in order to emphasize general patterns of civilian politics during the events leading to Suharto's fall, the following chapter argues that divisions between key civilian leaders and constituencies impacted significantly on the nature of the 1998 regime change and the format of Indonesia's post-authoritarian civil-military relations.

The intra-civilian fragmentation during the political upheaval in 1997 and 1998 had two important consequences for the democratic transition and the character of the post-New Order polity. To begin with, the inability of oppositional civilian forces to unite and form a powerful coalition against the weakening regime led to their exclusion from the first post-Suharto government. Stepan (1993, p. 67) asserted that "a crucial task for the active opposition is to integrate as many anti-authoritarian movements as possible into the institutions of the emerging democratic majority." Indonesia's "active opposition", if there was a movement worthy of that name, did not achieve this goal. Consequently, groups opposed to Suharto gained almost no executive and legislative positions in the early post-authoritarian state, leaving most decisions of structural reform to politicians (and military officers) associated with the New Order. The second crucial impact of the civilian infighting during the crisis related to the ability of military officers to exploit the weakness of their civilian counterparts and engineer a transition that protected their interests. Larry Diamond and Marc F. Plattner (1996, p. xxiv) suggested that "unity of democratic purpose among civilian political elites" is crucial to ending military intervention in politics and creating democratic civil-military relations in political transitions. If civilians do not succeed in establishing such unity, on the other hand, the armed forces typically are quick to regain the political initiative. For example, "the failure of civilian politicians and parties in Nigeria to unite against the annulment of the 12 June 1993 presidential election allowed the military to terminate the democratic transition" (Diamond and Plattner 1996, p. xxiv). Similarly, Indonesia's leading non-regime politicians did not manage to build an alliance to remove Suharto from office and install a transitional government; instead, the student movement and societal unrest damaged the president to an extent that encouraged the armed forces to negotiate his political exit and secure a controlled transfer of authority to his deputy.

In order to illustrate the repercussions of intra-civilian divisions for Indonesia's regime change, this chapter discusses the political interaction between Muslim organizations and other key non-regime groups in the crisis that led to Suharto's resignation. Influential authors on Indonesian Islam have provided largely favourable accounts of the role that moderate Muslim leaders played in the democratic transition. Robert Hefner (2000, p. 200), for example, suggested that "Soeharto galvanized moderate Muslim opposition to his rule." He claimed that this oppositional campaign "aligned Wahid with Amien Rais", and that "the two leaders coordinated their actions sufficiently that each reinforced the other" (Hefner 2000, pp. 199–200). Wahid, according to Hefner, was "at the forefront of those demanding reforms", and joined in the "call for Soeharto to step down" (Hefner 2000, p. 199). In Greg Barton's view (2002, p. 228), the Wahid of 1997 "was calling for reform and was one of the first major public figures to speak out about the need for Soeharto to resign". The following discussion will dispute such interpretations and argue that many Muslim leaders were reluctant to openly align with oppositional forces and demand Suharto's resignation; instead, they were at various stages prepared to help stabilize the regime in exchange for political concessions. The chapter focuses in particular on the political behaviour of the senior leadership of Nahdlatul Ulama, Muhammadiyah, and ICMI during the crisis, and also touches on their relationship with the secular-nationalist constituency led by Megawati Sukarnoputri. Driven by their decades-old competition over religio-political hegemony, it was the unwillingness of these groups to cooperate with each other that ultimately allowed officers around Wiranto to arrange Suharto's departure in a way that carried the least political risk for the armed forces.

## STABILITY FIRST: NAHDLATUL ULAMA AND THE CRISIS

As the largest organization of traditionalist Islam in Indonesia, Nahdlatul Ulama was certain to play an important role in deciding the fate of Suharto's regime in times of economic and political crisis. NU had in the past helped to establish and stabilize authoritarian regimes, but had also demonstrated in 1965 that it could be a decisive factor for regime change when it chose to withdraw its support for the incumbent government. For much of the New Order, however, the regime was sufficiently stable, and NU needed the regime more to secure its interests than the regime needed NU to consolidate its rule. Since 1984, Abdurrahman Wahid (who was popularly known as "Gus Dur") had navigated NU through the political minefield of the New Order, oscillating between strategies of accommodation and confrontation towards Suharto and his government. Using his lineage as the grandson of NU's founder Hasyim Asy'ari to legitimize his control over the organization, he promoted doctrinal and social reforms within the traditionalist community. Many of the *kiai* questioned Wahid's adaptation of secular ideas and were concerned about his close relationship with non-Muslim and pro-democracy groups, but they revered him for his deep knowledge of traditionalist culture and unrivalled political skills (Muhammad 1998). While Wahid's erratic and idiosyncratic leadership style had been subjected to regular criticism at NU conferences, his political longevity and frequent involvement in elite negotiations appeared to confirm the accuracy of his instincts.

The mounting problems confronting the government after 1996 and the widespread impression that the New Order had entered its political twilight presented NU once again with the choice of either backing or helping to unseat a faltering regime. In the 1997 elections, viewed as highly manipulated even by New Order standards, Nahdlatul Ulama faced two alternatives: first, the organization could try to establish itself as a moderate voice of protest against the anachronistic inflexibility of the Suharto government. This option would have led NU back to confrontation with the regime, with political cooperation and material support most likely cut off by a bureaucracy determined to secure another Golkar victory. The second alternative, namely extending its course of reconciliation with the regime pursued since late 1996, guaranteed NU a stable political environment and continued financial support for the *pesantren*, but put its claim to democratic credentials at risk. Confronted with this strategic dilemma, Wahid clearly chose to support the troubled regime. Even before the election campaign began, he invited Siti Hardiyanti Rukmana to visit a number of crucial *pesantren* in NU strongholds, courting her as a potential successor to her father and opening the NU constituency to Golkar's electoral machine.

## Opposing the Opposition: NU and the Regime in 1997

The decision of the NU chairman to collaborate with the regime undermined the prospects for a more united opposition against Suharto, whose support in the general populace was fading. In defining his course, Wahid was driven by three major considerations related to political strategy, personal ambition, and the socio-economic and religious interests of his community. First of all, Megawati's unsuccessful resistance against the regime had contributed to Wahid's conclusion that the New Order had a good chance of lasting much longer than the Suharto opponents were ready to admit. Given Suharto's increasingly repressive approach and the possibility that he could be in power for at least another five-year term, it appeared unwise to re-open the conflict with the president. Moreover, Wahid saw the disappointing performance of other political actors as a chance to locate himself and his organization once again in the centre of Indonesian politics:

> Many people looked to Megawati as a possible leader. But she did not have the courage to lead, and instead just sat at home. Let alone Amien Rais. He has become a victim of his own flip-flopping.... In this situation, I am called upon, and NU has a great chance. I can help Suharto to secure an orderly succession.[1]

The exact role he intended to play in Suharto's succession remained unclear, but some within the Muslim elite believed that he ultimately sought to assume the presidency himself.[2] The third element in Wahid's agenda was his concern for the religious and socio-economic interests of the Nahdlatul Ulama constituency. Many NU *kiai* were dependent on subsidies from the bureaucracy, and they pressured Wahid to view cooperation with the government as his priority.[3] Wahid himself was well aware of NU's economic backwardness, and he feared that other religio-political constituencies would develop faster than his own. One of the major themes in his addresses to NU crowds was "not to allow it to happen that others already take off, and the NU kids are left on the runway".[4] Good relations with the regime translated into access to the economic infrastructure of the state, and the memory of marginalization in the past served as a reminder not to confront Suharto again.

Wahid's support for the regime led to considerable irritation in pro-democracy circles, and even among many NU activists and *kiai*. Pro-democracy groups had hoped that Wahid would protest against the exclusion of Megawati's party from the elections scheduled for April 1997, and probably even support his long-time friend's veiled recommendation to boycott the vote. Instead, the NU chief not only ordered his followers to go to the ballot box — he also launched targeted attacks on PPP, trying to damage Golkar's only serious rival and effectively mobilizing NU members for the government party. Adam Schwarz (2004, p. 333) noted that Wahid's support for Golkar was motivated by his inclination to "put the NU's institutional interests ahead of the democratic agenda, and his credentials as a democratic reformer suffered as a result". For many within NU, however, it was more complicated than that. While most *kiai* supported Wahid's decision to ask NU members to participate in the vote in order to avoid confrontation with the regime, they criticized the open courtship of Siti Hardiyanti and Golkar. Habieb Syarief Mohammad, chairman of NU's West Java branch, recalled the perception among senior *kiai* that NU had become a "laughing stock" as a result of Wahid's closeness with Suharto's hugely unpopular daughter.[5] The doubts within NU about Wahid's strategy were also nurtured by the latter's own implausible explanations for his actions. Wahid insisted that he had supported Suharto's party in order to prevent an electoral victory for PPP, which he claimed would have been interpreted by the international community as an indication for the resurgence of radical Islam in Indonesia.[6] Many NU members appeared to disagree: in the elections, PPP gained significantly in traditional NU strongholds, suggesting that Wahid's dislike for the party was not necessarily shared at the grassroots level.

Despite the controversies over his leadership style, there was no doubt that the majority of *kiai* supported Wahid's determinaton to exclude NU from political initiatives towards a more united opposition against the regime. Most of the *kiai* enjoyed the newly obtained harmony with the government, and they shared Wahid's distrust in the reliability of oppositional figures such as Amien Rais. Thus the monetary crisis hitting the country in August 1997 could not have come at a more inconvenient moment for both NU and Wahid personally. The *kiai* feared that the economic crisis would affect their constituency seriously, with lower-class workers, peasants, and underemployed most exposed to the impact of inflation and food shortages. Although many economists initially predicted that the largely rural-based NU constituency would be shielded from the crisis by its strong network in the informal sector, imported inflation soon began to cross urban borders, causing severe loss of purchasing power in rural areas (Booth 2000, p. 159). In addition, much of rural Indonesia was affected by a severe drought related to El Niño, a specific climatic condition. The *kiai* therefore faced the prospect of increasing discontent within their constituency, possibly fuelling expectations that they take a more critical stand towards the government. A more confrontational approach, however, endangered the flow of subsidies facilitated by the strategy of accommodation, which in times of crisis played an even more crucial role than during the years of constant economic growth.

For that reason, the crisis presented itself to most NU leaders not as an opportunity to remove an unpopular authoritarian government, but as a disturbance in their search for a comfortable space in Suharto's polity. For Wahid personally, the crisis also threatened the consolidation of his position within Nahdlatul Ulama. After years of internal turmoil, he had aimed to strengthen his grip over the organization at an NU conference scheduled for November 1997 in Lombok, hoping that NU's smooth relations with the government would translate into increased support of Nahdlatul Ulama officials for his leadership. Previous conferences had seen enormous outbreaks of dissent against Wahid, with critics attacking both his tendency to make erratic statements and his lack of managerial skills. The last major NU gathering, the Cipasung Congress in 1994, had voted for Wahid only by a narrow margin.[7] Since then, he had changed his approach to the Suharto regime, and the Lombok conference was therefore viewed as the first internal test for Wahid's new policy of non-confrontation. The worsening crisis, however, shifted the focus of the conference from the issue of organizational consolidation to NU's views of the economic downturn and Suharto's future as president.

Nahdlatul Ulama's response to the crisis was defined by spiritual and political support for the embattled government (Mietzner 1998). Most importantly, NU echoed the assessment of the Suharto regime that the crisis was not a political phenomenon, but an unfortunate external shock. The NU leadership thus refrained from analysing the structural roots of the problem, asking its members instead to pray for the recovery of the economy. In addition, NU issued statements of support for Suharto's leadership, not only consolidating his position during the crisis but also assisting his re-election bid. The chairman of NU's religious advisory board, Kiai Ilyas Ruchiat, underlined in mid-September 1997 that the country still needed Suharto as its leader.[8] In the same vein, Wahid began to denounce Suharto's increasingly self-confident critics. After Amien declared in late September that he was ready to succeed Suharto, Wahid attacked the Muhammadiyah chairman as a publicity-seeking self-promoter with a hidden political agenda, and threatened to mobilize one million NU members against possible "unconstitutional moves".[9] Furthermore, Wahid demanded that Suharto alone be given the authority to arrange his succession, as too many participants in the debate would only produce a chaotic outcome.[10] Wahid's attacks on Amien and his repeated pro-regime statements appear to be at odds with Hefner's analysis that "the two leaders coordinated their actions" and were "aligned" against the regime. Wahid made little effort to hide his hostility towards the Muhammadiyah chairman, and used every occasion to demonstrate that his current interests lay in standing by the regime and not in trying to overthrow it.

NU's decision to distance itself from the growing opposition against the regime allowed it to hold its conference in Lombok in November 1997 without experiencing the high levels of government intervention so typical of previous events. In his opening speech, Ilyas Ruchiat mentioned the devastating impact of the crisis, but did not link the economic misfortune to questions about the quality of political leadership.[11] Ilyas had been a tacit supporter of Golkar in the past, and in a separate interview, described Suharto as " a great friend of NU", who "has made an extraordinary contribution to our country". Insisting that "NU can't desert Suharto now", Ilyias pledged that "we will do all we can to overcome this crisis, and assist Suharto in every possible way".[12] Wahid, for his part, told the delegates that "NU supports the leadership of President Suharto in organizing a safe and smooth succession."[13] He repeated his attacks on Amien, underlining that NU would not support anybody who promoted his candidacy in the press. With this, Wahid effectively ruled out the possibility of using the crisis to unite Indonesia's oppositional forces against the New Order, and exposed long-standing religio-political cleavages as the major reason for doing so. NU branches generally welcomed the de-escalation vis-à-vis the bureaucracy, reporting that they now faced the opposite problem of being accused of "collaboration".[14] Ultimately, a large majority of NU's regional chapters endorsed Wahid's leadership. A group of young activists, who had a more critical view of NU's support for the regime but hoped that it was only temporary, chose not to speak up at the conference.

## Wahid and the Struggle for Hegemony in NU

The cooperation between NU and the regime stabilized Wahid's leadership of the organization, but he was also aware of the negative side effects this strategy incurred. Wahid's manoeuvres had both damaged his reputation as a democratic reformer and isolated NU from those key forces of civil society that promoted political change. In order to counterbalance this trend, Wahid declared only a couple of days after the Lombok conference that NU was opposed to the status quo and demanded substantial political reform.[15] The escalating economic crisis had ultimately forced Wahid to adjust his public rhetoric, but he remained opposed to any form of organized challenge to the political framework of the New Order. Based on the news that Suharto had suffered a mild stroke in early December, Wahid now believed that the president could die soon, and left no doubt that NU would support Try Sutrisno as Suharto's constitutional successor. William Liddle (1999b, p. 67) asserted that Try had been Wahid's preferred presidential candidate for some time, expecting him to neutralize the threat of political Islam and "be less authoritarian, more consensual, and more attentive to the needs of ordinary Indonesians than Soeharto had been". The other alternative, a collective leadership of political, societal, and military leaders, as proposed by Amien Rais, was anathema to the NU chairman.[16] It was in this phase of the crisis that the foundations for an intra-systemic change of government were laid, with key societal leaders ruling out the possibility of forming an oppositional collective prepared to take over from the crumbling regime:

> What is in it for me if I joined Amien in bringing down Suharto and forming the next government? Amien and his friends are not to be trusted. They now suck up (*menjilat*) to myself and NU because they know we are important, but once Suharto is gone, they want power for themselves. I know them.... We are much better off by supporting Try. He is a good nationalist, and when he assumes power, everything will be according to the constitution. Amien, in contrast, wants chaos.[17]

In mid-January, Wahid declined an invitation to meet Amien and Megawati, holding political talks with Siti Hardiyanti instead in which he assured Suharto's daughter that he had no plans to join the opposition against the government.[18] Despite Suharto's waning political fortunes, Wahid preferred the benefits of cooperation with the regime to the uncertainty of building a coalition with his religio-political rivals.[19] The "unity of democratic purpose among civilian political elites", which Diamond and Plattner viewed as crucial for ending military-backed authoritarian rule, appeared impossible to achieve.

Ironically, Wahid's expectation that Suharto's death was imminent almost turned against him. On 19 January 1998, Wahid suffered a massive stroke, resulting in the complete loss of his already impaired eyesight and causing severe damage to his motor skills. During his convalescence, Wahid struggled to stay informed about political events, but he lost operational control over NU.[20] Given the previous concentration of power in Wahid's hands, however, no obvious replacement emerged to lead NU in the same authoritative way as the three-term chairman had done.[21] There were at least three groups competing for control of the organization: first, the religious leadership around Ilyas Ruchiat and Sahal Mahfudz, who were apolitical in the sense that they wanted to maintain close relations to the power centre in order to promote the interests of NU's *pesantren*. They publicly demonstrated loyalty to both Suharto and the military, opposing initiatives that were likely to lead NU on the path of opposition to the New Order. Second, the Wahid loyalists coordinated by Deputy Secretary-General Arifin Djunaidi, who wanted to integrate Nahdlatul Ulama into the discourse about political alternatives to Suharto, but refrained from openly antagonizing him. As Wahid recovered from the stroke at his residence in South Jakarta, the loyalists established a temporary office there to maintain control over the central board. The third group consisted of young NU activists, who staged open demonstrations against Suharto and demanded his resignation.[22] The various factions pursued their own strategies, but the majority still backed a policy of non-confrontation. Consequently, a leadership meeting in mid-February decided that NU would unambiguously support the president to be elected by the upcoming MPR session, i.e. Suharto.[23]

After Suharto's re-election in March 1998, Wahid developed a double strategy that was difficult to read for both his followers and his increasingly numerous critics. While blasting the Suharto government in interviews with foreign media and meetings with diplomats, he assisted the president in his efforts to consolidate power in the domestic context. After the formation of a cabinet widely seen as ridiculously nepotistic, Wahid contended that NU was satisfied with it as some NU members had been included. Asked who exactly these NU representatives were, he had to pass on the question.[24] In mid-April, he claimed that demonstrating students in Yogyakarta had been paid by certain parties, undermining the credibility of the protest movement at a time when radical elements within the regime were desperately looking for a pretext to crush the dissent (Nadjib 1998, pp. 161–62). Pressured by the growing societal dissatisfaction with Suharto, and fearful that Wahid's actions might damage NU's reputation irreversibly, NU officials from all three camps eventually took the initiative to restrain their chairman. Even Ilyas and Sahal, now sensing the shift in the power constellation, were worried that NU might ruin its prospects in the coming post-authoritarian era if it collaborated too closely with a doomed regime. A week after Wahid's heedless statement about the venality of the student movement, the NU central board issued a declaration supporting the demands of the protesters, and called on the military to listen to the aspirations of the people.[25] Wahid was deliberately excluded from the drafting of the press release.[26] Although contradicted by his subordinates, Wahid did not argue against the declaration, suggesting that he saw some benefit in his organization's undermining of Suharto while he personally continued to maintain good relations with the president.

NU's policy shift reflected the rapid decline of Suharto's authority. Even conservative *kiai* in the regions now strived to reconcile their traditionalist *fikih* with the popular demands for reform, indicating that Suharto's power base in Indonesia's rural society was crumbling.[27] The turn against the embattled ruler was not followed, however, by attempts to forge a broad coalition to prepare for possible succession scenarios. In this, the NU board shared the scepticism of its chairman. Like Wahid, many NU *kiai* still feared a possible backlash by the residual powers of the regime against their constituency, and they too had little interest in helping their modernist rivals to replace the faltering government. The *ulama* were concerned, however, that Wahid allowed NU's general policy to be defined by what Kevin O'Rourke (2002, p. 83) called "his determination to thwart Amien Rais". The majority in the NU board did not believe that Amien's leadership of the protest movement was sufficient reason for Nahdlatul Ulama to reject its goals. In the words of one NU deputy chair:

> Between Gus Dur and Amien, that was personal. Whenever Amien said "A", Gus Dur said "B". If Amien said "B", Gus Dur said "A".... We, however, had to defend the interests of NU. And by April and May, it was clear for everybody to see that the regime had no future.[28]

Despite Suharto's eroding power, however, the diversity of views within Nahdlatul Ulama still offered the president opportunities to divide the opposition against him. It was in particular Wahid's continued confrontation with Amien Rais and other modernists that fuelled Suharto's hope that the fragmentation of political Islam, used and nurtured since the late 1950s to sustain authoritarian rule, would also secure his survival in the crisis of 1998. So long as the goal of excluding competitors from power motivated non-regime forces to align with Suharto rather than with reformist groups, the president had a realistic chance to maintain his grip on the political elite and extend his decades-long rule.

## CHALLENGING SUHARTO: MUHAMMADIYAH, AMIEN, AND THE PRESIDENCY

Like Abdurrahman Wahid in Nahdlatul Ulama, Muhammadiyah's leader Amien Rais had experienced high levels of fluctuation in his relationship with the New Order regime. In his earlier years, he had criticized what he saw as anti-Islamic policies of the Suharto government, condemning the disproportionate representation of non-Muslims in the bureaucracy and economic privileges for the Chinese. His predilection for sharp, witty comments, often in defence of the modernist community, made him popular among Islamic intellectuals, but also consolidated his reputation as a "radical" in the eyes of traditionalist, secular, and non-Muslim constituencies. After Suharto's endorsement of the foundation of ICMI in 1990, however, Amien changed his attitude towards the government. He now believed that the interests of the Muslim community were best served by seeking representation in the regime, and thought that ICMI provided a political platform to achieve this goal. Subsequently, Amien built political networks with Muslim bureaucrats around Habibie and began to defend the Suharto government against accusations that it politicized Islam for the purpose of regime maintenance.

Amien's cooperation with the government also advanced the political interests of Muhammadiyah, which made sure that Amien played an increasingly important role in the organization. For most of the New Order period, Muhammadiyah had cultivated good relations with the regime, declaring itself a non-political organization in 1971 and thus complying with Suharto's official depoliticization strategy. As a result of that decision, many Muhammadiyah members were allowed to hold influential positions in the bureaucracy and Golkar. Against this background, most Muhammadiyah officials believed that Amien had all the necessary qualifications to lead the organization. On the one hand, he represented a new generation of Islamic intellectuals, promoting reforms and breaking with the conservative leadership style of the previous chairmen Fachruddin and Azhar Basyir. On the other hand, his easy access to government circles offered protection for the vast network of schools, hospitals, and social institutions run by Muhammadiyah throughout the archipelago. In 1994, Amien eventually became Muhammadiyah's general chairman.

Once in charge of Muhammadiyah, however, Amien began to question the effectiveness of his cooperation with the New Order. He acknowledged that the Muslim community had received a number of legal-political concessions, but also came to realize that the regime had not changed its repressive character. On balance, Amien concluded, the New Order had profited more from his regime participation than Muhammadiyah and the modernist Muslim constituency.[29] Thus in late 1996 and early 1997, Amien issued a series of statements critical of the regime, mostly focusing on the excesses of economic cronyism in Suharto's family and inner circle. The regime reacted by forcing Amien to resign from his senior position in ICMI, and it put pressure on the Muhammadiyah central board to distance itself from its chairman. Lukman Harun, a former Parmusi politician and *Dewan Dakwah* official who had joined Golkar in the 1990s, was the most prominent critic of Amien's confrontational course against the regime. The majority of Muhammadiyah activists, however, strongly supported their chairman. Muhammadiyah representatives reported from the regions that while the bureaucracy had issued continued warnings against the organization, there was no significant regime backlash against their social activities.[30] Apparently, the indispensability of Muhammadiyah's officials and socio-religious institutions for the political, educational, and medical infrastructure of the state made the organization much less vulnerable to regime sanctions than NU, protecting Amien effectively from regime-initiated punishment for his criticism.

## Between Crisis and Temptation: Amien and the Regime

Paradoxically, the crisis that began to unfold in August 1997 further consolidated Amien's authority within Muhammadiyah. In the eyes of many Muhammadiyah functionaries, the economic decline of the New Order confirmed the accuracy of Amien's earlier criticisms of the regime, which were now echoed in the standard commentaries of political observers. The crisis transformed Amien from a prominent Muslim leader into a key national figure, especially after he, rather spontaneously, declared his preparedness to run for the presidency in September 1997.[31] The challenge to Suharto's bid for re-election was a cultural revolution in a regime that had previously used its tools of repression and political engineering to secure the president's unanimous re-appointment. Megawati's ouster in 1996, following rumours she might officially declare her intention to replace Suharto, had underlined the ageing autocrat's insistence on undivided support for his rule. While Amien did not command a political party in the MPR, and could therefore not directly intervene in the electoral process, the crisis provided his candidacy with a psychological momentum difficult to control by the regime. Accordingly, in order to anticipate potential manoeuvres by Amien in the MPR, Suharto removed his name from a list of candidates for MPR membership.[32] This decision, while excluding Amien from the formal structures of the New Order regime, in fact strengthened his determination to undermine them from outside.

The regime criticism launched by the Muhammadiyah chairman was unique not only in its trenchant intensity, but also in its outreach to other socio-political constituencies. Among the leaders of Indonesia's major societal forces, Amien emerged as the only key figure working towards a united opposition against the authoritarian regime. Megawati, for example, had followed Wahid in rejecting active regime opposition because she felt responsible for the security of her followers. This reluctance was underpinned and aggravated further by her non-combative personal style. Believing that the New Order might crack down on a possible protest movement, Megawati avoided any public statement that her supporters or the regime could interpret as an appeal for active resistance against Suharto. Her husband contended that "these people who criticize Megawati for not doing more during the crisis have no idea how it's like to have the responsibility for millions of people — one wrong word, and there could have been a bloodbath".[33] Amien, on the other hand, was confident that the importance of Muhammadiyah's socio-religious institutions for the regime would grant them immunity from potential acts of retribution, allowing him to ignore advice by some of his sympathizers in the government to drive a less confrontational course.

Accordingly, instead of toning down his criticism, Amien developed strategies to build up a broad-based alliance against Suharto. By December 1997, he contemplated ways of cooperating with both Wahid and Megawati. A coalition between nationalist elements, traditionalist Islam, and modernist Muslims would have been a serious challenge to the crisis-ridden government, possibly overcoming the very disunity among Indonesia's civilian forces that had allowed non-democratic actors to establish and sustain decades of authoritarian rule. The response Amien received from Wahid, however, was negative. Wahid had no intention of aligning himself with anti-Suharto forces and thereby putting his good relationship with the regime at risk.[34] Megawati, for her part, was slightly more sympathetic. She was deeply suspicious of Amien because of the latter's reputation for Islamic exclusivism, but acknowledged his contribution to undermining the regime that had excluded her from political life since 1996.[35] Megawati agreed to two public appearances with Amien in January, which were designed to explore the possibility of a coalition between them.[36] The meetings failed, however, to overcome their mutual prejudices. Megawati saw no reason to revise her view of Amien as a political opportunist, and Amien felt that his perception of Megawati as an intellectually limited and politically overrated amateur had been confirmed (Tesoro 1998). By early February, the contact broke off.

The failure of Amien's efforts to forge an anti-regime alliance between influential elites reflected the fragmentation of Indonesia's civilian forces, and highlighted once again why the New Order had been able to survive for such a long time. The unwillingness of traditionalist and nationalist leaders to join him in eroding the regime had a profound impact on Amien, causing him to reconsider both his intention of mobilizing an oppositional movement against Suharto and the inclusivist character it was supposed to acquire. Furthermore, Suharto's decision to anoint Habibie as his vice-presidential candidate provided an additional incentive for Amien to revise his confrontational attitude towards the government. Indicating his shifting position, he returned to some of his political themes of the pre-crisis period. For example, Amien supported the president's attacks on Chinese conglomerates, identifying them as the source of the country's economic problems.[37] Evidently, the regime's increased use of Islamic sentiments in the crisis and the prospect of a Habibie presidency, under which Amien was likely to play a prominent role, softened the latter's criticism of the Suharto government. In mid-February, Amien told a Muhammadiyah gathering that Habibie had assured him Suharto would do all he could to overcome the economic crisis, suggesting that the president should be given more time. Moreover, Amien advised Emil Salim, a widely respected former minister and fellow ICMI associate, to drop his public candidacy for the vice-presidential nomination, which Emil had launched in protest against Suharto's monopolistic dominance over the political system.[38] For Amien, Emil's candidacy was a largely symbolic act, but it nevertheless carried the risk that Suharto could view the campaign as ICMI-driven and thus feel encouraged to cancel Habibie's nomination.

The opposition to Emil's candidacy indicated that Amien was about to redefine his political priorities. Amien's efforts to secure the rise of an Islamic ally to one of the top posts of the regime had obviously taken precedence over his support for expressions of protest against the non-democratic format of the New Order polity. Not surprisingly, speculation was rife that Amien had suspended his criticism of Suharto and thrown his support behind Habibie because he aimed at cabinet posts for Muhammadiyah.[39] The subsequent accusations of opportunism damaged Amien's reputation, and his critics appeared unconvinced by his assurances that he only followed the political advice of the former Masyumi leader Muhammad Natsir "to build up good communication channels with all segments of this state, but don't make commitments".[40] As Suharto was re-elected in March with Habibie as his vice-president, Amien called on his followers to remain calm and pray for the success of the new government. His fundamental opposition of the previous months, driven by the analysis that Suharto's continued rule was certain to result in Indonesia's political and economic collapse, seemed now far away.

## From Elite Politics to Populist Power: Amien and the Student Movement

Amien's sudden reconciliation with the regime raised questions about the reasons behind his previous demands for reform, and pointed to a general pattern of political motivations and strategic interests within the non-regime elite. Many of his critics suspected that Amien had sought to remove the regime only because it had broken its promises of increased political powers for Islamic leaders, and that he had hoped democratic change would bring the levels of regime participation for the Muslim majority that Suharto had not delivered. The prospect of a Habibie presidency, however, re-opened the possibility of achieving fair political representation for Muslims without replacing the foundations of the New Order polity. From this perspective, regime change was largely a function of serving sectoral interests of political elites, and not a rejection of non-democratic rule as such. Richard Robison and Vedi Hadiz (2004, p. 171) have suggested that Wahid, Megawati, and Amien "still considered that their ambitions could be achieved from within the regime", and that one of their main fears was "losing control to more radical and populist forces". While this observation is accurate for the political behaviour of both Wahid and Megawati throughout the crisis, it only partially captures the complexity of Amien's rapidly changing regime relations. The reason is that after only one month of conciliatory interaction, Amien did in fact conclude in March 1998 that Habibie was unable to serve his interests "from within the regime". Consequently, he aligned himself with the very "radical and populist forces" that Robison and Hadiz asserted were contradictory to his personal and political agenda. Hoping to combine his influence in elite politics with the moral authority and mass-driven force of popular protest, the chairman of Muhammadiyah linked up with the student movement in order to seek Suharto's removal from power.

Amien's abrupt switch from regime support to fundamental opposition was reflective of the many strategic choices and dilemmas that political actors faced in the constantly changing context of the crisis. But it also consolidated the view among Amien's critics in the elite that he was too unstable a partner to form a coalition with. The two main factors that led Amien to cancel his temporary support for Suharto underlined, in the eyes of his political rivals, that his interests were largely defined by tactical and constituency-based considerations. First, the announcement of what David Jenkins (1999, p. 32) called a "Caligulean" cabinet in mid-March convinced Amien that Suharto had no intention of granting Habibie greater political influence, let alone of preparing him as his successor. Instead of appointing critical Islamic figures from the activist faction of ICMI, Suharto had chosen a cabinet of cronies, with his Chinese business associate Bob Hasan taking the crucial trade portfolio. Second, popular protest had replaced elite politics as the main factor driving political change, leading Amien to believe that Suharto's fate would be decided on the streets rather than in political backroom deals.[41] After the cabinet line-up was made public, Amien started immediately to tour the campuses, ridiculing the quality of the ministers and gaining the sympathy of the students by mediating in their conflicts with the security forces.[42] He also stepped up his international media campaign against Suharto, and attempted to drive a wedge between the armed forces and the president by stating that the hope of the people now rested with the military.[43] With Wahid branding the students as paid agents of unnamed group interests, and Megawati refusing to play an active role in the opposition, Amien emerged as the *spiritus rector* of the student movement.

After his failure to build an elite-based alliance with central figures of other religio-political constituencies, Amien began to apply his pluralist strategy to the new coalition with students and grassroots groups. The student movement included significant non-Muslim and pluralist elements, and their leaders were apparently more prepared to believe in Amien's inclusivist turn than his traditional rivals in the political elite. Meeting with church figures and Chinese businessmen, Amien tried hard to alter his predominant image as an Islamic politician. But like his earlier attempts to forge a pluralist elite coalition, Amien's efforts to expand his grassroots support attracted accusations of opportunism from his political foes. His critics were quick to point out that Amien's courting of non-Muslim groups was a calculated move to enhance his position in the crisis negotiations and improve his political career prospects for the post-crisis period.[44] In addition, Amien's new pluralist outlook also appeared designed to polish his international image. The international community was likely to play an important role in determining both Suharto's fate and the shape of the political landscape in the post-New Order era, encouraging Amien to lobby Western capitals for their support. In the midst of the student demonstrations in early May, Amien travelled to the United States and Europe, presenting himself as the political alternative to Suharto and promoting his new pluralist agenda.[45]

The tension between Amien's Islamic image and the pluralist design of the coalition he tried to create was reflected in the continued use of Muhammadiyah as his political vehicle. While it provided him with the necessary operational resources, the explicit identification with his modernist home base also discouraged the leaders of other constituencies, most notably Wahid and Megawati, from joining his alliance. Members of the Muhammadiyah central board had for some time allowed Amien to use the Muhammadiyah offices in Yogyakarta and Jakarta for political purposes.[46] Moreover, since the beginning of the student demonstrations, Muhammadiyah universities had figured prominently in the protest movement, and banners supporting Amien's nomination as president were common on Muhammadiyah-affiliated campuses.[47] In institutional terms, the organization remained neutral, but prominent Muhammadiyah figures openly expressed their support for Amien. Deputy Chairman Malik Fajar was one of them, offering his house as "some kind of operational centre for Amien's campaign".[48] Returning from his overseas trip on 11 May, Amien announced at a gathering of 5,000 Muhammadiyah *santri* in Jakarta that he would establish a People's Leadership Council (*Majelis Kepemimpinan Rakyat*) by the end of May.[49] For Megawati and Wahid, the event represented the very combination of personal leadership ambitions, calculated pluralist outreach, and sectoral modernist interests that they had identified as the basis of Amien's political behaviour for some time. For that reason, they stayed away from the council although Amien had earlier claimed that he had secured their participation.

The refusal of important constituency leaders to support the protest movement against Suharto, while Amien had assumed its leadership, pointed to the continued divisions within Indonesia's non-regime elite. Amien's plan to forge an alliance of modernist Muslims, traditionalist Islam, and secular nationalism to challenge and ultimately replace the regime had failed. Wahid and Megawati harboured severe doubts about Amien's political sincerity, consistency, and reliability, leading them to believe that the chairman of Muhammadiyah pursued the goal of alliance-building and regime change largely to satisfy personal ambitions and constituency interests. As a result of their deep mutual suspicions, the initiative for overthrowing the New Order polity shifted from societal leaders to the student movement, with Amien playing an intellectual, but by no means operational leadership role. The absence of coordination between the main oppositional forces not only allowed the government to prolong its rule, but impacted also on the nature of the eventual regime change. With the civilian elite unprepared to seize power, and the student movement seeking a quick change of government, compromise-oriented elements in the armed forces took the lead in securing a negotiated, intra-systemic transfer of power. This handover of authority within the constitutional framework of the regime lifted its main beneficiaries into the limelight: B.J. Habibie and his ICMI associates.

## ICMI: BETWEEN REBELLION AND COLLABORATION

The difficulty of creating a united front against the regime was aggravated by the continued ability of the Suharto government to tie key civilian elites, including some Muslim leaders, to its fate. Amien's oscillation between support for the regime and fundamental opposition towards it was not a unique political phenomenon, but was also reflective of the debate within ICMI, the organization that had sidelined him in early 1997. ICMI had since its inception in 1990 accommodated a variety of divergent interests, balancing critical activists, government bureaucrats, and moderate Muslim intellectuals (Schwarz 2004, pp. 176–77). The activists around Adi Sasono, ICMI's secretary-general, had been highly critical of Suharto, especially of his economic policies. Despite their aversion to the president, they had hoped that cooperation with the regime would grant them greater access to the policy debates within the government elite and allow them to realize their strategic goal of redistributing Chinese-controlled economic assets to Muslim small-scale businesses.[50]

By 1997, however, many members of the activist faction were deeply frustrated with the limitations of their political influence. They filled only marginal posts in the lower bureaucracy as well as in think tanks and were largely excluded from the decision-making process in Suharto's power centre. Similar to Amien, the activist group in ICMI felt that the regime had failed to deliver on its promises of higher political representation for Muslims, but in contrast to the Muhammadiyah chairman, they had no power base of their own to launch independent political campaigns. In consequence, they continued to rely on Habibie's patronage and his appeals for patience. The bureaucrats in ICMI, on the other hand, had gained a number of important positions in cabinet, Golkar, and the armed forces. However, most government officials had shown little interest in ICMI's Islamic platform, aligning themselves with Habibie's group largely in order to improve their standing in the elite competition over crucial posts in the regime. ICMI-affiliated bureaucrats had very diverse agendas, ranging from the advancement of dubious high-technology projects to influence over military appointments.[51] It was the irrelevance of some of these goals for the social, cultural, and political needs of the Muslim community that encouraged the third ICMI faction, consisting of moderate Islamic intellectuals like Nurcholish Madjid, to almost completely disengage from the organization.

## Crisis and Exclusion: Habibie In or Out?

The attitudes of ICMI leaders vis-à-vis the New Order regime mirrored not only factional divisions within the organization, but were also defined by the fluctuating political fortunes of their main patron. For much of the 1990s, Habibie was considered a strong candidate for the vice-presidency. Despite his failure to win the nomination in 1993, he had continued to work ambitiously towards the 1998 anointment. Changes in the composition of the regime in the second half of the 1990s, however, had not always worked in Habibie's favour. Suharto's dislike of the critical comments on his government by ICMI activists had cast doubts over Habibie's prospects, and new political figures had entered the inner circle of the president. Suharto began to contemplate a dynastic solution to the succession problem, and other loyalists such as Hartono, Ginandjar Kartasasmita, or Wiranto were also mentioned as potential vice-presidential candidates. The impact of the economic crisis further added to Habibie's apparent decline. With Suharto forced to call for international help to acquire emergency credits, and Indonesia increasingly exposed to the fluctuations of the currency market and stock exchanges, the economic reputation of vice-presidential candidates attracted particular attention. Habibie's unorthodox view on economic mechanisms and industrial policy, in the better days of the New Order called "Habibienomics", now appeared as a heavy burden for the minister. International donor agencies and domestic critics viewed his import-substitution programme in the high-technology sector, with billions of dollars spent to develop national aircraft and other prestigious projects, as an irresponsible waste of funds. As Habibie's chances to become Suharto's deputy and possible successor appeared to wane, so did the loyalty of the ICMI group around Adi Sasono towards their patron.

The impression of Habibie's declining career prospects sharpened the factional divisions within ICMI and drove the activist group closer to regime opposition. While the camp associated with the bureaucratic and military elite still believed that Habibie had a realistic chance of becoming Suharto's deputy,[52] the activists around Adi Sasono were convinced that Habibie's campaign had been severely damaged.[53] In addition, Suharto had taken the names of Adi Sasono, Watik Pratikna, Jimly Assidiquie, and Dawam Rahardjo from the list of MPR candidates, further distancing the activist wing of ICMI from the New Order establishment. The feeling of exclusion from the regime and the expectation of Habibie's political demise led the ICMI activists to change their strategic goal from the penetration of state institutions to regime change. In line with Amien Rais, Adi Sasono now believed that only an alliance of Indonesia's leading societal figures could force Suharto to resign. In this coalition, ICMI was to be a major element, neutralizing its image of a collaborator with the regime and positioning itself for the post-authoritarian era. In early January 1998, Adi went public with the proposal for a national dialogue to overcome the economic crisis.[54] The dialogue was to engage Amien, Megawati, Wahid, and other relevant society leaders in a discussion forum, with regime change as the ultimate goal:

> We say generally that the goal is coalition-building for a better future, but I think everybody understands that our aim is to prepare the political landscape for the post-Suharto era.... It is clear that this country needs new leadership.[55]

Like Amien, however, Adi earned little more than suspicion from the socio-political leaders he sought to include in the coalition. Wahid ruled out his involvement in the dialogue, and Megawati sent no clear signals as to whether she would participate.[56] As the press still speculated about if and when the summit would take place, Adi suddenly called the meeting off.

The cancellation of the national dialogue pointed to the multitude of political interests and motives that drove oppositional forces during the crisis. It highlighted both the often tactical nature of their political considerations and the extreme uncertainty of the environment they operated in. ICMI had abruptly given up on the idea of the national dialogue because its position in the political landscape had changed dramatically, and literally overnight: Suharto had indicated that Habibie was his vice-presidential candidate for the upcoming MPR session in March 1998. With this, ICMI was transformed from an increasingly marginalized group with large oppositional elements into a political force with a substantial stake in defending the regime, at least until Habibie was securely installed. The unexpected turn of events surprised not only ICMI, but sent shock waves throughout the political system. Only days before, Suharto had signed a second agreement with the IMF, which political analysts believed had excluded Habibie from the vice-presidential competition as it increased pressure on Indonesia to deliver concrete evidence of economic and political reform. Suharto's political logic, however, worked contrary to the rationalism of the observers. Instead of bowing to the pressure, Suharto chose to defy the international finance community and demonstrate his unchanged control over domestic politics. In addition, the choice of a controversial vice-president allowed him to make the succession issue, in the words of John McBeth (1999, p. 22), "unpalatable". Had he anointed a candidate popular with both foreign governments and domestic political forces, the pressure on Suharto to resign in favour of his deputy might have become irresistible if the crisis continued.

Habibie's anointment led to the temporary revival of the concept of regime penetration that many modernist intellectuals had abandoned in the mid-1990s after it was considered a failure. The realistic chance of a Habibie presidency appeared to contradict their bitter assessment that Suharto had lured Muslim groups into backing his rule through false promises of greater regime participation. With Habibie a heartbeat away from the presidency, the strategy of cooperating with the regime appeared to have worked eventually.[57] Thus within days of the announcement of Habibie's endorsement by Suharto, Adi Sasono terminated his criticism of the government and began to bring ICMI back on the track of loyalty towards Habibie and, by implication, the New Order regime. In conceptual terms, Adi spoke now of an "accelerated evolution" instead of regime change.[58] The adjusted terminology tried to cover the fact that, once again, offers of increased representation in the New Order state had motivated a major religio-political force to suspend its opposition to the non-democratic nature of the regime. Most importantly, Adi and Achmad Tirtosudiro lobbied Amien Rais to end his policy of confrontation and put his trust in the prospect of a Habibie presidency.[59] They persuaded Amien to accept a truce with the regime, and for a while it seemed as if the promises of a prosperous era of Islamic politics under Habibie's leadership had reunited the Muhammadiyah chairman with his former companions in ICMI.

## ICMI's Dual Option: Defending or Overthrowing Suharto

Suharto's re-election and Habibie's installation as his deputy in March broadened ICMI's strategic options and anticipated yet another change in its relations with the regime. Before March, loyalty to Suharto's rule was essential in order to secure Habibie's ascension to the vice-presidency. After the MPR session, however, ICMI possessed two political options that were easily adjustable to the changing political environment: first, continued support for Suharto if the latter granted enough concessions to modernist Muslims in general and ICMI in particular; or, alternatively, joining the opposition, eroding Suharto's government, and working towards Habibie's constitutional rise to power. It was primarily the formation of the cabinet that pushed ICMI into endorsing the second option. After it had become known that Siti Hardiyanti was in charge of distributing the portfolios, Adi Sasono warned on 13 March that if the names rumoured to hold key posts in the government turned out to be true, Indonesia's international reputation was at risk. In response to the rumours, an ICMI leadership meeting asked Habibie to secure cabinet positions for several critical ICMI activists. At the same time, Achmad Tirtosudiro took over the acting chairmanship of the organization, increasing its autonomy vis-à-vis Habibie and preparing the group for its turn against the regime.[60] On the day before the cabinet announcement, Habibie accompanied Suharto to his Friday prayers to remind him of the importance of ICMI participation in the cabinet. The president, obviously unnerved, reprimanded his deputy in an unusually harsh tone.[61] When the line-up of the cabinet was revealed a day later, none of Habibie's nominees from ICMI's activist faction had been included. Instead, Suharto re-appointed the ICMI bureaucrat Haryanto Dhanutirto, whose questionable record had made him a controversial figure even within his own organization.[62]

The disappointment within ICMI over the composition of the cabinet drove the organization back to the course of opposing the regime. This high fluctuation in ICMI's attitudes exposed the volatility of the political context in which societal groups had to make quick and immensely consequential decisions for their constituencies. Amidst the collective uncertainty, however, a general pattern emerged that appeared to guide socio-political leaders in defining their position vis-à-vis non-democratic rule. Offers of participation in the regime were likely to silence concerns over its authoritarian nature, while exclusion from it led almost certainly to demands for democratic regime change. Suharto's omission of Islamic activists led the ICMI leadership to believe that the president had no intention of granting Habibie a significant role in running the government.[63] Within ICMI, it was now not only Adi Sasono and his critical associates who pushed for fundamental opposition towards the Suharto government, but also the senior leadership with bureaucratic and military backgrounds. Achmad Tirtosudiro began to sense that Suharto was about to lose control, and he feared that continued support for him might drag ICMI down into the political abyss. As the student demonstrations gained momentum, ICMI took concrete steps to dissociate itself from the Suharto government. At a leadership forum on 6 May, ICMI endorsed calls for a special session of the MPR to change the national leadership. This suggestion, however, presented Habibie with severe political problems. Balancing loyalty to Suharto and the institutional interests of ICMI, Habibie was forced to publicly disavow the statement of his own organization.[64]

Habibie's public rejection of ICMI's oppositional stand could not distract from the fact, however, that the vice-president was now the main beneficiary of the growing protest against the regime. Therefore, many within the political elite believed that Habibie actually encouraged ICMI's criticism of Suharto in order to promote his own succession to the presidency.[65] Wahid even suspected that Adi Sasono financed the student movement against Suharto in order to catalyze the downfall of his regime and facilitate Habibie's rise.[66] These widespread suspicions were mostly based on Habibie's unique constitutional position within Suharto's web of political patronage. For legal reasons, Habibie was the only central figure of the regime Suharto could not dispose of, and was therefore largely immune from potential reprisals for ICMI's increased criticism. In this context, Habibie's public distancing from ICMI's demands for leadership change appeared as nothing more than a tactical manoeuvre to avoid the impression that he actively worked towards replacing Suharto. In the same vein, the ensuing public dispute between Achmad Tirtosudiro and Habibie over the leadership of ICMI and its political course was widely seen as theatrically staged and thus politically inconsequential. Achmad asserted that it was he, not Habibie, who led the organization, and that the controversial call for an MPR session had been issued through proper channels and procedures.[67] Satisfied with this explanation, Habibie never raised the issue again.

## Islamist Groups and the Crisis

ICMI was not the only political force that had a strategic interest in Habibie's rise to the presidency, however. Most importantly, Prabowo believed that he had an arrangement with Habibie to make him chief of the armed forces once Habibie was in power. In Prabowo's entourage were a number of ultra-modernist Muslim groups with an Islamist religio-political agenda. Their political relevance was based less on numerical strength than their capacity to mobilize demonstrations, either for a particular issue or against selected institutions and individuals. KISDI (*Komite Indonesia untuk Solidaritas Dunia Islam*, Indonesian Committee for Solidarity with the Muslim World), founded in 1986, and DDII formed the core of this loose association of Islamist groups, with some senior PPP politicians offering protection and limited access to the political infrastructure. KISDI had participated in the demonstrations against Sofyan Wanandi in late January 1998, but otherwise appeared reluctant to formulate a clear position on the political crisis.[68] As their political affiliation with Prabowo was stronger than their ties with Habibie, the radical Islamic groups had difficulties in following ICMI's anti-regime turn after the March announcement of the cabinet. In contrast to Habibie, whose constitutional position protected him from possible Suharto-initiated reprisals, Prabowo was politically vulnerable. The competition between Wiranto and Prabowo exposed the latter to the risk of dismissal if Suharto concluded that Prabowo's political allies worked against him. Accordingly, the Islamist groups could not afford to confront Suharto in the way ICMI did. In fact, as Schwarz (2004, p. 331) observed, "their fervent support for Soeharto put them in a distinct minority of defenders of Soeharto's family". KISDI leaders knew, however, that Prabowo began promoting the possibility of a Suharto resignation in Habibie's favour, which in turn would result in increased political access for Islamist groups.[69] The leaders of KISDI and DDII therefore maintained a low profile for most of the crisis, but made political preparations for the increasingly likely scenario of a Habibie presidency.

## DIVIDED AGAINST SUHARTO

Political crises often provide traditionally divided civilian actors with an opportunity to forge the very coalitions that are essential for ending military-backed authoritarian rule. In Indonesia, the creation of a united front among Muslim groups would have gone a long way to remove Suharto from power and install a transitional government in his place. However, no such coalition emerged during the political crisis of 1998. Instead, Muslim-based and other civilian forces had highly divergent positions towards the troubled regime. Nahdlatul Ulama and Megawati's PDI were unwilling to become part of an aggressive oppositional movement, and the deterrent of Habibie's potential rise to power served as a further incentive to maintain their non-confrontational stance. By contrast, Amien and many Muhammadiyah functionaries had joined the student movement in demanding not only Suharto's resignation, but also a completely new political system. ICMI, finally, aimed at a controlled transfer of power from Suharto to Habibie. This confronted the organization with a delicate and seemingly contradictory task: while it had to damage the government severely enough to cause Suharto's removal, it also needed to ensure that the regime remained sufficiently functional to facilitate the orderly succession of Habibie.

The diametrically opposed interests of major societal forces obstructed the formation of effective elite opposition to Suharto and prevented the establishment of a political alternative to the faltering regime. Accordingly, the initiative for overthrowing Suharto shifted to the student movement and other non-elite actors, setting the country on a course of regime change driven by popular protest and mass violence rather than the institutional assumption of power by oppositional groups. Only when the nation-wide upheaval had rendered Suharto's resignation inevitable did most societal organizations eventually unite to call for the president's immediate withdrawal. By that time, however, it was too late for them to play any significant role in negotiating the terms of the ongoing regime change — this process had already been taken over by compromise-oriented military officers keen to preserve the interests of key New Order groups and individuals.

## Opposition after Medan: Strategic Options and Dilemmas

Not surprisingly, it was a major outbreak of street protest rather than elite-initiated activism that triggered the belated political consensus between Muslim and other civilian groups about Suharto's resignation. Highlighting the inevitability of Suharto's demise, the Medan riots of early May 1998 had a tremendous impact on the political behaviour of Indonesia's societal elite. The NU central board, for example, had cautiously declared its support for the student movement in mid-April, but the Medan incident accelerated its gradual desertion of Suharto. Shortly after Suharto's departure to Egypt, NU official Said Agil Siraj stated that NU would prepare its own reform proposals. He assigned special spiritual powers to these plans by stressing that the word "reform" was mentioned forty-one times in the Qur'an. On 12 May, leading NU *kiai* met in Surabaya and proclaimed their commitment to reform. In addition, two NU deputy chairmen, Fajrul Falaakh and Rozy Munir, became involved in efforts to establish a forum of opposition figures in order to maximize pressure on the regime. The preparatory meetings of the association, named *Forum Kerja Indonesia* (Forki, Indonesian Working Forum), were mostly held in the office of the NU-affiliated LKKNU (*Lembaga Kemaslahatan Keluarga Nahdlatul Ulama*, Institute for the Benefit of Nahdlatul Ulama Families).[70]

But while the establishment of Forki showed that most non-regime figures now agreed that Suharto had to go, it also underlined that they still found it impossible to cooperate with one another. Not only Wahid and Megawati appeared reluctant to engage in the forum; Amien too had at that stage concluded that an elite-based coalition with his rivals was neither possible nor necessary. Although Amien's private secretary Muhammad Najib took part in some of Forki's coordinating sessions, his boss preferred to focus on the preparations for his own opposition forum, the People's Leadership Council.

Amien's blueprint for the planned council reflected his belief that he no longer needed a broad elite coalition to achieve regime change. While still presented as a pluralist association of regime critics, the council now targeted intellectuals close to Amien rather than influential religio-political leaders. According to David Bourchier (1999a, p. 44), it was to consist "of people with moral authority" and form a "temporary repository of political power if need arose". The former editor of the banned news magazine *Tempo*, Goenawan Mohammad, assisted Amien in drafting a list of potential members, which included human rights activists Abdul Hakim Garuda Nusantara and Adnan Buyung Nasution, academic Arbi Sanit, and veteran politician Emil Salim. Involvement in the council was not without risks, however. After Amien had announced its imminent formation, the regime prepared to respond with its conventional catalogue of sanctions. Minister of Home Affairs Hartono questioned whether the council was a rival institution to the MPR, in which case the government would be forced to crack down on it. As Goenawan and Amien were preparing the official inauguration of the council, the killing of four students at Trisakti University on 12 May provided the plan with a new, significantly radicalized momentum. The subsequent chaos generated by mass protests, declining state authority, and open rifts within the regime prepared the stage for dramatic political change. The significance of the paradigmatic shift was captured in Amien's tour of the city on 13 May. As Amien passed the rioters, they applauded and shouted his name, and soldiers saluted him. The procedural insigniae of power, introduced and defended by the New Order for decades, were gradually transferred to those who challenged it.

With Suharto out of the country, and the security forces losing control over the capital, the induction of Amien's leadership forum on 14 May underscored the collective impression of imminent regime change. The name ultimately chosen for the forum was "Popular Mandate Council" (*Majelis Amanat Rakyat*, MAR), not coincidentally featuring Mohammad Amien Rais' initials. The organization was now tailored exclusively to the needs of the Muhammadiyah chairman, and its first press statement echoed Amien's political priorities. The release contained three major demands and appeals: first, Suharto had to step down immediately; second, the security forces had to exercise restraint in handling the riots; and third, the students and the broader population had to remain calm to ensure the unobstructed continuation of the reform process. Both in terms of its form and substance, the declaration of MAR constituted a further step in the disintegration process of Suharto's system of socio-political control. For much of its rule, the New Order had subjected all socio-political organizations in Indonesia to a regime of strict conformity, forcing them to obtain numerous licences and permits, adopt the national ideology, and accept their subordination to the ministry of home affairs. The creation of new groups without state approval demonstrated that the rules imposed by Suharto's state began to lose their power of intimidation, which in turn convinced oppositional forces to intensify their attacks on the regime.

The foundation of a pluralist association of regime critics not only widened the gap between Amien and the government, but also threatened to antagonize his long-time political allies in the modernist faction of Indonesian Islam. Only one hour after the MAR press conference had concluded, Adi Sasono asked Amien to visit him at ICMI headquarters. There, the two Muslim leaders engaged in a heated debate about both the strategy behind MAR's formation and the plurality of its composition. Adi objected to MAR's heterogeneous membership, which included Christians, secular nationalists, and even a gay activist. The ICMI secretary-general warned Amien that his core supporters in the modernist constituency felt increasingly alienated by his courtship of non-Muslim groups, and recommended that he reassert his Islamic image by speaking to a public gathering at the modernist Al-Azhar mosque a couple of days later (Najib 1998, p. 50). The invitation exposed Amien's structural dilemma that, in its various manifestations, had contributed to his reputation as a political chameleon: serving the interests of his own constituency while at the same time expanding his interaction with other religio-political groups was not only a delicate, but often impossible task. His cross-constituency approach led to confusion over his political and ideological positions, with Amien more often than not surrendering to the temptation of adopting the stance of the crowd he addressed or the person he debated with. In the discussion with Adi, he reassured his fellow modernist activist that the inclusion of Christians in MAR was inconsequential as he was determined to define the direction of the organization himself. He managed to excuse himself from the Al-Azhar event, but agreed to give a speech after the Friday prayers at the same place. Adi Sasono appeared satisfied, for the time being, and the two Muslim figures continued their exchange of views throughout the night as they awaited Suharto's return from Egypt in the early morning of 15 May (Najib 1998, p. 51).

Amien's temporary success in appeasing his core Islamic constituency confirmed his belief that he could bring down the regime without a broad-based coalition of key socio-political leaders. Although representatives from both ends of the political spectrum, such as the conservative Muslim politician Husein Umar and the leftist gay rights activist Dede Oetomo, eventually decided not to join MAR, Amien appeared confident that his popularity was sufficient to guarantee the success of the organization and the agenda it pursued. Thus he refused to cooperate when the idea of an alliance between Wahid, Megawati, and himself was revived by several civil society figures. Remaining conspicuously absent from the declaration ceremony of Forki on 15 May,[71] Amien signalled that he had given up on the idea of overthrowing the New Order government with an alliance of non-regime constituency leaders. Wahid and Megawati did not turn up either to the event, disappointing a crowd of domestic and international journalists who had hoped that the three national figures would finally come together and claim the leadership of Indonesia from the disintegrating regime. It was most likely the tangible inevitability of Suharto's departure, brought about by the student movement and widespread popular unrest, that convinced the three leaders that the regime's days were numbered even without their forming an alliance. In addition, Amien apparently saw Forki as an act of undeserved assistance for Wahid and Megawati who had kept a convenient distance to the popular protests and only emerged when the regime had almost collapsed.[72]

## Preparing for Post-Suharto Politics: Continuity or Radical Change?

Despite continued disunity among them, the major religio-political organizations began to prepare their constituencies for the end of Suharto's rule. NU issued a statement on 15 May that welcomed Suharto's contemplations in Egypt about resigning from office. Within Nahdlatul Ulama, the view was now prevailing that defending the lost cause of the regime would damage the organization more than taking the risk of a final retaliation from Suharto's side:

> We had a leadership meeting on that Friday (15 May), during which we were bombarded with phone calls from the regions, all pushing us to do something. Imron Hamzah [a respected *kiai* from Surabaya] shouted through the phone that he found it inconceivable that NU remained silent while everything fell apart. We said "yes, yes, be patient, we are working on it." ... At the end, we endorsed Suharto's alleged plan to resign.[73]

Wahid, by contrast, still preferred a negotiated settlement with Suharto to a chaotic transfer of power to a council of oppositional politicians. On 16 May, Wahid predicted that the student movement "will fade away like its predecessors, the 1974 and 1978 movements". He brushed aside calls for Suharto's resignation, saying that the president had been provided with strong legitimation from the MPR.[74] Van Dijk (2001, p. 199) claimed that Wahid made the remarks because he was "shocked by the violence in the middle of May". However, Wahid's comments followed an established pattern of his thinking that had its origins in much earlier periods of the crisis, and appeared to have more to do with his political strategy than with the distressing images of the riots. The prospects of either a populist transitional government dominated by Amien Rais or a constitutional handover of authority to Habibie were nightmares for both Wahid and the Nahdlatul Ulama constituency. Accordingly, he engaged with moderate elements in the armed forces that lobbied for a gradual withdrawal of Suharto from politics, but were prepared to leave the latter in charge of its details and schedule. In a meeting with Wiranto, Wahid underlined the necessity for close cooperation between NU and ABRI. Wiranto emerged from the encounter with the impression that Wahid was a loyal ally in his efforts to seek an orderly transition, and asked his staff in ABRI headquarters to draft a press release that emphasized the general importance of ABRI-NU relations.[75] It was this press release that led to considerable irritation on Suharto's part and, as described above, sparked a further escalation in the competition between Prabowo and Wiranto.

While key political forces now agreed on the necessity of Suharto's removal, they continued to differ about the form and composition of a possible post-New Order government. Amien aimed at the disposal of Suharto and the political system that carried him, while Wahid supported an orderly transition process largely controlled by the outgoing president. ICMI, on the other hand, began to promote Habibie's succession as the only constitutional solution to the crisis. On Sunday, 17 May, Adi Sasono suggested in a discussion with Amien that the most likely scenario was the handover of presidential powers from Suharto to Habibie.[76] Amien, however, was aware that a Habibie presidency was not what the students had been demonstrating for. The mere replacement of political leaders within the paradigmatic framework of the New Order system might have been satisfactory to the protesters only a couple of months ago, but the increased radicalism of the student movement after the Trisakti incident demanded nothing less than the complete reform of the political foundations of the state. While personally inclined to believe in Habibie's commitment to the interests of political openness in general and modernist Islam in particular, Amien felt that he could not promote an intra-regime solution to the crisis without jeopardizing his reformist credentials. But with Suharto still clinging to power, and the threat of a military crackdown hanging over the protesters, Amien conceded that removing Suharto had absolute priority over everything else.[77]

The dispute among major societal forces over the conditions of Suharto's withdrawal and the format of the post-New Order polity sparked a hectic search for compromise. Nurcholish Madjid, who was widely acknowledged as a mediator between traditionalist and modernist Islam and even respected by the New Order authorities, appeared to be an ideal candidate to offer solutions acceptable to all. On 14 May, Nurcholish had presented his ideas to ABRI headquarters, outlining the timetable for Suharto's gradual withdrawal from politics. The interaction over the following days with a large number of political leaders, however, convinced Nurcholish that his plan was unsustainable. It was most of all Amien whose arguments made Nurcholish conclude that the country could not afford taking the risk of allowing Suharto to set the terms for his own succession as the latter might well use the opportunity to consolidate his power. Nurcholish recalled that "at first, I thought Suharto could be given some time to organize the transfer of power — but Amien convinced me that Suharto might just want exactly that, and that he might come out on top again".[78] Unaware that Nurcholish had changed his mind, Suharto felt attracted to the idea of a controlled, loosely scheduled departure from the power centre. The Nurcholish initiative, in its initial form, provided Suharto with the chance of influencing the negotiations about his replacement, reach agreements over the legal aspects of his retirement, and seek long-term solutions for the business interests of his family. With the parliament demanding his resignation on Monday, 18 May, Suharto sent for Nurcholish to discuss the details of his plan.

As their discussion began, it quickly emerged that Suharto's main concern was to avoid a concrete time frame for his long-term withdrawal plans. Ignoring Nurcholish's opening remark that developments had overtaken his earlier proposals, and that the president's immediate resignation was now inevitable, Suharto insisted that general elections had to be held before he could resign in a constitutional and orderly fashion. Nurcholish, however, told him "that the elections and his resignation had to be completed within six months; he got irritated at that, and went off about how big Indonesia is and how long electoral preparations would take". Nurcholish then conveyed to him "that I was not convinced, so he tried to slightly increase his offer by proposing to step down 'as soon as possible' after general elections".[79] Clearly aware that his political credibility was exhausted, Suharto asked Nurcholish to assemble a team of Muslim leaders to announce his retirement proposals. As they went through the list of possible candidates for what Donald Emmerson (1999, p. 304) has termed Suharto's "Muslims of last resort", it emerged that the president intended to exploit the cleavages in the Islamic community for his agenda of a controlled political retreat: he nominated five representatives from NU, including Wahid and Ilyas Ruchiat, but insisted on the exclusion of Amien Rais. Mindful of NU's accommodative stance under Guided Democracy and much of the New Order, Suharto apparently hoped that the organization could be tempted to back his blueprint for the political transition. In this context, Amien's central role in the protest movement as well as the prospect of a Habibie presidency provided Suharto with deterrents potentially strong enough to lure NU into supporting his plans.

Suharto's courting of NU in order to outplay Amien Rais triggered an intense debate in Wahid's inner circle over the question whether to participate in the presidential meeting or not. For Suharto, Wahid's participation was crucial. His socio-political status equalled Amien's, and he was therefore potentially able to neutralize the latter's radicalism. In order to ensure Wahid's involvement in the gathering, Suharto asked Siti Hardiyanti and Hartono for help. Both had been politically aligned with the NU leader in the 1997 election campaign, and a loose personal contact had been maintained.[80] Siti Hardiyanti phoned Wahid in the early evening, explaining the reasons for the meeting. Wahid immediately agreed to take part, provided that his health allowed him to do so. Fearing that the NU chairman might finally back down from the event, Hartono visited Wahid two hours later. As the minister of home affairs left, he even asked Wahid's assistant to make sure that the NU leader showed up the following day.[81] While Wahid had made up his mind and was determined to participate, some of the younger intellectuals in his circle warned that he might be forced to lend moral legitimation to Suharto's consolidation plans. Muhaimin Iskandar, his nephew and a leader of PMII, suspected that the president had the draft for his political future already completed and only wanted Wahid's public blessing for it. Concerned about "Gus Dur's image and NU's reputation", Muhaimin warned Wahid that he was walking into a trap.[82] Others feared that rival political leaders participating in the meeting could overpower an unprepared Wahid with their scenarios for solving the crisis. However, with Wahid's younger brother Hasyim and Fajrul Falaakh arguing the case for participation, the NU chairman decided to go ahead as planned.[83]

Wahid was not the only Muslim leader who was inclined to grant Suharto a dignified, generously scheduled departure from politics. Wahid's Islamist opponents also felt that Suharto's withdrawal came at a time when they were profiting most from his regime. On Monday evening, when Nurcholish met Suharto, DDII patriarch Anwar Haryono sent for Amien Rais. In an attempt to deradicalize the Muhammadiyah chairman, the ailing *Dewan Dakwah* leader reminded him of Suharto's achievements in defending Muslim interests since the early 1990s: the foundation of ICMI, the establishment of Bank Muamalat, the publication of the Islamic newspaper *Republika*, the termination of the controversial state lottery SDSB, and the lifting of the ban on wearing headscarves in schools. In addition, according to Anwar, the number of non-Muslim ministers in the cabinet had been reduced to a minimum.[84] Based on his positive Islamic record, Anwar recommended that all Muslim groups support Suharto in the implementation of his reform project. Anwar's explanation highlighted the suspicions of Islamist forces concerning the political uncertainty that might succeed the authoritarian regime. While a Habibie presidency was viewed as a positive outcome, other scenarios were as likely: the military could take over and return to the anti-Muslim policies of the 1970s; a transitional government with representatives from diverse backgrounds could be installed, watering down Muslim demands; or, as in 1955, parliamentary democracy could split the Muslim forces and hand victory to the nationalists. Anwar's lecture, however, failed to convince Amien. When Amien left Anwar's house, he kissed his senior's hand, adding that he wanted to do so for Anwar, but "I won't do it for [Suharto]"(Najib 1998, p. 60).

## The Final Act: Suharto and his "Muslims of Last Resort"

The deep divisions within the civilian elite over Suharto's fate appeared to offer the president a final chance to play the various factions off against each other. The leaders of Nahdlatul Ulama and the Islamist groups were leaning towards a settlement with Suharto, while the modernist organizations Muhammadiyah and ICMI openly demanded his immediate resignation. That Suharto's efforts were ultimately in vain was not only due to the unstoppable force of the popular protest, but was also the result of Nurcholish's decision to include Amien in the preparations for the presidential meeting with the Muslim leaders. One hour before the meeting on Tuesday morning, 19 May, Nurcholish and Amien met with three modernist Muslim figures invited to the encounter with Suharto. Among them were Yusril Ihza Mahendra, an Islamist activist but also a speech writer in Suharto's state secretariat, and Muhammadiyah's Malik Fadjar. Addressing his modernist colleagues, Amien demanded that Suharto not be given a chance to consolidate his position, "warning us that we had to resist Suharto's charm".[85] The Muhammadiyah leader insisted on Suharto's resignation and elections within six months or, alternatively, the surrender of presidential authority through a decree similar to the 1966 letter that had transferred executive powers from Sukarno to Suharto. Equipped with Amien's proposals, Yusril, Malik, and Nurcholish left for the palace and met with the NU-affiliated participants. Nurcholish gave a short speech to the group before they entered the meeting room, stressing that it was Suharto who had invited them, and not the *ulama* who had sought the encounter. As Nurcholish conveyed Amien's message, he reminded the participants that they had to communicate the people's aspirations to Suharto, and these aspirations clearly demanded the president's resignation. Wahid and some military officers who listened to Nurcholish's words remained silent.[86]

The coordination between Nurcholish and Amien destroyed Suharto's hopes for a gradual withdrawal on his own terms. Nurcholish and former NU leader Ali Yafie made it clear from the beginning that Suharto's resignation was not negotiable. They also objected to Suharto's plans for the establishment of a "reform council" under his own coordination. Yusril raised concerns about the legality of the council, pointing out that "such a political-legal institution needed to be anchored in the constitution and related laws, and could not be established just like that".[87] Eventually, the participants agreed on the foundation of a "reform committee", elections at the earliest occasion possible, and Suharto's resignation afterwards. They added, however, that none of them was ready to sit either on the committee or in any reshuffled cabinet. They also declined Suharto's request to line up behind him during the announcement of his plans. Not only Suharto was taken aback by the intransigence of the Nurcholish-led team. Wahid, surprised about the extent of detailed coordination between Nurcholish and the modernist participants, expressed his discomfort with the way that Nurcholish had asked Suharto to resign.[88] Wahid's generous biographer, Greg Barton (2002, p. 242), explained Wahid's behaviour in the meeting in cultural terms, quoting him as saying that "now that the knife had been thrust deftly into Soeharto's side there was no need to twist it for it to accomplish its work". In addition, Barton also referred to Wahid's continued concerns over a possible regime backlash. It is more likely, however, that Wahid's indignation was triggered by his increasing fear of political marginalization. Amien and Nurcholish had taken the political initiative away from him, positioning themselves in the forefront of those deciding over the succession issue. When Wahid left the meeting, he called on the students to stop their demonstrations in order to give Suharto a chance to implement his reform programme.

Despite Suharto's failure to impose his initial agenda on the group of Muslim clerics, his announcement of a reform package created remarkable levels of irritation among its members and other societal leaders. Nurcholish and Amien, for example, had very different interpretations concerning the concessions that Suharto had made to the gathering. Nurcholish felt that he had resisted Suharto's attempts to push through a succession mechanism on his own terms, and viewed the result as the best possible outcome.[89] Amien, on the other hand, saw his fears confirmed that Suharto might use the meeting to consolidate his power. He questioned why Suharto had only invited Muslim leaders to the encounter, and criticized the use of Islamic symbols for political ends.[90] At the centre of his criticism was, of course, Suharto's failure to provide a clear date for his resignation. Accordingly, Amien decided to proceed with his preparations for a mass demonstration at the Monas Square on the following day, 20 May. Student leaders also emphasized that Suharto's announcement was insufficient to satisfy their demands, and that they were determined to continue their protest. It was once again the forceful initiative of the student movement that drove the process of regime change, exposing the elite debate over the quality and reliability of Suharto's offers as a hypothetical deliberation with limited political impact.

The most significant outcome of the palace gathering was that Suharto's efforts to sideline Amien and regain control of the political process had failed. Both in terms of his elite relations and his intellectual leadership of the student protest, the momentum remained with the Muhammadiyah chairman. This was reflected in public statements of student leaders that they intended to continue their protests, as well as in the political manoeuvres of elements within the regime struggling to save their career prospects. Amien's two operational centres, the Muhammadiyah office and Malik Fajar's house, were now crowded with ICMI leaders and prominent cabinet ministers keen on cutting their ties with the falling regime. Ministers Tanri Abeng, Fuad Bawazier, and Akbar Tandjung felt it necessary to demonstrate their presence in Amien's company on Tuesday evening, preparing the stage for their resignations on the following day. The cabinet ministers knew that Suharto's attempts to prolong his rule had no chance of succeeding. In Yogyakarta, students geared up for a huge demonstration protected by the Sultan, and despite Amien's cancellation of the Jakarta rally in the early morning of 20 May because of warnings from inside the armed forces, the disintegration of the regime proceeded at a rapid pace.[91] Even Wiranto viewed the banning of the protest not so much as an effort to sustain the regime, but as a final service to Suharto, allowing him to withdraw in dignity rather than going down in the chaos of a populist revolt.[92]

The last full day of the Suharto polity saw a stream of former loyalists turning their backs on the crumbling regime. With Yogyakarta witnessing one of the biggest rallies in its history, combining the power of the masses with the cultural strength of the sultanate, there was no hope that the protest would subside. In Jakarta, Amien made his way through the street blockades to the DPR building, where the students celebrated the third day of their occupation and showed no signs of declining enthusiasm for their cause. Fuelled by such images of unrelenting societal pressure, the internal erosion of the regime continued. As Suharto's assistants tried in vain to convince credible figures to sit on his reform committee, fourteen of his ministers handed in their resignations. Most importantly, Habibie now also accelerated his dissociation from his former patron. He had received information that in the meeting with the Muslim leaders, Suharto had used the prospect of a Habibie presidency as a political deterrent, asking them in a dismissive tone if they were aware that his resignation would automatically lead to Habibie's ascension.[93] Furthermore, in a subsequent meeting with Habibie, Suharto indicated that in the case of his resignation, he expected his vice-president to step down as well, clearing the way for a succession controlled by Suharto's cronies in the military and the political establishment (Habibie 2006, p. 37). Habibie refused to endorse this scenario, however, marking the end of their decades-long relationship of "filial responsiveness" (McIntyre 2005, p. 123) and provoking Suharto to break off all contact with the man he once believed to be a loyal student and supporter. Against all odds, Habibie was now determined to be president, eventually outsmarting his mentor who had put so much stress on his own political cleverness (McIntyre 2005, p. 116).

Habibie's insubordination provided Suharto with undeniable evidence for the extent of his isolation and decline. If it was impossible to secure the loyalty of a former minister who had famously called him "super genius" and "Professor Suharto", then there was nobody else to turn to. After Quraish Shihab, the minister of religious affairs, had made several unsuccessful attempts to talk Nurcholish into joining the president's reform team, Suharto dropped first hints to his aides about an immediate resignation. The desertion of key loyalists and the collapse of his reform ideas left Suharto trapped in a situation where only the military could keep him in power. Suharto knew, however, that the power constellation had irreversibly shifted to his disadvantage, and that military intervention was unlikely to prolong his rule, let alone restore the unchallenged authority he was used to exercise. When Wiranto suggested that the armed forces were not supportive of a military crackdown, Suharto concurred at once and asked his inner circle to prepare for the transfer of power to Habibie on the next day. In acknowledgement of the central role played by his main opponent, Suharto sent a personal message to Amien, informing him of his imminent resignation and asking him to refrain from further protests.[94]

Suharto's departure sparked highly diverse reactions in the various factions of Indonesia's Muslim community. While Amien was undoubtedly the central figure in the movement that convinced the long-time autocrat to leave, the Muhammadiyah leader was not completely satisfied with the details of the regime change. Habibie's presidency certainly offered rewards for the modernist Muslim constituency, but Amien suspected that the New Order power structures had a better chance of survival under Suharto's handpicked deputy than they would have had after a revolutionary disintegration of the regime.[95] Amien's friends from ICMI, on the other hand, were electrified by the opportunities that the new constellation provided. Only days after Suharto had used Habibie to fend off demands for his resignation, ICMI functionaries found themselves drafting Habibie's first speech as new president. The Islamist groups around DDII and KISDI, having failed to defend Suharto's presidency, swiftly redirected their pro-regime activism towards Habibie. Within hours, they led thousands of supporters to the parliament, fearing that the student movement might try to remove Habibie from power as well. The confrontation between student protesters and pro-regime demonstrators exposed the very vulnerable legitimacy that would become a dominant feature of the new government throughout Habibie's interregnum. Nahdlatul Ulama, for its part, also opposed the sudden transfer of presidential authority to Habibie. Some of Wahid's fiercest opponents were now likely to sit in government, possibly denying traditionalist politicians access to state resources. In short, Suharto's downfall had done little to overcome the divisions within Indonesia's Muslim community, but had sharpened them amidst increasing competition for the spoils of the evolving post-New Order polity.

## CIVILIAN DISUNITY, POPULAR PROTEST, AND THE END OF SUHARTO

Larry Diamond and Marc F. Plattner (1996, p. xxiv) maintained that militaries or authoritarian figures supported by them are able to seize power and sustain it over long periods of time when "civilian politicians are weak and divided". Indonesia's New Order has been an obvious example of this linkage between the level of democratic unity among civilian forces and the likelihood and duration of military intervention in politics. Cleavages in the civilian political sphere, and particularly within the Muslim community, allowed Suharto to seize, expand, and sustain authoritarian rule for more than three decades. This conclusion has led some analysts to explain Suharto's downfall with the reverse argument: that his demise was due to the sudden unification of civilian oppositional forces against him. Robert

Hefner (2000, p. 199), for example, argued that "for the first time, that opposition now united under Wahid's NU, Megawati's nationalists and the reform-minded modernists around Rais". The discussion in this chapter has shown, however, that no such coalition existed, and that the leaders of key socio-political organizations continued their long-standing, religio-political disputes throughout the crisis. Some of them appeared prepared to engage with the regime and secure its survival at various junctures of the evolving crisis, while others simply isolated themselves from the popular protest engulfing the New Order state. That they finally agreed that Suharto had to resign had to do less with a genuine political consensus between Indonesia's main societal groups than with the fact that the uncontrollable force of the student movement, combined with widespread social unrest, had driven the regime to the brink of collapse. The demands for Suharto's departure were, in most cases, post-factum endorsements of the inevitable.

The theory of a united opposition causing Suharto's fall has been challenged by several authors who stressed the non-involvement of major religio-political forces in the movement against the regime. Andrée Feillard (2002, p. 118), for example, conceded that "Nahdlatul Ulama was not a decisive factor in the 1998 political change", blaming the fact that Wahid was "quasi-absent" during the crisis as he was "lying in bed during most of this crucial time". Ken Young (1999, p. 120) concurred that Wahid's stroke had such an impact that "he and NU have not been at the forefront of the movement for change". These assessments, while contradicting the assumption of a united front against Suharto, still do not capture the systematic unwillingness of religio-political leaders to join forces with their rivals against the regime. Wahid's inclination to favour cooperation with the embattled autocracy over the agenda for democratic change predated his stroke, and was pursued consistently until the very end of Suharto's government. His endorsement of Golkar in the 1997 elections, the attacks on Amien Rais' candidacy, the public denunciation of plans to unite the opposition, and his calls to leave the succession to Suharto were perfectly compatible with the post-stroke criticism of the student movement and his lobbying for a negotiated settlement with Suharto. In fact, many NU leaders acknowledged in private that a healthy Wahid would probably have put even more effort into opposing the popular movement for Suharto's resignation than the ill chairman eventually did.[96] Wahid's political stance was defined by long-term considerations of strategy, religio-ideological convictions, constituency interests, and personal ambition that were largely immune to the effects of his medical condition. The NU central board, on the other hand, shared many of Wahid's sentiments, but felt overwhelmed by the force of popular protests and finally withdrew its support for Suharto when his position had become indefensible.

Wahid's fears that his support for a cross-constituency coalition against Suharto would open the door for the forces of modernist Islam to seize power turned him into one of the largest obstacles for a united opposition to the struggling New Order government. He was by no means the only civilian leader, however, who harboured deep suspicions about his religio-political rivals and thus refused to forge an anti-regime alliance. Megawati Sukarnoputri, the leader of the secular-nationalist segment of Indonesian politics, was equally reluctant to align herself with modernist Muslim figures and the populist force of the student movement. She too had concerns about the possible rise of Islam as a political factor, and she was not prepared to subject her constituency to the risk of retaliation by the troubled Suharto regime. Accordingly, she was hardly heard of throughout the crisis, except for a half-hearted declaration in January 1998 that she was ready to accept the presidency if it was offered to her. Amien Rais, for his part, saw himself confronted with accusations that he temporarily suspended his opposition to Suharto because Habibie had promised him increased regime participation for modernist Muslims. He also had little confidence in Wahid's reliability and Megawati's political skills, opting to link up with the student movement and critical intellectuals instead. In contrast to Wahid, Amien immediately understood the significance of the student protest. He was convinced that it would not just "fade away" like its 1974 and 1978 predecessors, but that it was to become the decisive political force in the crisis. Unlike Megawati, Amien put his personal safety and that of his followers at risk, earning him the respect of the students who subsequently allowed him to use their movement as his political vehicle. Established as the informal leader of the popular protest, Amien extracted himself from last-minute efforts to form a coalition with Megawati and Wahid. ICMI, finally, only supported a broad-based elite coalition against Suharto when it felt excluded from the regime, but turned to promote an intra-systemic transfer of power when its leader became the main beneficiary of such a solution.

This chapter has shown that deep divisions between crucial civilian forces were as important for the character of the 1998 regime change as developments within the armed forces. If intra-military conflicts gave rise to compromise-oriented officers willing to negotiate Suharto's resignation within the framework of the existing regime, then the inability of civilian groups to offer a credible alternative to Wiranto's plan made the succession of Suharto's deputy unavoidable. The material presented here has demonstrated that it was the anarchic force of popular protest, and not the effective coordination among key oppositional elites, that succeeded in removing Suharto from office. This, in turn, had significant implications for the way the power transfer took place as well as for the emerging political landscape of post-Suharto Indonesia. With the most influential societal forces unprepared and too fragmented to take Suharto's place, they had to surrender the political initiative to military officers and other New Order elements who arranged for a regime change that protected their interests. Instead of a non-regime alliance of societal leaders, it was Suharto's "student" who was put in charge of the first eighteen months of the post-authoritarian period. Under his tutelage, patronage networks and power structures of the New Order state, including those associated with the armed forces, managed to extend their influence into the new polity. The continuity of authoritarian structures and forces in the post-Suharto state was certain to complicate and delay the process of democratic consolidation, with the area of civil-military reforms particularly vulnerable to pressure from residual powers of the old regime. In addition, many of the religio-political cleavages that marked the pattern of elite conflicts during Suharto's fall were likely to persist after May 1998, with serious consequences for the prospects of democratic change.

## Notes

1    Interview with Abdurrahman Wahid, Mataram, Lombok, 16 November 1997.

2    Interview with Nurcholish Madjid, Jakarta, 28 May 1998.

3    In 1997, NU had 6,800 pesantren and 21,000 schools under its coordination. While money for development and civil society projects was increasingly coming through international channels (such as the Australian and American governments, UNICEF, or foundations like the Ford Foundation and The Asia Foundation), the majority of NU institutions remained dependent on funds from local governments. See "NU Kini Miliki 21,000 Sekolah dan 6,800 Pesantren", *Media Indonesia*, 21 October 1997.

4    "Gus Dur: Warga NU Jangan Tertinggal di Landasan", *Suara Merdeka*, 21 August 1997.

5    Interview with Habieb Syarief Mohammad, Lombok, 17 November 1997.

6    "Gus Dur Buka Rahasia Istigotsah Bersama Mbak Tutut", *Jawa Pos*, 15 October 1997.

7    Nahdlatul Ulama conducts congresses every five years, with mid-term conferences (*Konferensi Besar*, or *Konbes*) organized in between to evaluate the performance of the leadership elected at the congresses. The Lombok conference was one of these mid-term conferences.

8    "GM Trikora, KH Ilyas Ruchiat Mendukung Pak Harto", *Media Indonesia*, 17 September 1997.

9    "NU akan Gerakan Kekuatan Massa", *Kompas*, 7 October 1997.

10   "Suksesi Harus Lewat Satu Tangan, Jika Banyak Tangan Bisa Amburadul", *Tempo Interaktif*, 31 October 1997.

11   Rais Aam PBNU, "Khutbah Iftitah Rais Aam Pengurus Besar Nahdlatul Ulama Pada Pembukaan Munas dan Konbes NU", Bagu, 17 November 1997.

12   Interview with Ilyas Ruchiat, Mataram, 19 November 1997.

13   Abdurrahman Wahid during his accountability speech at the Konbes NU, Mataram, 19 November 1997, personal notes by the author.

14   PWNU Jawa Timur, "Laporan PWNU Jawa Timur Pada Konbes NU di Lombok", Mataram, 19 November 1997.

15   "Gus Dur: NU tidak Menghendaki Status Quo", *Kompas*, 24 November 1997.

16   Interview with Abdurrahman Wahid, Jakarta, 17 December 1997.

17   Interview with Abdurrahman Wahid, Jakarta, 17 December 1997.

18   "Resmi Diumumkan 'Kelompok 28 Oktober'", *Media Indonesia*, 16 January 1998.

19   In an interview with a Dutch radio station, Wahid added another reason: "So, if you ask me why NU is not mobilized to, let's say, topple Soeharto, then the answer is easy: I don't want my people to be slaughtered by the military." See "Gus Dur: Soeharto Harus Turun", *Kabar dari Pijar*, 13 January 1998.

20   Wahid spent more than two months in hospital, returning to his home on 22 March. See "Gus Dur Sudah Boleh Pulang", *Jawa Pos*, 20 March 1998.

21   NU's Deputy Chairman Hafidz Utsman was appointed acting chairman of NU on the day after Wahid's stroke, and Secretary-General Ahmad Bagdja was given the mandate to act as spokesman for the organization. Hafidz and Ahmad Bagdja were both low-profile functionaries without significant power bases. See "Hafidz Utsman Ditunjuk Pimpin NU Sehari-hari", *Media Indonesia*, 21 January 1998.

22   The activists were organized in three major NU-affiliated associations: IPNU (*Ikatan Pelajar Nahdlatul Ulama*, Nahdlatul Ulama Students Association), IPPNU (*Ikatan Pelajar Putri Nahdlatul Ulama*, Nahdlatul Ulama Female Students Association), and PMII (*Pergerakan Mahasiswa Islam Indonesia*, Indonesian Movement of Islamic Students). See "Generasi Muda NU: Krisis Ekonomi Akibat Mismanajemen", *Suara Pembaruan*, 22 February 1998; Forum Aliansi OKP/ LSM/MAHASISWA, "Seruan Suksesi Damai dan Terbuka Untuk Keselamatan dan Masa Depan Rakyat dan Bangsa Indonesia", Jakarta, 5 February 1998.

23   "NU Hanya Dukung Yang Dipilih MPR", *Jawa Pos*, 21 February 1998.

24   "Tinggalkan RSCM, Gus Dur Langsung Komentari Kabinet", *Media Indonesia*, 23 March 1998. Within the cabinet, only the Minister of Religious Affairs Quraish Shihab and the Minister for Women Affairs Tuti Alawiyah had NU backgrounds.

[25] "PB NU: ABRI Sebaiknya Dukung Reformasi", *Kompas*, 16 April 1998.

[26] Arifin Djunaidi attempted in vain to convince the central board to listen to Wahid before completing the draft, but his suggestion was ignored. Arifin engaged in a heated argument with NU Deputy Chairman Fajrul Falaakh, who was put in charge of writing the release in cooperation with senior *kiai* Mustofa Bisri. Fajrul reminded Arifin that it was unnecessary to carry Wahid's name for all purposes, and that the latter was sick anyway. Interview with Fajrul Falaakh, Yogyakarta, 22 November 2000.

[27] Nur Iskandar al-Barsany, one of Central Java's leading *kiai*, complained that NU should have popularized the ideas of reform much earlier: "If ideas like [those in the NU declaration in April] had been developed by NU headquarters earlier, and had those ideas become the theological foundation in the NU community, especially in the communities of the *kiai* and the *pesantren*, I am sure that in times when the state is facing a crisis like this, the culture of silence would not have been so evident" (Barsany 1998). He therefore demanded that the *kiai* immediately begin developing a theological foundation for the debate of politics in the *pesantren* (*fikih siyasah*), including the discussion of social issues (*al-fiqh al-ijtima'iy*).

[28] Interview with Fajrul Falaakh, Yogyakarta, 22 November 2000.

[29] Interview with Amien Rais, Yogyakarta, 25 November 1997.

[30] Interview with Muhammadiyah representatives from Padang and Makassar in the Muhammadiyah office in Yogyakarta, 28 November 1997. In addition, the chairman of the Muhammadiyah branch in Magelang described Amien's criticism as "sincere, clean, and without any pretension", and as such in line with Muhammadiyah's mission. See "Senat UMS Tolak Serahkan 'Kaos Dukungan'", *Bernas*, 4 October 1997.

[31] Amien's candidacy had begun with a question from famous soothsayer Permadi at a seminar at the Legal Aid Institute LBH (*Lembaga Bantuan Hukum*) in Jakarta in late September. Permadi had asked Amien if he was ready to take up the presidency if he were elected that day. Amien responded, "God willing, I'm ready." See "Calon Muhammadiyah dari Muhammadiyah", *Suara Independen*, October 1997.

[32] Amien interpreted his exclusion from the MPR as a rupture in the relations between the regime and Muhammadiyah. He stated that "A.R. Fachruddin was included [in the MPR], Ahmad Azhar Basyir was included, Amien Rais is not included." See "Amien Rais: 'Apakah Habibie itu Well Qualified? Jawaban Saya, Yes'", *Forum Keadilan*, 20 October 1997.

[33] Interview with Taufik Kiemas, Sanur, Bali, 10 October 1998.

[34] Interview with Abdurrahman Wahid, Jakarta, 17 December 1997.

[35] Interview with Laksamana Sukardi, senior PDI-P official, Sanur, Bali, 10 October 1998.

[36] "Opposition in Public Attack on Soeharto", *Sydney Morning Herald*, 26 January 1998.

37   "Amien Rais Imbau Warga Muhammadiyah Tetap Tenang", *Republika*,
     11 February 1998.

38   Amien Rais, "Emil Salim dan Duet Soeharto-Habibie", *Republika*, 25 February
     1998.

39   Amien offered to have his head shaved if it turned out later that he had sought
     cabinet seats for himself or his organization. He stated that "if he [Amien
     himself] has ambitions to get one of the ministerial seats, then it's not him
     anymore. If that happens, this is no *Amien* who is a *Rais* [leader] any longer. Or
     no *Rais* who is *Amien* [trusted] any longer. I receive bets for shaving my hair."
     See "Beri Pak Harto Kesempatan Lagi", *Jawa Pos*, 19 February 1998.

40   "Beri Pak Harto Kesempatan Lagi", *Jawa Pos*, 19 February 1998.

41   Amien openly acknowledged that he had previously underestimated the student
     movement as a political force. Speaking at the UI (*Universitas Indonesia*,
     University of Indonesia) campus on 12 March, Amien admitted that two months
     earlier, he thought that the young generation was already exhausted (*loyo*), but
     "obviously we, the older generation, were wrong. Yesterday, the students of
     Gadjah Mada organized similar protest activities, and I gave them eight out of
     ten. This time, I give eight and a half." See "Amien Tampil di Tengah Ribuan
     Mahasiswa UI", *Jawa Pos*, 13 March 1998.

42   "Amien: Nepotisme Tetap Berkonotasi Negatif", *Jawa Pos*, 19 March 1998.

43   On several occasions, Amien invited ABRI "to march together with the people
     while maintaining Pancasila, the Constitution, and Bhinneka Tunggal Ika
     [Indonesia's national motto, lit. "unity in diversity"]". By calling on the military
     to join the movement, and assuring it that the fundamentals of the state were
     not at risk if Suharto was to be deserted, Amien hoped that ABRI would finally
     conclude that supporting reform was a better choice than defending the president
     at all cost. Without ABRI's "green light", Amien declared on 21 March, a People's
     Power movement would never happen. See "Amien Rais: Reformasi Dari Kampus
     Jangan Dianggap Enteng", *Suara Pembaruan*, 19 April 1998; "Amien: Saya Siap
     Diperiksa 24 Jam", *Jawa Pos*, 22 March 1998.

44   Interview with Abdurrahman Wahid, Jakarta, 26 May 1998.

45   During a discussion in Washington on 30 April, Amien underlined that for
     the "last seven months, I have actively conducted dialogues with the leaders
     of other religions, like the bishops. They come to my house in Yogyakarta and
     have regular meetings with me. I am also invited to speak in front of Christian
     students. I am convinced that with meetings like these, we can cultivate a
     common understanding." See "Amien: Pemimpin Golkar Kehilangan Arah",
     *Jawa Pos*, 1 May 1998.

46   Amien often stressed that he criticized the government "as chairman of
     Muhammadiyah", and he frequently started his catalogue of demands with
     sentences such as "for Muhammadiyah, reform has to contain three aspects …".
     The reference to the organization he led added weight to his demands, but
     also strengthened the protection against possible punishment by the regime.

See "Amien Rais: Reformasi Dari Kampus Jangan Dianggap Enteng", *Suara Pembaruan*, 19 April 1998.

47   "Amien Rais: Orang Bisa Saja Mengeksploitasi Nama Saya", *Republika*, 8 February 1998.

48   Interview with Malik Fajar, Jakarta, 3 June 1998.

49   The supposed shape and function of the council changed frequently as Amien adjusted the idea to the rapid political developments. On 7 May, he had told a radio reporter in Germany that the "team" was to be formed by leading political figures of the country, including himself, Megawati, and Wahid. The task of the team was to meet with Suharto and his cabinet to discuss ways out of the crisis. On 8 May, Amien explained to a *Kompas* journalist in The Hague that the main agenda of the team was to work out a reform platform and then, interestingly, a power-sharing arrangement. After 11 May, Amien used the term "council", but Megawati's and Wahid's participation was no longer mentioned. Instead, he suggested the formation of a board of political and academic figures sympathetic to him, with the leadership of the council clearly in his hands. See "Amien Rais Ingin Bentuk Tim Kepemimpinan Rakyat", *Suara Pembaruan*, 8 May 1998, and "Amien Rais: Akan Dibentuk Majelis Kepemimpinan Rakyat", *Kompas*, 12 May 1998.

50   Adi wanted to develop "a national distribution system that reaches the whole society and reduces the risks of exclusive distribution as it happens these days". See "Sekum Adi Sasono: Unjuk Rasa itu Wajar dan Sehat", *Ummat*, 4 March 1998.

51   The military group in ICMI was led by Achmad Tirtosudiro, a retired lieutenant general with extensive experience in military business, bureaucratic jobs, and diplomatic postings, who had met Habibie in Germany in 1973 and had maintained a close relationship with him ever since. His closeness with Habibie also helped Tirtosudiro to become chairman of ICMI's Jakarta chapter (Sriwidodo 2002).

52   Tirtosudiro created severe tensions in Golkar in September 1997, when he stated that Habibie was ready to take up the vice-presidency. Supporters of Golkar Chairman Harmoko, who had vice-presidential ambitions himself, deplored the statement publicly, and Habibie finally had to distance himself from it. See "Golkar Merasa Di-Fait-a-compli ICMI", *Siar*, 19 September 1997. Z.A. Maulani, another retired general active in ICMI, was convinced that Habibie would surprise everybody and become the next vice-president. Interview with Z.A. Maulani, 11 December 1997.

53   Interview with Adi Sasono, Jakarta, 8 January 1998.

54   "Sudah Waktunya Dengarkan Pendapat Tokoh-tokoh Kritis", *Kompas*, 5 January 1998.

55   Interview with Adi Sasono, Jakarta, 8 January 1998.

56   "Gus Dur Tolak Dialog Nasional", *Kabar dari Pijar*, 13 January 1998.

57   Adi Sasono expressed ICMI's view that "the office of the vice-president in the upcoming term will be of strategic importance in the effort to change the economic and political system in Indonesia". Even Nurcholish Madjid was convinced that "if Habibie is elected vice-president, the future of Indonesian democracy will be brighter". Nurcholish had been one of the most vocal critics of ICMI's pro-regime approach. See "ICMI Siap Lepaskan Habibie Jadi Wapres", *Kompas*, 26 January 1998; "15 Tokoh Muslim Bertemu Habibie", *Republika*, 25 February 1998.

58   "Sekum ICMI Adi Sasono: Unjuk Rasa itu Wajar dan Sehat", *Ummat*, 4 March 1998.

59   "'Siapa Yang Lebih Baik daripada Habibie?'", *Jawa Pos*, 28 January 1998.

60   "Setelah Habibie Jadi Wapres: Emil Salim, Tirtosudiro, dan Azwar Calon Kuat Ketua Umum ICMI", *Surabaya Post*, 4 March 1998; "Pimpin Rapat ICMI, Pilih Pelaksana Harian", *Jawa Pos*, 13 March 1998.

61   Interview with Adi Sasono, Jakarta, 8 June 1998.

62   In late 1995, Haryanto had been in the centre of a corruption scandal, with the government's inspector-general accusing him of financial misconduct involving around US$3 million (van Klinken 1996).

63   "Adi Kecewa Susunan Kabinet", *Jawa Pos*, 16 March 1998.

64   "Perombakan Kabinet Hak Prerogatif Presiden", *Republika*, 9 May 1998.

65   Wahid, for example, was convinced that "this was all just a shadow play. In public Habibie said 'Don't be so harsh with poor old Suharto.' Behind the scenes he instructed them to demolish him so he could take his seat. Very predictable, but smart, I must admit.... But see, this is exactly why you can't work with these people. They always stab you in the back." Interview with Abdurrahman Wahid, Jakarta, 26 May 1998.

66   "Amien: Jangan Main Kucing-kucingan Lagi", *Suara Merdeka*, 13 April 1998.

67   "Pak Habibie Sebaiknya Konsentrasi sebagai Wapres", *Kompas*, 18 May 1998.

68   KISDI's pro-regime attitude also led to a rift with Amien Rais. KISDI distanced itself from Amien as much as Amien turned his back on the organization. In October 1997, Amien still spoke at a KISDI event in the Al-Azhar mosque, but afterwards Amien's confrontation with the regime and his lobbying of non-Muslim constituencies resulted in cool relations between the Muhammadiyah leader and the ultra-modernist group. See "Amien Rais: Ada yang tak Wajar dalam Kehidupan Nasional", *Kompas*, 6 October 1997; "Dibentuk Front Solidaritas Nasional Muslim Indonesia", *Kompas*, 9 February 1998.

69   The Cooperation Body of Indonesian Pesantren (BKSPPI, *Badan Kerja Sama Pondok Pesantren Indonesia*), which had close relations to DDII and KISDI, organized a prayer meeting for Habibie on 19 February. At the event, the complex of common interests between ICMI, Habibie, Prabowo, and the ultra-modernist Islamic groups became evident. Adi Sasono, Prabowo, and Jakarta military commander Sjafrie Sjamsoeddin gave speeches, and the event culminated in a prayer for Habibie's successful election. See "BKSPPI Doakan Habibie

Jadi Wapres", *Republika*, 20 February 1998. One week later, BKSPPI, DDII and KISDI leaders met Habibie to remind him of the hopes of the modernist Muslim constituency regarding his upcoming vice-presidency. See "15 Tokoh Muslim Bertemu Habibie", *Republika*, 25 February 1998.

70  The idea for Forki was born earlier in the year. It was conceptualized as a solidarity forum to organize food deliveries to poverty-stricken areas. After remaining inactive for a couple of months, the political dynamics of May provided Forki with a fresh momentum not only to implement its initial aims, but also to bring together political figures with different backgrounds to unite against Suharto. Interview with Fajrul Falaakh, Yogyakarta, 22 November 2000.

71  "Empat Anggota MAR dari Surabaya Mundur, Dede: Upaya Curi Panggung", *Surabaya Post*, 19 May 1998.

72  One of Megawati's advisers explained that Megawati refrained from visiting the campuses because she had been told by intelligence sources that she was the target of Prabowo-affiliated military units. The same applied to her brother Guruh. Interview with Mochtar Buchori, leading PDI official, Jakarta, 5 June 1998.

73  Wahid was neither involved in nor informed of the press release. Interview with Fajrul Falaakh, Yogyakarta, 22 November 2000.

74  "Ada Pembelokan Arah Reformasi", *Jawa Pos*, 17 May 1998.

75  Interview with General (ret.) Wiranto, Jakarta, 13 October 2000.

76  Some ICMI regional branches went public over the weekend with their demands for a special session of the MPR with the explicit agenda of replacing Suharto. The Central Java branch even demanded the resignation of DPR Chairman Harmoko for failing to follow up on the popular aspirations regarding Suharto's position. ICMI's central board would "only" call for the president's resignation on Monday, 18 May. See "ICMI Jateng Tuntut Ketua DPR/MPR Diganti", *Suara Merdeka*, 17 May 1998.

77  Interview with Nurcholish Madjid, Jakarta, 28 May 1998.

78  Interview with Nurcholish Madjid, Jakarta, 28 May 1998.

79  Interview with Nurcholish Madjid, Jakarta, 28 May 1998.

80  Wahid and Siti Hardiyanti had been scheduled to take part in an IPNU initiative to distribute money to poor school students on 25 May, before events determined otherwise. "PP NU dan Gerakan Berbagi", *Republika*, 6 May 1998.

81  Interview with Al-Zastrouw Ng, Jakarta, 26 May 1998.

82  Interview with Mohaimin Iskandar, Jakarta, 26 September 1999.

83  Interview with Hasyim Wahid, Jakarta, 14 November 1998. Fajrul compared the inter-elite politicking to a game of chess. As the game had already begun, and the major players already participated, NU had to play its part as well. Even if Wahid refused to attend, Fajrul continued, there was no guarantee that he would not be manipulated in his absence (Al-Zastrouw Ng 1999, pp. 41–42).

84  Interview with Anwar Haryono, Jakarta, 25 July 1998.

85 Interview with Malik Fadjar, Jakarta, 3 June 1998.
86 Interview with Nurcholish Madjid, Jakarta, 27 May 1998.
87 Interview with Yusril Ihza Mahendra, Jakarta, 25 August 1998.
88 Interview with Abdurrahman Wahid, Jakarta, 26 May 1998.
89 Interview with Nurcholish Madjid, Jakarta, 28 May 1998.
90 "Perihal Pernyataan Presiden Soeharto: Ada yang Berharap, Ada Pula yang Kecewa", *Kompas*, 20 May 1998.
91 In a TV address, Amien had called on his followers to pray at home. The cancellation apparently did not harm his image as the leader of the protest movement. Newspapers quoted students as saying that the decision had underscored Amien's stature as a rational and responsible politician. See "Amien Rais: Cegah Jatuhnya Korban Sia-Sia", *Surabaya Post*, 20 May 1998.
92 Interview with General (ret.) Wiranto, Jakarta, 13 October 2000.
93 Interview with Z.A. Maulani, Habibie's chief of staff, Jakarta, 5 June 1998.
94 Interview with Yusril Ihza Mahendra, Jakarta, 25 August 1998.
95 Interview with Amien Rais, Surabaya, 15 May 1999.
96 Confidential interview with a NU deputy chairman, Jakarta, 27 May 1998.

# PART THREE

# The Post-Authoritarian
# Transition, 1998–2004

# 5

# ADAPTING TO DEMOCRACY
# TNI in the Early
# Post-Authoritarian Polity

After Suharto's fall in May 1998, Indonesia embarked on a tumultuous political transition that was characterized by economic instability, security challenges, social fragmentation, and extensive experiments with new institutional concepts. It would take more than six years before an institutionally coherent framework for the new political system emerged, marking Indonesia's entry into the phase of democratic consolidation. In few areas was the political fluidity and uncertainty of the polity between 1998 and 2004 as tangible as in the field of civil-military relations. The assessments on the progress of military reform in that period differ immensely, ranging from Megawati's claim during the 2004 presidential campaign that democratic civilian supremacy had been firmly anchored during her rule to the reports of human rights groups and activists that the armed forces had in fact consolidated their political powers (East Timor Action Network/U.S. 2002). Writing in 2003, William Liddle tried to weigh the arguments put forward by the various camps. On the one hand, he asserted, the armed forces "did not attempt to prevent then Vice-President B.J. Habibie, a civilian disliked by the military, from becoming president" (Liddle 2003). They also refrained from undermining the "project to democratize Indonesia by holding free parliamentary elections, the first since 1955". In addition, the military "formally rescinded its twin-functions doctrine". Despite all these positive indicators, however, Liddle concluded that there is "a slowly dawning recognition that nothing fundamental has in fact changed since 1998". The armed forces, he maintained, "continue to hold a self-image and possess resources that predispose and enable them to intervene in national political life in a manner and at a time of their own choosing". Even within intellectual circles of the armed forces, there was acknowledgement that "while the post-New Order civilian governments ... managed to reduce some of the institutional privileges of the military, this reduction did not result in a significant decline in the political powers of the armed forces" (Yulianto 2002, p. 612).

The explanation for these contrasting characterizations of Indonesia's civil-military transition between 1998 and 2004 is partially rooted in the way the New Order regime transferred power to its successor government. Chapter 3 demonstrated that compromise-oriented military officers succeeded in negotiating the terms of the regime change, which secured a central place for the armed forces in the power constellation of the new polity. Chapter 4, for its part, showed how the inability of non-regime forces to assume government allowed important structures of the New Order to survive Suharto's fall. This intra-systemic transfer of power prefigured the post-authoritarian transition and caused many of its problems, but other factors appear to be important as well. Generally, the success of civil-military reforms depends on a number of variables, including the quality of civilian governance, the willingness of the armed forces to accept change, the appropriate selection of reform targets, the level of internal security threats and, to a lesser extent, a supportive international environment. In consequence, this chapter will analyse the impact of such factors on the nature of Indonesia's civil-military relations between 1998 and 2004. Given the highly diverse approaches of the Habibie, Wahid, and Megawati governments to the management of the armed forces, the chapter discusses their successes and failures in separate parts. In an additional section, it focuses on the post-Suharto career of Susilo Bambang Yudhoyono, exemplifying the gradual assimilation of military officers to the conditions of democratic political competition. In concluding, I argue that the political power struggles and security disturbances during the transition were as much caused by the ambiguity and instability of civil-military relations in the early post-authoritarian polity as by the specific circumstances of the preceding regime change in 1998.

## THE POLITICS OF GIVE AND TAKE: HABIBIE AND TNI, 1998–99

The ambivalent character of the 1998 regime change, which exhibited reformative and conservative features at the same time, had a profound impact on the development of the post-autocratic polity. Exposing sharp breaks with the authoritarian past but also strong lines of continuity, the new political system absorbed both democratic reformers and opportunistic New Order cronies. Against the backdrop of this general tension between radical change and the survival of parts of the old regime, post-Suharto civil-military relations acquired a distinctively hybrid nature as well.

The reformative aspects of the change in government led to considerable confusion within the armed forces. Habibie, under strong societal pressure to demonstrate his reformist credentials, launched a bold political reform programme within days of assuming office. He decided to lift the limitations on establishing political parties, allowed unrestricted freedom of the press, and promised free and fair elections for the near future (Liddle 1999c). Although observers such as Horowitz (2001, p. 147) believed that "Indonesian society is expecting — and is certainly ready for — a more complete democratization", the surprisingly swift liberalization of the political system had serious consequences for the military and its top brass. Most importantly, the press began to publish articles on past human rights abuses committed by the security forces, leading to a widespread sense that the political invulnerability of the military had come to an end. Moreover, political parties of all colours and ideologies sprang up between June and August 1998, colliding with the traditional military paradigm of societal control and its obsession with the perceived dangers of political pluralism. This new atmosphere of open political competition, which allowed all politico-ideological groups except for the communists to organize and participate in the struggle for power in the post-Suharto polity, disturbed many within the officer corps and left them in doubt about their role, function, and careers. From the military's perspective of self-preservation, Habibie's initiative to strengthen civilian groups and entrench them in the institutions of the new polity not only threatened to fundamentally alter the power relations in Indonesia's state structure, but also had the potential to marginalize the armed forces from political life for the first time since the late 1950s.

These elements of rapid change were balanced, however, by the strong lines of continuity that extended from the New Order into the new democratic polity. The government that took over from Suharto's last cabinet in May 1998 consisted largely of politicians and bureaucrats produced by the old regime. The legislature, established after the 1997 elections, remained in place until fresh polls could be held and a new parliament inaugurated. Thus the institutional structures of the immediate post-Suharto administration excluded those groups that had been in open opposition to the New Order. In the armed forces, Habibie opted to leave the majority of Suharto's top generals in their positions. The reasons for this decision were manifold. Most importantly, there was a widely held view in Habibie's circle and much of the political elite that the removal of the military hardliners was sufficient to satisfy initial public demands for change in the armed forces.[1] Personally, Habibie thought that Wiranto had to be rewarded for the orderly transition of presidential power, and as Harold Crouch (1999, p. 134) pointed out, both men had a joint interest in preventing investigations into the benefits they had received under authoritarian rule. Consequently, Wiranto held on to his control over the armed forces and the department of defence and security, and many of his associates retained their commands or were promoted to higher offices.[2]

This seemingly contradictory and confusing combination of change and continuity was strikingly evident in the political attitudes of the incumbent military elite towards the new polity. On the one hand, there was a strong sense of satisfaction within Wiranto's circle over its success in negotiating Suharto's resignation and assuming control over the post-New Order armed forces (Wiranto 2003, pp. 93–97). The compromise-oriented generals had — through their manoeuvring in the last days of the regime — avoided the example of countries such as South Korea that embarked on the reform of their post-authoritarian militaries by replacing large sections of the armed forces leadership (Jun 2001, p. 130). By contrast, the composition of Indonesia's top brass experienced only marginal changes, allowing senior officers attached to the old regime to defend their personal interests against demands for fundamental reform. The relief in the military elite over its continued grip on key positions was offset, however, by considerable discontent with the new political system. Comments made by senior generals on the character of Habibie's reform package illustrated this unhappiness. Agum Gumelar, for example, stated that

> now that the New Order is gone, we should think about why we had it. We had it because liberal democracy had failed. We had it because economic growth needs stability. We had it because many Indonesians are politically immature.... Let's not pull down all the fences we have erected to protect us. There was actually a reason why we had erected them.[3]

In the same vein, Susilo Bambang Yudhoyono warned that "we shouldn't suddenly have twenty-six, thirty-four, and so forth, political parties, because we have had experiences in the past".[4] Wiranto, for his part, spoke of the need to limit the scope of the reform efforts, and he defined those limits with the political terminology of the New Order: "Pancasila, the constitution, nationalism, and unity."[5] These cautioning statements highlighted the speed with which political developments threatened to overrun the armed forces and other political protagonists. Labelled as political moderates only weeks earlier for their implicit endorsement of Suharto's removal, key officers around Wiranto suddenly found themselves portrayed as opponents of further reform in the new democratic polity.

## Habibie's Supremacy

The military's reservations vis-à-vis the new political system were aggravated by the fact that for the first time since the end of Sukarno's rule in 1966 the armed forces had to receive orders from a president without a military background. While many officers had felt uncomfortable with Suharto's deep interference in military affairs, they had still viewed him as one of their own. Habibie, on the other hand, was not only a "pure" civilian, but he also had political priorities that differed significantly from those of his predecessor. Among Habibie's most immediate interests was convincing the military to refrain from sabotaging democratic reforms and, by implication, undermining the credibility of his rule. In Habibie's inner circle, there were substantial disagreements about how to approach this challenge, with some of the president's advisers recommending a more confrontational approach than Habibie was prepared to pursue. Adi Sasono, now minister for cooperatives and small enterprises, belonged to a group of close confidants who frequently warned Habibie of the "danger" that the military could potentially pose to his government.[6] For that reason, he had asked Habibie after his inauguration to replace Wiranto and his associates with generals more sympathetic to him, but Habibie had decided to stick with the incumbent. Apparently confident that Wiranto could be relied upon to support his democratic agenda, Habibie tried to assure Adi and other ABRI sceptics in his administration that their fear of military sabotage was exaggerated. Nevertheless, Habibie was determined to quickly establish his authority over the officer corps.

The protection of his democratic reforms was not the only motivation for Habibie to seek strong control of and cooperation with the armed forces, however. Given his political vulnerability, the new president had little choice but to integrate the military into his institutional and personal patronage network. Rejected by key societal forces and the emerging political parties, Habibie had to rely on the military as one of his major sources of power. With his authority over military appointments serving as an instrument of "persuasion", the president forced senior officers to assist him in consolidating his political position and in fending off challenges from opponents. There were three major events in which Habibie evoked his supremacy over the military to improve his political standing. To begin with, Habibie forced Wiranto on 23 May 1998 to dismiss the newly appointed Johnny Lumintang as commander of Kostrad. Some of Habibie's advisers had warned that a Christian in such a crucial military post could seriously undermine Habibie's popularity in the Muslim community.[7] Then, when Golkar held its congress in July 1998 to elect a new chairman, Habibie demanded that the military support the candidacy of his associate Akbar Tandjung.[8] Akbar's rival for the post was former ABRI commander Edi Sudradjat, a declared Habibie opponent and keen to end the latter's presidency as soon as possible. Edi was popular within the ranks, but Habibie's intervention with Wiranto secured Akbar's election. Finally, Habibie ordered the armed forces to help mobilize paramilitary groups (mostly thugs and urban poor) in defence of a special MPR session in November 1998, which was held to legitimate Habibie's presidency and his political programme.[9]

While Habibie's constitutional powers to hire and fire top military leaders goes a long way to explain ABRI's remarkable compliance with his orders in the early post-Suharto period, the evolving relationship between the president and the military was based on more than just hierarchically enforced authority. There was also a growing awareness on both sides that they had common interests on a variety of issues, largely relating to the protection of their powers and assets inherited from the New Order regime. Both Habibie and ABRI's senior officers had much to fear from the political changes that would inevitably lead to greater transparency, critical press reporting, and more credible legal proceedings. As former Suharto cronies, the new president and his generals shared concerns about possible investigations into their conduct under the New Order, which included illicit business deals and a long list of human rights abuses. Uniting against such threats therefore seemed to offer Habibie and ABRI a better chance of political survival than attempts to outplay each other. In consequence, Habibie granted a number of important concessions to the armed forces in exchange for supporting his rule. Most significantly, Habibie left the specifics of military reform to Wiranto and his advisers.[10] With this, the civilian government surrendered authority over one of the most crucial areas of structural reform and effectively allowed the armed forces to reform themselves. As one observer commented cynically, "this is like asking a bunch of incompetent and corrupt managers to develop a new business plan for the company they had previously bankrupted".[11]

Accordingly, in the first eighteen months of Indonesia's democratic transition, there were no executive orders by civilian authorities to the military elite as to how to revise its command system, doctrine, and political mindset. In fact, as David Bourchier (2000, p. 28) pointed out, the military of the Habibie period had arguably "more control over its own affairs than it had under Soeharto". Both in political and institutional terms, the military effectively supervised itself: Wiranto, in his double function as minister of defence and security and armed forces commander, represented the civilian government vis-à-vis the very military whose institutional interests he was determined to defend. The military's power to define its own reform process contrasted sharply with the emphasis Cottey, Edmunds, and Forster put on the importance of selecting the right reform targets when launching institutional changes to the defence sector. If allowed to set reform agendas for themselves, militaries are likely to focus on a large number of institutional areas that are of secondary importance to their interests in order to cover for the omission of more important issues. This omission of primary institutional targets from the reform agenda, in turn, is certain to cause long-term damage to the goal of establishing democratic control over the armed forces. As would soon become evident, that was precisely what occurred in the early period of Indonesia's political transition.

## Designing Self-Reform: Wiranto and the "New Paradigm"

The armed forces made extensive use of the authority to select their own reform targets by announcing a number of internal reforms between July 1998 and April 2000. While these reforms led to relevant and genuine institutional changes, they also protected the military's primary source of power. Most significantly, Wiranto proclaimed in July that the military was prepared to follow a "New Paradigm". This new concept, however, was in content and wording identical with the reform ideas formulated by moderate officers in 1996 and 1997 (Honna 2003, pp. 164–65). Like the drafts circulating at that time, Wiranto's post-Suharto paradigm consisted of four points: first, the military was content not to be in the forefront of all national affairs; second, the previous approach of occupying was changed into influencing; third, this influence was to be exerted indirectly rather than directly; and fourth, the armed forces acknowledged the necessity for role-sharing with other national forces.[12] The reuse of ideas developed in the context of the late New Order to address the challenges of the post-authoritarian transition dissatisfied some of the more progressive officers in Wiranto's circle. Agus Wirahadikusumah, for example, concluded that "the new paradigm wasn't new at all — it was the same concept that we had written up earlier in preparation for the time when Suharto would allow limited reforms". Bitter about the lack of enthusiasm for reform in ABRI, Wirahadikusumah stated that "now that Suharto had fallen, with a big bang, all we could come up with was to take that old paper out of the drawer; pretty saddening, actually."[13]

Despite its conservative attitude, however, the military leadership did eventually dispose of its Dual Function. Initially, senior officers had been reluctant to shelve their main doctrine, with Agus Widjojo recalling that "when I proposed scrapping *Dwi Fungsi* in September 1998, most generals thought that such a move was premature".[14] Consequently, Wiranto and his commanders experimented with several alternative terms for the Dual Function, among them "Combined Function" (*peran terpadu*). Such semantic distinctions failed to convince the public, though, forcing the military to declare the Dual Function officially terminated in April 2000.[15] The doctrinal change was accompanied by several measures designed to underline the military's determination to extract itself from active politics. In November 1998, a new policy was implemented that no longer allowed active officers to hold civilian positions in the bureaucracy. Moreover, in January 1999, the armed forces accepted a reduction of its legislative representation to 38 delegates in national parliament (down from 75) and 10 per cent of the seats in local legislatures. Wiranto also initiated the separation of the police from the military, which had been united under the institutional roof of armed forces headquarters since 1962. This split allowed Wiranto to rename ABRI as TNI, the term used for the armed forces during the "glorious" days of the revolution. In addition, the armed forces cut their formal ties with Golkar and pledged neutrality in the parliamentary elections scheduled for June 1999.[16]

The reform initiatives launched by Wiranto marked the early phase of what Cottey, Edmunds, and Forster have called the "first generation" of civil-military reforms. In this early phase of the post-authoritarian transition, the institutions of the old regime are reviewed, disbanded, and eventually replaced by new bodies that conform to the changed political conditions under democratic rule. Successful completion of first-generation reforms, however, is dependent on the accurate identification and substantial restructuring of those power foundations that enabled militaries to function as pillars of authoritarian rule. In Indonesia, the character and scope of reforms proposed by the armed forces suggested that the problem of military intervention in politics was created by and limited to the participation of senior officers in political institutions. Hence the armed forces concluded that the issue could be resolved by simply extracting the military from the political bodies it had penetrated; the macro-structures of military organization, on the other hand, were not to be affected:

> The main target of our reform program was to get out of politics. Militaries should not be involved in active politics. We left the government, disbanded our socio-political branches and gradually reduced our presence in the legislatures.... The Dual Function was over once we implemented those steps. The structure of our military itself has nothing to do with that. There is nothing wrong with that structure. It is needed for defence purposes.[17]

The exclusion of active military personnel from government and the gradual reduction of its representation in the legislature were important steps in the formal depoliticization of the armed forces. They led to a widespread sense of uncertainty and concern within an officer corps that for decades had viewed high-profile bureaucratic careers as part of its guaranteed professional benefits.[18] But the heavy emphasis on terminating military engagement in civilian institutions also distracted the attention of the public and political elite from other, more consequential areas of reform. Most importantly, the territorial command structure, the backbone of military presence in socio-political life in the regions, was left untouched for the entirety of Habibie's interregnum. This omission pointed to major conceptual flaws and shortcomings in Indonesia's military reform process.

The institutional and doctrinal dismantling of the Dual Function masked the fact that the political role of the armed forces had been the result of, rather than the reason for, the entrenchment of the military in Indonesia's society. The military had been granted direct participation in government in the late 1950s in acknowledgement of its capacity to stabilize (or destabilize) civilian governments. This capacity, in turn, was based on the military's territorial presence, its autonomy from central funding sources, and mediation in conflicts between political parties and other societal forces. The military reform measures initiated during the Habibie government, on the other hand, abolished the Dual Function without addressing the structural causes that had produced it. In the same vein, the massive outpouring of societal criticism of the military gave rise to the misleading impression that TNI's institutional strength was collapsing (Bourchier 1999, p. 166). However, such assessments tended to overlook the entrenched nature of the military's structure that enabled it, in spite of continuing institutional reform and sharp societal scrutiny of its history, to adjust effectively to the new democratic era. Critically, the increasing levels of competition between civilian groups offered the military opportunities of political mediation, and some of the structural reforms initiated by the Habibie government actually worked in its favour. The decentralization laws of 1999, for example, prepared the scene for a substantial transfer of political authority and financial resources into the regions, where the armed forces had a strong presence through their network of territorial units. With political parties, legislatures, and bureaucracies struggling to test their new powers in this early period of the post-Suharto years, the military stood out as the only institution with a deeply rooted, functioning infrastructure at the grassroots level.[19]

## TNI and the 1999 Elections

The adaptation of the military to the political system of the post-Suharto era was accelerated by the growing intra-elite tensions that accompanied the parliamentary and presidential elections in June and October 1999 respectively. Most importantly, this struggle for political hegemony led to fundamental changes in the relationship between the armed forces and the president in the second half of Habibie's term. In the early phase of his government, Habibie had been able to rein in the military elite by applying a combination of "persuasion" and compromise. The electoral process, however, substantially weakened Habibie's position and strengthened that of the armed forces. This was largely due to the fact that Habibie's Golkar party came only second in the parliamentary elections in June 1999, in which TNI had remained neutral both in rhetoric and in practice. By contrast, the party of opposition leader Megawati Sukarnoputri, PDI-Perjuangan (PDI-Struggle), finished first with 33.7 per cent of the votes, turning Megawati into the front-runner for the election of the president by the MPR in October. Furthermore, a number of political and financial scandals crippled the government throughout 1999, motivating even Golkar to consider alternatives to Habibie's nomination. Deserted by large segments of civil society and the political elite, Habibie's hopes for a second term thus rested on Wiranto's readiness to throw the full weight of the military behind the presidential campaign of the embattled incumbent. Wiranto, however, was in contact with other contenders as well, particularly with Megawati, but also with Abdurrahman Wahid, who was supported by a coalition of Muslim parties. Both politicians held regular meetings with Wiranto, trying to obtain the backing of TNI for their presidential bids. Evidently, the civilian actors of the post-preatorian polity still felt it necessary to lobby the armed forces for their political support.

The competition for the leadership of the first democratic government since the late 1950s ended with Habibie's defeat and the election of Wahid as Indonesia's fourth president in October 1999. Sensing that Habibie's chances were minimal, Wiranto had earlier publicly declined his offer to run as his vice-presidential candidate.[20] Instead, he decided to support Wahid. The armed forces chief had received assurances from Wahid that he would play a prominent role in the latter's government, and the NU leader had even raised the possibility of a Wiranto vice-presidency. Equally important were Wahid's guarantees that the military's interests would be "protected" if he won the election.[21] After intense last-minute lobbying, the armed forces leadership instructed its representatives to vote for Wahid, who subsequently beat Megawati by a margin of 373 to 313.[22] Wiranto's hopes for the vice-presidency were dashed, however, when Wahid decided to support Megawati for the post and, at the same time, Golkar leader Akbar Tandjung declined the general's request to be nominated by the former government party.[23] While Wiranto was furious that both Wahid and Golkar denied him a more influential position, the freshly elected president made sure that he and other influential commanders were integrated into the new administration. The disappointed TNI leader was consequently compensated with a key cabinet seat, while Susilo Bambang Yudhoyono and Agum Gumelar also obtained ministerial positions.

The inclusion of prominent military figures in the post-Habibie government pointed to the political transformation of the armed forces in the first eighteen months of the democratic system. Under the New Order, the military had been the main pillar of Suharto's regime, with the clearly defined and enforced agenda of prolonging the rule of the incumbent. By contrast, in the early post-authoritarian polity the armed forces operated as a largely independent actor with less institutional privileges, but more strategic flexibility, internal autonomy, and informal political influence. Shortly before his victory, Wahid admitted as much when he emphasized that "you still can't become president in Indonesia without the military; some people say they're out of the bureaucracy, and all of that, but that's nonsense". In reality, he continued, "they're still strong, and that's why I will seek and get Wiranto's support to become president".[24] Wahid's analysis reflected pride in his ability to use military support in outplaying his civilian opponents and assuming power, but it would also turn into a self-fulfilling prophecy affecting his own term in office. The events of the following two years would demonstrate that in addition to obtaining military support to gain the presidency, it was equally essential for the incumbent to maintain that support if he (or she) wanted to stay in power.

Apparently, the early phase of "first-generation reforms" initiated during Habibie's interregnum had changed the way the armed forces engaged in politics, but had produced rather mixed results as far as establishing democratic civilian control over the military was concerned. Besides the continued entanglement of the armed forces in the political competition between civilian actors, the main reason for the slow progress in the civil-military transition was the insulation of TNI's primary power base from the reform process. The military had successfully ensured that the territorial command system was not included in the reform agenda, allowing the generals not only to utilize their institutional strength at the grassroots level, but also to perpetuate the system of military self-financing. As was the practice under previous regimes since the 1940s, the military during Habibie's government remained largely independent from budget allocations provided by the state, enabling it to define its own operational and strategic agenda in spite of cuts to its political privileges. In addition, Richard Gunther (2001, p. 151) argued that TNI's continued representation in parliament, albeit reduced, endowed "the military with 'reserve powers' that might be invoked to frustrate a democratic mandate". However, the most striking evidence for the success of the armed forces in avoiding subordination to civilian control was its independent political operation in East Timor, where a referendum was to decide the future status of the territory occupied by Indonesia since 1975.

## OLD PRACTICES, NEW REALITIES: TNI'S DEBACLE IN EAST TIMOR

The attitude of the armed forces towards Habibie's decision in January 1999 to support a referendum in East Timor provided eloquent evidence for the gap between TNI's self-proclaimed institutional reform and the persistence of military power structures in the regions. Officially, Wiranto backed Habibie's plan, which offered the territory an opportunity to separate from Indonesia if the majority of East Timorese rejected a final offer of special autonomy in a "popular consultation" to be held by the United Nations. In a cabinet meeting on 27 January, Wiranto only insisted on three conditions: first, that the policy of intervening in East Timor in 1975 should not be repudiated; second, that the conduct of military operations in the province since then should not be criticized; and third, that the remains of Indonesian soldiers in the territory should be respected and returned to Indonesia if Jakarta lost the vote. These requests appeared to signal TNI's reluctant concurrence with the proposals of its civilian government; on the ground, however, the armed forces launched a massive intelligence operation to intimidate East Timorese into voting for Indonesia's offer.

The reason for Wiranto's endorsement of the ballot in cabinet has been the subject of an intense debate between analysts. The publicly expressed position of the TNI chief was particularly surprising since there was widespread opposition in the army mainstream to the referendum. Many within the senior military leadership had fought in East Timor at various stages of their careers, and they were well aware of the crucial importance of the annexed province for TNI's self-perception as the guarantor of Indonesia's territorial integrity. These sentiments within the officer corps led Kevin O'Rourke (2002, p. 256) to believe that "Wiranto adamantly opposed Habibie's ballot offer", in spite of cabinet records pointing to the contrary. Don Greenlees and Robert Garran (2002, p. 101), on the other hand, noted that Wiranto's endorsement was curious as "it is unlikely that Habibie could have overcome concerted opposition" to his decision. It seems that Wiranto's move was motivated by a combination of factors. To begin with, his relationship with Habibie was still in transition. Habibie's authority over the armed forces declined only when his chances of winning a second term began to falter amidst intense electoral competition from around March 1999. Thus when the East Timor decision was made in January, Wiranto did not feel sufficiently strong to oppose it without risking dismissal. In addition, Wiranto apparently believed that TNI's undiminished powers of territorial control would be able to deliver victory for both Indonesia and the armed forces. Misled by decades of manipulated intelligence reporting and by TNI's own propaganda, Wiranto thought that the East Timorese "appreciated the efforts of the government and the military in promoting economic growth in the province".[25] This misjudgement, combined with his belief that "we as military officers had a special relationship with East Timor", made Wiranto "confident that the people of East Timor would embrace Indonesia".

Against this background, the prospect of a popular poll presented itself not as a threat to TNI's interests, but as an opportunity to settle the East Timor issue once and for all. Accordingly, Greenlees and Garran (2002, p. 101) hit the nail on the head when they explained that the "attraction of an act of self-determination might have been to finally prove the legitimacy of Indonesia's claims to popular assent to its rule". But the prospect of a definite endorsement of East Timor's integration into Indonesia not only promised to vindicate TNI internationally and solve the country's most difficult diplomatic problem. At the same time, victory for Indonesia would have strengthened TNI's domestic position by demonstrating the indispensability of its territorial machinery for every civilian government, regardless of the outcome of the 1999 presidential election.

## "Culture of Violence": TNI and the Militias

In reaching his decision, Wiranto felt affirmed by reports from his assistants that conventional military methods of mass control and elite manipulation were certain to decide the ballot in favour of Indonesia. However, these assessments discounted the potential impact of diplomatic scrutiny and media reports on the credibility of the poll and ignored the wide-ranging political change that had occurred since Suharto's fall. Wondering "why the army should have been so blind to the counter-productive effects of its violence", Robert Cribb (2002, p. 240) pointed to the deep entrenchment of the officer corps in traditional paradigms of military doctrine and dominance as the most plausible explanation. One of Wiranto's closest associates offered some telling insights into this phenomenon when he claimed that

> East Timor was military territory. We had our people at every corner. People couldn't even cough without us knowing. We had spies in every pro-independence group. We knew everything, the central government knew nothing. There was no doubt that we could win this referendum or whatever they called it. Without the manipulation by the UN, we would have won.[26]

It appears that Wiranto's trust in the effectiveness of his apparatus was so high that no detailed instructions were issued to ensure the implementation of TNI policies on the ground. In this, Wiranto followed the example of Suharto, who rarely explained in concrete terms how he wanted to see his orders executed, but left it to the internal mechanism of the system he had created to produce the expected outcome. Geoffrey Robinson (2002, pp. 273–74) suggested that this "deeply embedded system of knowledge, discourse, norms, and behaviour within the TNI" was based on a highly institutionalized "culture of violence". This system "entails an almost reflexive, though constantly changing, understanding of a certain language, technology, and repertoire of violence and terror", and "arguably means that no explicit order or plan was necessary in order to trigger the actions that were observed". It was this non-institutional organism of the military's internal procedures that blurred the lines of command responsibility, making it impossible to identify the origin of TNI's plan for East Timor.

Therefore, Robinson concluded that the search for a "smoking gun" was (and will continue to be) "fruitless".

Despite its obscure origins, the pattern of TNI behaviour in East Timor that emerged soon after the announcement of Habibie's offer was of remarkable coherence and consistency. TNI officers stationed in the territory began in December 1998 — when Habibie's plan was not yet public but already internally discussed — to mobilize and expand their network of civilian militias that had previously assisted the military in its long-running guerrilla and intelligence operations. These militias had been built up, financed, equipped, and directed by local military leaders, and were now tasked with campaigning for the pro-integrationist cause and intimidating the supporters of independence. The militias clashed with pro-independence groups as early as February 1999, and soon launched a programme of systematic terror against prominent opponents of Jakarta's rule. Meanwhile, TNI falsely portrayed itself as a neutral mediator between the conflicting parties, calling for calm and peaceful negotiations. A brochure produced and distributed by Wiranto in 2000 claimed that

> on the one hand, TNI had to face the facts and see the horizontal conflict between the two fighting factions, and on the other hand, TNI had to provide full support and backing to the political decisions of the central government by placing itself in a position of complete neutrality.... TNI was now fully impartial and did not take sides with either of the fighting groups whatsoever (Wiranto, no date, p. 7).

The reality was, of course, strikingly different. The Task Force to Oversee the Popular Consultation in East Timor, set up by Wiranto and headed by former Prabowo ally Zacky Anwar Makarim, was the main institutional mechanism through which the military controlled the militias. Douglas Kammen (2001, p. 186) asserted that "by using controlled violence and terror, the Task Force and military personnel on the ground in East Timor hoped both to intimidate East Timorese into voting in favour of broad autonomy and to scare others away from the polls". Robinson (2002, p. 266), for his part, concurred that "despite efforts to conceal it ..., the direct link between the TNI and the militias remained clear".

## Indonesia's Exit from East Timor

Despite its continued optimism that military intelligence operations would be able to decide the referendum for Indonesia, the armed forces leadership began in June to prepare for a possible rejection of the autonomy package. The discussed options included directing the militias to protest against the outcome of the ballot, the partition of East Timor into two separate entities (with the Western districts to remain with Indonesia), and a large-scale relocation of pro-integration refugees to West Timor.[27] It was this emergency plan, more than anything else, that exposed the blatant disconnect between the policy directives given by civilian authorities in Jakarta and their translation by military officers on the ground. It is unlikely that Habibie raised serious objections to the military's efforts to win the ballot for Indonesia, and he may have even sympathized with them. But in contrast to the armed forces elite, he was prepared to let East Timor go in an orderly fashion if it rejected the autonomy offer. In fact, many within Habibie's circle of advisers had speculated that East Timor's peaceful separation would not only result in the disposal of a domestic trouble spot, but also in rising international sympathy for Indonesia and its president. Instead, military officers continued to contemplate violent ways of overturning a possibly negative result. Kammen (2001, p. 186) maintained that the plans made by these officers "lie at the root of the post-referendum events".

The massive destruction inflicted by militias on East Timor's infrastructure and population after the clear rejection of the special autonomy package in September 1999 was a consistent extension of the logic of violence that Robinson described as an inherent feature of TNI's thinking and behaviour. It also suggested that one and a half years of institutional military reforms had impacted only marginally on the way the armed forces conducted its operations. Despite its formal repositioning as an apolitical defence force, it appeared that the military, or at least influential elements within it, had decided to circumvent the civilian government's instructions, engineer a vote that was in TNI's institutional interests, and allow the militias to go on a rampage when that goal was not achieved. As a result, Indonesia suffered a major international embarrassment when it had planned to score a diplomatic victory, and the president — who was widely believed to have eyed the Nobel Peace Prize — was voted out of office one month after Australia and the United Nations moved into East Timor.[28] Dewi Fortuna Anwar, Habibie's spokesperson, made no secret of her view on TNI's insubordination:

> If you ask whether TNI's behaviour can be classified as insubordination towards the civilian government, I advise you to look at Habibie's instructions to Wiranto and other military leaders. There is nothing said about a militia build-up, nothing said about supporting one side in the ballot, nothing said about destruction if we lose. All it said was

stay neutral, contain violence, and make sure that the ballot proceeds peacefully. Now look at the outcome of this. Does that look like Habibie's instructions were implemented?[29]

The events in East Timor exhibited not only the weakness of Indonesia's civilian government, however. They were equally damaging for the military itself, painfully reminding the officer corps that the times in which it could use conventional intelligence operations to achieve political goals had irrevocably come to an end. Misguided by the false assumption that the referendum could be won with traditional New Order instruments, the TNI elite now had to come to terms with the fact that the increased public scrutiny into its actions after May 1998 had changed its interaction with society much more fundamentally than the generals had anticipated. In many ways, the failure to orchestrate the East Timor ballot in Indonesia's favour marked the end of the early civil-military transition, which had seen many New Order practices simply extending into the new democratic polity. By contrast, the next phase in post-authoritarian politics, which began with the election of Abdurrahman Wahid as Habibie's successor in October 1999, would force TNI to actively assimilate its political operations to the norms and rules of democratic competition.

## REFORM AND FAILURE:
## TNI UNDER THE WAHID PRESIDENCY, 1999–2001

After the Habibie interregnum had left the military in charge of its own reform process, the ascension of Abdurrahman Wahid to the presidency appeared to offer improved prospects for democratic consolidation in general and accelerated civil-military reforms in particular. To begin with, the establishment of the first democratically elected executive since 1955 removed large segments of the former New Order elite from government. Furthermore, the participation of most political parties in the cabinet provided, at least in theory, the very "unity of democratic purpose among civilian elites" that Diamond and Plattner (1996, p. xxiv) viewed as a precondition for successful military reform in democratic transitions. In addition, the armed forces had just suffered a humiliating defeat in East Timor, leading to increased external pressure on Indonesia to reform its military structures. Wahid, for his part, was widely viewed as a democratic reformer, despite his controversial role in late New Order politics. Kammen and Chandra (2002, p. 103) noted that Wahid's "strong Islamic credentials, political savvy, and wit were expected to tame the military beast". Consequently, the new president took office with a sound understanding of the depth of military intervention in Indonesian politics, and he lost no time in dismantling the network on which it was based. Starting with his immediate personal surroundings, he sought to marginalize armed forces officers from the palace bureaucracy (McBeth 2000).[30] Interestingly, this not only involved downsizing TNI's executive staff, but also included removing military tapping devices from the presidential residence and office.[31]

After trying to curb the influence of the armed forces on his inner circle, Wahid moved on to take a series of more general "measures to exert civilian control over the military and rein in the Army" (The Editors 2000, p. 126). For example, he appointed Navy Chief of Staff Admiral Widodo as TNI commander, drawing from the service that, according to Eric Heginbotham (2002, pp. 121–22), was "significantly more sympathetic to liberal political and economic positions" than the army. Moreover, by compensating Wiranto, Yudhoyono, and Agum with cabinet posts carrying considerable patronage potential, Wahid removed the army's most influential officers from central command positions and effectively ended their military careers. He also appointed a widely respected civilian as minister of defence (the first since the early 1950s), disbanded a military-coordinated security agency notorious for its political surveillance activities, and abolished the socio-political offices at the ministry of home affairs, a traditional military stronghold. In addition, he initiated negotiations with separatists in both Aceh and Papua, ignoring the warnings from conservative officers that only military force could quell the secessionist tendencies in the two conflict-ridden provinces. Wahid, it appeared, was determined to embark on a process of radical military reform and enforce civilian supremacy over the political sphere.

## Radical Reform and Military Factionalism

The replacement of several army generals who had risen to prominence under Suharto's rule aimed at the very break with the New Order military that Habibie had not achieved. Wahid had identified Wiranto as the biggest obstacle to further military reform and therefore decided to destroy the latter's patronage network spread throughout the TNI hierarchy. In this context, he asked his personal confidant Matori Abdul Djalil, the chairman of the NU-affiliated PKB (*Partai Kebangkitan Bangsa*, National Awakening Party), to come up with a list of reformist and anti-Wiranto military officers.[32] Topping the list was Agus Wirahadikusumah, one of the few military intellectuals in the final years of the old regime. In the conflict with Prabowo, Wirahadikusumah had sided with Wiranto, but he had since grown dissatisfied with the TNI chief's slow pace of internal reform. Moreover, he was bitter over Wiranto's decision to send him off to Sulawesi in November 1999 as regional commander there.[33] However, Wahid decided in January to bring Wirahadikusumah back to Jakarta. Believing that he "is exactly the right person to lead TNI", Wahid pledged to "make him army chief of staff soon, and then he can take over as TNI commander later on".[34] Smoothing the way for Wirahadikusumah, Wahid forced Wiranto to resign as coordinating minister for political and security affairs in February 2000. Shortly afterwards, in early March, he appointed Wirahadikusumah to head Kostrad, replacing close Wiranto associate Djadja Suparman. Simultaneously, several other reformist officers were rushed into crucial positions, among them Saurip Kadi as assistant for territorial affairs at army headquarters. Apparently, the president was about to take the same path as Taiwan's Lee Teng-hui who in the early 1990s had disposed of General Hau Pei-tsun, the country's military strongman, after long and difficult conflicts between the civilian executive and the leadership of the armed forces (Lo 2001, p. 156).

Beyond these major changes to TNI's leadership, the most important indication of Wahid's seriousness in pushing the reform of the armed forces forward was his encouragement of debates on the future of the territorial command structure. The command system, with its fund-raising capacities and opportunities of political intervention, was at the core of TNI's institutional interests, and had survived the post-authoritarian transition almost unchanged. Defence Minister Juwono Sudarsono (2000) estimated that "over seventy per cent of our defence spending are accrued from off-budget sources" at the national and local levels. Thus the vast majority of officers wanted to maintain the territorial concept and the benefits attached to it, with only a small number recommending its reform (Aribowo 2003, p. 117).[35] It was Agus Wirahadikusumah's trenchant criticism of the system — most eloquently presented at a parliamentary hearing in December 1999 — that had caught Wahid's attention and made him the president's choice to lead the military into a new phase of reforms. In Wirahadikusumah's view, the lower levels of the command structure were leftovers of the authoritarian past and therefore completely disposable:

> Why do we need a territorial unit in Wonosobo? Will the enemy attack us there? No, we have those units because lazy, inflexible officers have become complacent playing politics, making money, and retire on a nice civilian post out there. That has nothing to do with defence.[36]

The speed with which TNI headquarters adopted the reform rhetoric appeared to confirm Wahid's strategy of rapid and extensive change. In April 2000, a TNI leadership meeting endorsed Saurip Kadi's proposal for a pilot project aimed at the partial disbandment of the two lowest levels of the command system in selected urban areas. The project was designed as a starting point for a much larger effort, namely the gradual dismantling of the territorial structure from the *Korem* level downwards.[37] Wirahadikusumah had already begun in February to cooperate with several universities and think tanks on the development of such plans, and the official TNI endorsement seemed to clear the way for the most substantial reform of the armed forces since the late 1950s. Inspired by these developments, Wahid's biographer concluded that the president had "tamed" the military, calling it one of his "greatest successes" (Barton 2002, p. 384).

The unprecedented depth and scope of the reform effort triggered the most extensive fragmentation of the military elite since May 1998. The large circle of officers under Wiranto's patronage, which during the crisis had been united by its opposition to Prabowo and its interest in an orderly transition, had remained relatively solid during Habibie's interregnum. With the new government increasing its pressure on the armed forces to pursue structural change, however, the differences between the individual generals were brought into the open. The split was so severe that highly distinct and antagonistic factions emerged, each headed by former protégées of Wiranto. Wirahadikusumah led the faction of rapid reformers who, according to Bourchier and Hadiz (2003, p. 280), were "in favour of much more sweeping reforms than his commanding officers were prepared to countenance". Its goal was to accelerate the assimilation of military structures and norms to the conditions of the new democratic polity. To achieve this, Wirahadikusumah aimed to interact with politicians and state institutions, create a favourable public image in the media, and develop ties with civil society groups. "This is a new era", Wirahadikusumah explained, "in the past, an officer had to suck up to Suharto to get promoted and have influence, but now it is much more complicated."[38] As a result of the extensive changes since 1998, "the politicians must like you, the media must like you, only then you're a winner". Wirahadikusumah soon found himself labelled as a "multi-media officer", a term he took as a compliment rather than as an insult.

Chandra and Kammen (2002, p. 114) noted that the faction led by Wirahadikusumah consisted almost exclusively of members of the military academy class that graduated in 1973. Maintaining that the reformist attitude of the 1973 class was mostly due to its large size and its entanglement in an unsupportive promotion pattern, Chandra and Kammen offered a uniquely functionalist interpretation of military reform in Indonesia. In their view, the marginalized officers of 1973 simply used military reform as an instrument to break the monopolization of top positions by the 1970 and 1971 classes. However, this explanation is questionable for a number of reasons. First, the reformist thinking of Wirahadikusumah and some of his associates could be traced back at least to the 1980s, well before the reshuffle cycles of 2000 became apparent.[39] Second, many rapid reformers in the 1973 class, including Wirahadikusumah, were on track for promotions to senior positions when the split within the ranks occurred. Third, some prominent graduates of 1973 did not belong to the group of rapid reformers, such as Yudhoyono and Ryamizard, who both were members of different factions. Fourth, Chandra and Kammen's excessive emphasis on the technical aspects of promotion patterns ignores the political and personal attitudes of senior officers that reflect individual family backgrounds, educational paths, socio-economic conditions, and intellectual development. It appears that the latter combination of factors played a much larger role in determining conceptual positions than the inconclusive reference to reshuffle patterns.[40]

The second faction comprised reluctant reformers close to former TNI chief Wiranto. Sharing Wiranto's politically moderate, but institutionally conservative view on military reform, officers in this group believed that the changes introduced since 1998 had been sufficient, and that any further cuts to the military's privileges could threaten its functionality and mission. Under Wahid, the reluctant reformers felt marginalized by the removal of Wiranto from both the military leadership and cabinet. They were particularly unhappy with the ascension of the rapid reformers, whom they accused of sacrificing TNI's institutional interests to promote their own careers. Wirahadikusumah was passionately despised in these circles, both for his proposals for radical change in the armed forces and his "disrespectful" criticism of former superiors. It was thus not surprising that after Wiranto's dismissal, a declared opponent of Wirahadikusumah emerged as the informal leader of the reluctant reformers. Djadja Suparman had not only lost his Kostrad command to Wirahadikusumah, but was also the target of corruption charges initiated and publicized by his successor. Djadja felt that Wirahadikusumah had destroyed his reputation and career,[41] and many of the former's colleagues concurred that by leaking internal TNI material about Djadja to the press, Wirahadikusumah had expelled himself from the highly secretive community of military officers. It was this breach of the collectively accepted code of honour in the military that motivated many officers to join the ranks of the reluctant reformers and deny Wirahadikusumah their cooperation. Among the many senior officers in this faction, Endriartono Sutarto would soon become the most influential.

In accordance with their argument on the 1973 class, Chandra and Kammen (2002, p. 141) asserted that the opponents of further reform originated largely from the 1970 and 1971 classes, which had occupied the majority of command posts in the period leading up to Wahid's election. Their rejection of reform, Chandra and Kammen argued, was aimed at defending their positions and preventing the 1973 class from further rising through the ranks. Once more, this argument has several loopholes. Tyasno Sudarto, army chief of staff and a 1970 graduate, initially supported Wirahadikusumah's calls for reform in the hope that this support might improve his political standing. This shows that opposition to reform was not an inevitable choice for the 1970 and 1971 classes; in fact, there were certain political constellations under which backing reform could help their careers. On the other hand, some of the most vocal reform sceptics were graduates from the classes of 1972 and 1973, such as Djadja, Bibit Waluyo, and Ryamizard. Opposition to reform, therefore, appeared to have been rooted in much more specific circumstances than attachment to a particular class.

The resentment of Wirahadikusumah and his reform proposals aligned Djadja and his associates with the third faction in the armed forces, the gradual reformers. After Yudhoyono joined the cabinet, the most prominent officer in this group was Agus Widjojo, the new chief of staff of territorial affairs.[42] Widojo and Wirahadikusumah had been close associates in the 1980s and most of the 1990s, but their relationship had disintegrated with the latter's rapid ascent under Wahid. Widjojo believed that reform had to proceed at a faster pace than propagated by Wiranto but not as rapid and radical as that driven by Wirahadikusumah. In the short term, however, he viewed Wirahadikusumah's populism as a more immediate threat to the coherence and dignity of the armed forces: "Wirahadikusumah was like a politician; he looked at military reform from the perspective of his personal popularity, and was less interested in whether it promoted useful change."[43] Accordingly, Widjojo and his office refused to cooperate with the army's pilot project to disband segments of the territorial command structure, and began to develop counter-proposals instead.[44] Widjojo was not, however, "vehemently opposed to the liquidation" of territorial units, as some observers assumed (Sumarkidjo 2001, p. 143). His plan envisioned that territorial tasks previously carried out by the armed forces be handed over to provincial administrations within a time-frame of up to twenty years, accompanied by the gradual dismantling of the lower levels of the command structure (Mietzner 2003). This gradual approach, Widjojo argued, was designed to allow for institutional adjustments and to avoid uncertainty among military officers over possible consequences for their individual careers.

## The "Sudden Death" of Reform

The broad power base of the ruling coalition, the replacement of senior commanders affiliated with the old regime, and the launch of radical reform initiatives appeared to provide a solid foundation for the establishment of democratic control over the armed forces. Yet the reform drive began to stagnate only months after it had begun, and many of the initially planned projects never materialized. Agus Wirahadikusumah and his associates were removed from their positions by August 2000, the pilot project to disband parts of the territorial command system was abandoned, and opponents of further reform regained control over key posts in the armed forces. In the academic debate on the reasons for this abrupt termination of radical military reform, two divergent sets of propositions have been put forward. Damien Kingsbury (2003), on the one hand, argued that it was to a large extent the military that sabotaged Wahid's reform projects, working behind the scenes to orchestrate his downfall. Authors such as Jun Honna (2003, p. 184), on the other hand, focused more on the political blunders of the president that put him "in a position in which he was forced to make concessions to ensure the loyalty of the military, or at least to avert a show of defiance". In short, the controversy centred around the question of whether the failures of civilian governance caused the collapse of the military reform project, or whether the armed forces single-handedly engineered its abortion.

There is no doubt that the mainstream of the armed forces rejected the radical reform measures introduced in the early phase of Wahid's rule and that it used every opportunity to halt and overturn them. Kiki Syahnakri, then deputy army chief of staff, admitted that the military opposed Wahid's "tendency and attitude to break into technical military areas", which violated "mechanisms and strict procedures" (Syahnakri 2003). It was the president himself, however, who created the political context in which such opposition proved effective. In his study of the period, Malik Haramain (2004, p. 339) pointed to the "conflict between the president and parliament that provided TNI with the opportunity and self-confidence to show open opposition and insubordination to the president". From literally his first week in office, Wahid worked towards antagonizing the civilian support network that had facilitated his election. Falsely believing that Indonesia's presidential system granted him unlimited powers (McIntyre 2005, p. 225), he quickly fired ministers from Golkar, PDI-P, and PPP, the largest parties in parliament, and replaced them with personal loyalists. In addition, Wahid intervened in legal proceedings and the internal affairs of state enterprises, apparently in order to promote the political and economic interests of his major financial patrons. Moreover, the president appeared increasingly erratic, threatening to arrest his political adversaries and producing headlines with controversial statements and policies on an almost daily basis. Gradually excluded from power and disillusioned with the president's leadership, the parties that had promoted Wahid's election began to unite against him (Mietzner 2001, pp. 15–32). By mid-2000, the majority of the political elite had come to the conclusion that he had to go.

The erosion of Wahid's civilian support base removed one of the major preconditions for the successful implementation of radical military reform. The further the alienation between the president and key political parties and organizations progressed, the more conservative elements in the military elite felt encouraged to oppose additional reforms of the armed forces. In the lead-up to the annual session of the MPR in August 2000, during which Wahid had to account for his first ten months in office, the president was eventually forced to withdraw his support for Agus Wirahadikusumah and the reform ideas he represented. Wahid's concession was designed to secure political backing from the armed forces mainstream, compensating for his dramatic loss of support from civilian groups in and outside the legislature. In a major gesture of compromise directed at the generals, Wahid even agreed to delegate responsibility for internal TNI affairs to his deputy Megawati Sukarnoputri. Megawati was popular with conservative elements in the top brass, both for her nationalist credentials and her own growing frustration with Wahid. Using a rare chance to display her potential influence, she had joined forces with reform-sceptical officers in June and successfully pushed for the dismissal of Bondan Gunawan, Wahid's state secretary and a close civilian ally of Wirahadikusumah.[45] Shortly before the MPR session commenced, Wirahadikusumah himself was relieved of his Kostrad command and assigned to a desk job at TNI headquarters. Evidently, the opponents of further reform in the armed forces had successfully used the conflict between the presidency and the legislature to pursue their interests, and the initial rapid pace of military reform lost momentum as a result.

The political events surrounding the 2000 MPR session suggest that it was the president's loss of civilian support, rather than subversion by the armed forces, that caused the sudden stagnation in military reform. The overwhelming pressure on Wahid "to avoid antagonizing [military] hardliners if Indonesia's new democracy was to persist" (Case 2002, p. 73) was the logical consequence of his own actions. It is almost certain that sufficient levels of backing in the legislature would have allowed Wahid to isolate conservative officers effectively and continue with the rapid reform of TNI. Instead, he deliberately antagonized both friends and foes, leaving him vulnerable to the demands of officers trying to protect the privileges of the armed forces. Ironically, military reform had been one of the few policy initiatives that Wahid's civilian opponents supported, but they disagreed with him over almost everything else. As one senior parliamentarian put it, "Wahid's reform of the military is fine, we could all support him in that." But, he continued, "how can we allow him to monopolize political power, humiliate parliament, ridicule political parties, place his cronies in state enterprises, and talk nonsense almost every day?"[46] The armed forces, it appeared, were only in a position to oppose presidential authority when political circumstances allowed them to do so. Up until the months of February and March 2000, when the extent of Wahid's political decline was still unclear, the armed forces leadership felt institutionally obliged to comply with his instructions. By contrast, when the seriousness of the president's isolation from the political elite became fully tangible several months later, the military elite immediately grabbed the opportunity to launch highly effective attacks on his reform policies.

The dawning realization that his survival in the MPR depended on concessions to officers opposed to further military reform did little to convince Wahid that he had to rebuild his civilian support base. On the contrary, after the session was over, he apparently felt that his independence from the legislature and the political elite was greater than ever. In late August 2000, he reshuffled his cabinet once again without consulting Megawati, rushing in more personal loyalists and cutting his remaining ties to the political establishment. Among the dismissed cabinet members was Juwono Sudarsono, the minister of defence, who despite a mild stroke had effectively worked on enhancing civilian expertise and authority within his department. His poor health was cited as the official reason for his replacement, but the minister suspected a more politically motivated background:

> I think I fell out of grace because I insisted on a strictly institutional relationship with the president. I felt obliged to report issues related to my department and receive policy instructions if necessary. This relationship, however, became more and more blurred, with [Wahid] calling in ministers at any hour of the day to discuss political affairs, mostly related to his struggle with his opponents. I made it very clear that I did not view it as proper for me as the minister of defence to participate in after-office-hours discussions on matters not concerning my immediate authority.[47]

Juwono's replacement was Mahfud M.D., a professor of constitutional law. In a revealing indication of his political priorities, Wahid confessed that Mahfud had attracted his attention not by his expertise in defence matters, but by being one of the few legal observers who publicly supported the president's claim to political supremacy over parliament. In fact, Mahfud himself pointed out that he did not possess the necessary qualifications for the job, but had accepted the nomination only when Wahid insisted on it.[48] Mahfud's appointment signalled a significant shift in Wahid's policy towards the military — from trying to radically reform it at the beginning of his term to using it as a tool in his escalating conflict with the political elite.

Wahid's misperception that the MPR session and the cabinet reshuffle had consolidated his grip on power encouraged him to seek the reappointment of some of his loyalists to senior positions in the military. Dissatisfied with his lack of support in the officer corps, Wahid planned in October to dismiss the army chief of staff, General Tyasno Sudarto, and to replace him with Wirahadikusumah. In many ways, Tyasno's decline symbolized the rapidly disintegrating relationship between the president and the armed forces. Despite his conservatism, Tyasno had initially endorsed Wirahadikusumah's reform agenda because it enjoyed strong backing from the president and large sections of the political elite. After August 2000, however, Tyasno tried to dissociate himself from the rapid reformers and approach their opponents. His tactical shift not only attracted accusations of opportunism from fellow officers, but also highlighted the reality that presidential protection was no longer the main factor in the advancement of military careers.[49] Instead, it became crucial to gain the support of the majority of senior army officers, most of whom were members of the faction of reform sceptics. Consequently, Tyasno mobilized a large number of his colleagues to convene in Bandung in early October to oppose his planned replacement. The meeting decided to reject Wirahadikusumah's promotion and appeal to Megawati for support. Her disenchantment with the August cabinet reshuffle was sufficiently deep for her to confront the president on the issue, and she eventually succeeded in preventing Wirahadikusumah's appointment (Said 2001, p. 351). Tyasno, however, was unable to secure his own political survival. In his place, the armed forces leadership managed to have Endriartono Sutarto appointed as army chief of staff. Ultimately, Wahid's plan of reinstalling his personal associates in the military top brass had resulted in the army coming under the control of a staunch opponent of Wirahadikusumah and his reformist policies.

Isolated from the political elite and powerless to rein in the armed forces, Wahid resorted to increasingly irrational threats against his opponents. When parliament issued a memorandum in February 2001 to initiate a process aimed at his impeachment, the president threatened to "freeze" the legislature, declare a state of emergency, and use the security forces to execute his orders. Endriartono, however, indicated that the military would not carry out such instructions (Malley 2002, p. 132). Unintentionally, Wahid had provided the armed forces with the unique opportunity of proclaiming their successful self-transformation from Suharto's repressive instrument to a democratically aware and responsible defence force. TNI leaders maintained that their opposition to the emergency decrees provided evidence for their "consistency in implementing TNI's New Paradigm ..., its neutrality and non-involvement in practical and partisan politics and its refusal to be used as an instrument of power" (Markas Besar Tentara Nasional Indonesia 2001*b*, p. 57). Military opposition towards Wahid, previously widely described as defiance vis-à-vis civilian supremacy, now gained recognition as an act of protecting democratically legitimized institutions of the state. Wahid's associates were puzzled by the sudden change in public perceptions of the president, with his nephew and PKB secretary-general Muhaimin Iskandar wondering why "they had previously celebrated him as a radical military reformer, but now they say he's worse than Suharto, ..., authoritarian, a dictator, and so on; it's amazing".[50]

Like in previous periods of Indonesia's modern history, the high levels of political conflict among the civilian elite in 2000 and 2001 allowed the armed forces to depict themselves as an apolitical institution above partisan interests, a mediator between divided parties, and a defender of national (and now even democratic) interests. Most importantly, the public seemed to agree with TNI's self-assessment. Opinion polls showed that between September 2000 and October 2001 the percentage of respondents who had a favourable opinion of TNI rose from 28 to 58 per cent, while those who had an unfavourable view declined from 61 to 31 per cent (Simanungkalit 2002, p. 291). Beyond their rising popularity, the armed forces benefited from the intra-civilian chaos in several ways. To begin with, the military found its traditional sentiment against civilians and their alleged incompetence to govern confirmed. Moreover, Wahid's unreasonable demands to TNI made it possible for the generals to set a normative precedence for justified insubordination to a civilian president. Finally, only one year after Wahid's dramatic election, both the president and his opponents offered substantial concessions to the armed forces in order to convince TNI to take their side in the ongoing power struggle. Obviously, these facts were at odds with the proposition developed by Rabasa and Haseman (2002, p. xiv) that it was the military that was most disadvantaged by conflicts within the civilian elite.

For TNI, it appeared, intra-civilian fragmentation offered the possibility of gaining wide-ranging political benefits from all conflicting parties. In the words of one Australian observer, the military warmed up to the idea "that the longer the turmoil continues, the more Indonesians may come to see it as the last hope for stability" (Dibb 2001, p. 839).

## The Threat of Emergency Rule and Wahid's Fall

Wahid's attempt to use the security forces in his fight with the opposition not only damaged his reputation as a democratic reformer, but also catalyzed the impeachment proceedings against him. In May 2001, the DPR issued a second memorandum against the president. This move was part of the formal conditions for calling a special session of the MPR to decide on Wahid's impeachment should the latter not respond satisfactorily to parliament. Subsequently, the president stepped up his preparations for the declaration of a state of emergency and the dissolution of the legislature. With the military determined not to carry out such emergency regulations, however, Wahid turned to the police for support. In June, he tried to install the relatively unknown Chaeruddin Ismail as chief of police, replacing General Bimantoro, who was believed to be close to Megawati. But based on an MPR decree passed in 2000, the president had to seek the approval of parliament before appointing or dismissing a TNI commander or chief of police. In consequence, Wahid opted to only "suspend" Bimantoro and appoint Chaeruddin as deputy chief with full executive powers, a procedure not provided for by existing laws. Predictably, Bimantoro refused to leave office, and parliament continued to view him as the legitimate head of the police. With neither side showing any will to compromise, the constitutional conflict between the presidential office and parliament over the issue further aggravated political tensions.

At the height of the crisis, Wahid eventually threatened to bring thousands of fanatic supporters from his religious and political stronghold in East Java to Jakarta to defend him against the threat of impeachment. With this desperate step, the president managed to alienate his last ally: Megawati. On 18 July, she met with leading figures of the opposition and declared that a special session of the MPR was "unavoidable". According to one of her closest advisers, "Megawati had taken a lot from [Wahid], including the treachery in 1999, jokes on her private life, and many other humiliations; but when he led the country on a dangerous path of constitutional conflict, threats of mass violence, and abolition of democratic institutions, a line had been crossed."[51] Cornered by his usually restrained vice-president, Wahid named Chaeruddin as chief of police and asked his staff to draft a decree for the declaration of a state of emergency. Crucially, Chaeruddin's appointment was an open violation of existing constitutional requirements, and provided the DPR with the legal trigger to convene a special session of the MPR. The Assembly was opened on 21 July and immediately began hearing the impeachment charges. Within the political elite and the wider public, there was little doubt that the MPR would ultimately dismiss the president and authorize his deputy to serve out the remainder of his term.

The president's last chance for political survival rested with individual officers in the security forces potentially willing to carry out his orders.[52] Chaeruddin was one such officer, but he was effectively sidelined by Bimantoro and was never endorsed by the vast majority of the police top brass. On the military side, Wahid offered the post of deputy TNI commander to Johnny Lumintang, apparently trying to use the same mechanism with which he had aimed to impose Chaeruddin on the police. Wahid's manoeuvre caused considerable irritation in the TNI leadership, with Lumintang telling his superior officers that he was leaning towards accepting the offer. However, Endriartono argued that Wahid clearly intended to instrumentalize the military to confront the MPR, and it was finally decided that Widodo should convey TNI's official rejection of Lumintang's appointment on the grounds that the president himself had abolished the post of deputy commander before.[53] Wahid was furious when he was told of TNI's decision, aware that he had probably missed the last opportunity to secure military support for his planned declaration of emergency rule. Wahid's ultimate realization that the military could under no circumstances be convinced to back his move against the legislature became evident in a phone call to Endriartono on the day that the MPR impeachment proceedings began. Proudly announcing that one million of his supporters would encircle the MPR building and save him from dismissal, Wahid asked Endriartono not to interfere in the alleged popular uprising. If TNI tried to stop his followers, Wahid continued, Endriartono and other military leaders would be arrested.[54] The fact that Wahid apparently believed he could use NU mobs not only to dissolve the legislature, but also to arrest the military leadership, pointed eloquently to the extent of Wahid's isolation from political reality.

The NU crowds never made it to Jakarta, of course, and the impeachment session in the MPR was held without significant disturbances. In this situation, TNI decided to ensure that Wahid could leave office in dignity and with his personal safety guaranteed. Ryamizard Ryacudu, the commander of Kostrad, was therefore asked to place some of his troops in front of the palace and protect the president from protesters or other security threats. Wahid, however, misunderstood the gesture. He believed that Ryamizard had broken ranks with his fellow generals and was now prepared to side with him against the MPR. Consequently, Wahid associates immediately made the rounds to other senior military officers, trying to convince them that the political constellation was shifting in their favour. Muhaimin Iskandar, for example, even visited one of Wahid's most trenchant military critics, Djadja Suparman, and asked him to support his uncle.[55] However, it took Djadja only one phone call to Ryamizard to establish that the presence of his troops at the palace was not intended to strengthen Wahid's political position but to ensure the safety of the presidential compound. Ryamizard's clarification exposed the president's irreconcilable estrangement from the security forces that were formally under his command. By violating the constitution himself, Wahid had offered both the police and the armed forces strong arguments to defy his instructions and ignore his institutional authority. As Liddle (2003) put it, "the generals rejected Gus Dur's last-ditch attempt to save himself by staging a Sukarno-style coup against the MPR". On 23 July, the military and police faction in the MPR voted with most of the other parties to oust Wahid from office and appoint Megawati as his successor.

The fall of Wahid brought one of the most chaotic periods of Indonesia's post-authoritarian transition to an end. Launched with promises of radical political change, Wahid's presidency collapsed under massive conflicts within the elite and thus left highly mixed legacies for democratic consolidation and civil-military relations. On the one hand, the Wahid period witnessed some of the most innovative policy initiatives ever presented by an Indonesian executive, including offers of fresh negotiations with the separatist movements in Aceh and Papua and wide-ranging reform of the armed forces. On the other hand, the president regularly confronted his critics with authoritarian threats and saw nothing wrong with channelling state resources to his clientele. The ambivalence of Wahid's political character was visible even in the highly charged atmosphere of his final months in office: while he tried to utilize the armed forces against his opponents, small steps toward the institutional reform of the military continued. There were two main initiatives in this regard. First, the passing of two MPR decrees in 2000 that defined the task of the military as being exclusively focused on defence, while internal security was to be handled by the police. The same decrees also finalized the departure dates of TNI from parliament for 2004 and from the MPR for 2009 "at the latest".[56] Second, Wahid encouraged intensive civil society participation in the drafting of a new State Defence Bill, designed to replace the web of New Order laws that had legitimized the military's political role (Tim Propatria 2004). Such high levels of civil society engagement in deliberating defence legislation are typically found in post-authoritarian states that have already begun the second generation of civil-military reforms. That it was achieved in Wahid's Indonesia made his self-inflicted failure all the more tragic and regrettable.

## CONSERVATIVE REVIVAL: MEGAWATI AND HER GENERALS, 2001–04

The failed Wahid presidency underscored two major realities of civil-military relations in Indonesia's democratic transition: first, the political influence of the armed forces rose and fell proportionately to the level of conflict within the civilian elite. Backed by a large coalition of political parties, Wahid was able to launch an ambitious military reform programme at the beginning of his term. As this alliance fell apart, so did the prospect of substantially reforming the armed forces. Rizal Sukma and Edi Prasetyono (2002, p. 25) concluded that it was this "protracted tension and competition among civilian political forces and elites" that compromised the "bargaining position of the civilians" vis-à-vis TNI. A LIPI study on Wahid's rule concurred that "although there was a formal commitment to ending military engagement in politics, the requirements of real politics forced civilian politicians to be pragmatic and seek support from TNI ... to confront their political opponents" (Anwar 2002, p. 213). Second, the central role of the military in the struggle over Wahid's presidency revealed the limitations of the first generation of military reforms. The TNI elite was able to exert considerable political influence despite the ongoing institutional depoliticization of the armed forces, indicating that their powers rested more on their traditional security function than on the number of cabinet or parliamentary seats that they held. For the generals, this circumstance provided evidence that the shift from autocratic to democratic rule had not significantly undermined their ability to protect TNI's core interests, such as its internal autonomy and financial self-management. It appeared that in this period of the transition, neither incumbent governments nor oppositional groups could afford to alienate the armed forces, with both sides constantly approaching military leaders to recruit them for their cause. Whatever the outcome of political conflicts was, the armed forces were certain to profit from them.

## Megawati and Ideological Shifts in Society

Many observers of Indonesian military politics have discounted the legacy of the Wahid period when explaining the nature of civil-military relations under the presidency of Megawati Sukarnoputri. Instead, they have referred to Megawati's ideological disposition as the main factor behind the political consolidation of the armed forces after 2001. In their view, Megawati's political conservatism, her preoccupation with the territorial integrity of the state, and her indifference to intellectual discussions on human rights and individual freedoms made her a natural ally for conservative military officers. For example, Angus McIntyre (2005, p. 244) pointed to Megawati's "conservative populism", which "envisaged the armed forces presiding as guardian of her relationship with the people". Sidney Jones even referred to Megawati as a "sort of a mascot" of the armed forces.[57] Thus Megawati's ascension to power in July 2001 was seen as a watershed in civil-military relations, marking the return of the armed forces into the political arena and the end of military reforms. Despite Megawati's ideological and political affinity to the officer corps, however, her worldview alone is insufficient to explain the stagnation, and partial regression, in military reform efforts. This section will argue that it was mainly a combination of structural factors, both domestic and international, that changed the civil-military equation under Megawati's rule in favour of the armed forces. The origins of some of these factors lay in the political patterns of the pre-Megawati polity, while others reflected broader societal and even global change.

The first important factor behind the shifting civil-military relationship in the post-Wahid period were the concessions that Megawati granted to TNI in order to anticipate possible challenges to her rule. Deeply distrustful of the civilian alliance that had toppled Wahid and reluctantly handed her the presidency, Megawati viewed the military as an effective life insurance against a possible betrayal by parliament and the parties that dominated it. In extending more privileges to the armed forces, she continued and accelerated a trend started under the previous government. In order to arrest his rapid political decline, Wahid had begun to give concessions to the military since mid-2000, terminating the reform of the territorial command structure, removing controversial officers, ending the negotiations with separatists in Aceh and Papua, and ordering security crackdowns in both provinces.[58] Determined to keep the armed forces on her side, Megawati expanded these concessions to include greater institutional autonomy and increased influence on security affairs. Consequently, she approved a wide-ranging reshuffle of the armed forces leadership in 2002 that firmly installed opponents of further military reform in the TNI elite. Endriartono Sutarto, who was intellectually open-minded but also a fierce defender of the military's vested interests, reclaimed the TNI commandership for the army after a three-year interregnum by the navy. In addition, Megawati supported the promotion of Ryamizard Ryacudu to the position of army chief of staff. Ryamizard was known for his conservative ideological views and his stern rejection of the concept of civilian supremacy, making him politically controversial but popular with the army mainstream.

Besides appointing reform sceptics to key military positions, Megawati also reduced the authority of the department of defence as the executive's primary institution for controlling the armed forces. After the independent academics Juwono and Mahfud had confronted the officer corps on a variety of issues, Megawati deliberately selected a military-friendly and politically vulnerable party politician as minister of defence. Ignoring warnings from some of her advisers, she chose Matori Abdul Djalil, who had just lost the chairmanship of PKB over his involvement in Wahid's impeachment and was therefore without any significant political support base. Deprived of his patronage network and lacking knowledge of the conceptual and technical aspects of military affairs, Matori sought to compensate for his deficiencies by driving a course of accommodation towards the military elite.[59] Furthermore, Matori suffered a stroke in August 2003 after two ineffective years as minister, and Megawati did not fill the position again before the expiry of her term in October 2004. Not surprisingly, the military expressed satisfaction with the fact that it had no civilian oversight body to report to for an extended period of time, reminding it of the convenient arrangement under the previous regime when the TNI commander often had simultaneously held the position of minister of defence. The prolonged vacancy in the department of defence highlighted Megawati's disengagement from details of military management, which left the armed forces largely in control of their internal affairs throughout her rule.

Megawati's concessions to the armed forces coincided with significant shifts in the politico-ideological disposition of the civilian elite from the second half of 2001 onwards. Impatient with continued communal conflicts in Eastern Indonesia and the expanding influence of separatist movements in Aceh and Papua, many Jakarta-based politicians adopted an increasingly nationalist and security-focused rhetoric that exhibited remarkable similarities to that promoted by the New Order (Chauvel and Bhakti 2004, p. 52). Key party leaders viewed the "soft" approach of the Habibie and Wahid governments toward separatist groups as a massive blunder, and were eager to address the problems militarily. They also believed that the ongoing carnage in Ambon and Poso could only be ended by swift and harsh interventions by the security forces. This renewed prioritization of territorial integrity and repressive methods of conflict resolution favoured the armed forces in many ways. Most importantly, it restored the military's claim to a domestic security role and returned the armed forces to the centre of policy-making in areas affected by separatist movements and communal conflict (Crouch 2003, p. 20). In Maluku, the military assumed overall responsibility for security operations from the police in May 2002, after a joint command between the two forces had been unable to stop the religious violence that was devastating the province since 1999. While unsuccessfully demanding the declaration of martial law in Maluku and other conflict-prone areas, the military clearly reaffirmed its role in domestic security, which had been thrown into doubt by the MPR decrees of 2000. Even foreign observers now agreed with the rationale that "nationwide domestic disorder raise[s] the question of whether there is an appropriate domestic security role for TNI" (Weatherbee 2002, p. 28).

The change in civilian elite attitudes also supported TNI's efforts to promote the concept of "NKRI" (*Negara Kesatuan Republik Indonesia*, Unitary State of the Republic of Indonesia) as the new foundation of its doctrinal thinking. Before 1998, the protection of both the 1945 constitution and the state ideology Pancasila had formed major components of the military's doctrine, justifying its deep penetration of political institutions and society. After Suharto's fall, however, the armed forces had proven unable to shield the constitution from a series of amendments, and Pancasila had been largely discredited by decades of New Order propaganda. Against this background, the uncompromising defence of "NKRI" emerged as the core element of TNI's newly defined mission in the post-Suharto state. Amidst separatist threats and religio-ethnic conflicts, the goal of defending the territorial integrity of the unitary republic did not only appeal to conservative officers, but quickly attracted interest and support from the wider public. In consequence, what had started as an internal military discourse spread rapidly into the civilian realm, with party politicians, government officials, the media, and even civil society organizations integrating the term "NKRI" into their daily vocabulary. The introduction of "NKRI" as a dominant political theme of the democratic polity was probably the military's most successful public relations campaign after 1998. It enabled TNI to defend its continued claim on a prominent role in the governance of Indonesia, and allowed it to portray calls for further military reform as posing a risk to the maintenance of the unitary state.

Indeed, the effectiveness of the "NKRI" rhetoric eventually mixed with a general sense of reform fatigue to convince political decision-makers that they had to slow down or even halt ongoing processes of military reform. Fearing that further experiments with TNI reform could reduce the ability of the armed forces to crack down on separatist rebels, the majority of politicians agreed to suspend their reform efforts until the security situation had stabilized. As explained by one member of the DPR's commission I, which oversees defence and security affairs, "it is now not the time to play around with military reform — now is the time to support our military in their fight against separatists, in their fight to safeguard the territorial integrity of Indonesia."[60] Usually one of the more reformist members of the commission, he continued that "I'm sure we will be able to resume the reform effort in the future." In fact, the majority of the civilian elite appeared even more inclined to resort to traditional military paradigms of violent conflict resolution than Megawati. Throughout 2002 and early 2003, Megawati allowed her coordinating minister for political and security affairs, Susilo Bambang Yudhoyono, to seek a peaceful settlement of the Aceh problem through negotiations mediated by the Geneva-based Henry Dunant Centre (Huber 2004). The initiative resulted in a cessation of hostilities agreement in December 2002, but most political parties and the armed forces remained reluctant to endorse it. The military was widely suspected of sabotaging the peace deal by engineering attacks on monitors of the cease-fire, and in May 2003 the agreement collapsed. Unanimously supported by parliament and the vast majority of the public, Megawati declared martial law and launched one of the largest military campaigns in Indonesian history.

The military operation in Aceh provided important insights into the state of civil-military relations in Indonesia five years after Suharto's fall. The civilian government left the strategic and operational aspects of the campaign largely to the armed forces, and with no minister of defence in place since August 2003, executive oversight of the operations was particularly scant. Parliament limited its control function to infrequent meetings with the top generals, mostly expressing gratitude for the military's service in the war zone. Returning from a visit to Aceh, one of the deputy speakers of parliament, Sutardjo Surjoguritno, expressed his conviction that the military was doing a good job there because he had seen "more red and white flags in Aceh now than before the campaign".[61] Therefore, parliament injudiciously approved most of the financial requests made by the armed forces, attracting sharp criticism from officials in the Supreme Auditing Board. According to one auditor, "we told the DPR that TNI's reports are incomplete and questionable, but … parliament continued to grant new funds nevertheless".[62] Societal oversight of the operations was equally weak, with only a few critical non-governmental organizations interested in monitoring events and media coverage largely restricted to quoting official military sources. It was thus impossible for civilian control authorities and the public to verify military data related to the campaign, including the number and classification of victims.[63] In Aceh, the military established an emergency administration, filling vacant civilian posts in local government with army officers imported from TNI's vast territorial network. Accusing Aceh's civilian leaders of incompetence and corruption, TNI used martial law as a welcome opportunity to illustrate its alleged superiority over self-interested and unreliable politicians. In short, the operations in Aceh exposed the failure of the institutional control framework set up during the first generation of military reforms, and revealed how distant Indonesia still was from creating workable systems of democratic control.

## TNI and the War on Terror

Megawati's concessions to the armed forces and the renaissance of militaristic paradigms of conflict resolution were two important factors in TNI's political consolidation in the post-Wahid polity. An equally crucial element, however, were the fundamental changes in the international and domestic security environment after 11 September 2001. Since the 1990s, Indonesia's armed forces had been isolated by the United States and most of its Western allies for failure to address serious human rights violations committed by TNI officers, particularly in East Timor. Congress had prohibited the U.S. government from establishing full military-to-military ties with Indonesia, requiring TNI to meet certain reform benchmarks beforehand. The prospect of international rehabilitation and renewed access to modern military equipment had since then formed a secondary, but significant, incentive for the armed forces to pursue internal reforms. Prior to 11 September 2001, senior officers had asked the U.S. embassy in Jakarta to issue a statement that would acknowledge the success of military reform steps implemented so far, hoping that this might help lift the restrictions.[64] Their request had been turned down, but the terrorist attacks on New York and Washington changed the strategic priorities of the United States completely. Its focus was now on the creation of a global network of effective counter-terrorism forces to gather intelligence and carry out arrests, replacing what Catharin Dalpino (2002, p. 93) called the "free-floating post-Cold War idealism" behind "American support for Indonesia's democratization process". It was this new interest in establishing counter-terrorism cooperation with Indonesia's military, rather than a genuine interest in its structural reform, that provided "the main impetus to find a way to partially restore military-to-military ties" (Smith 2003, p. 3). International pressure to reform, an essential element of civil-military transitions according to Cottey, Edmunds, and Forster, was fading.

The Indonesian armed forces quickly grasped that the political fallout from the global war on terror carried, in Donald Emmerson's words (2002, p. 122), "more opportunity than danger". Senior officers instinctively understood that the United States and its allies needed strategic partners in their fight against terrorist networks, and that this new geopolitical constellation was likely to end TNI's international isolation. A senior official at the defence department admitted that "after East Timor we faced difficulties with our international reputation, and especially the U.S. was reluctant to engage with us, but ... the common interest of confronting the threat of terror creates completely new opportunities of cooperation, and makes the U.S. realize that TNI can be an important partner in this effort."[65] TNI's expectations were not disappointed. Soon after the 2001 events, the Bush administration called on Congress to review its sanctions on TNI, claiming that the Indonesian military had achieved satisfactory levels of success in its reform process.[66] Accordingly, the restrictions on military-to-military relations with Indonesia were gradually reduced and eventually lifted in 2005, citing the "national security interests" of the United States. This was all the more remarkable since the concrete contribution of TNI to the American anti-terror operations in Southeast Asia was minimal. Unlike in the Philippines, where the armed forces helped close terrorist training camps run by Islamist militants in Mindanao, the bulk of the anti-terror work in Indonesia was carried out by the police. While the military prepared for a possible aircraft hijacking or an attack on the trade ways in the Malacca Strait, no such terrorist incident had occurred by 2008. Apparently, the Indonesian armed forces profited politically from the counter-terrorism campaign without being involved in it.

The decline in international reform pressure on TNI as a result of the new terrorist threat was soon followed by similar trends in the domestic arena. The Bali bombings in October 2002, which killed more than 200 people and delivered negative headlines for Indonesia around the world, lifted the war against terror from an issue of largely diplomatic significance to an urgent political priority for Megawati's government. The Indonesian authorities reacted with a major crackdown on terrorist networks in the country, passed new anti-terrorism laws, and supported harsh and at times extra-judicial measures against suspects.[67] Again, the armed forces soon tried to profit from the new situation. Army Chief of Staff Ryamizard Ryacudu suggested that in response to the terrorist crisis, the government should "revive" and expand the intelligence-gathering capabilities of the territorial commands.[68] However, like in their negotiations with the United States, the armed forces reaped benefits from the counter-terrorism campaign without becoming engaged in its day-to-day operations. The responsibility for investigating terrorist crimes and arresting suspects remained in the hands of the police, with the military only serving as a standby force for possible larger attacks. But while it did not gain additional authority or resources, the military obtained politically important advantages. Crucially, the rise of terrorism as a serious internal security threat provided fresh ammunition to the generals in their effort to protect the territorial command structure from demands for reform. Adding to the public fear of separatism, communal violence, and national disintegration, the issue of terrorism was certain to serve as a new and effective disincentive against dismantling TNI's power base in the regions.

## General Election or Election of Generals?

The increased strategic value of the armed forces, boosted by their mediation in intra-civilian conflict and the emergence of new security threats, translated into direct political gains for the officer corps. Most importantly, the armed forces were now in a position to dispense with much of the reformist rhetoric it had reluctantly adopted since 1998. Using this welcome situation to further consolidate their power, the reform sceptics in the ranks moved quickly to marginalize the group of gradual reformers under Agus Widjojo. The chief of staff of territorial affairs had drawn criticism from his conservative colleagues by authoring a detailed policy paper on his ideas of reforming the territorial command structure (Markas Besar Republik Indonesia 2001a and 2001c).[69] Circulating widely in September 2001, the paper had led to open protest by those officers who were fiercely opposed to any changes to the territorial system. Consequently, Widjojo's office was disbanded in November 2001, and he was shifted to the less significant post of deputy chair of the MPR.[70] His removal marked the end of the internal military discourse on revamping the territorial command system and left the armed forces without influential proponents of reform. In addition to the rising self-confidence of TNI leaders to reject further military reform, the consolidation of the armed forces was also reflected in their increased popularity both within the civilian elite and among the wider public. Opinion polls showed that many Indonesians now favoured a president with a military background, reversing the trend of the early post-authoritarian period that had pointed to deep suspicions against officers in top political posts.[71] In practice, the improved image of the armed forces enhanced their bargaining position in the two most disputed political arenas of the Megawati polity: the struggle for executive positions in the regions and the preparations for the 2004 elections.

The election of new governors throughout Indonesia in 2002 and 2003 exposed the success of the armed forces in preserving their political powers despite a series of institutional reforms aimed at their depoliticization. In 1999, new bills on regional parliaments had been passed, allowing the legislatures to elect governors, mayors, and regents without interference by the central government. This was widely expected to discontinue the traditional grip of the armed forces on key governorships in Java and other crucial provinces. Writing before the elections took place, Michael Malley (2003, p. 111) noted that "the full impact of decentralisation is likely to be realised over the course of 2003 as the terms of governors appointed during the waning days of the Soeharto regime finally expire". The conflict between political parties over these positions was so intense, however, that many of them decided to back the incumbent or nominate other retired military officers to replace them. For instance, the retired three-star general Sutiyoso was re-elected as governor of Jakarta in 2002, nominated by PDI-P. Lieutenant General (ret.) Mardiyanto, governor of Central Java, won a second term in 2003, defeating another retired military officer backed by PAN. Lieutenant General (ret.) Imam Utomo of East Java also secured his re-election in 2003, beating a former general supported by PKB patron Abdurrahman Wahid.[72] In West Java, the governorship went to a leading figure of FKPPI (*Forum Komunikasi Putra-Putri Purnawirawan Indonesia*, Communication Forum of Sons and Daughters of Indonesian Veterans), while the former regional commander of Maluku was elected as new governor of the conflict-ridden province. Moreover, the brother of General Ryamizard Ryacudu became vice-governor of Lampung, and retired generals defended their governorships in East Kalimantan and North Sumatra. Explaining this phenomenon, Crouch (2003*a*) argued that political elites calculated that "it is better to re-endorse a military officer … than to risk the election of governors from rival parties".[73]

The prominence of retired officers in regional elections was replicated in the preparations for the national polls of 2004. Several former generals launched presidential candidacies, demonstrating once again how the armed forces as an institution as well as their individual members were able to offset the impact of structural reform by adjusting rapidly to the new democratic conditions. In August 2002, the MPR had passed the last of a series of constitutional amendments, which introduced direct presidential elections and removed the armed forces from the MPR. Initially, TNI headquarters had been opposed to both the military's departure from the MPR and the abolition of the latter's authority to elect the president, citing fears that a popular vote could lead to severe societal tensions. In reality, however, the armed forces were more concerned about preserving an electoral mechanism that in the past had allowed them to participate in backroom deals and exert influence on the composition of the national leadership. In the proposed direct elections, by contrast, the military was disadvantaged by its numerical insignificance, with its approximately 350,000 active members constituting only 0.7 per cent of the electorate. Thus there was widespread anxiety in the officer corps that the direct ballot could render the armed forces politically redundant, with serious consequences for their standing vis-à-vis the civilian elite.

It quickly became clear, however, that the new electoral mechanism did not necessarily undermine the political strength of the armed forces and their personnel. As candidates began to declare their intention to run for the presidency, it emerged that retired officers were among the most prospective contenders. To begin with, Susilo Bambang Yudhoyono supported the foundation of the Democratic Party in September 2002, which was widely seen as the unofficial launch of his presidential campaign. Wiranto and Prabowo competed for the nomination of the Golkar party, while Amien Rais approached several officers to become his vice-presidential candidate, among them Endriartono.[74] Hamzah Haz, chairman of PPP, recruited Agum Gumelar as his running mate. While retired military officers largely pursued their individual ambitions and thus did not directly represent the institutional interests of the armed forces, they were unlikely to substantially hurt the organization that had propelled them into national prominence. As one Indonesian commentator put it, "it has always been debated whether a retired military or police officer is considered a civilian or military man" (Razak 2004). But, he concluded, "it is difficult to believe that a retired military or police officer has no emotional links or organizational loyalty to their previous institutions". In addition, the courting of active military leaders by civilian politicians suggested that any elected president, whether former military or civilian, would seek the support of the armed forces and protect their fundamental interests in return.

The campaign for the presidential elections underscored that societal resentment of military engagement in politics — a pronounced feature of the early phase of the transition — had declined significantly since 1998. While student groups and critical civil society organizations staged occasional demonstrations against retired military officers participating in the elections, their protest no longer reflected general trends and sentiments in the larger population. Yudhoyono — who in 2001 had concluded that "Indonesians are not ready yet for a former general to become their leader" — established himself as the front-runner in the presidential race (Pereira 2004). His calm demeanour, charismatic appearance, and impeccable military credentials offered much needed reassurance to the Indonesian public, which after years of tumultuous reforms craved for political and economic stability. However, while his professional background helped him to evoke the image of a tough and decisive leader, his "softer" side was equally appealing to the electorate.

Known as a military reformer, Yudhoyono managed to convince voters that supporting a retired general did not necessarily mean endorsing a return to the repressive New Order period. Most importantly, this distinguished him from Wiranto, who had secured Golkar's nomination after beating its chairman Akbar Tandjung in a tightly contested party convention. Wiranto had been too close to Suharto to escape accusations that the former autocrat backed his campaign, and while he had played a largely constructive role in the 1998 regime change, his reformist credentials were much weaker than Yudhoyono's. In the competition between the two generals, Wiranto consequently never stood a realistic chance.

Riding on a wave of unprecedented popularity, Yudhoyono edged out Wiranto, Amien Rais, and Hamzah in the first round of elections in July 2004 and set up a showdown with Megawati in September. Megawati, trailing Yudhoyono by an average of thirty percentage points in opinion surveys, tried to tap into a largely eroded anti-military sentiment by allowing her campaign team to refer to her opponent as "General Yudhoyono".[75] Presented by her supporters as the candidate of civilian supremacy fighting against a possible resurgence in military power, Megawati appeared at odds not only with her previous image as a "mascot" of the armed forces, but also with the indifference of most voters toward the civilian-military dichotomy. Evidently, her declining electoral strength had other causes than her stance on military politics. Megawati had simply lost much of the trust that voters had put in her in 1999, having established a reputation for being aloof, inactive, intellectually and technically incapable, and out of touch with the concerns of a socially and economically troubled populace. The issue of civilian control of the armed forces was of negligible importance for most Indonesians who sought a change in government to improve the basic conditions of their daily lives. In consequence, Yudhoyono trounced Megawati in the second round of the elections with a margin of 60.9 to 39.1 per cent. His victory, while highlighting the successful adaptation of military leaders to the post-Suharto polity, also marked the end of Indonesia's transition. After six years of political experiments and institutional disorder, the country entered the stage of democratic consolidation — and with that, a completely new phase of its civil-military relations.

## YUDHOYONO AND POST-SUHARTO MILITARY POLITICS: A CASE STUDY

Susilo Bambang Yudhoyono's military and political career under three post-Suharto governments and his ultimate rise to the presidency reflect structural developments in Indonesian military politics since the fall of the New Order. They mirror the gradual adaptation of the armed forces to the early post-authoritarian polity, stretching from the disorientation of the officer corps in 1998 to the successful participation of retired generals in the presidential elections of 2004. A short analysis of Yudhoyono's career after 1998 can therefore help to illustrate the major arguments outlined in this chapter so far.

In the late New Order, Yudhoyono had skilfully managed to build a reformist image among his fellow officers and the political elite without drawing Suharto's anger. Despite his general loyalty to the regime, Yudhoyono had feared serious consequences for the armed forces if Suharto continued to deny political reforms or extended his stay in office indefinitely. Thus during the political crisis of 1998, Yudhoyono played a significant role in convincing other generals that clinging to Suharto would ruin the military's reputation, and he subsequently negotiated with civilian leaders over the terms for the president's resignation. Yudhoyono's reformist attitude in the final months of the New Order could not hide the fact, however, that he too was ill-prepared for the almost complete liberalization of the political system introduced by the Habibie government. Sharing many of the military's traditional sentiments against democratic practices and rules, he recommended in June 1998 that the government limit the number of political parties and strictly control their religio-ideological orientations. His suggestions were ignored by Habibie, however, leading to considerable confusion in the officer corps and increased pressure on the armed forces to assimilate more quickly to the conditions of the democratic polity. Eying the position of army chief of staff, Yudhoyono eventually began to build relationships with key figures in the government as well as with leaders of larger parties participating in the 1999 elections. For example, he cultivated special ties with Adi Sasono, who as minister of cooperatives and small enterprises ran a multi-million dollar credit scheme widely viewed as an effort to either support Habibie's re-election or his own rise to power.[76] Adi Sasono, however, fell out with Habibie shortly before the parliamentary elections and was therefore lost to Yudhoyono as a potential civilian ally in the government.

The circumstances of Yudhoyono's appointment to the first Wahid cabinet in October 1999 exposed the uncertainties and inconsistencies of TNI's transitional process. Yudhoyono initially rejected the post of minister of energy and mining and expressed his preference to remain in active military service. Only after Wahid insisted did Yudhoyono accept his nomination. With societal resentment of military officers in political positions still high, Yudhoyono's chances of succeeding in civilian-dominated democratic politics were indeed rather unpredictable. In contrast, the continuation of his military service would have almost certainly led him to the top post in the army and subsequently the armed forces. Yudhoyono has often spoken in bitterness about his aborted military career, and his actions after the appointment to cabinet provide evidence for his inner confusion. Although he himself had drafted the regulation that required military officers to retire when taking up civilian posts, Yudhoyono now postponed his own retirement for almost a year. Instinctively sensing the instability of the Wahid government, Yudhoyono apparently tried to keep the door open for a possible return to active service. He also resisted Wahid's courtship to become a leading figure in his party, PKB.[77] It was only in August 2000 that Yudhoyono began to warm up to the idea of a political career without finishing the military path he felt destined for. The political climate was changing in favour of military figures in civilian posts, and Wahid offered him a ministry in which he gained nominal supervision of Indonesia's security forces. Yudhoyono's appointment as coordinating minister for political, social, and security affairs marked his irrevocable entry into civilian elite politics, including the risks and complications associated with it.

In his new post, Yudhoyono was immediately drawn into the elite negotiations surrounding the conflict between Wahid and the legislature. Like the armed forces as an institution, Yudhoyono went through an extraordinarily stressful period of political turmoil but finally managed to emerge as one of its beneficiaries. The chaos of the Wahid presidency eroded the credibility of civilian politics, giving rise to a widespread sense that military officers may be needed to restore a minimal level of constitutional order. Wahid's dismissal of Yudhoyono in June 2001 only helped to cement this impression of failed civilian leadership, allowing the former general to portray himself as a victim of degenerate elite politics.[78] Subsequently, Yudhoyono's treatment by the political establishment not only boosted his poll ratings, but it also delivered a welcome theme for his further political career. The critique of elite-oriented and unaccountable party leaders developed into Yudhoyono's leitmotif as he planned his political future. Critically, it also helped him to explain and digest his unsuccessful candidacy for the vacant position of vice-president after Megawati's ascent to power in July 2001. Contemplating the reasons for his defeat in the first round of that election, he told his biographer that "the political process in the MPR sometimes does not mirror the reality outside of the MPR building" (Hisyam 2004, p. 451). Yudhoyono believed that he "was favoured by a number of polls [but] could not win the competition in the building of the people's representatives [because of] the games in the assembly". Concluding that "party leaders still determine the voice of the party", Yudhoyono bitterly complained that this is "not an ideal democracy".

Yudhoyono's dislike for elite politicians was reciprocal, however. Many of the party officials he had dealings with during his years as minister found him excessively cautious, politically vague, and unable to make concrete commitments. Not surprisingly, they too connected their negative image of him with his unsuccessful run for the vice-presidency in 2001. At the time, Yudhoyono was interested in being nominated, but he lacked sufficient support in the MPR. Accordingly, he approached a number of splinter parties, both nationalist and Islamic, and asked that his name be put forward. According to one party leader involved in the negotiations with Yudhoyono, the would-be candidate "openly stated that he actually was not interested in becoming vice-president, but only planned to use the publicity created by his nomination to regain his cabinet post".[79] In order to allow civilians to establish their hold on power, Yudhoyono even pledged that he would not seek the presidency "in the next three or four elections". Based on this promise, the party leaders "agreed to nominate Yudhoyono, and some of us even spoke to Megawati to get him back into the government — but only weeks later he broke his word and began to prepare his candidacy for president".[80] However, some of the politicians he invited to discuss his possible presidential run in 2004 were as irritated with Yudhoyono as those who nominated him in 2001. Aware that he needed his own political party to obtain a ticket for the presidential race, Yudhoyono encouraged his civilian allies to establish both the PPDK (*Partai Persatuan Demokrasi Kebangsaan*, United Party of National Democracy) in July 2002 and the Partai Demokrat (Democratic Party) in September of the same year. But despite being behind their creation, he initially refused to put any resources into either party, and was unwilling to be publicly associated with them.[81] More importantly, in mid-2003 Yudhoyono told officials of the two parties that he had doubts whether he should run for president at all, infuriating PPDK leader Ryaas Rasyid to such an extent that he broke off his political relationship with the unreliable contender.[82]

Yudhoyono's frequent conflicts with party officials pointed to the ongoing dilemma of his engagement in competitive elite politics. On the one hand, Yudhoyono needed to interact with the political class to build support networks for the upcoming campaign and tap into the resources attached to public office. Accordingly, after his reappointment to cabinet by Megawati in July 2001, he used his position to establish himself as a key figure in day-to-day government, intra-elite negotiations, and media-based policy discourses. In addition, he felt it necessary to cultivate Partai Demokrat as his potential electoral vehicle, despite his reluctance to help with its institutional development. However, his dependence on the instruments and rules of elite politics created an obvious problem for Yudhoyono: it stood in open contradiction to his plan to run his 2004 campaign on an anti-establishment platform, which emphasized that the entrenched political elites were incapable of overcoming Indonesia's problems. Ironically, it was Megawati who assisted Yudhoyono in solving this dilemma between having to attack elite politics and simultaneously enjoying the spoils it had to offer. Fearing that her minister would continue to use his office for the promotion of his candidacy, Megawati began to isolate Yudhoyono from government business. This, in turn, gave him the opportunity to stage a publicity-rich resignation from cabinet in February 2004. His dramatic resignation helped to create the public perception that Yudhoyono had once again fallen victim to brutal elite politicking, conveniently distracting from the fact that he was an integral part of this very elite. Ultimately, Megawati's move allowed Yudhoyono to present his elite-critical campaign slogans without accusations of hypocrisy and contributed to the unexpectedly good result of the Democratic Party at the parliamentary polls in April.[83]

The success of the party that he had helped to establish significantly increased Yudhoyono's self-confidence. With 7.5 per cent of the votes, Partai Demokrat had gone beyond the threshold required to file a presidential nomination, making negotiations with other parties unnecessary. Yudhoyono's awareness of his improved political standing was reflected first and foremost in the selection of his advisory team: he included a large number of retired military officers whom he trusted completely and who had developed an intimate understanding of his political thinking in years of joint service. After his landslide victory over Megawati in September, Yudhoyono appointed several of them to important government posts. Together, they had lived through the ups and downs of the military's transition from a pillar of authoritarian rule to a mediator and participant in democratic politics. Like Yudhoyono, these former generals had faced high levels of personal and professional uncertainty in the aftermath of Suharto's fall, had struggled to get accustomed to the new democracy, and had eventually found ways to pursue successful careers in a post-authoritarian environment. The problems of the political transition, with intense intra-civilian conflicts and overall political instability, had worked in their favour, allowing them to use widespread disappointment with party politics to gain power in a democratic fashion. However, Yudhoyono's election not only completed a messy transition, it also coincided with a number of structural reforms that would lead to a remarkable stabilization of Indonesia's political institutions and procedures after 2004. This political stabilization, in turn, was certain to make it much more difficult for the armed forces or their retired officers to use the dynamics of democratic politics to their advantage.

## CIVILIAN CONFLICT AND MILITARY REFORM

The period between Suharto's fall in 1998 and Yudhoyono's inauguration in 2004 witnessed highly fluctuating civil-military relations, with mixed results in terms of bringing the TNI under democratic control. There is no doubt that the armed forces lost some of their institutional privileges and became the target of intense public criticism, with civilian control authorities gaining powers they had not held since the 1950s. At the same time, however, the military managed to maintain enough of its political weight to shield itself from legal investigations into past abuses and prevent radical cuts into its territorial power base. It is this ambiguity that caused observers to express very divergent views on the state of civil-military relations in Indonesia, with many analysts exclusively focusing on either the reduction of military influence *or* the areas in which the armed forces have successfully defended their interests. Given the stagnation of military reform under Megawati's presidency, the majority of political commentators in 2003 and 2004 were in fact inclined to highlight the military's continued powers rather than its significant loss of control over the state and society.

There are several factors that account for the ambivalent development of Indonesia's civil-military relations in the early post-Suharto polity between 1998 and 2004. Most importantly, the balance between conservative and reformist features in Indonesian military politics was to a large extent the result of the pacted regime change in 1998. Ending thirty years of autocratic rule but avoiding the complete collapse of the regime, the intra-systemic transfer of power from Suharto to Habibie prefigured the hybrid pattern of the relationship between soldiers and the state in the early years of the post-authoritarian system. On the one hand, the conservative characteristics of Habibie's ascension to power were visible in the political survival of many New Order elites, including that of the military leadership. Unlike countries that embark on post-authoritarian transitions by replacing their military elite, Indonesia left Suharto loyalists in charge of the armed forces and their internal reforms. This allowed the military to successfully defend the territorial command structure against public demands for its reform and preserve significant political privileges. However, the reformist features of the 1998 regime change were as prevalent in the post-Suharto civil-military relationship as the conservative elements. The end of Suharto's sultanistic rule led to the gradual reduction of the military's role in formal politics and exposed the officer corps to unprecedented scrutiny by parliament, political parties, civil society, and the media. In short, this chapter has further consolidated one of the key hypotheses of this book, namely the assumption of a causal connection between the mode of regime change and the evolution of post-authoritarian military politics.

The intra-systemic nature of the 1998 regime change was not the only factor that shaped Indonesia's civil-military relations in the early post-Suharto years, however. The discussion above has pointed to a number of equally critical reasons for the mixed results of military reform efforts during the political transition. To begin with, the high levels of intra-civilian conflict between 1998 and 2004 allowed the armed forces to repair their image, request concessions from incumbent governments, and protect their institutional interests from further reform. During the 1999 elections, leading civilian contenders lobbied the military for its support, resulting in the inclusion of several officers in the first democratically elected government since 1955. Even more importantly, the constitutional crisis of 2001 caused a dramatic upsurge in the societal reputation of the military, and encouraged retired generals to engage more actively in politics. Arguably, the deep cleavages between civilian politicians and their consequent inability to agree on a common platform of military reform carried much of the responsibility for the ineffectiveness of democratic oversight of the armed forces in the early post-authoritarian period. With institutional mechanisms for political conflict resolution still in the making, most civilians turned to the military to decide the outcome of policy disputes and power struggles. During this vulnerable phase of its transition, Indonesia desperately lacked credible institutions that could assume the role of referee in political conflicts, such as a constitutional court or other similarly authoritative state bodies. Institutions of this kind would only establish their presence and authority after 2004, with considerable effects on the dynamics of civil-military relations.

Another important element of the protracted civil-military relationship before 2004 was the intensity of communal and secessionist violence in Indonesia's transition. Authors such as Michael Desch have frequently argued that states with high levels of internal armed conflict find it difficult to keep the military out of politics, and Indonesia between 1998 and 2004 appears to be a case in point. Encouraged by the temporary weakness of the central government, the separatist insurgents in Aceh and Papua exponentially increased their activity after Suharto's fall, with Aceh's rebels exercising effective control over much of the territory at the height of their power in 2001. In response, the government launched a full-blown military campaign against the Acehnese separatists in 2003, dramatically expanding the authority of the military in the conflict-torn province. Similarly, the proliferation of communal violence in Kalimantan, Maluku, and Central Sulawesi led to a resurgence of military influence on security policies between 2001 and

2004, reinforcing TNI's role as the main guardian of the territorial integrity of the unitary state. In addition, the military also used the newly emerging issue of Islamist terrorism as a pretext to warn against the possible negative effects of further military reform. Combined, the perceived and real threats of separatism, communal conflict, and terrorism provided the armed forces with formidable arguments to demand more resources, additional powers, and a halt to ongoing structural reform efforts.

The specific approaches of Indonesia's presidents to the armed forces also left their marks on the civil-military relationships of their respective periods. While often driven by macro-political considerations, the individual personalities of the three post-Suharto presidents between 1998 and 2004 were important as well. Habibie, for example, made the deliberate decision to leave Wiranto in charge of the armed forces, grant him freedom to define the military's reform agenda, and ask him for political support in return. These decisions were milestones of the early transition, and many of the developments in military politics after 1998 were direct results of Habibie's course of action. Wahid, for his part, launched a radical military reform programme that probably no other president would have dared to experiment with. However, his unique political character was not only the source of admirable courage, but also of strategic immaturity and erratic megalomania. Falsely believing that he could rule without the support of other civilian groups and take on the military at the same time, Wahid got lost in a self-created quagmire of constitutional conflict, threats of martial law, and attempts to bring both the military and police under his personal control. Wahid's adventurism and eventual failure triggered widespread disillusionment with the quality of civilian governance, helping the military to regain some of the societal trust lost under Suharto's regime. Megawati, finally, showed little inclination to exercise strong control over the armed forces, which was due to a mixture of disinterest, political pressure, and genuinely felt sympathy for the military's nationalist ideology. Her decision to leave the office of minister of defence vacant for more than a year enabled the armed forces to increase their autonomy from the central government and run their operations without much civilian oversight. Evidently, Habibie, Wahid, and Megawati had highly divergent strategies towards the armed forces, with each of them interpreting and practising civil-military relations in their own way.

Among the above-mentioned factors, this book has identified the level of intra-civilian conflict as a particularly critical element of the evolving relationship between soldiers and transitional states. While this chapter has touched on the high intensity of intra-civilian disputes in Indonesia's transition, the motivations, actors, and social settings of such conflicts deserve much more detailed attention. Accordingly, the following chapter will further explore the interrelation between intra-civilian competition for power and the quality and pace of military reform. As in Chapters 2 and 4, the socio-political tensions within the Muslim community are analysed as a case study for general trends of intra-civilian conflict in Indonesia.

# Notes

1   Interview with Z.A. Maulani, Jakarta, 5 June 1998.
2   Even ABRI's marginalized hardliners were able to sustain effective elite relationships, which helped them to pursue alternative careers. Despite their discharge from active military service in August 1998 after being found guilty of kidnapping regime dissidents, Prabowo and Muchdi continued to exert considerable influence. Prabowo went on to build a successful business empire and, in 2003, launched a political comeback in the Golkar party. Although he failed to gain Golkar's presidential nomination in 2004, he maintained his position in elite politics and thus ensured that investigators felt disinclined to investigate his operations under Suharto's regime. Muchdi, for his part, rose to become the deputy head of BIN (*Badan Intelijen Negara*, National Intelligence Agency) under the Megawati government. In addition, most of Prabowo's and Muchdi's military associates, such as Sjafrie Sjamsoeddin and Zacky Anwar Makarim, continued their service within the armed forces and were given influential posts and assignments. Sjafrie, despite losing his post as commander of the Jakarta garrison, later became spokesman of the armed forces and secretary-general of the department of defence, a three-star position. Zacky, who was replaced as head of BIA in January 1999, subsequently received important tasks in sensitive areas, most notably in Aceh and East Timor.
3   Interview with Agum Gumelar, Jakarta, 9 June 1998.
4   "Reformasi ABRI Batasi Masa Jabatan Presiden", *Republika*, 26 May 1998.
5   "Panglima ABRI: Kegiatan Politik Tanpa Batas Ganggu Reformasi", *Republika*, 4 June 1998, and Mabes ABRI, "ABRI dan Reformasi: Pokok-Pokok Pikiran ABRI Tentang Reformasi Menuju Pencapaian Cita-Cita Nasional", Jakarta, June 1998.
6   Interview with Adi Sasono, Jakarta, 11 June 1998.
7   Lumintang had replaced Prabowo after the latter's dismissal on 22 May, but held the post only for several hours. Wiranto's official explanation was that Lumintang had been installed as caretaker for Djamari Chaniago, the eventual commander, but both Lumintang and Djamari were surprised by the abrupt change. Lumintang had been actively coordinating the Kostrad troops when he was informed of his removal. In an interview, he bitterly referred to the length of his term as a "record" in Indonesian military history. Djamari, for his

part, was woken up at one o'clock in the morning to learn of his appointment. Interview with Lieutenant General Johnny Lumintang, Jakarta, 29 July 1999, and Lieutenant General Djamari Chaniago, Jakarta, 11 November 1998.

8 Wiranto's influence on Golkar's regional boards was significant as many of their chairmen were retired military officers.

9 According to an officer involved in the operation, Wiranto described the mobilization of the pro-government mob as "Habibie's order" (Zen 2004, p. 95). The mob was instructed to confront the anti-Habibie protesters, mostly students. On the last day of the MPR session, security forces killed several students demonstrating against Habibie at the Semanggi interchange close to the MPR building. The protesters had been particularly outraged by a clause passed by the MPR that guaranteed continued parliamentary representation to the armed forces.

10 Habibie asked the public on 23 June to "give ABRI time" to handle its "internal problems", suggesting that the reform of the armed forces was an internal military matter rather than a policy issue for the civilian government. See "Pangab: ABRI Harus Mereformasi Diri", *Kompas*, 24 June 1998.

11 Interview with Kusnanto Anggoro, Jakarta, 25 June 1999.

12 "Pangab: ABRI Kembangkan Empat Paradigma Peran Sosial Politik Baru", *Republika*, 18 July 1998.

13 Interview with Agus Wirahadikusumah, Jakarta, 12 November 1998.

14 Interview with Agus Widjojo, Jakarta, 15 August 2007.

15 "ABRI Lakukan Redefinisi atas Doktrin Dwifungsi", *Media Indonesia*, 23 September 1998; "Dwifungsi ABRI Dihapus, Diganti 'Peran ABRI'", *Republika*, 23 September 1998; "Dwifungsi tak Berkesudahan", *Media Indonesia*, 27 September 1998; and "Panglima TNI Pada Rapim TNI: Tinggalkan Sospol, Konsentrasi Pada Pertahanan", *Kompas*, 20 April 2000.

16 "Military Chiefs Told to Stay Distant from Parties", *Jakarta Post*, 17 October 1998.

17 Interview with Johnny Lumintang, deputy army chief of staff, Jakarta, 29 July 1999.

18 In July 1998, there were 6,899 active officers seconded to civilian posts in the government bureaucracy. If retired members of the armed forces were added, the total number was 12,446 (Bhakti et al., 1999, p. 143).

19 The strength of TNI's territorial network has motivated some observers to not only *predict*, but in fact *demand* a continued role of the armed forces in politics. Patrick Walters, for example, argued that the "military must continue to play an active role in national politics" as it "remains the only truly national institution in Indonesia with a cohesive and disciplined network that stretches down to the village level". Civilian institutions, Walters argued, were too weak to manage the transition. It was, of course, the territorial command structure that obstructed the establishment of strong civilian institutions in the regions, and the demand

for its maintenance was certain to perpetuate the problem rather than solve it (Walters 1999, pp. 59–60).

[20]   "Wiranto Tarik Diri Dari Calon Wapres", *Media Indonesia*, 19 October 1999.

[21]   Wiranto had initially favoured Megawati for the presidency, but had received no concrete offers as far as political concessions were concerned. Instead, senior PDI-P officials declared publicly that Megawati was unlikely to invite Wiranto to form a coalition, given the latter's unfavourable reputation with foreign governments. In response to the negative PDI-P attitude, Wiranto's assistants sponsored an organization named "Perkasa" to call for a Wahid-Wiranto leadership team. See "PDI Perjuangan 'Unlikely to Pick Wiranto as Partner'", *Jakarta Post*, 18 October 1999; interview with Subagio Anam, member of parliament for PDI-P, Jakarta, 5 October 1999; and Perkasa, "Rakyat Perintahkan Dwi Tunggal Gus Dur-Wiranto Selamatkan Bangsa Indonesia", Jakarta, 19 October 1999.

[22]   It remains unclear if the thirty-eight members of the military faction in the MPR voted en bloc for Wahid or whether the vote was split. Traditionally, the military faction in the legislature voted according to the instruction of armed forces headquarters, but the secret ballot may have allowed some members to vote for Megawati. Based on calculations of the voting behaviour of other factions, however, it seems likely that at least a majority of military members opted for Wahid.

[23]   Interview with Akbar Tandjung, 19 December 2006.

[24]   Interview with Abdurrahman Wahid, Jakarta, 18 October 1999.

[25]   Interview with Wiranto, Jakarta, 13 October 2000.

[26]   Confidential Interview, Jakarta, 17 May 2000.

[27]   East Timor District Commander Colonel Noer Muis said a few days before the referendum that "the security authorities would face a big problem if pro-independence forces won … as it would certainly incite harsh reactions from their opponents". The military, according to Noer, had made preparations to "evacuate people by air, sea and land". Atambua in West Timor was chosen as a "safe gate out of the territory". Noer added that "security personnel will be the last to leave the territory". See "Military Ready for 'Civil War' in East Timor", *Jakarta Post*, 26 August 1999.

[28]   "Ingin Nobel, Dapat Penjahat Perang", *Siar*, 2 October 1999; "Habibie Falls Into East Timor Quagmire", *Asia Times*, 10 September 1999.

[29]   Interview with Dewi Fortuna Anwar, Jakarta, 18 October 1999.

[30]   An edict of 1 December 1999 deprived the president's four adjutants of the right to monitor Wahid's visitors and outgoing correspondences. In addition, the number of senior military officers in the president's office was reduced from thirty-five to fifteen.

[31]   Interview with Ratih Harjono, former presidential secretary, Jakarta, 28 January 2003.

[32]   Interview with Matori Abdul Djalil, Jakarta, 28 February 2000.

33    Wirahadikusumah had been moved to Sulawesi in a reshuffle ordered by Wiranto shortly before he joined cabinet. Before the reshuffle, Wirahadikusumah had publicly demanded the removal of "status quo" officers from the ranks, which most observers interpreted as open criticism of Wiranto. Wirahadikusumah obviously believed that Widodo would be in charge of new military appointments, but Wiranto signed the reshuffle orders on his last day in office. "Asrenum Panglima TNI: Bersihkan TNI dari Pemimpin Status Quo", *Republika*, 24 October 1999; and interview with General (ret.) Wiranto, Jakarta, 13 October 2000, and Major General Agus Wirahadikusumah, Makassar, 23 February 2000.

34    Interview with Abdurrahman Wahid, Jakarta, 2 March 2000.

35    Field officers feared that the reform of the territorial structure could seriously affect their income opportunities and that of their soldiers: "Those who talk about abolishing the territorial commands, have they ever thought about what our soldiers should live on? And how TNI as an institution can survive?" Interview with Lieutenant Colonel Haryata, commander of district command 1008, Banjarmasin, 15 November 2000.

36    Interview with Agus Wirahadikusumah, Makassar, 23 February 2000.

37    The project aimed at the withdrawal of 33,000 personnel from the community level (*babinsa*). They were to be concentrated at the district commands (*kodim*), where they would have received training as members of regional defence units. As a result, 3,309 local commands (*koramil*) were also to be dissolved. Saurip's end goal was the establishment of multi-service bases with rapid deployment facilities (Kadi 2000, p. 79).

38    Interview with Agus Wirahadikusumah, Makassar, 23 February 2000.

39    According to Chandra and Kammen (2002, p. 111), particular classes tend to monopolize key posts at specific periods of time. These reshuffle and monopolization patterns are difficult to predict beforehand, however. In the case of the 1970 and 1971 classes, for example, Chandra and Kammen concede that "the monopolization by these classes was specific to the period of Indonesia's transition from authoritarian rule and the early phase of the democratic consolidation" between 1998 and 2000. This means that the allegedly unfavourable career prospects for the 1973 class only became apparent at a time when many of its members had already developed public profiles as rapid reformers. Consequently, the structural promotion pattern of 2000 cannot be cited as a decisive factor in forming their attitudes toward reform.

40    For example, it is evident that many of the reformist officers, including those from classes that graduated before and after 1973, served longer than their colleagues in positions at TNI's educational institutions. Most importantly, many members of the Wirahadikusumah faction had been lecturers in the staff and command schools of the armed forces in Bandung in the 1980s and 1990s. They were also much more likely to be recipients of international military

training than officers who opposed reform. Interview with Agus Widjojo, Jakarta, 15 August 2007.

[41] Interview with Djadja Suparman, Bandung, 15 January 2002.

[42] The office of the chief of staff of socio-political affairs had been renamed in November 1998, to become chief of staff of territorial affairs. Yudhoyono had held the position until his appointment to the Wahid cabinet in October 1999.

[43] Interview with Agus Widjojo, 15 August 2007.

[44] Djoko Mulono, Widjojo's assistant for territorial affairs, denied Saurip the authority to run the pilot project in territorial units. He maintained that Saurip's office was only responsible for technical planning and supply, while TNI headquarters held the right to determine long-term policies. Interview with Major General Djoko Mulono, Jakarta, 30 November 2000.

[45] Bondan Gunawan had been a personal friend of Wahid since their membership in the Democracy Forum in the early 1990s. Demanding political reforms and criticizing human violations of the military, the Forum comprised of activists who were prepared to challenge Suharto's supremacy over the political system. As state secretary under Wahid, Bondan continued his sharp criticism of the armed forces. In April 2000, he contended that "TNI is not prepared to see its political role reduced to defence tasks, and this is understandable, considering the privileges they have enjoyed so far" (Gunawan 2000).

[46] Interview with Djoko Susilo, member of parliament for PAN (*Partai Amanat Nasional*, National Mandate Party), the party led by Amien Rais, Jakarta, 10 August 2000.

[47] Interview with Juwono Sudarsono, Jakarta, 7 February 2002.

[48] Mahfud had received hints from the palace that he could expect the education portfolio, but was surprised to hear that he was appointed minister of defence. He first misunderstood the term *pertahanan* (defence) as *pertanahan* (land issues), and needed to confirm several times before he could comprehend what post he had been offered. See "Urutan Pangkat di Militer Pun Saya Tak Tahu", *Tajuk*, 31 August 2000.

[49] Confidential interview with a three-star general, Jakarta, 10 September 2000. This general reported that Tyasno was nicknamed the "rubber general" by his colleagues, alluding to his perceived political flexibility. There was particular resentment within the officer corps over a brochure distributed by Tyasno among the political elite. Instead of presenting TNI's reform agenda, it included Tyasno's personal views, biography, and family stories (Sudarto 2000).

[50] Interview with Muhaimin Iskandar, Jakarta, 6 June 2001.

[51] Interview with Cornelis Lay, Honolulu, 3 October 2001.

[52] Wahid's own security ministers advised him against declaring a state of emergency. In early June, the president dismissed Susilo Bambang Yudhoyono as coordinating minister for political, social, and security affairs for failing to

support his emergency plans. Subsequently, Wahid appointed Agum Gumelar to replace Yudhoyono, but the new minister offered the same advice. For this, Wahid called him a "transvestite" and "coward" (Kustiati and Effendi 2004, p. 208).

53   Interview with Endriartono Sutarto, Jakarta, 11 June 2007.
54   Interview with Endriartono Sutarto, Jakarta, 11 June 2007.
55   Interview with Djadja Suparman, Bandung, 15 January 2002.
56   The 1999 session of the MPR had already decided to exclude TNI from the DPR and local legislatures by 2004, but had granted the military continued representation in the MPR in exchange for dropping its opposition to leaving parliament.
57   "U.S. Warned Against Full Embrace of Megawati", *Inter Press Service*, 25 July 2001.
58   Jacques Bertrand argued that in Aceh, Wahid "adopted the more repressive approach favored by the armed forces" after his reconciliatory strategy had failed to produce results. His shift was, however, less a consequence of the situation in Aceh than of his declining political fortunes in Jakarta (Bertrand 2004, p. 181).
59   "Sebagai Menhan, Matori akan Menjembatani Dikotomi Sipil-Militer", *Kompas*, 9 August 2001.
60   Interview with Happy Bone Zulkarnaen, Jakarta, 30 March 2002.
61   "Darurat Militer Tak Menyimpang", *Sriwijaya Post*, 31 July 2003.
62   Interview with senior official, Supreme Auditing Board, Jakarta, 7 February 2004. See also "US$291 Million in Military Emergency Funds Missing", *Acehkita*, September 2004.
63   It was an apparent standard practice of the military in Aceh to declare almost all victims killed by its troops as supporters of the rebellious Free Aceh Movement (*Gerakan Aceh Merdeka*, GAM). Human rights groups pointed to numerous cases, however, in which the victims seemed to have been non-combatants. For instance, the discrepancy between the number of GAM members claimed to have been killed by TNI and the number of weapons seized from them suggests that at least some unarmed civilians were among the dead. By November 2003, TNI claimed to have killed 1,106 members of GAM, but had recovered only 488 of their firearms. "1106 Anggota GAM Tewas Selama Darurat Militer", *Kompas*, 19 November 2003; "Civilians in the Middle", *Acehkita*, September 2004.
64   Interview with senior U.S. defence official, Jakarta, 28 August 2001.
65   Interview with Major General Sudradjat, director-general for strategic defence planning at the department of defence, Jakarta, 25 September 2001.
66   "Powell Desak Pemulihan Hubungan Militer AS Dengan RI", *Detik.com*, 1 May 2002; "Rumsfeld Berharap Hubungan Militer AS-RI Terjalin Kembali", *Detik.com*, 2 May 2002.

[67]   Police officers were widely criticized for carrying out arrests without proper documents and without notifying family members of the suspects' whereabouts. See "DPR Minta Penjelasan Kapolri Soal Isu Penangkapan Aktivis Islam", *Kompas*, 16 September 2003.

[68]   "KSAD: Intelijen Militer Harus di Depan", *Suara Merdeka*, 20 August 2003. Ryamizard mentioned Israel as an example for effective counter-terrorism efforts based on territorial control.

[69]   See also "TNI Tak Ingin Lagi Tangani Fungsi Teritorial", *Kompas*, 22 August 2001; "Fungsi Teritorial Militer Sebagai Fungsi Pemerintahan", *Kompas*, 23 August 2001.

[70]   According to Widjojo, it was him who proposed the disbandment of his own office to TNI chief Widodo, partly because his possible replacement would have been a not-so-reformist general. Interview with Agus Widjojo, 15 August 2007.

[71]   In June 2004, 45 per cent of the electorate thought that an active or former general was best qualified for the presidency, as opposed to 14 per cent who favoured a religious leader and 9 per cent who wanted a human rights activist as president. Only 8 per cent of respondents believed a professional politician should become president (International Foundation for Election Systems 2004*a*).

[72]   "Enam Jenderal Berebut Jabatan Gubernur Jatim", *Kompas*, 8 June 2003.

[73]   Megawati's PDI-P also had other important reasons for supporting the re-election of incumbent governors. After 1999, PDI-P had suffered a series of embarrassing defeats in gubernatorial and *bupati* elections, with its candidates typically beaten by local strongmen who had gained the backing of other parties and renegade factions within PDI-P. After 2002, Megawati appeared to have given up on nominating PDI-P officials for key posts in local government, and instead backed powerful incumbents for a second term. This reduced the risk of more defeats, and appeared to secure the support of victorious candidates for Megawati's re-election bid in 2004. This particular element of Megawati's motivation is insufficient to explain, however, why other parties also nominated military figures as their candidates. Support for retired military officers came from the whole range of the political spectrum, pointing to the more general electoral pattern outlined above.

[74]   "Wiranto Diusulkan, Prabowo Cari Informasi", *Suara Pembaruan*, 16 July 2003; "Amien Rais Akui Pernah Bertemu Agum dan Sutarto", *Koran Tempo*, 15 April 2004.

[75]   "Hasyim: 'Saya Tahu Mega itu Lemah'", *Gatra*, 30 July 2004.

[76]   Confidential interview with a three-star general, Bandung, 19 May 1999.

[77]   Interview with Cholil Bisri, member of parliament for PKB, Surabaya, 25 July 2000.

[78] Yudhoyono sponsored the publication of a book that explained the reasons for his dismissal, indicating that he saw his departure from the faltering Wahid government not as the end of his political career but rather as the beginning of a new mission (Kurdi and Wahid 2003).

[79] Interview with Sutradara Gintings, Jakarta, 3 November 2006.

[80] Interview with Sutradara Gintings, Jakarta, 3 November 2006.

[81] Interview with Subur Bhudisantoso, former chairman of Partai Demokrat, Jakarta, 26 September 2006.

[82] Interview with Ryaas Rasyid, 7 November 2006.

[83] Yudhoyono's advisers admitted that "the dramatization of the events" surrounding his resignation "was the work of our team". Rachmat Witoelar, his leading campaign manager, described the decision to leave cabinet as "Yudhoyono's Sarajevo". See "Arsitek Politik Kampanye SBY", *Tempo*, 19 September 2004.

# 6

---

# NEW ERA, OLD DIVISIONS
## Islamic Politics in the Early
## Post-Suharto Period

Divisions within the political elite have traditionally played a major role in shaping Indonesia's post-independence civil-military relations. From the ideological conflicts in the 1950s that accompanied the rise of authoritarianism to the cleavages that prevented the formation of a united oppositional front against Suharto in 1998 — disputes between large societal forces have almost invariably benefited the armed forces and their quest for political power. Accordingly, one of the key hypotheses of this study has been that the level of political intervention of the armed forces rises and falls with the intensity of intra-civilian conflict. The previous chapter has pointed to several phases in Indonesia's post-authoritarian transition in which conflicts between civilian groups allowed the armed forces to improve their political standing: the 1999 elections, the constitutional crisis of 2001, and the campaign for the 2004 presidential ballot. However, as the chapter mainly focused on internal military developments, it did not discuss in detail the roots, actors, and social contexts of these intra-civilian conflicts. This chapter therefore analyses the dynamics of civilian politics in the early years of the post-Suharto polity, and explains how the disagreements, disputes, and personal rivalries between civilian leaders impacted negatively on the process of military reform between 1998 and 2004. As in previous chapters, the divisions within the Muslim community serve as a case study to illustrate general patterns of civilian conflict in Indonesia.

In this respect, the chapter concentrates on three main periods in the early political transition that witnessed severe conflicts between Islamic groups. To begin with, the chapter discusses the proliferation of Islamic parties in 1998 and its role in creating the fragmented political landscape of the Habibie interregnum. Demonstrating that old politico-ideological and religious cleavages prefigured the political fault-lines of the early democratic system, the analysis points to the failure of Muslim leaders to unite against the vested interests of residual New Order forces, including the military. Second, the chapter looks at the disputes between crucial Muslim constituencies over the Wahid presidency, arguing that both NU and other large Islamic groups placed their institutional interests above democratic principles. Finally, the discussion turns to the alliances between Islamic figures and retired military officers in the 2004 presidential elections. These alliances eloquently highlighted the crisis of civilian politics and the simultaneous resurgence of active and retired military officers as important political actors. In combination, these three sections show how long-standing conflicts between powerful Muslim groups extended from the New Order into the early phase of the democratic system, complicating and delaying the process of military reform. In an additional section, the chapter evaluates the impact of extremist Islamic movements on Indonesia's transitional civil-military relations. It concludes that in contrast to previous periods, the influence of post-Suharto Islamic militancy on the political strength of the armed forces has been marginal, with the repercussions of Muslim mainstream politics playing a much larger role.

## THE FORMATION OF ISLAMIC PARTIES AFTER 1998

The abrupt liberalization of the political system, announced by Habibie only days after Suharto's fall, came as a stunning surprise to the majority of Indonesia's societal and political leaders. The elite of the emerging post-authoritarian polity had not witnessed free competition between parties since the late 1950s, making democratic interaction a strangely foreign concept to the new political protagonists. For decades, they had organized their political activities within the limits set by tight regulations of authoritarian control, joining parties approved by the government or using their informal prestige to participate in elite negotiations. With the New Order's longevity paralysing the creative imagination of most civil society activists and established politicians, they considered it a useless utopian exercise to think about the kind of political party they would form in a free and democratic Indonesia. Even the growing demands for accelerated democratization and more individual rights in the late Suharto era, while envisioning a less regulated society, did not define complete freedom to form political parties as a realistic goal. Thus when Habibie lifted virtually all restrictions on establishing parties and promised to hold open and fair elections, many key figures were unprepared for the sudden task of creating new vehicles for their political careers.

This confusion was particularly evident in the Muslim community. Islamic leaders faced three major decisions concerning their political future. Most importantly, they had to make up their minds whether entering party politics was a viable option for them and their respective organizations. In all major Muslim groups, there was strong support for continuing the prioritization of social and religious activities adopted in the 1970s and 1980s. The departure of the largest Muslim organizations from formal politics during the New Order had left a compelling impression on many religio-societal leaders, and some of them doubted that returning to it would benefit their cause. The second challenge for Muslim politicians was to determine the role Islamic ideology would play in formulating their post-Suharto platforms. The New Order had outlawed the use of Islam as the ideological basis for political or societal organizations, promoting the religiously neutral Pancasila instead. The state ideology, while commonly viewed as a relic of authoritarian indoctrination, was so deeply entrenched in the political discourse that even Islamic activists were reluctant to completely abandon it. In addition, there was a residual fear that the new democratic polity might not last long, and that a possible military takeover could result in the purge of those Islamic leaders who hastily replaced Pancasila as their ideological guideline. Therefore, the ensuing debate within the Muslim community saw one faction arguing for an unrestricted use of Islam as its basis for engagement in democratic politics, while the other camp favoured the partial retention of Pancasila. Finally, Muslim leaders also had to decide to what extent they were prepared to seek cooperation with rival camps within the *umat* on the one hand, and other political forces on the other. The demands for an all-Islamic party were strong, but many leaders were inclined to form parties that represented the interests of their particular constituency only. Again others thought about joining forces with nationalist groups to establish cross-religious parties that would break long-standing constituency boundaries.

The decisions made by Muslim leaders for themselves and their various constituencies had a profound impact on the evolving post-authoritarian polity. The strategies that they pursued differed immensely, but a general pattern of post-Suharto Islamic politics quickly emerged. Critically, all major Islamic groups decided that they had to engage in party politics, whether in a direct or indirect manner. Some of them chose to use Islam as their ideological foundation, while others increased the emphasis on their Islamic identity but retained Pancasila as an over-arching principle. Most significantly, however, almost all major Muslim leaders opted to establish separate parties that appealed to their core constituencies rather than to an electorate spanning religious and ideological boundaries. Even those who declared their parties as ideologically open continued to rely on their respective communities as primary sources of support. Consequently, a large number of Islamic parties was established that served the interests of specific Muslim groups as well as the individual career plans of their leaders. The ideological and political fragmentation within the Muslim community, which had stretched from the colonial period to the final days of the New Order, was about to extend into the new political system. These intra-Islamic rivalries added to other traditional cleavages that divided the civilian realm along the entire political spectrum, weakening civilian leadership and creating substantial obstacles to the establishment of democratic control over the military.

## Defending Constituency Interests: Muslim Parties after 1998

The debate about the character and nature of their political engagement in the post-authoritarian transition caused serious conflicts within the various Muslim groups. In Nahdlatul Ulama, for example, internal disputes led to the formation of several parties that all claimed to represent the interests of the NU community. Initially, NU chairman Abdurrahman Wahid had rejected calls for the creation of an NU-based party, declaring his intention to defend the non-partisan stance that his organization had taken since 1984.[1] The pressure from prominent *kiai* in Central and East Java to establish a political party exclusively focused on NU's institutional interests was so strong, however, that Wahid had to change his position. By late June 1998, the process of defining the platform and structures of an NU-based party was under way (Panitia Deklarasi Partai Kebangkitan Bangsa 1998, p. 13). This decision ruled out two other possible formats of NU's participation in post-Suharto politics: rejoining PPP, of which NU had been a component until 1984, and the transformation of NU itself into a political party. In terms of its religio-political orientation, Wahid insisted that the new party refrain from portraying itself as explicitly Islamic but endorse Pancasila and secular-nationalist principles as well (Anam 2000, p. 14). This choice was expressed in the name chosen for the party, *Partai Kebangkitan Bangsa* (PKB, National Awakening Party), which also indicated Wahid's preferences in terms of future cooperation with other political forces.[2] Building on his relationships with pluralist groups and figures, Wahid evidently refused to integrate the NU constituency into the Islamic segment of Indonesian politics. Nevertheless, he was determined to enter upcoming elite negotiations backed up by an autonomous political power base rooted in his core constituency.

The secular-nationalist definition of PKB triggered fierce opposition from those elements within the traditionalist community that demanded a clearer Islamic image for the NU-based party. Senior *kiai* objected to Wahid's choice of Matori Abdul Djalil as party chairman, referring to his lack of religious credentials and frequent interaction with non-Muslim politicians.[3] The NU chairman was able to deflect such criticism, however, by granting numerous concessions to the *kiai*. For instance, the organizational structures of PKB were designed to mirror those of NU, with a religious advisory board exercising supreme authority over the political leadership of the party (Choirie 2002, p. 221). In addition, prominent NU *kiai* obtained key positions in the central board, giving them sufficient influence to protect the religious identity of PKB. Ma'ruf Amin, the chairman of PKB's advisory board, was satisfied that despite Wahid's formal endorsement of pluralist values, the party remained primarily a vehicle to represent the social, religious, and political interests of NU:

> Let [Wahid] talk about nationalism. He is the paramount politician, he has to think strategically. But the reality is here on the ground. Look at the party. The leaders are NU, the structures are NU, the procedures are NU, even the jokes are NU. There is no doubt that this is an NU party.[4]

However, not all *kiai* and NU-affiliated activists were prepared to accept this strategic dualism between a secular political outlook on the one hand and Islamic norms and values on the other. Accordingly, some supporters of more scripturalist interpretations of Islam, who had opposed Wahid's leadership throughout the 1980s and 1990s, decided to form separate NU-based parties with Islam as their sole ideological foundation. Estranged relatives of Wahid founded PKU (*Partai Kebangkitan Umat*, Party of the Awakening Umat), while the influential NU cleric Syukron Makmun formed the PNU (*Partai Nahdlatul Umat*, Revival of the Umat Party).[5] In addition to these new creations, many NU politicians and officials decided to remain in the parties they belonged to under the New Order, particularly PPP and Golkar. Given this fractured character of NU's post-Suharto engagement in politics, Suzaina Kadir (2000, p. 320) concluded that "the inherent inability of the

NU to act as an independent political force continues to weaken its overall bargaining position at the national level".

Muhammadiyah, NU's largest modernist counterpart, went through an equally intense discussion over the format of its engagement in the new democratic polity. Its leader, Amien Rais, was determined to enter formal politics, but he was aware that turning Muhammadiyah into a political party was not an option. The organization had withdrawn from party politics in the late 1950s, and the majority of its functionaries believed that re-entering it carried intolerable risks for Muhammadiyah's network of educational and social institutions. Amien therefore decided to quit as Muhammadiyah's leader and establish a political career outside of the organization.[6] His search for a party that fitted his strategic and ideological needs was tortuous, however, and damaged his relationship with potential political partners. Initially, Amien negotiated with ultra-modernist activists about a possible revival of Masyumi, but after no agreement was reached, he committed himself to taking over PPP from its discredited New Order leadership. However, some of his associates from the pluralist anti-Suharto forum MAR convinced him that chairing an exclusively Islamic party would reduce his chances of building a broad support base for his expected presidential bid. For that reason, Amien pulled out of the arrangement with PPP, and in August 1998 formed the secular-oriented *Partai Amanat Nasional* (PAN, National Mandate Party). While presenting itself as open to all religions, PAN's leadership was recruited largely from Muhammadiyah. This was particularly true of the regional boards. The dominance of Muhammadiyah leaders not only created conflicts between the majority of modernist party functionaries and the tiny minority of pluralists, but also affected PAN's external image. As one Indonesian observer commented, PAN was caught in a dilemma: for nationalist and non-Muslim constituencies, the strong Islamic character of the party's regional boards was a drawback; devout modernist Muslims, on the other hand, were concerned about the influence of pluralist elements on the policies of the party (Ghazali 2000, p. 188).

The establishment of a pluralist party by Indonesia's most popular modernist figure caused considerable disappointment on the part of those Muslim groups who had expected him to unite and lead the Islamic community through the democratic transition. Ultra-modernist activists from *Dewan Dakwah* and KISDI, who had offered Amien the leadership of a Masyumi-style party, felt a deep sense of betrayal over his choice of the pluralist option.[7] The man appointed to lead the party in Amien's stead, Yusril Ihza Mahendra, recalled that "we were already talking [with Amien] about a name for the party and who should be in it". But suddenly, Yusril continued, "we read in the papers that he also spoke with PPP and, finally, founded his own party — that was very bad behaviour, and we will certainly remember that for the future".[8] Yusril's party was eventually named *Partai Bulan Bintang* (Crescent and Star Party), a reference to Masyumi's symbol. Party officials aimed to portray Yusril as a "young Natsir", hoping to evoke the main elements of Masyumi's political profile in the early 1950s: strict adherence to Islamic values on the one hand, but intellectual modernity and professionalism on the other (Ghazali 1999, p. 5). In addition to Bulan Bintang, a number of other modernist parties sprang up, but most of them failed to grow. The only exception was *Partai Keadilan* (PK, Justice Party), which according to Elizabeth Fuller Collins (2003, p. 12) "marked the split between the younger generation of leaders" and older modernist figures in Bulan Bintang. The Justice Party consisted largely of Muslim activists recruited from a wide network of Islamic campuses. KAMMI (*Kesatuan Aksi Mahasiswa Muslim Indonesia*, Indonesian Muslim Student Action Union), a student organization that had supported Amien in the protest movement against Suharto, was its main component. KAMMI leaders had apparently hoped to join a political party led by Amien, but the latter's decision to pursue a pluralist strategy convinced them to form PK instead (Damanik 2002, pp. 196, 284). Espousing a puritanical view on Islamic culture and politics, PK presented itself as a bridge between traditionalist and modernist versions of the faith.[9]

## Coalitions and Conflicts: The 1999 Elections

The political fragmentation of the Muslim community in the early stages of the post-authoritarian transition reflected deeply rooted historical sentiments on the one hand and specific characteristics of the 1998 regime change on the other. Historically, the experiences of all-Islamic organizations had been largely negative, predisposing Muslim politicians to opt for parties that only represented their various core constituencies. The break-up of Masyumi in the 1950s had left bitter memories in both the traditionalist and modernist communities, and the conflicts within PPP throughout the New Order had served to confirm their prejudices. Besides the deterrent effect of previously failed all-Islamic experiments, the nature of the 1998 regime change supplied the second major reason for the proliferation of Muslim parties after Suharto's fall. Unable to unite against the struggling autocrat, Indonesia's Islamic and other societal forces had carelessly missed the opportunity that the political crisis had offered them. Linz and Stepan (1996, p. 71) indicated that in most declining dictatorial regimes, societal opposition to government repression can function as a catalyst for the creation of non-regime coalitions that have the potential to erode long-standing constituency boundaries. As explained in Chapter 4 of this study, however, no such coalition came to exist in Indonesia as its most influential civilian forces expressed highly divergent attitudes towards Suharto. Consequently, the regime was brought down not by effective elite opposition and cooperation, but by large-scale popular protest. Thus the experience of dictatorial rule did not, in Harold A. Trinkunas' words (2001, p. 166), "establish the basis for a broad civilian" coalition among different constituencies; instead, their fragmentation led to the formation of parties as distinct interest groups, producing "narrow opportunity structures" for further democratization. Even PAN, as one of the few parties born out of an oppositional forum, did not succeed in bringing key leaders together, but only assembled rather marginal community figures in support of the presidential aspirations of Amien Rais.

Processes of political fragmentation not only occurred in the Muslim community, however. The secular-nationalist segment of Indonesian politics was affected as well, albeit to a lesser extent. Megawati Sukarnoputri's party, which renamed itself into PDI-P in early 1999, was able to absorb most nationalist groups and currents, but some splinter parties with secular profiles emerged that represented particular ideological viewpoints or social classes. In addition, Golkar continued to appeal to secular and non-Muslim groups concerned over the possible rise of Islamic politics, challenging PDI-P's claim to speak for the majority of nationalist voters. The fierce competition between parties with overlapping target audiences gave rise to very peculiar conflict patterns in the Indonesian party system ahead of the 1999 elections. The campaign for the June 1999 ballot saw violent fights among Muslim parties on the one hand and secular-nationalist groups on the other, but rarely witnessed conflicts between the two large politico-ideological blocks. For example, PDI-P supporters frequently clashed with Golkar campaigners, PPP members were involved in street battles with PAN, and PKB faced angry opposition from NU politicians who had decided to remain in PPP (Mietzner 1999b, pp. 73–86). The latter rivalry cost four people their lives when the two sides engaged in brutal street fighting in Jepara in April 1999.[10] This conflict revealed the intensity of the differences within the *umat*, with PPP-affiliated clerics denouncing PKB leader Abdurrahman Wahid as a "blind infidel" and PKB campaigners warning that PPP intended to turn Indonesia into an Islamic state.[11]

The result of the parliamentary elections extended the fractures of Indonesia's political society into its formal institutions. PDI-P emerged as the largest party with 33.7 per cent, followed by Golkar with 22.4 and PKB with 12.6 per cent of the votes. PPP came in fourth with 10.7 per cent, PAN finished fifth with 7.1 per cent, ahead of Bulan Bintang and PK with 1.9 and 1.4 per cent respectively. Altogether, 21 out of 48 parties that contested the election gained seats in parliament. In terms of ideological affiliation, 28 secular-nationalist parties gained 62.5 per cent of the vote, while 20 Muslim-based parties (including PKB and PAN) received 37.5 per cent. Compared to the 1955 elections, the percentage of Islamic votes had dropped by 6 per cent, and if PAN and PKB were excluded from the pool of Muslim parties, the loss was 25.7 per cent (Suryadinata 2002, p. 106). This result sparked heated debates within the Muslim community over the causes and consequences of this "defeat". Many observers pointed out that the deep and often violent divisions between Islamic parties had driven Muslim voters to more solid and "moderate" options, particularly Golkar. Similarly, the conflicts among Muslim parties had made it impossible for their leaders to present a coherent concept of political Islam that could have attracted voters outside of their narrowly defined constituencies. Bahtiar Effendy (2003, p. 217) argued that "in so far they are diverse and unable to express and articulate the idea of political Islam in the light of public interests, then it will be difficult for Islamic political parties to be a dominant force on Indonesia's political stage". Accordingly, several Muslim intellectuals and politicians proposed the formation of an "Islamic faction" in the upcoming parliament. Aware of the overly optimistic nature of this proposition, Azyumardi Azra (1999, p. 307) asserted that such a pan-Islamic alliance would constitute a "breakthrough to overcome the acute fragmentation in the leadership of political Islam".

The frictions in the Muslim community did not bode well for the evolution of Indonesia's transitional civil-military-relations. With one of the most important segments of civilian politics marred by internal conflict, the efforts to establish democratic oversight of the armed forces became even more difficult than originally thought. Most theorists of military politics agree that a minimum amount of unity among civilian elites is a precondition for successful reformation of post-authoritarian armed forces. Indonesia, however, suffered from an obvious lack of such unity. Not only had the well-entrenched cleavage between traditionalist and modernist Muslims survived the fall of the New Order, but both communities had also splintered into numerous parties, groups, movements, and individual leaders. In the same vein, the personal tensions between Indonesia's most prominent Muslim politicians had not decreased, but escalated further. These intra-Islamic conflicts inevitably left their mark on the volatile civil-military relationship of the early post-Suharto years. Instead of cooperating on the development of a joint blueprint for military reform, key civilian leaders kept themselves busy with attempts to outplay their political rivals, both inside and outside their religio-ideological constituencies. This constellation came as a great relief to the military, which was struggling to find its place in the new democratic polity, initially fearing that civilian politicians would unanimously agree on and work towards its removal from the political arena. The assessments by Effendy and Azra cited earlier clarified that this was not the case, and the intellectuals' calls on Muslim elites to unite in the defence of "public interests" pointed to the damage that their infighting had done to the capacity of civilians to offer political visions and concepts to ordinary Indonesians. Beyond these long-term considerations, however, the need for Muslim parties to cooperate also had a more practical and urgent dimension: the presidential elections were approaching rapidly, and the inconclusive outcome of the June polls had thrown the race wide open.

## INTRA-ISLAMIC CONFLICT UNDER THE WAHID PRESIDENCY, 1999–2001

The election of a new president — scheduled for October 1999 — was widely expected to complete the first phase of Indonesia's post-authoritarian transition. The new head of state was to be elected by the MPR, which consisted of members of parliament, regional representatives, and functional groups. This indirect electoral mechanism, despite occasional criticism of its democratic deficiencies, finally forced the political elite to initiate talks on coalition-building and power-sharing — something it had tried very hard to avoid thus far. In this context, the negotiations among political parties offered the chance to mitigate the traditional antagonisms so evident during the parliamentary elections. Initially, however, it appeared as if the coalition-building efforts would only create alliances along the existing politico-ideological demarcation lines. PKB seemed prepared to support the presidential candidacy of Megawati, together with a number of smaller nationalist parties, the armed forces, and secular Golkar elements (Maulidin 1998, p. 28). On the other side of the political spectrum, most modernist Muslim parties pledged to prevent Megawati's rise to the presidency for a number of reasons, ranging from her gender to her secular political attitude (Platzdasch 2000; Parianom and Ariesdanto 1999). While leaning towards Habibie, these parties were reluctant to endorse him openly for fear of being labelled as forces of the political status quo. But despite being the clear favourite, Megawati failed to enter formal agreements with her potential coalition partners. Believing that the parliamentary polls had presented her with a non-negotiable claim to the presidency, she offered no concrete inducements to the parties expected to vote her into office. Wahid, returning from a meeting with Megawati during which he had hoped to secure detailed promises of cabinet appointments in exchange for PKB's support, felt so alienated by Megawati's non-committal stance that he decided on the spot to evaluate alternative options for his party.

Megawati's failure to consolidate her support base laid the foundations for the first coalition between rival Islamic parties in a democratic polity since the Ali Sastroamidjojo cabinet in 1956–57. Despite deep mutual suspicions, in June 1999 Amien Rais proposed Wahid as the presidential candidate of an alliance between traditionalist and modernist Muslim parties. Called the Central Axis, the coalition was designed to serve the shifting political interests of both sides (Suharsono 1999). For PKB and Wahid, on the one hand, the offer provided the unique chance of gaining the presidency for an NU leader. Earlier in the year, Wahid had speculated about becoming president, but PKB's modest performance in the June polls seemed to have put an end to his hopes. PAN, PPP, Bulan Bintang, and PK, on the other hand, found it increasingly difficult to maintain their support for Habibie. The president was engulfed in a number of political scandals, and even Golkar officials began to question openly whether Habibie was the best candidate. The nomination of Wahid thus promised to prevent Megawati's ascent to power and, at the same time, shield the modernist parties from charges that they intended to secure another term for Suharto's deputy. In spite of its obvious strategic benefits, functionaries of all parties harboured serious doubts over the coalition. Both sides had for decades traded ideological arguments and personal insults in a rivalry that Adam Schwarz (2004, p. 389) called "deep, long-lasting and bitter". In an eloquent and compelling speech in front of NU officials in July 1999, Amien admitted that it was "funny" that "I, as former chairman of Muhammadiyah, am offering the presidency to the boss of NU." He also revealed his awareness "that many of you don't believe me", but asked his audience to "please learn to trust me ... — we need to unite for the sake of the nation".[12]

Ironically, the doubts of NU officials towards Wahid's nomination were not only based on the fact that their modernist rivals had initiated it. Equally important were their own experiences with Wahid's erratic leadership style, poor health, and predilection for bombastic rumours and spectacular political manoeuvres.[13] Believing that Wahid was physically and mentally unfit for the presidency, many *kiai* privately expressed their hope that his candidacy would come to nothing. Ultimately, however, there were too many parties and individual politicians to whom Wahid's presidency appeared as the least damaging outcome of the presidential competition. With their short-term interest of denying Megawati the presidency outweighing most other considerations, the concerns over the workability of the proposed all-Islamic coalition and Wahid's competence to govern seemed temporarily negligible. In addition, Wahid was able to put on a remarkable display of his political skills. In a matter of weeks, the effectively blind NU chairman sidelined opponents of his candidacy within PKB, convinced ultra-modernists that he would represent their cause, won the support of the armed forces, and recruited the majority of Golkar members of the MPR for his campaign. On 20 October 1999, Wahid beat Megawati to become Indonesia's fourth president. Megawati, for her part, reluctantly accepted the vice-presidency and agreed to integrate PDI-P into Wahid's "rainbow" cabinet, which included ministers from all significant parties.

## The End of the Central Axis

In theory, the formation of a broad-based coalition government significantly improved the chances of consolidating Indonesia's democratic reforms and strengthening civilian control over the armed forces. Most importantly, the compromise between major Islamic groups appeared to bridge some of the differences that had caused deep political fragmentation in the past. Backed by a solid majority in the legislature, the government enjoyed the necessary preconditions for institutional stability and coherence in policy-making. In practice, however, these positive indicators for accelerated democratization evaporated as quickly as the multi-party alliance on which they were based. Wahid, it turned out, had no intention of maintaining the coalition that had paved his way to power. In interviews, the new president admitted openly that he had stitched together the alliance with the single purpose of facilitating his election, and expressed profound satisfaction that his modernist rivals had fallen for such a simple "trick".[14] For Wahid, who according to Angus McIntyre (2001, pp. 92, 94) was "convinced of his own superiority" and "omniscience", the electoral coalition had ceased to exist on the day of his inauguration. The country's presidential system, Wahid argued, guaranteed him an undisturbed five-year term, with or without the support of the legislature. Consequently, he began to systematically dispose of his former partners. Hamzah Haz, chairman of PPP, was sacked from cabinet only one month after his appointment. Wiranto was forced to resign in February 2000, and Jusuf Kalla from Golkar as well as Laksamana Sukardi from PDI-P lost their ministerial posts in April over unspecified corruption charges. Six months into his rule, Wahid had effectively dismantled the alliance through which he had pursued his presidential campaign.

The disintegration of the government coalition created fresh tensions between key political parties and the societal constituencies they represented. This was particularly the case in the Muslim community, where tensions between traditionalist and modernist groups grew substantially. The modernist side felt that Wahid had defaulted on his promises and was deliberately harming their interests. One modernist critic of the president's leadership complained that "although [Wahid] was elected through the Central Axis, namely the Islamic parties ..., he has not returned this favour of the Muslim community with pleasant expressions of gratitude." On the contrary, he continued, Wahid "increasingly enjoys himself by releasing statements that corner the Muslim community" (Jaiz 2000, p. 14). In addition to the removal of Islamic figures from cabinet, other issues that raised anger in modernist circles were Wahid's proposal to open trade relations with Israel, his initiative to lift an MPR ban on communism that dated back to 1966, a Christmas speech viewed as overly pro-Christian, and a series of statements that indicated lack of concern for the fate of Muslims in the ongoing religious conflicts in Maluku and North Maluku.[15] The latter topic motivated thousands of Muslim demonstrators to convene at the Monas Square in Jakarta in January 2000, where prominent Islamic leaders denounced the alleged insensitivity of the president towards the suffering of Moluccan Muslims (Schulze 2002, p. 67). Addressing the crowd, Amien Rais even called for a *jihad* to assist Muslims in the fight against their Christian opponents, to which Wahid responded that "I don't care if you want *jihad*, or you want *jahid* [asceticism], the bottom line is that if you threaten the stability of the state, we'll take action" (Zada 2002, p. 132). The event catalyzed the formation of modernist opposition against Wahid's rule and helped to turn what was essentially an elite conflict over power, resources, and privileges into a dispute among Muslim constituencies on the ground. The intra-Islamic "honeymoon" (Rais and Syah 1999), which had marked Wahid's election only months earlier, had come to an end.

The challenge launched by modernist Muslim leaders against Wahid mobilized traditionalist clerics to defend the embattled president. Before the election, many *kiai* had expressed serious reservations about Wahid's ability to lead a stable government, and they had even conveyed some of these concerns to the modernist proponents of his candidacy (Fraksi Kebangkitan Bangsa 2001, p. 1). Senior NU clerics and officials had warned their modernist counterparts that "you have no idea what you are getting yourself into",[16] reminding them also of the possible consequences for the relationship between their constituencies should Wahid's government fail. Thus the majority of *kiai* viewed it as inappropriate that only months after having been fully informed about the risks involved in Wahid's election, modernist leaders now attacked the president for a behavioural pattern about which they were already well apprised.[17] But for NU, the harsh criticism of Wahid not only provided proof of the hypocrisy of his opponents, it also put the material interests of the organization at stake. Critically, the prospect of Wahid's downfall threatened the institutional benefits that traditionalist clerics had enjoyed as a consequence of an NU leader holding the presidency. Since Wahid's election, there had been a considerable increase in payments to *pesantren* from local bureaucracies, and companies sought to recruit *kiai* close to the palace as business facilitators. In short, the possibility of a chaotic end to Wahid's presidency was likely to affect NU's social prestige, cause unrest in its strongholds, and result in the loss of lucrative privileges gained during his rule.

In the early period of the emerging presidential crisis, between April and December 2000, the approach of traditionalist leaders focused on mediation efforts and appeals for calm on both sides. Many *kiai* felt overwhelmed by the task, however, as the number of Wahid's opponents increased steadily. In addition to modernist politicians, the president also engaged in conflicts with the security forces, Golkar leaders, and his vice-president. Accordingly, NU officials arranged a series of meetings with groups that were seen as crucial for Wahid's survival. In April 2000, for example, the new NU chairman Hasyim Muzadi held a gathering with senior military officers at his *pesantren* in Malang to "demonstrate that there are no disturbances in the relationship between NU and the armed forces, despite recent reports to the contrary".[18] On the other side of the equation, senior *ulama* tried to convince Wahid that he had to improve his relationship with other societal forces if he wanted to stay in power. On most occasions, however, they found Wahid stubborn. Cholil Bisri, one of the most influential NU-affiliated *kiai*, insisted that "we tried a lot, believe me: we talked to him at *pesantren*, discussed with him in small circles, we visited him at the palace." Cholil and other senior *kiai* told Wahid "that he will go down if he continues like this, but mostly he just laughed and said that everything will be alright".[19] When Wahid did not point to his superior political instincts as the reason for his invincibility, he tried to assure his fellow NU leaders that his presidency was spiritually protected by the *wali songo*, nine saints revered by the traditionalist community for their role in Islamizing Java several centuries earlier.[20]

There was indeed little indication that Wahid listened to the advice from within NU. Most of the concessions that the president handed to his opponents were of a temporary nature and often followed by fresh attacks on their interests. To begin with, Wahid agreed to delegate some presidential powers to Megawati in August 2000 but subsequently reshuffled his cabinet without her consent and isolated her from important policy decisions. In addition, he recklessly destroyed his personal relationship with Megawati by frequently entertaining his visitors with jokes about her private life, intellectual deficiencies, and physical attributes. His interactions with other political parties were equally awkward and destructive. Wahid made numerous promises of increased cabinet representation to Golkar Chairman Akbar Tandjung, but regularly broke his word and continued to denounce Golkar as the major obstacle to further democratization. Besides failing to secure the support of political parties, he also made ill-considered advances to the security forces. For instance, in order to appease the military, he withdrew his initiative for radical military reform and reversed his stand on Aceh and Papua, but still insisted on the promotion of personal loyalists to top posts in the armed forces. As a result, key political groups alienated by Wahid forged a coalition against him, with parliament serving as its major institutional base.

## NU Between Power and Democracy

The growing tensions between Wahid and the oppositional coalition in parliament aggravated the conflict between traditionalist and modernist groups. From the many grievances against the president, the largest factions in the legislature had picked two cases of financial misconduct to launch formal impeachment proceedings against Wahid. The first case, referred to as "Buloggate", was concerned with an illicit transfer of money from the national logistics agency to the president's masseur, while the second case, "Bruneigate", related to a private donation from the Sultan of Brunei to Wahid. In January 2001, parliament issued its first memorandum, demanding an explanation from the president and initiating a long process aimed at his removal. The manoeuvre sparked angry reactions from traditionalist groups at the grassroots, particularly in East Java. The main target of PKB-affiliated militias such as *Gerakan Pembela Bangsa* (GPB, Movement of Defenders of the Nation) were offices and educational institutions associated with Muhammadiyah. Between February and July 2001, Muhammadiyah recorded attacks on 5 universities, 12 schools, 5 clinics, 4 mosques, 9 offices and at least 18 houses of its leaders (Feillard 2002, p. 127). In addition to locally limited violence, several groups sprang up that prepared to march on Jakarta to defend Wahid against what they viewed as unconstitutional moves to unseat him. According to O'Rourke (2002, p. 397), the president "tacitly endorsed such threats" as a deterrent to discourage parliament from continuing the impeachment proceedings. While Wahid distanced himself from individual acts of destruction, he pointed to the traditionalist outrage as evidence for his claim that several provinces would seek separation from Indonesia if he lost the presidency. The prediction of senior NU *kiai* that Wahid's election and subsequent removal from office could result in violence between traditionalist and modernist groups had turned into reality.

The extent to which NU *kiai* organized, encouraged, or tolerated some of the violence against modernist institutions and leaders remains unclear. Muhammadiyah officials certainly believed that NU clerics were responsible for the acts of their followers, and an offer by NU Chairman Hasyim Muzadi for financial compensation appeared to confirm that assumption.[21] There is no doubt, however, that senior *kiai* contributed to the emergence of an atmosphere in which violence was condoned as a legitimate instrument of political competition. In January 2001, one of Wahid's closest confidants, Nur Iskandar, declared that the blood of Akbar Tandjung and Amien Rais was *halal* (lit. "permissible"), which according to Islamic jurisprudence made it legal to kill them. In addition, a meeting in Sukabumi in April 2001, which was attended by some of NU's most respected clerics, decided that opponents of Wahid could be classified as *bughot*, or rebels against the legitimate government.[22] That categorization, in turn, made their violent suppression not only justifiable, but mandatory. In order to consolidate Wahid's presidential authority in religious terms, the *kiai* also called for the title of *waliyul amri dlaruri bissyyaukah* (legitimate interim ruler according to Islamic law) to be bestowed on him — the same title Nahdlatul Ulama had granted Sukarno in 1954. By implication, Muslims were obliged to defend the holder of that title against attempts to remove him. Such jurisprudential verdicts not only coincided with, but in fact provided legitimacy to, the creation of paramilitary pro-Wahid organizations such as *Pasukan Berani Mati* (PBM, Troops Ready to Die). According to Andrée Feillard (2002, p. 127), PBM volunteers were trained in several NU strongholds in East Java, and proclaimed that they were prepared to die "a martyr's death to defend [Wahid]".

Modernist groups reacted to the crisis with sharp critiques of traditionalist clerics and their religio-political concepts. Islamic intellectuals with modernist backgrounds pointed particularly to the ease with which *kiai* were prepared to use their jurisprudential authority to justify repressive action against Wahid's opponents. They also criticized the habit of NU figures to convey spiritual messages that they claimed to have received through exclusive communications with deceased saints. These messages predicted, not surprisingly, that Wahid would ultimately overcome his enemies.[23] The modernist rejection of supernatural discourses had been a point of contention between the two main Muslim constituencies for more than a century, but the current crisis provided the dispute with immediate political relevance. Feillard (2002, p. 134) argued that "NU's exacerbated feelings were now starting to play into the hands of [its] adversaries, always keen to criticize trends to *shirk* (associationism) and a lack of rationality among traditionalists."[24] Consequently, modernist leaders launched fierce attacks on what they interpreted as attempts by traditionalist *kiai* to protect Wahid with jurisprudential edicts and spiritual prophecies. Husein Umar, a prominent *Dewan Dakwah* figure, recalled how a *kiai* had reminded Akbar Tandjung that an angel located in Wahid's chest could observe whether the DPR chairman recited the al-Fatihah prayers 2000 times a day. Only then, the *kiai* asserted, would Akbar have the privilege of "encountering the soul of [Wahid]". Husein attacked these "irrational arguments" as attempts to "deify the ulama" and spread "slander" in the Muslim community. Feillard (2002, p. 134) called Husein's critique "a terrible slap for NU's respected kiais". Some modernists, however, did not limit themselves to intellectual "slaps". Islamist splinter groups like the Indonesian branch of *Ikhwanul Muslimin* (Muslim Brotherhood) and the *Front Pembela Kebenaran* (FPK, Front of Defenders of the Truth) established militias in anticipation of the announced PBM march on Jakarta.

Undeterred by criticism of their leadership, the majority of NU *kiai* continued their defence of the president and even supported his plans for disbanding the legislature. On 22 July 2001, one day before the MPR was scheduled to impeach Wahid and swear in Megawati as his successor, hundreds of *kiai* convened in Batu Ceper, just outside Jakarta, to discuss their response to the escalation of the crisis. Nur Iskandar, the host of the event, demanded in his opening speech that the clerics formulate a firm stand vis-à-vis "the maltreatment of [Wahid], the maltreatment of NU, and the maltreatment of the *kiai*".[25] He left no doubt that there was only one option for the *kiai*: to support the suspension of parliament and the declaration of a state of emergency, which Wahid had indicated would occur in the next couple of hours. Even more moderate NU officials concurred with the general view among the audience that the legislature had lost its right to exist. Hasyim Muzadi spoke at length about how "parliament has betrayed the people and engaged in unconstitutional moves to unseat the legitimate president".[26] The DPR, Hasyim maintained, could no longer claim to represent the electorate as it had violated commonly accepted democratic procedures. Encouraged by feisty speeches and messages conveyed from the palace, the NU clerics decided to ask the president to proceed with his emergency plans. Wahid's inner circle later claimed that it was this appeal by the *kiai* that convinced the president to issue the emergency decree in the evening of 22 July (Feillard 2002, p. 135). This is highly unlikely, however. Wahid had been threatening to make this move for several months, and he had told members of his cabinet that he was determined to realize his plan despite their opposition. In addition, presidential aides appeared to play an important role in the Batu Ceper gathering. The discussions were interrupted several times because the president had made special requests via telephone, mostly asking the *kiai* to recite specific prayers.

The impeachment of Wahid and the inauguration of a new government on 23 July 2001 came as an anticlimax to the presidential crisis. Family members and aides escorted the deposed head of state from the palace to a "vacation" in the United States, preventing him from launching further attempts to mobilize his supporters. Leading NU clerics, who just one day before had approved of disbanding the legislature, immediately established contacts with the new power holders and assured them of their cooperation. Even the PKB faction in parliament, which initially decided to boycott its proceedings, resumed full operations in the institution dissolved by Wahid's decree. Most importantly, however, the violence at the grassroots stopped once it had become clear that NU *kiai* had no intention of opposing the new government. It appeared that most clerics were prepared to defend Wahid as long as he was in office, but saw no benefit in post-factum challenges to his removal. In fact, many PKB and NU leaders seemed relieved that the burden of having to support Wahid had been taken off them. Nevertheless, Wahid's failure would turn into a traumatic legacy for NU's involvement in political affairs, with the public trust in the governing capacity of traditionalist Muslims severely damaged. After the chaos of the Wahid years, it seemed unlikely that any NU leader would be able to win the presidency again in the foreseeable future.

## Muslim Groups and the Challenges of Democracy

Despite the quick easing of tensions after Wahid's fall, the severe conflicts between Muslim mainstream organizations in the first half of 2001 calls into question some of the basic assumptions about their role in civil society and democratic consolidation. The literature on Nahdlatul Ulama and Muhammadiyah had since the early 1990s focused on their contribution to democratization at the grassroots level. Western observers in particular measured the democratic credentials of both organizations by their ability to contain the spread of groups with more Islamist agendas. Martin van Bruinessen (2003, p. 17), for instance, asserted that "moderation and tolerance have long been characteristic of the mainstream members of these organisations [as] both have resolutely opposed issues that could lead to the further polarisation of society (such as the Jakarta Charter)".[27] Bruinessen (2003, p. 6) concluded that NU and Muhammadiyah are "vehicles of a democratic climate" and "pillars of civil society", concurring with Hefner's notion (2000, p. 218) of centrist Muslim organizations as proponents of "civil Islam". Such classifications led many observers to downplay obvious cases of undemocratic behaviour in the two mainstream groups. Greg Barton (2001, p. 252), for example, explained NU's democratic deficiencies as resulting from the fact that "NU *ulama* are a rustic and eccentric group, being drawn primarily from rural stock." With significant non-democratic dispositions belittled as "rustic" and "eccentric", Barton maintained that NU leaders are generally "moderate" and "tolerant".

The competition between NU and Muhammadiyah for political hegemony in the early years of the post-Suharto system warrants a reassessment of their relationship with the state and civil society. During authoritarian rule, both organizations had created important niches for political activities outside of the formal institutions and norms imposed by the regime. Under constant pressure from Suharto, NU and Muhammadiyah were part of a civil society that was primarily concerned with protecting itself from intrusion by the control apparatus of the New Order. The 1998 regime change, however, fundamentally altered their relationship with the state. They decided to participate actively in the political structures of the post-authoritarian polity, supporting the creation of parties to defend the interests of their constituencies. Although NU and Muhammadiyah formally remained independent socio-religious organizations, their dominant role in PKB and PAN was undeniable. The vast majority of PKB and PAN functionaries were members of NU and Muhammadiyah respectively, and the voting patterns of the 1999 elections demonstrated that the public tended not to differentiate between the organizations and their affiliated parties (Ananta, Arifin, and Suryadinata 2004, p. 370; Iskandar 2001, p. 185).

In short, the post-1998 changes had turned NU and Muhammadiyah into electoral competitors and participants in the political negotiations over power, resources, and privileges.[28] Consequently, NU became an integral part of the regime when its chairman assumed the presidency in 1999, and it concentrated all its efforts on defending the incumbent against mounting opposition from society and the political elite. In doing so, leading NU officials and clerics exposed political attitudes that did not always focus on "inculcating civic values in their members" (Bruinessen 2003, p. 6). In fact, the edicts outlawing opposition to Wahid and calls for disbanding the legislature were neither supportive of a "democratic climate" nor did they accord with NU's self-image as a "pillar of civil society".

The social unrest and political instability associated with Wahid's removal pointed to the ambivalent contribution of the two largest Muslim mainstream organizations to the development of the early post-authoritarian state. Hefner and van Bruinessen were correct in lauding both sides for consistently opposing the formal Islamization of the state as demanded by some groups at the ultra-modernist fringes of the political spectrum. The promotion of moderate Islamic concepts of political organization supported the evolution of a pluralist party system and helped to reduce societal resistance to Western forms of democracy. This moderation did not extend to the norms and procedures of direct political competition among themselves, however. The attempts by modernist politicians to unseat a head of state they had voted into office only months earlier, and the willingness of traditionalist leaders to condone repressive measures in his defence, exposed a highly selective commitment to the upholding of democratic rules. Evidently, both currents of the Muslim community found it difficult to translate their civil society values developed under decades of authoritarian rule into a normative framework for their behaviour as political actors in the post-Suharto system.[29]

The political engagement of NU and Muhammadiyah in the early phase of the democratic transition did not only affect the relationship between Indonesia's largest Muslim organizations, however. The prolonged conflicts between its leading representatives, which resulted in violence at the grassroots level and political instability in the centre, also impacted negatively on public perceptions of civilian leadership qualities as a whole. In consequence, civilian politicians were confronted with a serious crisis of legitimacy, and the popularity of the armed forces and former generals active in politics increased considerably. Military officers, who had faced severe societal resentment in the aftermath of Suharto's fall, now blamed civilian leaders for "the complete mess they have created".[30] Particularly the communal violence in East Java and the mobilization of political militias assisted the armed forces in propagating their traditional prejudice that "if civilians are in charge, they do nothing but fight among themselves, even threaten to kill each other in God's name".[31] After two years of unprecedented political turmoil, an increasing number of Indonesians appeared to agree.

## COURTING THE GENERALS:
## ISLAMIC LEADERS AND THE 2004 ELECTIONS

The collapse of the Wahid government had important consequences for the relationship between Islamic groups and the constellation of power within them. The coalition that facilitated Wahid's election in 1999 had been designed to overcome memories of failed all-Islamic experiments since the colonial period, but the bitter conflicts that followed only deepened the existing divisions and sentiments. Although the chairmen of NU and Muhammadiyah, Hasyim Muzadi and Syafi'i Maarif, managed to rebuild their personal ties through a series of social and cultural initiatives, the political rift between the two largest Islamic constituencies was significant. Most importantly, it all but excluded the possibility of further coalitions between traditionalist and modernist Muslim parties in the coming years, particularly in the run-up to the 2004 elections. In addition to the widening gap between key Islamic groups, the events surrounding Wahid's removal also created new divisions within Nahdlatul Ulama. Loyalists of the deposed president accused leading NU and PKB functionaries of not doing enough to defend Wahid and of reconciling too quickly with his opponents. The chairman of the PKB branch of East Java, Choirul Anam, claimed that thousands of his supporters had been ready to flock into the capital and confront Wahid's adversaries, but Matori Abdul Djalil and Hasyim Muzadi had prevented them from taking action (Feillard 2002, pp. 136–37). Indeed, Matori had participated in the MPR session that impeached Wahid, despite PKB's official boycott, and Hasyim had made it clear that NU acknowledged the legitimacy of the new government.[32] Consequently, Wahid insisted on Matori's replacement as PKB chairman, and his relationship with Hasyim Muzadi was damaged irreparably. Like the split between the largest Islamic constituencies, the factionalism within NU was certain to impact on the process of coalition-building for the 2004 polls.

The political elite began to prepare for the 2004 elections as soon as Megawati took office, despite the fact that her term was scheduled to last for more than three years and thus longer than that of any other democratic government in Indonesian history. There were several reasons for this. To begin with, the largest political parties had agreed after Wahid's fall that they would allow Megawati to serve out the remainder of the presidential term without major challenges to her rule. According to Amien Rais, leading politicians signed an agreement that guaranteed Megawati "that she will not be brought down halfway into her presidency, because if she were impeached too, that would be a joke for Indonesia's democracy".[33] This decision diverted the focus of political competition from active opposition against the incumbent to the issue of succession. Crucially, Megawati also fulfilled her side of the contract with the political elite. She supported the election of PPP leader Hamzah Haz as her vice-president, included members of most political parties in her government, and largely refrained from conflicts with the legislature. During her three years in office, she did not dismiss a single minister, compared to fifteen cabinet reshuffles involving more than thirty cabinet members under Wahid's rule (Simanjuntak 2003, p. 432). In terms of policy, the Megawati government stayed away from controversial initiatives for change, turning it into "something of a holding operation" under which political actors concentrated their resources for the 2004 race (Crouch 2003*b*, p. 15). Finally, the upcoming elections were also the main subject of inter-elite negotiations over amendments to the constitution. In August 2002, the MPR decided that the president and vice-president would be elected in a direct ballot, encouraging party leaders and political figures to position themselves within the new electoral framework.

## Islamic Groups and Electoral Politics

The divisions between and within Islamic groups impaired their ability to find prospective candidates for the presidential contest. Given the conflicts under the Wahid government, the nomination of a joint candidate representing both traditionalist and modernist parties like in 1999 was out of the question. Wahid refused to meet Amien Rais for more than two years after his fall, and even after he agreed to an encounter in July 2003, he ruled out the possibility of political cooperation. Pledging publicly not to "fall into the same hole twice", Wahid insisted that "Amien has proven that he is not trustworthy."[34] On the modernist side, support for the renewal of an all-Islamic alliance was equally weak. Many modernist politicians viewed the failure of Wahid's presidency as evidence of the political immaturity of traditionalist leaders. They contended that NU-affiliated clerics in politics "believe that running the state is like running a *pesantren* — all the authority, all the funds are in the hands of the *kiai*, and there is no accountability".[35] In addition to these mutual sentiments, the all-Islamic option lacked credible candidates. Some youth leaders in both NU and Muhammadiyah mentioned Nurcholish Madjid as a possible nominee, but his candidacy never gained political momentum. After scoring high levels of support in opinion polls, Nurcholish considered participating in the convention held by the Golkar party to select its presidential candidate. He finally withdrew from the contest in protest against Golkar's internal convention procedures, and fell seriously ill shortly afterwards. In July 2004, just as Indonesians cast their votes for the next president, Nurcholish underwent liver transplant surgery in China, and he eventually died in August 2005.

Traditionalist and modernist groups not only faced insurmountable difficulties in nominating a joint candidate, but they were also divided internally over the best nominee for their respective constituencies. Amien Rais was determined to run for the presidency again, but as an ICG report (2003, p. 11) noted, it was "barely imaginable that the Islamic parties would join to nominate him". His relationship with PPP and Bulan Bintang was tense since Amien had failed to fulfil his promise to lead these parties in 1998. Accordingly, PPP officials were leaning towards a renewed alliance with Megawati, and Yusril made it clear that Bulan Bintang would not support Amien's nomination. Even Partai Keadilan, which formed a joint faction in parliament with PAN, appeared reluctant to back up its former patron. That left PAN and Muhammadiyah as the only organizational vehicles for Amien's campaign. PAN, however, was unlikely to receive much more than the 7.1 per cent of the votes it had gained in 1999, casting doubts on its effectiveness as an independent electoral machine for the presidential ballot. Given PAN's weakness and the non-committal attitude of modernist parties, Muhammadiyah leaders promised Amien full institutional support for his 2004 candidacy, departing from their 1999 position that had ruled out such direct electoral assistance.[36] In the traditionalist community, the search for a candidate was similarly difficult and divisive. Despite strong reservations on the part of senior *kiai*, Wahid insisted on competing in the popular ballot.[37] He was certain that he could regain the presidency for NU and provide ultimate proof that his 2001 ouster had been the work of a tiny elite. NU leaders around Hasyim Muzadi believed, however, that their organization would have a much better chance of participating in the next government if it nominated a vice-presidential candidate to pair up with one of the key contenders. The split caused heated debates between the two camps, with one group suggesting that the former president was unfit for office and the other accusing Hasyim of having received bribes from Megawati.[38]

Before the campaign for the 2004 presidential ballot began, however, the elections of new governors in several Indonesian provinces in 2002 and 2003 offered the political parties ample opportunities to test possible alliances and electoral strategies. Reflecting the deep divisions within the civilian elite, these local polls ultimately led to the emergence of new patterns of coalition-building. At the centre of these new electoral dynamics was a remarkably high number of retired military officers — presenting themselves as partners for civilian forces keen to deny their opponents important bureaucratic posts. In East Java, for example, the PDI-P leadership decided in 2003 to support the re-election of incumbent governor Imam Utomo, a retired two-star general and former commander of the province. PDI-P was locked in a paralysing power balance with PKB in the East Java legislature, with each party controlling one third of the seats. From PDI-P's perspective, Imam's nomination promised to hand the governorship to a neutral mediator and thus helped to prevent a possible PKB victory. Wahid, for his part, responded to PDI-P's move by pushing for another retired general, Abdul Kahfi, to be named PKB's nominee.[39] Kahfi's nomination stirred opposition from some leading *kiai* who favoured PKB secretary-general Saifullah Yusuf for the post.[40] Wahid prevailed, however, setting up a contest between two retired generals for one of Indonesia's most crucial governorships.

The outcome of the gubernatorial election in East Java was a foregone conclusion, however. Kahfi had been virtually unknown in East Java before Wahid suddenly presented him as PKB's candidate, and he was also a marginal figure in the national military hierarchy. In consequence, he found it difficult to turn himself into a credible contender. Imam, by contrast, had used his governorship effectively to manoeuvre himself into a formidable electoral position. One member of East Java's election commission predicted an easy victory for Imam, saying that "he has prepared his re-election for years, paying off the right people, including in the parties and religious organizations; this will be an easy ride for him."[41] Imam indeed won the election in the East Java legislature by a large margin. Beside his military background, the access to state resources and other privileges associated with incumbency had given him a decisive advantage over his competitor. Imam's victory reflected a new pattern of electoral behaviour within the elite that evoked memories of the pre-1971 period of Suharto's rule when, according to Sundhaussen (1978, p. 52), "many provincial and district assemblies favoured the appointment of colonels and generals, even ... when political parties still had an important say in these assemblies". The major reason for this phenomenon was "the reluctance of party politicians to back a candidate from a rival party; they would rather vote for someone who is considered 'neutral' in party politics". Despite the stark differences between the early New Order and the post-Suharto polity, Sundhaussen's assessment could well be applied to describe the character of provincial politics in 2002 and 2003.

East Java was not the only case in which retired military officers profited from civilian divisions to defend or gain top bureaucratic positions. In Central Java, PKB nominated a local NU leader to run as vice-governor on the ticket of the incumbent, retired two-star general Mardiyanto. PDI-P also decided to support Mardiyanto's re-election bid, despite the party's electoral predominance in the province and consequent strong pressure from its rank and file to nominate a party figure for governor. PAN, for its part, recruited the one-time commander of Jakarta, retired Major General Kirbiantoro, as its nominee for the gubernatorial election. Although neither candidate had any prior party affiliation, the PDI-P leadership celebrated Mardiyanto's eventual win against his former military colleague as proof of its impressive negotiation skills.[42] Several local PDI-P chairmen disagreed, however, and left the party in dismay. In West Java, PKB sent retired general Tayo Tarmadi into the elections for governor, facing an experienced bureaucrat nominated by Golkar, Danny Setiawan. The Golkar candidate, who was a leading figure in FKPPI, won the ballot.[43] In Lampung, incumbent governor Oemarsono, also a former officer, ran with Army Chief of Staff Ryamizard Ryacudu's brother as his candidate for the vice-governorship. The pair was backed by the PDI-P central board, but lost against a local businessman who had obtained the support of local legislators. The governor-elect was arrested on corruption charges, however, leading to the annulment of the vote by the central government and a re-run of the election. Subsequently, Ryamizard's brother joined forces with a new candidate for governor and, this time, emerged as part of the winning team. In addition, victories for retired military officers were recorded in North Sumatra, Jakarta, East Kalimantan, and Maluku.[44]

The success of former generals in a series of local elections provided additional evidence for the interrelationship between divisions in the civilian elite and the political engagement of the armed forces and its personnel. With parties unable to form alliances and agree on joint civilian candidates, retired officers dominated the electoral scene easily. The fragmentation in the Muslim community was particularly consequential in this regard. After Wahid's fall, traditionalist and modernist Muslim parties found it impossible to cooperate on joint nominations, and ex-generals reaped the benefits from this ongoing antagonism. In the same vein, Wahid's antics as president had severely damaged the historically good relationship between traditionalist Muslims and nationalist parties. Megawati's PDI-P was still bitter over Wahid's empty promises of support in the 1999 presidential campaign, and the deposed president himself believed that his former deputy had helped to engineer his downfall in an unconstitutional manner. These personal animosities prevented PDI-P and PKB from working together in most gubernatorial elections, and led to the re-election of incumbents with a military background in the parties' strongholds in East and Central Java. Their victories exposed the weakness of civilian politics in the early period of the post-Suharto transition and indicated that the armed forces and their retired officers had successfully recovered from their low societal reputation in 1998 and 1999. Most importantly, the electoral trends emerging from the local ballots prefigured the national political landscape ahead of the 2004 polls, with former generals once again taking centre stage.

## Building Civil-Military Alliances for the 2004 Polls

With electoral deals between civilian parties and retired military officers in local ballots proving highly successful, national politicians tried to replicate this pattern in their presidential campaigns. Amien Rais was the first party leader and presidential hopeful who publicly lobbied senior generals, both active and retired, to become his running mate. After his failure to enlist the backing of modernist parties, the presentation of a popular military figure appeared as the next best strategy to broaden his support base. In September 2003, the former Muhammadiyah chairman introduced the idea of a civilian-military alliance as the key message of his campaign. He argued that the expertise of former generals was needed to secure the territorial integrity of the state against separatist threats and other security disturbances.[45] In Amien's view, the blend between his image as a reform-minded civilian with the nationalist credentials of a retired military leader was certain to attract substantial support from a society unsettled by six years of political transition. Consequently, he offered Susilo Bambang Yudhoyono the vice-presidential nomination on his ticket, but was turned down.[46] Yudhoyono was not the only military retiree who rejected Amien's advances, however. After PAN's disappointing performance in the 2004 legislative elections,[47] Amien asked both Endriartono and Agum Gumelar if they were interested in the vice-presidential candidacy, but received negative responses.[48] By the time Amien had to make a definitive decision in May, there were already three other tickets with civilian-military pairs in the race. He ultimately chose former minister Siswono Yudohusodo, a civilian, as his partner for the elections and turned his earlier concept on its head: what had been planned as an integrated civilian-military ticket was now popularized as the only genuinely civilian duo confronting the dominance of retired officers in the presidential competition.[49]

Many of the modernist Islamic parties that had refused to endorse Amien's candidacy eventually built alliances with retired military officers as well. Bulan Bintang declared its support for Yudhoyono early on in the nomination process, becoming one of the three parties that formed the core of his coalition. Party chairman Yusril Ihza Mahendra was the driving force behind Bulan Bintang's support for Yudhoyono, having grown close to him during their time together in several post-Suharto cabinets. Some elements of the party opposed Yudhoyono's nomination, however. Ahmad Sumargono, a former KISDI figure and one of Bulan Bintang's most prominent ultra-modernist figures, declared his resignation from the party and threw his support behind Amien Rais.[50] Equally, a large number of branches in the regions chose to join Amien's campaign and risk open conflict with the central board. PPP witnessed similar conflicts. Hamzah Haz had initially sought the vice-presidential slot on Megawati's ticket, but after she had picked Hasyim Muzadi, PPP decided to nominate its chairman for the presidency and Agum Gumelar as his running mate. The move sparked protest from some factions within PPP, which declared their support for Amien as well. Partai Keadilan Sejahtera, for its part, was split between supporters of Amien and Wiranto, who had won the nomination of the Golkar party in an internal ballot. The sympathy for Wiranto within PKS surprised many, but appeared to have originated from his personal protection of KAMMI leaders during the 1998 student protests.[51] The pro-Wiranto group caused a deadlock in the internal party deliberations about the question of which candidate to recommend to its voters, delaying the decision to the final phase of the campaign. Although the party ultimately opted for Amien, 21 per cent of PKS's supporters still voted for Wiranto, the highest percentage for the former TNI commander among those major parties that did not officially campaign for him (IFES 2004b).

Former generals also played important roles in the search for presidential nominees who could represent the traditionalist Muslim community. In Nahdlatul Ulama and PKB, there was both strong support for and fierce opposition against another candidacy of Abdurrahman Wahid. Even after the Election Commission indicated that Wahid was likely to be excluded from the presidential ballot for health reasons, the prospect of finding a candidate acceptable to all NU factions remained remote. The former president made it clear that he would not endorse any NU nominee considered disloyal to him, mentioning Hasyim Muzadi by name. Therefore, the recruitment of a retired military leader as a compromise candidate appeared to many as an attractive solution, offering to bridge internal differences and improve the electoral standing of the traditionalist constituency. PKB officials thus consulted in late 2003 with Yudhoyono about the possibility of him running as the party's presidential candidate.[52] Partai Demokrat, however, won enough votes in the April elections to nominate Yudhoyono for the presidency on its own, and PKB leaders felt that his interest in PKB as a possible electoral vehicle declined as a result.[53] The negotiations over Yudhoyono's possible nomination by PKB were broken off in late April, and when the Election Commission officially excluded Wahid from the poll in May, the party was acutely conscious of its lack of a candidate. As expected, Wahid categorically ruled out supporting Hasyim Muzadi, who had joined Megawati's campaign as her vice-presidential nominee.[54] Finally, the ex-president threw his support behind Wiranto and allowed his younger brother, Solahuddin Wahid, to run as the deputy of the former TNI chief. Despite his initial intention to boycott the ballot in protest against his disqualification, Wahid campaigned actively for the pair. Senior *kiai* loyal to Wahid also called on their *santri* to elect Wiranto, arguing that voting for Hasyim Muzadi constituted a violation of Islamic norms as he had teamed up with a female presidential candidate.[55] Evidently, the divisions within a major civilian constituency had once more served the interests of a politically active ex-general.

## Yudhoyono and the Elections of 2004

The first round of presidential elections in July 2004 highlighted the successful adaptation of former military leaders to the new democratic framework. With Yudhoyono, Wiranto, and Agum, three protagonists of Suharto's military competed for political power in the post-authoritarian state, just a few years after the armed forces seemed to have been irrevocably discredited by their involvement in the New Order regime. Using the fragmentation of civilian politics to their advantage, the former generals had emerged as welcome alternatives to the chronic infighting between and within the political parties. However, there were significant differences in their electoral appeal. Yudhoyono eventually defeated his former TNI colleagues because he effectively combined the traditional features of a military leader with the images of post-Suharto reform. Ranking first with 33.6 per cent, Yudhoyono was viewed by voters as firm yet consensus-oriented, consistent yet open-minded, conservative yet liberal. Wiranto, on the other hand, was largely identified with the political inflexibility of the New Order (NDI 2004, pp. 6, 12). In addition to an unfavourable reputation, the confusion within the traditionalist Muslim community and Golkar over which candidate to support also undermined the electoral chances of the former TNI chief. Wahid, despite calling on his supporters to vote for Wiranto, gave interviews in which he predicted that the retired general had no chance of winning.[56] The same ambivalence applied to Golkar's attitude. By most accounts, the party machinery was not fully mobilized to support its candidate. Golkar Chairman Akbar Tandjung had little interest in a Wiranto victory, and a lot of local party leaders who had spent all their resources on the parliamentary elections were reluctant to raise further funds for an uncertain cause. Thus Wiranto only came in third with 22.2 per cent, behind Megawati who claimed second place with 26.6 per cent and qualified for a second-round encounter with Yudhoyono in September. Amien Rais finished fourth, while Hamzah Haz and his running mate Agum took bottom place.

The second round of the presidential elections saw key Muslim groups and parties once again deeply divided. In the modernist camp, Partai Keadilan Sejahtera declared its support for Yudhoyono, while PAN was clearly leaning towards the former general despite officially remaining neutral.[57] The two parties joined forces with Bulan Bintang, which had been part of Yudhoyono's campaign since May 2004. PKS, PAN, and Bulan Bintang were opposed to what was widely perceived as Megawati's secularist attitude to political affairs, and certainly were not in favour of a traditionalist Muslim in the vice-presidency. They were also highly critical of Megawati's lackluster performance since 2001, insisting that a change of the national leadership was inevitable. These ideological and political considerations were of such importance that they overcame concerns over Yudhoyono's military background, particularly in PKS. On the other hand, PPP and one of its splinter parties, PBR, became members of the Nationhood Coalition (*Koalisi Kebangsaan*), which pledged to secure Megawati's re-election. Other members of the coalition included PDI-P, Golkar, and a number of smaller secular-nationalist parties. PPP leader Hamzah Haz felt that his party had received a fair share of resources and positions under Megawati's rule and sought to continue this arrangement, while PBR joined the coalition with the explicit notion of defending civilian supremacy against the danger of a resurgent military.[58] With modernist Muslim parties supporting different candidates, the elections offered fresh proof that shared Islamic beliefs and values were insufficient as common denominators when it came to building effective political coalitions.

On the traditionalist side, efforts to reconcile Wahid and Hasyim Muzadi in order to unite the Nahdlatul Ulama vote behind its chairman were unsuccessful.[59] The former president assigned one of his daughters to accompany Yudhoyono to important *pesantren* and campaign for him, effectively neutralizing Hasyim Muzadi's call on traditionalist voters to support him as the only NU cadre left in the presidential race. In addition to the effects of Wahid's manoeuvres, many *kiai* also believed in the inevitability of Yudhoyono's victory and therefore began to distance themselves from Megawati and Hasyim, who according to opinion polls had no realistic chance of winning the contest. For many traditionalist clerics, the attraction of being on the winning side was stronger than their loyalty to the NU chairman, highlighting the pragmatism inherent in Nahdlatul Ulama's political ideology. Ultimately, amidst the chaos surrounding the tactical decisions of their respective parties, the majority of modernist and traditionalist Muslim voters supported Yudhoyono. He won the election in a landslide against Megawati, who could only defend her strongholds in predominantly non-Muslim areas such as Bali, Maluku, and East Nusa Tenggara. Yudhoyono's victory was a bittersweet experience for many Muslim politicians, both modernist and traditionalist: they had succeeded in replacing Megawati, but had failed again to place a credible Islamic figure in the presidency. The idea of pan-Islamic unity in Indonesian politics seemed as utopian as ever.

Yudhoyono's victory completed a series of electoral successes by retired military officers in provincial and national polls. This phenomenon occurred despite the introduction of new electoral mechanisms that, in theory, provided civilian political parties with the instruments to secure important government posts for their cadres. In provincial legislatures, parties that held large numbers of seats still felt it necessary to select non-party figures, mostly former generals, as their nominees for executive posts. At the national level, the first direct presidential ballot in Indonesia's history — which had been designed to empower civilian politicians — had three retired officers competing in the race. There are two interrelated explanations for this. First, the deep divisions within and between civilian constituencies encouraged their leaders to seek former generals as partners in order to resolve internal conflicts and improve their electoral chances vis-à-vis other participants in the polls. The fragmentation of Muslim politics was most illustrative in this regard. The conflict in Nahdlatul Ulama, for example, demonstrated that many civilian leaders were willing to use military figures to outplay their internal rivals, with Wahid supporting Wiranto and Yudhoyono to undermine the vice-presidential nomination of the NU chairman. The second explanation relates to the improved public image of the armed forces and its retired personnel since the constitutional crisis of 2001. The surge in societal support for notions of political stability and the corresponding decline of trust in civilian leadership qualities created incentives for politicians to integrate former generals into their campaigns. As a result, by late 2004 retired officers had been installed in crucial posts in local administrations and in the presidency. Democratic elections, previously viewed as an obstacle to the participation of both active and retired military figures in politics, had evolved into one of its most effective vehicles.

## ISLAMIC RADICALISM AND THE MILITARY, 1998–2004

The increasing fragmentation of the Muslim mainstream was not the only development in Indonesian Islam between 1998 and 2004 that had the potential of playing into the hands of the military. Earlier chapters of this book have also highlighted the way in which a small, but violent segment of extremist Islam helped to underpin the claim of the armed forces to political privileges from the 1950s to the 1990s. This section discusses the role of militant Muslim groups in the early post-New Order polity as well as their impact on the position of the military in Indonesian society. It shows that while the issue of violent Islamist radicalism allowed officers to pursue some of their political and economic interests, it was nowhere as important for TNI's institutional agenda as similar threats under pre-1998 regimes, and did not match the significance of "conventional" Muslim politics for the evolution of Indonesia's transitional civil-military relations.

In the early post-Suharto era, violent Islamic extremism was manifested in three different types of groups: terrorist cells, "anti-vice" militias, and paramilitary groups that intervened in communal conflicts. To begin with, the leaders of terrorist cells were largely Islamic militants who had fled Indonesia in the 1980s and returned to their homeland after the regime change of 1998 (Fealy 2004; Bruinessen 2002).[60] The most prominent among them was Abu Bakar Ba'asyir, a cleric from the city of Solo in Central Java. He headed *Jemaah Islamiyah* (JI), which functioned as an umbrella organization for militant cells across the archipelago and, in fact, Southeast Asia. Beginning in 2000, *Jemaah Islamiyah* carried out a series of bombings in several Indonesian provinces. Initially, the attacks focused mostly on Christian churches and institutions,[61] but after 11 September, the terrorists increasingly chose targets associated with the United States or its Western allies. In January 2002, the Singaporean government announced that it had arrested members of a JI cell that had planned to blow up the U.S. embassy in the city-state, and that the intelligence gathered from the suspects pointed to Ba'asyir's involvement. The Indonesian authorities appeared unwilling to confront Ba'asyir, however, fearing a backlash from the Muslim community, which viewed foreign demands for counter-terrorism operations as part of an anti-Islamic campaign by the West. Only after the Bali bombings of October 2002 did Megawati order her ministers to take action, resulting in the arrest of Ba'asyir and new anti-terrorism legislation.

Despite their domestic and international repercussions, the terrorist attacks launched by JI at no point constituted a serious threat to the authority and stability of the government. Unlike the *Darul Islam* rebellion in the 1950s, JI's activities did not require the political elite to initiate extensive military operations and expand the resources of the armed forces. The hunt for JI terrorists was, for the most part, a challenge for police investigators rather than military strategists. Nevertheless, military officers still managed to use the issue of Islamist terrorism to their benefit. Most significantly, by offering the United States cooperation in its "war against terror", TNI leaders advanced their international rehabilitation after years of sanctions and isolation. As a result, existing restrictions were gradually lifted, with Western governments now prioritizing the development of TNI's counter-terrorism capacities over its structural adaptation to the democratic system (Mietzner 2002). Moreover, officers argued that the threat posed by jihadist terrorists justified a larger role for TNI in domestic security. Ryamizard, for example, declared it "impossible" for the police to handle terrorism on its own, and suggested that the military's territorial units be at the "forefront" of the anti-terror campaign.[62] While his pleas did not result in more resources or authority for the armed forces, they strengthened the doubts within the political elite about ongoing military reforms. Already irritated by growing separatist sentiments in Aceh and Papua and communal violence in Kalimantan, Maluku, and Sulawesi, politicians in the executive and legislature interpreted the new terrorist threat as an additional reminder that the process of institutional change in the military should not affect its capacity as an effective security force. Accordingly, the emergence of Islamic terrorism served less as a trigger for new military powers than as a strong disincentive against continuing structural reforms in the armed forces.

In contrast to the underground operations of JI that aimed at killing alleged enemies of Islam, the "anti-vice" militias were largely concerned with imposing Muslim morals through violent acts of intimidation. The most prominent such group was FPI (*Front Pembela Islam*, Front for the Defenders of Islam), which was formed in August 1998 and carried out raids on nightclubs, prostitution venues, and gambling facilities (Purnomo 2003, p. 31). Police and military officers were widely suspected of backing FPI as they profited from increased security payments from the attacked sites. However, in 2002 the police began to take action against FPI and its leaders. FPI Chairman Habib Muhammad Rizieq Syihab was arrested in October of that year, forcing him to temporarily suspend the activities of his organization.[63] FPI resumed operations in February 2003, but found it difficult to regain its previous influence. Finally, the third type of militant Islamist groups specialized in training paramilitary fighters to assist the Muslim side in communal conflicts. Established in January 2000, *Laskar Jihad* (LJ) sent thousands of its members to Maluku and Poso to support Muslims in the religious violence raging there (Hasan 2002 and 2006; Hefner 2003). Like in the case of FPI, individual military and police officers seemed to extend assistance to LJ, for a variety of reasons (ICG 2001, p. 13).[64] Most importantly, it was alleged that a group of officers dismissed by Wahid in 2000 intended to destabilize his presidency by nurturing violent conflicts among societal groups. Their support for LJ was discontinued after Wahid's fall, however, pointing to the contingent character of the cooperation. Second, it was also obvious that ongoing communal clashes created additional income opportunities for officers, with their protection services, vehicles, and arms in high demand. But while the conflict economy provided incentives for the troops to prolong the violence, LJ was by no means the only instrument to achieve that goal. For example, the military in Maluku was also known to have close contacts with a gang of Christian criminals that stirred up violence through arbitrary bomb attacks. Therefore, most cases of military support for radical Muslims appeared to have been motivated by distinctly pragmatic rather than ideological considerations.

## Muslim Politics, Radicalism and Transitional Civil-Military Relations

In general terms, developments at the extremist fringes of Indonesian Islam after 1998 provided only limited opportunities for military officers to expand their political and economic space. In contrast to the role of militant Islam under pre-1998 regimes, extremist Muslim groups in the early post-Suharto era were of secondary importance for the position of the armed forces in society. The threat posed by Islamist terrorists to the Indonesian authorities after 1998 was on a much smaller scale than that launched by the *Darul Islam* rebellion against the political leadership of the 1950s. Similarly, the manipulation of post-1998 Islamist groups by individual officers for short-term political and economic gains had significantly less impact on the role of the military in politics than the New Order intelligence operations in the 1970s on the legitimacy of the military-backed regime. In the 1970s, the creation of radical Islamist groups had been crucial for the Suharto government in order to compensate for the declining role of communism as a credible ideological deterrent. By contrast, the rise of jihadist terrorism was only a marginal element in the military's search for a new identity after 1998. Instead, the armed forces put their main stress on the defence of the unitary state, with separatist movements identified as the military's most important political and ideological adversaries. Even as partners for shadowy operations in conflict areas, militant Islamic groups were only of little relevance for the armed forces. There were other groups with diverse religious, ethnic, and social backgrounds that could be mobilized to serve the same purpose, with their specific use depending on the location, character, and duration of the planned operation.

Clearly, developments in the Islamic mainstream played a much larger role in influencing the dynamics of the early civil-military transition than the security threats from the Islamist fringes. As argued in this chapter, serious divisions between Indonesia's most influential Muslim groups contributed to the fractured state of civilian politics during the post-authoritarian transition between 1998 and 2004. These conflicts encouraged major political forces to turn to the military for assistance in an effort to sideline their opponents. The political infighting during much of the early post-Suharto period — demonstrated most vividly in the constitutional crisis of 2001 and the subsequent collapse of the Wahid government — delivered crucial posts in local administrations to retired generals and assisted the armed forces in repairing their public image damaged during decades of repressive rule. This surge in the military's societal reputation and political significance prepared the way, finally, for Susilo Bambang Yudhoyono's rise to the presidency in 2004. With Islamic leaders unable to define a joint platform for political action, their prediction in the early phase of the democratic transition that there would be "a new era of Indonesian politics dominated by a united, purposeful alliance of Muslim parties" (Fealy 2003, p. 151) remained unfulfilled. It was only after 2004 that intra-Islamic relations began to stabilize, coinciding with considerable improvements in the effectiveness of Indonesia's political system and the quality of democratic control over the armed forces.

## Notes

[1] Interview with Abdurrahman Wahid, Jakarta, 26 May 1998.

[2] Wahid explained that "*Kebangkitan Bangsa*" was derived from "*Nahdlatul Ulama*" (lit. "Revival of the Religious Scholars"). The important difference in this respect, however, was the replacement of *ulama* by *bangsa* (nation).

[3] Interviews with Rozy Munir, deputy chairman of the NU central board, Jakarta, 22 July 1998; Musthafa Zuhad Mughni, deputy chairman of the NU central board, Jakarta, 23 July 1998; Muchith Muzadi, senior *kiai* and one of the five members of the PKB founding committee, Jakarta, 22 July 1998; see also Asmawi (1999, p. 71).

[4] Interview with Ma'ruf Amin, Jakarta, 23 July 1998. In a series of letters sent by the NU central board to its branches, the organization left no doubt that PKB was its political arm. In a letter dated 22 June, the central board reminded its officials that the new party was designed to "pool the political aspirations of Nahdlatul Ulama members". On 24 July, NU called on its followers to "support and take care of Partai Kebangkitan Bangsa as the only party owned by Nahdlatul Ulama citizens". See "Surat Tugas No. 925/A.II.03/6/1998", 22 June 1998, and "Keputusan Rapat Pleno PBNU ke-IV", 24 July 1998.

[5] Abu Hasan, Wahid's challenger at the 1994 congress, added another NU-based party by establishing SUNI (*Solidaritas Uni Nasional Indonesia*, Solidarity of the National Indonesian Union). Hasan's motivations appeared to be more personal

than ideological, however, with SUNI endorsing Pancasila as well. Wahid referred to PKU, PNU, and SUNI summarily as the "chicken shit" of NU, while PKB was its "egg". See "Koalisi Tahi Ayam Merebut Suara NU", *Aula*, Volume 21, Issue 5, 1999; see also Mietzner (1999*a*).

6    Before his resignation, Amien had considered staying on as Muhammadiyah chairman, in which case he would have asked his long-time associate Syafi'i Maarif to establish a Muhammadiyah-affiliated party. Ultimately, however, it was Amien who formed the party, and Syafi'i who took over as Muhammadiyah leader (Sutipyo and Asmawi 1999, p. 116).

7    An anti-Amien Rais booklet published in late 1998 provided interesting insights into the bitterness of many ultra-modernists vis-à-vis the Muhammadiyah chair and his new party: "If we were to follow Amien Rais' thinking (non-sectarian and non-discriminating), and the electoral system is a proportional one ..., then Muslim voters will engage in an act of gambling when voting for their leaders. It may well be that their choice falls on Amien Rais who is Muslim, the Christian figure Albert Hasibuan, the Christian activist Pius Lustrilanang, or the priest Th. Sumartana. This means, if not *haram* [outlawed], PAN can be considered *syubhat* or questionable." The last three names referred to non-Muslim members of PAN (Jaiz 1998, p. 15).

8    Interview with Yusril Ihza Mahendra, Jakarta, 25 August 1998.

9    Interview with Nur Mahmudi Ismail, president of Partai Keadilan, Jakarta, 26 November 1998.

10   Interview with Muhammad Rois, deputy chairman of the PKB Jepara branch, Jepara, 29 May 1999.

11   Interviews with Abdullah Astofa, chairman of the PPP Tegal branch, Tegal, 28 May 1999; Mahmud Mazkur, chairman of the PPP Pekalongan branch, Pekalongan, 28 May 1999; Faris Sulchaq Basori, chairman of the PKB Brebes branch, Brebes, 28 May 1999; M. Mokhtar Noer Jaya, chairman of the PKB South Sulawesi chapter, Makassar, 3 May 1999; and Matori Abdul Djalil, Jakarta, 10 and 22 July 1999.

12   Amien Rais during a speech at a meeting of Ansor, NU's youth organization, Jakarta, 24 July 1999, personal notes by the author.

13   Interview with Saifullah Yusuf, NU youth leader and Wahid's nephew, Jakarta, 12 September 1999.

14   Interview with Abdurrahman Wahid, Jakarta, 2 March 2000.

15   Conflicts between Christians and Muslims had broken out in Ambon in January 1999, quickly spreading to other parts of the Maluku archipelago, particularly Halmahera. By the end of 1999, the Christian side appeared to have gained the upper hand in the conflict, which cost thousands of lives and was portrayed by both parties as an "onslaught" at the hands of their respective adversaries.

16   Interview with Ahmad Anas Yahya, member of PKB central board, Jakarta, 10 October 1999.

17   Interview with Sahal Mahfudz, chair of NU's religious advisory board, Malang,

16 April 2000.

18   Interview with Hasyim Muzadi, Malang, 17 April 2000.

19   Interview with Cholil Bisri, Surabaya, 25 July 2000.

20   Masduki Baidlawi, "Memahami Tiga Langkah Gus Dur", *Aula*, Volume 21, Issue 9, 1999.

21   Hasyim acknowledged in February 2001 that the hierarchical culture of *pesantren* made it unlikely that followers of *kiai* would run important operations without seeking their approval. Thus Hasyim stated that if so many *santri* were participating in violent protests to defend Wahid, the conclusion was unavoidable that the *kiai* "tolerated" these actions. The *kiai* did so, according to Hasyim, because "they are really angry now". See "Hasyim Muzadi: 'Para Kiai di Jawa Timur Sudah Marah'", *Kompas*, 7 February 2001.

22   "Hasyim Muzadi: 'Bughot Dibahas dengan Pendekatan Fikih dan Ketatanegaraan'", *Koran Tempo*, 15 April 2001.

23   Interview with Cholil Bisri, Jakarta, 25 May 2001.

24   "Shirk" describes a concept that considers the powers or attributes of people or inanimate things as being of equal or higher status than those possessed by God.

25   Speech by Nur Iskandar in Batu Ceper, 22 July 2001, personal notes by the author.

26   Speech by Hasyim Muzadi in Batu Ceper, 22 July 2001, personal notes by the author.

27   There have been few serious attempts to re-introduce the *syariat* clause of the Jakarta Charter after 1998. Radical Muslim groups that demonstrated for its reinstatement, typically at annual sessions of the MPR, have received little societal support. In the political arena, only PPP, PK, and Bulan Bintang sympathized with the idea, with the vast majority of parties firmly opposed.

28   Benyamin Fleming Intan maintained that only by remaining in the realm of civil society can religious groups avoid the conflicts associated with the fight for hegemonic control of social and political institutions. Once the line is crossed from engagement in civil society to political competition with rival constituencies, conflicts are almost inevitable (Intan 2004).

29   The problem was not, as Howard Federspiel suggested, that NU and Muhammadiyah "have become more energized in political affairs with their cadre and members actively recruited for the newly formed political parties" (Federspiel 2002, p. 110). Rather, NU and Muhammadiyah — despite official declarations to the contrary — were turned from civil society organizations into political interest groups.

30   Confidential interview with a one-star general, Bandung, 21 September 2001.

31   Confidential interview with a one-star general, Bandung 21 September 2001.

32   Hasyim, for his part, blamed the PKB faction in parliament for failing to stop the impeachment proceedings against Wahid. In a brochure that compiled reports on his leadership and was distributed at an NU event in 2002 in Jakarta, it

was maintained that "NU as a grassroots-oriented organization was hit by the political mud flying around as a result of the less than optimal role played by the PKB elite." The brochure stated that the "capability of every single member of parliament from the PKB faction was still appalling" (Lembaga Kajian dan Pengembangan Informasi Media 2001, pp. x, xii).

33    "Saya Sangat Menikmati Memimpin MPR", *Koran Tempo*, 3 October 2004.
34    Abdurrahman Wahid on TV7, 20 April 2004.
35    Interview with Djoko Susilo, Jakarta, 30 March 2001.
36    "Sikap Muhammadiyah Berdampak Positif Pada Perolehan Suara PAN", *Sinar Harapan*, 12 February 2004.
37    "Tarik Ulur Pencalonan Gus Dur", *Gatra*, 12 March 2004.
38    "Abdurrahman Wahid: Ada Dana Pelicin Rp. 3 Milyar", *Kompas*, 28 July 2002.
39    Wahid had earlier mentioned three retired generals who could potentially represent PKB in the election for governor: Kahfi, a former deputy governor of Jakarta, and the two former military commanders of East Java, Haris Sudarno and Djoko Subroto. "PKB Mengajukan Tiga Jenderal", *Suara Merdeka*, 4 June 2003.
40    "Pencalonan Kahfi tak Lewat Rapat Resmi", *Suara Merdeka*, 3 July 2003.
41    Interview with Aribowo, deputy chairman of East Java's election commission, Surabaya, 23 June 2003.
42    "Mardiyanto Menang Mutlak", *Suara Pembaruan*, 24 July 2003.
43    Despite his connection with a military-affiliated organization, some press reports praised Setiawan as a "civilian governor in an era of reform". See "Danny Setiawan, Gubernur Sipil di Era Reformasi", *Pikiran Rakyat*, 13 June 2003.
44    However, ballots at the district level exhibited different electoral patterns. Only very few retired military officers were nominated as candidates for the posts of *bupati* or mayor. This suggests that the inclination of political parties to nominate ex-military candidates was directly linked to the significance of the contested post for national politics. The more important a particular position was to the interests of the central party leadership, the more likely the latter was to intervene in the nomination process and favour a candidate with a military background.
45    "Amien Rais Pilih Wapres dari Kalangan TNI", *Kompas*, 13 September 2003.
46    "Cawapres dari Kalangan Militer Jadi Pilihan Amien Rais", *Kompas*, 22 February 2004.
47    In the elections in April, Golkar finished first with 21.6 per cent of the votes, followed by PDI-P with 18.5, PKB with 10.5, PPP with 8.2, as well as Partai Demokrat and PKS (*Partai Keadilan Sejahtera*, Prosperous Justice Party) with 7.5 and 7.3 per cent respectively. PAN received 6.4 per cent of the votes, ahead of Bulan Bintang and PBR (*Partai Bintang Reformasi*, Reform Star Party) with 2.6 and 2.4 per cent respectively. PKS had been formed out of the old PK as the latter had failed in 1999 to reach the two per cent threshold required to compete in the 2004 ballot. PBR, for its part, was founded by the Muslim leader

Zainuddin MZ after his departure from PPP.

[48] Interview with Endriartono Sutarto, Jakarta, 11 June 2007; see also "Politicians Courting Military Criticized", *Jakarta Post*, 21 April 2004.

[49] "Siswono: Negara Aman Tidak Harus Dipimpin Militer", *Kompas*, 25 June 2004.

[50] "PBB Gelar Rakornas, Sosialisasi Dukungan atas SBY-Kalla", *Koran Tempo*, 16 May 2004.

[51] I am grateful to Greg Fealy for providing this information. A PKS-sponsored publication praised Wiranto, among others, for participating in the presidential elections in a democratic way and thus "using constitutional means to receive the sympathy of the people" (Furkon 2004, p. 255).

[52] "PKB Juga Lirik SBY", *Surya*, 28 January 2004.

[53] "Gus Dur Mengaku Tidak Pernah Beri Restu SBY", *Jawa Pos*, 21 April 2004.

[54] "Gus Dur Tak Dukung Muzadi Jadi Cawapres", *Kompas*, 24 April 2004.

[55] "Kiai Khos Haramkan Umat Islam dan NU Pilih Mega-Hasyim", *Koran Tempo*, 3 June 2004.

[56] "Gus Dur Writes Off Wiranto", *Laksamana.Net*, 3 June 2004.

[57] "Susilo and Kalla Win PKS's Support", *Jakarta Post*, 27 August 2004.

[58] PBR Deputy Chair Zainal Maarif asserted that "this doesn't mean that we think [Yudhoyono] is militaristic, maybe he is a military man who can be democratic, but it is better to leave civilian supremacy in civilian hands". See "SBY: Pada Akhirnya Rakyatlah Yang Menentukan Pilihannya", *Surabayawebs*, 23 August 2004.

[59] "Gus Dur Tak Akan Dukung Hasyim Muzadi", *Koran Tempo*, 27 July 2004.

[60] In exile, these leaders had participated in guerrilla wars in Afghanistan and the Philippines or received extensive training in jihadist doctrine and practices in Malaysia, Pakistan, and the Middle East. Upon their return, they organized themselves in small groups and cells in various Indonesian regions, but maintained a well-functioning communication network established under decades of authoritarian rule and exile. Most of the older leaders had links to the NII rebellion of the 1950s, and many of their recruits originated from families associated with Islamist insurgencies in the past.

[61] In May 2000, a bomb exploded at a Protestant church in Medan, injuring at least forty-seven people. The incident set the tone for a string of similar attacks, culminating in the Christmas eve bombings of 2000 that hit churches in ten Indonesian cities in six provinces. Eighteen people were killed and thirty-six were badly injured.

[62] "KSAD: Intelijen Militer Harus di Depan", *Suara Merdeka*, 20 August 2003.

[63] "Ketua Umum FPI Habib Rizieq Ditahan", *Kompas*, 17 October 2002.

[64] In April 2000, LJ had faced no difficulties in shipping its troops to Maluku, suggesting that police and military officers approved of the operation. Subsequently, LJ leader Jafar Umar Thalib claimed that he had several meetings with TNI officers to discuss the presence of his men in Maluku, and according to his account, none of the military leaders wanted LJ to withdraw (Shoelhi

# PART FOUR

# Democratic Consolidation, 2004–08

# 7

# YUDHOYONO AND THE DECLINING ROLE OF STATE COERCION

Susilo Bambang Yudhoyono's election as president in 2004 marked, in many ways, the end of Indonesia's democratic transition. Naturally, the transitional process between 1998 and 2004 had been of an experimental character, resulting in political compromises, institutional improvisations, and ambiguous legal frameworks. The transition had also been marred by serious security disturbances, with several waves of communal violence reflecting the general instability of Indonesia's social and political fabric during that time. But many of these typical phenomena of political transitions began to phase out in 2004 and 2005, with new democratic procedures taking root and most of Indonesia's key institutions settling into their post-authoritarian functions (Aspinall 2005*a*). The first direct presidential election in Indonesia's history was a watershed in this regard, providing the head of state with a strong popular mandate — and thus much better prospects of serving out a full term than his predecessors, who had come to power either through Suharto's appointment (Habibie), an indirect vote that included non-elected legislators (Wahid), or a controversial impeachment process (Megawati). The new electoral mechanism at the national level was followed by similar innovations in local politics, with governors, mayors, and district heads directly elected from June 2005 onwards (Mietzner 2005). At the same time, the intensity of communal conflict declined, with even some of the most volatile areas returning to almost normal political conditions. Overall, the political process began to stabilize significantly after 2004, and Indonesia entered into the phase of democratic consolidation.

This book has argued that the quality of democratic governance and the level of conflict between civilian groups have a considerable impact on the extent of military involvement in politics and, more specifically, on the pace of military reform in transitional societies. Accordingly, given the improving stability of the political process after 2004, we should expect a significant decline in military participation in Indonesian politics and, corresponding to this, improved democratic civilian control over the armed forces. To a large extent, this has indeed occurred. Yudhoyono sidelined the most conservative elements in the armed forces, creating a degree of effective authority over the military that none of his post-Suharto predecessors had been able to achieve. The government settled the Aceh conflict peacefully without heeding objections raised by senior generals, and — contrary to previous predictions — active and retired officers performed poorly in Indonesia's first direct local elections. In addition, the government targeted TNI's businesses for the first time, and although the reform drive was deficient in many aspects, it led to considerable irritation in the officer corps (Human Rights Watch 2006; Rieffel and Pramodhawardani 2007). Moreover, civilian politicians overcame the resistance of the military elite to a new law that will permit TNI personnel to be tried in civilian courts, providing a classic example of the power of civilian groups vis-à-vis the armed forces if the former take a united stand on issues related to military reform. In short, Indonesia under Yudhoyono moved a step closer towards completing the first-generation reform agenda, despite ongoing and complex difficulties.

In the following, Chapters 7 and 8 explore the dynamics in military politics and intra-Islamic affairs that contributed to the improved state of civil-military relations after 2004. Chapter 7 begins by analysing the reasons behind Yudhoyono's success in marginalizing several key officers who had been the main obstacles to further reform in the pre-2004 period. It then proceeds to explain how the government managed to implement a negotiated settlement with the separatist rebels in Aceh, something most observers were certain would fail due to fierce military opposition. Subsequently, the chapter discusses the government's efforts to control TNI's off-budget funds, and other military reform initiatives after 2004. The latter included the reform of the military justice system, which took significant steps forward because of the initiative and obstinacy of civilian politicians in the legislature. Finally, the chapter reviews the continuing deficiencies and shortcomings of the institutional military reforms carried out under Yudhoyono, arguing that more structural changes need to occur for the reform effort to be sustainable. Chapter 8 then focuses on developments within civilian politics in general and political Islam in particular, illustrating the correlation between the decline of military influence and the consolidation of the civilian polity.

## SIDELINING THE MILITARY CONSERVATIVES

Yudhoyono's rise to power in October 2004 constituted a crucial turning point in Indonesia's post-authoritarian civil-military relations. Both in institutional and personal terms, Yudhoyono's presidency was markedly different from that of his three predecessors since 1998. Institutionally, he commanded a much stronger mandate than the other post-Suharto presidents. Habibie had succeeded Suharto only because the latter had engineered his election as vice-president by the discredited MPR two months before his resignation. Abdurrahman Wahid, for his part, had skillfully exploited the indirect electoral mechanism in the MPR in 1999 to gain the presidency, and Megawati Sukarnoputri had risen to the national leadership after Wahid's controversial impeachment two years later. Under all three presidents between 1998 and 2004, TNI had used the weak legitimacy of the incumbents to seek concessions from them, offering protection and support in return. Yudhoyono, by contrast, was the winner of Indonesia's first direct presidential elections, in which he had soundly beaten his opponents. This provided him with an unprecedented level of popular legitimacy, and added to other innovations introduced during the 2002 constitutional amendments that aimed to strengthen the presidency. For example, presidential impeachments were made much more difficult than at the time of the proceedings against Wahid, creating high obstacles to the removal of the head of state during his five-year term (King 2004).

But Yudhoyono differed from his predecessors not only because of the new electoral rules that had brought him to office. He was also equipped with a political character that starkly contrasted with the personality traits of the other post-Suharto presidents. Rather uniquely, Yudhoyono combined a strong sense of pragmatism with intellectual curiosity and a deep knowledge of how the armed forces worked (Haseman 2006, p. 113). Neither Habibie nor Wahid and Megawati had ever acquired the intimate familiarity with military affairs that Yudhoyono naturally possessed, leaving them with a significant disadvantage in dealing with the armed forces. Habibie never fully understood the secret machinations of Indonesia's military, and was consequently unable to grasp and prevent the developments in East Timor, which occurred not only under his watch, but under full international scrutiny. Wahid, on the other hand, felt so confident of his own political position that he falsely believed he could push through radical military reforms while at the same time alienating his civilian support base — in the end, he was overthrown by a large civil-military coalition of his enemies. Megawati, finally, left all details of military management to her top brass, either out of genuine disinterest or a misguided belief that the military would not work against her. Yudhoyono, by contrast, knew the ins and outs of military politics. He not only understood the potential threats of military opposition to his rule, but also the vast opportunities available if the officer corps could be pulled to his side. Thus removing his military opponents and appointing personal loyalists to key positions in the armed forces was an immediate priority for Yudhoyono when taking up the presidency.

The identification of his main opponents in the military was no difficult task for Yudhoyono. Many of those within TNI who viewed his ascension to the presidency with dismay had been among Yudhoyono's critics for more than three decades. They included fellow graduates from the class of 1973, who believed that Yudhoyono owed his meteoric rise more to his marriage to the daughter of Sarwo Edhie, an influential general in the 1960s, than to distinction on the battlefield (Wandelt 2004). Despite Yudhoyono's comprehensive military career, which included service in East Timor, teaching positions at military colleges, a regional commandership, and international assignments, Yudhoyono was often seen as a military outsider by his foes. They portrayed him as "bookish" and too distant from the culture and ideological dispositions of the army mainstream, and when Yudhoyono emerged as a prominent proponent of military reform in the mid-1990s, they saw their suspicions confirmed.[1] After 1998, officers such as Wiranto, Ryamizard Ryacudu, and Bibit Waluyo watched Yudhoyono's political ambitions with little sympathy. They openly opposed Yudhoyono's reconciliatory policies on Aceh and Papua when he was coordinating minister of political and security affairs, insisting that military action was the only appropriate answer to separatism. Ryamizard, as army chief of staff, played a particularly significant role in the failure of the 2002–03 Aceh truce agreement, which Yudhoyono had negotiated (Aspinall and Crouch 2003, p. 24).[2] Against this background, the showdown between Yudhoyono and Wiranto in the 2004 presidential elections highlighted the deep divisions between Yudhoyono's gradual reformers and the supporters of Wiranto, who believed that military reforms had gone too far and that the government was too soft on the opponents of the Indonesian unitary state.

Thus when Yudhoyono took office, he had a very good understanding of where his opponents and supporters in the military were located. The biggest threat to his rule was undoubtedly Ryamizard Ryacudu, who was still army chief of staff at the time of Yudhoyono's inauguration. With Ryamizard at the helm of the army, it was self-evident that Yudhoyono would find it extremely difficult to enforce any policy that prioritized negotiations with rebels over straightforward security crackdowns. In the presidential campaign, Yudhoyono had attracted remarkable support from Acehnese and Papuans, who trusted his promises of a new policy approach to the two conflict-ridden areas.[3] In consequence, removing Ryamizard from office must have been on Yudhoyono's mind, but ironically it was his predecessor Megawati Sukarnoputri who forced Yudhoyono to act more quickly than initially planned. In her last days in office, Megawati accepted the "resignation" of the TNI commander, Endriartono Sutarto, much to the surprise of the latter, who claimed that he had not asked to be relieved of his duties at that particular time.[4] In Endriartono's stead, Megawati appointed Ryamizard as TNI chief, sending shockwaves through the political arena and triggering expressions of concern by the foreign media and diplomats. Fortunately for Yudhoyono, however, the appointment needed to be confirmed by the parliament, which was in the middle of handing over its business to the newly elected legislature. There was considerable support for Ryamizard in the DPR, but when Yudhoyono sent a letter to its freshly installed leadership and withdrew Megawati's request to confirm the appointment of a new TNI chief, the legislators chose not to challenge the president's decision.[5] Ryamizard's takeover of the armed forces was aborted, and Endriartono remained in office.

The withdrawal of Ryamizard's nomination signalled the beginning of a larger move against the most vocal conservatives in the armed forces. In conversations with Endriartono, Yudhoyono made it clear that he needed reliable military leaders to pursue his agenda, which included peace in Aceh and TNI's continued political neutrality.[6] Accordingly, in early 2005 the president expressed his wish to reshuffle all three chiefs of staff, which conveniently also affected Ryamizard. Endriartono concurred with Yudhoyono's assessment and handed him a list of possible replacements — none of whom were known for being vocal or ultranationalist. In all three cases, Yudhoyono endorsed the candidates submitted by Endriartono. Thus Ryamizard was replaced as army chief of staff in February 2005, forcing him to spend his last year of active service without a functional job. Previously, the commander of Kostrad, Bibit Waluyo, had already been sent into retirement — precisely one week after Yudhoyono's convincing victory over Megawati in the presidential elections.[7]

Ryamizard and Bibit had been prototypes of the kind of politicized military officers that Megawati had allowed to blossom under her rule: not only did they hold very conservative views on the role of the military in political affairs, but they also had no reservations about expressing them regularly in public. Both Ryamizard and Bibit had openly criticized government policies on such matters as the ongoing separatist conflicts in Aceh and Papua, and they were strongly opposed to legal proceedings against soldiers and officers involved in human rights abuses. Ryamizard had famously called the killers of Papuan independence leader Theys Eluay "heroes", slamming the judges who had handed down (very light) sentences against the Kopassus officers responsible for the crime.[8] Bibit, for his part, made a point of attending numerous trials of military personnel, often appearing in court with a huge entourage of soldiers to support the defendants. Although he denied that his presence had an intimidating effect on judges, witnesses, and prosecutors, many observers felt that way. Their provocative statements and actions had turned Ryamizard and Bibit into embodiments of the self-confidence prevalent in the post-Wahid officer corps, with most generals agreeing that the time of military soul-searching had to come to an end. Therefore, Ryamizard and his circle believed that instead of engaging in intellectual reflections on the armed forces' dark history, officers should aggressively propagate traditional military sentiments against the alleged civilian incapacity to rule, which in their view had been confirmed by the events since 1998.

## The Post-Ryamizard Military Elite

In terms of their ideology, the officers promoted by Yudhoyono to replace Ryamizard and his associates were not that much different from their predecessors. They too were socially conservative and believed that civilians were weak and divided. However, they distinguished themselves from Ryamizard's group in two important aspects: first, they accepted the constitutionally anchored authority of elected leaders to set government policies, and defined the military as an executive tool of the administration. While not especially enthusiastic about this arrangement, these officers understood that the post-Suharto polity left them with no other choice than to endorse the political reality or to be swept away by it. Djoko Santoso, one of the post-Ryamizard military leaders, expressed this awareness in June 2005 when clearing the way for the government to proceed with the peace negotiations with Acehnese rebels: "This [decision] belongs into the political arena — the government carries out this process, and if the government has made a decision, we will support and implement it."[9] Secondly, the post-Ryamizard officers largely kept their political views to themselves. Where Ryamizard and Bibit had made headlines with controversial statements on an almost daily basis, their successors avoided the media. Even if pushed by journalists to express their opinion, they typically issued standard endorsements of government policies.

Whether this new approach reflected a broader trend of depoliticization within the military or simply the fear of senior officers of being fired by Yudhoyono is difficult to ascertain. Nevertheless, the socio-political implications of this partial withdrawal of military leaders from the public sphere were tremendous (Ramage 2007). The press significantly reduced its coverage of the activities and opinions of generals in leadership positions, up to a point where members of the public were no longer aware of their names. During the New Order and the immediate post-Suharto period, newspapers had been full of information about upcoming military reshuffles, complete with class affiliations and previous postings. Back then, the patronage relations of officers among each other, with senior politicians, and with religious organizations had been the subject of heated discussions even among ordinary Indonesians, who believed that understanding intra-military rivalries and alliances would give them a sense of the general direction in which the country was heading. In the post-Ryamizard military, by contrast, reshuffles became much less scrutinized affairs, and TNI officers, except for the very top brass, gradually lost their status as political celebrities. Knowing the names of military commanders and their political leanings was no longer deemed a matter of public interest, with the press increasingly concentrating their political coverage on party politicians, who delivered much more controversial and juicy opinions and statements than the officer corps under Yudhoyono's grip.

Besides promoting officers with little ambition to appear in the public spotlight, Yudhoyono also made sure that personal loyalists were placed in strategic positions. Djoko Santoso, a long-time personal friend, replaced Ryamizard as army chief of staff, while a fellow graduate from Yudhoyono's 1973 military academy class, Djoko Suyanto, followed Endriartono Sutarto as TNI commander in 2006. Thus unlike Habibie, Wahid, or Megawati, Yudhoyono could rely on close personal relationships to control the armed forces. As both Djoko Santoso and Djoko Suyanto were well liked by the public for their low-key personalities, these appointments raised almost no opposition from the political or societal elite. Rather more controversial were Yudhoyono's attempts to ensure the rise of family members to important posts in the army. His brother-in-law Erwin Sudjono was appointed as TNI's chief of staff of general affairs in September 2007, while another in-law, Pramono Eddy Wibowo, became chief of staff of the Diponegoro command in Central Java. In addition, the military career of Yudhoyono's son Agus

Harimurti Yudhoyono also received significant public attention. While still in the early stages of his career, Agus obviously was much more influential than his rank suggested, and there were frequent rumours of preferential treatment by his superiors. For example, when Agus was assigned to TNI's battalion serving under the UN mission in Lebanon in November 2006, almost the entire military leadership appeared at the airport to send him off.[10] Other presidential family members in the military elite and influential public positions included his brother-in-law Hadi Utomo, a retired colonel who took over the chairmanship of Partai Demokrat in 2005.[11]

The combination between a more predictable institutional system, a better understanding of the internal dynamics of the armed forces, and an intellectually grounded political realism put Yudhoyono in a stronger position than his predecessors to enhance government control over the military. In contrast to Habibie and Wahid, he possessed the necessary legitimacy and civilian support base to protect himself from potential military challenges to his rule, and unlike Megawati, he was aware of the importance of effective oversight of TNI for the quality of Indonesia's politics, economy, society, and diplomatic relations. Paradoxically, it was Megawati who helped Yudhoyono to overcome his single most important weakness: his legendary hesitancy and predilection for long deliberations before taking action. It is improbable that Yudhoyono would have moved so quickly against Ryamizard had Megawati not forced her successor's hand by appointing the army chief of staff as TNI commander. Given Yudhoyono's indecisive personality, it is more likely that he would have postponed Ryamizard's removal until a time when he could be absolutely certain that Ryamizard was incapable of successful retaliation. Pre-empted by Megawati, however, Yudhoyono took immediate action, solving one of the most crucial problems of his early presidency much faster than initially planned. Ryamizard's removal not only eliminated the biggest obstacle to military reform. More importantly, it established Yudhoyono's authority over the armed forces, signalling that he was prepared to sack generals unwilling to support government policies. Thus by the time Yudhoyono began to tackle one of the key issues of his reform agenda, i.e. the Aceh problem, the military found it impossible to undermine the government's strategy of peaceful negotiations, as it had done in the past.

## THE ACEH PEACE AGREEMENT

In many respects, the government's handling of the Aceh problem after 1998 reflected the changing political moods at various stages of Indonesia's transition. Under Presidents Habibie and Wahid, it appeared that most elements of Jakarta's political elite wanted to settle the separatist conflict in the province in a peaceful way, having failed to quell the rebellion militarily since its latest outbreak in the late 1970s. After Megawati's half-hearted attempt at a settlement with GAM in 2002 and the subsequent breakdown of the accord in 2003, however, the central government launched an all-out war against the rebels. As explained in Chapter 5, Jakarta's move then was supported by a vast majority of politicians and ordinary Indonesians, pointing to the growing conservatism in the elite and the general public. Nevertheless, after his election as president, Yudhoyono was determined to restart peace negotiations to end the conflict, aware that the 2002 process had failed largely because Ryamizard had actively undermined it and Megawati had no genuine interest in its success.[12] At that time, Yudhoyono had been one of the few defenders of the settlement in cabinet, and he had not forgotten who the main spoilers in the military and the bureaucracy were. Thus settling the Aceh conflict under his presidency provided an opportunity for him to prove his critics wrong and to demonstrate the superiority of his moderate approach over the iron-fisted security ideology of Ryamizard and other military conservatives. Moreover, Yudhoyono indicated in interviews with Michael Morfit that solving the Aceh problem had larger implications for his presidency and the process of Indonesia's democratization (Morfit 2006, pp. 13, 19).[13] As long as Aceh remained a battlefield, the military was unlikely to subordinate itself to democratic rule, budget transparency standards, and internationally acknowledged human rights codes. Yudhoyono, it appears, hoped to advance military reform by removing one of the hotbeds of military abuses, insubordination, and exploitation.

Like in the case of Ryamizard's dismissal, however, Yudhoyono needed external pressure to overcome his inherent hesitancy. There were two major factors that drove Yudhoyono to take action faster than his usually prolonged deliberative approach would have allowed: first, his vice-president, Jusuf Kalla, who did not share Yudhoyono's dislike for rapid political moves, had been engaged in secret negotiations with GAM even before he had taken office. Renowned as an effective mediator in the communal conflicts of Maluku and Poso, Kalla was eager to add Aceh to his list of resolved security problems and therefore insisted on a speedy solution. While Yudhoyono found it hard to keep up with Kalla's pace, he endorsed his deputy's manoeuvres, which ultimately led to plans for informal talks with GAM in Helsinki in January 2005. Before these negotiations could be convened, however, the devastating tsunami of December 2004 provided the second impetus for Yudhoyono to catalyze the peace process in Aceh. With international aid agencies and militaries supporting the relief efforts, there was increasing pressure by foreign powers on the Indonesian government and GAM to settle their differences and allow the reconstruction process to go ahead without further security disturbances. Pushed by Kalla and international encouragement, the peace negotiations in Helsinki between Jakarta and GAM reached agreement in only six months of intensive talks. In the accord signed in August 2005, GAM agreed to give up its demands for independence, while the Yudhoyono government conceded a partial withdrawal of security forces and GAM's participation in Aceh's electoral process (Aspinall 2005*b*).

## The Helsinki Accord: TNI Support and Opposition

The signing of the Helsinki accord was greeted by domestic and foreign observers with profound skepticism.[14] The collapse of the 2002 agreement was still a fresh memory, and as outlined in Chapter 5, the military campaign between 2003 and 2005 had been a discouraging example of ineffective civilian oversight of a major security operation. There appeared to be little reason to believe that things would be fundamentally different this time around, and bets were taken on whether TNI would bring down the agreement first or allow GAM to undermine it beforehand. But it quickly emerged that both sides were determined to honour the treaty, albeit for different reasons. To begin with, GAM's strength had declined significantly since 2003, not the least as a result of the military campaign. The separatist organization simply did not have many options left, forcing it to swallow the bitter pill of abandoning its goal of independence.[15] Moreover, the Indonesian government had made wide-ranging concessions that had not been granted during the 2002 negotiations, making it easier for GAM to sell the accord to its followers. TNI, for its part, was certainly not happy about the agreement, but Ryamizard's sacking had sent an unambiguous message to the officer corps that disloyalty would be harshly dealt with by the government. Faced with the choice between dogmatic insistence on their ideological beliefs and the pragmatic pursuit of their individual careers, most officers chose to adopt the government's line. In fact, senior officers seemed to outbid one another in their positive statements about the accord, often sounding more supportive than their civilian counterparts in the cabinet and the legislature.

Besides the prospect of dismissal in case of disobedience, there were several other factors that led senior officers to endorse the 2005 peace treaty. First of all, Yudhoyono had taken a personal interest in the technicalities of the military's partial withdrawal from the province, meeting on several occasions with top generals to explain the government's policies and the rationale behind them. Moreover, in his efforts to overcome opposition in the armed forces, Yudhoyono could rely on the strong support of Endriartono Sutarto. Although he was a military conservative himself and had presided over the collapse of the 2002 agreement, Endriartono was also a pragmatist with a tremendous grasp for changing political dynamics. He had been locked in a notoriously bad relationship with Ryamizard, whose blunt rhetoric he viewed as a liability for the reputation of the armed forces. After Yudhoyono had retained him and dismissed Ryamizard, Endriartono defined securing TNI's loyalty towards Yudhoyono's Aceh policy as his last major task before retirement. In discussions with his generals, Endriartono faced down fierce criticism from conservative officers who wanted TNI to clearly express its objection to the Helsinki accord:

> These were tough meetings. Some of my generals said that TNI had an obligation to fight for the nation's territorial integrity, even if that meant violating instructions by the government or the MPR. I told them that they were wrong. I made it crystal clear that if the MPR decided to let Aceh go, TNI would have to accept that because it's a political decision. I said, 'look if we follow your logic, we would have to be in East Timor now and try to get it back. Are we doing that? No.' As a result of that discussion, some generals called me the most unpatriotic TNI chief in history, but I did not care.[16]

Subsequently, Endriartono personally reprimanded officers whose actions or statements were seen out of line with those of the government, leading to public endorsements of the Helsinki accord even by officers previously known for their staunchly nationalist views (Morfit 2006, p. 19).

Another factor in TNI's support for the peace agreement was the money made available to the military in the course of the troop withdrawal and post-tsunami reconstruction process. Many observers had feared that TNI would try to obstruct the peace agreement because of its financial interests in the province, which to some extent depended on the continuation of the conflict.[17] It was Kalla in particular who understood that TNI needed to be compensated for these losses for it to remain supportive of the peace accord. Thus the budget for the troop withdrawal was set at an unusually high level (526 billion rupiah, or around US$58.4 million),[18] and the allocations for the reconstruction effort included large sums for security and rebuilding of military barracks. For example, in the 2005 budget of the Aceh-Nias Rehabilitation and Reconstruction Agency, over 400 billion rupiah (or US$44.4 million) were earmarked for the military and police, officially to rehabilitate their facilities destroyed by the tsunami.[19] In October 2007, parliament approved another 225 billion rupiah (US$25 million) for the armed forces in Aceh, stressing that the money was allocated for "non-combat" activities.[20] Furthermore, local officers soon discovered the profitability of the service industry that catered to expatriate aid and construction workers in Aceh. Opening car rentals, pizza restaurants, and retailers, military rent-seekers began to enjoy significant peace dividends that increased their allegiance towards the Helsinki accord.[21]

The TNI leadership continued to support the peace process even after GAM leader Irwandi Yusuf won the first direct gubernatorial elections in Aceh in December 2006. The image of a GAM rebel being sworn in as Aceh's governor had been the ultimate nightmare for TNI officers, but when it became reality, most generals kept a cool head. There is no doubt that even Yudhoyono was shocked by GAM's victory in Aceh, but he called in TNI Commander Djoko Suyanto immediately after the results were announced to issue guidelines for a joint government response to the media. That response was that Irwandi had won in a democratic contest, and that the government and its executive agencies would therefore respect the result. In their public statements, TNI leaders repeated that line to the letter, pointing once more to the effectiveness of Yudhoyono's threat of sanctions in case of non-compliance. TNI's moderate response to Irwandi's election triggered equally considered reactions on the other side: Irwandi paid a highly publicized visit to army headquarters shortly before his inauguration in February 2007, declaring that he was committed to overcoming the old rivalries between Indonesia's military and GAM.[22] Stating once again that GAM had given up on the idea of independence, he assured the generals that they had nothing to fear from his rule over Aceh.[23]

## Aceh and Civil-Military Relations

The success of the Aceh peace process so far has had ambiguous implications for Indonesia's civil-military relations. On the one hand, the military's endorsement of a negotiated settlement with separatist rebels constituted a novelty in post-Suharto politics and thus appeared to reflect significant progress in Indonesian efforts towards military reform. After the military's torching of East Timor in 1999, its undermining of Wahid's negotiations with Papua in 2000, and its sabotaging of the Aceh peace process in 2002, Yudhoyono finally demonstrated that it was possible to rein in the armed forces — even on an issue considered essential to their interests. Yudhoyono's unchallenged political authority, his grasp of military affairs, and his quick move against the most vocal conservatives in the armed forces had been the key to this success, which earned him a nomination for the 2006 Nobel Peace

Prize. By settling one of Indonesia's longest-lasting insurgencies, Yudhoyono narrowed the political space available to the armed forces, providing evidence for Desch's and Alagappa's proposition that the level of military intervention in politics tends to decline in those states that manage to reduce both the intensity of internal conflict and the use of state coercion in governance (Desch 1999; Alagappa 2001*a*). Indonesia's resolution of the Aceh conflict was an eloquent example of such a reduction in the use of state coercion to address political disputes, and as the main agency typically authorized to exercise coercion, the armed forces saw their role decline accordingly.

This point was further underscored by reverse experiences in Thailand and the Philippines, which saw — at the same time that the Aceh conflict was resolved — the role of their militaries in politics increasing, largely due to intensifying insurgencies in both countries. Thailand experienced unprecedented separatist violence in its Muslim provinces since early 2004 (McCargo 2007, p. 4), while the Philippines faced similar challenges in Mindanao and a reinvigorated communist rebellion in the whole country. As a result of these developments, the frequency of human rights violations by security forces in Thailand and the Philippines increased, and the militaries of both countries expanded their political role. The Thai army launched a coup in September 2006, ousting Prime Minister Thaksin Sinawatra, and subsequently revised the constitution to consolidate its authority over domestic security politics. In the Philippines, President Arroyo became increasingly dependent on the armed forces, which were widely accused of intervention in the 2004 elections in order to secure Arroyo's victory. Consequently, Freedom House in 2006 downgraded both Thailand and the Philippines in their annual country ratings of freedoms and liberties from "free" to "partly free", while Indonesia was rated as "free" for the first time (Freedom House 2006). Significantly, Indonesia was the only Southeast Asian country in 2006 to receive such a classification.

But it was precisely this celebration of the Aceh case as an indicator of Indonesia's progress in reforming its armed forces that harboured significant dangers for the ongoing reform process. The success in Aceh papered over unaddressed problems in the field of institutional reform, with the territorial command structure, military self-financing, and continued legal impunity still obstructing the subordination of Indonesia's military to firm democratic control. As demonstrated above, Yudhoyono had established his authority over the military more through personal interventions and relationships than through an established institutional system of oversight. Thus while on the surface the military appeared to be reformed and subjugated to civilian control, there was no effective institutional framework in place to sustain democratic authority over the armed forces beyond Yudhoyono's presidency. In fact, the events in Aceh led to a significant reduction in the pressure on TNI to further reform its structures, with many international and domestic politicians falsely believing that the armed forces no longer constituted a threat to Indonesia's democratic consolidation.[24] This consequent decline in reform pressure was not only reflected in the restoration of military-to-military ties with the United States and other Western powers in 2005, but also in the rather mixed results of the reform initiatives launched by Minister of Defence Juwono Sudarsono.

## HALF-HEARTED REFORMS?
## INSTITUTIONAL CHANGE UNDER YUDHOYONO

Reducing the use of state coercion in governance is an important element in improving the quality of democratic civilian control over the military. The less the military is needed to quell internal violent conflicts, the better the chances for strong democratic oversight of the armed forces. In Indonesia, the decline in the intensity of communal conflicts after 2003 and the peaceful settlement of the Aceh dispute have contributed to the marginalization of the armed forces from political affairs. This, in turn, led to a considerable improvement in the effectiveness of civilian control over the military. As Cottey, Edmunds, and Forster have pointed out, however, the institutional entrenchment of oversight mechanisms is an equally important factor in this process. The use of state coercion in governance can fluctuate significantly, with sudden outbreaks of violence having the potential of bringing the military back into the political spotlight within a very short period of time. Accordingly, the introduction of strong institutional oversight mechanisms is necessary to shield states in civil-military transitions from such fluctuations in the level of internal (or in some cases, external) conflict. In the Indonesian case, the success in Aceh provided a good opportunity to introduce further institutional changes to the armed forces and the mechanisms that control their affairs. As it turned out, however, the government made only limited use of this unique chance.

The reason for this failure is partly due to Yudhoyono's famous predilection for risk aversion which had become obvious long before his presidency. Despite his reputation as a progressive officer in the 1990s, Yudhoyono had paid surprisingly little attention to institutional military reform during his two terms as coordinating minister for political and security affairs between 2000 and 2004. None of the pieces of security-related legislation passed in that period carried his signature, although he had nominal oversight over their drafting processes. The 2002 State Defence Act had been initiated by Ministers of Defence Juwono Sudarsono and Mahfud M.D., and their successor Matori Abdul Djalil had finalized the bill with parliament. The discussions on a new TNI Act had also begun under Matori, but after his stroke in August 2003, the ministry had been vacant, leaving the draft for the new law unfinished. Yudhoyono, who had direct authority over the defence department, apparently did not view the Act as an urgent matter, while civil society organizations and even the armed forces pushed for its enactment.

Supporters of Yudhoyono maintained that he did not take action on structural reform matters as minister because Presidents Wahid and Megawati had restricted him. However, this appears implausible, particularly in the case of Megawati.[25] Disinterested in issues of day-to-day governance, Megawati granted her ministers much room to launch their own policy initiatives, and with no minister of defence in place after August 2003, Yudhoyono would have had considerable opportunities to leave his mark on the military reform process. The potential powers of the office of coordinating minister were demonstrated impressively by Yudhoyono's successor Hari Sabarno, who picked up the unfinished draft of the TNI Act shortly after taking office in March 2004. Hari immediately asked his team to complete the bill, submitted it to parliament in June, and personally negotiated it with a special committee of legislators until the Act was passed in September 2004. In consequence, the only significant legacy of Yudhoyono's three and a half years as coordinating minister was the failed Aceh peace process of 2002. Institutional change, on the other hand, had been driven by others.

Yudhoyono's silence on structural military reform had also extended into his 2004 presidential campaign. Pushed by panelist Ikrar Nusa Bhakti during the televised debate with his rivals to explain his plan for reforming the armed forces, Yudhoyono remained uncommitted.[26] Sidestepping questions about concrete policy initiatives he might take as president, Yudhoyono only pledged to continue military reforms in a "balanced and considered" manner. This vagueness stood in stark contrast to his opponents Wiranto and Agum Gumelar, who both offered detailed blueprints for their potential handling of the armed forces if elected president or vice-president respectively. Predictably, Wiranto provided a conservative vision for TNI's future, insisting that he would not subordinate the armed forces structurally to the department of defence, which had been one of the key demands of military reformers. He also stated that the territorial command structure would stay in place, and even considered expanding its functions. Agum Gumelar, on the other hand, committed to placing the military under the civilian department of defence, and also pledged to carefully review the existence of the territorial commands.[27] With both extremes of military reform offered to the electorate, Yudhoyono refused to make his own stance public, consolidating his reputation as a moderate, but excessively hesitant politician.

## The Lightning Rod: Juwono and Military Reform

Even after Yudhoyono's election as president, there was no indication that he intended to personally lead a new initiative for structural military reform. Therefore, the task of pushing for institutional changes in the armed forces fell to Juwono Sudarsono, who was appointed to his second stint as minister of defence.[28] A political science professor with a long history in government, Juwono was a highly intellectual and analytical figure, enabling him to identify the weaknesses and strengths of Indonesia's military organization with clinical clarity. However, he was also a pragmatist, who often warned his NGO-based critics that military reform was a long-term project of fifteen to twenty years, and that expectations of a quick fix were not only unrealistic, but also dangerous. It was this unique combination of a critical mind with an almost paternalistic sympathy for the shortcomings and concerns of the officer corps that made Juwono, in Yudhoyono's eyes, the ideal candidate for the job. On the one hand, Juwono was certain to pursue the reforms that he had recognized as crucial for the modernization and professionalization of the armed forces. On the other hand, however, Juwono's understanding of and respect for the interests of the military made it unlikely that he would alienate Yudhoyono's top generals. In short, Juwono's political character mirrored Yudhoyono's own predispositions, which prioritized deliberative collaboration over quick and unilateral action. But while Yudhoyono, as president, could afford to limit himself to general policy statements, Juwono did not enjoy such a luxury. He was expected to design and implement the very military reform blueprint that Yudhoyono had been unable or unwilling to provide. This expectation forced Juwono onto a slippery slope of trial and error, often with disappointing results.

The first of such trial-and-error initiatives was Juwono's idea of a National Security Act. Initially, Juwono had only planned to revise existing laws to subordinate the armed forces more firmly to the department of defence. Having studied the jungle of current laws and government regulations, however, Juwono concluded that the problem of his department's unclear authority over the military could not be solved without addressing a host of other issues at the same time. Consequently, Juwono proposed to draft a new National Security Act, which would not only clarify the position of the armed forces and the police vis-à-vis the presidency and related ministries, but also regulate the relationship between all state security agencies in the instance of domestic unrest and external attacks. Juwono set up a team in his ministry to work on a draft, and in February 2005 he announced that he would be able to send the bill to parliament "within the next two months".[29] This proved an unrealistically optimistic estimate, however. Not only had Juwono misjudged the effectiveness of his own department, but he had also underestimated the institutional resistance of state agencies that were affected by the bill but excluded from its drafting. Most importantly, the police felt that Juwono's initiative was a military-driven plot to subordinate the police to the department of home affairs, which has traditionally been headed by retired military generals.[30] In late 2006, after two years of slow deliberations, the press published parts of the bill, confirming some of the police's suspicions and throwing Juwono's drafting effort into disarray. A public dispute between the police, the military, and Juwono ensued, which only ended after Yudhoyono ordered all parties involved to refrain from discussing the topic with the media. Yudhoyono did not say, however, how he wanted to resolve the substantial issues at the heart of the dispute. Instead, he told Juwono and others engaged in the controversy to "put the matter on hold".[31]

The case of the National Security Act reflected both the general pattern of Juwono's relationship with Yudhoyono and the character of military reform initiatives launched under their watch. In the absence of clear directives from the president, Juwono often pushed ahead with his own ideas, but when those were challenged by the public or other state agencies, the palace offered no political protection:

> In front of several other ministers the president once said that I'm his lightning rod, drawing all the public criticism [on military reform issues] away from him. I'm fine with that, because I believe in him. Yudhoyono is the most decent, untainted, and educated president we've ever had, and he deserves all the support he can get.[32]

Another case in point was the planned takeover of military businesses by the government, which had been mandated by the TNI Act passed in 2004. According to the law, all businesses owned directly or indirectly by the military had to be handed over to the state by 2009. In 2005, then TNI Commander Endriartono Sutarto even declared that he wanted to bring the schedule forward and complete the transfer within only two years. From the beginning, however, there was great confusion over what exactly qualified as a military business. Yudhoyono apparently had no opinion on the matter, leaving Juwono uncertain about how far the president wanted this potentially deep cut into the military's economic interests to go. Therefore, the definition of the term "military business" and the inventory of all military assets were left to an inter-departmental team, which included active military officers as well.

In the negotiations within the team, the secretary-general of the department of defence, Sjafrie Sjamsoeddin, who was still an active general, played a particularly important role. He insisted that cooperatives and most foundations be excluded from the takeover plan, announcing that only six or seven out of more than 1,520 reported economic units under military management would eventually be transferred to the state.[33] Endriartono supported this interpretation, and neither Juwono nor Yudhoyono countered the military's definition. At the same time, the armed forces began to sell off their most profitable assets before the government could assess their value, and refused to transfer the proceeds to the state coffers.[34] In fact, Juwono issued statements that legalized these sales during the inventory period, leading to widespread speculation that the government wanted to solve the problem of military businesses by tacitly encouraging their spin-off before the actual handover could take place.[35]

Like in the case of the National Security Act, Yudhoyono eventually expressed dissatisfaction with the overall effort, but provided little insight into how he wanted the issue to be resolved. The department of defence had drafted a presidential decree in late 2006 that outlined the institutional framework for the management of the businesses, which was remarkably vague for a legal document of such political importance. One key paragraph simply stated that the task of a new supervisory team for military assets would be to "settle" the problem of military businesses, without offering any further details.[36] The draft was rejected by Yudhoyono as insufficient in February 2007, returning it to the department for substantial revisions. But once again, he did not point to specific weaknesses that he objected to, nor did he issue binding guidelines for the required revisions. Sjafrie Sjamsoeddin found it difficult to disguise his irritation over the matter, admitting publicly that he did not know what the president's instructions were, and when Cabinet Secretary Sudi Silalahi was pressed to comment, he could only guess that Yudhoyono probably wanted more coordination between the departments potentially involved in the takeover.[37] Juwono, for his part, believed that Yudhoyono simply did not want to deal with the subject:

> When I took office, the president talked in very general terms about
> a number of issues that he wanted to see pursued, but the military
> businesses were not one of them. He probably knew that this would be

a sensitive issue, particularly for his former colleagues in the army, so he tried to stay away from the topic. I think he wanted me to take care of it — hence he did not give specific instructions. He only said "please bring this in order".[38]

The chaos surrounding the definitions, parameters, and technical details of the transfer of military businesses tainted what otherwise could have been presented as a major achievement of the Yudhoyono government in institutional military reform. Instead, the public witnessed a confusing display of diverse opinions within the administration, with Yudhoyono unwilling to use his presidential prerogative to set the policy priorities. Given that Yudhoyono had utilized his authority extensively during the Aceh negotiations, his abstinence during the debates on military businesses seemed especially curious.

## Reform Against Yudhoyono: The Military Justice Bill

With the government lacking a clear blueprint for institutional change in the armed forces, it effectively surrendered the initiative for military reform to other state institutions, most notably the parliament. Intriguingly, the legislature could not only claim credit for some significant reforms in the security sector, but it achieved those reforms against fierce opposition by the government. The most prominent case in this regard was the reform of the military justice system. The DPR had initiated a bill during its 1999–2004 term that aimed to substantially revise the rules and procedures of military justice, hoping to end the impunity that most members of the armed forces still enjoyed in military courts. Since the fall of Suharto, not a single general had been imprisoned for human rights abuses, and lower-ranking personnel were typically sentenced to mild prison terms. Moreover, civil society organizations and the media frequently questioned whether these convicts actually served their sentences in the military's correction facilities or simply spent some leisure time in their barracks. For example, in 2007 it emerged that several officers who had been formally convicted to prison terms and discharged from the military for the kidnapping of activists in 1998 did in fact continue to develop successful military careers, reaching senior territorial command positions.[39] In other cases, suspects and convicts had mysteriously disappeared before being sent to prison.

In order to rectify these serious flaws in the military justice system, the DPR proposed in one of the bill's most important articles that military members involved in off-duty crimes should stand trial in civilian courts.

This stipulation reflected the large number of cases in which soldiers and officers committed crimes while moonlighting for other employers, whether as drug couriers, bodyguards, security staff, or even assassins. In addition, the proposal sought to deal with the many instances in which military personnel were involved in brawls with civilians. The local sections of popular tabloids were regularly filled with stories of soldiers beating up clients of bars or discotheques over minor quarrels or, alternatively, using their guns to settle traffic disputes. Thus the DPR initiative addressed a demand long held by society leaders and the public, and while the civilian justice system was deeply problematic itself, it certainly offered slightly better chances of securing reasonable sentences for TNI-affiliated suspects involved in off-duty crimes than its military counterpart.

In its deliberations with parliament, which began in August 2005, the government rejected this proposed change to the military justice system. Juwono argued that the military was "psychologically unprepared" to accept civilian jurisdiction, which of course was more a description of the problem rather than an explanation for why he opposed its suggested solution.[40] The idea of putting civilian police and prosecutors in charge of trying military personnel was premature, Juwono said, given the traditional rivalries between the armed forces and the police, which had only been institutionally separated in 1999. Juwono was so insistent in his opposition that the deliberations deadlocked. For months, both sides did not move at all from their various positions, making the failure of the talks a real possibility. Legislators were so annoyed at Juwono's stance,[41] however, that they increased the pressure on the minister by public advocacy campaigns and direct communication with the president. Most importantly, parliament decided that it would not move forward with the deliberations of the whole bill until agreement on this particular issue had been reached. The DPR argued that without a breakthrough in this critical area of military justice reform, it was impossible to negotiate other aspects of the proposed law. With this move, the legislators had skilfully prevented the government's attempts to postpone the discussion of this controversial section until the end of the deliberations, at which point the media probably would have lost interest in the topic. In addition, the parliament's decision had manoeuvred Juwono into a position in which the politically aware public would blame him, and not the DPR, for the potential breakdown of the negotiations.

In its conflict with the government, parliament benefited from the expertise and unconventional strategies of some of its younger members, who often had postgraduate degrees from foreign universities. The chairman of the DPR committee deliberating the bill, the Germany-trained political scientist

Andreas Pareira from PDI-P, played a key role in mobilizing the political elite, NGOs, and the public against the government's intransigence:

> We invited NGOs over to get them on board. I also briefed journalists, and it helped that some of them followed the story regularly, so there was continuity in their reporting. Equally important was the fact that even parties that were undecided at the beginning of the deliberations could be convinced to fully back our initiative. At the end, the public viewed the government as anti-reformist on this issue, and the pressure became unbearably high for them.[42]

Believing that Juwono had formed his view because the military elite had imposed it on him, senior parliamentarians turned the issue into a test case for the general state of military reform in Indonesia. Eventually, the outrage in parliament over the military's position helped to produce a cross-factional stance on the subject, something civilian forces had rarely been able to achieve as far as post-1998 military reforms were concerned. In a letter to the president, which was accompanied by mounting pressure in the media, the DPR leadership took the unusual step of complaining about Juwono's performance in the deliberations and asking what the president's position on the matter was. Initially reluctant to respond, Yudhoyono in November 2006 replied that the government agreed with the DPR's proposal to transfer off-duty cases to civilian courts.[43] The affair once again exposed the lack of coordination between Juwono and Yudhoyono, and the minister could only save face by successfully asking the DPR for a two-year transition period during which other laws and government regulations would have to be adjusted to the new policy.[44] While the negotiations on the overall bill are unlikely to be completed before 2009, the landmark decision to allow civilian courts to try TNI personnel significantly boosted the reform of the military justice system; sadly for the government, this important step forward was taken against its initial opposition.

## Doctrinal and Strategic Shifts

While Juwono found it difficult to deal with the protracted details of concrete and short-term military reform, and thus often appeared defensive when explaining his policies in public, he was much more comfortable at laying out his long-term vision for Indonesia's armed forces and the political system as a whole. This is where Juwono could apply his extraordinary analytical skills much more effectively than in the nitty-gritty debates with his own ministry,

other security agencies, the president, and parliament. Consequently, it is in
the field of doctrinal and strategic groundwork where Juwono's achievements
were most evident. Under his leadership, TNI headquarters finally issued
its new doctrine in early 2007, which had been drafted since 2002. The
new doctrine summarized the post-Suharto military reforms in one large
document, defining the military as an apolitical defence force carrying
out the orders of democratically legitimized governments.[45] In addition,
Juwono launched several new concepts that set the parameters for change in
Indonesia's armed forces in the next two decades. At the core of his proposals
was the creation of an essential minimalist force capable of responding quickly
to crises throughout the archipelago.[46] This planned force would still rely on
the army's territorial command network, but is expected to increasingly use
the navy and the air force in defence operations, civic missions, and disaster
relief. In this regard, Juwono envisioned the establishment of new regional
command centres, which would no longer consist exclusively of army combat
units, but integrate all three services.[47]

Despite the long-term nature of Juwono's plans, he tried to carry out
some of them during his term as minister. To begin with, Juwono started
the process of shifting military resources from the army to the navy and the
air force, eroding the land-based territorial ideology that had dominated
TNI's thinking since the 1940s.[48] Although he stopped short of questioning the army's territorial structure, Juwono's open promotion of navy and
air force interests constituted a significant departure from past practices.
Moreover, in the equipment purchase plans developed by his ministry,
Juwono prioritized transport planes and ships over fighter jets and frigates.
This was in response to the experience of the Aceh tsunami, where the
government had been forced to call in foreign militaries to provide the
transportation vehicles that TNI lacked.[49] While it remains to be seen if
Juwono's plans will be carried out as prescribed by his ministry (the three
services, the finance ministry, and parliament still have a significant say in
the purchasing process),[50] Juwono seems to have initiated a paradigmatic
shift away from the tradition of land-based defence organization. The
other major policy initiative started by Juwono concerned the budget.
With the exception of the 2008 fiscal year, Juwono secured considerable
budget increases for the armed forces. Between 2004 and 2008, the defence
budget grew from around 19 trillion rupiah (US$2.1 billion) to around
33.7 trillion rupiah (US$3.7 billion), an increase of 73 per cent.[51] Juwono
correctly viewed these increases as a precondition for closing TNI's
off-budget sources, and while the progress on transferring military businesses
to the state was sluggish at best, Juwono's efforts to obtain more funds for

the military at least slightly reduced the dependency of the armed forces on illicitly raised monies.

In summary, Yudhoyono's personal success in sidelining military conservatives and reining in the armed forces over Aceh was not matched by similar progress in institutional military reform. Many of the initiatives launched under Yudhoyono's presidency were fragmentary and poorly coordinated, creating the impression that no coherent blueprint for reform existed that could guide the government's actions. In particular, there appeared to have been only very vague directives given by Yudhoyono to his Minister of Defence Juwono Sudarsono, leading at several occasions to contradictory statements by the two men over military reform issues. The deep confusion over the National Defence Act, the planned handover of TNI businesses, and the reform of the military justice system left the public wondering what exactly the government's plan for the military was. It was only in the field of long-term doctrinal strategizing where Juwono could highlight some innovative ideas, but because many of his plans have yet to be fully implemented, they have attracted neither much attention by the public nor institutional resistance from vested interests in the security sector. Thus his well-argued vision of Indonesia's military as a multi-service force with rapid deployment capabilities has yet to stand the test of scrutiny by the political elite and the non-governmental defence community, and it is unclear if Juwono will stay in power long enough to witness this debate as minister of defence.[52]

## CONTINUED CHALLENGES

Despite its mixed record in institutional military reform, the Yudhoyono government has done more to improve Indonesia's post-authoritarian civil-military relations than most of its predecessors. The resolution of the Aceh conflict in particular constituted an unprecedented achievement. Before the signing of the Helsinki agreement, Aceh had been the arena with the most eloquent display of the shortcomings of military reform in Indonesia: rampant human rights violations, ranging from arbitrary raids on whole villages to targeted extrajudicial executions; extortion of businesses, commercial kidnappings, and other forms of military involvement in the conflict economy; and widespread violence triggered by TNI's proxy militias, combined with intimidation ahead of elections to secure satisfactory levels of voter participation (McCulloch 2003; Davies 2006). The successful implementation of the Helsinki accord put an end to most of these practices, depriving the armed forces of one of the few territories in which it had been able to engage in pre-democratic habits without fear of public scrutiny and sanction. Since 2005, the only area that still offers opportunities to the military to carry out operations without much control by the press and civil society organizations is the interior of Papua (McGibbon 2006). But even Papua has seen a significant reduction in the number of serious human rights violations, with the International Crisis Group (2006, p. 1) remarking that gross violations under the New Order have given way to "chronic low-level abuse". Yudhoyono has issued orders to security forces to exercise maximum restraint in the province, and that instruction seems to have been upheld in the urban centres. However, there are continued concerns over TNI operations in the highlands and in the border area with Papua New Guinea.

The considerable decline of military involvement in Indonesia's conflict-prone areas has provided the government with the opportunity to turn these short-term gains into sustainable institutional reforms. However, as we have seen in the previous section, the Yudhoyono administration has made less than optimal use of this unique chance; instead, the government has been content with playing the role of a largely passive actor in structural military reform, presenting surprisingly few concrete policy ideas. This, to be sure, is not for a lack of institutional deficiencies and problems that need to be addressed. Despite the fundamental changes to the military's presence in politics and society since Suharto's fall, the Indonesian armed forces remain a highly problematic institution, and further reform is and will be necessary (Haseman 2006). The following parts of the chapter list some of the continuing problems in Indonesia's post-New Order military affairs, arguing that unless these issues are addressed, the country will find it difficult to proceed from the basic first-generation of military reforms to the second-generation changes typically associated with established democracies. In turn, the persistence of serious defects in its civil-military relations could undermine and slow down the process of Indonesia's democratic consolidation, with wide-ranging implications not only for the political arena, but the economy and society as well.

The largest obstacle to moving Indonesia to the crucial stage of second-generation military reforms is the outdated territorial command system of the army. Besides being incapable of fending off external attacks effectively, the territorial structure continues to provide the military with considerable residual powers, both political and economical. These powers could potentially be mobilized in times of socio-political instability to propel the military back into the political arena, following the example of the Thai armed forces, which staged their 2006 coup after almost fifteen years of relative political inactivity. While a military coup in Indonesia seems highly unlikely at this stage and would have to overcome much higher societal hurdles than in Thailand, the territorial web of army units could supply the Indonesian military with the logistic facilities to quickly establish nationwide control.

Despite its formal depoliticization after 1998, the territorial system still allows the military to tap into the local political infrastructure. Military commanders remain ex-officio members of informal local leadership circles called Muspida (*Musyawarah Pimpinan Daerah*), which comprise the local governor or *bupati*, senior legislators, the police chief, the head of the prosecutor's office, the head of the local court, and other influential society leaders. In these elite discussions, key decisions are being made outside of formal institutional channels, keeping the military at the centre of high-level political negotiations.[53] In order to remove the armed forces completely and irreversibly from political affairs, and make it impossible for them to use their existing institutional network for future interventions in politics, the reform of the territorial command system needs to be addressed urgently and comprehensively. This would require the most wide-ranging institutional reform of the armed forces since 1945, and would have to take consideration of budgetary issues as well as the capacity of the police to handle internal security. In spite of Juwono's attempts to shift resources from the army to the navy and the air force, and despite preliminary discussions among his advisers about reforming the territorial command structure, there have been no serious policy initiatives targeting the system since Agus Wirahadikusumah's failed pilot projects in 2000.[54]

In addition to its continued political relevance, the territorial command structure has also been essential in perpetuating the military's self-financing practices. As the government team tasked with drafting the inventory of TNI businesses found out in 2006, the vast majority of military enterprises are not large conglomerates, but small cooperatives attached to the territorial units at each level.[55] Moreover, it is mostly military personnel in territorial commands who engage in off-duty activities such as smuggling, business protection, and illegal logging. Accordingly, reforming the territorial command structure would not only reduce the military's potential to stage a coup in times of social upheaval, but would also shut down many of the off-budget income opportunities that currently allow the armed forces to raise a substantial amount of their total expenditure from sources outside official state channels. The refusal of the army leadership to include cooperatives and foundations in the pool of military businesses to be handed over to the government by 2009 is an indication of their importance for military self-financing, making it even more urgent to phase them out. At this point, however, the government seems unwilling to move seriously against the military's rent-seeking activities, which have traditionally compensated the armed forces for their low levels of state funding. Juwono's declaration in early 2007 that his ministry had already "completed" the job of "transferring assets of all units of cooperatives, foundations and businesses" to the government does not augur well for further executive initiatives on this issue (Sudarsono 2007). The efforts in this regard are far from "completed"; in fact it would be an overstatement to say that they have already begun in any meaningful way.

Another area that remains deeply problematic is the legal accountability of military officers for human rights abuses and other transgressions. The government has not only been hesitant to initiate further reform in this respect, but has actively blocked attempts to investigate violations by active and retired generals. In 2007, then Attorney-General Abdurrahman Saleh insisted that he could not investigate the 1998 shootings of demonstrators by the military at the Semanggi interchange, using legalistic arguments that most experts believed were groundless. Furthermore, political parties supporting the government voted in parliament against the reopening of the Semanggi case, which would have left Saleh with no other choice but to launch a full investigation.[56] The government's stance on the issue reflected Yudhoyono's general disinclination to prosecute past abuses, which the president had made explicit on a number of occasions. Believing that Indonesia should look ahead and not waste energy on lengthy debates about the past, Yudhoyono had little appreciation for the fact that abuses not properly prosecuted can instil a sense of impunity in the officer corps, with serious consequences for the behaviour of field troops in current crisis situations. Yudhoyono also happily aborted the establishment of the already legislated Truth and Reconciliation Commission, arguing that its creation could trigger societal tensions.[57] The absence of a clear government concept of how to deal with past gross human rights abuses in Aceh, Papua, East Timor, and other parts of the country has not only helped some of the suspects to pursue respectable post-Suharto political careers, but has also allowed the officer corps to have confidence in its continued protection from legal prosecution.

The 2007 decision by parliament — against initial government opposition — to have off-duty crimes tried by civilian courts was an important step towards greater military accountability, but the problems are unlikely to end there. Civilian courts are less inclined to give light sentences to TNI personnel than the military justice system, but past experience has shown that civilian judges often lack courage and expertise when dealing with cases that involve the armed forces. Between 2002 and 2004, the special human rights courts that tried the East Timor cases, the Tanjung Priok massacre, and a shooting incident in the Papuan town of Abepura consisted largely of civilian judges, who handed down some convictions but even more acquittals. The very few sentences imposed on senior generals were eventually overturned by the Supreme Court, which also comprised mostly civilian judges. In the same vein, the transfer of overall responsibility for the administration of the military justice system from TNI headquarters to the Supreme Court in 2004 was of a largely symbolic nature. TNI headquarters retained its managerial authority over military judges, with civilian Supreme Court officials arguing that they were unable to exercise proper supervision of military personnel because of the different promotion systems in the civilian and military bureaucracies. Further, the structural supervision of the military justice system at the Supreme Court was handed to veteran military judge German Hoediarto, who had previously gained some prominence for freeing Suharto's son Tommy from corruption charges in 2001.[58] In August 2007, he also notoriously ordered the news magazine *Time* to pay more than US$100 million in damages to Suharto for allegedly defaming him over his illicitly obtained wealth. In short, none of the post-New Order governments has managed to install the appropriate system and personnel necessary to uphold fair and effective procedures of military justice, leaving a huge task for the incumbent Yudhoyono administration to tackle.

The strengthening of civilian institutions overseeing the armed forces constitutes another important challenge for the Yudhoyono government. Military reformers have since 1998 demanded that TNI headquarters be subordinated firmly to the department of defence, which in turn would have to undergo a process of "civilianization" in order to exercise effective control. At the moment, TNI headquarters is hierarchically at the same level as the department of defence, with both institutions directly answering to the president. The 2002 State Defence Act and the 2004 TNI Act have handed the ministry some authority of coordination over the armed forces, largely in the field of long-term planning and strategic equipment purchases. But TNI chiefs have invariably insisted that their direct superior is the president, not the minister.[59] Moreover, the department itself is still under the control of military officers. While there has been a succession of civilian ministers of defence since 1999, the key bureaucratic posts in the department have continuously been held by active TNI generals.[60] Most importantly, the secretary-general of the department has traditionally been a three-star officer nominated by TNI headquarters. The government has argued that existing laws on bureaucratic organization prevent it from appointing more civilians to senior posts in the ministry, but it has done little to change the regulations accordingly. Thus only high-ranking civil servants are eligible for such positions, but they tend to lack the specific education and expertise to deal with military affairs. On the other hand, civilians with qualifications in defence matters are usually not top civil servants and are therefore barred from taking up posts in the department. Creating the legal framework for better supervision of TNI by the department of defence, and the posting of more civilians in the latter, remain crucial issues on the way to improved civil-military relations.

By the same token, parliamentary oversight of the armed forces continues to be sketchy. While some parliamentarians have made good use of the new powers of the legislature over the military such as budget control, the majority of DPR members have not acquired the necessary skills to exercise oversight properly. Even in commission I, which is in charge of security, defence, and foreign policy, most members have only very limited knowledge of military affairs, making it impossible for them to ask the right questions or read budget proposals critically (Muradi 2006). Most legislators simply have no interest in such technical matters, but there is a larger underlying problem of a lack of institutional capacity as well. Indonesian parliamentarians have very few advisory staff that could collect material, prepare briefs, and provide input on key policy decisions. While the factions and commissions have a number of underpaid and often insufficiently qualified advisors, they are rarely able to provide meaningful assistance (Sherlock 2003).[61] The provision of more expert staff and research resources would thus go a long way to improve the conditions of parliamentarians tasked with overseeing the armed forces. Of course the high levels of rotation among commission members, the massive corruption in the legislature, and the vested interests of politicians in dealing with the military have a complicating effect on such long-term reforms to parliamentary oversight mechanisms. Like their counterparts in many other democracies, DPR members are often more interested in searching for additional income opportunities or manoeuvring themselves into politically advantageous positions than getting good advice on policy matters.

There are plenty of unresolved issues in military reform, but the government has shown little inclination to address them any time soon. This reluctance is a reflection of Yudhoyono's legendary hesitancy, but also of the declining societal pressure for further change in the armed forces. Unlike in 1998 and 1999, the military is no longer seen as an immediate threat to Indonesian democracy, given the dramatic changes that have occurred since the end of the New Order. Opinion polls in 2006 and 2007 have demonstrated that military reform is no longer a policy priority for the Indonesian electorate, with economic development, unemployment, education, food supply, domestic security, and natural disaster relief ranking much higher than previously crucial items of political reform (Lembaga Survei Indonesia 2006).[62] The resolution of the conflict in Aceh, the decline in human rights violations, and the military's withdrawal from formal politics all seem to suggest to Indonesian citizens that military reform is less urgent than in the past. In addition, given the vast budgetary resources required to revamp the territorial system, replace it with a highly mobile multi-service force, and boost the capacity of the police to absorb all domestic security responsibilities from the army, most Indonesians apparently prefer to spend available state funds on improving the country's infrastructure, health system, or public schools (Ramage 2007).[63] The experience in Thailand has shown, however, that militaries with a long history of politicization can stage sudden comebacks even after extended periods of political abstinence, especially if the power structures that underpin the military's strength remain unreformed. Thus, despite the predominant impression that the military has completely extracted itself from politics, further delays in reforming the Indonesian armed forces may prove costly, particularly in the event of unexpected political or social instability.

## PRELIMINARY CONCLUSIONS: BETWEEN STAGNATION AND REFORM

The dynamics of Indonesian civil-military relations between 1998 and 2008 were anything but a linear process. There have been some steps forward and some steps back, often leaving observers confused about the extent of change that has occurred since Suharto's fall. It is thus imperative to assess Indonesia's civil-military relationship against comparative data and explanatory frameworks. Only by comparing it to other countries at similar stages of their post-authoritarian transition or democratic consolidation is it possible to judge Indonesia's progress in a fair and objective manner. In this regard, the two-generation model of civil-military reforms developed by Cottey, Edmunds, and Forster provides an analytical tool for assessing the performance of particular states in establishing democratic control over their post-authoritarian militaries. Based on a number of qualitative indicators, Cottey et al. evaluated the measures taken by a group of selected countries in Europe and Asia to achieve structural military reform. This evaluation, in turn, allowed for the location of these states on a comparative scale of civil-military transitions. The highest level of progress was reached by those states that had completed the first-generation reforms but experienced problems in implementing the second. At the bottom of the scale, several states had not even started serious efforts to address first-generation issues.

Applying the model to Indonesia, it appears that while significant first-generation military reforms have been achieved, the persistence of basic structural problems has prevented the country from proceeding to the second generation of reforms. In consequence, the almost complete extraction of the armed forces from formal politics was counterbalanced by continued military privileges in state and society, most notably the *de facto* legal impunity enjoyed by TNI officers and soldiers. This ambivalence affected the credibility of the reform package as a whole, even if from an institutional and procedural perspective it looked impressive. For example, the electoral reforms carried out under the Habibie government meant that the executive and legislative institutions overseeing the armed forces were democratically legitimized. Parliament was formally empowered to exercise control functions vis-à-vis the military, ranging from budget allocation to defence planning. The department of defence was led by civilian ministers for the first time since the 1950s, and the 2002 State Defence Act and the 2004 TNI Act handed it authority over the strategic and logistical aspects of military management. MPR decrees defined the role of the armed forces as being focused on defence, while the police was separated from the military and charged with maintaining internal security. Human rights courts were established in 2000 to put security officers on trial for gross violations, and the civilian government was able to settle the Aceh conflict peacefully, against opposition from conservative military officers. There were even some "leaps" into second-generation reforms: the participation of civil society groups in drafting the State Defence Bill and other similar legislative initiatives hinted at the development of what Cottey et al. called a "civilian defence community", an indicator of a state already at a very late stage of successful transition.

These obvious successes were tainted by Indonesia's inability to remove what was widely identified as the main obstacle to effective and sustainable military reform: the army's territorial command structure. The persistence of this command system allowed the practice of military self-financing to remain operational, with serious implications for the political and legal accountability of the armed forces to the newly established civilian control bodies. The failure to tackle the single most important item on the first-generation military reform agenda was aggravated by other problems typical of civil-military transitions. Civilian defence officials lacked the expertise and political clout to professionally review strategic, technical, and operational questions of military management and present alternative ideas. In addition, the continued influence of the military discouraged civilian politicians from seeking to exercise their control function properly. Instead, they sought the support of the armed forces to settle conflicts within the civilian elite, particularly at the height of political tensions between 1999 and 2002. At the same time, human rights courts acquitted almost all officers indicted for violations in East Timor and the 1984 massacre of Tanjung Priok, extending what Robert Cribb (2002, p. 239) called the "triumphalist culture of impunity". Apparently, the institutions produced by the first generation of reforms, while equipped with formal authority and legal instruments, often proved toothless when confronted with the entrenched network of political relationships cultivated by the armed forces.

In order to explain the different stages of progress that states have reached in their civil-military transitions, Cottey et al. introduced five explanatory propositions. If applied to the case of Indonesia, they help to illustrate the mixed results of its military reform process. First, Cottey and his associates look at historical legacies, focusing particularly on the depth of the military's entanglement with the authoritarian order that preceded the democratic transition. In Indonesia, the loyalty of the post-authoritarian military elite towards the old regime was considerably higher than in other countries where military-backed regimes fell. The composition of the armed forces in the first eighteen months of the democratic polity reflected appointments and promotions Suharto had made in his last years of office, causing a strong inclination for senior officers to protect the residual interests of the fallen regime. The second criterion evaluated by Cottey et al. is the quality of civilian governance and the extent to which major forces support the existing democratic form of state organization. Indonesia's post-Suharto elite has largely accepted democracy as the most viable political system, providing the country with a better chance of achieving progress in civil-military relations than other states in which the foundations of government remain widely disputed.[64] However, in the period between 1998 and 2004, the level of conflict within the elite over the rules and norms of democratic interaction was so high that some important reforms of the armed forces could not be pursued.

Third, in terms of international factors that influenced military reform efforts in Indonesia, their impact on the transition has been largely negative. To be sure, it was the external shock of the Asian economic crisis that caused Suharto's regime to collapse in the first place. During the transition itself, however, the post-911 security environment reduced the international pressure on TNI to reform, rehabilitating the armed forces as an important player in the "war against terror". In addition, Indonesia's increasing orientation towards China, India, and Eastern Europe as sources of defence procurement made the government less dependent on Western countries that set strict conditions for military cooperation. Fourth, Cottey and his colleagues analysed the quality of institutional reform as an indicator for the solidity of the reform process and the prospects of future change. In Indonesia, the failure to include the territorial command structure in the programme of institutional reform increased, in the terminology of Cottey et al. (2000, p. 3), the "vulnerability of civil-military relations to the vagaries of domestic political change". Thus in spite of the significant successes in its civil-military transition, and despite the general political stability after 2004, Indonesia still cannot rely on sufficiently strong institutional mechanisms to fend off possible military interference in politics in the future. Finally, Cottey, Edmunds, and Forster discuss the role of "military cultures" as catalyzing or obstructing factors in the reform process. In this regard, the specific "military culture" in Indonesia, nurtured by decades of self-financing, operational autonomy, and legal impunity, proved mostly unsupportive of fundamental changes to the foundations of the armed forces. Even ten years after Suharto's fall, the mindset of military officers remains dominated by a deep sense of political entitlement, and although the officer corps does not openly oppose the democratic polity, it still has not developed a natural affinity with it either.

The mixed results of its efforts to establish democratic control over the armed forces grants Indonesia a medium ranking in the field of states at comparable stages of their post-authoritarian transitions. Indonesia has fared better than a large number of Eastern European and Central Asian countries researched by Cottey, Edmunds, and Forster, and compares increasingly well to its neighbours in the Southeast Asian region, most notably Thailand and the Philippines. Some of the countries analysed by Cottey et al. have not even begun their first generation of civil-military reforms, such as Turkmenistan and Belarus (Herd and Tracy 2006, pp. 552–53). Indonesia has also achieved more stable results than states that addressed both first and second-generation reforms, but saw their reform processes collapse due to the weakness of the state. Such countries include Armenia, Bosnia-Herzegovina, and Tajikistan. Among the countries studied by Cottey and his fellow researchers, Russia and the Ukraine are the most similar to Indonesia as far as their current state of civil-military relations is concerned. In those states, problems with the first generation of reforms persist, and the armed forces remain a highly politicized and privileged institution despite formal changes to their organizational framework. Indonesia lags behind states, however, that have seen successful first and second-generation reforms while still experiencing sporadic problems in the process. Cottey et al. identified eleven countries belonging to this group, including Bulgaria, Estonia, the Czech Republic, and Hungary.

Despite its illustrative strength, however, the scheme developed by Cottey et al. remains fragmentary. It has been argued throughout this book that the model needs to add the character of regime change and the level of conflict in civilian politics as major factors determining the fate of civil-military reforms in post-authoritarian states. Chapter 6 of this study has discussed the struggle between major civilian forces for hegemony over the post-Suharto polity between 1998 and 2004, and has pointed to the disruptive impact of these conflicts on military reform efforts. The following final chapter will, by way of contrast, highlight the increasing stability of the Indonesian polity after 2004, and it will argue that important gains made in the field of democratic control of the armed forces were a direct result of this reduction in political uncertainty and intra-civilian conflict. As in previous chapters, the focus of the analysis will be on the competition and interaction between Muslim forces, which will expose general trends in civilian politics in Indonesia after 2004.

## Notes

[1]   The derogative terms for Yudhoyono that circulated in the officer corps ranged from "air conditioner general" during his time of active military service to "minister for discourse" after his appointment to the cabinet. Not surprisingly, many of the criticisms implied in these terms — alleged isolation from hard realities on the ground, predilection for intellectual debates, and political indecisiveness — became popular critiques of Yudhoyono's presidency after 2004.

[2]   Ryamizard and Yudhoyono had openly clashed before and during the internationally mediated peace process, with Yudhoyono telling a U.S. general in 2002 that talks would continue, to which Ryamizard responded that "fundamentally, there is no dialogue" (Aspinall and Crouch 2003, p. 29). After the signing of the "cessation of hostilities" agreement in December 2002, Ryamizard toured Aceh, using his radical anti-GAM rhetoric to destabilize the accord. The agreement finally collapsed in May 2003, followed by a full-blown military campaign to end GAM's insurgency by force.

[3]   In Aceh, Yudhoyono received four times as many votes as Megawati in the first round of the election, and attracted about 80 per cent support in the second. In Papua, a traditional PDI-P stronghold, Yudhoyono obtained more than double of Megawati's vote in the first round, and reached slightly more than his national average of 60 per cent in the second.

[4]   Interview with Endriartono Sutarto, Jakarta, 11 June 2007.

[5]   "SBY Tetap Mempertahankan Sutarto Sebagai Panglima TNI", *Pikiran Rakyat*, 28 October 2004.

[6]   Interview with Endriartono Sutarto, Jakarta, 11 June 2007.

[7]   "Tugas Pangkostrad Diserahkan ke KSAD", *Kompas*, 28 September 2004.

[8]   "Jenderal Ryamizard: Pembunuh Theys Hiyo Eluay Adalah Pahlawan", *Tempo Interaktif*, 23 April 2003. Shortly after the trial, Rymamizard remarked that

"I don't know, people say they did wrong, they broke the law. What law? Okay, we are a state based on the rule of law, so they have been punished. But for me, they are heroes because the person they killed was a rebel leader."

9    "Tuntaskan Kasus Aceh, TNI AD Dukung Keputusan Politik Pemerintah", *Media Indonesia*, 6 June 2005.

10   In March 2007, it emerged that Agus had taken some time off to go shopping with his celebrity wife in London and Paris, sparking a debate in Indonesia about whether Agus had received special privileges. Yudhoyono personally intervened in the affair, clarifying that Agus had enjoyed the same number of vacation days as other soldiers. See "Cuti Lettu Agus Harimurti Sah", *Kompas*, 31 March 2007.

11   Hadi Utomo's predecessor as chairman of Partai Demokrat, Subur Budhisantoso, suggested that Hadi was chosen as party leader at the insistence of Yudhoyono's mother-in-law, the widow of Sarwo Edhie. Arguing that both Erwin and Pramono had been promoted under Yudhoyono's leadership while Hadi had gained nothing, Yudhoyono's mother-in-law allegedly proposed to hand the chairmanship of the party to Hadi in order to maintain some kind of "balance" within the family. Interview with Subur Budhisantoso, Jakarta, 28 September 2006.

12   Only one month after the Megawati government had launched the military campaign against GAM in May 2003, Yudhoyono told a group of visiting foreign scholars, of which the author was a member, that "ultimately, we know that military action alone won't bring a solution to the problem". He stated that he was thinking about ways to re-open the dialogue, but admitted that this was difficult "under the current circumstances". Group discussion with Yudhoyono Bambang Yudhoyono, notes by the author, Jakarta, 18 June 2003.

13   Although Yudhoyono did not specifically state that he wanted to end the Aceh conflict in order to improve state control over the military, he hinted in the conversations with Morfit that this was one of the welcome outcomes of the peace process. Interview with Michael Morfit, Jakarta, 3 May 2007.

14   "Fears As Aceh Peace Deal Signed", *The Standard*, 16 August 2005.

15   At the height of its power in 2000 and 2001, GAM was estimated to have controlled around 60 per cent of Aceh's territory. Its officials managed local government offices, issued business and marriage licences, and collected taxes. After the military campaign in 2003, however, GAM largely had to withdraw to the hills, isolating it from its income sources and logistical supply lines. Its declining military position subsequently led to discussions within the GAM elite about new approaches to the Indonesian government (Kingsbury 2006).

16   Interview with Endriartono Sutarto, Jakarta, 11 June 2007.

17   Endriartono had indicated in August 2005 that giving up economic interests in Aceh was a serious sacrifice for TNI. Asked by reporters about TNI's economic stake in the province, Endriartono replied that "preventing future bloodshed and preventing the death of my men is a consideration that overrides all others".

See "Hope for Peace as Drums Welcome Aceh Deal", *The Age*, 15 August 2005.

18  "Pemerintah Bahas Dana Penarikan di Aceh", *Media Indonesia*, 4 August 2005.

19  "BRR Slammed for Funding Aceh Military Operations", *Jakarta Post*, 12 August 2006.

20  "Anggaran Non-Perang", *Kompas*, 18 October 2007.

21  Interview with local businessmen, Banda Aceh, March 2007.

22  "Mendagri Akan Lantik Irwandi-Nazar — Irwandi Temui Kasad", *Waspada*, 6 February 2007.

23  Irwandi's reconciliatory approach after the elections stood in sharp contrast to the much more aggressive attitude he had displayed during the campaign for the governorship. Before the ballot, he had threatened to "rock the boat" if elected to head the province, distancing himself from other candidates who emphasized their good relations with Jakarta. Interview with Irwandi Yusuf, Banda Aceh, 9 October 2006.

24  "Rice Defends Resuming Military Ties With Indonesia", *The Sydney Morning Herald*, 16 March 2006.

25  "SBY Mundur, Mega Tersenyum", *Suara Merdeka*, 12 March 2004.

26  Ikrar had been asked to put this question forward by his colleagues and friends in the Indonesian Working Group for Security Sector Reform, a team of civilian academics and activists that had since 2001 worked on several bills regulating the security sector. Interview with Ikrar Nusa Bhakti, Jakarta, 5 July 2004.

27  "Mencerdaskan, Dialog Antarcapres", *Pikiran Rakyat*, 3 July 2004.

28  After Juwono's dismissal as minister of defence by then President Wahid in 2000, Megawati had appointed him as ambassador to London in June 2003. However, Juwono returned frequently to Indonesia for political discussions and maintained his deep interest in military affairs.

29  "TNI-Polri akan Disatukan", *Suara Merdeka*, 16 February 2005.

30  "Kapolri Tolak 'Diperintah' Mendagri", *Harian Komentar*, 20 December 2006.

31  Interview with Juwono Sudarsono, Jakarta, 1 May 2007.

32  Interview with Juwono Sudarsono, Jakarta, 1 May 2007.

33  "Menkeu Tolak PPA 'Dititipi' Bisnis Militer", *Kompas*, 2 August 2006.

34  The assets sold by TNI included its share in the Artha Graha bank, which had previously served as the major investment arm of the armed forces. By selling the share, the military made it impossible for the state to treat Artha Graha's investments as military assets. In addition, the army also sold the previously Kostrad-owned airline Mandala, which in the past had been an important cash cow for senior military officers. The proceeds of these sales were not handed over to the state; instead, TNI announced that they would be used for "educational" purposes. See "Penjualan Saham TNI di Artha Graha Disorot", *Bali Post*, 8 September 2005.

[35]   I am indebted to Lex Rieffel for pointing this out to me.

[36]   "Peraturan Presiden Republik Indonesia Nomor ... Tahun ... Tentang Badan Pengelola Bisinis Tentara Nasional Indonesia", no date. The stipulation mentioned above can be found in paragraph 4, article 1.

[37]   The best documentation on this dispute was presented in the internet news portal *detik.com*. It covered the discussion over several days: "SBY Minta Draf Produk Transformasi TNI Diperbaiki" (9 February 2007); "Dephan Siap Revisi Perpres Transformasi Bisnis TNI" (13 February 2007); "Harmonisasi Institusi Pengambil Alih Bisnis TNI" (13 February 2007).

[38]   Interview with Juwono Sudarsono, Jakarta, 1 May 2007.

[39]   "Panglima TNI Akui Tim Mawar Punya Hak Yang Sama", *Kompas*, 15 May 2007.

[40]   "Patuhi Saja Presiden", *Kompas*, 30 November 2006.

[41]   Slamet Effendi Yusuf, a legislator from Golkar, remarked sarcastically that Juwono was a "real asset" for TNI, and he believed that the armed forces were gradually turning their back on many of the reforms launched after 1998. Interview with Slamet Effendi Yusuf, Jakarta, 27 September 2006.

[42]   Interview with Andreas Pareira, Jakarta, 7 May 2007.

[43]   "Presiden Setuju Anggota TNI Diadili di Pengadilan Umum", *Republika*, 26 November 2006.

[44]   According to Pareira, even this transitional period was not Juwono's idea, but had previously been proposed by the DPR. Interview with Andreas Pareira, Jakarta, 7 May 2007.

[45]   "TNI Terapkan Doktrin Baru", *Suara Karya*, 25 January 2007.

[46]   "Menhan: Indonesia Dipertahankan dengan Mukjizat", *Gatra*, 9 September 2006.

[47]   Interview with Juwono Sudarsono, Jakarta, 1 May 2007.

[48]   "Panglima TNI : Mau Perang Pakai Pisau Dapur?", *Koran Tempo*, 13 May 2006.

[49]   "Indonesia to Purchase more Hercules from U.S.", *Jakarta Post*, 26 November 2005.

[50]   Only defence purchases above 50 billion rupiahs are currently controlled by the department of defence, with contracts below that sum still handled by the various services of the armed forces. Rather predictably, the military has used this regulation to split bigger equipment purchases into a number of smaller contracts, allowing it to maintain managerial control over a large proportion of the purchases.

[51]   "Menteri Juwono: Anggaran Pertahanan 2008 Tak Dipotong", *Koran Tempo*, 18 August 2007.

[52]   There has been frequent speculation about Juwono's possible resignation or replacement, with his allegedly fragile health mentioned as the main reason. On several occasions, it was predicted that either the head of Lemhannas, Muladi, or the chairman of parliament's commission I, Theo Sambuaga, (both Golkar politicians) would replace Juwono. However, Yudhoyono had promised

Juwono in 2004 not to appoint a party politician as minister of defence, and when the president announced a cabinet reshuffle in May 2007, Juwono was indeed allowed to stay in his position. Interview with Juwono Sudarsono, Jakarta, 1 May 2007.

53　In November 2006, a number of NGOs launched an initiative to disband the Muspida. But the ministry of the interior insisted that the legal basis for the Muspida, a presidential decree dating back to 1986, was still in place. The only change since 1998 has been the discontinuation of special funding for the forum and a less regular meeting schedule. See "Muspida Itu Peninggalan Orba", *Kompas*, 27 November 2006.

54　According to Andi Widjajanto, a security expert often consulted by the department of defence, there have been debates in the department in 2006 and 2007 about how to approach possible changes to the territorial command system. Widjajanto said that one school of thought wants to see the structure disbanded from above (i.e. *Kodam* and *Korem*), leaving the lower levels intact. The opposite view is that the system should be revamped from below, with the lower-level units (*Koramil, Babinsa*) abolished, while the higher levels remain untouched. When asked for confirmation, however, Juwono stated that these discussions were rather informal and did not yet reflect a new policy debate in the department. Discussion with Andi Widjajanto, Manila, 8 March 2007, and interview with Juwono Sudarsono, Jakarta, 1 May 2007.

55　"Daftar Inventarisasi Badan Usaha Yayasan/Koperasi di Bawah TNI AL/TNI AD/TNI AU/Mabes TNI (Sebelum Diaudit), Berdasarkan surat Panglima TNI Nomor: B/3385-05/15/06/Spers Tanggal, 28 September 2005."

56　The 1999–2004 parliament had voted against classifying the Trisakti and Semanggi shootings as "gross and systematic human rights violations", a decision that prevented the establishment of a special human rights court. Some factions tried to overturn this agreement in 2007, but the majority of parties, mostly those supporting the government, rejected the proposal. See "Mayoritas Fraksi DPR Menolak: Pengungkapan Kasus Trisakti dan Semanggi Tampaknya Bakal Tamat Riwayatnya", *Kompas*, 7 March 2007.

57　The Truth and Reconciliation Commission, mandated by a 2004 law, would have provided for a mechanism to investigate and, in some cases, recommend sanctions against human rights abusers. Yudhoyono, however, delayed the process of selecting commission members beyond the deadline set by the law, and amidst increasing legal uncertainty, the Constitutional Court in December 2006 declared the law invalid. The president then terminated the selection process. Vice-President Kalla echoed Yudhoyono's position, saying that focusing on the past was an unproductive, "emotional" exercise. See "Seleksi KKR Dihentikan", *Kompas*, 19 December 2006.

58　"Ketua MA Seharusnya Tinjau Susunan Majelis PK", *Kompas*, 5 October 2001.

59　In November 2004, TNI commander Endriartono Sutarto declared that, "I have never rejected the idea of TNI being under the department of defence, but the TNI Act really did not mandate this. … There, it is only stated that in administrative and strategic matters, TNI is under the coordination of the department of defence, but not structurally. … At the moment, TNI is in a transitional process of depoliticization. Only if that process is over, we will design an ideal structure." See "Panglima TNI Tidak Menolak di bawah Dephan", *Pikiran Rakyat*, 3 December 2004.

[60]  "Menhan Akan Melalukan Pergantian Pejabat", *Suara Merdeka*, 15 December 2004.

[61]  In early 2007, each of the 550 DPR members had one personal assistant (mostly for administrative affairs), and the total number of expert staff at the commissions and factions was 155. As monthly salaries, they received 3.5 and 7.5 million rupiah (US$389 and 833) respectively, but staff often complained about delayed or incomplete payments. See "Gaji Staf Ahli DPR Belum Dibayarkan", *Kompas*, 1 March 2007.

[62]  In the same survey, TNI received the highest public satisfaction score out of all government agencies and departments. It received 3.86 out of 5 possible points, with the forestry ministry obtaining the lowest score (3.26). In a similar opinion poll by the news magazine *Tempo* in October 2007, TNI was also the institution with the highest satisfaction rate (84 per cent). The coordinating ministry for the economy finished last with 52.4 per cent. See "Dulu 8, Sekarang 5", *Tempo*, 29 October 2007.

[63]  NGOs, politicians, and teachers organizations have, for example, consistently demanded that the government spend twenty per cent of its budget on education, as mandated by the constitution. The Constitutional Court reminded the government in May 2007 that it needed to fulfil this requirement if it did not want to be seen in violation of the constitution. See "Harus Dipenuhi, 20% Anggaran Pendidikan", *Pikiran Rakyat*, 2 May 2007.

[64]  The high levels of elite support for the democratic polity were also reflected in the wider public. In 2006, 74 per cent of Indonesians believed that democracy was the best system for Indonesia, up from 68 in 1999 (Mujani 2006).

# 8

## STABILIZING THE CIVILIAN POLITY
### Muslim Groups in Yudhoyono's Indonesia

The decline in the intensity of violent conflict and the consequent reduction in the use of state coercion in governance were important factors in the increasing political marginalization of the Indonesian armed forces after 2004. The end of the communal violence in Maluku, North Maluku, and Poso as well as the resolution of the Aceh conflict reduced the political intervention opportunities for the military and strengthened the hand of the civilian government. In addition, President Yudhoyono's openly declared preference for peaceful negotiations with separatists and other state dissidents left the proponents of repressive military action without much influence to pursue their cause. Sidelined by Yudhoyono at the beginning of his term, the most prominent conservatives in the armed forces had no choice but to keep a low profile and prepare for retirement. In the meantime, the leadership of the armed forces shifted to politically moderate officers with a strong dislike for appearances in the media, contrasting sharply with the publicity-seeking and controversial nature of the statements made by officers such as Ryamizard Ryacudu and Bibit Waluyo during Megawati's presidency.

But the improvement in the quality of democratic civilian control over the military after 2004 was not only related to developments within the armed forces and the lower intensity of violence in the regions. As argued in previous chapters, the level of conflict between key civilian groups plays a significant role in determining the extent of military interference in politics, with intra-civilian fragmentation typically allowing the armed forces to defend their institutional interests and shield themself from demands for reform. By contrast, broad consensus among civilian groups on the form of state organization and important policy issues often leads to the marginalization of the military from political affairs. In Indonesia, conflicts between major civilian forces had marked the transfer of power from Suharto to Habibie, assisting protagonists of the New Order to remain in government and extend their influence into the democratic era. In the same vein, fierce competition between civilian constituencies over the posts and resources of the new polity brought the state to the brink of constitutional collapse in 2001, with the military emerging from the crisis largely rehabilitated and with new self-confidence. This chapter demonstrates, however, that the level of conflict between important civilian groups declined significantly after 2004, and that this decline had a stabilizing impact on security sector governance in general and the control of the armed forces in particular.

The following chapter, like the preceding ones on Muslim politics, analyses developments within political Islam in order to illustrate trends and patterns of civilian politics as a whole. The discussion focuses on five areas in which certain dynamics of Muslim politics have contributed to the post-2004 stabilization of the civilian polity and the consequent reduction in military influence on political affairs. To begin with, the political reforms implemented in 2004 have clarified the rules and norms of democratic competition, removing most of the ambiguities that had fuelled the power struggles of the immediate post-Suharto period, including that between key Muslim groups. Secondly, new leaders in the two largest Islamic organizations, NU and Muhammadiyah, managed to de-escalate the tensions built up in the early phase of the transition. The third section of this chapter discusses the centrist tendencies among Islamic parties, which gave up some of their dogmatic demands in order to gain votes from the political mainstream. As a result, many of the contentious issues that had previously raised tensions between Indonesia's main political forces were defused in the process. Fourth, the chapter analyses the results of the direct local elections held after 2005, which saw intensive cooperation between political parties across the ideological spectrum. Finally, the chapter concludes with a short overview of developments in "fundamentalist" Islam, highlighting the decline in militant activity after 2005. This decline, like other parallel developments in political Islam, led to a further stabilization of the civilian polity and, by implication, eroded the political clout of the armed forces.

# THE STABILIZATION OF THE CIVILIAN POLITY

The intensity of intra-civilian conflict is one of the major factors that determine the level of military engagement in political affairs (Finer 2002). States with traditionally high measures of intra-civilian fragmentation have been prone to frequent interventions by their armed forces, and Indonesia has been a case in point. The deep divisions between Muslim forces in particular have helped to sustain forty years of military-backed authoritarian rule, and the early post-New Order transition saw the fault-lines of these divisions extending into the new democratic polity. After 2004, however, the ferociousness of these conflicts appears to have declined, although substantial differences between the various Islamic groups remain. The most important reason for this decline has been the implementation of wide-ranging political and institutional reforms shortly before and after 2004, which established the rules and procedures for democratic competition. This set of new norms and institutions filled the very gap in which the conflicts of the early transitional period had spread and damaged the democratic system.

At the core of the institutional reforms was the introduction of direct presidential elections in 2004. Previously, the president had been elected by the MPR, which consisted of a large proportion of non-elected members (including from the police and the armed forces). The election of Abdurrahman Wahid in 1999 had been the result of political deals within the elite rather than popular support for the blind Muslim cleric, and when Wahid began to dismantle the coalition that had voted for him, his legitimacy evaporated rapidly. Similarly, Megawati Sukarnoputri replaced Wahid in 2001 through a controversial impeachment process, leaving a considerable stain on her credibility. Thus, much of the early post-Suharto transition was spent on negotiations over a mechanism for presidential elections that would establish a strong presidency, but avoid the possibility of renewed authoritarian rule (Clear 2005). A compromise was finally reached in 2002, based on which the first direct presidential polls in Indonesia's history were to be held in 2004.[1] This reformed electoral system not only provided the new president with an unambiguous popular mandate, but also created additional hurdles for his or her impeachment. Learning from the Wahid debacle, the conditions for dismissing a sitting president were clarified and tightened, making a repetition of the 2001 constitutional crisis unlikely.[2] In short, the fight for political power was now codified in strict procedural rules, replacing the previous chaos of multi-interpretable regulations.

Equally crucial for the stabilization of the civilian polity was the implementation of new electoral rules for local government heads. From

June 2005 onwards, all governors, *bupatis*, and mayors had to be directly elected by the people, as opposed to their election by local legislatures under the previous system (Mietzner 2005). Between 1999 and 2004, the chiefs of local governments had often bribed their way into office, exploiting the splits within and between political parties to pay off enough parliamentarians for a majority of the votes. As demonstrated in Chapter 6, retired military officers benefited from this inability of parties to settle on joint candidates, offering themselves as compromise nominees and ultimately retaining key governorships across Indonesia. However, incumbents elected through this process found it difficult to rule effectively, with legislatures frequently turning against local government heads shortly after their election. Trying to extort more money from them, parliaments threatened to impeach incumbents, and because the rules and regulations on this matter were ambiguous, local administrations were often paralysed while the two sides insisted on their positions. To make matters worse, both parties to the conflict typically mobilized their supporters, leading to violent clashes that needed to be contained by local security forces.

The new electoral framework made it impossible for candidates to simply buy office, instead requiring them to seek popular support from grassroots voters (Gross 2006). Consequently, the direct mandate from the people made incumbents less dependent on local legislatures, which could no longer threaten to overthrow officials unwilling to distribute money and other benefits among parliamentarians. In the new law on local government passed in 2004, the procedure for impeaching governors, *bupatis*, and mayors was spelled out in detail, avoiding the regulatory confusion that had fed many of the pre-2004 conflicts.[3] After the direct elections were introduced, protracted and violent controversies over disputed incumbents were a much less common phenomenon than before.[4] Obviously, disagreements over election results still occurred after 2005 as well, but those were mostly settled in a very short time and rarely affected the long-term ability of local administrations to govern.

The fresh institutional arrangements were watched over by the newly created Constitutional Court (*Mahkamah Konstitusi*, MK), which was established in August 2003. The court had the authority to rule on the compatibility of laws with the constitution, decide conflicts between state institutions, disband political parties, and issue verdicts on disputed election results (Wrighter 2005). Most importantly, it played a crucial role in the impeachment of presidents, evaluating whether the actions of the head of state were indeed in violation of the constitution. The court quickly established itself as a respected referee in state affairs, playing the role that the Supreme

Court had been unable to fulfil in the turbulent transition after 1998. In the 2004 elections, the Constitutional Court ruled on complaints submitted by presidential candidates, political parties, and individual legislative nominees, and all sides accepted its decisions. Similarly, while some of its verdicts were heavily criticized (Butt 2007), the court's rulings on disputes between state agencies were almost invariably accepted and enforced.[5] The existence of the new court had a stabilizing impact on Indonesia's political process, offering conflicting parties an avenue for peaceful mitigation that previously was not available. Arguably, some of the controversies brought before the court would have been resolved in the past by mass mobilization of supporters, intimidation of opponents, or the deliberate deadlocking of parliamentary and executive proceedings until one of the parties relented.

The reforms of electoral mechanisms and the creation of new bodies in charge of political conflict mediation strengthened the civilian polity and reduced the powers of the military. In the early phase of the transition, civilian groups had still turned to the armed forces as both powerful allies and mediators in intra-civilian disputes. In 1999, civilian presidential candidates lobbied the armed forces for their votes and informal support in the elections held in the MPR, and the military elite was offered significant benefits in return. In 2001, both Wahid and his foes struggled to drag the armed forces to their sides, with the president trying to convince TNI to arrest his opponents, and the latter pleading to the generals to desert him. The military's move to side with the leaders of the impeachment initiative decided the conflict in their favour, and the armed forces consequently gained substantial concessions from Wahid's successor, Megawati Sukarnoputri. After 2004, such lobbying of the armed forces became much less important for civilian groups. While some parties still tried to recruit retired generals as vote-getters, they no longer needed the support of the institution to get elected. In the same vein, after 2004 conflicts between state institutions were much more likely to be resolved by the Constitutional Court or in inter-elite negotiations than by approaching the military for advice and mediation. Even in the conflict that erupted between Yudhoyono and parliament in June 2007 over the right of the DPR to summon the president, neither side asked the armed forces to take a stance on the issue.[6] Before 2004, by contrast, TNI would have been forced to make its position public as it still had legislators in the DPR.

Despite continuing problems in the relationship between Indonesia's state institutions, the post-2004 reforms have brought a great measure of order to a previously erratic political system (Aspinall 2005a). The clarification of the rules and procedures of democratic competition has provided badly needed stability to the government and its prospects of serving out a full term. This greater predictability of the political process has not only defused tensions within the elite, but also between key socio-religious constituencies. With courts now in charge of resolving disputes between political leaders, the latter find it more difficult to justify calling on their supporters to fight for their cause in the streets. The de-escalation in the relationship between NU and Muhammadiyah, which had come head to head in the constitutional crisis of 2001, is a good example of this improvement of inter-constituency relations as a result of the stabilizing civilian polity.

## NU AND MUHAMMADIYAH: DEPOLITICIZING THE DIVIDE

The socio-religious divide between traditionalist and modernist Islam — and between their main representatives NU and Muhammadiyah — has had a deep impact on Indonesia's political history. As explained in previous parts of this book, both Sukarno and Suharto exploited this intra-Muslim division to consolidate and prolong their rule. More recently, the profound distrust between the two main currents in Indonesian Islam prevented them from cooperating in the 1998 regime change, allowing key figures of the New Order to retain power instead. The split within Islam also extended into the post-authoritarian era, with traditionalists and modernists (as well as their various sub-currents) sponsoring the establishment of distinctly antagonistic political parties after 1998. The lowest point in the relationship between NU and Muhammadiyah was eventually reached in 2001, when during the crisis over the Wahid presidency fanatic NU activists attacked Muhammadiyah schools and offices, believing that the modernist organization was involved in efforts to overthrow Wahid. Although leaders of NU tried to de-escalate the situation after Wahid's fall, the relationship with its modernist counterpart remained fragile.

After the elections of 2004, however, there was a significant improvement in the atmosphere between the two largest Muslim groups. One obvious reason for this was the fact that neither Muhammadiyah- nor NU-affiliated candidates were successful in the presidential elections. Amien Rais and Wiranto's vice-presidential nominee Solahuddin Wahid dropped out in the first round, while NU chairman Hasyim Muzadi failed as Megawati's running mate in the second. Thus neither constituency had to be mobilized to keep one of theirs in the presidency in the way that the NU community had been called upon in 2001 to rally around Wahid at all cost. With both NU and Muhammadiyah only marginally represented in the Yudhoyono government (some ministers in the cabinet had links to the organizations), their stakes in national elite politics were considerably lower than during the Wahid presidency or Amien's 2004 bid. In addition, the clarified institutional procedures left leaders of both groups little room to challenge their electoral defeats by mass protests or clashes with opponents. While Amien believed that the elections had been flawed, he decided not to file a complaint with the Constitutional Court because he knew that he would not be able to provide the necessary legal proof for his claims. By contrast, Solahuddin and Wiranto challenged the election result in court, but their case was dismissed.[7] Finally, Hasyim Muzadi and Megawati, learning from this experience, accepted their defeat by Yudhoyono without taking legal action.

## The Marginalization of Wahid and Amien

The elections and their aftermath also marked the end of the dominance of Amien Rais and Abdurrahman Wahid over their respective organizations. Their rivalry and personal dislike for each other had marked NU-Muhammadiyah relations at least since the 1990s, peaking in Amien's presiding over Wahid's impeachment in 2001. In the post-2004 period, however, both groups sidelined their previous patriarchs, rushing in a new generation of leaders less interested in highlighting the differences between traditionalist and modernist Islam. At the 2004 NU congress in Solo, Wahid had tried to regain control over the organization by nominating himself as *Rais 'Aam*, the religious leader of NU with directing authority over the executive board. His bid ended with a crushing defeat, however, and with Hasyim Muzadi's re-election as general chairman.[8] Hasyim had been Wahid's hand-picked successor in 1999, but after 2001 the relationship between the two had deteriorated sharply. One of the main reasons for this was Hasyim's policy of distancing NU from PKB, and when Hasyim accepted Megawati's invitation to run as her vice-presidential partner, Wahid pledged to remove Hasyim from the NU chairmanship. Wahid's failure demonstrated that most NU branches had grown tired of his combative leadership style, preferring the much more soft-spoken and consensus-seeking Hasyim in his stead.[9] Bitterly attributing his defeat to Hasyim's alleged "money politics", Wahid consequently cut off his ties with most NU officials and concentrated on managing PKB, which he still chaired.

Muhammadiyah went through a similar, albeit less spectacular transformation. Under the leadership of Syafi'i Maarif since 1998, Muhammadiyah had extended barely veiled assistance to PAN and its leader Amien Rais. The Syafi'i-led central board had allowed Muhammadiyah officials to help with the creation of PAN's institutional infrastructure in 1998, and it also expressed unambiguous support for Amien's presidential bid in 2004.[10] At the 2005 Muhammadiyah congress in Malang, however, Amien's hegemonic influence over the organization came to an end. Prior to the congress, Amien had played with the idea of running for the Muhammadiyah chairmanship again.[11] Much to his surprise, however, there was very little enthusiasm in Muhammadiyah for his return. Abd. Rohim Ghazali, an influential Muhammadiyah youth leader, summarized the widespread sentiments in the organization against another term for Amien:

> Many believe that if Amien returned to Muhammadiyah, this would constitute a setback…. Of course it would be a big risk for Muhammadiyah if he was still tempted to run for the presidency in 2009. Like during the previous presidential election, Muhammadiyah would once again be dragged deeply into practical politics. While this is not necessarily negative, it is a worrying thought (Ghazali 2005).

After testing the waters for several weeks, Amien decided not to continue his candidacy. His main competitor, Din Syamsuddin, had prepared his own nomination for a number of years, travelling to Muhammadiyah offices throughout Indonesia to mobilize support. As the nominations from the local branches reached the Muhammadiyah headquarters in mid-2005, it emerged that Din, who maintained a difficult personal relationship with Amien, had acquired an unassailable lead. Din was ultimately elected chairman in Malang, terminating Amien's informal grip over Muhammadiyah in the same way that the NU congress in Solo had ended Wahid's dominance over NU.

The marginalization of Amien Rais and Aburrahman Wahid from Muhammadiyah and Nahdlatul Ulama respectively was accompanied by efforts of both organizations to disengage from the political parties that their two former patrons had founded. At its Solo congress, NU decided to keep an equal distance from all parties, departing from its earlier stance that it should cultivate a special relationship to parties that it had helped to establish — effectively meaning PKB.[12] Muhammadiyah, for its part, also issued a statement in May 2007 that formalized its disentanglement from party politics, sending a clear signal to PAN that it no longer viewed the party as its natural political ally; instead, it recognized the fact that Muhammadiyah members were active in all political parties.[13] These parallel decisions marked a significant policy change for both Muslim groups: following the breakdown of the authoritarian regime in 1998, they had concluded that building up their own parties was the best avenue to advance the interests of their constituencies. After a decade of experience with democratic rule, however, the disadvantages of direct engagement in party politics were all too obvious.[14] The Wahid presidency had damaged NU's relations with almost all other socio-political groups, and it took years for the organization to restore its reputation. Similarly, Muhammadiyah leaders felt that the involvement of its cadres in elite politics had stirred up social tensions at the grassroots level, and that PAN had failed to represent Muhammadiyah's interests effectively.[15] Thus the withdrawal from institutional party politics presented itself as the inevitable conclusion from this disappointment.

## New Cooperation and New Ambitions

The formal depoliticization of both NU and Muhammadiyah did not mean that its new leaders had no political ambitions, however. In fact, both Hasyim Muzadi and Din Syamsuddin were widely believed to be interested in participating in some capacity or other in the 2009 presidential elections. But unlike in the early phase of the post-New Order polity, they could no longer count on the support of their organizations. Hasyim Muzadi, for example, was forced to sign a contract (*kontrak jamiyah*) at the Solo congress that barred him and his entire central board from running for any legislative or executive office — a clear expression of discontent over his 2004 nomination. The contract, which had been drafted on the insistence of the staunchly apolitical *Rais 'Aam* Sahal Mahfudz, also did not allow Hasyim to represent NU in any political forum without the explicit approval of the whole NU leadership (Satrawi 2006). In Muhammadiyah, it was a poorly kept secret that Din had political ambitions, but he fully understood that he could not use the organization as a vehicle to run for public office in the same way as Amien had done in the past. And while Din encouraged Muhammadiyah cadres to seek leading positions in parties, parliaments, and executive institutions, he ruled out that Muhammadiyah would ever again enter into an exclusive political relationship such as the one with PAN before 2005.[16]

The generational change in the leadership of both organizations and their gradual extraction from party politics coincided with a significant reduction in their doctrinal differences. Ironically, this de-escalation of religio-ideological divisions was achieved by a shift of both NU and Muhammadiyah towards more conservative interpretations of the Muslim faith (Olle 2006, p. 11). In NU, Wahid's marginalization weakened the young liberal activists within the traditionalist group who had promoted cross-religious cooperation and modern understandings of Islamic scripture.[17] Under Hasyim Muzadi, NU reiterated its commitment to conservative Islamic values, denouncing liberal exegeses of theological texts as deviations from the faith. The same trend was visible in Muhammadiyah. Syafi'i had been an unorthodox Muslim leader, who was open to liberal views of Islamic teachings and equal collaboration with other faiths. Din, on the other hand, had established a reputation for consistently defending the purity of the scripture and promoting the rights of Indonesia's Muslim majority vis-à-vis religious minorities (Burhani 2005). Reflecting their doctrinal shift, for the first time in decades the top leaders of Muhammadiyah and NU were represented on the conservative Muslim coordination body MUI (*Majelis Ulama Indonesia*, Indonesian Council of Muslim Scholars): Sahal Mahfudz as chairman and Din Syamsuddin as his deputy. Previously, both Wahid and Amien Rais had avoided (and even attacked) the council whenever they could (Olle 2006, p. 8).

The declining tensions between NU and Muhammadiyah led to an unprecedented level of cooperation between them. According to Din, his relationship with Hasyim was "much better than that between previous chairmen of both organizations".[18] A member of the NU central board confirmed that

> Din and Hasyim go along very well. They are both graduates from the modern *pesantren* Gontor in East Java, so there is a bond there. They often meet. And really, many of the things that separated NU and Muhammadiyah only a few years ago are becoming less and less relevant.[19]

Din and Hasyim cooperated on anti-corruption initiatives, represented their organizations on international religious forums, and issued joint declarations on pressing socio-political matters.[20] Apparently, with NU no longer tied to Wahid's erratic leadership of PKB, and Muhammadiyah distancing itself from PAN, the relationship between the two Muslim groups had been successfully isolated from the volatility of day-to-day politics. Cases such as the failed cooperation between PKB and PAN in the gubernatorial election in Jakarta in June 2007, in which Wahid withdrew his support for the already agreed PAN-PKB ticket at the last minute and thus triggered the breakdown of the coalition, could no longer harm the overall relationship between NU and Muhammadiyah. Instead, the climate between the two groups was determined by their cooperation on social and religious affairs, with both organizations assuming similarly conservative positions on key doctrinal and contemporary issues. And while substantial differences between them remained, by 2008 they appeared to be far away from the extreme tensions and clashes of the 2001 crisis.

## THE NEW CENTRISM OF MUSLIM PARTIES

The disentanglement of the largest Muslim organizations from the political parties they had created improved their institutional relations, both among their elites and at the grassroots level. In fact, they now shared a common goal: defending their social and religious roles in society against the intrusion by political parties. This meant not only demarcating themselves from those parties that claimed to represent their constituencies, i.e. PKB and PAN, but also countering the efforts by other parties to mobilize traditionalist and modernist Muslim voters through religious programmes in their communities. In particular, Muhammadiyah was annoyed at the "aggressive and penetrative"[21] attempts of the puritanical Muslim party PKS (*Partai Keadilan Sejahtera*, Prosperous Justice Party) to establish itself as a *dakwah* organization, apparently aiming to take over Muhammadiyah's and NU's proselytizing activities in both urban and rural areas. In a letter signed by Din Syamsuddin and circulated to all branches in December 2006, the Muhammadiyah chairman reminded his members that all political parties, "including those that claim to carry out or have established wings to carry out *dakwah* activities like the PKS, are really political parties".[22] As such, Din continued, they were vehicles for political power, from which Muhammadiyah needed to stay clear. In many ways, the disengagement of NU and Muhammadiyah from party politics had restored their role as civil society organizations, including their distrust of interference by the state and other vested interests.

The significant reduction in tensions between the two largest Muslim groups reflected a similar trend in Islamic party politics. However, the process of political and ideological rapprochement among Muslim parties took the opposite direction to that taken by NU and Muhammadiyah. While the two socio-religious organizations disengaged from party politics by concentrating on their Islamic core values, the Muslim parties moved increasingly to the political centre. Trying to present a more pluralistic and inclusive image, most Islamic parties disposed of overly dogmatic elements of their ideology. In a major strategic shift, they now sought to gain votes in the moderate and largely secular political mainstream, which remained suspicious of mixing Islamic dogma and state affairs. The following sections analyse how individual Islamic parties have gradually adopted more moderate positions on the role of Islam in politics, and how this has helped to defuse tensions in the party system. Most significantly, Indonesia's Muslim parties in the current polity endorse democracy as the only viable form of state organization, unlike their counterparts in the 1950s, which had called for an

Islamic state and the introduction of *syariat* in place of the existing political system (Nasution 1992). In consequence, the stabilization of the rules and procedures of democratic competition after 2004 was complemented by a considerable trend toward moderation among the parties that participated in it, strengthening the civilian polity even further.

## PAN and PKB: The Catch-All Parties

The parties sponsored by NU and Muhammadiyah had been founded with pluralistic platforms in 1998, appealing to both devout *santri* and more secularly oriented Muslims. After their "mother" organizations began to distance themselves from "their" parties after 2004, however, PAN and PKB moved even further to the centre. Amien Rais retired from the PAN chairmanship in 2005, and while his replacement Sutrisno Bachir had a Muhammadiyah background, he was more of a political entrepreneur than an ideologically motivated leader. Consequently, Bachir opened up PAN to all constituencies, believing that its narrow concentration on Muhammadiyah-affiliated voters had damaged the party.[23] His rather simplistic calculation was that if PAN previously could obtain fifty seats in the DPR with Muhammadiyah support, it could easily get one hundred if it broadened its appeal. Much to the surprise of senior party functionaries, Bachir made the recruitment of national film and music celebrities into PAN a major element of his strategy, proudly proclaiming in June 2007 that his party was now widely called "Partai Artis Nasional" (Party of National Celebrities).[24] In addition, Bachir often emphasized the need to establish PAN as a party of and for entrepreneurs, encouraging businesspeople to enter party politics as a way of fixing the national economy.

The centripetal orientation of PAN under Bachir's leadership was so strong that some of its key officials began to caution him not to severe all ties with the party's original constituency. The trigger for this warning was the founding of a new party by Muhammadiyah activists in December 2006. Named *Partai Matahari Bangsa* (PMB, Party of the National Sun), the party was led by former PAN figures disappointed with its new course. While Bachir initially insisted that PBM posed no threat to PAN, the continuously bad poll results of the latter forced him to change that perception. Suddenly concerned that his centrist strategy might drive Muhammadiyah elements away from PAN, Bachir in early 2007 tried to improve his relationship with Din Syamsuddin. Bachir asked Din to re-engage with the party, but Din had invested too much into Muhammadiyah's withdrawal from party politics to reverse his stance.[25] Although Din agreed to appear at a PAN event in Palembang in June 2007, he made it clear there that the days of Muhammadiyah's institutional support for PAN were over.[26] Accordingly, despite heated discussions within the party about its course and ideological orientation, at this point there appear to be few alternatives to Bachir's plan to turn PAN into a classic catch-all party.

In the traditionalist Muslim community, PKB went through a similar process of opening and moderation. In 1998, Wahid had determined the pluralist orientation of the party against objections from several senior *kiai*, who insisted that PKB primarily serve as NU's political wing. However, in 2005 and 2006 a large number of these revered Islamic leaders left PKB in protest against Wahid's erratic and belligerent leadership style.[27] With the most influential *kiai* outside the party, Wahid was free to define its agenda at will and move PKB further to the centre. Not only did he ensure that all three top positions in PKB were in the hands of his family, but he also took concrete steps to prove that the party was indeed pursuing a pluralist agenda. Under Wahid's direction, non-Muslims were elected as chairmen of the PKB branches in North Sulawesi and Nusa Tenggara Timur, and the non-NU women's activist Nursyahbani Katjasungkana was put in charge of PKB's Jakarta branch (before being fired by Wahid for alleged disloyalty in August 2007). But like Bachir in PAN, Wahid could not completely severe his ties with NU. In order to compensate for the departure of the most senior *kiai*, Wahid began to mobilize thousands of village-based junior *kiai* (*kiai kampung*) to work for PKB (Asfar 2007). By this, he intended to consolidate PKB's core constituency while at the same time opening the party for non-Muslim groups and other segments in the political mainstream.

## The Modernist Parties: Abandoning the Jakarta Charter

While PAN and PKB had begun their gradual shift to the political centre from fairly pluralistic platforms adopted in 1998, other Muslim-based parties commenced their journeys to moderation and openness from explicitly Islamic party programmes. PPP, for example, had pledged in 1998 to free itself from all secular restrictions imposed on it by the New Order and return to its true Islamic identity. Accordingly, at its first post-Suharto congress in December 1998, PPP restored the *Ka'abah* as its party symbol and changed its basic ideological guideline from Pancasila to Islam.[28] Since then, however, the party found it difficult to maintain this ideological rigidity in the day-to-day politics of negotiations and compromise. In 2001, after having argued for years that Islam barred women from becoming president, PPP Chairman Hamzah Haz accepted the post of vice-president under Megawati Sukarnoputri — who previously had also been criticized by PPP leaders for her secular attitude and her occasional partaking in prayers at Hindu temples.[29] Apparently, the drive for opportunities to participate in government was stronger than ideological concerns, forcing the party to alter some of its core dogmatic positions. Most importantly, in 2002 PPP dropped its demand for the inclusion of the Jakarta Charter into the amended constitution. Having realized that most other parties were opposed to it, PPP decided not to pursue the issue any further.

The new centrism of PPP was codified in the party statutes at its congress in 2007. There, the party affirmed its commitment to *ummatan wasathan*, a stance that "avoids the political left as well as the right" (Partai Persatuan Pembangunan 2007, p. 22). This message was designed to convince those voters who still associated PPP with the "extreme right" — Suharto's euphemism for Islamist militancy that the New Order had frequently (and successfully) thrown at PPP. In order to erase that stigma among ordinary Indonesians, the freshly elected party chairman Suryadama Ali, a moderate NU politician, described the new inclusivism of PPP in somewhat populist terms:

> Generally, we open up the understanding of Islam. Basically, if he or she is of Muslim faith, we integrate him or her — including Muslim youths who wear mini skirts or torn jeans, and men with earrings or coloured hair.[30]

This was a significant departure from PPP's previous image as the party of and for the devout *santri*. While still defining itself as an Islamic party, it now appealed to the full spectrum of Indonesia's Muslim population. This included ideologically liberal Muslims, who in the past had supported parties such as Golkar and PDI-P because they feared possible restrictions on their secular lifestyles if an Islamic party came to power.

Another Islamic party that moved increasingly to the political centre was Partai Bulan Bintang (PBB). Founded in 1998 as the successor party to Masyumi, it initially claimed to represent devout modernist *santri* and pledged to fight for a greater role of Islam in political affairs. Like PPP, however, it had to quickly compromise its ideological position in order to participate in government. In 2001, then party chairman Yusril Ihza Mahendra accepted an appointment to the cabinet of Megawati, the very woman that PBB had fiercely campaigned against in 1999. In addition, PBB gave up its fight for the restitution of the Jakarta Charter in the face of overwhelming opposition from other parties,[31] and in 2004, it formed a coalition with the staunchly secular-nationalist PKPI (*Partai Keadilan dan Persatuan Indonesia*, Party of Indonesian Justice and Unity) in order to nominate Susilo Bambang Yudhoyono as president. Opposing Muslim leaders Amien Rais and Hamzah Haz in the presidential polls, the party helped Yudhoyono to gain political credibility in Islamic circles. After Yudhoyono's victory, PBB was rewarded with two cabinet seats — a disproportionate share, given that it had only obtained around 2 per cent of the votes in the 1999 and 2004 elections. When Yudhoyono dismissed Yusril from the cabinet in 2007 over a corruption scandal, PBB briefly considered withdrawing from cabinet and sharpening its Islamic profile in opposition. But PBB's determination to maintain its access to state resources once again overrode ideological considerations: the party remained in government and continued its course of political moderation.[32]

Even PKS, the most puritanical and ideologically consistent of the Indonesian Muslim parties, saw the need to give itself a more moderate image. Founded by Islamic elements of the 1998 student movement and urban *dakwah* groups, the party and its cadres had quickly built up a reputation for honesty, strict adherence to Muslim ethics, and fierce opposition to corrupt practices in elite politics. However, many party strategists wanted PKS to be more than merely a small constituency-based party for urban *santri* at the modernist fringes of the Islamic spectrum; instead, they envisaged PKS's growth into one of the dominant forces in Indonesian politics, with a long-term perspective of gaining the presidency and the majority of seats in parliament. In order to achieve this goal, the party had to attract the many voters who were suspicious of its dogmatic agenda and would only support PKS if it pledged not to turn Indonesia into an Islamic state. Thus after its remarkable performance in the 2004 elections, in which it had quintupled its 1999 result, PKS started to take aim at even greater gains by presenting itself as an inclusive, flexible, and modern party. In the direct local elections that began in June 2005, and which will be discussed in some detail in the next section, PKS entered into coalitions with parties from highly diverse ideological origins, including Christian parties. In addition, it nominated non-party bureaucrats for governorships and other key posts in local government, partly in order to receive substantial payments from them in exchange for the nomination, but also to show that PKS "now wants to capture the middle ground".[33]

In their efforts to portray PKS as moderate, senior functionaries even denied that PKS was an Islamic party. Former PKS president and chairman of the MPR, Hidayat Nurwahid, for example, insisted that "PPP and PBB are Islamic parties, unlike us — we have always been in the centre."[34] Hidayat maintained that contrary to PPP and PBB, his party had not supported the reintroduction of the Jakarta Charter in 2002. Instead, it had proposed a compromise based on the Madinah Charter, which guaranteed religious freedom and equality before the law for everyone, regardless of their faith. In contrast to PPP and PBB, Hidayat's party had not withdrawn its proposal when it became clear that it would not find a majority — PKS allowed it to be voted down. Despite these signs of moderation, however, many observers and politicians from other parties remain convinced that PKS's centrist course is little more than a tactic to achieve political power. They point to opinion polls among PKS cadres that highlight the persistence of scriptualist interpretations of Islamic teachings within the party, ranging from negative perceptions of non-Muslims to the belief that women should not become president (Mujani 2005). However, it is significant to note that despite these "darker sides" of the PKS (Bubalo and Fealy 2005, p. v), the party accepts the fact that in order to expand its support base, it needs to moderate its image — which in itself is an acknowledgement of Indonesia's extreme religious and social heterogeneity. As one PKS parliamentarian explained, "maybe it's best to put it this way: our ideology is only important for our internal coherence as a party; but when it comes to coalition-building and governance, the practical needs of Indonesian society gain priority."[35]

The centripetal shift of most Muslim parties in recent years has defused many of the ideological tensions that had emerged in the early phase of the post-Suharto transition. While the level of inter-party rivalry remains high, this competition no longer affects fundamental questions of state organization. The issue of establishing an Islamic state or introducing Islamic law in Indonesia was buried in 2002 during the last round of constitutional amendments, and no Muslim party has seriously raised it again ever since.[36] In those negotiations in 2002, many Muslim politicians had become aware that upholding exclusive Islamic doctrines at all cost was not a suitable strategy in a political system as diverse as Indonesia's. Initially, there had been unrealistic hopes in Muslim circles that the fall of the authoritarian regime would result in a resurgence of Islamic ideology in Indonesian politics (Fealy 2004). However, in the first few years of the democratic system, it became clear that it was not only the Suharto government that had imposed restrictions on political Islam; it now emerged that even under democratic rule, the political scope of Islamic politicians and their ideology was limited by the pluralism of views in Indonesia's party system and civil society. Thus the only way to make the voice of Islam heard was by engaging in compromise-oriented negotiations with all parties and groups, including those opposed to the politicization of the Islamic faith. After most Muslim parties came to recognize this reality, the way was free for their gradual shift to the political centre and, at the same time, unprecedented cooperation between political parties across the ideological spectrum.

## "CIVILIANIZING" POLITICS: LOCAL ELECTIONS AFTER 2005

The unwillingness of political parties to cooperate with one another had been a major factor in the re-election of retired military officers to key governorships all over Indonesia in 2002 and 2003. More determined to deny their competitors access to important government posts than to capture those positions for themselves, many parties had turned to former generals as compromise candidates who could bridge the deep divisions within the civilian party system. The indirect electoral mechanism through local legislators had offered parties and retired officers the opportunity to make backroom deals without having to test the candidate's popularity at the ballot box. From June 2005 onwards, however, governors, *bupatis*, and mayors had to be popularly elected in a direct vote. Following the example of the direct presidential polls in 2004, nominees for top local government positions now needed to convince the electorate rather than bribe legislators to succeed. While parties still reserved the right to nominate candidates, and almost invariably demanded hefty fees from them in return, the reformed electoral system completely changed the dynamics of gaining executive office. This included new patterns of alliance-building among political parties, and a significant decline in the importance of retired generals as alternative nominees.

## More Inter-Party Cooperation, Fewer Military Candidates

The centripetal strategies of most Muslim parties, which coincided with similar trends among their secular-nationalist counterparts, opened up vast opportunities for inter-party cooperation in the direct local elections. Consequently, parties showed a high degree of ideological and political flexibility when entering into coalitions to nominate joint candidates. In fact, the majority of alliances were built between parties of opposing ideological platforms, while exclusive coalitions between Islamic parties were rare. Data collected by an election-monitoring network revealed that 37 per cent of all coalitions featured Islamic and nationalist parties. On the other hand, only 2.4 per cent were forged exclusively between Muslim parties.[37] Evidently, this highly pragmatic coalition-building stood in sharp contrast to the deadlocks in inter-party collaboration that had marred the 2002 and 2003 elections. As a result of this increased flexibility in the party system, retired generals were less likely to succeed with their attempts to offer themselves as mediators and alternative candidates. After 2005, civilian nominees clearly dominated the elections, both at the provincial and district level, sidelining the retired generals who had dominated the scene in 2002 and 2003. Most importantly, these new electoral tendencies also occurred in the politically and economically crucial provinces on Java as well as North Sumatra, South Sulawesi, and East Kalimantan.

The other reason for the increasing marginalization of military officers from electoral politics at the local level related to the selection criteria used by political parties to appoint their nominees. First of all, parties were keen to find candidates who had enough cash to not only finance their own campaigns, but also to give contributions to the party board in exchange for the nomination (Choi 2005; Mietzner 2005). The 2004 national elections, with three costly polls in five months, had left many parties cashed-strapped, making payments from nominees more important than in the 2002–03 period. This emphasis on monetary resources disadvantaged retired generals, because despite their considerable wealth, they were not as rich as many of their civilian opponents. Entrenched bureaucrats and well-connected businesspeople often controlled huge financial networks, dwarfing the assets owned by military retirees, with only very few exceptions. The second selection criteria considered by parties was popularity among the electorate. Particularly after the first wave of local elections in 2005, parties began to conduct pre-election opinion polling to determine their nominees (Mietzner 2006). Golkar, for example, made it mandatory for all its branches to take opinion surveys into account before appointing their candidates for local elections.[38] In those polls, civilian figures with a long attachment to their area often did significantly better than military officers who may have been born in the province or district concerned, but had not lived there for decades because of the frequent shifts required by their military careers.

The new trends in local elections were reflected in the statistics on the socio-political and economic backgrounds of the candidates. Based on a sample of fifty local elections in 2005, career bureaucrats made up 36 per cent of all nominees, followed by 28 per cent entrepreneurs, and 22 per cent party politicians (Mietzner 2005). A mere 8 per cent of the candidates were active or retired officers from the armed forces and the police, forming the second-smallest group of nominees. Only the civil society leaders, media figures, and grassroots activists sent even less nominees into the race, constituting 6 per cent of the total. While these numbers primarily pointed to the weakness of the political parties and the dominance of affluent bureaucrats and businesspeople, they also exposed the shifting balance between civilian and military power brokers in the regions. In the early days of the New Order, 80 per cent of all local government heads had been military officers. That figure dropped to 40 per cent in the late 1980s, and now was below 10 per cent less than a decade after Suharto's fall. Clearly, the new electoral dynamics were undermining the grip of the armed forces (or to be more precise, that of retired military officers) on key government posts at the local level.

While the number of candidates with military backgrounds was low, their performance in the elections was even less impressive. In May 2005, there had been a heated public debate over six active military officers that TNI headquarters had allowed to participate in district head elections in Sumatra, Java, Kalimantan, Papua, and Nusa Tenggara Barat. Some observers had claimed that this move signalled TNI's intentions to force its way back into the political arena, betraying its own reform agenda.[39] However, the results of the elections indicated that these concerns were exaggerated. None of the six candidates approved by TNI won the contest in his electoral area, and retired officers did only slightly better. Even in conflict-prone districts, where voters tended to prioritize security issues over other political considerations, the electorate often favoured retired police officers over their military counterparts.[40] In Poso, for example, retired police officer Piet Inkiriwang won the district election in June 2005 after making security and stability the central topics of his campaign. In August 2006, TNI finally reacted to the poor performances of active TNI officers and the controversy over their candidacies. Based on a decree signed by new TNI Chief Djoko Suyanto, active officers were no longer allowed to stand in local elections. If they were still interested in running, they had to hand in their resignations.[41]

## The Jakarta Elections: Residual Military Influence

Despite the strengthening of the civilian elements in local politics, some of the old patterns of inter-party tensions and their exploitation by retired military officers survived the introduction of the new electoral system in 2005. This was less visible at the district level, where typically lower-ranked retired officers entered the race and found themselves outplayed by influential and resourceful civilian power brokers. At the provincial level, however, some former top generals believed the stakes were high enough for them to get involved. In Jakarta, for instance, almost a dozen ex-generals applied to political parties to be nominated for the gubernatorial elections in 2007. At the end, however, only former police general Adang Daradjatun and Vice-Governor Fauzi Bowo, a civilian bureaucrat, obtained nominations. Adang teamed up with a PKS functionary as his running mate, while Fauzi decided to select a retired military officer as his candidate for deputy governor. There were six or seven candidates for the job, however, each supported by different parties in Fauzi's coalition.[42] Irritated by the large number of former generals who wanted to run with him, Fauzi asked Army Chief of Staff Djoko Santoso for permission to nominate an active military leader, hoping that this would end the dispute. Ultimately, the army's Assistant for Territorial Affairs Prijanto, an active major-general, was chosen as Fauzi's running mate. But while Prijanto immediately retired from active service, many observers questioned the deep involvement of the army in his selection.

The emergence of a military general as a key player in the Jakarta ballot was closely related to the electoral politics among Muslim parties at the local level. PKS was the strongest party in Jakarta and could nominate a gubernatorial candidate on its own, without having to recruit coalition partners. This strength of PKS had a polarizing effect on the party system in Jakarta and discouraged other parties, even those ideologically close to PKS, from joining its campaign. Suspecting that PKS intended to monopolize the Jakarta administration for its purposes if its candidate was elected, a total of nineteen parties came together in the "Coalition for Jakarta" and threw their support behind Fauzi Bowo.[43] In order to counterbalance Adang's reputation as a capable security manager, the coalition (and Fauzi) decided that his deputy needed to be a retired military officer. As explained above, the parties failed to agree on a name, leading to lengthy debates and, eventually, Prijanto's nomination. The example of Jakarta showed that while the post-2005 local elections were marked by a high degree of flexibility in coalition-building which typically benefited civilian candidates, in some cases nominees with military backgrounds still found entry points arising from intra-civilian fragmentation.

In spite of such residual pockets of military influence, the increasing willingness of parties to cooperate with one another has significantly reduced the political space for the armed forces and their retired personnel. Even Jakarta, with all its ideological divisions and highly dynamic political manoeuvrings, witnessed the election of its first non-military governor since the communist-leaning artist Henk Ngantung was replaced in 1965. The political trends in other provinces are similar. The increasingly centrist leanings of Muslim parties have contributed to this process, with new options for civilian alliances undercutting the opportunities of retired generals to present themselves as compromise candidates in electoral contests. Civilians now control the vast majority of local governments in Indonesia, and while many observers have lamented their poor quality and lack of responsiveness, the gradual marginalization of active and retired military officers from local politics constitutes a remarkable achievement in itself — and one which few commentators would have predicted in 2002 and 2003, when a large number of New Order-affiliated ex-generals had successfully defended their grip on the most lucrative governorships in the country.

## ISLAMIC MILITANCY UNDER YUDHOYONO

The rise of Islamic militancy and terrorism during the transition between 1998 and 2004 had provided the military with welcome arguments for its claim that it needed to maintain a role in domestic security. The terrorist bombings in Bali in 2002, at the Marriott Hotel in Jakarta in 2003, and at the Australian embassy in 2004 had invariably been followed by TNI requests to get involved in counter-terrorism, which the government had largely entrusted to the police. Indeed, each time an attack occurred, the government indicated that it was prepared to grant the military a greater role in fighting jihadist militants. In terms of concrete concessions such as additional authority or resources, however, the armed forces gained very little. The police remained in charge of capturing, interrogating, and processing terrorist suspects (with significant assistance from the Australian Federal Police), and BIN continued to be the major centre for intelligence collection and analysis. Thus unlike in the 1950s and early 1960s, when the *Darul Islam* movement had provoked massive military interventions, the Islamist militants of the post-Suharto era never managed to launch a full-blown insurgency that would have compelled the government to bestow emergency powers on the armed forces. Instead, *Jemaah Islamiyah* (JI), the main terrorist group with an Islamist agenda, carried out its operations through a network of small, but effective cells spread across the archipelago, requiring the deployment of trained investigators and high-technology surveillance equipment rather than the use of military force (International Crisis Group 2007b, p. 15).[44]

This pattern of JI's terrorist activities (regular high-profile attacks but very limited impact on national security as a whole) initially seemed to experience little change after Yudhoyono took power in 2004. In October 2005, Bali was hit by a second bomb blast, killing twenty people and bringing the island's slow economic recovery to an abrupt end. In the same vein, terrorism remained a significant problem for the local population in Poso, where militants tried to reignite communal clashes between Christians and Muslims that had largely subsided after 2002. In May 2005, twenty-three people were killed when a bomb exploded at a market place mostly frequented by Christians, and in October terrorists beheaded three Christian schoolgirls in an attempt to provoke the Christian community of Poso into another round of religious violence. Thus it appeared as if the general stabilization of political affairs under Yudhoyono's government had not led to a decline in Islamist terrorist attacks, despite occasional arrests and the circumstance that JI's actions had inspired very little sympathy among the public for its political agenda. In fact, 2005 turned out to be the year with the highest number of terrorist victims since 2002, and there were few indications that the following years would see considerable improvements.

However, the second Bali bombings and the beheadings in Poso, both in October 2005, marked a turning point in the fortunes of Islamist terrorism in Indonesia. Both actions failed to achieve their goals and instead triggered major police operations against key JI figures. In Poso, the beheadings did not lead to fresh fighting between the two religious camps; rather, they helped to delegitimize JI, even in the eyes of Muslim hardliners.[45] The public outrage over these crimes also convinced the police that it had to do more to destroy JI's network in Poso and put an end to the constant attacks. Finally, the police's anti-terror unit Detachment 88 stormed a hide-out of terrorists in Poso in January 2007, killing several of them and arresting others. After the arrests, the number of terrorist incidents in Poso dropped sharply, allowing the area to return to some degree of normalcy. In Bali, the suicide bombings killed "only" five foreigners, much less than planned and way below what the 2002 attack had achieved. Moreover, many of the Indonesian victims were Muslims, leading to heated debates even within JI about the purpose of such acts. Like the Poso beheadings, the Bali bombings motivated the police to intensify their search for the organizers behind the carnage. Only one month later, in November 2005, police besieged a house in a mountain village in East Java where Azahari Husin, the chief bomb-maker of JI, had been in hiding. In the ensuing shoot-out with police, Azahari was killed. Several of his assistants were apprehended later, and in June 2007, police managed to capture JI's military chief Abu Dujana, then Indonesia's most-wanted terrorist. In addition, the nominal head of JI, Zarkasih, was also arrested. In consequence, JI's capacity to launch further attacks had been seriously diminished.

Even before the arrests of its key leaders, there had been widespread reports about JI's fragmentation into a number of splinter groups. Rejecting JI's tactics and its organizational structure, several leading Islamist terrorists operated independent cells without formally reporting to the JI leadership. Noordin Mohammed Top, for example, who had been Azahari's closest associate, was widely believed to have run his own operations, which focused on killing as many non-Muslim citizens of Western countries as possible

(International Crisis Group 2007*b*). Opposing this approach, Zarkasih, who had taken up the JI leadership in 2005, argued that it was much more important for the organization to focus on the domestic enemies of Islam in Indonesia, intensify JI's proselytizing activities, and recruit new cadres.[46] The serial arrests in 2007 interrupted these internal debates within JI, and highlighted the dramatically improved counter-terrorism capacity of the Indonesian state after 2005. In Poso, for instance, the police had known the identities and whereabouts of the main suspects for quite some time, but had been reluctant to act because the local Muslim community protected them. In 2007, however, the government managed to convince important Muslim leaders in Poso and at the national level to revise their stance and throw their support behind the police, isolating the militants from the Islamic mainstream and paving the way for their arrests.

The military was largely a bystander in these developments, much to its dismay. TNI was particularly disappointed because it had been promised a greater role in counter-terrorism at several occasions, including by President Yudhoyono. Shortly after the second Bali bombings in October 2005, Yudhoyono delivered a speech at TNI's anniversary celebrations in which he called on the armed forces to get involved in counter-terrorism activities.[47] Then TNI Chief Endriartono Sutarto immediately followed up on this order by instructing his territorial commands to set up counter-terrorism intelligence bureaus at all levels. These offices were established in a relatively short period of time, and they began collecting intelligence in their various areas. But the resources for this programme were shifted from already existing military budgets, and its personnel was recruited from other organizational units rather than newly hired. In addition, TNI received no new institutional authority to carry out counter-terrorism functions — it was given neither power of arrest nor the right to interrogate suspects. It was also not clear how the police and BIN used the data collected by TNI in their pursuit of JI terrorists. In short, the counter-terrorism role of the armed forces remained largely nominal, denying them the opportunity to request additional resources and reclaim some of their former rights in domestic security.

The significant weakening of the jihadist terror groups coincided with a further fragmentation of the "anti-vice" militias, which had radical, but much less violent Islamist platforms. As explained in Chapter 6, FPI had never fully recovered from its temporary disbandment in 2002, and its influence continued to decline after 2004. In Jakarta, where it had concentrated most of its forces, FPI gradually lost ground to other militias that put more emphasis on local ethnic sentiments and commercial interests than religious convictions.

The FBR (*Forum Betawi Rempug*, Betawi Brotherhood Forum) rose to become the dominant militia in the capital, offering its thugs to businesspeople and politicians for protection in exchange for regular payments (Wilson 2005*a* and 2005*b*). The militia could be hired to intervene in land disputes, control parking lots, and organize demonstrations for or against a certain issue, group, or individual. The Islamist militias, by contrast, were much less centrally controlled than at the height of FPI's power in 2000 and 2001. Local groups often sprung up spontaneously and concentrated on a specific topic, such as the closure of a neighbourhood church or entertainment venue. In addition, the resolution of the communal conflicts in Maluku, North Maluku, and Central Sulawesi gave radical Muslim groups little justification to send their fighters to battlegrounds across the archipelago. Laskar Jihad (LJ), which was disbanded in 2002, has so far not been replaced by any organization of similar size or political significance (Hasan 2006).

The arrests of important JI leaders and the declining influence of the large Islamist militias both reflected and reinforced the stabilization of general security conditions under the Yudhoyono government. As Noorhaidi Hassan (2006, p. 221) noted in his study of LJ, the group could only blossom because of the "state's inability to carry out its primary role as the guardian of social order and the enforcer of the law". Consequently, LJ's demise in 2002 pointed to the increasing stability of the state and its institutions as the democratic transition came to an end.

This stabilization, in turn, has offered the armed forces much fewer chances to use the issues of terrorism and Islamic militancy to their advantage. At the peak of the terrorist attacks between 2002 and 2005, TNI had frequently asked for increased powers to address the threat, and although the government did not meet these demands with concrete concessions, the topic of terrorism as such had served as an excuse to leave the territorial command structure in place. However, after the series of arrests in 2007, carried out by special units of the police, the military found it difficult to argue that it was absolutely essential to expand its role in counter-terrorism. In the same vein, there had been widespread reports of cooperation between Laskar Jihad and disgruntled officers in the armed forces in 2000 and 2001, aiming to destabilize the Wahid government. By contrast, such opportunities for rogue military elements no longer presented themselves after 2002 and 2003, when the intensity of communal conflicts began to decline. This does not mean, however, that jihadist groups and Islamist militias no longer pose a security threat. JI has proven in the past that it can adjust quickly after arrests of key personnel, and the "decentralization" of Islamist militias after the decline of FPI has led to the emergence of hundreds of smaller groups that the government may find difficult to control. But the times of simultaneous security disturbances by FPI, LJ, and JI, as witnessed at the height of the tumultuous transition, appear to be largely over.

## Muslim Groups and the Stabilization of the Civilian Polity

The ideological and political fragmentation within the Muslim community has for long been one of the most serious challenges for the establishment of a modern democratic state in Indonesia. In the 1950s, the conflict between the Islamic and the secular-nationalist camp on the one hand, and the split between traditionalist and modernist Muslims on the other, contributed significantly to the decline of parliamentary democracy. Subsequent authoritarian regimes managed to play the various Muslim groups off against one another, and even the restoration of democratic rule in 1998 initially saw the continuation of old disputes and tensions. The fall of President Wahid in 2001 was accompanied by grassroots conflicts between traditionalist and modernist groups, leading to several years of cold relations between the two constituencies. But changes in the leadership of both groups, and the institutional clarification of the rules and norms of democratic competition after 2004, have helped to improve intra-Muslim relations. In addition, Muslim political parties have perceptibly moved to the centre, increasing their flexibility in building coalitions among themselves and with secular-nationalist counterparts.

The declining tensions within the Muslim community have had considerable implications for Indonesia's civil-military relations. While the armed forces in the early period of the post-authoritarian transition benefited from serious divisions between civilian groups, this was not the case after 2004. By then, many of the ideological disputes of the early transition had subsided, and most civilian groups, both Muslim and secular, accepted the existing democratic polity as the only game in town. Consequently, the armed forces and their retired personnel found it difficult to use political disputes to their advantage. The concurrent developments of improving intra-civilian relations and declining political intervention opportunities for the Indonesian armed forces highlighted the continued relevance of the theoretical propositions introduced by Samuel Finer. Finer had pointed to the close relationship between the quality of civilian governance and the level of military engagement in political affairs. Post-Suharto Indonesia has been an example of this interrelationship in many ways: first, the tumultuous transition between 1998 and 2004, with high levels of intra-civilian conflict and institutional uncertainty, saw frequent interventions of the military in politics — both as an institution and through its officers. By contrast, military politicking was much less significant in the post-2004 period, which enjoyed improved relations between civilian groups and, corresponding to that, much greater institutional stability.

Despite these positive trends after 2004, it is important to note that none of them are irreversible. Indonesia's civilian politics remain vulnerable to external shocks, changes in the leadership of key groups, and suddenly escalating conflicts of interest. For example, the election of a senior NU or Muhammadiyah figure as president or vice-president could reignite the tensions between traditionalist and modernist Muslims. Both constituencies would almost certainly rally around their representative in times of political crisis, and view his or her critics as potential enemies. This could end the currently well-functioning cooperation between NU and Muhammadiyah, which has been possible since 2004 precisely because none of their leaders was in a leading position of government. By the same token, renewed serious conflicts between state institutions are not inconceivable. A popularly elected president without backing in parliament could potentially run into the same problems that Wahid faced in 2001, despite the tightened impeachment regulations. The fight between Yudhoyono and the DPR in June 2007 over the Iran dispute, while far from threatening the stability of the political process, gave an indication that such constitutional controversies are still a possibility. In addition, parties can quickly change their ideological and political orientation if they are excluded from or included in cabinet, or if their leadership suddenly changes. Accordingly, however supportive the political trends after 2004 may have been for the stabilization of the civilian polity, there are no guarantees that some of the old divisions in Indonesian society will not erupt again.

## Notes

[1]  The negotiations over the direct presidential elections had been the longest and most protracted in the process of amending the constitution. Golkar had been the leading proponent of the change, while PDI-P seemed determined to prevent it. During the 2001 amendments, PDI-P had agreed in principle to direct elections, but insisted that the MPR should choose between the two strongest contenders if no candidate reached more than 50 per cent in the popular vote. It was only in the last round of constitutional amendments in 2002 that PDI-P finally gave in and agreed to a direct election without the involvement of the MPR.

[2]  Under the new constitutional rules, a president can no longer be dismissed simply because he or she has lost majority support in the DPR. Instead, he or

she must have been found to be in violation of the constitution or other laws — a judgment no longer left to the DPR but to the Constitutional Court. Only if the Constitutional Court states that such violations have indeed occurred, can the DPR call for a special session of the MPR to impeach the president. In that session, which has to be attended by three-quarters of all MPR members, a two-third majority is necessary to dismiss the president.

3 Similar to the new constitutional rules on impeaching the president, the 2004 law on local governments made it impossible for regional parliaments to dismiss local government heads simply because they no longer enjoyed a legislative majority. Heads of local administrations had to be in clear violation of existing laws to qualify for impeachment, and the final say over possible dismissals rested with the minister of home affairs as the representative of the president.

4 One of the few cases in which the leadership of a province or district continued to be disputed after 2005 was the mayoral election in Depok, West Java, which was eventually settled by the Constitutional Court in January 2006. See "Sidang Pilkada Depok Perdebatkan Kewenangan MK", *Kompas*, 25 January 2006.

5 In some cases, the court opted to issue ambivalent verdicts that appeared to please both conflicting parties, but eventually failed to resolve the dispute at hand. One such verdict was the court's decision in late 2004 on the legal status of the province of West Irian Jaya. The judges found that its creation had violated existing laws, but they nevertheless endorsed the legal existence of the province because its infrastructure had already been so well developed. Consequently, both sides felt that they had won the case, and the conflict continued.

6 The conflict had emerged after President Yudhoyono refused to appear personally before parliament to explain why Indonesia had voted for a UN Security Council resolution on Iran that threatened the country with sanctions if it did not comply with UN regulations on nuclear enrichment. See "President vs. Lawmakers: Who Will Blink First?", *Jakarta Post*, 26 May 2007.

7 Wiranto and Solahuddin simply claimed that approximately 5.4 million of their votes had not been counted — coincidentally, that was around the number of votes the team needed in order to overtake Megawati and Hasyim and claim the second place in the run-off with Yudhoyono in September 2004. The judges needed only a short time of deliberation to rule that the lawsuit was baseless. See "Putusan MK Tutup Peluang Wiranto", *Kompas*, 13 August 2004.

8 In the elections for the position of *Rais 'Aam*, Wahid did not even receive enough votes to make it beyond the qualification stage. The statutes required candidates to obtain 99 votes in the nomination process to participate in the elections. Wahid, however, only received 75 votes, against Sahal Mahfudz's 363. As only Sahal had achieved sufficient support to qualify for the elections, he was declared the winner by acclamation. See "Gus Dur Gagal Raih Angka Minimal, Duet Sahal-Hasyim Kembali Pimpin NU", *Pikiran Rakyat*, 3 December 2004.

9 Interview with Mustafa Zuhad Mugni, deputy chairman of the NU central board, Jakarta, 12 June 2007.

10 "Muhammadiyah Dukung Amien Rais", *Kompas*, 10 February 2004; "Sikap Muhammadiyah Berdampak Positif pada Perolehan Suara PAN", *Suara Pembaruan*, 12 February 2004.

11 Amien declared that political events had "interrupted" his term as Muhammadiyah chairman in 1998, and that he now felt the "moral obligation" to complete what he had not finished. See "Amien Rais Bersedia Pimpin Muhammadiyah", *Pikiran Rakyat*, 28 April 2005.

12 In his opening speech at the Solo congress, *Rais 'Aam* Sahal Mahfudz demanded that "the modified result of the thirtieth congress in Lirboyo which still pushed NU members into that area [of practical politics] needs to be annulled; in addition, NU officials at all levels should under no circumstances be allowed to engage in practical politics, let alone to take up positions as functionaries of political parties." See "NU Harus 'Disapih' dari Politik Praktis", *Pikiran Rakyat*, 28 November 2004.

13 In its May 2007 meeting, Muhammadiyah decided to "confirm the direction and measures of Muhammadiyah as an Islamic movement which engages in *dakwah* ..., and is not involved in practical politics". It also stated that Muhammadiyah had been infiltrated by "political party activity, which has weakened the commitment to the mission, interest, identity, and principles of Muhammadiyah". See "Pimpinan Pusat Muhammadiyah, Surat Keputusan Pimipinan Pusat Muhammadiyah Nomor: 53/KEP/I.0/B/2007, Tentang Tanfidz Keputusan Tanwir Muhammadiyah Tahun 1428 H/2007 M", Yogyakarta, 17 May 2007.

14 In his speech in Solo, Sahal stressed that "ultimately, the involvement in practical politics is wasting our energy, and even creates conflict among NU members themselves — at the same time, other urgent needs of the Muslim community and society are ignored". See "NU Harus 'Disapih' dari Politik Praktis", *Pikiran Rakyat*, 28 November 2004.

15 Interview with Din Syamsuddin, chairman of Muhammadiyah's central executive board, Jakarta, 27 June 2007.

16 Interview with Din Syamsuddin, chairman of Muhammadiyah's central executive board, Jakarta, 27 June 2007.

17 After 2004, Wahid used his self-founded Wahid Institute to attack NU and Muhammadiyah for their growing conservatism. In a supplement for the news magazine *Gatra* in October 2005, the Wahid Institute accused both organizations of having betrayed the young generation of Muslim liberal thinkers. See "Dua Simpul Satu Nasib: Kisah Generasi Hibrida NU dan Muhammadiyah", *Gatra*, 31 October 2005.

18 Interview with Din Syamsuddin, chairman of Muhammadiyah's central executive board, Jakarta, 27 June 2007.

19  Interview with Mustafa Zuhad Mugni, Jakarta, 12 June 2007. The *pesantren* Gontor in Ponorogo, founded in 1926, integrates elements of modern school curricula into classic religious education. Its *santri* often wear ties and trousers instead of traditional Muslim clothing. Besides Hasyim and Din, Nurcholish Madjid also graduated from this particular boarding school.

20  The cooperation between NU and Muhammadiyah on anti-corruption programmes had already begun under Din's predecessor Syafi'i Maarif in 2003 and 2004, but Din had often represented Syafi'i in the coordination meetings between the two organizations on the subject. See "NU-Muhammadiyah Ajak Negara Aktif Berantas Korupsi", *Suara Pembaruan*, 2 December 2003; "NU dan Muhammadiyah Dorong Kebersamaan", *Kompas*, 4 February 2006.

21  Interview with Din Syamsuddin, chairman of Muhammadiyah's central executive board, Jakarta, 27 June 2007.

22  Pimpinan Pusat Muhammadiyah, "Surat Keputusan Pimpinan Pusat Muhammadiyah Nomor 149/KEP/I.0/B/2006, Tentang: Kebijakan Pimpinan Pusat Muhammadiyah Mengenai Konsolidasi Organisasi dan Amal Usaha Muhammadiyah", Yogyakarta, 1 December 2006.

23  "Gandeng Nahdliyin dan Kaum Marhaen", *Suara Merdeka*, 28 January 2007.

24  "Dari Rakernas II PAN di Kota Empek-Empek Palembang", *Jawa Pos*, 6 June 2007.

25  Interview with Rizal Sukma, chairman of the international relations division, central executive board of Muhammadiyah, Bandung, 24 January 2007.

26  "Muhammadiyah Sees Parties Equally: Din", *Jakarta Post*, 5 June 2007.

27  The so-called *kiai khos* (the "venerable" *kiai*), a select circle of senior Islamic scholars around the Lamongan-based cleric Abdullah Faqih, had in the past been among the strongest supporters of Wahid, and the PKB chief had in turn made sure that their spiritual influence was widely accepted in the NU community. However, when Wahid sacked the PKB General Chairman Alwi Shihab in late 2004 and had his nephew Muhaimin Iskandar elected to that position at a controversial congress in Semarang in 2005, most of the *kiai khos* withdrew their support for Wahid. They supported a rival party leadership under Choirul Anam, and decided in 2006 to establish their own party (PKNU, *Partai Kebangkitan Nasional Ulama*, Party of the Islamic Scholars' National Awakening).

28  The *Ka'abah* is a small shrine in the centre of the Great Mosque in Mecca, and is considered by Muslims the most sacred site on the globe.

29  "PPP Tak Lagi Permasalahkan Piagam Jakarta dan Gender", *Koran Tempo*, 27 July 2001. After his election as vice-president, Hamzah was visited by representatives of the militant Islamist militia Laskar Jihad, who declared that Megawati's presidency constituted a sin committed by all Indonesian Muslims. In response, Hamzah asked the LJ leaders to give up their support for militancy and violence (Hasan 2006, pp. 204–05).

30  "Target 20 Persen, harus Eksis jadi Partai Islam", *Jawa Pos*, 13 May 2007.

[31] PBB's official position was that it "did not participate" in the decision of the MPR to reject the inclusion of the Jakarta Charter in the constitution. However, its faction took part in the MPR session to note its non-participation. Its spokesman said that "we have no intention to withdraw, although we have no power to overcome this wall [of opposition by the other parties, M.M.]; we only wait for the right moment to continue this journey." See "Final Pasal 29 UUD 45 Kembali ke Naskah Asli", *Sriwijaya Post*, 11 August 2002.

[32] "PBB Kecewa, Tapi Tidak Tarik Dukungan", *Kompas*, 7 May 2007.

[33] Interview with Zulkieflimansyah, member of parliament for PKS, Jakarta, 19 September 2006.

[34] Interview with Hidayat Nurwahid, Jakarta, 7 November 2006.

[35] Interview with Nasir Jamil, member of parliament for PKS, Jakarta, 15 September 2006.

[36] There were, of course, occasional statements by Muslim parties after 2002 that reasserted their commitment to the Jakarta Charter. These were largely of a rhetorical nature, however. When the DPD (*Dewan Perwakilan Daerah*, Regional Representative Council) demanded a new round of constitutional amendments in 2007 to gain additional rights, the response by most Muslim parties was unenthusiastic. Had the Islamic parties been serious about the Jakarta Charter, they would have welcomed the DPD's initiative as an opportunity to call for a special session of the MPR and start fresh debates on changes to the constitution and its preamble.

[37] This data was collected by JPPR (*Jaringan Pendidikan Pemilih Untuk Rakyat*, People's Voter Education Network), an association of civil society groups engaged in election monitoring and voter education. I am grateful to Jeremy Gross, programme manager at The Asia Foundation in Jakarta, for sharing the data, which reflects elections held up to June 2007.

[38] Golkar took this step after many of its nominees had failed to get elected in the first wave of local elections in 2005. After evaluating the reasons for these serial defeats, the party concluded that many local Golkar chairpersons had claimed the nomination for themselves without paying attention to their level of popularity with the electorate. In order to address this problem, Golkar's central board increased its authority to determine the candidates for local elections. After 2006, the central board held 40 per cent of the votes in local conventions to select nominees, and it pledged to make its choice based on the mandatory opinion surveys. Interview with Rully Chairul Azwar, deputy secretary-general of Golkar, Jakarta, 18 September 2006.

[39] "Pencalonan TNI Dimotivasi Kemenangan SBY", *Suara Merdeka*, 2 May 2005.

[40] Under the new electoral mechanism, two retired officers gained governorships in 2006: in West Irian Jaya and Central Sulawesi. In both cases, however, the candidates had been governor before, and voters arguably based their choice

more on their performances while in office rather than their affiliation with TNI. In Papua, the neighbouring province of West Irian Java, a recently retired TNI officer finished last.

41   "Maju Pilkada, Prajurit TNI Harus Pensiun Dulu", *Kompas*, 23 November 2006.

42   Each general paid bribes to the political parties that promised to secure the nomination. However, after learning that despite those payments somebody else was nominated, several of the former generals demanded their money back and sent thugs to party offices to collect the debt. See "Ongkos Politik Para Jenderal", *Tempo*, 25 June 2007.

43   Some parties had considered other candidates, but Fauzi's strong standing in the polls and the large payments he offered for nominating him convinced most party leaderships that supporting Fauzi was a safer choice than backing a nominee with fewer resources and a smaller chance of winning.

44   The International Crisis Group estimated in 2007 that JI consisted of around 900 cadres in its various local cells. By contrast, the *Darul Islam* rebellion in West Java had around 13,000 followers in 1957, while the Islamist insurgency in South Sulawesi was supported by between 10,000 to 15,000 rebels (International Crisis Group 2007*b*, p. 1; International Crisis Group 2005, p. 3).

45   One of the most conservative Muslim leaders in Poso, Adnan Arsal, who had links with some of the terrorists, commented that if it was true that Muslims from his circle were responsible for the beheadings, their heads should be taken in return (International Crisis Group 2007*a*, p. 10).

46   I am indebted to Greg Fealy for pointing this out to me.

47   Yudhoyono asked TNI in his speech to "play its part in stopping, preventing, and taking action against terrorism, in an effective way". However, he gave no concrete instructions or hints as to how he wanted this involvement of TNI to be formalized. See "Koter Akan Dihidupkan Lagi?", *Pikiran Rakyat*, 6 October 2005.

# CONCLUSION

## CONTROLLING THE MILITARY
## Conflict and Governance in Indonesia's Consolidating Democracy

> My military friends say that they would bow under civilian supremacy
> only when civilians are of supreme quality.[1]

This book has presented a detailed account of Indonesia's civil-military
relations during and after the downfall of Suharto's New Order regime in
1998. It has portrayed the ups and downs in this relationship, both from the
perspective of internal military developments and the dynamics within civilian
politics. In very broad terms, the discussion has distinguished between two
highly diverse periods in the country's transitional civil-military affairs: first,
the phase between 1998 and 2004, when deep divisions between civilian
groups allowed the armed forces to extend some of their privileges into the
new democratic, but unstable polity. By contrast, the period of democratic
consolidation after 2004 witnessed firmer government control of the military,
facilitated by the stabilization of civilian politics and, more specifically, a
significant decline in the level of conflict between key societal forces. By
2008, the Indonesian military had come a long way from its past as the
regime-stabilizing instrument of Suharto's repressive rule or, subsequently,
the mediator between rival civilian groups in the early transition. Although
they retained some of their social and political privileges, the armed forces
were no longer a "veto player" (Tsebelis 2002) in Indonesia's consolidating

democracy; their power to determine the course of political affairs had diminished considerably.

The following conclusion assesses the role of the armed forces in post-Suharto politics on the basis of the analytical tools and empirical material presented in this book. It will begin with an evaluation of the extent to which the Indonesian armed forces after 1998 intervened in the four classic areas of military interests. The discussion of the military's involvement in political institutions, the economy, the management of its internal affairs, and the socio-cultural sector confirms that the position of the armed forces in the democratic transition was, in Larry Diamond's terms, of a "hybrid" character (Diamond 2002). On the one hand, the military was largely extracted from formal politics and lost its status as the country's most dominant socio-political force. On the other hand, however, the armed forces maintained a relatively privileged position in social and political life, enjoying impunity from legal investigations and continuing their practice of self-financing through TNI's territorial structure. As illuminated in the subsequent sections, the reasons for this mixed assessment of military influence in Indonesia a decade after Suharto's fall are related to, among others, deeply entrenched historical legacies, the nature of the 1998 regime change, and the level of conflict in the civilian polity. Integrating these explanations into the two-generation model of civil-military relations developed by Cottey, Edmunds, and Forster, the chapter concludes by highlighting the lessons learnt from the Indonesian case for the scholarly debate on the role of the armed forces in post-authoritarian transitions.

## Adapting to the Post-Suharto Polity: TNI after 1998

As explained in the introduction to this book, militaries tend to involve themselves in four areas that are of pivotal interest to them: political affairs, the economy, institutional military management, and the socio-cultural sector. The assessment of their involvement in these fields allows for a comparative analysis of their role in politics and society as a whole. To begin with, the Indonesian armed forces after 1998 had to accept a drastic reduction of their participation in formal political institutions. Their representation in the national and local legislatures was reduced in 1999 and ultimately terminated in 2004. In addition, active officers were no longer allowed to hold cabinet posts and other key positions in the bureaucracy. There were, however, residual pockets of formal military engagement in political institutions. The TNI chief, for example, remained an ex-officio member of cabinet, giving him access to and influence on important policy decisions made by the government. Senior officers were also entitled to hold influential positions in the coordinating ministry for political and security affairs and the department of defence, obstructing the urgently needed "civilianization" of political and bureaucratic posts in the defence sector. Thus despite its extraction from parliament and most executive institutions, the military maintained a number of strongholds in the infrastructure of the state.

The military's withdrawal from formal politics was also counterbalanced by the fact that prominent TNI figures often started successful political careers after retirement. Although former officers were no longer subject to the orders of the TNI chief and pursued a variety of political interests and personal ambitions, they were widely viewed as representatives of the military and its core values. Most importantly, retired generals defended key governorships in 2002 and 2003, became leading executives in political parties, and gained a significant number of seats in the national and regional legislatures. Moreover, the victory of Susilo Bambang Yudhoyono in the presidential elections of 2004 opened the door for many of his retired associates to take up posts in the new government. He appointed five ministers with military and police backgrounds, equalling the number of retired generals in the last Suharto cabinet. Ironically, however, it was precisely under Yudhoyono's leadership that the influence of the military began to recede. Probably in order to mitigate concerns that his rule may facilitate the return of the military to politics, Yudhoyono in fact tightened control over the armed forces after years of loose oversight by Megawati. Simultaneously, electoral reforms that took roots under his rule made it more difficult for retired personnel to gain top positions in local government. The direct local elections after June 2005, while still witnessing some involvement by retired generals in important provinces, saw an overall decline in the political influence of military retirees at the local level. The drop in the number of governors, *bupatis*, and mayors with a military background from 80 per cent in the early New Order to below 10 per cent in 2005 pointed to the profound change that has taken place.

The character of military intervention in the economy also underwent substantial change after 1998. The large military conglomerates built up during thirty years of stable growth under the New Order suffered greatly in the economic crisis of 1997 and 1998, leading to a considerable drop in revenues. Academics Lex Rieffel and Jaleswari Pramodhawardani (2007, p. 103) estimated in 2007 that the contribution of military-owned enterprises to Indonesia's defence budget was only between US$8 and 28 million a year, and while their research methodology was highly problematic, there is no doubt that the importance of formal military businesses for the overall financial interests of the armed forces has declined sharply since the end of authoritarian rule. Confirming this finding, audit reports of institutional military businesses after Suharto's fall showed that most of them were technically bankrupt, and that those that still operated with a profit had severe cash-flow problems.[2] However, despite the decline of its large businesses, the military remained determined to defend its extensive web of small business units that contributed to the maintenance of the territorial command structure across the archipelago. When the government began in 2005 to draft an inventory of all military businesses for eventual handover to the state, the armed forces lobbied successfully for the exclusion of cooperatives and foundations from that list. In addition, the TNI leadership also managed to sell off some of the few assets that were still profitable, cashing in the proceeds without reporting them to state authorities.[3]

In addition to the declining significance of the military's business empire, many of the key ethnic Chinese entrepreneurs who under Suharto had paid large sums to the military and its individual leaders now experienced serious financial difficulties and had to suspend or reduce their contributions. Liem Sioe Liong, Eka Tjipta Widyaya, and other important military financiers with ethnic Chinese backgrounds had piled up huge debts during Indonesia's banking crisis in 1997 and 1998, making it impossible for them to set more money aside for the armed forces. In order to escape from their financial and legal obligations in Indonesia, some of the biggest debtors even relocated their core businesses to Hong Kong or Singapore. After their departure from the scene, the post-authoritarian business elite developed a fundamentally different approach to the military. Given the reduction in TNI's political influence and the emergence of alternative power centres in parliament, political parties, and local government, the new class of business leaders that entrenched itself after 1998 did not feel the necessity to cultivate the military in the same way as their predecessors had done. Moreover, the military also faced an increased number of competitors in one of its main commercial areas — the protection business. The police, security forces of political parties, ethnic and religious militias, and criminal gangs became major players in providing "security services" to businesses and entertainment venues, absorbing payments previously reserved for military officers.

The reduced cash flow threatened the ability of the armed forces to maintain their practice of self-financing and thus led officers to intensify their more "informal", and often questionable, fund-raising activities. It is this sector that has seen almost no reform since 1998, with the government undertaking very little to effectively curb these politically dangerous and economically damaging operations. For instance, local officers continued (and even increased) their collusion with bureaucrats in illegal logging and smuggling activities, and soldiers regularly got engaged in trading drugs, backing up prostitution, or protecting gambling dens. There has been no reduction in the frequency with which local newspapers report about the involvement of military officers and soldiers in such crimes, suggesting that the underlying structural problems remain unaddressed. The only regions in which considerable change has occurred are the conflict areas — although "change" in these territories merely described the return to normal levels of illegal activity after a dramatic increase during the course of the conflicts. Throughout the transition between 1998 and 2004, soldiers stationed in conflict areas such as Aceh, Maluku, West and Central Kalimantan, North Maluku, Papua, or Central Sulawesi profited from selling weapons, offering services in the transportation sector, and engaging in commercial hostage-taking. However, the decline in communal violence after 2002 and the resolution of the Aceh conflict in 2005 drastically reduced the number of conflict economies from which soldiers could gain profit. Today, Papua appears to be one of the few areas in which some of these conflict-related practices still persist.

Besides the clearly illegal fund-raising methods by its individual officers, TNI also continued to engage as an institution in income-generating activities that violated existing laws and regulations but were tolerated by the government. For example, senior officers rented out many of the vast military-owned properties to investors who subsequently used the land to build shopping malls and supermarkets. From a legal perspective, these were questionable deals, as TNI's pieces of land were technically considered state assets managed by the military for defence purposes. However, such schemes provided considerable income opportunities for the military and the officers who signed the contracts, making doubts over their legality a matter of secondary concern. Finally, despite regulations that did not allow the military to receive income outside of official state allocations, the armed forces still profited from security payments made by companies that believed only experienced soldiers or mobile police could be entrusted with securing their sites. The U.S.-based gold and copper mining company Freeport McMoRan, for instance, had paid a total of US$66 million to the military and police by the end of 2005, and spent an additional US$8.5 million in 2006.[4] Several other large gas and mining projects all over Indonesia offered similar forms of compensation. In 2006, the police began to gradually assume sole responsibility for security at Freeport, but the military's local territorial unit continued to receive support from the company.

In terms of managing its internal matters, the military experienced highly fluctuating levels of autonomy from the central government. Under Habibie, the military had been able to negotiate a delicately balanced deal by which it supported his presidency in exchange for the right to run its own affairs. During the Wahid years, however, the president frequently interfered in the military's promotion system, trying to fire generals at will and sometimes even "to appoint lieutenant-colonels to two-star positions".[5] Besides many other grievances, it was this regular meddling in the military's internal management that fuelled opposition in the officer corps to Wahid. By contrast, during Megawati's term, the armed forces had almost complete control over their personnel affairs. In fact, TNI was arguably more autonomous under Megawati than in the late phase of the New Order, when many military officers had complained about Suharto's repeated interventions. During Megawati's presidency, the military enjoyed remarkable freedom in running the Aceh military campaign in 2003 and 2004, and had no minister of defence to report to for fourteen months. Making the most out of this vacancy, the chiefs of the various services procured expensive military hardware without the necessary approval of the ministry.[6] At a hearing with legislators, TNI Chief Endriartono Sutarto joked that he was "happy" not to have a minister of defence, and when Juwono took over the department for a second time in October 2004, Endriartono welcomed him with the warning not to "talk about issues related to the armed forces".[7] However, Juwono was not prepared to simply stay out of TNI-related matters, and President Yudhoyono made it clear that the days of lax civilian control over the military during Megawati's rule were over. Thus after 2004, Yudhoyono established the firmest control over the armed forces of all post-Suharto presidents.

In Indonesia's post-New Order polity, the presidency remained the state institution with the greatest powers to limit the military's ambition for internal autonomy. The president's authority to appoint the TNI chief and the chiefs of staff of the services gave him considerable means to enforce loyalty to the government within the officer corps. Accordingly, the quality of civilian democratic control over the military was often a function of the president's determination or ability to exercise that control effectively. Beyond the executive powers of the presidency, however, there were other structural and institutional factors that often proved unsupportive of the attempts to reduce TNI's drive for self-regulation. For example, throughout the transition and the period of democratic consolidation, the military has successfully defended its territorial command structure against occasional attempts to reform it, allowing the armed forces to partly sustain their financial self-sufficiency. In addition, the military was also able to escape more intensive scrutiny by the legislature. Staffed with politicians who lacked technical knowledge of military affairs, the parliamentary commission on defence and security only rarely fulfilled its control function properly. The department of defence, for its part, did not establish meaningful mechanisms of civilian democratic control either. Despite its separation from TNI headquarters in 1999, the department's upper echelons remained largely controlled by active military officers, leading to the popular joke that there were only two civilians in the ministry — the minister and his chauffeur. Consequently, despite Yudhoyono's strongly demonstrated will to impose a tight control regime on the armed forces, the military has been able to maintain residual areas of self-management into which civilians find it difficult to intrude.

In the fourth area of traditional military interactions (i.e. that with society, the cultural sector, and the media), TNI also experienced major changes after 1998. To begin with, the military faced unprecedented scrutiny by the press, with investigative journalists uncovering many of its human rights abuses since 1965. The constant stream of critical reporting by hundreds of new print media, radio stations, and TV channels proved overwhelming for TNI officers used to favourable coverage under Suharto. Furthermore, civil society leaders launched sharp attacks on the armed forces and their unwillingness to support faster and more wide-ranging reforms. With the conventional instruments of intimidation and state-imposed censorship increasingly ineffective, officers had to adapt their public relations strategies to the requirements of an open democratic climate. In this respect, they used several approaches. For instance, they increasingly influenced journalists with financial inducements rather than threats of sanctions. Reporters who previously feared serious consequences if called in by military units were now greeted with envelopes containing money, encouraging them to "improve" the quality of their reporting on TNI. In addition, officers also paid writers to publish articles in influential papers that promoted the viewpoint of the armed forces or individual military leaders. They also began to "groom" academics who were seen as important allies in propagating a positive image of the armed forces. Identifying young researchers with the potential to influence public opinion, generals frequently offered them scholarships for further education or other forms of assistance.[8]

Besides adopting new approaches to the media, the officer corps also increased its cooperation with groups in society that could be called upon to support the armed forces in times of crises. For example, whenever TNI was confronted with public calls for legal investigations into past human rights abuses, it could almost invariably count on sympathetic pressure groups to stage demonstrations against such demands. As the leading human rights activist Munir reported, there were regular protests in front of his office every time he raised the issue of military human rights abuses in public.[9] While the names of the demonstrating organizations changed constantly, the participants were mostly the same. Sometimes these groups would give themselves Islamic names to attract support from the Muslim community, while at other occasions the particular name of the group had a more nationalist and patriotic appeal. In addition to fending off the demands for legal inquiries into the military, these groups could also be mobilized to oppose policy initiatives aimed at reducing TNI's privileges. However, the armed forces were not the only institution using paid crowds to demonstrate for or against certain issues. The post-Suharto era saw the emergence of a highly sophisticated protest industry, which offered demonstrators, vehicles, and banners to everybody who was prepared to pay professional fees for the service.[10] The fact that the armed forces engaged in such practices provided further evidence that the post-1998 military was forced to replace its traditional concept of repressive social control with more modern practices of strategic communications.

The above analysis of the military's involvement in key socio-political sectors after 1998 has highlighted significant changes and continued problems. On the one hand, it is impossible to argue that no transformation has taken place and that the armed forces remain as powerful as during previous periods of Indonesia's post-independence history. On the other hand, however, it is obvious that the military has been able to defend considerable social and political privileges, and that effective democratic control over the armed forces has yet to be fully established. Applying the model developed by Cottey, Edmunds, and Forster, there is sufficient evidence that Indonesia has made substantial progress in the first generation of reforms, but has faced difficulties in entering the stage of second-generation changes. In other words, the almost complete extraction of TNI from formal politics was counterbalanced by persisting structural defects in the oversight mechanisms established by the post-Suharto polity. The best indication of these shortcomings is the fact that the quality of oversight still depends to a great extent on the strategic approach of individual presidents to controlling the military. The extreme differences between the oversight regimes imposed by Habibie, Wahid, Megawati, and Yudhoyono exposed the absence of an institutional process that could guarantee democratic control of the armed forces regardless of changes in the political leadership. In order to create such "effective systems of security sector governance" (Cottey, Edmunds, and Forster 2001, p. 5), the territorial command structure would have to be reformed, civilian control institutions strengthened, the practice of military self-financing discontinued, and legal accountability for officers introduced and upheld.

Having provided a mixed picture of Indonesia's progress in establishing democratic civilian control over its military after 1998, we now need to examine the factors that led to the successes and failures in this process. In the following sections, several explanatory propositions developed by Cottey, Edmunds, and Forster are tested against the Indonesian case. These propositions, which underscore elements that typically shape the pace and scope of civil-military reform processes, include the role of historical legacies, the quality of democratic governance, international factors, the depth of institutional reform, and specific military cultures. However, the discussion throughout this book has also pointed to the mode of regime change and the extent of fragmentation between key civilian constituencies as important factors that have determined the direction of the reform effort. Accordingly, the discussion below integrates these additional factors into the model presented by Cottey, Edmunds, and Forster, using the lessons learnt from the Indonesian case to enrich the scholarly literature on post-authoritarian military reform projects.

## Historical Legacies

The first potential factor in civil-military transitions considered by Cottey, Edmunds, and Forster is historical legacy. In this context, the level of political engagement of the armed forces with the fallen authoritarian regime is of particular interest. In Indonesia, the military had developed an exceptionally long and deep attachment to two successive authoritarian governments between 1959 and 1998. In fact, out of the fifty-three years of post-independence history until 1998, the armed forces had been sidelined from politics for only seven — during the time of parliamentary democracy in the early 1950s. Obviously, the period of the New Order between 1965 and 1998 had seen the most intensive military participation in politics, with the armed forces forming the backbone of Suharto's regime. Given this long history of military entanglement in politics and society, it was to be expected that Indonesia's transition from a military-backed autocracy to a democratic system would be significantly more difficult than in other countries with less historical baggage. Accordingly, many of the delays and setbacks in military reform after Suharto's fall could be attributed to the fact that neither the military nor Indonesian society found it easy to imagine a polity without involvement of the armed forces. The military's privileges had been so deeply entrenched in the country's laws, social norms, and economic practices that simply terminating them in 1998 was not an option. Instead, they needed to be phased out in a complex and lengthy process of institutional reform and social change. And while the importance of historical legacies for the contemporary political process began to wane after six years of turbulent transition, many ideological and institutional remainders of past Indonesian polities continue to influence military politics to this day.

Ideologically, a strong sense of entitlement and superiority still marks the world-view of many officers. TNI leaders have traditionally interpreted the origin of the army in the country's war for independence as an eternal mandate for engagement in political affairs. The formal abolition of the Dual Function in 2000 did little to change this mindset of the officer corps, with most of its members still convinced that the armed forces have the right to define and defend national interests against the alleged selfishness and incompetence of civilian elites. To be sure, some authors have argued that military officers around the world tend to hold significantly more conservative views than their civilian counterparts, even in developed democracies. They stress that this "civil-military divergence" is manageable as long as strong mechanisms of civilian democratic oversight are in place to keep excessive political ambitions by military leaders at bay (Russett and Hanson 1975; Holsti 1997 and 2001; Feaver 2003). In Indonesia, however, such mechanisms are not yet fully established. In addition, the conservatism of mainstream TNI officers does not only feature anti-liberal social values — it is dominated by deep distrust of civilian leadership and the system that selects it. In order to function properly, consolidated democracies need militaries that not merely tolerate, but genuinely endorse the democratic system. Indonesia's military, by contrast, still seems far away from such an unambiguous endorsement. The last graduates of New Order military academies will only retire in around 2031 — until that time, it appears inevitable that concepts of military superiority will circulate in the officer corps.

Similarly, some institutional legacies of military involvement in pre-1998 politics had a significant impact on the shape of civil-military relations during the transition. The territorial command structure is probably the most important of these institutional legacies, having been established in the 1950s and left largely unchanged throughout the post-New Order period. As the new polity consolidated, the structure ensured that TNI remained present at all levels of Indonesia's political administration, from the centre down to the village level. The principle of territorial defence was so deeply anchored in the political culture of both the military and civilian leaders that the system survived all half-hearted attempts at its reform. Since an aborted pilot project in 2000, there have been no more initiatives to seriously revamp the territorial system, and the current political and military leadership has openly stated that it sees no urgency to address the issue. Closely related to the territorial structure is the practice of military self-financing, another influential institutional legacy from the early days of the Indonesian republic. Begun in the guerrilla war and maintained throughout the New Order, the unofficial fund-raising channels of the armed forces allowed them to maintain a large degree of autonomy from civilian control authorities. It took until 2004 for civilian politicians to begin discussing the problem, but the subsequent plan to transfer military businesses to the state failed to address the underlying structural weaknesses of military financing in Indonesia. Ten years after Suharto's fall, the state still openly admits that it is not the sole provider of funds for the military, suggesting that Indonesia's elite views this issue as an unavoidable, but not immensely worrying disturbance.

Besides legacies directly related to the pre-1998 role of the armed forces, the history of intra-civilian relationships also left a deep mark on the post-Suharto military reform process. The level of fragmentation between key civilian forces has been identified in this book as an influential factor in shaping civil-military relations, both in Indonesia's history and in its current affairs. The more recent aspects of internal civilian conflict will be discussed in detail in the section on the quality of democratic governance, but given its rootedness in long-standing divisions in Indonesian society, the complex of intra-civilian hostility forms an important historical legacy as well. In this study, the main analytical focus has been on tensions within the Muslim community as an example of broader trends in the evolution of protracted conflicts in civilian politics. Throughout Indonesia's modern history, the controversy between secular-oriented Muslims and proponents of a formal role for Islam in state affairs on the one hand, and the deep antagonism between traditionalist and modernist groups on the other, have caused serious divisions in the civilian political realm. These cleavages contributed to the destabilization of the democratic polity in the 1950s, and opened opportunities for the armed forces to justify and enforce their claim to a permanent political role. Subsequently, the divisions between Muslim groups also extended into the post-Suharto polity, leading to a highly fragmented political landscape that served as an obstacle to quick and wide-ranging military reform efforts in the early phase of the transition.

It is important to emphasize, however, that the role of historical legacies in influencing post-authoritarian military politics has been significantly more profound during the political turbulence between 1998 and 2004 than in the period of democratic consolidation following Yudhoyono's election. For example, the territorial command structure was of tremendous importance for the military in the early years of the transition, when political parties, local legislatures, and government executives found it difficult to establish their authority at the grassroots level. However, after a series of elections and a significant expansion of political parties even to remote areas of the archipelago, the political relevance of the territorial system has declined accordingly. After 2005, direct elections have equipped local government heads with strong popular mandates, further empowering them vis-à-vis the territorial units in their area. Thus while the territorial structure remains an important leftover from previous regimes, and could potentially provide the logistic infrastructure for the military to intervene in times of political crisis, its powers are currently restricted by newly emerging forces in local politics. In the same vein, the continued practice of self-financing had a much larger impact on society under the weak oversight regimes of Habibie, Wahid, and Megawati than under the relatively tight control exercised by Yudhoyono. Consequently, while the military's continued fund-raising outside official state allocations is still a structural defect in Indonesia's security sector, the ability of the armed forces to run independent operations has been diminished by the stricter control through the executive. Finally, the intensity of intra-civilian conflict has declined considerably after 2004, showing that while history can be a strong structural determinant, it is the political and social actors who ultimately decide the course of current affairs.

## Intra-Systemic Regime Change

Another important factor in the development of civil-military relations in political transitions is the character of regime change from authoritarian to democratic rule. Cottey, Edmunds, and Forster have not included this element in their explanatory model, but the discussion in this book has pointed to its crucial importance in the Indonesian case. In 1998, power was transferred from Suharto to his deputy within the institutional framework of the existing regime, resulting in a post-authoritarian government that consisted largely of politicians groomed by the fallen New Order. Unlike in other autocratic and sultanistic states, where oppositional forces often take power amidst the tumultuous breakdown of the old system, former Indonesian regime dissidents were largely excluded from the executive and legislative institutions of the immediate post-1998 polity. This intra-systemic regime change was the result of important dynamics in the military as well as in civilian elite politics.

In terms of internal military politics, the outcome of the serious factional struggles within the armed forces during Suharto's fall played a significant role in determining the nature of the power transfer. The victory of Wiranto and his circle of compromise-oriented officers over Prabowo and other hardline generals allowed the former to negotiate an orderly handover of authority from Suharto to Habibie. By contrast, had Prabowo decided the intra-military competition in his favour, and had martial law been declared as he had demanded, the inevitable result would have been further violence and, ultimately, the complete collapse of the regime. In this scenario, executive power would not have been transferred to New Order figures, but to a transitional government consisting of oppositional groups, however divided they may have been. In this sense, the triumph of Wiranto's group in the armed forces avoided a Tienanmen-style bloodbath, but also prevented the very implosion of the authoritarian regime that may have provided Indonesia with better prospects of achieving a radical break with its past.

In addition to internal military developments, the continued fragmentation within the civilian elite also contributed to the intra-systemic regime change. Even as rapid economic decline and mounting societal unrest eroded the power of the regime, many key civilian forces refused to work together toward a democratic alternative to the faltering government. The mutual distrust among the civilian elite was so deep that some leaders preferred the continuation of Suharto's rule to the uncertainty associated with its replacement. Unwilling to present a coherent concept for a future without Suharto, civilian figures surrendered the momentum for regime change to the student movement and violent popular protest. When the May riots and the stubbornness of the students had finally brought the regime to the brink of collapse, there was no coalition of crucial societal leaders standing ready to take its place. Instead, the power vacuum was filled by the negotiation efforts of military officers around Wiranto, who succeeded in organizing a transfer of power within the structures and procedures of the New Order. This regime change arranged by major beneficiaries of Suharto's patronage network allowed important elements of the old elite to take charge of the post-authoritarian government and define its reform agenda, creating huge hurdles for the establishment of effective control over the military in the early period of the transition.

Similar to the historical legacies, the intra-systemic character of regime change had a delaying and complicating effect on the transition, but its influence began to wane as the political process stabilized after 2004. To be sure, the fact that so many figures of the New Order had been able to entrench themselves in the new democratic system goes a long way to explain why it took Indonesia six years to establish the main pillars of its new institutional framework. The survival of old authoritarian power structures and political procedures was also responsible for many of the crises of the early transition, ranging from the East Timor debacle to Wahid's failed presidency. However, after a lot of protracted debates, experiments, and compromises, Indonesia managed to build a reasonably stable democratic polity by 2004, which positively impacted on the quality of civil-military relations. Accordingly, while many of today's remaining problems in establishing democratic control over the armed forces are indirect results of the pacted transition in 1998, the inaction of the current government on these issues can no longer be attributed to the intra-systemic regime change alone. The apparent reluctance of Indonesia's ruling elite to tackle problems like the ongoing impunity of the officer corps, the practice of military financing, or the territorial command system is as much the product of old entrenched patronage structures as of the newly emerging political, economic, and social dynamics of the post-authoritarian state.

## Democratic Politics and Civilian Conflict

Complex historical legacies and the intra-systemic regime change predisposed Indonesia to a difficult transition path as far as the establishment of democratic civil-military relations was concerned. Deeply entrenched military mindsets and institutional features, combined with the smooth transfer of influential New Order power brokers into the post-authoritarian polity, made attempts to subordinate the armed forces to democratic civilian control a very challenging task. Aguero (1995, p. 39) has emphasized the importance of such "initial conditions" of a transitional state for the further process of democratization, and Indonesia is a case in point. However, not all developments in political transitions are historically predetermined. The situational decisions made by key leaders, unforeseen political incidents and trends, and economic booms or downturns can be equally essential for the transition outcome. Thus Cottey, Edmunds, and Forster, in discussing the various factors that shape civil-military relations in post-autocratic states, put the greatest emphasis on the contemporary contexts of transitional processes. In particular, they draw attention to the level of acceptance of the democratic polity within the elite and the general public, the political and economic stability of the state, and the quality of democratic governance. In addition to that, the extent of conflict between civilian groups also needs to be counted among the possible causes for the successes and failures of military reform processes in transitional states.

Cottey, Edmunds, and Forster have argued that the delegitimization of alternatives to the democratic system is an important condition for reducing the level of military intervention in politics. States in which the democratic polity is constantly challenged by proposals for other forms of governance have a smaller chance of successful transition than those where the vast majority of citizens endorse the principle of democratic government. Despite widespread frustration with its deficiencies, Indonesia's post-1998 polity has only been opposed by numerically small elements at the extremist fringes.[11] The democratic amendments to the constitution were the result of elite negotiations involving all key parties and groups, and did not cause severe ruptures in the political process. It is this broad consensus on the principle of democratic governance that has given Indonesia's transition a better chance of succeeding than the experiment with liberal democracy in the 1950s, when a wide variety of alternative concepts of governance were in circulation and undermined the stability of the parliamentary system. Significantly, the fact that Indonesia's past negative experience with democracy had no lasting impact on the course of the reform process after 1998 exposed the limited relevance of historical predispositions for the transition outcome. In fact, the collective awareness that the democratic breakdown in the 1950s had produced forty years of authoritarian rule was probably to some extent responsible for the absence of any serious challenge to the democratic system since Suharto's fall.

In more general terms, Cottey, Edmunds, and Forster point to the politico-economic stability of the state and the quality of democratic governance as important factors that influence transitional civil-military relations. Indonesia's state, while diffusing some of its powers in the process of decentralization, remained relatively strong throughout the transition. Applying Joel Migdal's scheme of strong and weak states (Migdal 1988), post-Suharto Indonesia could not be described as "weak", let alone as in danger of becoming a "failed state". The Fund for Peace's Failed State Index in 2007 listed Sudan, Iraq, and Somalia as the top three states at the brink of failure, with Indonesia coming in a distant fifty-fifth.[12] Except for a small number of conflict areas, the authority of the Indonesian state remained unchallenged during the transition, and its administration continued to function fairly well. In the same vein, Indonesia's post-New Order economy avoided further contraction after the meltdown of 1997 and 1998, growing at an average of 4 to 5 per cent each year. While this failed to trigger an economic boom comparable to the 1990s, it was enough to hold back social unrest that could have undermined the stability of the democratic system. It was also sufficient to provide for largely tolerable levels in the quality of democratic governance, particularly after 2004.[13] The post-2004 democratic state was based on a carefully designed system of checks and balances, and while substantial defects persisted, its quality was much improved over the experimental polity of the early transition. Thus overall, the Indonesian state after 1998 delivered the basic economic, political, and social stability that Cottey, Edmunds, and Forster view as an essential precondition for any military reform process to take place.

While the fundamental stability of the state was secured throughout the transition, there were noteworthy fluctuations that provided evidence of the close link between the quality of democratic rule and the level of military engagement in political affairs. Whenever the civilian polity was in crisis, the armed forces found entry points to increase their participation in politics. This was most obvious during the constitutional turmoil over Wahid's presidency in 2001, which was arguably the time when Indonesia's transition was closest to failure. In the first half of 2001, both the executive and the legislature had all but stopped carrying out their functions, focusing on gaining the upper hand in the escalating conflict instead. The military assumed the role of referee in this dispute, ultimately deciding the conflict in favour of Wahid's opponents and gaining important concessions in return. By contrast, the most stable government of all post-Suharto administrations — that of President Susilo Bambang Yudhoyono — has seen the lowest levels of military engagement in politics. When Yudhoyono took office in 2004, the rules and norms of democratic competition had been newly codified through wide-ranging constitutional amendments. These amendments introduced alternative avenues of institutional conflict resolution (most notably the Constitutional Court), narrowing the opportunities for the armed forces to offer themselves as an emergency negotiator between rival state bodies. These fluctuating dynamics make Indonesia a highly illustrative example of the positive correlation between the stability of the democratic polity and the degree of military intervention in governance.

Another aspect of democratic governance that tends to influence the level of military participation in politics is the extent to which states use coercion to settle disputes with regime opponents or between societal groups. This element does not figure prominently in Cottey, Edmunds, and Forster's model, although some of the states they researched (Russia, for example) had high levels of internal conflict. Other analysts, however, have placed the intensity of violent domestic conflict, and the state's response to it, at the core of their theoretical thinking on the quality of democratic civilian control over the armed forces. Michael Desch (1999), for instance, proposed that states with a high degree of internal conflict are unlikely to see strong institutional control over their armed forces. In the same vein, Muthiah Alagappa (2001a, p. 4) has suggested that "as the weight of coercion in governance rises (or declines), so does the political power and influence of the military". Once more, Indonesia is a good test case for this hypothesis. The country witnessed extended periods of internal violence between 1998 and 2005, reaching its peak with the escalation of communal clashes in several provinces in around 2000–01. Not coincidentally, this period of sectarian wars and the time of the 2003 military campaign against GAM were also the phases in the political transition with the weakest government control over the armed forces.

By contrast, after Yudhoyono settled the Aceh conflict in 2005, the level of internal conflict dropped substantially, leading to an equally significant decline in the political role of the armed forces. Most importantly, Yudhoyono had achieved this without using the government's "weight of coercion", opting for peaceful conflict resolution instead. As a consequence of the Helsinki agreement, Aceh was "lost" for TNI as the territory where it had interfered most deeply in political, economic, and social affairs, and where it had been able to run military operations without effective control by the civilian government. However, Yudhoyono's success questioned another of Alagappa's premises, namely that "the weight of coercion in governance declines with increasing levels of economic development" (Alagappa 2001a, p. 4). Economic development does not appear to have played a role in Yudhoyono's decision to negotiate with the rebels rather than to continue the military offensive. The economic growth rates under Megawati and Yudhoyono were roughly the same — Yudhoyono simply opted for a different approach to resolving Indonesia's long-standing internal conflicts, highlighting the importance of individual agency in spite of the continuously strong influence of structural factors.

It is not only the level of armed conflict that has implications for civil-military relations, however. The extent of deeply entrenched social, ideological, and religio-political divisions in the civilian polity can have similarly powerful impacts. Cottey, Edmunds, and Forster (2003, p. 12) have made cursory references to this issue, but it does not seem to figure prominently in their explanatory framework. In Indonesia, however, these divisions were a major factor in deciding the quality of the military reform process. Between 1998 and 2004, the degree of intra-civilian tension was high, largely reflecting traditional cleavages in Indonesian society and the fact that most groups opted to participate in the democratic system by establishing their own political parties. This book has pointed to the divisions within Indonesian Islam as an example of intra-civilian disputes, but other social groups were affected as well: nationalist parties, labour unions, grassroots movements, and liberal civil rights groups. While there was a stable consensus on the political character of the state, parties and societal forces differed immensely over the norms and procedures of open democratic competition. The constitutional crisis of

2001 revealed that even civilian figures and religio-political organizations with reputable democratic credentials were prepared to condone mass violence as a legitimate instrument of intra-civilian competition, providing opportunities for the armed forces to mediate and repair their image damaged by decades of authoritarian repression.

The intensity of these splits between major civilian forces began to decline after 2004, however. As the post-Suharto polity consolidated, the norms of democratic competition were clarified in new sets of legal regulations, providing alternative institutional mechanisms to resolve disputes not only between state institutions, but also between powerful civilian groups. This, in turn, helped to reduce the tendency of civilian leaders to mobilize their masses against opponents, and consequently undermined the position of the armed forces as conflict mediators. This stabilization of the civilian polity formed the backdrop for improvements in the relationship between key societal forces, most notably between Muslim organizations. Critically, a new generation of leaders in the traditionalist Nahdlatul Ulama and the modernist Muhammadiyah seemed determined to overcome the long-established hostility between them, and both organizations began to gradually withdraw from party politics. The party landscape, for its part, witnessed a significant shift of parties to the political centre, ending most of the ideological disputes of the early post-Suharto transition. This increased strategic flexibility of political groups was also visible in the direct local elections after 2005, with parties forming alliances across the ideological spectrum and retired military officers thus finding it increasingly difficult to use intra-civilian divisions to their benefit. Overall, Indonesia provided interesting insights into the causal link between divisions in the civilian polity and the quality of civil-military relations, both in terms of a negative impact during the turbulent transition and strong improvements after 2004.

## The International Context

In their studies on civil-military reforms in the post-authoritarian societies of Eastern Europe and Central Asia, Cottey, Edmunds, and Forster (2002, p. 13) concluded that the incentive to join important international organizations was "by far the single greatest external factor" in removing opposition to structural change in the armed forces. The prospect of becoming a member of NATO (North Atlantic Treaty Organization) or the European Union, with privileged access to development funds and soft loans, has succeeded in overcoming even the strongest objections from conservative generals to reforms of the military. NATO and the EU made it very clear that if candidates for membership did not adjust their mechanisms of military control to standards established by their organizations, no admission was possible. Faced with the potential loss of billions of dollars in aid and other forms of assistance, civilian governments forced their militaries to comply. Turkey, for example, which in the past had experienced levels of military participation in politics very similar to those in Indonesia, pressured its generals to accept substantial cuts to their privileges. In Indonesia, however, no such dynamics were at work. Although the regime change itself had been triggered by an external economic shock, the impact of international organizations on the civil-military transition after 1998 was negligible. APEC (Asia-Pacific Economic Cooperation) and ASEAN (Association of Southeast Asian Nations), the two main multilateral associations in which Indonesia engages, are organizations that do not require their members to meet particular democratic standards. The IMF and the World Bank, on the other hand, missed the chance to use their extensive economic powers during the monetary crisis to demand more wide-ranging reforms of Indonesia's security sector. Prioritizing changes in economic policy and the restructuring of the banking system, IMF and World Bank officials did not view military reform as a matter of immediate urgency. Although they later began to raise the issue as an important instrument to reduce corruption and remove obstacles to further investment, by 2003 the IMF's emergency loan programme had been largely phased out and the window of opportunity had closed.

If there were any international factors impacting on Indonesia's post-1998 civil-military relations, they were largely unsupportive of the reform process. First of all, sanctions imposed on TNI by the United States and other Western countries after the East Timor events did not succeed in convincing the armed forces to introduce more reforms. In fact, the restrictions on equipment purchases and educational exchanges hardened the resolve of conservative officers and fuelled anti-Western sentiments in the military mainstream. The rise of India and China as global economic powerhouses and Russia's resurgence as an international security player allowed Indonesia to ignore most of Washington's demands and establish closer ties with alternative military partners instead. By 2008, Indonesia was purchasing significant percentages of its military equipment from Russia, South Korea, and Eastern European countries, reducing its dependence on the United States and demonstrating that it was unimpressed by the threat of sanctions. The United States largely lifted its restrictions on military-to-military cooperation in November 2005, although Indonesia had fulfilled very few of the American conditions previously set for resuming the ties. Apparently, the Bush administration had great concerns about

Indonesia's improving military relationships with China and Russia, mindful of TNI's shift in the 1960s from U.S. defence hardware to equipment procured from the Soviet Union. Thus after 2005, the U.S. Government no longer threatened to restrict equipment purchases, but in fact lobbied TNI to buy from American companies rather than their rivals in Asia or Europe.

Besides being led by regional security interests, the United States and the West also reduced their reform pressure on TNI because they needed Indonesia's assistance in the "war on terror". After 11 September 2001, the U.S. government began to radically revise its global strategic priorities, subordinating its concern for democratic governance to the more pressing need to capture Islamist terrorists around the world. The example of Pakistan was most illustrative in this regard. When General Pervez Musharraf seized power there in a military coup in 1999, the United States initially implemented sanctions and demanded the immediate return to the democratic system. After the 2001 terrorist attacks, however, the American government courted Musharraf as an important ally in its fight against Islamic radicalism in Asia. Washington even lent tacit support to Musharraf when he controversially engineered his election to a second presidential term in October 2007. Indonesian officers followed such developments with great interest, and learnt that defaulting on reform benchmarks did not necessarily cause negative reactions from the United States. In order to qualify for American assistance, it was evidently sufficient for TNI to pledge its commitment to suppressing Islamist terrorism in Indonesia — a pledge it had made anyway to serve its domestic political interests. In summary, international factors played only a secondary role in Indonesia's civil-military relations after 1998. There were no reform standards imposed by regional organizations, and Western sanctions were lifted after they had failed to achieve their goal. At best, international developments added slight nuances to the military reform process, but it remained a predominantly domestic affair.

## Institutional Factors and Military Culture

The final two factors proposed by Cottey, Edmunds, and Forster relate to the extent of institutional reform and the persistence of specific military cultures. The depth of institutional change is an important explanatory indicator for the long-term prospects of civil-military relations; it reflects the quality of institutional processes rather than the performance of individual governments or leaders. The case of Indonesia demonstrates the relevance of this distinction. Most importantly, Yudhoyono's relatively tight control over the military was established by a number of personal decisions rather than by strong institutional mechanisms of oversight. His moves to sideline conservative officers from the TNI leadership and to seek a peaceful resolution of the Aceh conflict were watersheds in the civil-military relations during his presidency, but they were not followed up by further institutional changes. Accordingly, with institutional reform incomplete, there is no guarantee that Yudhoyono's successor will exercise the same firm control over the armed forces. In order to create a stable and enduring system of security sector governance, Indonesia has to progress beyond its first generation of already implemented institutional reforms, which "only" led to the extraction of the military from political institutions, the formal granting of oversight authority to the department of defence and the DPR, as well as a series of laws and regulations. In consequence, it is essential that Indonesia launch a new initiative for institutional change, addressing the two most important remaining reform targets: the military's financing system and the army's territorial command structure. Without this, the institutional process of overseeing the military will continue to be exposed to the uncertainty of Indonesia's erratic day-to-day politics and the highly diverse leadership styles of its presidents.

Finally, Cottey, Edmunds, and Forster pointed to specific military cultures that can be either supportive or unsupportive of military reform processes. In this context, the level of professionalism in the armed forces received their particular attention. In the Indonesian case, however, the explanatory proposition of military cultures seems to overlap significantly with that of historical legacies. Indonesia's armed forces had since their inception defined themselves as a domestic security force and a political supra-institution, making the idea of "military professionalism" a foreign concept for their officers. From the very beginning, TNI's doctrine was marked by expressions of political entitlement, superiority over civilian leaders, and a missionary sense of guarding both the constitution and the territorial integrity of the state. This complex military culture formed a difficult legacy for the post-Suharto polity, and it continues to influence the thinking of officers to this day. In fact, the problem for the contemporary political system is not only that the erosion of the old military culture within the officer corps is painfully slow, but also that some of TNI's militaristic values have spread to the civilian sector. After 1998, political parties expanded their security forces and developed them into paramilitary groups with ranks and codes similar to those used by TNI. Ethnic and religious groups also established militias. This cultural militarization of Indonesian society made changing the anachronistic values of the military even more difficult. Accordingly, non-state militias need to be disarmed and demilitarized if the government wants to seriously improve the professionalism of the armed forces and adapt their value system to the new democratic framework (Sebastian 2006, p. 358).

## Post-Authoritarian Civil-Military Relations: The Case of Indonesia

The evaluation of Indonesia's civil-military relations after Suharto's fall in 1998 has led to important descriptive and analytical findings. First of all, it has demonstrated that Indonesia has made significant progress in addressing the first generation of military reforms, which is related to institutional changes in security sector governance. Indonesia has largely extracted its military from formal politics, has empowered civilian control bodies to exercise more oversight, and has introduced new legislation for the management of its armed forces. However, the omission of two key items from the reform agenda (i.e. the ongoing practice of military self-financing and the territorial command structure) has prevented the country from fully entering the stage of second-generation reforms, which is concerned with the creation of meaningful and enduring institutional mechanisms of democratic civilian oversight. The quality of the government's control over the armed forces has improved considerably after 2004, but this was largely due to the personal leadership of President Yudhoyono rather than consolidated institutional control. Thus if Indonesia wants to turn the reforms achieved so far into irreversible institutional norms and procedures, it will have to address a number of remaining reform issues. This does not only include the territorial system and the military's off-budget sources, but also the continued legal impunity for military officers, the lack of expertise in civilian institutions tasked with overseeing the armed forces, and the absence of regular assessments of Indonesia's security threats and their implications for TNI's force structure and allocation of resources.

Weighing the factors that have shaped Indonesia's post-authoritarian civil-military relations, this book has highlighted a number of structural and agency-driven influences. To begin with, historical legacies have had a significant impact on the process of military reform in the early phase of the transition, delaying and complicating the efforts to remove the military from politics. In addition, the character of the 1998 regime change, which had avoided the implosion of the New Order and secured the political survival of many of its protagonists, also left a deep mark on the immediate post-Suharto period. The strength of these structural predispositions began to decline after 2004, however, when the transition came to an end and Indonesia entered into the phase of democratic consolidation. The post-2004 dynamics also provided evidence for the powerful influence of two other factors for the quality of civil-military relations: the extent of armed internal conflict and the degree of intra-civilian divisions. In both areas, Indonesia registered high levels of tensions before 2004, allowing the armed forces to continue their engagement in political affairs. Discussing cleavages in the Muslim community as an example of general patterns of intra-civilian disputes, this book has outlined in detail how irreconcilable differences between key societal groups in the 1998–2004 period served to pull the military back into politics. After 2004, the degree of both internal armed conflict and intra-civilian fragmentation declined, and the armed forces saw their political role eroding as a consequence of these developments. By contrast, international events seem to have played no significant part in Indonesia's military reform process after May 1998.

Thus contrary to many of the cases researched by Cottey, Edmunds, and Forster, Indonesia's transitional civil-military relations were a largely domestic affair, driven by both structural predeterminations and the situational decisions by key leaders. International incentives and pressure were almost insignificant, and the strength of historical legacies began to wane as the transition progressed. The most important influences were clearly the quality of democratic governance, the intensity of communal and separatist violence, and the level of conflict between civilian socio-political actors. The level of military participation in politics was high whenever democratic governance was in crisis, armed violence escalated, and civilians engaged in extended periods of bickering. On the other hand, when democratic governance was effective, its rules and procedures widely accepted, and the extent of both violent and political conflict low, the armed forces found it difficult to intrude into the civilian polity. This positive correlation between the stability of the democratic system and the political role of the military provides both hopeful prospects and crucial warnings to Indonesia as it seeks to move forward in the process of reforming its military. If the country can maintain and consolidate the relative stability of its post-2004 political system, then Indonesia should be able to gradually address the remaining challenges of its security sector reform agenda. If, on the other hand, Indonesia returned to another phase of political instability — whether caused by economic decline, renewed intra-civilian tensions, or external shocks — then its chances of proceeding to the second generation of military reform would be limited at best.

# Notes

1   Minister of Defence Juwono Sudarsono in an interview with the *Jakarta Post* in November 2004. See "Transparency will be Instituted in Defense Ministry", *Jakarta Post*, 4 November 2004.

2   In 2000, the international consulting firm Ernst & Young conducted an audit of the businesses run by the army's main foundation *Yayasan Kartika Eka Paksi*. It concluded that the net loss of the foundation in that year was 8.21 billion rupiah (around US\$892,000). For the detailed figures, see Ernst & Young (2001).

3   Rieffel and Pramodhawardani used a 2003 report by a Jakarta-based strategic communications firm and TNI's official disclosure of its business profits as the basis for their calculation. Obviously, this does not provide a reliable foundation for making serious estimates of all the assets and profits, which traditionally have been managed through private holding companies, the relatives of generals, and a large network of cronies. None of these external holdings would show up in TNI's books. Nevertheless, Rieffel and Pramodhawardani are correct with their claim that the relevance of the formal business has often been overestimated.

4   These figures are based on official filings by Freeport McMoRan to the Securities and Exchange Commission (SEC). I am grateful to Lisa Misol from Human Rights Watch, New York, for providing information on these payments.

5   Interview with Endriartono Sutarto, Jakarta, 11 June 2007.

6   "Indonesia Segera Beli Korvet dari Belanda", *Kompas*, 1 July 2004.

7   "Mega Manja Militer, Biarkan Kursi Menhan Kosong", *Duta Masyarakat*, 27 February 2004; "Panglima TNI Keberatan TNI Diletakkan di Bawah Dephan", *Kompas*, 9 November 2004.

8   Confidential interview with a three-star general, Bandung, 15 January 2002.

9   Interview with Munir, Jakarta, 23 May 2004.

10  "Rent a Mob for as low as \$4 a Head", *Straits Times*, 22 February 2003.

11  Despite the belief of many Indonesians that their economic conditions were better under the New Order, the majority continues to support democracy. In the second quarter of 2007, 69 per cent of Indonesians polled by the Roy Morgan Good Governance Monitor thought that "democracy is working in Indonesia", which was only slightly lower than in 2005 and 2006, when most quarterly polls had shown figures above 70 per cent (Guharoy 2007).

12  The survey lists 177 nations and divides them into four categories, which indicate the probability that they could turn into failed states — 32 states were put under "alert", 97 received a "warning", 33 were seen as "moderate" and only 15 as "sustainable". For details of the survey, see the Fund for Peace's website at <http://www.fundforpeace.org/web/index.php?option=com_content&task=vie w&id=229&Itemid=366> (accessed on 10 July 2007).

13  In the Roy Morgan Good Governance Monitor survey cited above, slightly below 60 per cent of Indonesians said in the second quarter of 2007 that "the government is doing a good job in running the country" (Guharoy 2007).

# BIBLIOGRAPHY

## A. Book Chapters, Articles, Doctoral Dissertations and Seminar Papers

Alagappa, Muthiah. "Introduction". In *Coercion and Governance: The Declining Political Role of the Military in Asia*, edited by Muthiah Alagappa, pp. 1–28. Stanford: Stanford University Press, 2001. Cited as Alagappa 2001*a*.

———. "Investigating and Explaining Change: An Analytical Framework". In *Coercion and Governance: The Declining Political Role of the Military in Asia*, edited by Muthiah Alagappa, pp. 29–68. Stanford: Stanford University Press, 2001. Cited as Alagappa 2001*b*.

———. "Military Professionalism: A Conceptual Perspective". In *Military Professionalism in Asia: Conceptual and Empirical Perspectives*, edited by Muthiah Alagappa, pp. 1–19. Honolulu: East-West Center, 2001. Cited as Alagappa 2001*c*.

Anwar, M. Syafi'i. "Politik Akomodasi Negara dan Cendekiawan Muslim Masa Orde Baru: Sebuah Retrospeksi dan Refleksi". In *ICMI: Antara Status Quo dan Demokratisasi*, edited by Nasrullah Ali-Fauzi, pp. 227–48. Bandung: Mizan, 1995.

Aribowo. "Koter dan Kepentingan TNI (AD) di Daerah". In *Wacana Penghapusan Koter: Pengembalian Fungsi Teritorial dari TNI ke Pemerintah Daerah*, edited by Muhammad Asfar, pp. 115–38. Surabaya: Pusat Studi Demokrasi dan HAM, 2003.

Asfar, Muhammad. "Gus Dur dan Kiai Kampung". *Suara Merdeka*, 22 February 2007.

Aspinall, Edward. "Opposition and Elite Conflict in the Fall of Soeharto". In *The Fall of Soeharto*, edited by Geoff Forrester and Ron May, pp. 130–53. Bathurst: Crawford House Publishing, 1999.

———. "Political Opposition and the Transition from Authoritarian Rule: The Case of Indonesia". Ph.D. dissertation, The Australian National University, 2000.

———. "Elections and the Normalization of Politics in Indonesia". *South East Asia Research* 13, no. 2 (2005): 117–56. Cited as Aspinall 2005*a*.

Azra, Azyumardi. "Fraksi Islam". In *Mengapa Partai Islam Kalah? Perjalanan Politik Islam dari Pra-Pemilu '99 Sampai Pemilihan Presiden*, edited by Hamid Basyaib and Hamid Abidin, pp. 307–10. Jakarta: AlvaBet, 1999.

Baidlawi, Masduki. "Memahami Tiga Langkah Gus Dur". *Aula* 21, no. 9 (1999).

Ball, Nicole. "Transforming Security Sectors: The IMF and World Bank Approaches". *Conflict, Security, Development* 1, no. 1 (2001): 45–66.

Barsany, Nur Iskandar al-. "Ulama, Santri dan Reformasi". *Suara Merdeka*, 21 April 1998.

Barton, Greg. "The Prospects for Islam". In *Indonesia Today: Challenges of History*, edited by Grayson J. Lloyd and Shannon L. Smith, pp. 244–55. Singapore: Institute of Southeast Asian Studies, 2001.

Baswedan, Anies. "Sirkulasi Suara dalam Pemilu 2004". Unpublished Manuscript, 2004.

Bland, Douglas. "Patterns in Liberal Democratic Civil-Military Relations". *Armed Forces and Society* 27, no. 4 (2001): 525–40.

Bodden, Michael H. "Seno Gumira Ajidarma and Fictional Resistance to an Authoritarian State in 1990s Indonesia". *Indonesia* 68 (1999): 155–63.

Booth, Anne. "Development: Achievement and Weakness". In *Indonesia Beyond Soeharto: Polity, Economy, Society, Transition*, edited by Donald K. Emmerson, pp. 109–35. Armonk and London: M.E. Sharpe, 1999.

———. "The Impact of the Indonesian Crisis on Welfare: What do We Know Two Years On?". In *Indonesia in Transition: Social Aspects of Reformasi and Crisis*, edited by Chris Manning and Peter van Diermen, pp. 145–62. Singapore: Institute of Southeast Asian Studies, 2000.

Bourchier, David. "Why Indonesia had to Explode". In *The Last Days of Suharto*, edited by Edward Aspinall, Herb Feith, and Gerry van Klinken, pp. 42–44. Clayton: Monash Asia Institute, 1999. Cited as Bourchier 1999*a*.

———. "Skeletons, Vigilantes and the Armed Forces' Fall from Grace". In *Reformasi: Crisis and Change in Indonesia*, edited by Arief Budiman, Barbara Hatley, and Damien Kingsbury, pp. 149–72. Clayton: Monash Asia Institute, 1999. Cited as Bourchier 1999*b*.

———. "Habibie's Interregnum: Reformasi, Elections, Regionalism and the Struggle for Power". In *Indonesia in Transition: Social Aspects of Reformasi and Crisis*, edited by Chris Manning and Pieter van Diermen, pp. 15–38. Singapore: Institute of Southeast Asian Studies, 2000.

Brömmelhörster, Jörn and Wolf Christian Paes. "Soldiers in Business: An Introduction". In *The Military as an Economic Actor: Soldiers in Business*, edited by Jörn Brömmelhörster and Wolf Christian Paes, pp. 1–17. New York: Palgrave Macmillan, 2003.

Bruinessen, Martin van. "Traditions for the Future: The Reconstruction of Traditionalist Discourse Within NU". In *Nahdlatul Ulama, Traditional Islam and Modernity in Indonesia*, edited by Greg Fealy and Greg Barton, pp. 163–89. Clayton: Monash Asia Institute, 1996.

————. "Genealogies of Islamic Radicalism in Post-Soeharto Indonesia". *South East Asia Research* 10, no. 2 (2002): 117–54.

————. "Post-Soeharto Muslim Engagements with Civil Society and Democratisation". Paper Presented at the Third International Conference and Workshop "Indonesia in Transition". Universitas Indonesia, 24–28 August 2003.

Burhani, Ahmad Najib. "Muhammadiyah's New Chairman and the Future of its Liberalism". *Jakarta Post*, 12 July 2005.

Butt, Simon. "The Constitutional Court's Decision in the Dispute Between the Supreme Court and the Judicial Commission: Banishing Judicial Accountability?". In *Indonesia: Democracy and the Promise of Good Governance*, edited by Ross H. McLeod and Andrew McIntyre, pp. 178–99. Singapore: Institute of Southeast Asian Studies, 2007.

Chandra, Siddharth, and Douglas Kammen. "Generating Reforms and Reforming Generations: Military Politics in Indonesia's Democratic Transition". *World Politics* 55, no. 1 (2002): 96–136.

Clear, Annette. "Politics: From Endurance to Evolution". In *Indonesia: The Great Transition*, edited by John Bresnan, pp. 137–88. Lanham, Boulder, New York, Toronto and Oxford: Rowman & Littlefield Publishers, 2005.

Cohen, Margot. "'Us' and 'Them'". *Far Eastern Economic Review*, 12 February 1998. Cited as Cohen 1998*a*.

————. "The Vanishings". *Far Eastern Economic Review*, 7 May 1998. Cited as Cohen 1998*b*.

Collins, Elisabeth Fuller. "*Dakwah* and Democracy: The Significance of Partai Keadilan and Hizbut Tahrir". Unpublished Paper, 2003.

Cottey, Andrew, Timothy Edmunds, and Anthony Forster. "Soldiers, Politics and Defence: Some Initial Conclusions on the Democratisation of Civil-Military Relations in Post-Communist Central and Eastern Europe". Civil-Military Relations in Central and Eastern Europe Project, Unpublished Paper, 2000.

————. "The Second Generation Problematic: Rethinking Democratic Control of Armed Forces in Central and Eastern Europe". Civil-Military Relations in Central and Eastern Europe Project, Unpublished Paper, 2001.

————. "Introduction: The Challenge of Democratic Control of Armed Forces in Post-Communist Europe". In *Democratic Control of the Military in Post-Communist Europe: Guarding the Guards*, edited by Andrew Cottey, Timothy Edmunds, and Anthony Forster, pp. 1–20. New York: Palgrave, 2002.

Cribb, Robert. "From Total People's Defence to Massacre: Explaining Indonesian Military Violence in East Timor". In *Roots of Violence in Indonesia*, edited by Freek Colombijn and J. Thomas Lindblad, pp. 227–42. Singapore: Institute of Southeast Asian Studies, 2002.

Crouch, Harold. "Wiranto and Habibie: Military-Civilian Relations since May 1998". In *Reformasi: Crisis and Change in Indonesia*, edited by Arief Budiman, Barbara Hatley, and Damien Kingsbury, pp. 127–48. Clayton: Monash Asia Institute, 1999.

————. "Professionalism in Southeast Asian Militaries: Indonesia". Unpublished Paper, 2003. Cited as Crouch 2003*a*.

————. "Political Update 2002: Megawati's Holding Operation". In *Local Power and Politics in Indonesia: Decentralisation and Democratisation*, edited by Edward Aspinall and Greg Fealy, pp. 15–34. Singapore: Institute of Southeast Asian Studies, 2003. Cited as Crouch 2003*b*.

Dalpino, Catharin E. "Indonesia's Democratic Difficulty: The Center Will Not Hold". *The Brown Journal of World Affairs* 9, no. 1 (2002): 85–94.

Diamond, Larry. "Introduction: Political Culture and Democracy". In *Political Culture and Democracy in Developing Countries*, edited by Larry Diamond, pp. 1–27. Boulder and London: Lynne Rienner Publishers, 1994.

————. "Thinking About Hybrid Regimes". *Journal of Democracy* 13, no. 2 (2002): 21–35.

Diamond, Larry and Marc F. Plattner. "Introduction". In *Civil-Military Relations and Democracy*, edited by Larry Diamond and Marc F. Plattner, pp. ix–xxxiv. Baltimore and London: Johns Hopkins University Press, 1996.

Dibb, Paul. "Indonesia: The Key to South-East Asia's Security". *International Affairs* 27, no. 4 (2001): 829–42.

Djiwandono, J. Soedjati. "Civil-Military Relations in Indonesia: The Case of ABRI's Dual Function". In *Civil-Military Relations: Building Democracy and Regional Security in Latin America, Southern Asia, and Central Europe*, edited by David R. Mares, pp. 45–58. Boulder: Westview Press, 1998.

Editors, The. "Changes in Civil-Military Relations since the Fall of Soeharto". *Indonesia* 70 (2000): 125–38.

Elson, R.E. "In Fear of the People: Soeharto and the Justification of State-sponsored Violence Under the New Order". In *Roots of Violence in Indonesia: Contemporary Violence in Historical Perspective*, edited by Freek Colombijn and J. Thomas Lindblad, pp. 173–95. Singapore: Institute of Southeast Asian Studies, 2002.

Emmerson, Donald K. "Exit and Aftermath: The Crisis of 1997–98". In *Indonesia Beyond Soeharto: Polity, Economy, Society, Transition*, edited by Donald K. Emmerson, pp. 295–343. Armonk and London: M.E. Sharpe, 1999.

————. "Whose Eleventh? Indonesia and America since 11 September". *The Brown Journal of World Affairs* 9, no. 1 (2002): 115–26.

Fealy, Greg. "The 1994 NU Congress and Aftermath: Abdurrahman Wahid, Suksesi and the Battle for Control of NU". In *Nahdlatul Ulama, Traditional Islam and Modernity in Indonesia*, edited by Greg Fealy and Greg Barton, pp. 257–78. Clayton: Monash Asia Institute, 1996.

————. "Indonesian Politics, 1995–1996: The Making of a Crisis". In *Indonesia Assessment: Population and Human Resources*, edited by Gavin W. Jones and Terrence H. Hull, pp. 19–38. Singapore: Institute of Southeast Asian Studies, 1997.

————. "Ulama and Politics in Indonesia: A History of Nahdlatul Ulama, 1952–1967". Ph.D. dissertation, Department of History, Monash University, Melbourne, 1998.

———. "Divided Majority: The Limits of Political Islam in Indonesia". In *Islam and Political Legitimacy*, edited by Shahram Akbarzadeh and Abdullah Saeed, pp. 150–68. London and New York: RoutledgeCurzon, 2003.

———. "Islamic Radicalism in Indonesia: The Faltering Revival?". In *Southeast Asian Affairs 2004*, pp. 104–21. Singapore: Institute of Southeast Asian Affairs, 2004.

Federspiel, Howard. "Indonesia, Islam, and U.S. Policy". *Brown Journal of World Affairs* 9, no. 1 (2002): 107–14.

Feillard, Andrée. "Traditionalist Islam and the Army in Indonesia's New Order: The Awkward Relationship". In *Nahdlatul Ulama, Traditional Islam and Modernity in Indonesia*, edited by Greg Fealy and Greg Barton, pp. 42–67. Clayton: Monash Asia Institute, 1996.

———. "Traditionalist Islam and the State in Indonesia: The Road to Legitimacy and Renewal". In *Islam in an Era of Nation-States: Politics and Religious Renewal in Muslim Southeast Asia*, edited by Robert W. Hefner and Patricia Horvatich, pp. 129–56. Honolulu: University of Hawai'i Press, 1997.

———. "Indonesian Traditionalist Islam's Troubled Experience with Democracy (1999–2001)". *Archipel* 64 (2002): 117–44.

Feith, Herbert. "Dynamics of Guided Democracy". In *Indonesia*, edited by Ruth McVey, pp. 309–409. Second Revised Printing. New Haven: HRAF Press, 1967.

Gross, Jeremy. "Direct Local Elections Truly Change the Political Culture". *Jakarta Post*, 22 June 2006.

Hernandez, Carolina G. "Controlling Asia's Armed Forces". In *Civil-Military Relations and Democracy*, edited by Larry Diamond and Marc F. Plattner, pp. 66–80. Baltimore and London: Johns Hopkins University Press, 1996.

Finer, Samuel E. "The Retreat to the Barracks: Notes on the Practice and the Theory of Military Withdrawal from the Seats of Power". *Third World Quarterly* 7, no. 1 (1985): 16–30.

Fitch, J. Samuel. "Military Attitudes Toward Democracy in Latin America: How Do We Know If Anything Has Changed?". In *Civil-Military Relations in Latin America: New Analytical Perspectives*, edited by David Pion-Berlin, pp. 59–87. Chapel Hill and London: University of North Carolina Press, 2001.

Ghazali, Abd. Rohim. "Dilema Hubungan PAN-Muhammadiyah". In *Islam di Tengah Arus Transisi*, edited by Abdul Mu'nim D.Z., pp. 185–90. Jakarta: Penerbit Kompas, 2000.

———. "Amien Pasca-PAN". *Koran Tempo*, 7 April 2005.

Guharoy, Debnath. "Can Corporates Influence 'Good Governance' in Indonesia?". *Jakarta Post*, 10 July 2007.

Gunawan, Bondan. "Reformasi TNI dalam Kabinet Gus Dur". Paper Presented at the Halqah Nasional "Hubungan Ulama-Tentara untuk Indonesia Baru". Malang, 17 April 2000.

Gunther, Richard. "Opening a Dialogue on Institutional Choice in Indonesia: Presidential, Parliamentary and Semipresidential Systems". In *Crafting Indonesian Democracy*, edited by R. William Liddle, pp. 149–78. Bandung: Mizan, 2001.

Habir, Ahmad D. "Conglomerates: All in the Family?". In *Indonesia Beyond Soeharto: Polity, Economy, Society, Transition*, edited by Donald K. Emmerson, pp. 168–204. Armonk and London: M.E. Sharpe, 1999.

Hadad, Toriq. "Mengapa ABRI-Golkar?". In *ABRI Punya Golkar?*, edited by Santoso, pp. 69–74. Jakarta: Institut Studi Arus Informasi, 1996.

Hamid, Syarwan. "Kepemimpinan ABRI dalam Perspektif Sejarah". In *Visi ABRI Menatap Masa Depan*, edited by Djoko Subroto, pp. 125–47. Magelang: Gadjah Mada University Press, 1997.

Harvey, Barbara S. "Diplomacy and Armed Struggle in the Indonesian National Revolution: Choice and Constraint in a Comparative Perspective". In *Making Indonesia: Essays in Honor of George McT. Kahin*, edited by Daniel S. Lev and Ruth MvVey, pp. 66–80. Ithaca, New York: Cornell University, 1996.

Hasan, Noorhaidi. "Faith and Politics: The Rise of the Laskar Jihad in the Era of Transition in Indonesia". *Indonesia* 73 (2002): 145–69.

Haseman, John. "Indonesian Military Reform: More Than a Human Rights Issue". In *Southeast Asian Affairs 2006*, pp. 111–28. Singapore: Institute of Southeast Asian Studies, 2006.

Hatley, Barbara. "Constructions of 'Tradition' in New Order Indonesian Theatre". In *Culture and Society in New Order Indonesia*, edited by Virginia Matheson Hooker, pp. 48–69. Oxford, Singapore and New York: Oxford University Press, 1993.

Hefner, Robert W. "Islamization and Democratization in Indonesia". In *Islam in an Era of Nation-States: Politics and Religious Renewal in Muslim Southeast Asia*, edited by Robert W. Hefner and Patricia Horvatich, pp. 75–128. Honolulu: University of Hawai'i Press, 1997.

———. "Civic Pluralism Denied? The New Media and *Jihadi* Violence in Indonesia". In *New Media in the Muslim World: The Emerging Public Sphere*, edited by Dale F. Eickelman and Jon W. Anderson, pp. 158–79. Bloomington and Indianapolis: Indiana University Press, 2003.

Heginbotham, Eric. "The Fall and Rise of Navies in East Asia: Military Organizations, Domestic Politics, and Grand Strategy". *International Security* 27, no. 2 (2002): 86–125.

Herd, Graeme P. and Tom Tracy. "Democratic Civil-Military Relations in Bosnia and Herzegovina: A New Paradigm for Protectorates?". *Armed Forces and Society* 32, no. 4, (2006): 549–65.

Hill, Hal and Jamie Mackie. "Introduction". In *Indonesia's New Order: The Dynamics of Socio-Economic Transformation*, edited by Hal Hill, pp. xxii–xxxv. St. Leonards: Allen & Unwin, 1994.

Holsti, O.R. "Of Chasms and Convergences: Attitudes and Beliefs of Civilians and Military Elites at the Start of a New Millennium". In *Soldiers and Civilians: The*

*Civil-Military Gap and American National Security*, edited by Peter D. Feaver and Richard H. Kohn, pp. 15–99. Cambridge: MIT Press, 2001.

Honna, Jun. "Military Ideology in Response to Democratic Pressure During the Late Suharto Era: Political and Institutional Contexts". In *Violence and the State in Suharto's Indonesia*, edited by Benedict R. O'G. Anderson, pp. 54–89. Southeast Asia Program Publications. Ithaca, New York: Cornell University, 2001.

Horowitz, Donald L. "The Draft Laws on Indonesian Political Parties, Elections, and Legislative Bodies: An Analysis". In *Crafting Indonesian Democracy*, edited by R. William Liddle, pp. 137–48. Bandung: Mizan, 2001.

Huntington, Samuel P. "Reforming Civil-Military Relations". In *Civil-Military Relations and Democracy*, edited by Larry Diamond and Marc F. Plattner, pp. 3–11. London and Baltimore: Johns Hopkins University Press, 1996.

Intan, Benyamin Fleming. "'Public Religion' and the Pancasila-based State of Indonesia: A Normative Argument within a Christian-Muslim Dialogue (1945–1998)". Ph.D. dissertation, Boston College, 2004.

International Foundation for Electoral Systems (IFES). "Results from Wave XIII Tracking Surveys". 23 June 2004. Cited as IFES 2004*a*.

———. "Results from Wave XV Tracking Surveys". 4 August 2004. Cited as IFES 2004*b*.

Jenkins, David. "Suharto Digs In With His All-Crony Cabinet". In *The Last Days of Suharto*, edited by Edward Aspinall, Herb Feith, and Gerry van Klinken, pp. 31–33. Clayton: Monash Asia Institute, 1999.

Jun, Jinsok. "South Korea: Consolidating Democratic Civilian Control". In *Coercion and Governance: The Declining Political Role of the Military in Asia*, edited by Muthiah Alagappa, pp. 121–42. Stanford: Stanford University Press, 2001.

Kadir, Suzaina. "Contested Visions of State and Society in Indonesian Islam: The Nahdlatul Ulama in Persepective". In *Indonesia in Transition: Social Aspects of Reformasi and Crisis*, edited by Chris Manning and Peter van Diermen, pp. 319–35. Singapore: Institute of Southeast Asian Studies, 2000.

Kahin, Audrey R. "Introduction". In *Regional Dynamics of the Indonesian Revolution: Unity from Diversity*, edited by Audrey R. Kahin, pp. 1–20. Honolulu: University of Hawaii Press, 1982.

Kammen, Douglas. "The Trouble with Normal: The Indonesian Military, Paramilitaries and the Final Solution in East Timor". In *Violence and the State in Suharto's Indonesia*, edited by Benedict R. O'G. Anderson, pp. 156–88. Southeast Asia Program Publications. Ithaca, New York: Cornell University, 2001.

King, Blair Andrew. "Empowering the Presidency: Interests and Perceptions in Indonesia's Constitutional Reforms, 1999–2002". Ph.D. dissertation, The Ohio State University, 2004.

Klinken, Gerry van. "Clash of Interests". *Inside Indonesia* 46, March 1996.

Koonings, Kees and Dirk Kruit. "Military Politics and the Mission of Nation Building". In *Political Armies: The Military and Nation Building in the Age of*

*Democracy*, edited by Kees Koonings and Dirk Kruit, pp. 9–34. London and New York: Zed Books, 2002.

Koonings, Kees. "Political Orientations and Factionalism in the Brazilian Armed Forces, 1964–85". In *The Soldier and the State in South America: Essays in Civil-Military Relations*, edited by Patricio Silva, pp. 127–50. New York: Palgrave, 2001.

Kroef, Justus M. van der. "Instability in Indonesia". *Far Eastern Survey* 26, no. 4 (1957): 49–54.

Langenberg, Michael van. "The New Order State: Language, Ideology, Hegemony". In *State and Civil Society in Indonesia*, edited by Arief Budiman, pp. 121–50. Monash Papers on Asia no. 22. Clayton: Monash University, 1990.

Lasswell, Harold D. "The Garrison State". *American Journal of Sociology* 46, (January 1941): 455–68.

Leclerc, Jacques. "Amir Sjarifuddin, Between the State and the Revolution". In *Indonesian Political Biography: In Search of Cross-Cultural Understanding*, edited by Angus McIntryre, pp. 1–42. Monash Papers on Southeast Asia no. 28. Clayton: Monash University, 1993.

Lev, Daniel S. "On the Fall of the Parliamentary System". In *Democracy in Indonesia: 1950s and 1990s*, edited by David Bourchier and John Legge, pp. 39–42. Monash Papers on Southeast Asia no. 31. Clayton: Monash University, 1994.

Liddle, R. William. "*Media Dakwah* Scripturalism: One Form of Islamic Political Thought and Action in New Order Indonesia". In *Toward a New Paradigm: Recent Developments in Indonesian Islamic Thought*, edited by Mark R. Woodward, pp. 323–56. Tempe: Arizona State University, Program for Southeast Asian Studies, 1996.

———. "Indonesia's Unexpected Failure of Leadership". In *The Politics of Post-Soeharto Indonesia*, edited by Adam Schwarz and Jonathan Paris, pp. 16–39. New York: Council on Foreign Relations Press, 1999. Cited as Liddle 1999*a*.

———. "Regime: The New Order". In *Indonesia Beyond Soeharto: Polity, Economy, Society, Transition*, edited by Donald K. Emmerson, pp. 39–70. Armonk and London: M.E. Sharpe, 1999. Cited as Liddle 1999*b*.

———. "Indonesia's Democratic Opening". *Government and Opposition* 34, no. 1 (1999): 94–116. Cited as Liddle 1999*c*.

———. "Indonesia's Army Remains a Closed Corporate Group". *Jakarta Post*, 3 June 2003.

Limbagau, Daud. "Keterlibatan TNI dalam Perdagangan di Sulawesi Selatan dari Masa Revolusi Sampai Tahun 1970-an". In *Dunia Militer di Indonesia: Keberadaan dan Peran Militer di Sulawesi*, edited by Edward L. Poelinggomang and Suriadi Mappangara, pp. 321–44. Yogyakarta: Gadjah Mada University Press, 2000.

Lo, Chih-cheng. "Taiwan: The Remaining Challenges". In *Coercion and Governance: The Declining Political Role of the Military in Asia*, edited by Muthiah Alagappa, pp. 143–64. Stanford: Stanford University Press, 2001.

Luckham, Robin. "Democratic Strategies for Security in Transition and Conflict". In *Governing Insecurity: Democratic Control of Military and Security Establishments in Transitional Democracies*, edited by Gavin Cawthra and Robin Luckham, pp. 3–28. London and New York: Zed Books, 2003.

MacIntyre, Andrew. "Political Institutions and Economic Crisis in Thailand and Indonesia". In *Politics of the Asian Economic Crisis*, edited by T.J. Pempel, pp. 143–62. Ithaca, New York: Cornell University Press, 1999.

Mackie, Jamie. "Inevitable or Avoidable? Interpretations of the Collapse of Parliamentary Democracy". In *Democracy in Indonesia: 1950s and 1990s*, edited by David Bourchier and John Legge, pp. 26–38. Monash Papers on Southeast Asia no. 31. Clayton: Monash University, 1994.

Malley, Michael S. "Indonesia in 2001: Restoring Stability in Jakarta". *Asian Survey* 42, no. 1 (2002): 124–32.

———. "New Rules, Old Structures and the Limits of Democratic Decentralisation". In *Local Power and Politics in Indonesia: Decentralisation and Democratisation*, edited by Edward Aspinall and Greg Fealy, pp. 102–16. Singapore: Institute of Southeast Asian Studies, 2003.

Mandan, Arief Mudatsir. "H.M. Subchan Z.E. — Sang Maestro: Politisi Intelektual dari Kalangan NU Modern". In *Subchan Z.E.: Sang Maestro, Politisi Intelektual dari Kalangan NU Modern*, edited by Arief Mudatsir Mandan, pp. 19–102. Jakarta: Pustaka Indonesia Satu, 2001.

Maulidin, "Peta Koalisi PKB". In *Pro-Kontra Partai Kebangkitan Bangsa*, edited by Munid Huda Muhammad, pp. 23–28. Jakarta: Fatma Press, 1998.

McBeth, John. "Shadow Play". *Far Eastern Economic Review*, 23 July 1998. Cited as McBeth 1998*a*.

———. "Twilight Zone". *Far Eastern Economic Review*, 16 April 1998. Cited as McBeth 1998*b*.

———. "Political Update". In *Post-Soeharto Indonesia: Renewal or Chaos?*, edited by Geoff Forrester, pp. 21–32. Singapore: Institute of Southeast Asian Studies, 1999.

———. "Wahid's Coming Clash". *Far Eastern Economic Review*, 3 February 2000.

McCargo, Duncan. "Introduction — Behind the Slogans: Unpacking Patani Merdeka". In *Rethinking Thailand's Southern Violence*, edited by Duncan McCargo, pp. 3–10. Singapore: NUS Press, 2007.

McCulloch, Lesley. "Greed: The Silent Force of the Conflict in Aceh". Occasional Paper, 2003 <www.preventconflict.org/portal/main.greed/pdf> (accessed 5 December 2005).

McIntyre, Angus. "Middle Way Leadership in Indonesia: Sukarno and Abdurrahman Wahid Compared". In *Indonesia Today: Challenges of History*, edited by Grayson J. Lloyd and Shannon L. Smith, pp. 85–96. Singapore: Institute of Southeast Asian Studies, 2001.

McLeod, Ross. "Indonesia". In *East Asia in Crisis: From Being a Miracle to Needing One?*, edited by Ross McLeod and Ross Garnault, pp. 31–48. London: Routledge, 1998.

Mietzner, Marcus. "Between Pesantren and Palace: Nahdlatul Ulama and its Role in the Transition". In *The Fall of Soeharto*, edited by Geoff Forrester and R.J. May, pp. 179–99. Bathurst: Crawford House Publishing, 1998.

———. "Nationalism and Islamic Politics: Political Islam in the Post-Soeharto Era". In *Reformasi: Crisis and Change in Indonesia*, edited by Arief Budiman, Barbara Hatley, and Damien Kingsbury, pp. 173–200. Clayton: Monash Asia Institute, 1999. Cited as Mietzner 1999*a*.

———. "Nahdlatul Ulama and the 1999 General Election in Indonesia". In *Pemilu: The 1999 Indonesian Election*, edited by Susan Blackburn, pp. 73–86. Annual Lecture Series no. 22. Clayton: Monash Asia Institute, 1999. Cited as Mietzner 1999*b*.

———. "From Soeharto to Habibie: The Indonesian Armed Forces and Political Islam during the Transition". In *Post-Soeharto Indonesia: Renewal or Chaos?*, edited by Geoff Forrester, pp. 65–104. Singapore: Institute of Southeast Asian Studies, 1999. Cited as Mietzner 1999*c*.

———. "Personal Triumph and Political Turmoil: Abdurrahman and Indonesia's Struggle for Reform". In *The Presidency of Abdurrahman Wahid: An Assessment after the First Year*, edited by Damien Kingsbury, pp. 15–32. Annual Lecture Series no. 23. Clayton: Monash Asia Institute, 2001.

———. "Politics of Engagement: The Indonesian Armed Forces, Islamic Extremism, and the 'War on Terror'". *Brown Journal of World Affairs* 9, no. 1 (2002): 71–84.

———. "Business as Usual? The Indonesian Armed Forces and Local Politics in the Post-Soeharto Era". In *Local Power and Politics in Indonesia: Decentralisation and Democratisation*, edited by Edward Aspinall and Greg Fealy, pp. 245–58. Singapore: Institute of Southeast Asian Studies, 2003.

———. "Local Democracy". *Inside Indonesia* 85 (2005): 17–18.

———. "Opportunities, Pitfalls of RI's New Democracy". *Jakarta Post*, 16 October 2006.

Morfit, Michael. "Staying on the Road to Helsinki: Why the Aceh Agreement was Possible in August 2005". Paper Prepared for the International Conference on "Building Permanent Peace in Aceh: One Year after the Helsinki Accord", sponsored by the Indonesian Council for World Affairs, 14 August 2006.

Moskos, Charles C., John A. Williams, and David R. Segal. "Armed Forces after the Cold War". In *The Postmodern Military: Armed Forces after the Cold War*, edited by Charles C. Moskos, John A. Williams, and David R. Segal, pp. 1–13. New York: Oxford University Press, 2000.

Mujani, Saiful. "Analisis Parpol: PKS, Tantangan Baru Politik Indonesia". *Media Indonesia*, 28 July 2005.

Muradi. "Pembelian Panser dan Kontrol DPR". *Pikiran Rakyat*, 21 September 2006.

National Democratic Institute for International Affairs (NDI). "The People's Voice: Presidential Politics and Voter Perspectives in Indonesia". Report on a Series of

Focus Groups Conducted during May in Seven Indonesian Provinces Ahead of the July 2004 Presidential Elections, June 2004.

Pereira, Derwin. "A General and an Intellectual". *Straits Times*, 21 October 2004.

Philip, George. "Military Governments: Continuity and Change in Twentieth-Century South America". In *The Soldier and the State in South America: Essays in Civil-Military Relations*, edited by Patricio Silva, pp. 71–86. New York: Palgrave, 2001.

Pion-Berlin, David. "Introduction". In *Civil-Military Relations in Latin America: New Analytical Perspectives*, edited by David Pion-Berlin, pp. 1–35. Chapel Hill and London: University of North Carolina Press, 2001.

Platzdasch, Bernhard. "Islamic Reaction to a Female President". In *Indonesia in Transition: Social Aspects of Reformasi and Crisis*, edited by Chris Manning and Peter van Diermen, pp. 336–49. Singapore: Institute of Southeast Asian Studies, 2000.

Rais, Amien. "Emil Salim dan Duet Soeharto-Habibie". *Republika*, 25 February 1998.

Ramage, Douglas. "A Reformed Indonesia". *Australian Financial Review*, 12 October 2007.

Razak, Imanuddin. "Retired Officers in Cabinet: Assets or Liabilities?". *Jakarta Post*, 28 October 2004.

Robinson, Geoffrey. "Indonesia: On a New Course?". In *Coercion and Governance: The Declining Political Role of the Military in Asia*, edited by Muthiah Alagappa, pp. 226–56. Stanford: Stanford University Press, 2001.

———. "The Fruitless Search for a Smoking Gun: Tracing the Origins of Violence in East Timor". In *Roots of Violence in Indonesia*, edited by Freek Colombijn and J. Thomas Lindblad, pp. 243–76. Singapore: Institute of Southeast Asian Studies, 2002.

Robison, Richard. "What Sort of Democracy? Predatory and Neo-Liberal Agendas in Indonesia". In *Globalization and Democratization in Asia: The Construction of Identity*, edited by Catherina Kinnvall and Kristina Jönsson, pp. 92–113. London and New York: Routledge, 2002.

Said, Salim. "Presiden Abdurrahman Wahid dan TNI: Bulan Madu yang Singkat". In *Militer Indonesia dan Politik: Dulu, Kini dan Kelak*, pp. 333–64. Jakarta: Pustaka Sinar Harapan, 2001.

Samson, Allan A. "Conceptions of Politics, Power and Ideology in Contemporary Indonesian Islam". In *Political Power and Communications in Indonesia*, edited by Karl D. Jackson and Lucian W. Pye, pp. 196–228. Berkeley, Los Angeles and London: University of California Press, 1978.

Samudavanija, Chai-Anan. "Old Soldiers Never Die, They Are Just Bypassed: The Military, Bureaucracy, and Globalisation". In *Political Change in Thailand: Democracy and Participation*, edited by Kevin Hewison, pp. 42–57. London and New York: Routledge, 1997.

Sasono, Adi. "ICMI Itu Dari Menteri Sampai Sri Bintang, Kok". In *Mereka Bicara Tentang ICMI: Sorotan 5 Tahun Perjalanan ICMI*, edited by Lukman Hakiem, Tamsil Linrung and Mahmud F. Rakasima, pp. 25–35. Jakarta: Penerbit Amanah Putra Nusantara, 1995.

Schulze, Kirsten E. "Laskar Jihad and the Conflict in Ambon". *Brown Journal of World Affairs* 9, no. 1 (2002): 57–70.

Schwarz, Adam. "Hunting for Scapegoats in Indonesia". *Wall Street Journal*, 3 February 1998.

Shiraishi, Takashi. "The Indonesian Military in Politics". In *The Politics of Post-Suharto Indonesia*, edited by Adam Schwarz and Jonathan Paris, pp. 73–86. New York: Council on Foreign Relations Press, 1999.

Silva, Patricio. "The Soldier and the State in South America: Introduction". In *The Soldier and the State in South America: Essays in Civil-Military Relations*, edited by Patricio Silva, pp. 1–12. New York: Palgrave, 2001.

Smith, Anthony L. "U.S.-Indonesia Relations: Searching for Cooperation in the War Against Terrorism". *Asia-Pacific Center for Security Studies* 2, no. 2 (2003): 1–4.

Smith, Chris. "Security Sector Reform: Development Breakthrough or Institutional Engineering?". *Conflict, Security, Development* 1, no. 1 (2001): 5–19.

Stepan, Alfred. "The New Professionalism of Internal Warfare and Military Role Expansion". In *Armies and Politics in Latin America*, edited by Abraham F. Lowenthal and J. Samuel Fitch, pp. 134–50. New York: Holmes and Meier, 1986.

———. "On the Tasks of a Democratic Opposition". In *The Global Resurgence of Democracy*, edited by Larry Diamond and Marc F. Platter, pp. 61–69. Baltimore: Johns Hopkins University Press, 1993.

Sudarsono, Juwono. "The Military and Indonesia's Democratic Prospects". Transcript of Remarks at The United States-Indonesia Society (USINDO) Open Forum, Washington, D.C., 11 April 2000.

———. "TNI Enlists in Nationwide War Against Poverty". *Jakarta Post*, 15 March 2007.

Sumarkidjo, Atmadji. "The Rise and Fall of the Generals". In *Indonesia Today: Challenges of History*, edited by Grayson J. Lloyd and Shannon L. Smith, pp. 136–45. Singapore: Institute of Southeast Asian Studies, 2001.

Sundhaussen, Ulf. "The Military: Structure, Procedures, and Effects on Indonesian Society". In *Political Power and Communications in Indonesia*, edited by Karl D. Jackson and Lucian W. Pye, pp. 45–81. Berkeley, Los Angeles and London: University of California Press, 1978.

Supriatma, A. Made Tony. "Politik Genealogis dan Cita-Cita 'ABRI diatas Semua Golongan'". In *ABRI Punya Golkar?*, edited by Santoso, pp. 158–69. Jakarta: Institut Studi Arus Informasi, 1996.

Susanto, Budi. "Siapa Cendekiawan Modern Indonesia?". In *ICMI: Kekuasaan dan Demokrasi*, edited by Ahmad Bahar, pp. 29–58. Yogyakarta: Pena Cendekia, 1995.

Syahnakri, Kiki. "Gus Dur versus Militer: Dikotomi Semu atau Riil?". Paper Presented at the book launch of "Gus Dur versus Militer". Jakarta, 10 March 2003.

Tesoro, Jose Manuel. "Forging a Shaky Alliance". *Asiaweek*, 6 February 1998.

————. "The Scapegoat?". *Asiaweek*, 3 March 2000.

Trinkunas, Harold A. "Crafting Civilian Control in Argentina and Venezuela". In *Civil-Military Relations in Latin America: New Analytical Perspectives*, edited by David Pion-Berlin, pp. 161–93. Chapel Hill and London: University of North Carolina Press, 2001.

Wahid, Abdurrahman. "ICMI Memang Sektarian, Kok". In *Mereka Bicara Tentang ICMI: Sorotan 5 Tahun Perjalanan ICMI*, edited by Lukman Hakiem, Tamsil Linrung and Mahmud F. Rakasima, pp. 15–23. Jakarta: Penerbit Amanah Putra Nusantara, 1995.

Waldman, Peter, Raphael Pura, and Marcus W. Brauchli. "Changes Put Soeharto on Outside, Looking In". *Asian Wall Street Journal*, 25 May 1998.

Walters, Patrick. "The Indonesian Armed Forces in the Post-Soeharto Era". In *Post-Soeharto Indonesia: Renewal or Chaos?*, edited by Geoff Forrester, pp. 59–64. Singapore: Institute of Southeast Asian Studies, 1999.

Weatherbee, Donald. "Indonesia: Political Drift and State Decay". *Brown Journal of World Affairs* 9, no. 1 (2002): 23–34.

Wilson, Ian. "From Criminal to Contractor: Free-Market Racketeering and the Struggle for Control Over Jakarta's Streets". *AsiaView* (December 2005): 1–2. Cited as Wilson 2005*a*.

Wrighter, Selina. "Questions of Judgement: The New Constitutional Court Combines Law and Politics". *Inside Indonesia* 81 (2005).

Young, Ken. "Local and National Influences in the Violence of 1965". In *The Indonesian Killings 1965–1966: Studies from Java and Bali*, edted by Robert Cribb, pp. 63–100. Centre of Southeast Asian Studies. Clayton: Monash University, 1990.

————. "The Crisis: Contexts and Prospects". In *The Fall of Soeharto*, edited by Geoff Forrester and Ron May, pp. 104–29. Bathurst: Crawford House Publishing, 1999.

## B. Books, Monographs and Other Publications

'Ulum, Bahrul. *"Bodohnya NU" Apa "NU Dibodohi"? Jejak Langkah NU Era Reformasi: Menguji Khittah, Meneropong Paradigma Politik*. Yogyakarta: PW IPNU Jawa Tengah — Lembaga Pers dan Penerbitan, 2002.

Abd. Rohim Ghazali, *Yusril Ihza Mahendra — Sosok Politisi Muda Muslim: Pandangan dan Harapan tentang Indonesia Masa Depan*. Jakarta: RajaGrafindo Persada, 1999.

Abdillah, Masykuri. *Demokrasi di Persimpangan Makna: Respons Intelektual Muslim Indonesia terhadap Konsep Demokrasi (1966–1993)*. Yogyakarta: Tiara Wacana, 1999.

Abrahamson, Bengt. *Military Professionalism and Political Power*. Beverly Hills: Sage, 1972.

Aguero, Felipe. *Soldiers, Civilians, and Democracy: Post-Franco Spain in Comparative Perspective*. Baltimore: Johns Hopkins University Press, 1995.

Aleana, Badrun. *NU, Kritisisme dan Pergeseran Makna Aswaja*. Yogyakarta: Tiara Wacana, 2000.

Alfian. *Muhammadiyah: The Political Behaviour of a Muslim Modernist Organization under Dutch Colonialism*. Yogyakarta: Gadjah Mada University Press, 1989.

Al-Zastrouw Ng. *Gus Dur, Siapa Sih Sampeyan?: Tafsir Teritik atas Tindakan dan Pernyataan Gus Dur*. Jakarta: Penerbit Erlangga, 1999.

Anam, Choirul. *2 Tahun PKB Jawa Timur*. Surabaya: DPW PKB Jawa Timur, 2000.

Anam, Choirul. *Gerak Langkah Pemuda Ansor: Sebuah Percikan Sejarah Kelahiran*. Surabaya: AULA, 1990.

Ananta, Aris, Evi Nurvidya Arifin, and Leo Suryadinanta. *Indonesian Electoral Behaviour*. Singapore: Institute of Southeast Asian Studies, 2004.

Anderson, Benedict R. O'G. *Language and Power: Exploring Political Cultures in Indonesia*. Ithaca and London: Cornell University Press, 1990.

Andreski, Stanislav. *Military Organization and Society*. London: Routledge & Paul, 1954.

Anwar, M. Syafi'i. *Pemikiran dan Aksi Islam Indonesia: Sebuah Kajian tentang Cendekiawan Muslim Orde Baru*. Jakarta: Paramadina, 1995.

Anwar, Dewi Fortuna et al. *Gus Dur versus Militer: Studi Tentang Hubungan Sipil-Militer di Era Transisi*. Jakarta: Gramedia and Pusat Penelitian Politik — Lembaga Ilmu Pengetahuan, 2002.

Aritonang, Diro. *Runtuhnya Rezim Soeharto: Rekaman Perjuangan Mahasiswa Indonesia 1998*. Bandung: Pustaka Hidayah, 1999.

Asmawi. *PKB: Jendela Politik Gus Dur*. Yogyakarta: Titian Ilahi Press, 1999.

Aspinall, Edward. "The Helsinki Agreement: A More Promising Basis for Peace in Aceh?". Policy Studies 20. Washington: East West Center Washington, 2005. Cited as Aspinall 2005*b*.

―――. *Opposing Suharto: Compromise, Resistance and Regime Change in Indonesia*. Stanford: Stanford University Press, 2005. Cited as Aspinall 2005*c*.

Aspinall, Edward and Harold Crouch. "The Aceh Peace Process: Why It Failed". Policy Studies 1. Washington: East West Center Washington, 2003.

Awwas, Irfan Suryahardi. *Dakwah dan Jihad Abubakar Ba'asyir*. Yogyakarta: Wihdah Press, 2003.

Azra, Azyumardi. *Islam Substantif: Agar Umat Islam Tidak Jadi Buih*. Bandung: Mizan, 2000.

Barton, Greg. *Gus Dur: The Authorized Biography of Abdurrahman Wahid*. Jakarta and Singapore: Equinox Publishing, 2002.

Basalim, Umar. *Pro-Kontra Piagam Jakarta di Era Reformasi*. Jakarta: Pustaka Indonesia Satu, 2002.

Butabutar, Benny S. *Soeyono: Bukan Puntung Rokok*. Jakarta: Ridma Foundation 2003.

Bertrand, Jacques. *Nationalism and Ethnic Conflict in Indonesia.* Cambridge: Cambridge University Press, 2004.

Betz, David. "Comparing Frameworks of Parliamentary Oversight: Poland, Hungary, Russia, Ukraine". Working Paper Series no. 115. Geneva: Centre for the Democratic Control of Armed Forces, 2003.

Bhakti, Ikrar Nusa et al. *Tentara Yang Gelisah: Hasil Penelitian Yipika tentang Posisi ABRI dalam Gerakan Reformasi.* Bandung: Mizan, 1999.

Boland, J.B. *The Struggle of Islam in Modern Indonesia.* The Hague: Martinus Nijhoff, 1982.

Bourchier, David and Vedi R. Hadiz, eds. *Indonesian Politics and Society: A Reader.* London and New York: RoutledgeCurzon, 2003.

Born, Hans, ed. *Parliamentary Oversight of the Security Sector: Principles, Mechanisms and Practices.* Geneva and Belgrade: Centre for the Democratic Control of Armed Forces, 2003.

Born, Hans, Marina Caparina, and Karl Haltiner. "Models of Democratic Control of the Armed Forces: A Multi-Country Study Comparing 'Good Practices' of Democratic Control". Working Paper Series no. 47. Geneva: Centre for the Democratic Control of Armed Forces, 2002.

Bresnan, John. *Managing Indonesia: The Modern Political Economy.* New York: Columbia University Press, 1993.

Brooks, Risa. *Political-Military Relations and the Stability of Arab Regimes.* Adelphi Papers 324. New York: International Institute for Strategic Studies, 1998.

Bruinessen, Martin van. *NU: Tradisi, Relasi-relasi Kuasa, Pencarian Wacana Baru.* Yogyakarta: LkiS, 1994.

Bubalo, Anthony and Greg Fealy. "Between the Local and the Global: Islamism, the Middle East, and Indonesia". Analysis Paper 9. Washington: Brookings Institution, 2005.

Cahyono, Heru. *Soemitro dan Peristiwa 15 Januari '74.* Jakarta: Pustaka Sinar Harapan, 1998.

Callaghan, Jean and Jürgen Kuhlmann. "Measuring the Civil-Military Complex: Tools and Some Empirical Evidence". Working Paper Series no. 46. Geneva: Centre for the Democratic Control of Armed Forces, 2002.

Case, William. *Politics in Southeast Asia: Democracy or Less.* Richmond: Curzon, 2002.

Chauvel, Richard and Ikrar Nusa Bhakti. "The Papua Conflict: Jakarta's Perceptions and Policies". Policy Studies 5. Washington: East-West Center Washington, 2004.

Chauvel, Richard. *Nationalists, Soldiers and Separatists: The Ambonese Islands from Colonialism to Revolt, 1880–1950.* Verhandelingen van het Koninklijk Instituut voor Taal, -Land-en Volkenkunde 143. Leiden: KITLV Press, 1990.

Cheema, Pervaiz Iqbal. *The Armed Forces of Pakistan.* Crows Nest: Allen & Unwin, 2002.

Choi, Nankyung. "Local Elections and Democracy in Indonesia: The Case of the Riau Archipelago". IDSS Working Paper 91. Singapore: Institute of Defence and Strategic Studies, 2005.

Choirie, Effendy. *PKB — Politik Jalan Tengah NU: Eksperimentasi Pemikiran Islam Inklusif dan Gerakan Kebangsaan Pasca Kembali ke Khittah 1926*. Jakarta: Pustaka Ciganjur, 2002.

Chrisnandi, Yuddy. *Reformasi TNI: Perspektif Baru Hubungan Sipil-Militer di Indonesia*. Jakarta: LP3ES, 2005.

Cribb, Robert. *Gangsters and Revolutionaries: The Jakarta People's Militia and the Indonesian Revolution, 1945–1949*. Sydney: Allen & Unwin, 1991.

Crouch, Harold. *The Army and Politics in Indonesia*. Revised Edition. Ithaca and London: Cornell University Press, 1988.

Daman, H. Rozikin. *Membidik NU: Dilema Percaturan Politik NU Pasca Khittah*. Yogyakarta: Gama Media, 2001.

Damanik, Ali Said. *Fenomena Partai Keadilan: Transformasi 20 Tahun Gerakan Tarbiyah di Indonesia*. Bandung: Penerbit Teraju, 2002.

Danopoulos, Costas. "Civil-Military Relations in the Post-Communist World". Working Paper Series no. 38. Geneva: Centre for the Democratic Control of Armed Forces, 2002.

Davies, Matt. *Indonesia's War Over Aceh: Last Stand at Mecca's Porch*. London and New York: Routledge, 2006.

Decalo, Samuel. *Civil-Military Relations in Africa*. Gainesville and London: FAP Books, 1998.

Denny J.A. *Democratization from Below: Protest Events and Regime Change in Indonesia*. Jakarta: Sinar Harapan, 2006.

Desch, Michael C. *Civilian Control of the Military: The Changing Security Environment*. Baltimore: Johns Hopkins University Press, 1999.

Dhakidae, Daniel. *Cendekiawan dan Kekuasaan dalam Negara Orde Baru*. Jakarta: Gramedia Pustaka Utama, 2003.

Dhofier, Zamakhsyari. *The Pesantren Tradition: The Role of the Kyai in the Maintenance of Traditional Islam in Java*. Tempe: Arizona State University, 1990.

Dijk, Kees van. *A Country in Despair: Indonesia Between 1997 and 2000*. Verhandelingen van het Koninklijk Insituut voor Taal, -Land-en Volkenkunde no. 186. Leiden: KITLV Press, 2001.

Dirdjosanjoto, Pradjarta. *Memilihara Umat: Kiai Pesantren — Kiai Langgar di Jawa*. Yogyakarta: LkiS, 1999.

Effendy, Bahtiar. *Islam dan Negara: Transformasi Pemikiran dan Praktik Politik Islam di Indonesia*. Jakarta: Paramadina, 1998.

———. *Islam and the State in Indonesia*. Singapore: Institute of Southeast Asian Studies, 2003.

Eklöf, Stefan. *Indonesian Politics in Crisis: The Long Fall of Suharto, 1996–98*. Copenhagen: Nias Press, 1999.

Elson, R.E. *Suharto: A Political Biography*. Cambridge: Cambridge University Press, 2001.

Fananie, Zainuddin and Atiqa Sabardila. *Sumber Konflik Masyarakat Muslim Muhammadiyah — NU: Perspektif Keberterimaan Tahlil*. Surakarta: Muhammadiyah University Press, 2000.

Feaver, Peter D. *Armed Servants: Agency, Oversight, and Civil-Military Relations.* Cambridge, Massachusetts, and London: Harvard University Press, 2003.

Fedorov, Yuri E. "Democratic Transformation of the Security Sector in Russia: A Sad Saga of Failure". Working Paper Series no. 98. Geneva: Centre for the Democratic Control of Armed Forces, 2002.

Feith, Herbert. *The Indonesian Elections of 1955.* Ithaca, New York: Cornell Modern Indonesia Project, 1957.

————. *The Decline of Constitutional Democracy in Indonesia.* Ithaca, New York: Cornell University Press, 1962.

Finer, Samuel. *The Man on Horseback: The Role of the Military in Politics.* With a new introduction by Jay Stanley. New Brunswick and London: Transaction Publishers, 2002.

Freedom House. *Freedom in the World 2006: The Annual Survey of Political Rights and Civil Liberties,* edited by Aili Piano, Arch Puddington, and Mark Y. Rosenberg. New York and Washington, D.C.: Freedom House and Rowman & Littlefield Publishers, 2006.

Friend, Theodore. *Indonesian Destinies.* Cambridge and London: The Belknap Press of Harvard University Press, 2003.

Furkon, Aay Muhammad. *Partai Keadilan Sejahtera: Ideologi dan Praksis Politik Kaum Muda Muslim Indonesia Kontemporer, Refleksi Masyarakat Baru.* Bandung, 2004.

Geertz, Clifford. *The Religion of Java,* Glencoe: Free Press, 1960.

Greenlees, Don and Robert Garran. *Deliverance: The Inside Story of East Timor's Fight for Freedom.* Crows Nest: Allen & Unwin, 2002.

Gunawan, Hendra. *M. Natsir dan Darul Islam: Studi Kasus Aceh dan Sulawesi Selatan Tahun 1953–1956.* Jakarta: Media Da'wah, 2000.

Habibie, Bacharuddin Jusuf. *Detik-Detik Yang Menentukan: Jalan Panjang Indonesia Menuju Demokrasi.* Jakarta: THC Mandiri, 2006.

Hadikoemoro, Soekismo. *Tragedi Trisakti 12 Mei 1998.* Jakarta: Penerbit Universitas Trisakti, 1999.

Hafidz, Tatik S. *Fading Away? The Political Role of the Army in Indonesia's Transition to Democracy, 1998–2001.* Singapore: Institute of Defence and Strategic Studies, 2006.

Haidar, M. Ali. *Nahdlatul Ulama dan Islam di Indonesia: Pendekatan Fikih dalam Politik.* Jakarta: Gramedia, 1994.

Hamid, Syarwan. *Dari Orde Baru ke Orde Reformasi.* Jakarta: Mutiara Sumber Widya, 1999.

Haramain, Malik. *Gus Dur, Militer dan Politik.* Yogyakarta: LkiS, 2004.

Haris, Syamsuddin. *PPP dan Politik Orde Baru.* Jakarta: Gramedia, 1991.

Hefner, Robert W. *Civil Islam: Muslims and Democratization in Indonesia.* Princeton and Oxford: Princeton University Press, 2000.

Hidayatullah, Syarif. *Intelektualisme dalam Perspektif Neo-Modernisme.* Yogyakarta: Tiara Wacana, 2000.

Hill, David T. *The Press in New Order Indonesia*. Perth: University of Western Australia Press, 1994.

Hindley, Donald. *The Communist Party of Indonesia, 1951–1963*. Berkeley and Los Angeles: University of California Press, 1964.

Hisyam, Usamah. *Feisal Tanjung: Terbaik Untuk Rakyat Terbaik Bagi ABRI*. Jakarta: Dharmapena Nusantara, 1999.

———. *SBY: Sang Demokrat*. Jakarta: Dharmapena, 2004.

Hodgson, Marshall. *The Venture of Islam: Conscience and History in a World Civilization*. Chicago: University of Chicago Press, 1974.

Holsti, O.R. "A Widening Gap Between the Military and Society? Some Evidence, 1976–1996". Working Paper no. 13. Olin Institute, Harvard University, 1997.

Honna, Jun. *Military Politics and Democratization in Indonesia*. London: RoutledgeCurzon, 2003.

Huber, Konrad. "The HDC in Aceh: Promises and Pitfalls of NGO Mediation and Implementation". Policy Studies 10. Washington: East-West Center Washington, 2004.

Human Rights Watch. *Too High a Price: The Human Rights Cost of the Indonesian Military's Economic Activities*. New York: Human Rights Watch, 2006.

Hunter, Wendy. *State and Soldier in Latin America: Redefining the Military's Role in Argentina, Brazil, and Chile*. Washington, D.C.: United States Institute of Peace, 1996.

Huntington, Samuel P. *The Soldier and the State: The Theory and Politics of Civil-Military Relations*. Cambridge: Harvard University Press, 1957.

Huser, Herbert C. *Argentine Civil-Military Relations: From Alfonsin to Menem*. Washington, D.C.: National Defense University Press, 2002.

Idris, Kemal. *Bertarung dalam Revolusi*. Jakarta: Pustaka Sinar Harapan, 1997.

International Crisis Group. "Indonesia: Violence and Radical Muslims". Indonesia Briefing. Brussels, 2001.

———. "Al-Qaeda in Southeast Asia: The Case of the 'Ngukri Network' in Indonesia". Indonesia Briefing. Brussels, 2002.

———. "Indonesia Backgrounder: A Guide to the 2004 Elections". Asia Report no. 71. Brussels, 2003.

———. "Recycling Militants in Indonesia: Darul Islam and the Australian Embassy Bombing". Asia Report no. 92. Brussels, 2005.

———. "Papua: Answers to Frequently Asked Questions". Asia Briefing no. 53. Brussels, 2006.

———. "Jihadism in Indonesia: Poso on the Edge". Asia Report no. 127. Brussels, 2007. Cited as International Crisis Group 2007*a*.

———. "Indonesia: Jemaah Islamiyah's Current Status". Asia Briefing no. 62. Brussels, 2007. Cited as International Crisis Group 2007*b*.

Iskandar, Muhaimin. *Manajemen Komunikasi Partai Kebangkitan Bangsa dalam Pemilu 1999*. Jakarta: Pustaka Bumi Selamat, 2001.

Isre, M. Saleh, ed. *Tabayun Gus Dur: Pribumisasi Islam, Hak Minoritas, Reformasi Kultural.* Yogyakarta: LkiS, 1998.

Iswandi. *Bisnis Militer Orde Baru: Keterlibatan ABRI dalam Bidang Ekonomi dan Pengaruhnya Terhadap Pembentukan Rezim Otoriter.* Bandung: Remaja Rosdakarya, 1998.

Jaiz, H. Hartono Ahmad. *Kekeliruan Logika Amien Rais.* Jakarta: Darul Falah, 1998.

————. *Menyakiti Hati Umat: Bahaya Pemikiran Gus Dur II.* Jakarta: Pustaka Al-Kautsar, 2000.

Jamhuri, Said. *Gus Dur: Pemimpin NU Kharismatik Kontroversial.* Jakarta: Yayasan Lembaga Pemelihara Moral Masyarakat, 1998.

Jenkins, David. *Suharto and his Generals: Indonesian Military Politics 1975–1983.* Monograph Series (Publication no. 64). Ithaca, New York: Cornell Modern Indonesia Project, 1984.

Jenkins, Gareth. "Context and Circumstance: The Turkish Military and Politics". Adelphi Paper 337. New York: International Institute for Strategic Studies, 2001.

Kadi, Saurip. *TNI-AD. Dahulu, Sekarang, dan Masa Depan.* Jakarta: Grafiti, 2000.

Kahin, Audrey R. and George McT. Kahin. *Subversion as Foreign Policy: The Secret Eisenhower and Dulles Debacle in Indonesia.* Seattle and London: University of Washington Press, 1995.

Kahin, George McTurnan. *Nationalism and Revolution in Indonesia.* Ithaca, New York: Cornell University Press, 1952.

Kammen, Douglas and Siddharth Chandra. *A Tour of Duty: Changing Patterns of Military Politics in Indonesia in the 1990s.* Ithaca, New York: Cornell Modern Indonesia Project, 1999.

Karim, M. Rusli. *Negara dan Peminggiran Islam Politik: Suatu Kajian Mengenai Implikasi Kebijakan Pembangunan Bagi Keberadaan "Islam Politik" di Indonesia Era 1970an dan 1980an.* Yogyakarta: Tiara Wacana, 1999.

Kasdi, Aminuddin. *Kaum Merah Menjarah: Aksi Sepihak PKI/BTI di Jawa Timur 1960–1965.* Yogyakarta: Jendela, 2001.

Kingsbury, Damien. *Power Politics and the Indonesian Military.* London and New York: RoutledgeCurzon, 2003.

————. *Peace in Aceh: A Personal Account of the Helsinki Peace Process.* Jakarta: Equinox Publishing, 2006.

Kurdi, Mustafa and A. Yani Wahid. *Susilo Bambang Yudhoyono Dalam 5 Hari Mandat Maklumat.* Jakarta: Aksara Kurnia, 2003.

Kustiati, Retno and Fenty Effendi. *Agum Gumelar — Jenderal Bersenjata Nurani.* Jakarta: Pustaka Sinar Harapan, 2004.

Legge, J.D. *Central Authority and Regional Autonomy in Indonesia: A Study in Local Administration.* Ithaca, New York: Cornell University Press, 1961.

————. *Sukarno: A Political Biography*. Second edition. Sydney, Wellington, London and Boston: Allen & Unwin, 1990.

Lembaga Kajian dan Pengembangan Informasi Media. *Kiprah PBNU 2000–2001: Analisa dan Evaluasi Pemberitaan tentang Kepeminpinan K.H. A. Hasyim Muzadi*. Malang: elKapim, 2001.

Lembaga Survei Indonesia. "Prospek Kepemimpinan Nasional: Evaluasi Publik Atas Kinerja Presiden dan Wakil Presiden — Survei Nasional Nov. 2004 — Oktober 2006". Jakarta, 11 October 2006.

Lev, Daniel S. *The Transition to Guided Democracy: Indonesian Politics, 1957–1959*. Ithaca, New York: Cornell Modern Indonesia Project, 1966.

Liddle, R. William. *Pemilu-Pemilu Orde Baru*. Jakarta: LP3ES, 1992.

Linz, Juan J. and Alfred Stepan. *Problems of Democratic Transition and Consolidation: Southern Europe, South America, and Post-Communist Europe*. Baltimore and London: Johns Hopkins University Press, 1996.

Lowry, Robert. *The Armed Forces of Indonesia*. St Leonards: Allen & Unwin, 1996.

Luhulima, James. *Hari-Hari Terpanjang: Menjelang Mundurnya Presiden Soeharto dan Beberapa Peristiwa Terkait*. Jakarta: Penerbit Kompas, 2001.

Luwarso, Lukas, ed. *Jakarta Crackdown*. Jakarta: Alliance of Independent Journalists (AJI), Asian Forum for Human Rights and Development (FORUM-ASIA) and Institute for the Studies on Free Flow of Information (ISAI), 1997.

Ma'shum, Saifullah. *Karisma Ulama: Kehidupan Ringkas 26 Tokoh NU*. Bandung: Mizan, 1998.

Maarif, Ahmad Syafii. *Islam dan Politik: Teori Belah Bambu — Masa Demokrasi Terpimpin (1959–1965)*. Jakarta: Gema Insani Press, 1996.

Mackie, J.A.C. *Konfrontasi: The Indonesia-Malaysia Dispute 1963–1966*. London, New York, and Melbourne: Oxford University Press, 1974.

Madjid, Nurcholish. *Islam: Kemodernan dan Keindonesiaan*. Bandung, 1987.

Maliki, Zainuddin. *Birokrasi Militer dan Partai Politik dalam Negara Transisi*. Yogyakarta: Galang Press, 2000.

Mangunwijaya, Y.B. *Tentara dan Kaum Bersenjata*. Jakarta: Penerbit Erlangga, 1999.

McDonald, Hamish. *Suharto's Indonesia*. Blackburn: Fontana Books, 1980.

McFarling, Ian. *The Dual Function of the Indonesian Armed Forces: Military Politics in Indonesia*. Canberra: Australian Defence Studies Centre, 1996.

McGibbon, Rodd. "Pitfalls of Papua: Understanding the Conflict and its Place in Australia-Indonesia Relations". Lowy Institute Paper 13. Double Bay: Lowy Institute for International Policy, 2006.

McGregor, Katharine. *History in Uniform: Military Ideology and the Construction of Indonesia's Past*. Singapore: Asian Studies Association of Australia and NUS Press, 2007.

McIntyre, Angus. *The Indonesian Presidency: The Shift From Personal Toward Constitutional Rule.* Lanham, Boulder, New York, Toronto, and Oxford: Rowman & Littlefield, 2005.

Migdal, Joel. *Strong Societies and Weak States: State-Society Relations and State Capabilities in the Third World.* Princeton: Princeton University Press, 1988.

Mrazek, Rudolf. *Sjahrir: Politics and Exile in Indonesia.* Ithaca, New York: Cornell University, 1994.

Mujani, Saiful. "Mengkonsolidasikan Demokrasi Indonesia: Refleksi Satu Windu Reformasi". Jakarta: Lembaga Survei Indonesia, 2006.

Muhaimin, Yahya A. *Perkembangan Militer dalam Politik di Indonesia 1945–1966.* Cetakan Kedua. Yogyakarta: Gadjah Mada University Press, 2002.

Muhammad, Munib Huda, ed. *Kiai Menggugat, Gus Dur Menjawab: Sebuah Pergumulan Wacana dan Transformasi.* Jakarta: Fatma Press, 1998.

Najib, Muhammad. *Amien Rais — Sang Demokrat: Dilengkapi Catatan Harian Sampai Jatuhnya Soeharto.* Jakarta: Gema Insani, 1998.

Nashir, Haedar. *Perilaku Politik Elit Muhammadiyah.* Yogyakarta: Tarawang, 2000.

Nasution, A.H. *Menudju Tentera Rakjat: Hasil Karya dan Pikiran Djenderal Dr. A.H. Nasution.* Jakarta: Jajasan Penerbit Minang, 1963.

Nasution, Adnan Buyung. *The Aspiration for Constitutional Government in Indonesia: A Socio-Legal Study of the Indonesian Konstituante, 1956–1959.* Jakarta: Pustaka Sinar Harapan, 1992.

Noer, Deliar. *Gerakan Moderen Islam di Indonesia 1900–1942.* Cetakan Ketujuh, Jakarta: LP3ES, 1994.

Nordlinger, Eric A. *Soldiers in Politics: Military Coups and Governments.* Prentice-Hall, 1977.

Nwagwu, 'Emeka. *Taming the Tiger: Civil-Military Relations Reform and the Search for Political Stability in Nigeria.* Lanham, New York, and Oxford: University Press of America, 2002.

Nyman, Mikaela. *Democratising Indonesia: The Challenges of Civil Society in the Era of Reformasi.* Copenhagen: Nias Press, 2006.

O'Donnell, Guillermo and Philippe C. Schmitter, eds. *Transitions from Authoritarian Rule: Tentative Conclusions from Uncertain Democracies.* Baltimore: Johns Hopkins University Press, 1986.

Olle, John. "The Campaign Against 'Heresy': State and Society in Negotiation in Indonesia". Paper Presented to the 16th Biennial Conference of the Asian Studies Association of Australia, Wollongong, 26–29 June 2006.

O'Rourke, Kevin. *Reformasi: The Struggle for Power in Post-Soeharto Indonesia.* Crows Nest: Allen & Unwin, 2002.

Page, Edward. *Political Authority and Bureaucratic Power.* Second edition. New York and London: Harvester Wheatsheave, 1992.

Pangaribuan, Robinson. *The Indonesian State Secretariat, 1945–1993.* Jakarta: Pustaka Sinar Harapan, 1996.

Parianom, Bambang and Dondy Ariesdanto, eds. *Megawati and Islam: Polemik Gender dalam Persaingan Politik.* Surabaya: Antar Surya Jaya bersama LSK, 1999.

Pattiradjawane, Rene L. *Trisakti Mendobrak Tirani Orde Baru: Fakta dan Kesaksian Berdarah 12 Mei 1998.* Jakarta: Gramedia dan Yayasan Trisakti, 1999.

Perlmutter, Amos. *The Military and Politics in Modern Times.* New Haven: Yale University Press, 1977.

Purdey, Jemma. *Anti-Chinese Violence in Indonesia, 1996–1999.* Singapore: Asian Studies Association of Australia and Singapore University Press, 2006.

Pour, Julius. *Jakarta Semasa Lengser Keprabon: 100 Hari Menjelang Peralihan Kekuasaan.* Jakarta: Gramedia, 1998.

Purnomo, Alip. *FPI Disalahpahami.* Jakarta: Penerbit Mediatama Indonesia, 2003.

Pusat Studi dan Pengembangan Informasi. *Tanjung Priok Berdarah: Tanggung Jawab Siapa? Kumpulan Data dan Fakta.* Jakarta: Gema Insani Press, 1998.

Rabasa, Angel and John Haseman. *The Military and Democracy in Indonesia: Challenges, Politics, and Power.* Santa Monica: RAND, 2002.

Rais, Amien and Zarman Syah. *Bulan Madu NU-Muhammadiyah.* Jakarta: Madjid Press Solo, 1999.

Ramage, Douglas. *Politics in Indonesia: Democracy, Islam and the Ideology of Tolerance.* London and New York: Routledge, 1995.

Ricklefs, M.C. *Polarising Javanese Society: Islamic and Other Visions (c. 1830–1930).* Singapore: NUS Press, 2007.

Rieffel, Lex and Jaleswari Pramodhawardani. *Out of Business and On Budget: The Challenge of Military Financing in Indonesia.* Washington: Brookings Institution Press and U.S. Indonesian Society, 2007.

Rinakit, Sukardi. *The Indonesian Military After the New Order.* Singapore: Nias Press and Institute of Southeast Asian Studies, 2005.

Robison, Richard and Vedi R. Hadiz. *Reorganising Power in Indonesia: The Politics of Oligarchy in an Age of Markets.* London and New York: RoutledgeCurzon, 2004.

Robison, Richard. *Indonesia: The Rise of Capital.* Sydney: Allen & Unwin, 1986.

Roestandi, Achmad. *Masuk Letnan, Keluar Letnan: Sisi Jenaka Pengemban Dwi Fungsi ABRI.* Yogyakarta: Kreasi Wacana, 2003.

Roosa, John. *Pretext for Mass Murder. The September 30ᵗʰ Movement and Suharto's Coup d'Etat in Indonesia.* Madison: The University of Wisconsin Press, 2006.

Russet, Bruce M. and Elizabeth C. Hanson. *Interest and Ideology: The Foreign Policy Beliefs of American Businessmen.* San Francisco: Freeman, 1975.

Said, Salim. *Genesis of Power: General Sudirman and the Indonesian Military in Politics, 1945–49.* Jakarta and Singapore: Pustaka Sinar Harapan and Institute of Southeast Asian Studies, 1992.

———. *Militer Indonesia dan Politik: Dulu, Kini dan Telak.* Jakarta: Pustaka Sinar Harapan, 2001.

Samego, Indria, et al. *Bila ABRI Berbisnis: Buku Pertama yang Menyingkap Data dan Kasus Penyimpangan dalam Praktik Bisnis Kalangan Militer.* Bandung: Mizan, 1998.

Satrawi, Hasibullah. "NU, Kontrak Jamiyah dan Bara Politik". *Media Indonesia,* 6 December 2004.

Schwarz, Adam. *A Nation in Waiting: Indonesia's Search for Stability.* Third Impression. Singapore: Talisman, 2004.

Sebastian, Leonard. *Realpolitik Ideology: Indonesia's Use of Military Force.* Singapore: Institute of Southeast Asian Studies, 2006.

Shambaugh, David. *Modernizing China's Military: Progress, Problems, and Prospects.* Berkeley, Los Angeles, and London: University of California Press, 2002.

Sherlock, Stephen. "Struggling to Change: The Indonesian Parliament in an Era of Reformasi — A Report on the Structure and Operation of the Dewan Perwakilan Rakyat (DPR)". Canberra: Centre for Democratic Institutions, Research School of Social Sciences, Australian National University, 2003.

Sidel, John. *Riots, Pogroms, Jihad: Religious Violence in Indonesia.* Singapore: NUS Press, 2007.

Simanjuntak, P.N.H. *Kabinet-Kabinet Republik Indonesia Dari Awal Kemerdekaan Sampai Reformasi.* Jakarta: Penerbit Djambatan, 2003.

Simanungkalit, Salomo. *Indonesia dalam Krisis, 1997–2002.* Jakarta: Penerbit Buku Kompas, 2002.

Sinansari Ecip, S. *Kronologi Situasi Penggulingan Soeharto: Reportase Jurnalistik 72 Jam yang Menegangkan.* Bandung: Mizan, 1998.

Sinansari Ecip, S. *Siapa "Dalang" Prabowo.* Bandung: Mizan, 1999.

Srengenge, Sitok, ed. *Surat Rakyat Tentang Pemilu 1997.* Jakarta: Institut Studi Arus Informasi, 1998.

Sriwidodo, Rayani. *Jenderal dari Pesantren Legok: 80 Tahun Achmad Tirtosudiro.* Jakarta: Pustaka Jaya, 2002.

Stepan, Alfred. *Rethinking Military Politics: Brazil and the Southern Cone.* Princeton: Princeton University Press, 1988.

Suharsono. *Cemerlangnya Poros Tengah: Terpilihnya Gusdur Terobosan Besar Elite Politik Islam.* Jakarta: Prenial Press, 1999.

Sujuthi, Mahmud. *Politik Tarekat: Hubungan Agama, Negara dan Masyarakat.* Yogyakarta: Galang Press, 2001.

Sukamto. *Kepemimpinan Kiai Dalam Pesantren.* Jakarta: LP3ES, 1999.

Sukma, Rizal and Edi Prasetyono. "Security Sector Reform in Indonesia: The Military and the Police". A Study Report Prepared for the Conflict Research Unit of the Netherlands Institute of International Relations. Clingendael: Netherlands Institute of International Relations, 2002.

Sukmawati, Carmelia. *Subagyo HS: KASAD dari Piyungan.* Jakarta: Aksara Karuna, 2004.

Sulistyo, Hermawan. *Lawan: Jejak-Jejak Jalanan di Balik Kejatuhan Soeharto.* Jakarta: Pensil 324, 2002.

Sundhaussen, Ulf. *The Road to Power: Indonesian Military Politics, 1945–1967.* Kuala Lumpur: Oxford University Press, 1982.

Supriyatmono, Hendri. *Nasution, Dwifungsi ABRI dan Kontribusi ke Arah Reformasi Politik.* Surakarta and Yogyakarta: Sebelas Maret University Press, 1994.

Suryadinata, Leo. *Elections and Politics in Indonesia.* Singapore: Institute of Southeast Asian Studies, 2002.

————. *Military Ascendancy and Political Culture: A Study of Indonesia's Golkar.* Monographs in International Studies, Southeast Asia Series no. 85. Athens, Ohio: Ohio University Center for International Studies, 1989.

Suryohadiprojo, Sayidiman. *Mengabdi Negara Sebagai Prajurit TNI: Sebuah Otobiografi.* Jakarta: Pustaka Sinar Harapan, 1997.

Sutipyo R. and Asmawi. *PAN: Titian Amien Rais Menuju Istana.* Yogyakarta: Titian Ilahi Press, 1999.

Syaifullah. *Gerak Politik Muhammadiyah dalam Masyumi.* Jakarta: Pustaka Utama Grafiti, 1997.

Taylor, Alastair M. *Indonesian Independence and the United Nations.* London: Stevens & Sons Limited, 1960.

Thaba, Abdul Azis. *Islam dan Negara dalam Politik Orde Baru.* Jakarta: Gema Insani Press, 1996.

Thoyibi, Mohammad. *Menentang Arogansi Kekuasaan: Kasus Mega Bintang.* Solo, 1999.

Tim Propatria. *Reformasi Sektor Keamanan Indonesia.* Jakarta: Propatria, 2004.

Tjokropanolo. *Jenderal Soedirman: Pemimpin Pendobrak Terakhir Penjajahan di Indonesia: Kisah Seorang Pengawal.* Jakarta, 1993.

Tsebelis, George. *Veto Players: How Political Institutions Work.* Princeton: Princeton University Press, 2002.

Turmudi, Endang. *Perselingkuhan Kiai dan Kekuasaan.* Yogyakarta: LKiS, 2004.

Uhlin, Anders. *Indonesia and the "Third Wave of Democratization": The Indonesian Pro-Democracy Movement in a Changing World.* Richmond: Curzon, 1997.

Uhrowi, Zaim. *Mohammad Amien Rais: Memimpin dengan Hati Nurani — An Authorized Biography.* Teraju, Jakarta: The Amien Rais Center, 2004.

Vatikiotis, Michael R.J. *Indonesian Politics Under Suharto: Order, Development and Pressure for Change.* London and New York: Routledge, 1994.

Wahid, Marzuki, Abd. Moqsith Ghazali, and Suwendi. *Dinamika NU: Perjalanan Sosial dari Muktamar Cipasung (1994) ke Muktamar Kediri (1999).* Jakarta: Kompas dan Lakpesdam-NU, 1999.

Wahid, Nusron. *Membongkar Hegemoni NU: Di Balik Independensi PMII (1966–1972).* Jakarta: Bina Rena Pariwara, 2000.

Wahyudi, Andi. *Muhammadiyah Dalam Gonjang-Ganjing Politik: Telaah Kepemimpinan Muhammadiyah Era 1990-an.* Yogyakarta: Media Pressindo, 1999.

Wandelt, Ingo. "Die Neuen Militärzivilisten". *Watch Indonesia! Information und Analyse.* Berlin: Watch Indonesia!, 2004.

Ward, Ken. *The Foundation of the Partai Muslimin Indonesia.* Ithaca, New York: Cornell Modern Indonesia Project, 1970.

———. *The 1971 Election in Indonesia: An East Java Case Study.* Melbourne: Centre of Southeast Asian Studies, Monash University, 1974.

Weeks, Gregory. *The Military and Politics in Postauthoritarian Chile.* Tuscaloosa and London: The University of Alabama Press, 2003.

Wilson, Ian. "The Changing Contours of Organized Violence in Post New Order Indonesia". Working Paper no. 118. Perth: Asia Research Center, Murdoch University, 2005. Cited as Wilson 2005*b*.

Wiranto. *Bersaksi di Tengah Badai: Dari Catatan Wiranto, Jenderal Purnawirawan.* Jakarta: IDe Indonesia, 2003.

———. "Strive for Peace in East Timor: The Events in East Timor Prior to and Post August 30, 1999 Popular Consultation Period". No place, no date.

———. "Redefinisi, Reposisi dan Reaktualisasi Peran ABRI Dalam Kehidupan Bangsa: Merupakan Pokok-pokok Kebijakan Menhankam/Pangab yang Melandasi Reformasi Internal ABRI". Edisi II, *Widya Dharma*, Majalah Sesko ABRI, Edisi Khusus 1999, pp. 81-106. Bandung: Sesko ABRI, 1999.

Yulianto, Arif. *Hubungan Sipil Militer di Indonesia Pasca Orba ditengah Pusaran Demokrasi.* Jakarta: Rajawali Pers, 2002.

Zada, Khamama, ed. *Neraca Gus Dur di Panggung Kekuasaan.* Jakarta: Lakpesdam, 2002.

Zayd, Nashr Hamid Abu. *Imam Syafi'i: Moderatisme, Eklektisisme, Arabisme.* Yogyakarta, 1997.

Zen, Kivlan. *Konflik dan Integrasi TNI-AD.* Jakarta: Institute for Policy Studies, 2004.

Zon, Fadli. *Politik Huru-Hara Mei 1998.* Jakarta: Institute for Policy Studies, 2004.

## C. Official and Other Primary Sources

"Analisis Perkembangan Sosial-Politik Menjelang Pemilu 1997 dan SU-MPR 1998". Unpublished Paper.

Departemen Pertahanan. "Daftar Inventarisasi Badan Usaha Yayasan/Koperasi di Bawah TNI AL/TNI AD/TNI AU/Mabes TNI (Sebelum Diaudit), Berdasarkan Surat Panglima TNI Nomor: B/3385-05/15/06/Spers Tanggal 28 September 2005".

Dinas Sejarah TNI Angkatan Darat. *Sejarah TNI AD 1945–1973, Jilid 8: Sendi-Sendi Perjuangan TNI-AD.* Bandung, 1979.

East Timor Action Network/US. "Indonesian Activists Urge U.S. Congress To Block Military Training". Press Release, 7 October 2002.

Ernst & Young. "Yayasan Kartika Eka Paksi: Strategic Review Report Phase II". Jakarta, 2001.

Forum Aliansi OKP/LSM/MAHASISWA. "Seruan Suksesi Damai dan Terbuka Untuk Keselamatan dan Masa Depan Rakyat dan Bangsa Indonesia". Jakarta, 5 February 1998.

Fraksi Kebangkitan Bangsa. *Menegakkan Kebenaran: Kesaksian Fraksi Kebangkitan Bangsa DPR RI Tentang Dana Yanatera Bulog dan Bantuan Sultan Brunei*. Jakarta: FKB DPR RI, 2001.

Kodam VII/Diponegoro. *Sedjarah Tentara Nasional Indonesia — Komando Daerah Militer VII Diponegoro (Djawa Tengah)*. No date.

Mabes ABRI. "ABRI dan Reformasi. Pokok-Pokok Pikiran ABRI Tentang Reformasi Menuju Pencapaian Cita-Cita Nasional". Jakarta, June 1998.

Markas Besar Tentara Nasional Indonesia. "Ceremah Kepala Staf Teritorial TNI Pada Workshop Pusat Studi Demokrasi dan HAM tentang: Penyelenggaraan Fungsi Teritorial Sebagai Fungsi Pemerintahan". Surabaya, 14 November 2001. Cited as Markas Tentara Nasional Republik Indonesia 2001*a*.

———. "Implementasi Paradigma Baru TNI Dalam Berbagai Keadaan Mutakhir". Jakarta, 2001. Cited as Markas Tentara Nasional Republik Indonesia 2001*b*.

———. "Penyelenggaraan Fungsi Teritorial Sebagai Fungsi Pemerintahan". Jakarta, October 2001. Cited as Markas Tentara Nasional Republik Indonesia 2001*c*.

Nasution, A.H. "Angkatan Bersendjata — Orde Baru — Sapta Marga — Undang-Undang 1945 (Coaching Ketua Madjelis Permusjarawatan Rakjat Sementara Dr. A.H. Nasution kepada para Instruktur Akademi Angkatan Bersendjata Repubik Indonesia di Magelang pada achir September 1966)". In *Ketetapan-Ketetapan M.P.R.S.: Tongggak Konstutusionil Orde Baru*, published by A.H. Nasution, pp. 21–85. Jakarta: Pantjuran Tudjuh, 1966.

Panitia Deklarasi Partai Kebangkitan Bangsa. *Menyambut Deklarasi Partai Kebangkitan Bangsa*. Jakarta, 1998.

Partai Persatuan Pembangunan. *Rancangan Materi Muktamar ke VI*. Jakarta: Partai Persatuan Pembangunan, 2007.

Perkasa. "Rakyat Perintahkan Dwi Tunggal Gus Dur-Wiranto Selamatkan Bangsa Indonesia". Jakarta, 19 October 1999.

Pengurus Besar Nahdlatul Ulama. "Surat Tugas No. 925/A.II.03/6/1998". Jakarta, 22 June 1998.

———. "Keputusan Rapat Pleno PBNU ke-IV". Jakarta, 24 July 1998.

"Peraturan Presiden Republik Indonesia Nomor ... Tahun ... Tentang Badan Pengelola Bisinis Tentara Nasional Indonesia". No place, no date.

Pimpinan Pusat Muhammadiyah. "Surat Keputusan Pimipinan Pusat Muhammadiyah Nomor: 53/KEP/I.0/B/2007, Tentang Tanfidz Keputusan Tanwir Muhammadiyah Tahun 1428 H/2007 M". Yogyakarta, 17 May 2007.

———. "Surat Keputusan Pimpinan Pusat Muhammadiyah Nomor 149/KEP/I.0/B/2006, Tentang: Kebijakan Pimpinan Pusat Muhammadiyah Mengenai Konsolidasi Organisasi dan Amal Usaha Muhammadiyah". Yogyakarta, 1 December 2006.

PWNU Jawa Timur. "Laporan PWNU Jawa Timur Pada Konbes NU di Lombok". Mataram, 19 November 1997.

Rais Aam PBNU. "Khutbah Iftitah Rais Aam Pengurus Besar Nahdlatul Ulama Pada Pembukaan Munas dan Konbes NU". Bagu, 17 November 1997.

Sekretariat Negara Republik Indonesia. *Risalah Sidang Badan Penyelidik Usaha-Usaha Persiapan Kemerdekaan Indonesia (BPUPKI): Panitia Persiapan Kemerdekaan Indonesia (PPKI), 28 Mei 1945–22 Agustus 1945.* Jakarta: Sekretariat Negara Republik Indonesia, 1995.

Seskoad. *Doktrin Perdjuangan TNI-AD: Tri Ubaya Cakti.* Jakarta: Angkatan Darat, 1966.

Sudarto, Tyasno. "Tekad Moral Jenderal Tyasno Sudarto — Kembali Diterima". Yogyakarta, 2000.

# INDEX

**A**

*abangan*, 69
  view on inclusion of *syariat*, 73
Abd Rohim Ghazali, 336
Abdul Hakim Garuda Nusantara, 171
Abdullah Faqih, 357
Abdurrahman Saleh, 316
Abdurrahman Wahid, 4, 83
  armed forces, approach towards, 242
  attacks on Amien Rais, 152
  defending constituency interests,
    254
  fall of, 222–25
  fear for regime backlash, 178
  Gus Dur, 93
  health of, 182
  hostility towards Muhammadiyah's
    chairman, 152
  intra-Islamic conflicts during
    Presidency of, 260–80
  isolation from political reality, 223
  leadership style, erratic, 261
  marginalization, 335–37
  opposition to state support for
    Islamization, 85
  political talks with Siti Hardiyanti,
    153
  support for orderly political
    transition process, 174
  support for Suharto regime, 150

TNI under, 211–25
  end of reform, 217–22
  reform and military factionalism,
    212–17
  threat of emergency, 222–25
ABRI (*Angkatan Bersenjata Republik
  Indonesia*), 64
  crisis of declining regime, 109–10
  damage to reputation, 123
  support for calls for Suharto's
    resignation, 130
  headquarters, 55
  view of itself, 39
Abu Bakar Ba'asyir, 88–89
  leader of Jemaah Islamiyah, 281
Abu Dujana, 350
Abu Hasan, 284
Abdul Kahfi, 274
Aceh
  civil-military relations in, 302–04
  peace agreement, *see* Aceh Peace
    Agreement
  resolution of conflict, 329
  Yudhoyono's reconciliatory policies,
    294
Aceh Peace Agreement, 298–304
  efforts of Jusuf Kalla, 299
  Helsinki Accord, 300–02
Aceh-Nias Rehabilitation and
  Reconstruction Agency, 301

Achmad Tirtosudiro, 166, 188
Adang Daradjatun, 347
Adi Sasono, 82, 163–66
  meeting with Amien Rais, 172
Adnan Arsal, 359
Adnan Buyung Nasution, 171
Agum Gumelar, 63, 117, 124, 234
Agus Widjojo, 104, 202
Agus Wirahadikusumah, 67, 104, 246,
  315
Ahmad Anas Yahya, 285
Ahmad Sumargono, 276
Akabri
  officers graduating from, 54
Akbar Tandjung, 179, 265
  elections (2004), 278
al-Baghdadi, 71
al-Ghazali, 71
al-Jamiyatul al-Wasyliah, 72
al-Mawardi, 71
Alagappa, Muthiah, 20, 57
Ali Murtopo, 88, 141
Ali Yafie, 178
Alwi Shihab, 357
Ambon, 227
  prevalence of Christianity, 74
Amien Rais, 2, 32, 93, 271
  address at public hearing at
    parliament, 131
  attempt to forge anti-regime
    alliance, 159
  cancellation of Jakarta rally, 179
  chairman of Muhammadiyah, 84,
    256
  challenging Suharto, 156–63
  criticism of regime, 158
  elections (2004), 273, 334
  intellectual leader of reform
    movement, 122
  marginalization, 335–37
  meeting with Adi Sasono, 172
  Partai Amanat Nasional (PAN), 256
  retirement from, 340

  pluralist outlook, 161
  resignation from ICMI, 85
  student movement, 160–63
  support of Muhammadiyah leaders,
    163
  transformation into key national
    figure, 157
Amir Shakib Arsalan, 72
Amir Sjarifuddin
  at enforcing civilian control, 39
Andi Widjajanto, 327
Anwar Haryono, 176
Arbi Sanit, 171
Argentina, 22
Arifin Djunaidi, 154
armed forces
  cash flow, reduced, 363
  change in societal perceptions of,
    59
  decline in influence, 61
  deep divisions, 41
  institutional autonomy, 40
  management of own affairs, 40
Armenia, 27
Artha Graha bank, 325
Asia-Pacific Economic Cooperation,
  378
Aspinall, Edward, 61
Association of Southeast Asian Nations
  (ASEAN), 378
Azahari Husin, 350
Azhar Basyir, 156
Azyumardi Azra, 259

B
Babinsa (Bintara Pembina Desa), 65
Badan Intelijen Negara (BIN), 243
Bahtiar Effendy, 259
Bali bombings, 281, 350
Bandung Institute of Technology
  (ITB), 143
Bangladesh, 12
Bank Duta, 58

Bank Muamalat, 177
Barton, Greg, 147
Belarus, 27
Benny Murdani, 60, 141
BIA
    military intelligence agency, 115
Bibit Waluyo, 216
Bimantoro (General), 222
BKSPPI (*Badan Kerjasama Pondok Pesantren Indonesia*), 142
Bob Hasan, 161
Bondan Gunawan, 218
Brawijaya
    military unit, 99
Bresnan, John, 83
Bruneigate, 265
Buddhism, 70
*bughot*, 266
Bulgaria, 27
Buloggate, 265
bureaucracy, 6
Burma, 12
business elite, 53

**C**
Center for Strategic and International Studies (CSIS), 115
Central Axis
    end of, 262–65
Chaeruddin Ismail, 222–23
China
    orientation towards, 321
    global economic powerhouse, rise as, 378
Chinese conglomerates
    relations with Suharto's family, 63
Chinese entrepreneurs, 363
Choirul Anam
    PKB branch of East Java, 271
Christians
    prevalence in certain areas, 74
civil servants
    prohibition from joining political parties, 92
civil society
    engagement, 26
civil-military alliances
    elections (2004), 276–78
civil-military reforms, 26
civil-military relations, 2, 29
    Aceh, in, 302–04
    post-authoritarian, 381
    rejection of term, 38
    transitional, 382
civilian conflict, 373
    legacies, 68–91
    military reform, and, 240–43
civilian control, 5–8
    traditional theories on, 7
civilian defence community, 320
civilian groups
    emphasis on gaining representation, 86
civilianizing politics, 345–49
Clausewitz, Karl von, 46
companies
    established by military, 54
conglomerates
    military-owned, 9
Constitution
    rewriting of, 2
Constitutional Court (*Mahkamah Konstitusi*), 328, 330, 375
    function, 333
cooperatives
    military-owned, 9
Cottey, Andrew, 24
Cribb, Robert, 321
cultural Islam, 82
Czech Republic, 27

**D**
Darul Islam, 87–88, 283, 349, 359
    rebellion in West Java, 90, 281
Dawam Rahardjo, 165
Decalo, Samuel, 33

Dede Oetomo, 172
democratic control, 5–8
  concepts, 7
democratic governance
  quality of, 3
Democratic Party (*Partai Demokrat*),
  239
democratic politics, 373
democratic transitions, 2
  "hybrid" character, 361
department of religious affairs, 75
Desch, Michael, 16, 90, 241, 375
*Dewan Dakwah Islamiyah Indonesia*
  (DDII), 81, 90, 256
Dewi Fortuna Anwar, 210
Dhakidae, Daniel, 66
*Dharmais*, 58
Diamond, Larry, 33, 361
Dibyo Widodo, 108
Din Syamsuddin, 336–37, 340
Diponegoro
  military unit, 99
divisive dynamics, 57
Djadja Suparman, 105
Djamari Chaniago, 129
Djoko Mulono, 247
Djoko Santoso, 296
Djoko Suyanto, 297, 347
DPD (*Dewan Perwakilan Daerah*),
  358
DPR (*Dewan Perwakilan Rakyat*)
  removal of armed force from, 2
Dual Function, 46, 49, 52
  evolution, 63
  leading guideline, 56
  official termination of, 202
Dutch
  attack on Yogyakarta, 48
*Dwi Fungsi* (Dual Function), 38
  see Dual Function

**E**
East Timor

acquittal of officers indicted for
  violations, 321
Indonesia's exit from, 209–11
TNI's handling of, 206–08
Eastern Europe, 24
economic powers
  armed forces, 55
economy
  military intervention, 362
Edi Sudradjat, 141
Edmunds, Timothy, 24
Eka Tjipta Widyaya, 363
El Niño, 151
elections
  local (after 2005), 345–49
elections (1997)
  post-election landscape, 107–09
  traditionalist and modernist Islam
    diametrically opposed, 85
elections (1999)
  coalitions and conflicts, 257–60
  TNI, role of, 204–06
elections (2004), 232–35
  civil-military alliances, 276–78
elite politics, 82
elites
  military, *see* military elite
electoral mechanisms
  reforms, 333
emergency rule
  threat of, 222
Elson, Robert, 45
Emil Salim, 159
Endriartono Sutarto, 133, 220–21
  setting up of counter-terrorism
    intelligence, 351
  TNI commandership, 226
era of openness, 62
Estonia, 27
European Union, 28

**F**
Fachruddin, 156

facilitation, 53
Fadli Zon, 141
Fajrul Falaakh, 170, 186
Fauzi Bowo, 347–48
Fealy, Greg, 71
Feaver, Peter D., 10
Federspiel, Howard, 286
Feisal Tanjung, 103
    rejection of study by LIPI, 106
Feith, Herbert, 45, 49, 51
*fikih* discourse, 72
financial autonomy, 49
Finer, Samuel E., 8
Ford Foundation, 184
*Forum Kerja Indonesia* (Forki), 170
*Forum Komunikasi Putra-Putri
    Purnawirawan Indonesia* (FKPPI),
    233
Forster, Anthony, 24
*Forum Betawi Rempug* (FBR), 352
Free Aceh Movement, 248
    see also *Gerakan Aceh Merdeka* (GAM)
Freeport McMoRan, 364, 383
*Front Pembela Islam* (FPI), 282
*Front Pembela Kebenaran* (FPK), 267
Fuad Bawazier, 179
Fund for Peace, 383

**G**
Gadjah Mada University
    attack by security forces on, 123
Geertz, Clifford, 70
Georgia, 27
*Gerakan Aceh Merdeka* (GAM), 248
    Irwandi Yusuf, 302
*Gerakan Pembela Bangsa* (GPB), 265
    targeting of Muhammadiyah
        premises, 265
German Hoediarto, 317
Ginandjar Kartasasmita, 164
Goenawan Mohammad, 171
Golkar
    Akbar Tandjung, 265

appeal to secular and non-Muslim
    groups, 258
Sekber, 65
governance
    reduced military participation in,
        61
guerilla war
    subject of intensive debates, 41
guerilla warfare
    against Dutch, 38
Guided Democracy, 44, 82
    dismantling of political structures
        of, 79
    dissatisfaction, 50
    height of, 49
    imposition of, 77
Gus Dur, *see* Abdurrahman Wahid

**H**
Habibie, 4
    armed forces, approach to, 242
    ascension to presidency, 134
    lifting of restrictions on political
        parties, 253
    opposition against nomination of,
        114
    refusal to step down together with
        Suharto, 180
    rejection of ICMI's oppositional
        stand, 168
    supremacy, 199–201
    TNI, relations with, 196–99
Habibienomics, 164
Habieb Syarief Mohammad, 150
Hadi Utomo, 324
Hafidz Utsman, 185
*Hajj*
    pilgrimage to Mecca, 91
Hamengkubuwono IX, 42
Hamzah Haz, 234, 341
    elections (2004), 277
Harmoko, 107
Happy Bone Zulkarnaen, 248

Hari Sabarno, 305
Hartono (General), 103
    appointed Minister of Home
        Affairs, 122
Haryanto Dhanutirto, 167
Hasibuan, Albert, 285
Hasyim Asy'ari, 92, 148
Hasyim Muzadi, 264, 266, 337
    elections (2004), 271, 334
    offer of compensation to
        Muhammadiyah, 266
    general chairman of Nahdlatul
        Ulama, 335
Hatley, Barbara, 56
Hatta, Mohammad, 44
Hau Pei-tsun, 213
Hefner, Robert, 72, 112, 147
hegemony
    armed forces, 54
    competition for, 73–75
Helsinki Accord, 300–02
Hendropriyono, 89
Henk Ngantung, 348
Henry Dunant Centre, 229
Hidayat Nurwahid, 343
Hill, Hal, 51
Hinduism, 70
Hungary, 27
Huntington, Samuel, 13–14, 33
    performance dilemma, 19
Husein Umar, 172
Huser, Herbert C., 22


I
Ibn Jama'a, 71
Ibn Khaldun, 71
Ibnu Sutowo, 54
ICMI (*Ikatan Cendekiawan Muslim
    se-Indonesia*), 84, 163–69
    option of defending or
        overthrowing Suharto,
        166–68
Idham Chalid, 92

*ijtihad*
    promotion of modernists, 70–71
*Ikhwanul Muslimin* (Muslim
        Brotherhood), 267
Ikrar Nusa Bhakti, 305
Ilyas Ruchiat, 152, 154
Imam Utomo, 233
    re-election as governor, 273
Imron Hamzah, 173
independence
    TNI's role, 38–42
India
    orientation towards, 321
    global economic powerhouse, rise
        as, 378
Indonesian Communist Party (*Partai
        Komunis Indonesia*) (PKI), 50
Indonesian Institute of Sciences (LIPI)
    study by
        rejection by Feisal Tanjung, 106
Indonesian Working Group for
        Security Sector Reform, 325
Indonesians
    growing dissatisfaction, 62
Inkiriwang, Piet, 347
Intan, Benyamin Fleming, 286
intellectual reform movement, 82
inter-party cooperation, 345
International Crisis Group, 314, 359
International Monetary Fund (IMF),
    21
intra-civilian fragmentation, 3
intra-Islamic conflict
    during Wahid's presidency, 260–80
    stabilisation after 2004, 284
intra-military debate
    1997 elections, 101–02
    Golkar, on, 105
intra-systemic regime change, 137
Irwandi Yusuf, 302
Islamic democracy, 82
Islamic groups
    differences from secular groups, 86

divisions within, 272
electoral politics, 272–75
engagement in politics, 253
militant, 90
standing during Suharto crisis,
168–69
Islamic jurisprudence
study of, 72
Islamic leaders
elections (2004), 270–80
Islamic militancy, 86–91, 349–54
declining influence of militias, 352
Islamic parties
constituency interests paramount,
254
elections (1955), 74
formation after 1998, 252–60
Islamic politics
conflict and decline (1950s and
1960s), 75–78
post-Suharto period, 251–88
Islamic platform, 163
Islamic radicalism
military, and, 280–83
Islamic theology
call for depoliticization of, 82
Islamic youth organizations, 79
Islamist groups, *see* Islamic groups

**J**
J. Kristiadi, 142
Jafar Umar Thalib, 288
Jakarta Charter, 74, 342
abandoning, 341
attempts at re-introducing *syariat*
clause, 286
Jakarta Elections, 347–49
*Jaringan Pendidikan Pemilih untuk
Rakyat* (JPPR), 358
Jemaah Islamiyah, 88, 349
Bali bombings, 281
violent activities, 281
Jimly Assidiquie, 165

Jusuf Kalla, 262
Aceh peace agreement, role in,
299–300
Juwono Sudarsono, 213, 305, 311,
313
military reform, 306–09

**K**
Kahin, George McTurnan, 41, 64
Kammen, Douglas, 209
KAMMI (*Kesatuan Aksi Mahasiswa
Indonesia*), 257
Kartosuwirjo, 87
*kekaryaan*
doctrinal concept of, 52
*kekaryaan* positions, 66
Khin Nyunt, 20
*kiai*, 70
concern for rapid expansion of PKI,
79
definition, 91
dependence on subsidies from
bureaucracy, 149–50
fear outcome of economic crisis,
151
KISDI (*Komite Indonesia untuk
Solidaritas Dunia Islam*),
168–69
*kitab kuning*, 83
reservations on Wahid's ability to
lead, 263
responsibility for spiritual well being
of followers, 71
*kiai khas*, 357
Kiki Syahnakri, 217
Kirbiantoro (Major General), 274
*kitab kuning*, 71
KNIL (*Koninklijk Nederlandsch-Indisch
Leger*), 43, 64
*Kodam (Komando Daerah Militer)*, 65
*Kodim (Komando Distrik Militer)*, 65
*Komando Jihad*, 88
campaign in (1977), 90

*Komando Wilayah Pertahanan*, 55
Kopassus, 103
Kopkamtib, 93
*Koramil* (*Komando Rayon Militer*), 65
*Korem* (*Komando Resort Militer*), 65
Kostrad (Army Strategic Reserve), 50

**L**
Laksamana Sukardi, 262
Laskar Jihad, 282, 352
Lay, Cornelis, 247
LBH (*Lembaga Bantuan Hukum*), 186
Lee Teng-hui, 213
liberal democracy
    unsustainability, 45
Liddle, William, 153, 195
Liem Sioe Liong, 363
LKKNU (*Lembaga Kemaslahatan
    Keluarga Nahdlatul Ulama*), 170
local elections
    after 2005, 345
lower ranking personnel
    retirement packages, 55
Lowry, Robert, 53
Luckham, Robin, 21
Lukman Harun, 157
Lumintang, Johnny, 200, 243

**M**
Ma'aruf Amin, 255
Mackie, Jamie, 45, 51
Madinah Charter, 344
Mahfud M.D., 220
*Majelis Kepemimpinan Rakyat* (MKR),
    126
Malaysia, 50
Malik Fajar, 162, 179
Maluku
    communal violence, end of, 329
    martial law, 228
    religious conflict in, 263
Mandala airline, 325
Mardiyanto, 144, 233, 274

Mares, David R., 61
martial law
    Maluku, 228
Masyumi, 91
    destruction of, 78
    formation, 76
    regional uprisings, role in, 77
Mathlaul Anwar, 73
Matori Abdul Djalil, 212, 227, 255
    finalization of State Defence bill,
        305
    participation in MPR session to
        impeach Wahid, 271
*mazhab*, 70
    rejecting or adopting aspects of, 71
Medan
    violent demonstrations in, 125
media
    criticism from, 55
medieval Sunni jurisprudence
    commentaries, 71
Mega-Bintang movement, 107
Megawati Sukarnoputri, 2, 4, 102
    armed forces, approach towards,
        242
    elections (2004), loss in, 235
    failure to consolidate support base,
        261
    guarantee signed by leading
        politicians regarding her
        presidency, 271
    ideological shifts in society, 225–30
    mascot of armed forces, as a, 226
    public appearances with Amien
        Rais, 158
    relations with Generals, 225–35
    reluctance to join modernist
        Muslim figures, 183
    support for PPP leader Hamzah
        Haz, 271
Merapi, 47
Middle Way, 46–47
    development of, 48

militant Islamic groups, 90
military
claim to national leadership, 51
establishment of companies, 54
financial autonomy, 49
guardian of Pancasila, 51
participation in politics, increase in
certain times, 382
transitional states, 22–24
military budget
cut in, 48
military candidates
elections (after 2005), 345–47
military conservatives
sidelining of, 293–98
post-Ryamizard military elite,
296–98
military cultures, 322
institutional factors, 379–81
military elite
post-Ryamizard, 296–98
military engagement
areas, 8–12
economic sector, 9
institutional and organizational
autonomy, 9–10
participation in political
institutions, 8
socio-cultural sector, 11
military equipment
purchase from Russia and South
Korea, 378
military factionalism, 97–138
(1997) elections, 102–05
declining regime, in, 109
military intelligence, 20
military intervention, 8
analytical explanations, 13–19
typological models, 12–14
partipicant-ruler, 12
praetorian rule, 12
Military Justice Bill, 309–11
military professionalism, 14

military reforms
civilian conflict, and, 240–43
doctrinal and strategic shifts,
311–13
first generation, 320
issues, unresolved, 318
Juwono Sudarsono, 306–09
outdated territorial command
system, 314
military regimes
fall of, 19–22
international factors, 21
military self-financing activities
persistence of, 320
military-owned business, 9
militias
culture of violence, 208–09
Minahasa
prevalence of Christianity, 74
modernist Muslims
integration into regime, 84
modernists
Outer Islands, 71
promotion of *ijtihad*, 70–71
Monas Square, 263
mass demonstration at, 179
Morfit, Michael, 299
Moskos, Charles, 25
MPR (*Majelis Permusyawaratan
Rakyat*)
removal of armed forces from, 2
Muchdi Purwopranjono, 118
Muhaimin Iskandar, 176
Muhammad Ma'ruf, 104
Muhammad Najib, 170
Muhammad Natsir, 76
Muhammad Rizieq Syihab (Habib)
Chairman of radical FPI, 282
Muhammadiyah, 73, 81, 84
anti-corruption programmes, 357
challenging Suharto, 156–63
competition with Nahdlatul Ulama,
269–70

congress 2005, 336
de-escalation of conflict with
    Nahdlatul Ulama, 330,
    333–38
distancing itself from PAN, 338
entrance into politics, 256
premises targeted by PKB-affiliated
    militias, 265
MUI (*Majelis Ulama Indonesia*), 338
multinational associations, 28
Muslim activists
rising influence of, 60
Muslim community
declining tensions, 353
Muslim demonstrators
clash with troops at Tanjung Priok,
    89
Muslim groups, 34
challenges to democracy, 268–70
cooperation between, 80
divided against Suharto, 146–84
stabilization of civilian polity, 353
Yudhoyono's presidency, during,
    329–59
Muslim organizations, 50
interaction with other key
    non-regime groups, 147
Muslim politics
transitional civil-military relations,
    283–84
Muspida (*Musyawarah Pimpinan
    Daerah*), 315
M. Yusuf, 141

**N**
Nahdlatul Wathan, 73
Nahdlatul Ulama, 81, 83
anti-corruption programmes,
    357
call to ABRI to support reform
    process, 123
competition with Muhammadiyah,
    269–70

de-escalation of conflict with
    Muhammadiyah, 330, 333–38
effect of economic crisis, 151
Gus Dur and struggle for hegemony
    within, 153
merge into PPP, 80
policy shift during Suharto's decline,
    155
reconciliation with regime, 84
relations with Suharto regime,
    149–53
reluctance to support Guided
    Democracy, 78
role in Suharto's fall from power,
    148–56
role in Sukarno's political demise,
    79
traditionalist organization, 72
Nasakom, 92
Nasution, A.H., 43, 47
consolidation of leadership, 44
defeat of rebellion, 48–49
extra-constitutional powers, 48
participation of military in politics,
    47
National Council, 47
national logistics board, 52
National Security Act, 306–07
Nationhood Coalition (*Koalisi
    Kebangsaan*)
elections (2004), 279
North Atlantic Treaty Organization
    (NATO), 28, 377
*Negara Islam Indonesia* (NII), 87
*Negara Kesatuan Republik Indonesia*
    (NKRI), 228
New Order
attitudes towards, 80
indoctrination, 56
late, 59–63
TNI's participation in government,
    38
Noer Muis, 245

non-Muslim nationalists
view on inclusion of *syariat*, 73
Noorhaidi Hassan, 352
Noordin Mohammed Top, 350
Nurcholish Madjid, 8, 130, 175,
178
possible nominee in elections
(2004), 272
Nur Iskandar al-Barsany, 186
declaration on political opponents,
266
support for Abdurrahman Wahid,
267
Nur Mahmudi Ismail, 285
Nursyahbani Katjasungkana, 341

**O**
O'Rourke, Kevin, 207
October 17 Affair, 64
Oemarsono, 275
organizational autonomy, 55
Outer Islands
Masyumi, 77
modernists, 71

**P**
*Pancasila*
first principle of, 74
protection by military, 51
retention by Islamic groups, 254
Papua
Yudhoyono's reconciliatory policies,
294
paramilitary groups, 50
parliament
officers delegated to, 52
parliamentary democracy, 42–46
parliamentary oversight, 6
*Partai Amanat Nasional* (PAN), 247,
256
*Partai Bintang Reformasi* (PBR), 287
*Partai Bulan Bintang* (PBB), 257,
342

Masyumi, as successor to, 342
*Parmusi* (*Partai Muslimin Indonesia*),
81
*Partai Demokrasi Indonesia* (PDI), 53
*Partai Demokrat*, 324
*Partai Keadilan*, 257, 273
*Partai Keadilan dan Persatuan
Indonesia* (PKPI), 343
*Partai Keadilan Sejahtera* (PKS), 287,
339
*Partai Kebangkitan Bangsa* (PKB), 254
non-Muslims elected as chairmen in
certain areas, 341
*Partai Kebangkitan Umat* (PKU), 255
*Partai Matahari Bangsa* (PMB), 340
*Partai Nahdlatul Umat* (PNU), 255
*Partai Persatuan Demokrasi Kebangsaan*
(PPDK), 238
past connections
use of, 54
*Pasukan Berani Mati* (PBM)
pro-Wahid paramilitary group, 266
People's Leadership Council (*Majelis
Kepemimpinan Rakyat*), 162
People's Liberation Army, 14, 42
Papua New Guinea, 314
Pareira, Andreas, 311
performance dilemma, 19
*pesantren*
financial support of, 149
hierarchical structure of, 286
*pesantren* Gontor, 338
Persatuan Tarbiyah Indonesia, 73
Pertamina, 53
Philippines, 12
Pion-Berlin, David, 23
Pius Lustrilanang, 285
PKB-affiliated militias, 265
PKI (*Partai Komunis Indonesia*)
threat of, 86
PNI (*Partai Nasional Indonesia*), 76
political activists
kidnapping of, 112

political parties
  interests, 43
  lifting of restrictions on formation
    of, 253
politics
  civilianizing, 345–49
Popular Mandate Council (*Majelis
  Amanat Rakyat*, MAR), 171
Poso, 227, 351
  beheadings in, 350
  communal conflict, end of, 329
post-authoritarian transitions, 3
post-Ryamizard military elite,
  296–98
post-Suharto governments, 2
post-Suharto military politics,
  235–39
post-Suharto period
  Islamic politics, 251–88
post-Suharto polity
  TNI adapting to, 361–68
Prabowo Subianto, 90
  mobilization of Muslims against
    Chinese conspiracy, 115
  relief from duties, 135–36
  strategy of radicalization, 114–15
  suspicions against, 127–28
Praetorian Rule, 49–56
presidency
  weakening, 1
presidential elections, 354
pribumization of Islam, 93
pro-Wahid paramilitary group
  *Pasukan Berani Mati* (PBM), 266
PSI (*Partai Sosialis Indonesia*), 113

**Q**
Quraish Shihab, 180

**R**
radicalism
  transitional civil-military relations,
    283–84

Ramage, Douglas, 64
Ratih Harjono, 245
rationalization programme, 41
reforms
  electoral mechanisms, 333
  radical, 212–17
  sudden death of, 217–22
reform council
  establishment of, 132
reform movement, 82
regional commanders
  business alliances with, 53
  facilitation service, 53
  relations with local entrepreneurs,
    53
regional rebellions
  effect on Nasution's leadership, 44
  end of, 44
*Republika*, 177
Robison, Richard, 24, 54
Roy Morgan Good Governance
  Monitor, 383
Rozy Munir, 170
Russia, 27
Ryamizard Ryacudu, 129, 226
  aborted appointment as TNI chief,
    295
  clash with Yudhoyono, 323

**S**
Sahal Mahfudz, 154, 285, 337–38
Saifullah Yusuf, 274
Salim Said, 145
Said Agil Siraj, 170
Samson, Allan A., 86
*santri*, 69
Saurip Kadi, 213
scholarships
  Suharto's foundations, 58
second-generation reforms, 26
second-generation measures
  military reforms, 28
security community, 20

security sector
  concepts, 7
  effect of reforms on, 2
  governance, 26
  reforms, 6
Sekarmadji Maridjan Kartosuwirjo,
  87
self-reform
  Wiranto and the "new paradigm",
  201–04
senior officers
  special treatment, 55
Setiawan, Danny, 275
*shirk* (associationism), 267, 286
Siliwangi
  military unit in, 99
Siliwangi division, 87
Silva, Patricio, 37
Siti Hardiyanti Rukmana, 61, 103
  visits to *pesantren*, 149
Siti Hartinah, 101
  death of, 101
Siswono Yudohusodo, 276
Sjafrie Sjamsoeddin, 115, 308
Slamet Effendi Yusuf, 326
social services
  Suharto's foundations, 58
Soeyono, 63, 104
Sofian Effendi, 140
Sofyan Wanandi, 114
Solahuddin Wahid
  claims of votes not counted, 355
  elections (2004), 277, 334
Solo, 128
South America
  divisions between military and
    civilians, 37
South Korea, 12
Sriwijaya
  military unit, 105
state coercion
  declining role, 291–328
State Defence Act, 317, 320

initiation by Juwono Sudarsono,
  305
Stepan
  notion of "new professionalism", 15
student activists
  occupation of parliament complex,
  131
student groups, 58
student movement, 160–63
Subagyo, 108
Subchan ZE, 92
Sudirman, 64
  defiance of civilian orders, 41
  directly elected by fellow officers,
  40
Sudjono Humardhani, 141
Sudomo, 93
Sudrajat, 66
Sugiono, 108
Suharto
  announcement of resignation, 134
  autocracy and the military, 57–59
  broadening of power base, 38
  control of administration, 52
  dependence on Muslim leaders
    during last days, 176
  direct control over military
    commands, 58
  dismissing Benny Murdani, 60
  establishment of an independent
    network of financing sources
    for political operations, 58
  expansion of personal economic
    empire, 58
  fall of, 97–138
  final exit, 133–36
  inability to reform, 119–21
  increasing Muslim participation in
    regime, 89
  laws to strengthen Islamic courts
    and educational institutions, 84
  Muslims of last resort, and, 177–81
  negotiation for exit of, 125–27

no united opposition against, 169–81
re-election to third presidential
term, 59
removal of NU members from
cabinet, 80
resignation, path to, 129–33
role in military campaign, 42
view of armed struggle, 41
Suharto's inner circle
divisions with armed forces, 57
reshuffling, 59
Sukarno, 39
announcement of five ideological
principles, 65
capture by Dutch, 40
concept of functional groups, 64
Guided Democracy, 44
Sultan of Yogyakarta, 42
Sumitro, 66
SUNI (*Solidaritas Uni Nasional
Indonesia*), 284
Sunni law schools (*mazhab*), 70
Sunni theorists
political experience of, 71
Supersemar foundations, 58
Supreme Auditing Board, 229
Susilo Bambang Yudhoyono, 104, 235
Aceh, votes garnered in, 323
challenges, continued, 313–19
civilian polity, stablization of,
331–34
conflicts with party officials, 238
control over armed forces, 2
declining role of state coercion,
291–328
dislike for elite politicians, 238
fight with DPR, 354
first directly elected President, 293
elections (2004), 278–80
victory, 280
institutional changes, 304–13
military, knowledge of, 294
military reforms, silence on, 305

Papua, handling of, 314
post-Suharto military politics,
235–39
pragmatism, sense of, 293
presidential mandate, strong, 293
reconciliatory policies on Aceh and
Papua, 294
Ryamizard, clash with, 323
support for foundation of
Democratic Party, 234
Truth and Reconciliation
Commission, abortion of,
316
Sutardjo Surjoguritno, 229
Sutiyoso (General), 233
Suwisman, 63
Syafi'i Maarif,
elections (2004), 271
leadership of Muhammadiyah,
335
Syamsir Siregar, 140
*syariat*
recognition in Constitution, 73
Syarwan Hamid, 111
Syukron Makmun, 255

**T**
Tajikistan, 27
Tanjung Priok
acquittal of officers indicted for
violations, 321
clash with Muslim demonstrators,
89
Tanri Abeng, 179
Tarub (Lieutenant General), 116
Tayo Tarmadi, 275
*Tentera Islam Indonesia* (TII), 87
territorial command system, 48, 315
outdated, 314
perpetuating military's self-financing
practices, 315
The Asia Foundation, 184, 358
theory of strategic action, 23

theory of united opposition, 182
threat level theories, 17
Tien Suharto, *see* Siti Hartinah
TKR (*Tentara Keamanan Rakyat*), 39
TNI (*Tentara Nasional Indonesia*)
    adapting to post-Suharto polity,
      361–68
    East Timor, issue of, 206–08
    elections (1999), 204–06
    fight against Dutch colonial forces,
      38
    Helsinki Accord, support and
      opposition for, 300–02
    historical legacy, 37–38, 368–71
    Indonesian independence, 38–42
    intra-systemic regime change,
      371–73
    militias, handling of, 208–09
    name change, 64
    news media and press, interactions
      with, 366
    relations with Habibie, 196–99
    territorial network, 244
    war on terror, and, 230–32
TNI Act, 317, 320
    discussions for new, 305
    takeover of military businesses,
      307
traditionalist organizations, 72–73
traditionalists
    interpretation of Quranic
      injunction, 72
transfer of authority
    from Sukarno to Suharto, 51
Trinkunas, Harold A., 258
Trisakti University, 127
    death of students, 171
Truth and Reconciliation Commission,
    327
    abortion of, 316
Try Sutrisno, 62, 141
Turkmenistan, 27
Turkey, 13, 378

Tyasno Sudarto, 216, 220
Two-Generation Model, 25–29

**U**
Uhlin, Anders, 63
Ukraine, 27
*ulama*, 70
    avoidance of conflict, 71
    fikih discourse, 72
    definition, 91
*umat*, 91
UNICEF, 184
United Nations
    West Irian issue, 47

**V**
Vietnamese People's Army, 42

**W**
Wahab Chasbullah, 92
Wahid Institute, 356
*wali songo*
    spiritual protection from, 264
Watik Pratikna, 165
war on terror
    TNI, role of, 230–32
West Irian, 46–47, 355
Widodo (Admiral), 212
Wirahadikusumah, *see* Agus
    Wirahadikusumah
Wiranto, *see* Wiranto (General)
Wiranto Arismunandar
    appointed Minister of Education,
      122
Wiranto (General), 47, 54
    claims of votes not counted, 355
    dispute in favour of, 146
    East Timor
      recollection of civilian interference,
        40
    soft-line element in political
      character, 116
    view of ABRI, 39

Wiranto-Prabowo rivalry, 110–13

**Y**
Yogyakarta, 41, 48
Yudhoyono, *see* Susilo Bambang
    Yudhoyono
Yudhoyono administration, 86
    declining role of state coercion,
        291–328

Yunus Yosifah, 114
Yusril Ihza Mahendra, 177, 342

**Z**
Z.A. Maulani, 141
Zacky Anwar Makarim, 115, 209
Zainuddin MZ, 287
Zarkasih Nur, 125, 350
Zulkarnaen, Happy Bone, 248

www.ingramcontent.com/pod-product-compliance
Lightning Source LLC
Chambersburg PA
CBHW030634150426
42811CB00048B/94